Fourth Edition

COURTS
and
JUSTICE

Fourth Edition

COURTS
and
JUSTICE

A Reader

G. Larry Mays
New Mexico State University
Peter R. Gregware
New Mexico State University

WAVELAND
PRESS, INC.
Long Grove, Illinois

For information about this book, contact:
    Waveland Press, Inc.
    4180 IL Route 83, Suite 101
    Long Grove, IL 60047-9580
    (847) 634-0081
    info@waveland.com
    www.waveland.com

To Otis H. Stephens—mentor and friend—
the person who first sparked my interest in the courts.

GLM

To Nancy, whose caring and ongoing support has made my life
so much better and, thus, this effort so much easier.

PRG

Preface

As long-time criminal justice educators, the editors of this book believe that the greatest disservice we can do for our students is to bore them. Therefore, over the years as this book has evolved we have tried to include new and "classic" works that are designed to both inform students and to challenge some of their strongly held assumptions. In preparing the fourth edition we really struggled with what to keep and what to replace. When we sought contemporary replacement pieces, we went to some of the leading experts in the field of courts and solicited their input and submissions. The result was a reduction of one article (from 27 to 26) from the third edition to the fourth edition.

The new articles added to this edition include an overview of the courts in the United States written by one of the book's editors (Mays) and an article by Frances Bernat on the impact of one U.S. Supreme Court decision (*Ring v. Arizona*, which removed the right of judges to impose capital punishment on their own without input from a jury) on the operations of a state supreme court. Additionally, David Orrick revised and updated his submission on court administration. Furthermore, four very provocative new pieces have been added on the following topics: (1) the impact of wrongful convictions (Marvin Zalman), (2) the processing of "normal homicides" (David Keys), (3) the role of gender in the courtroom work group (Susan Lentz), and (4) the effects of policy, law, and democratic influences on sentencing (Matthew Crow and Marc Gertz). Finally, Nancy Baker and Peter Gregware revised their contribution, which was introduced in the third edition of the book, asking once again: "Who owns the courts?"

Dropping some selections that appeared in the earlier editions of the book seems a little like saying goodbye to old friends. However, the courts are not a static area when it comes to both practice and research, so we had to make some hard choices. We believe that the composition of this fourth edition will be both informative and thought provoking. It should prove useful in a number of different courses and social science disciplines. In fact, a reviewer of an earlier edition characterized the book as an "indispensable reference work" that was kept near his desk at all times. We hope we can continue to live up to that challenge.

Acknowledgements

There are a number of people to whom we owe a great debt of gratitude for making a fourth edition of this book possible. First, we would like to thank the many professors who have adopted this book over the years, and to their students who have thought it worth the purchase price. Second, we would like to thank our students and colleagues at New Mexico State University and their support for our projects like this over the years. Third, we would like to thank the journal editors who have allowed us to reprint previously published articles and the authors who kept their commitments to submit unpublished works for our consideration. Finally, the cast and crew at Waveland are always a joy to work with. Special mention needs to go to Gayle Zawilla (our editor from previous editions) who started the project with us but who had to hand us off to the very capable Diane Evans and, of course, Neil and Carol Rowe have continued to be very kind to us over the years.

Contents

Section V
Politics in the Decision-Making Process   319

Section VI
The Future of Courts: Thinking Outside the Lines   421

Introduction
Trying to Make Sense of It All

It has become clear to many of us who toil in the vineyards of academic teaching and research related to courts that most students (and citizens in general) do not understand much about courts, and what they do know is often based on inaccurate media representations. Many people cannot articulate basic civic theories about the role of court personnel, such as lawyers and judges, and about the role of courts in enhancing the social good. Aside from emotional responses about the adequacy of government institutions, few can discuss with any specificity how well our current legal institutions actually meet the goals of our social and political theories. When institutions fail to meet our goals, it seems to us imperative that we begin to understand the underlying stresses and conflicts that any concerned citizen, either within or outside the court system, must understand in order to keep government functions that work and reform those that do not.

The first goal of this text is to provide information on the function of courts and on the underlying conflicts that must be resolved if we are to increase the level of justice that courts can contribute to our society. We seek to challenge what are often incorrect assumptions about the role or functions of courts. Second, we seek to provide in-depth material on often overlooked areas of court study, which hopefully will ensure the clear understanding that can be gained by a multifaceted perspective. Third, by providing an analysis of court function and problems, we hope to provide a useful framework for class and small-group discussion. The interactive and personal dynamic provided by such discussion has continually impressed educators with its ability to break down rigid assumptions and inspire deeper levels of discernment. It is to such increasing levels of understanding and insight that we dedicate this book.

Two major related themes run throughout these articles. The first is the political nature of courts; courts are political institutions just as much as the legislative or executive branches of government, although the political nature of courts is usually more hidden from the public eye. The second

1

theme is really a question: In a democratic society within a constitutional framework, who owns the courts? That is, do we entrust the operation of our dispute management system to the discretion of professional legal experts, or do citizens have an ongoing and ultimate say in how this essential part of their government operates? Alternatively, to what extent should either the executive or legislative branches of government have control over the courts, especially given the "separation of powers" assumptions on which our constitutional democracy was based? The fact that the operation of courts is political helps to explain the ongoing conflict between citizens, professionals, and now primarily the executive branch, over who should control our courts. It also helps us to assess our own responsibility for understanding this conflict and making a choice about such ownership.

The first section begins by examining these themes, and in the process asks why approximately one-third of Americans report little or no confidence in our legal system and why this opinion seems to be growing (1999 University of Chicago National Opinion Research Center).[1] The articles in this section locate courts in the broader social and political process, looking at the distrust professionals feel toward citizens; the distrust many citizens feel toward both the legal professional and the courts; and the extent to which courts are increasingly becoming drawn into, or captured by, the larger national political process.

While on one level we increasingly acknowledge the importance of courts, much of what courts do remains hidden from public view. The second section explores this shadow world, asking questions about judicial accountability, where judges preside over an institutional world with relatively little public awareness or participation. Here we begin to investigate the political culture of judicial and prosecutorial decision making, asking who should be responsible and whether they can be made accountable for making societal choices. In the ongoing debate between the values of efficiency and justice, how are these values being balanced, and who does the balancing?

Sections III and IV continue this citizen/professional debate by first focusing on citizen/juror participation in the court process: What should the role of citizens be in deciding issues of social concern? To what extent has this role been limited by professional groups wielding the power to do so? Section IV then explores the record of the legal profession's management of our courts. Is the record one of just stewardship or one of turf battle between "insiders" and "outsiders"? Regardless of the record, how do we now resolve the conflict between the need for some level of judicial independence and the need for accountability to reduce abuses of power?

Section V directly addresses the issue of politics in the courts. Contrary to popular impressions, politics is not a dirty word. The articles in this section reiterate the fact that we cannot escape from politics in the operation of our political institutions. They challenge us not to eliminate politics but rather to seek a balance by harnessing the wisdom acquired through the political process while limiting the prejudices of our human foibles. They also suggest that the more we collectively organize our decision-making processes, the more we can provide accountability in pursuing the goal of justice.

The last section focuses on two contested areas that will be with the courts for awhile—gender inclusion/bias and the struggle over which segment of our society controls our courts. Both incorporate the politics and control themes of this text and provide rich examples appropriate for further dialogue. Both issues illustrate how the courts are part of our society and part of the larger political process. Our political and social culture strongly influences our courts, and in turn what happens in our courts influences whether we see each other as equals and how we view our relationship with our government.

Each effort at reform must cope with the larger political context, which may at times assist but more often may impede these attempts. Additionally, those who work in the court process may actively resist change because it may threaten self-interest or accepted methods of behavior. It is difficult to control these interacting elements, much less anticipate the variety of responses to any reforming intervention. It is our hope that by expanding our understanding of both underlying problems and potential conflicts, we not only can increase our ability to formulate appropriate policy but also can implement such policies successfully.

Endnote

[1] Joan Biskupic, "Veto by Jury," *Washington Post National Weekly Edition*, March 29, 1999.

Section I
Overview of Courts

In the first selection, Larry Mays provides an introductory overview. This chapter is not meant to be a comprehensive discussion of court organization and operations but is offered to help refresh the memories of those who may have taken a course or read a text on courts some time ago. It will be very useful to those who are studying courts for the first time. It can be used as a reference guide for many of the terms and concepts that one may encounter in all of the chapters that follow.

Frances Zemans then lays the ground work for many of the themes you will find in this book by highlighting a variety of the issues underlying the study of courts, such as the relationship of courts to the political process and the inherent conflicts in mass-production justice. We (the outsiders) gain a vital perspective on courts by attempting to understand our own view of courts and how it might differ from those of professionals (the insiders) who work within the court system.

Citizen outsiders often have some experience with the court process but still feel less informed about the judicial system than about legislative and executive systems. In an era of growing concern about the operations of government, evidenced by anti-incumbency feelings and disillusionment with administrative operation, there is also increased criticism of judges and decreasing perceptions that courts are places to obtain justice.

While the media clearly have provided a distorted picture of court processes, some of the blame must be placed on insiders, the court personnel who have exhibited some disdain for the public and their ability to participate in and understand the judicial process.

This indictment of courts is echoed by John Langbein, who describes how lawyers and judges limit public involvement in court functions by limiting jury trials. He argues that many of these limitations on juries have been, and are, compounded by the historical decision to adopt an adversary system that gave lawyers the power to control court proceedings. Abuse of this power led in turn to demands that lawyers be controlled, resulting in more and more power being given to lawyers who have been elevated to the rank of judge. Now judges referee a clumsy and time-consuming court process that leads many to seek reductions in the use of jury trials, thus reducing public involvement in court processes as envisioned by constitutional framers.

If we are to have an informed citizenry that not only respects the role of courts in society but also is willing to use courts to seek justice, how can exclusion of citizens from the process improve levels of understanding and respect? What changes must be made in the way courts function and in the way court professionals view public involvement?

Crow and Gertz take a slightly different track on this interaction between the public and professionals. While acknowledging the impact of popular culture on individual judges and their decisions, they seek to find ways to balance or filter this influence through such methods as sentencing guidelines. Does such a detailed, research-oriented approach offer ways to significantly improve the court system or can we at best just influence such a socially entrenched system at the margins?

Finally, Chaires and Lentz help us to address the seeming complexity of our court system that the preceding articles have uncovered by placing courts in a broader political and cultural context. They provide insightful categories that help us understand what we see going on, such that readers may wish to revisit these categories as they proceed through this text. They help us to appreciate why our society increasingly relies on courts to resolve our disputes; and we become amused, enlightened, and sometimes a bit depressed at the many ways courts participate in the myths and foibles of the larger political process. Yet the authors also provide the necessary tools for further inquiry, pragmatic methods to separate the ideal from the real, and give incentives to read on.

Quite simply, these articles reveal that there is intellectual power in understanding law in ways that law schools are often unwilling to explore. We can begin to understand how courts really work and that they are part of the larger political process in which we all participate. We can cut through the legal jargon often used by lawyers and judges; we need no longer be mystified by law.

1

A Brief Introduction
to Courts

G. LARRY MAYS

This chapter is designed to do two things. First, it will serve as a refresher for those of you who have already had an introductory course on the courts and the justice system in the United States. Second, for some of you this will be your first exposure to the world of courts, and this chapter will provide you with information on the basic terminology, concepts, actors, and processes of the courts. For both groups, this introduction will prepare you to understand better the group of readings that follow.

Introduction

In every course that provides an introduction to the criminal justice system, the three parts of the system are characterized as police, courts, and corrections. It would seem, based on this simple description, that the courts are coequal partners along with the police and correctional agencies in dispensing justice in the United States. However, a little research will demonstrate that while the courts are important, they are anything but coequal partners.

For example, data provided by the Bureau of Justice Statistics demonstrate something of the disparity among the three components of the criminal justice system. In 2003 justice system expenditures in the United States totaled $185 billion dollars. The criminal justice system employed 2.4 million people at all levels of government and had a March 2003 payroll of $9 billion.

Written especially for *Courts and Justice*.

Of the total expenditures, $83 billion went to police protection, $60.8 billion went for corrections, and $41.5 billion were devoted to judicial and legal functions—this includes both courts and prosecutors' offices (Hughes 2006:4). In examining the March 2003 payroll expenditures, again police protection represents the largest category: 1.1 million employees and a one-month payroll of $4.55 billion. Correctional agencies constitute the second largest category with 748,250 employees and a one-month payroll of $2.52 billion. Judicial and legal services represent the smallest component with 494,007 employees and a $1.97 billion payroll (Hughes 2006:6).

The differences in relative status are illustrated further by examining the percent of state and local justice employees by function. In 2003 44.7 percent of state and local justice employees worked in police protection, 35.0 percent worked in corrections, and 20.4 percent served in judicial and legal services (Hughes 2006:8). The presentation of all of these numbers is to illustrate a simple point: The courts are vital to the operation of the justice system in the United States. However, they do not employ equivalent numbers of personnel in comparison with police and corrections, and they are not allocated budgets of equivalent sizes.

Federalism and Comity

A point frequently made in discussing courts in this country is that we have multiple court systems. Indeed, there are at least 51 organizational patterns with a court system for the national government, each state having a unique arrangement, and some local governments having their own systems (Neubauer 2008). Understanding two legal/political principles is essential to comprehending the way courts are organized and the ways in which they operate in this country. First, is the principle of *federalism*. In simplest terms, federalism means that we have chosen a system where some courts hear matters arising under the U.S. Constitution and as a result of congressional statutory enactments. These are what we normally call the federal courts. Second, states are allowed to have their own courts that hear matters related to state constitutional interpretations, state statutes, and even county and municipal ordinances. These two systems do not exist one on top of the other, but rather side-by-side.

Under our federalist system, federal courts and state courts have their own particular jurisdictions, although they are very similar in nature.[1] Each is able to adjudicate cases without the other, although in some ways they are mutually interdependent. As an illustration, in certain types of cases there is "concurrent" jurisdiction over criminal matters. Thus, in bank robbery cases the federal courts may have jurisdiction as a result of the robbery of a federally insured institution. Nevertheless, state courts may have jurisdiction as a result of statutes dealing with armed robbery.

The second legal/political principle that we must consider is that of *comity*. Comity means that one set of courts will recognize the jurisdiction of another set of courts and, in some instances, defer both to the other jurisdiction's ability to decide a case and any resulting decisions (see Champion 2005). Unless there are compelling reasons to do otherwise, federal courts and state courts often will defer to one another when there are questions about jurisdiction.

Court Organization in the United States

With this background, we now turn our attention to the ways in which state courts and federal courts are organized. Given the wide range of state court organizations, they can best be understood using very broad categories.[2]

State Courts

At the most basic level, state courts can be divided into two categories: courts of original or trial jurisdiction and courts of appellate jurisdiction. Every state has these two types of courts, but the types of courts within these two categories may vary from state to state. For instance, some states (South Dakota, for example) have one level of trial courts while other states have two levels.

In those states with two levels of trial courts, the lowest level typically is characterized as the courts of limited or inferior jurisdiction. These courts may be called municipal courts, magistrate courts, or a variety of other designations (see Rottman et al. 2000). The courts of limited jurisdiction hear misdemeanor cases, preliminary hearings for felony cases, and civil cases below a certain dollar amount ($5,000, for example). In 2005, the state courts of limited jurisdiction in the United States disposed of 5,451,078 civil cases and 6,670,742 criminal cases for a total of 12,121,820 dispositions (Schauffler et al. 2006).

States may require the judges of these courts to be licensed attorneys or they may permit lay or nonlawyer judges in these courts. The courts of limited jurisdiction may be courts of nonrecord—that is, they do not keep verbatim transcripts of proceedings—and the use of juries may be limited. They may use a small number of jurors (for example, six) or they may not have jury trials at all. They hear traffic cases and other minor offenses, and they frequently dispense rapid and "rough" justice (Robertson 1974); in many instances neither side of the case appears with an attorney. Courts of limited jurisdiction process the bulk of cases heard in the United States. They often typify the process known as "assembly line justice" (Packer 1968), and they are found in one form or another in virtually every state.

Above the courts of limited jurisdiction are the courts of general trial jurisdiction. These courts are what most people think of when they think of a case "going to court." In 2005 state general trial courts disposed of 4,382,200 civil cases and another 2,570,034 criminal cases for a total of 6,952,234 dispositions (Schauffler et al. 2006).

General trial courts hear felony cases. They also adjudicate civil cases above a specified monetary amount (such as $5,000). The trial courts require judges to be licensed attorneys, they are courts of record, attorneys are almost always present for both sides, juries typically are used to try cases, and all of the pomp and ceremony associated with trials is present in these courts. In some jurisdictions, the courts of general trial jurisdiction also can perform an appellate function. For example, since limited jurisdiction courts routinely do not keep verbatim transcripts, when a case is appealed from these courts it will go to the general trial jurisdiction courts on what is known as a trial *de novo* (in other words, a whole new trial).

Each state also has an appellate court system. In 2005, state intermediate appellate courts disposed of 288,614 cases (Schauffler et al. 2006). Appellate courts review convictions any time an error of law is alleged to have occurred. The majority of states have more than one level of appellate court: a court of last resort as well as an intermediate appellate court, sometimes called the court of appeals. The intermediate appeals courts may meet in one location (such as the state capital) or they may be divided up into panels that meet regionally to review cases. Intermediate appellate courts frequently hear the cases that are mandatory appeals. Mandatory appeals are those required by the constitution or state statutes and the courts may not have discretion in hearing these appeals. In most states the vast majority of cases do not proceed past this point.

All 50 states have a high court or court of last resort, and two states (Oklahoma and Texas) have divided courts of last resort, one for civil cases and the other for criminal cases. The most common designation (48 states) for these courts is the state supreme court or some variation of this title. However, this is not universally the title used. For example, in Maryland the general trial court is the circuit court and the court of last resort is known as the court of appeals. Also, in New York State the general trial jurisdiction courts are known as supreme courts and in that state the court of last resort also is known as the court of appeals (Rottman et al. 2000). State supreme courts may hear some mandatory appeals, but the bulk of their caseload is composed of discretionary appeals, or those in which the judges have discretion over whether to accept the case. This means that unlike the intermediate appellate courts, state courts of last resort have substantial control over their dockets, and in 2005 they disposed of 87,804 cases (Schauffler et al. 2006).

Federal Courts

Like their state court counterparts, the federal courts also have trial and appellate distinctions. However, unlike many states, the federal judicial system has only one level of trial courts. There are 505 full time and 45 part time U.S. magistrate judges attached to the federal courts (U.S. Courts 2007b), and they perform many of the routine functions that must be discharged, such as bail and evidentiary hearings, misdemeanor trials, etc. However, they do not function as independent courts of limited jurisdiction (see Christopher Smith's article in this volume).

The trial courts in the federal system are called district courts, and nationwide there are 94 federal court districts (U.S. Courts 2007a). Some states (principally in the Rocky Mountain region) contain only one federal court district, and some states have three (Florida, North Carolina, Oklahoma, and Tennessee, for instance) or four (California and Texas) such districts depending on the state size and population. Federal district courts have jurisdiction over misdemeanors—occasionally tried by U.S. magistrate judges—and felonies committed under federal law (the United States Code). They also have jurisdiction over civil cases that involve at least $75,000 in dispute. Furthermore, they have jurisdiction over cases between persons or companies from different states, or the so-called "diversity of citizenship" cases.

District courts serve as the workhorses for the federal court system. As an example, in 2006 there were 66,860 criminal cases and 259,541 civil cases filed in federal district courts (U.S. Courts 2007b). This provides a significant caseload for most of the nation's 645 active district court judges.

Cases that are appealed from the federal district courts go to one of the U.S. courts of appeals. Often these are called the circuit courts. This results from the early tradition of having Supreme Court justices "ride circuit" and hear appeals in various locations. This tradition has been continued by naming each of these courts the U.S. Court of Appeals for the Fourth Circuit (as one example). Currently, there are 11 numbered circuits (see figure 1.1) plus the courts of appeals for the District of Columbia and the federal circuit (both of which meet in Washington, DC).

These federal intermediate appellate courts hear cases originally tried in the federal district courts and nationwide in 2006 there were 179 judgeships authorized and 165 active judges sitting on the courts of appeals (U.S. Courts 2007b). Unlike their state court counterparts—which disposed of nearly 210,000 cases in 2005—the federal courts of appeals disposed of 29,913 cases in 2005 and 34,580 cases in 2006 (Mecham 2006, 2007).

The court of last resort in the federal judicial system, and probably the court with the highest profile in the nation, is the United States Supreme Court. Article III of the U.S. Constitution provides that "the judicial Power

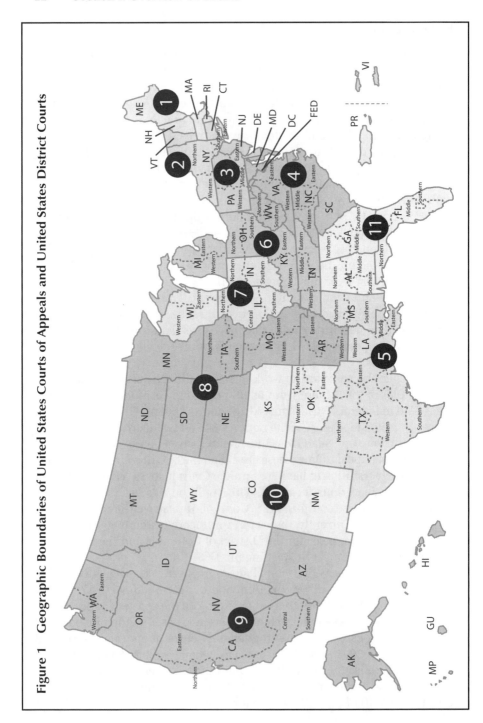

Figure 1   Geographic Boundaries of United States Courts of Appeals and United States District Courts

of the United States, shall be vested in one supreme Court, and in such inferior Courts as the Congress may from time to time ordain and establish." The judicial article defines in very broad terms the jurisdiction of the Supreme Court. However, the Constitution is silent on the number of justices that shall compose the Court and the qualifications of those justices; these are decisions that are left to the discretion of Congress. Thus, the first court to be seated in 1789 had a chief justice and four associate justices. This number was increased to six justices total in the 1790–91 term. In 1807 the number was expanded to seven, and beginning in 1837 until the Civil War the number fluctuated between eight and nine. At one point during the Civil War (1863–65) there were 10 Supreme Court justices. Since that time the number settled on has been nine, comprised of eight associate justices and the chief justice.

Unlike Congress or the president, there are no formal requirements to serve as a justice of the Supreme Court. The reality, however, is that in recent history all of the nominees have been licensed to practice law and they generally have had long and distinguished careers as attorneys, judges, or law school professors (see Rehnquist 2001). When a vacancy occurs on the Supreme Court—or any federal court, for that matter—the president of the United States has his staff begin the search for a suitable nominee. In most instances, the nominees for federal judgeships come from the president's own party, and a key consideration for Supreme Court candidates is the "judicial philosophy" that the nominee has expressed (Schmidhauser 1979).

Each nominee to the Supreme Court will have a background investigation completed by the U.S. Justice Department to ensure that there are no legal impediments to the nomination. After this, the American Bar Association will rank the nominees according to their qualifications and suitability for the position. Once these hurdles have been cleared the Judiciary Committee of the United States Senate will schedule confirmation hearings. Especially in the case of Supreme Court nominations, the hearings are televised on C-SPAN and the major national news outlets will run excerpts from the nomination hearings. Nominees who clear the Judiciary Committee must have their appointments confirmed by the entire U.S. Senate, and once confirmed the justices (and other federal judges) will serve life terms "during good behavior."

The Supreme Court has original jurisdiction defined by the Constitution. These are cases in which the Court can act as a trial court over a limited number of legal issues; it seldom exercises this jurisdiction. For the most part, the cases that are received and reviewed come to the Court under its discretionary appeals jurisdiction. In fact, the vast majority of the cases reviewed by contemporary Courts have resulted from the granting of writs of certiorari. A writ of certiorari is a command from the Court to the highest level state court to "send up the record" of the case in order for it to be considered for possible review. In making decisions about which cases to accept, the Supreme Court meets in conference to review summary documents that have been prepared by the justices' law clerks (Rehnquist 2001). At least four of the justices must vote to grant certiorari, but even this does not guarantee that a case will make it to the Court's docket. For instance, at some later point the justices may reconsider their votes and reject the case on the grounds that certiorari was "improvidently granted."

A small number of the Court's landmark cases will make the news every few years, but most of what the Supreme Court does largely goes unnoticed by members of the general public. In fact, even with its relatively high level of visibility, most members of the general public would be hard pressed to name the current chief justice of the Supreme Court and more than one or two of the associate justices.[3] Nevertheless, the Supreme Court continues to have great symbolic significance in American government, and a few of its more famous cases (such as *Mapp v. Ohio* [1961] and *Gideon v. Wainwright* [1963]) have significantly impacted the processes of the criminal justice system in the United States.

Subject Matter Jurisdiction and Court Specialization

Already in this chapter we have referred to the jurisdiction exercised by courts. Briefly, jurisdiction is the legal authority a court has to decide a case (see, for example, Black 1991; Champion 2005). In some states (for example, Texas) courts have very specialized jurisdictions and there are numerous specialized courts. In other states courts have very broadly defined jurisdictional boundaries and there are fewer types of courts. The latter states have what often are called unified court systems. A few examples will suffice.

First, some states have courts that only hear criminal cases. Other states (those with unified systems) have courts that hear both civil and criminal cases. Second, some states (Arkansas, Delaware, Mississippi, and Tennessee) have separate law and equity (chancery) courts. The law courts decide cases based on constitutional provisions, statutes, and local ordinances. By contrast, equity courts decide what is "right" or "fair," often in the absence of written law. Calvi and Coleman (2008:365) say that equity is "a branch of law that provides for remedies other than damages and is therefore more flexible than common law." Today most states have merged their law and equity jurisdictions. Third, 12 states have separate juvenile courts or families courts that have juvenile cases as part of their jurisdiction. In all other states, juvenile cases are heard in a court of general trial jurisdiction, commonly the same court that handles adult criminal cases.

Finally, a number of states have courts that hear very specialized types of cases (Rottman et al. 2000). For example, 15 states have probate courts that hear matters relating to wills and inheritances. Other specialized courts include: tax court or court of tax review (Arizona, New Jersey, Oklahoma, and Oregon), water court (Colorado and Montana), small claims (Indiana), orphans court (Maryland), housing court (Massachusetts), land court (Massachusetts), workers' compensation court (Montana, Nebraska, and Rhode Island), surrogates court—for adoptions and estates (New York), court of claims (Ohio), and environmental court (Vermont).

The general trend over the past half century has been for states to move away from court specialization toward the use of specialized judges within courts of general jurisdiction (Ashman and Parness 1977; Neubauer 2008). However, given the strong influences of legal tradition, several states still have one or more specialized courts.

Actors in the Courts

There are a number of people associated with the processing of cases in the judicial systems of the United States. For purposes of simplicity, we will divide the actors in the criminal courts into two broad categories: (1) the courtroom work group and (2) ancillary actors. The courtroom work group is a notion that has been around for some time (see Eisenstein and Jacob 1977; Glick 1984). It is a shorthand reference to the three principal actors in any criminal courtroom setting: the judge, the prosecuting attorney, and the defense attorney. In this section we will look at the roles and functions of the members of the courtroom work group, as well as other actors commonly encountered in the courts.

Judges

Judges are the indispensable actors in the courts. Cases can be processed without the presence of attorneys—as they often do in courts of limited jurisdiction—but they cannot proceed without judges. Briefly we will examine the functions performed by judges, the qualifications for judges, the different mechanisms for choosing judges (what is often called judicial selection), and how different levels of government can discipline judges.

Trial court judges function in three arenas relative to case processing: pretrial, trial, and posttrial (including sentencing). During the pretrial stages judges in inferior courts set bail and conduct initial appearances and preliminary hearings. If the state is able to establish probable cause to the satisfaction of the judge, the case will be bound over to the grand jury for review in roughly half the states that utilize grand juries (Neubauer 2008).

In the remaining states, a more thorough preliminary hearing is conducted and this suffices to establish probable cause that the case should move forward to trial.

In those states that utilize grand juries, if probable cause is established, the grand jury will return an indictment or a "true bill." Unlike trial court juries in most states, grand juries do not require unanimous decisions in order to hand down an indictment.

At this point, the formal charges have been established and the case is scheduled for arraignment in a court of general trial jurisdiction. Again, the judge has a variety of responsibilities at this stage. For example, the issue of bail may be revisited for those defendants who have not been able to secure their release. The judge also will make sure that adequate representation by counsel has been provided, either privately or through a court-appointed attorney. The charges will be presented once again to the defendant, and perhaps for the first time the defendant will be asked to enter a plea. If the defendant enters a plea of not guilty or, in rare instances, stands mute before the court, the judge will schedule the case for trial.

Prior to commencing a trial, many defendants will begin plea negotiations with the prosecuting attorney's office. The level of plea bargaining and outright guilty pleas is somewhat astounding. In fact, most estimates are that upwards of 90 percent of the criminal cases in the United States are resolved without ever going to trial (Levine 1992; Rosett and Cressey 1976). The facts are not in dispute in many of these cases, and the negotiation process revolves around the defendant trying to obtain some measure of leniency. In reality, plea bargaining does not involve bargaining over the plea itself, but rather involves discussions about the charge(s), the number of times the offense occurred (counts), and the sentence. The prosecutor and the defense attorney conduct these discussions in most states, and the judge may play little or no role in the process other than sanctioning the final recommendation from the attorneys. Nevertheless, the recommendation will be within a range that is acceptable to all parties as a result of the widespread agreement over what Walker (2006:47–67) calls the "going rate." This concept explains the widely held understanding within the courtroom work group about what a case is worth.

Judges may also consider a number of pretrial motions before trials can commence. The most common of these are motions to reduce bail, motions for evidentiary hearings or to suppress physical evidence or confessions, motions to dismiss some or all of the charges, motions for discovery, and motions for a change of venue (Kamisar, LaFave, and Israel 1990:18). Many of these are handled (and dismissed) in summary fashion, but addressing these issues takes some of the judge's time.

When defendants plead not guilty their case is set for trial. As the trial date approaches, the court clerk, jury commissioner, or similar official works behind the scenes to assemble a potential jury pool (Levine 1992). In many state court systems, and for the federal courts as well, people summoned for jury duty may serve a specified term (for example, 30, 60, or 90 days), they may be called for a certain number of "jury days," or simply serve in one trial. There are various ways of identifying potential jurors, and some jurisdictions use property tax rolls, voter registrations, or lists of licensed drivers (with an under 18 years of age disqualifier). The pool of potential jurors is called the *venire*, and those summoned to appear in the pool of potential jurors are called *veniremen*. From this group of 30 to 45 people the two attorneys and the judge will select a group of 12 jurors and normally one or two alternates. However, before going further it is important to say something about jury size.

Under Anglo-American legal tradition juries have been composed of 12 members. No one knows exactly why that is. In the U.S. Supreme Court case of *Williams v. Florida* (1970) Justice Byron White wrote that this "particular feature of the jury system appears to have been a historical accident, unrelated to the great purposes which gave rise to the jury in the first place." He concluded that "the fact that the jury at common law was composed of precisely 12 is a historical accident, unnecessary to effect the purposes of the jury system and wholly without significance, 'except to mystics'" (103). As a result of *Williams* and other cases, the Supreme Court has allowed juries of less than 12 members, but not less than six. However, in capital cases, the Court has insisted on 12 person juries.

The jury selection process is known as the *voir dire*. This is a French term meaning "to speak the truth," and the official purpose of this process is to eliminate bias in the trial process. Courts vary in their practices in conducting *voir dires*. In some the custom is that the attorneys submit questions to the judge and the judge actually conducts the questioning of prospective jurors. Other courts allow the attorneys to do the questioning. Typical questions deal with whether prospective jurors have had law enforcement experience, whether they know any of the parties involved in the case, whether they have personal knowledge of the case, and whether they have formed any opinions about the defendant's guilt or innocence. Both sides will be given an unlimited number of exclusions (or "strikes") for cause, with the permission of the judge. The principal cause for exclusion is prejudging or prejudice. Additionally, each side will be given a certain number of *peremptory challenges* or strikes that do not require a stated justification.[4]

Two facts are very clear concerning the *voir dire* of jurors. First, unlike what most people would assume, some attorneys are not trying to pick a neutral jury. In fact, a few attorneys would like to find 12 jurors already inclined to vote for their position. The result, of course, is that the most predisposed veniremen get eliminated in the selection process (Levine 1992). Second, attorneys—and especially prosecuting attorneys—cannot use their peremptory challenges in such a way as to systematically exclude certain classes of people. This is especially true for exclusions based on race (see *Batson v. Kentucky*, 1986).

Once the jury has been selected, the judge's responsibility shifts to presiding over the trial. In a number of ways, this function resembles something of a referee in a sporting event. The judge is there to make sure both sides obey the rules, and also to make rulings during the trial when particular issues or objections are raised by the lawyers.

After both sides have presented their cases and the defense rests, the judge will prepare the instructions to the jury (sometimes called the jury charge). Most states have developed standardized jury instructions, but the prosecutor and the defense attorney may submit issues to the judge in areas they want to see included in the instructions. This is particularly the case when the defense has raised an affirmative defense such as insanity, duress, entrapment, or alibi. In most instances the judge will simply read the various instructions to the jury and dismiss them to begin their deliberations.

Much like the requirement of 12 jurors, most jurisdictions (both state and federal) have required unanimous verdicts. This, like jury size, is something of a historical artifact, but it is one way in criminal cases that we can establish guilt "beyond a reasonable doubt." Nevertheless, in the cases of *Apodaca v. Oregon* (1972) and *Johnson v. Louisiana* (1972), the U.S. Supreme Court allowed states to use nonunanimous verdicts with three stipulations: (1) six-member juries must return unanimous verdicts, (2) 12-member juries can convict on 10–2 or 9–3 votes, and (3) in capital cases jury verdicts must be unanimous.

When the jury reaches a decision, the members will return to the courtroom and announce their verdict. If the verdict is guilty, the judge has two major remaining responsibilities. The most obvious of these is to order the probation department to prepare a presentence investigation report and to set a date for sentencing.[5] Additionally, the judge will be asked to review and rule on postconviction motions that may be the basis for an appeal.

When considering what judges do, it is important to mention the qualifications required to be a judge. Essentially, there are two groups of judges based on qualifications: lay (or nonlawyer) judges and judges that have been licensed to practice law. In the courts of limited jurisdiction in the United States, lay judges are common. For example, some states still have elected justices of the peace and, for the most part, these individuals are not licensed to practice law. This is also true in some states in municipal or magistrate's courts.

By contrast, judges in courts of general trial jurisdiction and appellate courts universally are required to be licensed attorneys. In fact, some states stipulate further requirements such as the individual must have practiced law in the state for a specified period of time, such as five years (Rottman et al. 2000).

Consideration of methods of judicial selection is also important. At the most basic level, there are three methods of selecting judges in the United States: (1) appointment, (2) election (partisan and nonpartisan), and (3) merit selection, or the Missouri Plan (Canon 1977). We will examine each of these briefly in turn.

Judicial appointments take two forms: permanent (such as federal judges) and interim or limited term. As we have mentioned previously, all of the so-called Article III federal judges (district court, courts of appeals, and Supreme Court) are appointed by the president, confirmed by the Senate, and they then have life tenure. Thus, the appointive system is used by the federal courts, but state governors also may have the constitutional authority to make interim appointments when judicial vacancies suddenly occur. This may be the result of a judge retiring before his or her term expires, the unexpected death of a sitting judge, or judges being removed from the bench as a result of impeachment, recall, or conviction of a crime. Interim appointments allow the governor to temporarily place someone on the bench. In elective systems, judges who receive interim appointments must later run for office if they want to retain the position.

In many local and state courts judicial vacancies are filled through elections. This tradition dates back to the presidency of Andrew Jackson and use of the "long ballot," where every political office was filled through election. Some states utilize nonpartisan elections. In these states the candidates' political party affiliations may be known, but they do not appear on the ballot. Nonpartisan elections are common in local elections for a variety of offices, including that of judge. By contrast, most states traditionally have selected judges in partisan elections. These states clearly place the candidates' political party labels on the ballot.

One of the primary justifications for electing judges is that this helps hold them accountable to the electorate. The feeling is that if we elect them, we can "un-elect" them if we disagree with the ways in which they discharge their duties. The truth, however, is that once a person is elected judge voters tend to reelect this person time and again. This tendency demonstrates the power of incumbency in all aspects of American political life.

The third method of choosing judges is merit selection. This system is often called the Missouri Plan after the state that pioneered this system in 1940 (Berkson 2007). The American Judicature Society (2007) has long been a proponent of the merit selection of judges, and in its official position it calls merit selection "the best way to choose the best judges."

In merit selection systems, when a vacancy occurs a judicial nominating commission is convened to take nominations and applications from potential candidates. After reviewing the applications the nominating commission will send forward an unranked slate of candidates (typically three) to the governor who then appoints one of the three or rejects the whole slate, giving a justification in writing. The person appointed to the judgeship will serve until the next general election at which time he or she must run for election against anyone else who chooses to run. After being elected the first time, the judge subsequently runs for reelection in retention elections in which the ballot reads, "Shall Judge Jane Smith be retained in the office of District Court Judge?" Voters are then given a yes or no option and most of the judges are routinely reelected.

Merit selection is supposed to minimize the costs of elections and the necessity of fund-raising by judges. The system is also designed to minimize the influence of the local bar association and local politics in judicial selection. In reality, it shifts the political influence from the local level to the state level. Currently, about two-thirds of the states utilize merit selection for selecting some or all of their judges (Berkson 2007).

Finally, at times it is necessary to discipline judges for misconduct in office, including potentially removing them from office. Much like the systems of judicial selection, there are at least three methods of judicial discipline. As was mentioned previously, with elective systems judges can be voted out of office at the next election. Additionally, most states provide for recall elections where a certain number of voters can sign a petition asking to have political officials (including judges) stand for election at any point in the term of office. In effect, these are votes of confidence or no confidence.

A second way of imposing judicial discipline is through impeachment. Some states have provisions for impeachment, and this is the only way to remove sitting federal judges from office, even if they have been convicted of bribery or corruption in office (Ashman 1973; Jacob 1984). The impeachment process is a cumbersome one, but it is designed to insulate judges from retribution over politically unpopular decisions (like the death penalty, school desegregation, and abortion).

The way most states have moved to sanction judges—up to and including removal from office—is through the creation of judicial disciplinary commissions. These commissions frequently are composed of lawyers, judges, and sometimes citizens who review complaints against judges and decide the appropriate sanctions. These can include a private reprimand, a public reprimand, censure, or removal from office. The judicial discipline commission may make its recommendations to the state supreme court for action, and states utilize the state supreme court as the body sitting as the judicial discipline commission. Whatever system is employed, relatively few judges ever are sanctioned for misconduct, but when they are the cases tend to attract much public attention.

Prosecuting Attorneys

Nationwide, the attorneys representing the government operate at the local, state, and federal levels. State and local prosecutors are known by a variety of titles, including county attorney, state's attorney, commonwealth attorney, and district attorney general or simply district attorney (see Perry 2006). At the highest level in a state is the state attorney general. In the federal system there also are two levels of prosecutors: the 94 U.S. attorneys that work in each of the federal court districts, and the U.S. attorney general who sits on the president's cabinet and oversees the Department of Justice. For the sake of simplicity, in this section we will use the generic designation of "prosecuting attorney."

At the local and state levels, prosecutors in the United States are typically elected, for the most part, in partisan elections. They represent their level of government in criminal prosecutions, and for many this position is a springboard to higher political office (judge, state attorney general, governor, U.S. attorney, or member of Congress). George Cole, for one, has described this position as existing at the center of an "exchange system" that places the prosecutor in perhaps the most powerful position within the courtroom work group (Cole 2004).

As an illustration of this, the prosecutor has the ultimate decision over whether to take a case at all, or whether to carry it forward to trial. Even after a grand jury indictment, the prosecutor can petition the court to have the charges dismissed through a *nolle prosequi* (no prosecution) motion. Additionally, prosecutors have power over charging certain crimes given a wide range of options and, with determinate sentencing, to set the punishment by what is charged.

Prosecutors work with police officers, crime victims, and other witnesses to prepare their cases for trial. However, as previously mentioned, most cases are settled prior to trial so much of the prosecutor's time is devoted to crafting plea agreements. Every guilty plea is entered into the prosecutor's track record or "batting average" as a win. As a result, many prosecutors running for reelection will tout their better than 90 percent winning record.

Defense Attorneys

Standing in opposition to the prosecutor and the resources of the state are the defense attorneys and, while they are not completely powerless, they certainly are at a disadvantage in comparison with the judges and prosecutors. Defense attorneys represent a much more diverse group of individuals than do judges and prosecutors. This is the case because there are two distinct ways in which defendants can procure the services of an attorney.

Defendants with the economic resources can hire their own attorneys. By contrast, indigent defendants cannot afford counsel, and they must rely on the courts (supported by the Sixth Amendment of the U.S. Constitution) to appoint attorneys for them. Indigent defense now has a long history of constitutional development, including the following cases:

- *Powell v. Alabama* (1932)—the famous "Scottsboro Boys" case held that under the Sixth Amendment's "right to counsel" provision the state was obligated to provide attorneys to indigent defendants in capital cases.

- *Gideon v. Wainwright* (1963)—*Gideon* expanded the right to counsel protection to state felony cases that were not capital cases when the defendant was indigent.

- *Argersinger v. Hamlin* (1972)—this case extended the guarantee of the right to counsel to all nonpetty offenses, which would include many misdemeanors (where there was the possibility of incarceration).

- *Douglas v. California* (1963)—the Supreme Court also found that the right to counsel should include state defendants who were indigent when they filed their first appeal "as of right," but later the Court refused to extend this right to second or discretionary appeals (*Ross v. Moffitt*, 1974).

Nationwide indigent defense is provided in a variety of ways (DeFrances and Litras 2000). For instance, the system that has almost become synonymous with indigent defense is the *public defender system*. Public defender representation was first utilized in Los Angeles County, California, in 1914. Today there are public defenders in over 1,100 counties (about one-third of the total) and these counties represent about 70 percent of the nation's population (Cole, Gertz, and Bunger 2004:175; see also Neubauer 2008). For the most part, this means that public defenders are found in the most urban counties, although 19 states have statewide public defender systems (DeFrances 2001).

Public defenders are the defense counterparts to the prosecuting attorneys. They are state-funded employees who routinely handle a high volume of indigent defense cases. Many of the assistant public defenders are recent law school graduates who have passed the bar exam and this position is their first taste of real "lawyering." A very small number will stay in public defense work their whole professional careers, but most will get some courtroom experience and move on to private law firms.

The second most common method for indigent defense is known as the *appointed counsel system*. The appointed counsel system is present in the majority of counties in the United States. However, since many of these counties are small and rural, the population represented by this system is much smaller than that covered by public defenders (Cole et al. 2004; Neubauer 2008).

Courts that utilize the appointed counsel system may vary in their approach. For example, in many jurisdictions judges will ask for attorneys to volunteer to take appointed cases on an occasional basis. The result often is that the least experienced attorneys and those with declining practices (perhaps as a result of health problems) volunteer to take cases. The alternative is for judges to compile lists of all attorneys in the local bar association, with the understanding that each must bear an equal burden in providing counsel for indigents.

The attorneys appointed to represent indigent defendants are compensated by the county or the state at modest rates depending on the seriousness of the case. And while it is difficult to make a living taking appointed cases, it does provide the least experienced lawyers an opportunity to get more courtroom experience. As a result, there is a question about the adequacy of legal representation or comparative justice with paid attorneys.

A third system of indigent defense involves contract attorneys (see Worden's article in this volume). The jurisdictions that utilize this approach issue requests for proposals from law firms willing to provide indigent defense. A contract might call for the firm to provide 1,000 hours of legal defense work in a given year and the bidders will submit proposals saying how much they will charge for each hour of service rendered.[6] Bidders may submit one rate for the first 1,000 hours of service, and a higher bid if the work exceeds the proposed amount. In most jurisdictions, the contract must go to the firm that submits the lowest, best bid to perform the services. In this way the private sector is involved in the indigent defense process and the governmental body knows in advance what the services will cost.

Finally, there are a few other ways that indigent defense can be provided. For instance, in cities that have universities with law schools, second- and third-year law students get practical experience taking a "legal clinic" course and as part of the requirements of this course they work with indigent clients on minor civil and criminal cases where the state would not normally provide representation. Additionally, some cities have Legal Aid Societies where members of the local bar association can do *pro bono publico* (Latin for "the public good") work. Attorneys can donate their services freely for a certain number of hours per year.

All-in-all, providing legal services for those people who cannot afford them is a sizable undertaking in the United States. By some estimates, 60 percent or more of the criminal defendants in the United States cannot afford an attorney (Spangenberg et al. 2000). Many typically cannot make bail either. Therefore, based on the Supreme Court's interpretation of the Sixth Amendment, state and local governments must plan for ways to provide adequate legal assistance for indigent defendants.

Ancillary Actors

In addition to the core members of the courtroom work group, typically there are several other individuals who participate before, during, and after a trial. For example, in most court systems there is an elected or appointed court clerk. Court clerks have a variety of responsibilities, but one of the chief ones they perform in many states is assembling the pool of potential jurors (see Mays and Taggart 1986). Depending on state law or local customs, court clerks also may be responsible for maintaining court records and for docketing or calendaring cases.

Court reporters also will be present in the courts of general trial jurisdiction. They are responsible for maintaining a verbatim transcript of proceedings. This is important so that lawyers and judges can review what was said by whom at various points in the trial. Transcripts also become the mechanism by which an appeal can be filed. Throughout much of the twentieth century court reporters recorded what was said manually on machines that typed shorthand. Today, much of the recording is done with audio recording equipment or, in some courts, with video recorders.

Perhaps one of the most visible groups of ancillary actors in courts includes the bailiffs. Bailiffs are sometimes called court officers, and they may be members of the sheriff's department assigned to the courts, or perhaps retired law enforcement officers. They announce the arrival and departure of the judge and maintain security and decorum in the courtroom. In the federal courts, these functions frequently are performed by deputy U.S. Marshals.

A final group of actors that often are seen in courts today are interpreters. These specially trained individuals may be required to assist deaf defendants and witnesses, or they may be foreign language specialists. In effect, they have to be fluent in at least three languages: English, a foreign language or American Sign Language, and the court's language ("legalese"). In the federal courts and many state courts interpreters must pass a rigorous examination, and they must prove their ability to do simultaneous translations while court proceedings are moving along.

Critical Issues Facing the Courts

In some ways, there are an almost limitless number of critical issues facing the courts in the United States. However, in this section three of the most visible issues will be examined: workload demands on the courts, judicial selection and accountability, and judicial independence.

As was mentioned previously in this chapter, the courts in the United States have been looked to even more frequently to be the arbiters of society's problems. The criminal caseload has continued to grow in most courts around the country. However, the size and demands of their civil caseload are threatening the ability of some courts to dispose of criminal cases in a timely manner. We are facing additional demands from both sides (Rosenberg 1977). On the criminal side, we are dealing with what has been called a "crisis of over-criminalization" (Kadish 1967). Each year legislative bodies add more laws to the nation's criminal codes. On the civil side, courts are flooded with litigants who believe the courts are the most appropriate forums for resolving every imaginable social problem (Rosenberg 1977). The result is that courts are being asked to process more cases of all types, often with few additional resources.

In terms of judicial selection and accountability, a few examples will illustrate the dilemmas facing the courts. First, there is an ongoing controversy surrounding the methods of judicial selection, and this is directly related to the question of accountability. If we continue to use partisan or nonpartisan election systems, then judges are presumed to be more accountable to the citizens. However, election systems require judges to raise funds to run for office and often donations come from elite citizens such as lawyers and corporations that might come before them at later dates. As a result, the American Judicature Society has been a long-time advocate of the merit selection system (or the so-called Missouri Plan). Merit selection does not remove politics from the judicial selection process, but merely shifts it from the local level to the state level. While local political parties and professional associations may lose power, state bar associations, judicial nominating commissions, and the executive all gain power in the process. The bottom line is that no one system of judicial selection produces inherently better candidates (Canon 1977). In fact, we can say that any system is likely to select well-qualified or poorly qualified judges. Nevertheless, the next few decades will see additional calls to change the methods of judicial selection as political races get increasingly more expensive.

Finally, one of the "hot button" issues of the early twenty-first century is the degree to which courts are masters of their own fates (see, for example, Baker and Gregware in this volume). Several challenges are apparent in this area. For example, beginning with the presidential administration of Bill Clinton (and some would say before) and continuing through the two terms of George W. Bush, Congress has used its power to delay nominations to the benches of federal courts at all levels. At times, it seems like the president and Congress have played a game of "who blinks first" in terms of nominating favored judicial picks that have a difficult time making it through the senatorial confirmation process. Additionally, the "war on terror" has seen the creation of a judicial system—the Foreign Intelligence Surveillance Court—that is virtually beyond the normal review of civilian courts in the United States (Mays and Ruddell 2008). As a result, some have asserted that the courts have been co-opted or taken hostage by the executive branch (Baker and Gregware 2008).

The Future

So as we conclude this chapter, we are faced with the question: Where does this leave us? In some ways, the readings that follow will answer this question. However, as a foundation for these readings five summary statements seem appropriate:

- Throughout our nation's history there has been a dynamic tension between the courts and the general public, and between the courts and the "political" branches of government (executive and legislature). This is not likely to change. The judiciary has been described as the least democratic branch of government, and as a people we often are suspicious of imperious appearing offices.

- Our system of justice often is characterized as adversarial, but the reality is that much of what courts do is bureaucratic, routine, and administrative. The basis of the courtroom work group's functioning is that it can process cases in a cooperative way based on the "going rate" for cases.

- Juries seem to be the major way the public can interact with the courts, but people maintain a certain sense of ambivalence toward juries. For example, the average person would bristle at the suggestion that juries be eliminated from the criminal justice system (see Adler 1994). By the same token, many people ignore summonses to jury duty or they try their best to get out of jury service. Even when cases go to jury trial, the general public often second guesses the verdicts rendered by juries.

- The judicial system in the United States is an inherently political system. We can maintain a certain myth that impartial juries decide cases before disinterested judges, on the basis of clear evidence, but every part of the judicial system is imbued with politics (Levine 1992). In fact, political influence is apparent throughout the criminal justice system (and the civil justice system as well).

- In an effort to address more social ills, the courts will be forced to change some of their traditional procedures. This may involve less adversarial forums for settling disputes (so-called alternative dispute resolution) as well as specialized courts that focus on specific social problems.

As you read this book you may get answers to some of the questions that you have about courts. However, it is equally likely that you will have a lot more questions once you finish the book and whatever course in which you are enrolled. That is the fascinating and frustrating aspect about studying courts and the creative challenge we all have in working with courts to help them be better servants of the public good.

Notes

[1] The word jurisdiction has a number of different applications. However, in its simplest form it simply means the legal authority to hear and decide certain types of disputes.

[2] For more specific information see the volume by Rottman et al. (2000) or the Web site for your particular state. An outline of federal courts is provided by the Administrative Office of U.S. Courts at the following Web site: www.uscourts.gov/understand03/.

[3] I have made this statement many times over the years, and several years ago a group of students who were going to Washington, DC on a field trip decided to accept my challenge. They stood on the plaza in front of the Supreme Court building and asked people in line to enter the Court if they knew how many justices there were on the Supreme Court, if they could name the chief justice, and if they knew the name of one (or more) of the associate justices. Nearly two-thirds of those entering the building were not able to accurately answer the questions.

[4] The number of peremptory challenges allowed may be set by state law, or it may vary based on the type of case and the amount of pretrial publicity that has occurred.

[5] In most jurisdictions in the United States the judge is responsible for imposing the sentence. The major exception to this pattern is in death penalty cases where the jury rather than the judge must decide the sentence (see *Ring v. Arizona*, 2002).

[6] In some jurisdictions (Phoenix, Arizona, for example) law firms bid on the number of days of representation they will provide. In this system they represent all of the indigent defendants that appear for court on those days. Thus, they may represent many or few people who cannot afford a lawyer.

References

Adler, Stephen J. 1994. *The jury: Disorder in the court*. New York: Doubleday.

American Judicature Society. 2007. Merit selection: The best way to choose the best judges. Retrieved November 8, 2007, from http://www.ajs.org/js/ms_descrip.pdf.

Apodaca v. Oregon, 406 U.S. 404 (1972).

Argersinger v. Hamlin, 407 U.S. 25 (1972).

Ashman, Allan and Jeffrey Parness. 1977. The concept of a unified court system. Pp. 103–13 in *Managing state courts*. Editors Larry C. Berkson, Steven W. Hays, and Susan J. Carbon. St. Paul, MN: West Publishing Co.

Ashman, Charles R. 1973. *The finest judges money can buy*. Los Angeles: Nash Publishing.

Batson v. Kentucky, 476 U.S. 79 (1986).

Berkson, Larry C. (updated by Rachel Caufield). 2007. *Judicial selection in the United States: A special report*. Retrieved from http://www.ajs.org/js/Berkson.pdf.

Black, Henry C. 1991. *Black's law dictionary*. St. Paul, MN: West Publishing Co.

Calvi, James V. and Susan Coleman. 2008. *American law and legal systems*, sixth edition. Upper Saddle River, NJ: Prentice-Hall.

Canon, Bradley C. 1977. The impact of formal selection processes on the characteristics of judges—reconsidered. Pp. 126–38 in *Judicial administration*. Editors Russell R. Wheeler and Howard R. Whitcomb. Englewood Cliffs, NJ: Prentice-Hall.

Champion, Dean J. 2005. *The American dictionary of criminal justice*, third edition. Los Angeles, CA: Roxbury Publishing Co.

Cole, George F. 2004. The decision to prosecute. Pp. 178–88 in *The criminal justice system: Politics and policies*, ninth edition. Editors George F. Cole, Marc G. Gertz, and Amy Bunger. Belmont, CA: Wadsworth Publishing Co.

Cole, George F., Marc G. Gertz, and Amy Bunger. 2004. The adversarial process. Pp. 169–77 in *The criminal justice system: Politics and policies*, ninth edition. Editors George F. Cole, Marc G. Gertz, and Amy Bunger. Belmont, CA: Wadsworth Publishing Co.

DeFrances, Carol J. 2001. *State-funded indigent defense services. 1999*. Washington, DC: U.S. Department of Justice.

DeFrances, Carol J. and Marika F. X. Litras. 2000. *Indigent defense services in large counties, 1999*. Washington, DC: U.S. Department of Justice.

Douglas v. California, 372 U.S. 353 (1963).

Eisenstein, James and Herbert Jacob. 1977. *Felony justice: An organizational analysis of criminal courts*. Boston: Little, Brown and Co.

Gideon v. Wainwright, 372 U.S. 335 (1963).

Glick, Henry R. 1984. *Courts, politics, and justice*. New York: McGraw-Hill.

Hughes, Kristen A. 2006. *Justice expenditure and employment in the United States, 2003*. Washington, DC: U.S. Department of Justice.

Jacob, Herbert. 1984. *Justice in America: Courts, lawyers, and the judicial process*, fourth edition. Boston: Little, Brown and Co.

Johnson v. Louisiana, 406 U.S. 356 (1972).

Kadish, Sanford H. 1967. The crisis of over-criminalization. *Annals* 374 (November):157–70.

Kamisar, Yale, Wayne R. LaFave, and Jerold H. Israel. 1990. *Basic criminal procedure*, seventh edition. St. Paul, MN: West Publishing Co.

Levine, James P. 1992. *Juries and politics*. Pacific Grove, CA: Brooks/Cole Publishing Co.

Mapp v. Ohio, 367 U.S. 643 (1961).

Mays, G. Larry and Rick Ruddell. 2008. *Making sense of criminal justice: Policies and practices*. New York: Oxford University Press.

Mays, G. Larry and William A. Taggart. 1986. Court clerks, court administrators, and judges: Conflict in managing the courts. *Journal of Criminal Justice* 14(1):1–7.

Mecham, Ralph. 2006. Annual report of the director. Administrative Office of U.S. Courts. Retrieved December 3, 2007, from http://www.uscourts.gov/judbususc/judbususc.html.

———. 2007. Annual report of the director. Administrative Office of U.S. Courts. Retrieved December 3, 2007 from http://www.uscourts.gov/judbususc/judbususc.html.

Neubauer, David W. 2008. *America's courts and the criminal justice system*, ninth edition. Belmont, CA: Wadsworth Publishing Co.

Packer, Herbert. 1968. *The limits of the criminal sanction.* Stanford, CA: Stanford University Press.

Perry, Steven W. 2006. *Prosecutors in state courts, 2005.* Washington, DC: U.S. Department of Justice.

Powell v. Alabama, 287 U.S. 45 (1932).

Rehnquist, William H. 2001. *The Supreme Court*, revised edition. New York: Alfred A. Knopf and Co.

Ring v. Arizona, 536 U.S. 584 (2002).

Robertson, John A. 1974. *Rough justice: Perspectives on lower criminal courts.* Boston: Little, Brown and Co.

Rosenberg, Maurice. 1977. Let's everybody litigate? Pp. 270–79 in *Judicial administration.* Editors Russell R. Wheeler and Howard R. Whitcomb. Englewood Cliffs, NJ: Prentice-Hall.

Rosett, Arthur and Donald R. Cressey. 1976. *Justice by consent: Plea bargains in the American courthouse.* Philadelphia: J.B. Lippincott Co.

Ross v. Moffitt, 417 U.S. 600 (1974).

Rottman, David B., Carol R. Flango, Melissa T. Cantrell, Randall Hansen, and Neil LaFountain. 2000. *State court organization 1998.* Washington, DC: U.S. Department of Justice.

Schauffler, Richard Y., Neal B. Kauder, Robert C. LaFountain, William E. Raftery, Shana M. Strickland, and Brenda G. Otto. 2006. State court caseload statistics, 2005. Retrieved on December 3, 2007, from http://www.ncsconline.org.d_research/csp/CSP_Main_Page.html.

Schmidhauser, John R. 1979. *Judges and justices: The federal appellate judiciary.* Boston: Little, Brown and Co.

Spangenberg, Robert L., Marea L. Beeman, David J. Carroll, David Freeman, Evelyn Pan, David J. Newhouse, and Dorothy Chan. 2000. *Contracting for indigent defense services.* Washington, DC: U.S. Department of Justice.

U.S. Courts. 2007a. *District courts.* Washington, DC: Administrative Office of U.S. Courts. Retrieved October 29, 2007, from http://www.uscourts.gov/district-courts.html.

———. 2007b. *Judicial facts and figures.* Washington, DC: Administrative Office of U.S. Courts. Retrieved October 29, 2007, from http://www.uscourts.gov/judicialfactsfigures/2006.

Walker, Samuel. 2006. *Sense and nonsense about crime and drugs*, sixth edition. Belmont, CA: Wadsworth Publishing Co.

Williams v. Florida, 399 U.S. 78 (1970).

2

In the Eye of the Beholder
The Relationship Between the Public and the Courts

FRANCES KAHN ZEMANS

Courts as Institutions of Government

In considering the courts' relationship to the public it is appropriate to view the courts as institutions of government and to consider the public's relationship to those institutions more generally. For, as viewed by political scientists, courts very much qualify as political institutions.

The relationship between courts and the public is one of dynamic equilibrium much like that between citizens and other institutions of government. As diagrammed below, the public translates its desires and wants into demands on government.

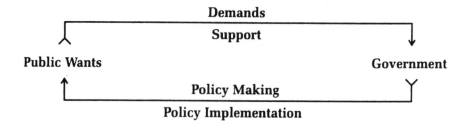

Reprinted by permission of the *Justice System Journal* from vol. 15, no. 2 (1991), pp. 722–740.

Government institutions (including courts) respond by developing policies and taking actions. Outcomes from government activity constitute the feedback to the public that they can evaluate to determine whether their demands have been satisfied. Satisfaction or lack thereof is then expressed in support for that government and/or in further demands upon it.

In practice of course, both support and demands are likely to occur simultaneously. On a day-to-day basis and under most circumstances the public is largely quiescent in relation to its government, thereby providing inactive support. As noted in a classic text on American government, "effective leadership indeed requires compliance with the leaders' decisions from the bulk of the members [of society] . . . most of the time" (Easton, 1975:185). In American society that compliance and support has generally been forthcoming. Political Scientist David Adamany has applied that concept to courts, noting that the public is generally supportive and "permissive." That is to say, the public is largely content to leave both the "agenda and initiative" for court reforms to those most involved in the daily operations of the courts (Adamany, 1978).

There have, however, been times in our history when the citizenry has become more vocal and active, demanding change to better satisfy their desires and wants. Public support for government is not a constant, but rises and falls over time, and the judiciary, as part of that government, is affected by those general shifts in public regard for political institutions. Thus, for example, in recent years we have observed a general decline of public support for government as evidenced in lower voter turnouts, a growth of ballot propositions by which citizens appropriate the legislative function, and widespread discussion of term limitations for office holders. This declining support affects the judiciary as well. For example, in 1990 Missouri's judges were retained in office by the lowest margins since merit selection was adopted in 1940 (Birkes, 1990). In other instances, public dissatisfaction has focused more specifically on the judicial arena.

One example has been society's periodic demands for greater access to justice for the legal claims of ordinary people, claims that are seen as too small to justify the time, money, and complexity involved in normal litigation. One institutional response to this demand was the creation and then national dispersion of small claims courts.[1] The growth of the legal services movement can similarly be viewed as an institutional response to demands by the public for greater access to the judicial system. The recent development of extensive alternative dispute resolution programs is another response, although it is not yet clear whether the public views this as satisfying their current demands for access to justice. (Compare this *Journal*, Volume 14, No. 2 [1990]).

By and large, however, the public has been, and continues to be, extraordinarily supportive of the judicial branch of government. An oft-cited example of this phenomenon was the Supreme Court's 8–0 decision that required then-President Nixon, despite his insistence otherwise, to cooperate in a criminal investigation by turning over his presidential tapes to prosecutors. Two messages of that decision were very clear and widely accepted. First, under a system that operates within the rule of law, even the rulers are subject to that law. Second, and more closely related to our concerns here, is that when it comes to a determination of whether the law applies even to the individual who has been elected by the people at large, it is the courts (and in this instance unelected courts) who are accepted as the appropriate decision-makers.

Courts are also significantly different from other political institutions. They are different in two very important ways that are worth addressing here. First, the courts are in many ways the institutions with which individual citizens most directly interact, or at least have the potential for interacting. Unlike other institutions of government where citizen action is most typically engaged in as a group activity (and indeed is most effective as a group activity), interaction with a court is by and large an individual enterprise. There are, of course, group actions in court and we continue to see attempts by organizations with particular interests to use the courts to achieve their goals. Still, that remains a relatively small proportion of the work of the courts. By and large the courts respond to the demands of individual citizens; it is indeed the one governmental institution for which a demand by a single individual is sufficient to evoke a full hearing. Such a hearing in some cases may even result in governmental policy-making with wide and long-term implications. The classic example is the case of Clarence Gideon whose pencil-written note to the Supreme Court complaining of a lack of a fair hearing because of his inability to pay for a lawyer resulted in a Sixth Amendment guarantee of free counsel in all felony cases (*Gideon v. Wainwright*, 372 U.S. 335 (1963)).

Second, and as we will see later, the public still considers the courts the place to go to get what is their due. In the aggregate these individual interactions with a large proportion of the citizenry provides courts with both a burden and an opportunity. Courts have an opportunity to engender a broad base of support that is necessary to the operation of governmental institutions; at the same time, that extent of interaction also opens the courts to demands for accountability and for responsiveness from a broad base of the society. We will return later to the implications of the double-edged sword of citizens' interaction with their courts.

Courts are also distinctive among the branches of government in the extent to which they are dependent on others for setting their agendas.

It is true that appellate courts by the nature and content of their decisions often send signals as to the kinds of cases and arguments that they would be receptive to hearing. Indeed even trial courts by the pattern of their decisions send signals that help generate the many settlements that occur in our legal system (see Mnookin, 1979). Still, as compared to other institutions courts are truly at the mercy of others for setting their agenda and determining their workload. One need look no further than the contemporary influx of drug cases in both state and federal courts to observe this phenomenon.

Courts are expected to continue their normal operations to satisfy demands of the populace over a wide range of issues and yet still handle the geometric growth in drug cases. Unfortunately, though perhaps predictably, political demands for the investment of more and more resources in drug enforcement almost always overlook the need to increase court resources in a like manner. Indeed, the courts are often projected in political rhetoric as part of the problem rather than part of the solution.

As Alexander Hamilton noted in *The Federalist Papers* No. 78, the courts have neither the power of the sword nor the power of the purse to enable them to address some of their most serious needs. While, according to Hamilton, that made the judiciary the least dangerous of the three branches of government, it also left it vulnerable to the support of others. It is often noted in the literature that courts must rely on general public grants of authority and legitimacy and that such grants are critical to their power and the role they play in our system of government. But relying on that kind of support can be hazardous, for unlike the other branches, the judiciary has few natural supporters. Most critically, the support the courts enjoy is diffuse support, that is, spread throughout the society as opposed to narrowly organized in the kinds of special interest groups that are so effective in generating both funding and support for particular governmental programs.

Public debate on issues like the exclusionary rule and judicial salaries is conducted largely in a substantive vacuum. Whatever one's view of the exclusionary rule, to be understood at all, it requires comprehension of the adversary system that structures our judicial process. Such understanding is clearly not widespread. The same can be said regarding the public debate over judicial salaries. The public support necessary for the courts to function is directly related to public knowledge and the level of public debate about our judicial institutions. Court personnel have a central role to play. For communication between the courts and the citizenry can help build the constituency necessary to support the courts and enhance the perceived and actual quality of justice.

Public Knowledge of the Courts

A treasury of anecdotes could be offered to make the point that this theme might well be public ignorance, not knowledge, of the courts. There is also considerable systematic documentation of the breadth of public misunderstanding of the courts. The results of a survey commissioned by the *National Law Journal* and LEXIS to mark the 200th anniversary of the establishment of the Supreme Court is a recent case in point. The survey found that less than a quarter of Americans over the age of 18 knew the number of justices on the United States Supreme Court (*National Law Journal* 1990:1). Close to two-thirds of the respondents could not name a single justice (a note of interest is that the best known justice was Sandra Day O'Connor). Such ignorance of the judicial system has been documented more than once. A 1978 survey by Yankelovich, Skelly and White revealed the public's self-perceived lack of familiarity with the federal, state, and local courts. From 63 percent to 77 percent of the respondents reported knowing very little or nothing about the courts (Yankelovich, 1978). "The American public, the Media and the Judicial System," a national survey sponsored by the Hearst Corporation in 1983, had similar results. The survey revealed that the public feels least informed about the judicial system as compared to other branches of government; responses to other questions indicate the validity of that perception. For example, 77 percent of the respondents believe that every decision by a state court can be reviewed and reversed by the U.S. Supreme Court, and less than half (44%) know that federal judges are appointed for good behavior. Unfortunately, most undergraduate curricula do little to address this problem.

Several years ago the American Judicature Society surveyed major American government textbooks and a more limited number of state government and urban politics texts and discovered that despite the co-equal formal status of the judicial branch of government, it is accorded only limited attention in the teaching of American government. Moreover, it is typically treated as a separate module without integration with other topics. The presentation goes something like this. A brief reference to Article III of the United States Constitution is followed by a short discussion of the United States Supreme Court. The Court, students are told, decided *Marbury v. Madison* and *Brown v. Board of Education*, among other cases. After the appropriate discussion of the relevance of these to judicial review and the civil rights movement respectively, little more is said about the third branch of government. The not very subliminal message conveyed by this brief coverage and quick progression to other topics is that the courts are not very important to understanding our system of government.

Some years ago A. Bartlett Giamatti, then President of Yale University, in a speech before the Second Circuit Judicial Conference expressed the need for general education in the law:

> I think America's ignorance about the law is neither inevitable nor trivial; I also think it is a scandal. And so must anyone who believes that the rule of law in a democracy must assume first comprehension on the part of the citizenry in order then to be effective on behalf of the citizenry. (Giamatti 1983:34)

What is to be done about this reality? And who is to do it? It will be a theme addressed later that it is in the self-interest of those intimately involved in the operation of the courts to attempt to fill this gap. But lest we think this job is an easy one, we need recognize not only that there has been a gap in education about the courts, but that the public is regularly exposed to misrepresentation of the judicial process that makes the job significantly more difficult.

The Courts and the Media

Media coverage of the courts takes two distinct forms, although it is not always clear which form contributes more to public misunderstanding of the courts. First, there is the entertainment side of the media, which devotes a significant amount of time to the administration of justice. Clearly, television networks and cable channels have discovered that the American public has an enormous appetite for this topic. There are the early entries like "The Defenders" and "Perry Mason," the latter of which remains popular in reruns and now is broadcast in a new and updated version. There is "Miami Vice," it too in continuous reruns in which almost every potential defendant is "taken care of" before entering the judicial process at all. There is, of course, "L.A. Law," the popular weekly night-time soap that is credited by many law school deans with having contributed significantly to the recent upsurge in law school applications. One can only wonder whether it is the intricacies of the law or the lifestyle of Arnie Becker that is the major attraction. "Equal Justice" appears to be the latest entry, modeled after "L.A. Law," but set in a metropolitan prosecutor's office.

And then there is the ubiquitous Judge Wapner who, as noted in a devastating review by D.C. circuit federal appeals court Judge Abner Mikva, may be the most troubling of all. Precisely because of the "veneer of realism" that exists in Judge Wapner's courtroom, the clear implication is that this is how the administration of justice works in this country, and how it ought to work (Mikva, 1989). The veneer of realism to which he refers and which he finds most troubling is that it "offers itself up as a slice of real law" (at 14). It has real people with real controversies. It has a real judge—or at least a real former judge, sporting the real trappings of a judge: a high bench and a black robe. After documenting a number of legal errors in Wapner's courtroom, Judge Mikva expresses particular concern about Judge Wapner's judicial temperament or lack thereof. In one example, Wapner ends the argument between two dog owners by announcing "there will be no more testimony. I'm leaving now." Judge Mikva notes that most real trial judges would be delighted to know that they could stop testimony whenever they felt like it. He concludes with his verdict that the show "does for law what Dynasty does for monogamy" (at 14).

The media, of course, do not have to rely on dramatic representations or fictional stories to present the judicial process in a way that will be appealing to the average viewer. As noted in a recent critique of television coverage, "trials that earn the most attention from local news and magazine shows, not to speak of docudramas, have all the elements of the nation's prime-time favorites: sex and violence, conflict and commotion" (Goodman, 1990: B1 and B6). Missing from this coverage, Goodman goes on to note, are the subtleties that are also involved in such major trials. The typical report conveys very little understanding of the law or judicial process. Goodman actually asks quite a bit more when pointing out that trials, in addition to being inherently dramatic, are "tests of the society, and the way those tests are conducted can reveal its strengths and weaknesses. That aspect rarely makes it to the tube" (Goodman, 1990:B1).

With the trend toward cameras in the courtroom (44 states allow cameras in some courtrooms and an experiment is being conducted in selected federal courts), there is an opportunity to do more; whether that opportunity will be pursued is as yet an open question. It is certainly the case that the trials that have received gavel to gavel coverage have, in most instances, also been the most sensational. Still it could be argued that gavel-to-gavel coverage will in and of itself bring out some of the subtleties and complexities that are inherent in any real trial. That opportunity is now being explored by a new cable channel devoted exclusively to the judicial process and the legal system. The channel will rely heavily on coverage of actual trials. What remains to be seen is whether it will do what it promises and use coverage of the courtroom to convey a true understanding of the judicial process.

As noted by Steven Brill, publisher and editor-in-chief of The American Lawyer Magazine and founder and president of the new cable channel, "the irony of the debate over cameras in the courtroom is that, of the three branches of government, the judiciary's work is clearly meant to be public and is clearly the most amenable to television coverage" (1990:3). Brill goes on to point out that the clarity of the judiciary's work is in stark contrast to coverage of the floor of the United States Congress or television speeches of the President. The bulk of the work of those branches of government goes on behind closed doors. What you see is decidedly not what you get. With the judiciary, what you see is precisely what you get. ABC Network News legal affairs reporter Tim O'Brien, in a speech at the Mid-year Meeting of the American Judicature Society, stated that the best kept secret in our government is just how well the judiciary works (1990:341). Perhaps done well, day-to-day coverage of trials with appropriate commentary will make that less of a secret.

There is more to news about of the judicial system than even that revealed in the coverage of sensational trials; it has to do with coverage that seeks to contribute to public understanding of how the process works and to examine the courts as institutions of government. It may be here that the journalists' lack of understanding is perhaps the most damaging and the most subject to manipulation by interested parties. News coverage of an unpopular ruling is illustrative of the problem.

Unlike other public office-holders, judges are little known to the citizenry at-large. If a mayor, governor, or legislator does something that enrages constituents, it can be put in the context of other information that is known and other policies that are attached to that governmental actor. For judges it is typically only the individual controversial decision that is the measure of performance. The public has no broader context within which to evaluate the judge.

It is almost unheard of for news reports on these kinds of decisions to include any reference to the fact that making unpopular decisions is part of the job of being a judge. That the role of the judge is to be faithful to the Constitution and the law even if the result reached is not the one preferred by the judge. There was, for example, virtually nothing in the very extensive coverage of the flag-burning case that in any way suggested that this decision did not mean that the United States Supreme Court was condoning flag-burning. While the media certainly have no obligation to address the institutional role of the courts, the reality is that it is not done elsewhere. Public reliance on the media for such information does at a minimum provide an opportunity for them to inform the public more broadly.

This is not to suggest that if only there were better media coverage of the courts the result would be strong public support for the courts. But better coverage and more information would be beneficial by generating respect for those aspects of the system worthy of respect, and generating demands for change in those aspects of the system that clearly bear changing.

Citizens' Experience with the Courts

Public opinion on any topic is influenced both by personal experience and by what one learns from others. As has been made clear elsewhere, attitudes about personal experiences may vary significantly from views about the operation of institutions more generally. For example, Curran (1977) has documented that members of the public have much more positive attitudes toward their own lawyers based on actual experience with those lawyers than they do toward the legal profession as a whole. To the extent that the same may be true with regard to the judiciary, it is worth considering some recent studies that examine public views about the courts based on personal experience.

The first is a study conducted by psychologist Tom Tyler based on a survey of Chicago residents. Close to 1,600 respondents were first interviewed by telephone in 1984; a subsample of more than 800 respondents was subsequently reinterviewed in 1985. Focusing particularly on the courts and the police, the study examined personal contacts that citizens had with authorities where they had a "personal stake in the situation." The research indicates that the attitudes of the citizens who have participated in the judicial process is not so much a matter of whether they have won or lost, but very much a matter of how they perceive they have been treated. People seem to care most about having neutral, honest authorities who allow them to state their views and who treat them with dignity and respect. Interestingly, judgments of that fairness are independent of success in the courtroom. The study demonstrates that people comply with the law if they feel that legal authorities are legitimate, and views of that legitimacy are linked to the perceived fairness of the procedures used by those legal authorities (Tyler, 1990). The message to judges and court administrators may be that the treatment of judicial system clients will have a major impact on how those people view that system. In the aggregate those experiences may bear on the extent to which the public will grant the authority and legitimacy that the judicial system needs to fulfill its role.

Another recent study may shed some interesting light on the findings of the 1978 Yankelovich survey referred to earlier. It was found in the earlier study that courts dealing with minor criminal and juvenile matters receive more unfavorable ratings than civil and major criminal courts (Mahoney, et al., 1978:83). To some extent that may be a reflection of Tyler's findings that attitudes are particularly influenced by perceptions of fair treatment. For it is precisely in the high-volume minor criminal and juvenile courts where the formal procedures that may generate a sense of fairness are sometimes short-circuited in the interests of moving the caseload. But it also may be that those somewhat more negative views reflect a significant variance between court personnel and the public as to what it is that courts can and should achieve in dealing with what the system views as relatively minor matters.

Merry (1990) recently examined the use of courts for help with personal problems such as protection from violence, controlling neighbors and relatives, or managing rebellious teenagers. What she found was that plaintiffs come to court with a very different view from the one with which they are received. They come with a sense of entitlement and a desire to assert legal claims. They want to get the zero-sum game that they view on television dramatizations of the courtroom. They want a winner and a loser; they want an assertion of who is right and who is wrong and they want those deemed wrong to be punished. The courts, in contrast, receive these claims with great ambivalence. Court personnel try to provide help for what they see as problems rather that to focus on underlying legal claims. Many complaints are seen by the courts as frivolous, with lectures or direction to social service agencies deemed appropriate responses. Yet what the plaintiffs want is protection or punishment. The fact that many or most of these claims are interpersonal in nature does not diminish the plaintiffs' perceptions of legal entitlement.

This discontinuity between what the claimants seek and the way in which the courts respond may help explain why burgeoning alternative dispute resolution mechanisms are still a supply largely in search of a demand. For there remains an enormous reservoir of public trust in the courts and a belief that the courts are responsible to citizens as Americans to protect their rights to property and their safety (Merry, 1990:2). These claimants over so-called minor issues find it easy to get into court, but much more difficult to get a hearing before a judge; and they find it even more difficult to get punishment for an adversary or an abusive spouse (Merry, 1990:3).

It is in this context that nonjudicial court personnel exert great influence on public perceptions of the courts. According to Merry, the courts these people get are not those of elaborate procedures and complex rules. Rather they are exposed to informality and the attention of lesser court actors. Yet the working poor she studied "share the common American understanding that all members of society are entitled to ask the courts for help in protecting their fundamental rights" (Merry, 1990:17).

Whose Courts Are They Anyway?

In 1979 the Wingspread Conference on Contemporary and Future Issues in the Field of Court Management was held in Racine, Wisconsin. The goal was to review developments in court administration and to consider contemporary and future issues in the field. According to the conference reporters, one conferee characterized the public view of the courts as "a private game preserve in which judges, lawyers and frequent litigants romp playfully while those who foot much of the bill watch from over the fence" (Nejelski and Wheeler, 1979:10). There are many who would suggest that little has changed since then.

The *Report of the Federal Courts Study Committee* unfortunately reflects the same reality. The report proposed an extraordinary number of substantive changes in the operation of the courts that were clearly designed to enhance the administration of justice in the United States. Yet the work of the Committee as reflected in the report looked inward. The Committee gave little cognizance to the important link between the courts and the public they were created to serve. The suggested designation of a media contact person for each of the federal circuits (*Report*, 1990:164) does not serve this purpose, for it focuses on improving the image of the courts rather than enhancing public understanding. In reflecting upon its burdensome caseload the *Report* goes on to comment that "many . . . people do not realize, however—or do not care—that the demands they place on the system make it less able to serve the needs of other groups, or even their own needs in the long run" (*Report*, 1990:4). At the same time, however, the Committee fails to acknowledge that the taxpayers are unlikely to foot the bill for a system they do not see as closely tied to their own lives.

Another recent example of a similar attitude toward the public is found in *The Report of the Twentieth Century Fund Task Force on Judicial Selection* (1989), which made a number of suggestions to enhance our system of selecting federal judges. The attitude toward the public is expressed in two ways in the report. First, and to its credit, the task force recommends the following: bipartisan nominating commissions to screen and recommend nominees, advance announcement of confirmation hearings on nominees, and open Senate subcommittee hearings in the locale of the vacancy (*Report*, 1989). Unfortunately, the task force fails to mention any role that the public could appropriately play in this process. Instead they emphasize the importance of participation by leaders of state and local bar associations and of announcing the upcoming confirmation hearings in legal newspapers and periodicals. While that is certainly proper, the report would have done well to consider the role that non-lawyer members of the general public should play in the selection of federal judges and how notice of hearings for that consideration might be communicated to them.

When it came to Supreme Court nominations, the task force, (although with some dissent) suggested that to depoliticize the process nominees should no longer appear before the Senate Judiciary Committee. While depoliticization of that process may be a worthy goal, Senate confirmation is intended to be a democratic check on a non-democratic branch of government. To exclude the populace from that process smacks of an elitism that is untenable in a democratic society.

There are a whole host of other examples that reflect a disdain for the public and their ability to participate in and understand the judicial process. These include objections to juror participation in complex trials, a hesitancy (if not outright objection) to allowing cameras into public courtrooms, and a hesitancy (if not outright objection) to more active juror participation in trials through both note-taking or jurors asking questions of witnesses. It should be noted that judicial experience with cameras in the courtroom, juror note-taking, and juror question-asking tends to make judges more positive toward these mechanisms. Still, they are resisted in a way that the public can certainly interpret as a closing of ranks and containment of the judicial process for professionals only.

Language in the courtroom continues to be a problem both for jurors and litigants. The oft-quoted Will Rogers observation makes the point: "the minute you read something that you can't understand, you can almost be sure it was drawn up by a lawyer" (Wilde, 1987). A humorous example of this phenomenon in operation is quoted by 2nd Circuit federal appeals court Judge Roger Miner in a recent law review article. The courtroom exchange goes something like this:

Q. Mrs. Jones, is your appearance pursuant to a deposition notice which I sent to your attorney?

A. No, this is how I dress when I go to work. (Miner, 1989:6 quoting Lederer, 1987:33).

In addition, despite the yeoman efforts of many, by and large jury instructions continue to be written for appellate courts and not for jurors.

Closing out the public in the long run will not enhance the status of the judiciary or its capacity to make its unique contribution to our system of government. Public frustration is high, and we are seeing some of its results in efforts to limit the powers and prerogatives of the courts. Judicial responses to these efforts are too often framed in a rather simplistic separation of powers argument that sounds to the public suspiciously like "we are above it all; trust us, we will do the right thing." There are better and more articulate responses that can and should be made, but without greater public understanding of the process it is difficult to make them effectively.

Capacity of the Public to Know and Participate

Broad ignorance of the courts does not necessarily indicate a lack of capacity on the part of the public to better understand the American judicial system. There are numerous examples of direct public participation in the operation of the judicial system that suggest that not only does the public have the ability to understand and participate, but that they bring a very special and important perspective to a system that is otherwise operated by insiders. The most obvious example is the jury, even though as mentioned above there are continuing efforts to eliminate the right to a jury trial in highly-complex cases. Yet time and time again in very complicated and controversial cases juries exhibit the capacity to understand and to do justice. Several examples come to mind.

First is the now somewhat infamous Chicago Seven trial that was the federal government's attempt to establish criminal responsibility for the demonstrations and subsequent rioting that occurred surrounding the 1968 Democratic national convention. In that case the defendants, the defense counsel, the prosecutors, and even the judge each made their own individual contributions to generating a circus-like atmosphere that has no place in the courtroom. Despite that atmosphere, extraordinary media coverage, and the simultaneous prosecution of seven quite distinct defendants, the jury of ordinary citizens did a remarkable job fashioning different verdicts for each of the seven defendants. While the judge's contempt rulings were overturned on appeal, all of the jury's verdicts were upheld.

The next example is the well-reported Texaco-Penzoil case. One of the arguments made by Texaco in the trial was that there were industry standards and complex issues that jurors could not understand. But the jury understood rather clearly. Their conclusion was that "a deal is a deal." As intended in our common-law system the jury brought community notions of fairness and justice to bear in their decision making.

A third and final case appropriate to mention in this context is the prosecution of Imelda Marcos. There in the glare of a highly-public prosecution with the investment of enormous amounts of government resources, the jury stood their ground and entered a not guilty verdict.

Other examples of public participation in the judicial process include non-lawyer membership in judicial nominating commissions in merit selection states and in judicial conduct commissions in all 50 states and the District of Columbia. In both of these contexts, non-lawyers bring a very special perspective to selecting and evaluating candidates for judicial office and then determining whether or not judges should be subject to discipline. The experience of the American Judicature Society working with both judicial nominating commissions and judicial conduct commissions suggests that non-lawyers take their roles in those processes extremely seriously. The role of lawyers, and in some case judges, on those bodies is certainly critically important. But non-lawyers often see things quite differently and bring a public perspective that is invaluable. Such public participation may also generate broad support for the institution.

What Can Be Done and Who Is to Do It?

More than a decade ago at the Wingspread Conference a sharp distinction was drawn between "taking the courts' case to the public and recognizing communication as an organic relationship from which courts can learn as well as teach" (Nejelski and Wheeler, 1979:10). There was a call for dialogue between the judiciary and other segments of the society emphasizing that "improved communications is a two-way street: courts must be prepared to listen to 'outsiders' as well as to convey information about themselves" (Mahoney, et al., 1978:91).

A true dialogue requires a degree of mutual respect between participants. Such respect for the public must pervade the system if the courts wish the larger society to believe that they are in the business of providing justice. Despite this, our mechanisms for selecting and evaluating those seeking positions as judges, court managers, or other court personnel give scant attention to these issues.

We neither train nor provide incentives for court personnel to treat the public with respect or to view them as having worthy ideas to improve the administration of justice. It may well be that the courts could learn from private industry how to best serve their customers, to learn what they want and to shape their behavior accordingly. Viewing the public as consumers to be satisfied is not at all natural for institutions that have had a traditional monopoly on services. But as is clear for courts, schools, prisons, and other institutions, competitive alternatives are emerging that are challenging public monopolies. For all of these it is not only a question of losing "customers" but of losing the public support necessary if the courts are to fulfill their role in our system of government.

Much communication with the public necessarily occurs through the media. Here too, the courts are capable of doing much more. While public information officers for court systems may be a good idea, they can play only a small part in the important process of communication. Courts can work with the press and make it easier for them to find answers to their questions. A simple "no comment" is neither required by standards of judicial ethics nor is it very effective. It serves only to enhance public perceptions that this is a system closed to them. Judge Nat Hentel of the Supreme Court of New York, appearing on a panel devoted to "[j]udges, critics and the public interest: balancing competing values," suggested that judges take the responsibility of educating journalists and use them as surrogates to educate the public (*Judicature*, 1989:231). Such efforts, however, cannot be postponed until election time. There must be more general accessibility if genuine communication is to be achieved.

The argument for the courts to increase their interaction with the media is not based solely on the courts' need to be understood. More importantly, the public needs to know what their courts are doing. Ongoing communications also provide opportunities to move from a discussion of an individual case to consideration of the judicial process more generally; it allows an opportunity to clarify the limits that the people, through their legislators, place on judicial decision making. At the appellate level, for example, reporters can be given advance notice of decisions and the date that they will be announced, allowing reporters the opportunity to give more time and thoughtful analysis to the case at hand. Availability to the press and public will of course increase accountability and produce predictable moments of discomfort. Caution is advisable so as to provide appropriate information without violating ethical restraints. But it is unacceptable and dysfunctional for judges to hide behind those restraints and thereby contribute to public misunderstanding of the judicial process.

Many courts are not only aware of a need for increased and better communications with the public, but many have acted upon that belief by developing a variety of creative programs. For example, the Administrative Office of the California Supreme Court has set up public meetings with judges around the state. The meetings last three hours and invite the public to ask general questions about the operation of the courts in that jurisdiction and to get answers directly from their judges. Response has been favorable among the citizens as well as the judges. The State of Colorado has two groups active in giving information about the courts to the public, the Colorado Judicial Planning Council Forum and the Colorado Judicial Institute. The Planning Council Forum, appointed by the Chief Justice, provides a speakers' bureau to citizens' groups. The Judicial Institute provides in-service teacher training, mock trial competition, publications, and public forums for discussion of matters involving the courts. In addition, the Colorado Supreme Court itself holds oral arguments at selected high schools around the state after first supplying teachers with the briefs in the cases to assist them in preparing their students. The State of Nebraska publishes a book for the public on the organizational structure of the Nebraska courts, and in Hawaii there is a simple but effective booklet on the judicial selection method used in that state.

What else can be done? The answer is many things indeed. At a May, 1990 conference on "The Future and the Courts," co-sponsored by the American Judicature Society and the State Justice Institute, participants were required to look into the future and see the justice system as they envisioned it would become. Upon establishing a variety of possible futures, participants were asked to choose their preferred vision and then to develop strategies that would be most likely to achieve it. The range of suggestions reflects a strong preference for judicial proactivity in relationship to the American public.

Suggestions included the following:

- develop a response office to answer questions from the public and interpret the process for them, to refer complainants to appropriate agencies and services, and to develop emergency legal triage;
- create a court ombudsman;
- develop programs to identify the functionally illiterate who could not possibly successfully manage their way through the judicial system as it is currently structured;
- create citizen advisory panels;
- expand court hours to nights and weekends;
- develop courthouses on wheels;
- open court proceedings to real-time media coverage;
- increase use of lay advocates;
- simplify language and procedures; and
- conduct market surveys of the consumers of court services. (1990:17)

While not every suggested strategy constituted efforts to increase the dialogue with the public and/or make the courts more user-friendly, many of those involved in the conference were struck by the consistency of support for more proactive efforts to achieve genuine communication with and provide service for the public at large.

How do we get the public to identify independence and intellectual honesty as virtues to be supported in our judicial system? How do courts get the public support they need if they are to act effectively on behalf of the public? These are difficult questions and we have only scratched the surface of possible answers; but several things are clear. It will take effort and it will take time, and it will take a willingness to accept the criticism and increased demand for accountability that will come with more understanding. Most of all, it will take commitment on the part of those involved in the courts.

Endnote

[1] For a discussion of the emergence of small claims courts see Steele (1981: 293).

References

Adamany, David (1978) *The Implementation of Court Improvement.* Williamsburg, VA: National Center for State Courts.

Birkes, Keith (1990) "Conversation with Kathleen M. Sampson," November.

Brill, Steven (1990) "Watching the Drama of Justice," *The American Lawyer,* July.

Curran, Barbara (1977) *The Legal Needs of the Public.* Chicago: American Bar Foundation.

Dator, James A. and Sharon J. Rodgers (1990) *The Future and the Courts Conference Executive Summary.* Chicago: American Judicature Society.

Easton, David (1975) *The Political System.* Chicago: University of Chicago Press.

Giamatti, A. Bartlett (1983) "The Law and the Public," 38 *The Record of the Association of the Bar of the City of New York* 34.

Goodman, Walter (1990) "TV and the Irresistible Melodrama of America's Legal System of Action," *New York Times,* July 26, B1 and B6.

Judicature (1989) "Judges, Critics and the Public Interest: Balancing Competing Values," 72/4 *Judicature* 226.

Lederer, R. (1987) *Anguished English: An Anthology of Accidental Assaults upon our Language.*

Mahoney, Barry, Austin Sarat and Steven Weller (1978) "Courts and the Public: Some Further Reflections on Data from a National Survey," in *State Courts: A Blueprint for the Future,* T. Fetter (ed.). Williamsburg, VA: National Center for State Courts.

Merry (1990) *Getting Justice and Getting Even, Legal Consciousness Among Working-Class Americans.* Chicago: University of Chicago Press.

Mikva, Abner (1989) "The Verdict on Judge Wapner," *TV Guide,* April 22, 13.

Miner, Roger J. (1989) "Confronting the Communication Crisis in the Legal Profession," 34 *New York Law School Review* 6.

Mnookin, Robert and Lewis Kornhauser (1979) "Bargaining in the Shadow of the Law: The Case of Divorce," 88 *Yale Law Journal* 950.

National Law Journal (1989) "Don't Mess with the Mouse," July 31, 1.

_____ (1990) "How Americans View the High Court," February 26, 1.

Nejelski, Paul and Russell Wheeler (1979) *Conference Report,* Wingspread Conference on Contemporary and Future Issues in the Field of Court Management. Institute for Court Management.

O'Brien, Tim (1990) "The Best Kept Secrets of the Judiciary," 73/6 *Judicature* 341.

Report of the Federal Courts Study Committee (1990).

Report of the Twentieth Century Fund Task Force on Judicial Selection (1989).

Steele, Eric H. (1981) "The Historical Context of Small Claims Courts," *American Bar Foundation Research Journal* 293.

Toward More Active Juries: Taking Notes and Asking Questions (1990) Chicago: American Judicature Society.

Tyler, Tom R. (1990) *Why People Obey the Law.* New Haven, CT: Yale University Press.

Wilde, L. (1987) *The Ultimate Lawyer's Jokebook.*

Yankelovich, Skelly and White (1978) "Highlights of a National Survey of the General Public," *State Courts: A Blueprint for the Future*, T. Fetter (ed.). Williamsburg, VA: National Center for State Courts.

3

On the Myth of Written Constitutions
The Disappearance of Criminal Jury Trial

JOHN H. LANGBEIN

We are accustomed to viewing the Bill of Rights as a success story. With it, the American constitution-makers opened a new epoch in the centuries-old struggle to place effective limits on the abuse of state power. Not all of the Bill of Rights is a success story, however. While we are celebrating the Bill of Rights, we would do well to take note of that chapter of the Bill of Rights that has been a spectacular failure: the Framers' effort to embed jury trial as the exclusive mode of proceeding in cases of serious crime.

I. The Constitutionalization of Jury Trial

The Sixth Amendment says: "In *all* criminal prosecutions, the accused shall enjoy the right to a speedy and public trial, by an impartial jury of the State and district wherein the crime shall have been com-mitted. . . ."[1] "All" is not a word that constitution-makers use lightly. The drafters of the Sixth Amendment used it and meant it. Indeed, the Framers of the Constitution had already used the same word for the same

Reprinted with permission of the *Harvard Journal of Law and Public Policy* from vol. 15, no. 1 (winter, 1992), pp. 118–127.

end when speaking to the same subject two years earlier. Article III of the Constitution insists: "The Trial of *all* Crimes, except in Cases of Impeachment, shall be by Jury. . . ."[2]

Two hundred years later, this Constitution and its Bill of Rights continue to govern our criminal justice system. Indeed, because the Sixth Amendment has been treated as incorporated by the Fourteenth Amendment, the federal jury guarantee now governs not only in the federal courts that the Framers had in mind, but also in the state systems where we process the bulk of our criminal caseloads.[3]

Although the texts mandate jury trial for "all" criminal cases, the reality is far different. In place of "all," a more accurate term to describe the use of jury trial in the discharge of our criminal caseload would be "virtually none." Like those magnificent guarantees of human rights that grace the pretended constitutions of totalitarian states, our guarantee of routine criminal jury trial is a fraud.

This article discusses the astonishing discrepancy between what the constitutional texts promise and what the criminal justice system delivers.

II. Non-Trial Procedure

Why did the Framers call for jury trial in "all" criminal cases? They prescribed "all" because they experienced "all." In the world in which they lived, on both sides of the Atlantic, cases of serious crime systematically went to full jury trial. Jury trial was the routine dispositive proceeding of Eighteenth-Century Anglo-American law. We have historical records from the English sources of a few Eighteenth-Century cases in which some pathetic accused, caught in the act or otherwise sensing the hopelessness of his case, attempted to plead guilty. In these cases, the trial judge resisted accepting the guilty plea. Time and again the judge urged the accused to plead "not guilty" and to take his case to the jury.[4] The great historian of English criminal law, John Beattie of Toronto, has studied this question closely in the surviving Eighteenth-Century records of the county of Surrey, south of London. He reports: "Virtually every prisoner charged with a felony insisted on taking his trial, with the obvious support and encouragement of the court. There was no plea bargaining in felony cases in the eighteenth century."[5]

Return now from the Framers' world of routine jury trial to the practice of our own day. The Constitution has not changed, the Bill of Rights remains in force, and jury trial lives on in the law books as our prototypical mode of discharging cases of serious crime. Furthermore, were you to form your impression of modern American criminal procedure from our popular culture, as nonlawyers and foreigners tend to do, you would scarcely have occasion to notice that anything has changed. Television is busy broadcasting courtroom dramas that culminate in the verdict of a criminal jury trial.

Those who understand our criminal justice system know better. Criminal jury trial has all but disappeared in the United States. Can you find it? Of course, you can find it. You can find it in the show trials of the day, Oliver North, General Noriega, or whatever. But jury trial no longer typifies our system. Can you find a hippopotamus in the Bronx? Yes, there's one in the Bronx Zoo, but it has nothing to do with life in the Bronx. It's a goner. And so, too, stunningly, is criminal jury trial, which has ceased to typify American criminal justice. The criminal justice system now disposes of virtually all cases of serious crime without jury trial, through the plea bargaining system. This non-trial procedure has become the ordinary dispositive procedure of American criminal justice.[6]

The plea bargaining system operates by threat. The authorities who administer our non-jury and non-trial procedure tell the accused in effect: "So you want your constitutional right to jury trial? By all means, be our guest. But beware. If you claim this right and are convicted, we will punish you twice, once for the offense, and once again for having displayed the temerity to exercise your constitutional right to jury trial." Our authorities are, of course, more circumspect in their discourse. They do not need to convey this threat in the bald fashion that I have just expressed it. There is no doubt, however, that plea bargaining works precisely in this way. Whether plea bargaining takes the form of charge bargaining (a lesser offense in exchange for a guilty plea) or sentence bargaining (a reduced sanction in exchange for a guilty plea), the object is to coerce the accused to surrender his right to jury trial by threatening him with a materially greater sanction if he exercises that right.

In observing that the Framers spoke of jury trial in "all" cases of serious crime—that jury trial was their norm—I do not mean to say that they mandated jury trial. Jury trial was indeed waivable. Then as now, the defendant had the option to plead guilty. What he lacked was the inducement. Because prosecutorial authorities were not yet in the business of pressuring people to decline trial, the Framers did not forbid practices that they had no reason to foresee.

III. The Disappearance of Jury Trial

How did criminal jury trial disappear? There is much we do not know, but the historical outline seems tolerably clear.[7] The starting point is to understand that criminal jury trial as the Framers observed it on both sides of the Atlantic in the second half of the Eighteenth Century was a summary proceeding.

The trial that the Framers thought they were constitutionalizing was, by our standards, shockingly brusque and deficient in safeguard. In the Old Bailey in London, the principal court for the trial of serious crime in the Anglo-American world, a dozen or more cases of felony jury trial went forward in a single courtroom in a single day.[8] The procedures were crude. Lawyers were infrequently involved for prosecution or defense.[9] There was almost no law of evidence. The "beyond-reasonable-doubt" standard of proof was neither precisely formulated nor routinely announced.[10] There was no *voir dire* of jurors; challenge rights were virtually never exercised. Jurors sat on many trials during a single session, and many of them were experienced veterans who had sat at previous sessions. They received little judicial guidance and may not have needed much.[11] The accused conducted his own defense, usually without aid of counsel, and without being allowed to testify under oath. There was virtually no appellate review of trials. Indeed, capital convicts were usually executed within days of trial, unless the trial judge took the special step of reprieving the convict in order to allow post-verdict proceedings. Because the system effectively lacked appellate redress, there was no occasion for those features of modern trial practice that are associated with the enterprise of provoking and preserving error for appeal.[12]

We understand that a criminal procedural system so brusque could not have endured. The procedural system that the Framers presupposed when they constitutionalized jury trial was grievously deficient. No one can yearn for the good old days when an Old Bailey judge could try a dozen felons a day. The movement for greater safeguard in criminal procedure that intensified in the later Eighteenth Century and across the Nineteenth and Twentieth Centuries was benign in spirit, and it was in a deep sense inevitable. But there are many ways to increase the level of safeguard and, in the light of hindsight, one can see that the path taken in Anglo-American law was catastrophic. Whereas the Europeans of this period were refining the techniques of an increasingly trustworthy, officialized system of impartial evidence-gathering and prosecuting, the Anglo-American systems turned for safeguard down the path of partisan lawyerization. We came to experience the capture of the criminal trial by lawyers—lawyers for the defense and for the prosecution. The rise of the adversarial system led to the loss of the accused as a testimonial resource, and to the vast elaboration of the law of evidence and of trial procedure that was undertaken in a forlorn effort to regulate adversary combat. Jury trial was redefined as adversary jury trial. The explosive combination of adversary procedure and criminal jury trial produced a system so clumsy, so time-consuming, and so costly that, in the end, Americans found it intolerable to honor the Framers' promise to use jury trial in "all" criminal cases. As a result, the pressure to subvert adversary jury trial has grown ever more intense across the last century.

IV. Evils of Non-Trial Procedure

What is so bad about plea bargaining? A good way to approach that question is to ask why the Framers so valued jury trial. Plea bargaining suppresses both the jury and the trial. There are important virtues to each. The jury disperses power away from the officers of the state. Because the sanctions applied in the criminal justice system are so ominous, the danger of abuse of state power in criminal procedure is serious. Plea bargaining achieves just what the Framers expected the jury to prevent, the aggrandizement of state power. Plea bargaining transfers the power of condemnation to a low-visibility decisionmaker, the prosecutor. Because negotiation replaces trial, plea bargaining substitutes an essentially concealed procedure for the salutary openness of public jury trial. The prosecutor who operates the negotiated plea system exercises awesome powers, powers that were meant to be shared with judges and jurors. As a practical matter, plea bargaining concentrates both the power to adjudicate and the power to sentence in the hands of the prosecutor.

Plea bargaining is also wrong because it is coercive. A legal system that comes to depend upon coercing people to waive their supposed rights is by definition a failed system. The system can no longer function by adhering to its own stated principles. Plea bargaining puts the accused under ferocious pressure to bear false witness against himself.[13] As the disparity grows between the sentence offered for confession and the sentence threatened for conviction upon trial, the inducement to confess becomes ever more intense. I do not think that large numbers of innocent people are confessing themselves guilty to crimes committed by strangers. At the margin, however, such cases do indeed arise.[14]

The want of trial is also costly in another way. There is an important civic interest in having public inquiry and adjudication take place in cases of serious crime—a positive externality, the economists would say. Plea bargaining prevents the citizenry from learning about the circumstances of the crime and punishment. There is, for example, a lingering distaste among substantial sections of the American people about the way that James Earl Ray was sent off to prison in Tennessee. Without trial, we do not feel adequately informed about whether our institutions have responded fully and fairly to events.

In the end, however, the worst aspect of plea bargaining is simply the dishonesty. Charge bargaining has made our criminal statistics into hash. The person who committed murder is pretended to have committed manslaughter; the person whose real crime was child molesting is convicted of loitering around a schoolyard.[15] Not only has this willful mislabelling turned our criminal statistics into a pack of lies, it has also forced us into the widespread practice of preferring arrest records over conviction records for a host of purposes. Continental observers find our reliance upon bare arrest records in matters of sentencing and employment to be incredible.[16] And looming over the whole of the saga of plea bargaining is the lie that has to be lived to escape the Constitution and the Bill of Rights—the lie that persons accused of serious crime really do not want a jury trial.

V. Markets

The Supreme Court's justification for plea bargaining, though wholly unprincipled, possesses the virtue of candor. In *Santobello v. New York,*[17] Chief Justice Burger explained that plea bargaining is to be encouraged because "[i]f every criminal charge were subjected to a full-scale trial, the States and the Federal Government would need to multiply by many times the number of judges and court facilities."[18] Translation: We cannot afford the Constitution and the Bill of Rights. Sheer expediency is rationale enough for disregarding the constitutional texts.

The most prominent academic effort to justify plea bargaining is Frank Easterbrook's chilling paper, "Criminal Procedure as a Market System."[19] Easterbrook correctly observes that the behavior of actors in the plea bargaining system is market-like. Under the constraints of the system, they behave rationally, maximize their utiles, allocate their resources, and so forth.[20] It is indeed quite a glorious Turkish rug market that we have created in lieu of what the Framers designed. Easterbrook's paper assumes away the vital question, which is what purpose the Framers ascribed to jury trial. Did they mean for this entitlement to be sold at the Turkish market with the other rugs? I think not. They had public purposes in mind when envisioning that "all" serious criminal cases would go to jury trial. To say that we have constructed a market in criminal procedural rights is a condemnation, not a justification.

VI. The Fragility of the Written Texts

The disappearance of criminal jury trial offers as telling a lesson as one could wish about the myth of written constitutions. Constitutional texts do not enforce themselves. They require the adherence and support both of the social and political order and of the legal system and legal professionals. Plea bargaining has defeated the Constitution and the Bill of Rights because legal professionals—especially judges, prosecutors, and defense attorneys—have preferred the convenience of doing deals to the rigor of trying cases.

I am left to say that much more attention should be given to how we handle criminal adjudication. I believe that concessionary non-trial procedure is wrong. Condemnation without adjudication, which is effectively what we practice in the plea bargaining system, is wrong. On the other hand, we do not want to recover the procedural world that the Framers envisioned, the world of summary jury trial. Nor can we afford the routine adversary jury trial that is the norm of our formal law.

Events that we cannot foresee but whose happening we can predict with serene certainty will one day force us to rethink our failed system of criminal procedure. We will be driven to re-introduce some component of genuine adjudication into our criminal procedure, perhaps on the platform of the existing Rule 11 hearing that is at present mostly a formalism.[21] When we do, I hope that we might pay attention to the Continental model. More than a century ago, Europeans came to look at Anglo-American criminal justice. They took back with them the notion that lay participation in criminal adjudication is profoundly important, but they also came to the conclusion that systems of mass justice appropriate to urban industrial democracies could not use laypersons in the clumsy, time-consuming, costly fashion of the adversary jury trial. The Europeans devised ways of combining laypersons with professional judges in streamlined procedures that guarantee significant lay participation in every case of serious crime.[22] The result is that they have perpetuated more of our jury tradition than we have. They have a system of routine lay participation in every case of serious crime, whereas we have a system of full-dress adversary jury trial so complex that we must deny it to almost all defendants.

Endnotes

[1] U.S. Const. amend. VI (emphasis added).

[2] Id. art. III, § 2 (emphasis added).

[3] See *Duncan v. Louisiana*, 391 U.S. 145, 149 (1968). State constitutions contain similar guarantees.

[4] See John H. Langbein, "The Criminal Trial before the Lawyers," 45 *U. Chi. L. Rev.* 263, 278–79 (1978) (reporting cases).

[5] John M. Beattie, *Crime and the Courts in England: 1660–1800*, at 336–37 (1986); see id. at 446–47.

[6] In the state courts that handle most of the criminal caseload, 95 percent of felony convictions occur without jury trial; 91 percent are plea bargained; 4 percent occur at bench trial. See United States Dep't of Justice, Bureau of Justice Statistics, *Felony Sentences in State Courts: 1988*, at 1 (1990). Bench trial is a latter-day American novelty. See Susan C. Towne, ''The Historical Origins of Bench Trial for Serious Crime,'' 26 *Am. J. Leg. Hist.* 123 (1982).

[7] See Albert W. Alschuler, ''Plea Bargaining and Its History,'' 79 *Colum. L. Rev.* 1 (1979); see also Lawrence M. Friedman & Robert V. Percival, *The Roots of Justice: Crime and Punishment in Alameda County, California, 1870-1910* (1981); John H. Langbein, ''Understanding the Short History of Plea Bargaining,'' 13 *Law & Soc'y Rev.* 261 (1979); Mary E. Vogel, ''Courts of Trade: Social Conflict and the Emergence of Plea Bargaining in Boston, Massachusetts, 1830-1890'' (1988) (unpublished Ph.D dissertation, Harvard University, Univ. Microfilms No. 8901664).

[8] See Langbein, supra note 4, at 277.

[9] See id. at 282-83.

[10] See id. at 284.

[11] See id. at 276, 284.

[12] See generally Beattie, supra note 5, at 348-50 (describing the ''old'' form of trial); Langbein, supra, note 4, at 263.

[11] See John H. Langbein, ''Torture and Plea Bargaining,'' 46 *U. Chi. L. Rev.* 3 (1978).

[14] See Albert W. Alschuler, ''The Prosecutor's Role in Plea Bargaining,'' 36 *U. Chi. L. Rev.* 50, 61 (1968) (discussing an example of coercive plea bargaining).

[15] See David Sudnow, ''Normal Crimes: Sociological Features of the Penal Code in a Public Defender Office,'' 12 *Soc. Probs.* 255, 258-59 (1965).

[16] See Mirjan Damska, ''Evidentiary Barriers to Conviction and Two Models of Criminal Procedure: A Comparative Study,'' 121 *U. Pa. L. Rev.* 506, 533 (1973).

[17] 404 U.S. 257 (1971).

[18] Id. at 260.

[19] 12 *J. Legal Stud.* 289 (1983).

[20] See id. at 308-09.

[21] See *Fed. R. Crim. P.* 11.

[22] See John H. Langbein, ''Mixed Court and Jury Court: Could the Continental Alternative Fill the American Need?,'' 1981 *Am. B. Found. Res. J.* 195.

4

Legal and Democratic Subcultures
Understanding How the Law and Political Forces Shape Criminal Sentencing

MATTHEW S. CROW and MARC GERTZ

Introduction

The determination of punishment for individuals convicted of crimes is among the most important responsibilities of American courts. This sentencing decision affects more than the lives of offenders. It also impacts their families, victims, and oftentimes the community and society in general. The manner in which we choose to punish law violators and the criteria on which we base sentencing decisions speak to the integrity and legitimacy of our judicial system. This chapter discusses the effect of policy, law, and democratic influences on sentencing. By examining how these various factors interact to shape sentencing decisions, we are able to see that courts make important choices based on more than just the law. Instead, the law is one of several issues contributing to judicial decision making.

Judges and other judicial decision makers face a variety of influences and constraints on their sentencing discretion. Efforts to limit, control, and analyze discretion and disparity in sentencing outcomes are long-standing (Mitchell, 2005; Spohn, 2000). These efforts have had numerous consequences for the judicial branch of government (Tonry, 1996). They have also led to policy change across the nation. For example, in 1994 the U.S. Congress offered billions of federal dollars to states that transformed their

Written especially for *Courts and Justice*.

sentencing systems into determinate policies (Tonry, 1996). The goal of these determinate policies was to make sentencing more uniform, less biased, and more predictable. By 2003, 25 states, the District of Columbia, and the federal government had either implemented or were considering sentencing commissions and sentencing guidelines (Gillespie, 2003). Thus, the effort to implement determinate sentencing met with great success.

Throughout this time, research on sentencing has also contributed to a vastly greater understanding of the complex nature of judicial decision making. Researchers continue to analyze the sentencing process and the sources of disparity. This research contributes to a greater understanding of the complexities of judicial decision making (Albonetti, 1997; Johnson, 2005; Kramer & Steffensmeier, 1993). This chapter examines the effects of policy transformation on sentencing decisions. It also incorporates the perspective of lower court decision making developed by Richardson and Vines (1970) within the existing theoretical traditions within sentencing.

Strong theoretical traditions have been established by Albonetti (1991, 1997) and Steffensmeier and several colleagues (Johnson, 2005; Steffensmeier & Demuth, 2001; Steffensmeier, Kramer, & Streifel, 1993; Steffensmeier, Ulmer, & Kramer, 1998; Ulmer & Johnson, 2004; Ulmer & Kramer, 1996). Albonetti developed what has been termed the *uncertainty avoidance/bounded rationality* perspective to explain the diverse influences on sentencing decisions. According to this perspective, judges have limits regarding both time and the information they receive about each case. Because of these limits, they are unable to eliminate uncertainty regarding the appropriateness or consequences of their sentencing decisions. They attempt to reduce this uncertainty by developing *patterned responses* based on the legal information available to them. They also tend to associate certain groups of offenders with future criminal involvement (Albonetti, 1991).

Similarly, the *focal concerns perspective* also recognizes the limits on decision makers' time and information. According to this perspective, judges are guided by three main focal concerns when making sentencing decisions. The first focal concern is the offender's blameworthiness (culpability). The second is the need to protect the community (dangerousness of the offender). The third concern is practical constraints and consequences (is there enough prison space and whether the offender is capable of doing time in prison). Judges have limited time and information when making decisions. This requires them to base decisions on incomplete information. In response, judges develop a *perceptual shorthand* to help determine culpability, dangerousness, and constraints. Perceptual shorthands are based primarily on factors such as offense seriousness and prior record. However, stereotypes about certain groups are sometimes used to fill in the gaps of information regarding the focal concerns.

Existing sentencing research has examined the effect of both individual and contextual factors on sentencing outcomes. Individual influences include factors such as the race and gender of the offender. Contextual factors involve things such as characteristics of the surrounding community and the organization of the courts. In addition to examining individual and contextual factors, there is a need within the sentencing literature to analyze the impact of policy change. During the late twentieth and early twenty-first centuries, states and the federal government developed several sentencing reforms (Tonry, 1996). From a research standpoint, there is still relatively little that is known about the effects of these changes. Before we consider how individual, contextual, and policy factors influence sentencing decisions, we will explain the idea of legal and democratic subcultures.

Competing and Overlapping Subcultures

This chapter examines criminal sentencing by applying the perspective of lower court decision making developed by Richardson and Vines (1970). Richardson and Vines describe the influences on the judicial branch of government as stemming from a continual interaction between two subcultures. The complex interplay between these two subcultures shapes the judicial process and its outcomes. The relationship between the two cultures involves both conflict and synthesis. Conflict occurs when the two subcultures call for different things. Synthesis involves incorporating ideas from both subcultures through compromise. This interplay between the two subcultures can help to explain decision makers' use of *patterned responses* and *perceptual shorthands* as well as contextual influences in sentencing. We will return to this relationship shortly, but first we should discuss the differences between the two subcultures.

The *legal subculture* consists of the "rules and norms governing the judicial process." This includes "the sorts of guidelines judges should use in arriving at decisions" (Richardson & Vines, 1970, p. 8). Court actors are trained and socialized in this subculture through institutions such as law schools, bar associations, and judicial training. These institutions teach judges about the value of the rule of law and judicial self-restraint. This socialization results in a relatively stable set of perceptions and opinions regarding the role and operation of the judiciary. While differences certainly exist, the influence of the legal subculture operates to produce judges and other lawyers who think and act like lawyers. In other words, through formal training and socialization within the legal subculture, most judicial decision makers approach the law and the operation of the courts in a relatively similar way. The legal subculture emphasizes its "own unique methods, procedures, and logic" that set judges and other judicial decision makers somewhat apart from other political actors (Glick, 1983, p. 3).

The other subculture, the *democratic subculture*, is shaped by society's values and norms. Democratic inputs into the judicial system include public opinion and attitudes, the election of decision makers, and local and regional customs (Atkins & Gertz, 1983; Richardson & Vines, 1970). The democratic subculture includes the factors that affect politics and members of society in general. People of all walks of life are impacted by popular passions. This public opinion is shaped by historical and contemporary developments within democratic society. The courts can only survive in the evolving American democratic system by responding and reacting to democratic forces. For example, legislatures control budgeting, jurisdiction, and organization of the courts. Furthermore, judicial actors are selected through political means. Judges, prosecutors, and court clerks are popularly elected officials in many states. In fact, popular election or political appointment of judges is the norm in state courts.[1] This need to obtain public support helps to explain why judges and the courts often react to popular opinion.

According to Richardson and Vines (1970) the two subcultures interact to produce a judicial process influenced by both legal and political forces. In addition, the cultures oftentimes overlap. For example, changes in the democratic subculture can lead to adjustments within the legal subculture. The law and other aspects of the legal subculture are not developed in a static environment and are responsive to democratic influences. For example, legislation is often enacted in response to news-making events that result in public outcries and demands. Examples include "three strikes laws," sex offender registries, and drunk driving statutes. Similarly, alterations within the legal subculture allow for variations in the impact of democratic factors within the judiciary. Appellate court decisions often motivate popular movements supporting different sides of an issue. This can be seen with regard to issues such as abortion, same-sex marriage, and separation of church and state. As Richardson and Vines note, "in the performance of their role, the courts combine the features of both the legal and democratic subcultures, responding to the demands of both in a continuing dialectic of political conflict" (1970, p. 174).

This framework of legal and democratic subcultures is reflected in Savelsberg's (1992) discussion of formal and substantive rationality in the law and sentencing guidelines. *Formal rationality* in the law exists when judicial decisions are based on the legal criteria set forth by the rules governing the process. Formally rational law provides consistency, predictability, and uniformity. By contrast, *substantive rationality* in law involves the tailoring of judicial decisions to individual and social circumstances. It allows judges to partly base decisions on social rather than legal criteria. In other words, formal rationality in the law is associated with the cues from the legal subculture, whereas substantive rationality is connected to the democratic subculture.

Savelsberg (1992) and others (Johnson, 2005; Ulmer & Kramer, 1996) view contemporary sentencing policies as an attempt to restore formal rationality in the law. Under this reasoning, sentencing guidelines "attempt to cure several dilemmas" (Savelsberg, 1992, p. 1347) that emerged during the twentieth century, including sentencing disparity. Sentencing guidelines represent formal restrictions on judges' discretion. Guidelines are intended to drastically reduce or eliminate the harms associated with substantive rationality. The harms include bias in sentencing. These scholars argue that guidelines have failed to completely restore formally rational decision making into sentencing. This failure is due to problems relating to the design and implementation of the policies.

In our view, sentencing policy represents neither legal nor democratic subculture. Instead, sentencing policy serves as a filter through which the values of the democratic and legal subcultures compete and are synthesized. This process of competition and synthesis shapes the policies themselves. Sentencing policies are an effort to establish the legal values of consistency, predictability, and impartiality in the sentencing process. Yet, the guidelines themselves reflect popular democratic sentiments such as increased punitiveness or the reduction of disparity. Changes in policy can be viewed as alterations in the balance and blend of the two cultures. Some sentencing policies, such as Florida's 1994 sentencing guidelines, provide more restrictions on judicial discretion, thus reflecting a tilt toward the legal values of consistency, predictability, and impartiality. Other policies, such as Florida's Criminal Punishment Code, allow greater judicial discretion. This facilitates a greater role for democratic values of decision makers and of the communities that elect and potentially influence them. The inclusion of both legal and democratic values into the sentencing process should not be viewed as a failure of policy to formally rationalize the law. Instead, the mixture and synthesis of these two cultures is evidence of the judicial institution accommodating both legal and democratic values in an effort to adapt and persist in changing environments.

According to sentencing scholars, formally rational sentencing would consist of outcomes that are determined almost exclusively by legal factors (Dixon, 1995; Johnson, 2005). Measures of offense seriousness and criminal history are representative of these legal factors. These factors can be viewed as cues from the legal subculture. Substantive rationality in sentencing is indicated by the inclusion of extralegal or nonlegal factors as determinants of outcomes. These extralegal factors reflect the democratic subculture. According to Albonetti's (1991, 1997) *bounded rationality/uncertainty avoidance* theory, extralegal factors come into play in sentencing decisions as a result of *patterned responses* that link "specific defendant groups to future criminal involvement" (1997, p. 797). Similarly, Steffensmeier and associates argue that the influence of both legal and extralegal attributes in sentencing result from decision makers' consideration of the three focal concerns (Steffensmeier & Demuth, 2001; Steffensmeier et al., 1993). Legal factors help to inform decision makers about these focal concerns. They do not always provide enough information though. Since time and information are limited, judges often use stereotypical assessments of blameworthiness and dangerousness. Thus, judges' *perceptual shorthand* is based on cues from both subcultures.

Sentencing policy acts as a filter and should have an effect on the influence of legal and extralegal factors. A policy whose synthesis of the legal and democratic subculture dialectic tilts toward the legal subculture would likely reduce the influence of cues from the democratic subculture. Conversely, sentencing policies that allow greater discretion are likely to allow a greater influence for cues from the democratic subculture.

Sentencing Policy and the Legal Subculture

Judges are socialized through the legal subculture to uphold a certain respect for the law and legal procedure (Richardson & Vines, 1970). Thus, it follows that the law should affect judges and other judicial decision makers. As noted earlier, the formal legal cues available to judges in the sentencing decision include information regarding offense seriousness and criminal history. The legal subculture emphasizes the importance of these legal factors. Nevertheless, the discretion available to judicial decision makers varies depending on the sentencing policy. Some policies instruct judges to sentence offenders within narrow ranges of possible sanctions. Other policies permit broader ranges of sentences. For example, indeterminate sentencing systems are characterized by wide judicial discretion to decide sentences. Determinate systems limit the available sentencing options. It is generally argued that racial and other extralegal disparities in sentencing should be less likely under determinate systems (Wooldredge, Griffin, & Rauschenberg, 2005). This position asserts that determinate policies reduce the impact of personal and societal biases associated with the democratic subculture. This is thought to produce greater equity in punishment decisions (Blumstein, Cohen, Martin, & Tonry, 1983; Tonry, 1996; for a competing perspective, see Mauer, 1999).

Previous research provides some evidence of the effect of sentencing policy on sentencing decisions. For example, Miethe and Moore (1985) found that a shift from an indeterminate to a determinate sentencing system in Minnesota resulted in greater weight being placed on legal factors.

Miethe and Moore also reported that the effects of race were diminished under the sentencing guidelines. Similarly, Crow and Bales (2006) found that a complete restructuring of the sentencing guidelines in Florida had a direct impact on sentencing outcomes. The change also influenced how both legal and extralegal factors influenced sentencing outcomes. Their study reported that the transition from relatively loose guidelines to the more restrictive 1994 sentencing guidelines resulted in a stronger effect for many legal factors. The change also reduced the impact of race on sentencing outcomes.

Wooldredge and colleagues (2005) also examined the effects of moving from an indeterminate to a determinate sentencing system. The authors found only modest support for the contention that the shift affected sentencing decisions. Specifically, they reported that the change led to slight differences in how judges interpreted legal and democratic cues. Nevertheless, each of these studies indicated that the sentencing policies affect sentencing decisions.

While not extensive, the prior literature on the effects of changes in sentencing policy reflects the modification that occurred during the 1980s and 1990s. The synthesis of the legal and democratic subcultures experienced a transition in many jurisdictions during that time. Law makers drafted statutes and developed commissions to shift from systems characterized by high levels of judicial sentencing discretion to policies that curtailed that discretion (Tonry, 1996; Wicharaya, 1995). The three studies previously discussed shed light on the impact of restricting judicial sentencing discretion through policy transformation. It is interesting to note that in each study the policy transformation changed the effect of extralegal factors, but did not eliminate their influence. Instead, the courts adapted to the alteration in the balance between the legal and democratic subcultures while remaining accommodating to both.

Public Opinion, Race, and the Democratic Subculture

While the legal subculture provides an enduring influence on judicial decision making, these decisions are not made in a legal vacuum. Decision makers are not "judicial computers who take in a volume of facts, law, and legal doctrines and spew out 'correct' rulings—determinations that are virtually independent of the judges' values and characteristics as human beings" (Carp & Stidham, 2001, p. 284). Instead, judges react to and are influenced by democratic and societal pressures. In fact, Richardson and Vines (1970) argue that the courts have survived as an American political institution through their connection to popular sentiment. Judges must be somewhat responsive to the public will. This is particularly evident when one considers the fact that many judges throughout America face popular election of some sort. This is unlike the judicial selection process in nearly all other countries. In the United States, the courts are oftentimes considered the least democratic of American political institutions. Nevertheless, it is widely recognized that the judicial branch relies heavily on public opinion and support to establish and maintain its legitimacy (Caldeira, 1986; Overby, Brown, Smith, & Winkel, 2004; Tannenhaus & Murphy, 1981). Recent research has shown the importance of both diffuse support and specific support. *Diffuse support* involves positive public opinion for courts generally. *Specific support* relates to public opinion regarding particular judicial decisions (Rottman & Tomkins, 1999; Wenzel, Bowler, & Lanoue, 2003). In other words, individual judicial decisions and overall assessments of judges and courts influence public opinion and support for the courts.

When considering public opinion regarding the courts and judges it is important to understand what the public desires from the courts and the criminal justice system. Consider that Americans tend to have punitive attitudes toward crime and criminals (Beckett, 1997; Roberts & Stalans, 1997). Perceived leniency toward criminals is often a criticism of the judicial branch (Rottman & Tomkins, 1999). For example, approximately 80 percent of the American public believes that the courts are too lenient (Warr, 1995). Cullen and colleagues (2000) describe a 1997 survey that found that nearly 90 percent of adults were in favor of tougher sentences for criminals. The authors report similar findings from a 1998 poll in which "78 percent of the respondents 'strongly agreed' that 'we should toughen and strengthen penalties for convicted criminals'" (p. 27). Furthermore, the public tends to associate their desires for harsh punishment with prison sentences. According to Warr, "Americans overwhelmingly regard imprisonment as the appropriate form of punishment for most crimes" (cited in Cullen et al., 2000, p. 28). The public's desire for more punitive sanctions for offenders indicates a relatively clear message to the courts from the democratic subculture. Trial court judges need the courts to maintain institutional legitimacy. They also have the individual desire to get reelected. This could lead to judges feeling pressured by these democratic forces to increase sentence severity. While the implications of this input from the democratic subculture are straightforward, there may be less transparent consequences in addition to more severe sentences in general.

Several commentators argue that in American culture, crime is often associated with race (Beckett & Sasson, 2000; Russell, 1998; Szykowny, 1994). This association has been termed the "racial typification of crime" (Chiricos, Welch, & Gertz, 2004, p. 363). According to this argument, our culture tends to connect crime with racial minorities (Chiricos et al., 2004; Eschholz, Chiricos, & Gertz, 2003). According to Roberts, "race is used both to identify criminals and to define crime" (1993, p. 1947). Punitive attitudes are also related to this racial typification of crime. Notably, individuals who associate crime with minorities are likely to have stronger punitive attitudes toward crime (Chiricos et al., 2004).

We should also note that deviant and criminal behavior is also more often associated with men (LaGrange & Silverman, 1999; Liu & Kaplan, 1999). In addition, most research finds that males are punished more severely than females (Albonetti, 1997; Nobiling, Spohn, & DeLone, 1998; Spohn & Holleran, 2000; Ulmer & Kramer, 1996). While several explanations for these gender differences exist, some authors have advanced "paternalism" or "chivalry" hypotheses. It can be argued that sentencing women more leniently based on paternalism or chivalry is due to cues from the democratic subculture.

The public's fear of crime, the racial typification of crime, and the associated support for more punitive punishments may have implications in the form of unwarranted disparity in sentencing. Judicial decision makers are not only influenced by contemporary political and social pressures. They are themselves products of their social and political environments. Judicial scholars have long argued that judges are norm enforcers for their communities (Jacob, 1978). There is also evidence that their background characteristics affect their decisions (Nagel, 1962; Ulmer, 1973). As such, it is likely that the combination of fear, racial typification, and punitiveness in society will be partially reflected in the sentences of judges. Increased severity in sentencing policy could translate into more punitive sentences. It could also result in a greater likelihood of more severe sentences for racial minorities compared to whites. The race, ethnicity, and gender of the offender serve as cues from the democratic subculture regarding the culpability and dangerousness of the individual. The fact that many in the public associate racial minorities and males with crime suggests that judges' perceptual shorthand and patterned responses will incorporate these factors as indicators of blameworthiness and the need to protect the community.

Local Democratic Subculture and Sentencing Policy

One of the major aspects of Richardson and Vines' (1970) framework is their contention that trial courts are susceptible to local democratic forces. As Glick (1983) explains, "The content of court decisions also is likely to depend upon the *social context* in which the courts operate and the major values of people in the area" (p. 4; emphasis in original). It follows that community characteristics should play a role in shaping sentencing decisions. Several previous studies have examined the effects of community contextual variables on sentencing outcomes. While the findings are mixed, research suggests numerous contextual characteristics influence sentencing decisions. For example, unemployment rates (Myers & Talarico, 1987), racial composition, crime rates (Britt, 2000; Crawford, Chiricos, & Kleck, 1998; Johnson, 2005; Ulmer & Johnson, 2004), and political context (Helms & Jacobs, 2002) are all shown to affect sentencing outcomes.

In addition to these contextual factors, politics are a key to the democratic subculture. Political party representation in a community is one way to measure the cues from the democratic subculture. Several scholars have noted that Republicans and conservatives tend to show higher levels of support for harsher punishment (Barkan & Cohn, 1994; Borg, 1997; Whitehead, 1998). This association may be partly due to the Republican party campaigning on the crime issue and positioning itself as the law and order party since the 1960s (Beckett, 1997).

To examine these issues more closely, we analyzed sentencing in the felony trial courts of Florida. The analysis looks at sentencing outcomes under two distinct sentencing policies. The goal is to gain a better understanding of how several factors from each subculture affect authorities' sentencing decisions. We also aimed to determine how policy filters these factors to shape outcomes. Before we discuss the findings, it is helpful to gain a better understanding of sentencing policy in Florida.

Policy Transformation in Florida

Florida's sentencing policies have changed substantially over the past 30 years. Until 1975, the state operated under an indeterminate sentencing system (Griswold, 1985). That year, Florida implemented its first determinate sentencing measures in the form of mandatory minimum sentences for crimes involving the use of firearms (Griset, 1996). By 1983, Florida moved to its first sentencing guidelines system. These guidelines remained in effect until 1994 (Handberg & Holten, 1993).

The second system of sentencing guidelines is known as the 1994 Sentencing Guidelines. This was the guiding sentencing policy until 1998 (Griset, 1999). The 1994 policy was designed to be a highly deterministic sentencing system. It set relatively narrow ranges for sentencing discretion. It also drastically limited prison release discretion (Florida Department of Corrections, 2003; Griset, 1999). The guidelines utilized a point system based primarily on the seriousness of the current offense and an offender's prior criminal record. Point values determined the recommended sentence (Florida Department of Corrections, 1996). Within the policy, limited discretion was still available to court authorities. For example, judges could adjust sentence length by 25 percent and could depart from the recommended sentences. Although judges maintained a level of discretion over punishments, sentences that differed from the recommended sentence required written justification. These sentences were also subject to appellate review at the request of either the prosecutor or defense (Griset, 1999).

The Florida legislature transformed the state's sentencing policy once again in 1998. The move to the Criminal Punishment Code (CPC) in 1998 maintained the basic structure of the 1994 Sentencing Guidelines (Florida Department of Corrections, 1999; Griset, 1999). The new policy still calculated sentencing points in the same manner. The change occurred primarily in the severity of recommended sentences and the level of discretion permissible under the CPC. While the point calculations determined the recommended sentence, the policy gave judges the discretion to increase the sentence as they saw fit (Florida Department of Corrections, 1999). Moreover, the policy lowered the point threshold for mandated prison sentences. Thus, the maximum prison sentences allowed under the CPC were much more severe compared to the 1994 Sentencing Guidelines (Florida Department of Corrections, 1999; Griset, 1999, 2002). Upward sentencing discretion was virtually unbounded. The discussion below is based on an analysis of the 1994 guidelines and the CPC.

Legal and Democratic Subculture Effects in Sentencing

In Florida, there is ample evidence of a complex interplay between the legal and democratic subcultures with regard to sentencing outcomes. Sentencing policy also appears to operate as a filter that helps to shape how legal actors translate cues from each subculture into sentences. In the following sections, we will discuss how cues from the legal subculture and the democratic subculture influence sentencing in Florida. We will also discuss how different sentencing policies filter these cues.

Legal Subculture and Sentencing in Florida

The most obvious indication of an important role for the legal subculture in sentencing is the influence of the offense committed by the individual and his or her prior criminal record. The law dictates that judges more severely punish crimes that are more serious. Our research in Florida shows that the law is translated into harsher sentences for people who are convicted of more serious offenses. For example, individuals convicted of murder are generally more likely to go to prison and receive longer sentences than those convicted of burglary. Specifically, all else being equal, someone convicted of second-degree murder is 13 times more likely to receive a prison sentence than someone convicted of burglary of a dwelling. Likewise, if both offenders were sentenced to prison, the offender convicted of second-degree murder would receive an average sentence 23 years longer than the one sentenced for burglary. While this may seem to be an obvious outcome, it is still important evidence that the legal subculture works to influence sentencing. Sentencing authorities do follow the cues from the legal subculture when making their decisions.

Similarly, we find that offenders in Florida with longer and more serious prior criminal records are also punished more severely than those without a criminal history or with a less serious prior record. For example, offenders who were previously incarcerated one time are 61 percent more likely to receive a prison sentence than those who have never been in prison. For offenders sentenced to prison, those who have been in prison once before will receive sentences over three years longer than an offender who has never been incarcerated. Likewise, someone who has a violent crime in his or her criminal history is sentenced more severely than someone with a history of drug or property crimes. Once again, the law in Florida states that repeat offenders should be punished more severely than first-time offenders should. The fact that this is found to be the practice in the courts indicates that judges and other authorities are following the cues from the legal subculture.

The influence of offense severity and prior criminal record on sentences is a prime example of how the legal subculture affects sentencing. The law sets forth that more serious and repeat offenders should be punished more severely. Having been trained and socialized to adhere to the rule of law judges look to the law to help determine the proper sentences to impose. If the legal subculture were not a significant basis for sentencing, then we might find evidence that nonviolent burglars with no prior record were regularly sentenced more severely than violent sexual offenders with lengthy criminal histories. Fortunately, that is not the case. Our research confirms that the law matters.

The impact of offense severity and criminal history on sentencing also offers clues about the interaction between the legal and democratic subcultures. The law is not developed in a vacuum. Instead, humans who are subject to the same societal influences as everyone else draft laws. Thus, the severity of crimes and the laws that set forth how to deal with law violators partly are shaped by the democratic subculture. For example, armed robbery is deemed a more serious crime than forgery because most people in American society view it as having greater negative consequences on the victim and society. In addition, laws are often changed due to democratic pressures. For example, the statutory punishments for DUI were increased in many jurisdictions following pressure from groups such as Mothers Against Drunk Driving (MADD). Here we see the interplay between the legal and democratic subcultures. There is also evidence that the democratic subculture exerts its own independent influence on sentencing.

Democratic Subculture and Sentencing in Florida

Our analysis of sentencing in Florida found strong evidence that cues from the democratic subculture influence sentencing outcomes. First, it is important to note that the democratic subculture differs based on location. Different communities have differing norms, values, and mores. In Florida, despite the fact that the same criminal and procedural laws govern all jurisdictions, we found evidence that sentencing outcomes differ depending on where an offender is sentenced. In counties with more registered Republicans, offenders are more likely to be sentenced to prison. Political conservatism is often associated with more punitive attitudes toward crime. A community's level of conservatism influences the sentence severity within that jurisdiction. Similarly, a county's unemployment rate is also related to more punitive sentences. Unemployment rate is sometimes used as a measure of economic threat and a loosening of informal social controls. Thus, we see the democratic subculture influencing sentencing outcomes across the state.

We discussed earlier that American society tends to associate crime with racial minorities. It is logical to derive that the cues from the democratic subculture may support harsher sentences for minority offenders. These cues are translated by sentencing authorities into more severe sentences for blacks and Hispanics compared to whites. All else being equal, blacks in Florida are 51 percent more likely to be sentenced to prison compared to whites. Prison sentences for black offenders average two years longer than sentences for whites. Similarly, Hispanic offenders are 31 percent more likely to be sentenced to prison than white offenders. In other words, stereotypical assessments of dangerousness associated with blacks and Hispanics serve as cues from the democratic subculture. Judges and other sentencing authorities seem to be influenced by these cues and deliver more punitive sentences to racial minorities for the same offenses.

The results of the Florida sentencing analysis also show that males are sentenced much more severely than females. All else being equal, men are more than twice as likely as women to be imprisoned. Compared to females who are imprisoned, incarcerated men receive sentences nearly five years longer. These findings support the argument that decision makers are influenced not only by the law and legal subculture, but also by common stereotypical views that associate minorities and males with dangerousness and criminality. These results show that cues from the legal subculture affect sentencing outcomes, but cues from the democratic subculture also play a part.

Sentencing Policy as a Filter for Subcultural Cues

The preceding discussion demonstrates that both subcultures influence sentencing decisions. Legal cues in addition to stereotypical cues from the democratic subculture each play a role in determining outcomes. Sentencing authorities synthesize these cues when making their sentencing decisions. Our analysis of sentencing in Florida across two distinct sentencing policies indicates that this synthesis is partly shaped by the policy guiding the decisions.

As mentioned earlier, Florida transitioned from the 1994 sentencing guidelines to the CPC in 1998. This policy transformation is an example of the interplay between the legal and democratic subcultures. The policy was changed in response to public sentiments supportive of more punitive punishments for criminals. The legal and democratic subcultures interacted to influence sentencing.

Specifically, our analysis shows that sentencing was more punitive under the CPC. All else being equal, offenders sentenced under the CPC were 63 percent more likely to receive a prison sentence compared to those sentenced under the 1994 guidelines. Of those offenders sent to prison, those sentenced under the CPC received sentences nearly three years longer than those sentenced under the 1994 guidelines. While this result is perhaps not surprising, it illuminates how the two subcultures can interact to affect outcomes.

This analysis also shows the way policy seems to operate as a filter for the synthesis of the cues from the two subcultures. Compared to the 1994 guidelines, the CPC provided judges with considerably more discretion for deciding sentences. In effect, this change loosened the legal restrictions placed on judges' sentencing decisions. The shift in policy had several interesting consequences for how cues from the legal and democratic subcultures were translated into sentencing outcomes. When judges were given more discretion under the CPC there was greater racial and ethnic disparity in sentence severity. When the legal restrictions on judges' ability to tailor sentences to individual offenders were loosened, the decision makers' *perceptual shorthand* was more likely to be influenced by cues from the democratic subculture. When judges had less discretion under the 1994 guidelines there was still racial and gender disparity in sentencing, but it was to a lesser extent than under the CPC.

Similarly, the effect of community characteristics was greater under the CPC. Conversely, under the 1994 guidelines the effect of offense severity and prior record on sentencing outcomes was stronger than under the CPC. When their discretion was limited, sentencing authorities tended to rely more heavily on cues from the legal subculture compared to when they had more discretion.

These results support the conception of sentencing policy as a filter. Filters serve to allow certain material through while keeping other material out. More porous filters allow more material, some of which may be undesirable, to pass through. If we view sentencing policy as a filter, when the filter is more porous (i.e., more discretion is permitted to be utilized), cues from the democratic subculture are better able to affect the process. This includes the negative stereotypes associated with certain groups. By contrast, when the filter is less permeable (i.e., discretion is limited), the cues from the democratic subculture have less influence while cues from the legal subculture are afforded greater weight.

This chapter contributes to our understanding of American courts by showing that more than just the law and legal factors influence important aspects of the judicial process. The courts are not immune to, or set apart from, politics and democracy. They are a vital component of our democratic society. As such, they maintain their legitimacy by synthesizing signals from two competing, yet overlapping forces: the legal and democratic subcultures. If the courts were entirely unresponsive to cues from the democratic subculture, they would not maintain public support. This could undermine and eventually erode their legitimacy. Unfortunately, at times the signals from the democratic subculture support negative stereotypes. The challenge for policy makers is to develop an effective filter that allows courts to respond to democratic forces without rendering biased justice. While certainly imperfect, there are signs that sentencing guidelines are a positive contribution to this goal. It is important to continue to develop new policies in an effort to strike a proper synthesis of democratic and legal values in sentencing. By responding to democratic cues and legal cues, the courts preserve the authority associated with the rule of law and also the flexibility to evolve with the politics of democracy.

Note

[1] According to the American Judicature Society's publication entitled "Judicial Selection in the United States: A Special Report," by Larry C. Berkson and Rachel Caufield, 38 states use appointment for selection of at least some judges, while 31 states use election for at least some judicial positions (see http://www.ajs.org/js/berkson_2005.pdf).

References

Albonetti, C. A. (1991). An integration of theories to explain judicial discretion. *Social Problems* 38:247–266.

Albonetti, C. A. (1997). Sentencing under the federal sentencing guidelines: Effects of defendant characteristics, guilty pleas, & departures on sentence outcomes for drug offenses, 1991–1992. *Law & Society Review* 31:789–822.

Atkins, B. & Gertz, M. G. (1983). The local politics of judicial selection: Some views of law enforcement officials. *Judicature* 66:39–44.

Barkan, S. E. & Cohn, S. F. (1994). Racial prejudice and support for the death penalty by whites. *Journal of Research in Crime and Delinquency* 31:202–209.

Beckett, K. (1997). *Making Crime Pay: Law and Order in Contemporary American Politics*. New York: Oxford University Press.

Beckett, K. & Sasson, T. (2000). *The Politics of Injustice: Crime and Punishment in America*. Thousand Oaks, CA: Pine Forge Press.

Blumstein, A., Cohen, J., Martin, S. E., & Tonry, M. (Eds.). (1983). *Research on Sentencing: The Search for Reform* (Vol. 1). Washington, DC: National Academy Press.

Borg, M. J. (1997). The southern subculture of punitiveness? Regional variation in support for capital punishment. *Journal of Research in Crime and Delinquency* 34:25–45.

Britt, C. L. (2000). Social context and racial disparities in punishment decisions. *Justice Quarterly* 17:707–732.

Caldeira, G. (1986). Neither the purse nor the sword: Dynamics of public support for the United States Supreme Court. *American Political Science Review* 80:1209–1226.

Carp, R. A. & Stidham, R. (2001). *Judicial Process in America*. Washington, DC: CQ Press.

Chiricos, T., Welch, K., & Gertz, M. (2004). Racial typification of crime and support for punitive measures. *Criminology* 42:359–389.

Crawford, C., Chiricos, T., & Kleck, G. (1998). Race, racial threat, and sentencing of habitual offenders. *Criminology* 36:481–511.

Crow, M. S. & Bales, W. (2006). Sentencing guidelines and focal concerns: The effect of sentencing policy as a practical constraint on sentencing decisions. *American Journal of Criminal Justice* 30:285–304.

Cullen, F. T., Fisher, B. S., & Applegate, B. K. (2000). Public opinion about punishment and corrections. *Crime and Justice: A Review of Research* 27:1–79.

Dixon, J. (1995). The organizational context of criminal sentencing. *American Journal of Sociology* 100(5):1157–1198.

Eschholz, S., Chiricos, T., & Gertz, M. (2003). Television and fear of crime: Program types, audience traits, and the mediating effect of perceived neighborhood racial composition. *Social Problems* 50:395–415.

Florida Department of Corrections. (1996). *Sentencing Guidelines 1995–1996 Annual Report*. http://www.dc.state.fl.us/pub/sg_annual/9596/i_intro.html.

Florida Department of Corrections. (1999). *Florida's Criminal Punishment Code: A Descriptive Assessment (FY 1998–1999)*. http://www.dc.state.fl.us/pub/sg_annual/9899/intro.html.

Florida Department of Corrections. (2003). *Historical Summary of Sentencing and Punishment in Florida*. http://www.dc.state.fl.us/pub/history/index.html.

Gillespie, W. L. (2003). State sentencing policy: Review and illustration. *Justice System Journal* 24:205–210.

Glick, H. R. (1983). *Courts, Politics, and Justice*. New York: McGraw-Hill.

Griset, P. L. (1996). Determinate sentencing and administrative discretion over time served in prison: A case study of Florida. *Crime & Delinquency* 42:127–143.

Griset, P. L. (1999). Criminal sentencing in Florida: Determinate sentencing's hollow shell. *Crime & Delinquency* 45:316–333.

Griset, P. L. (2002). New sentencing laws follow old patterns: A Florida case study. *Journal of Criminal Justice* 30:287–301.

Griswold, D. B. (1985). Florida's sentencing guidelines: Progression or regression? *Federal Probation* 49:25–32.

Handberg, R. & Holten, G. N. (1993). *Reforming Florida's Sentencing Guidelines: Balancing Equity, Justice, and Public Safety.* Dubuque, IA: Kendall/Hunt.

Helms, R. & Jacobs, D. (2002). The political context of sentencing: An analysis of community and individual determinants. *Social Forces* 81:577–604.

Jacob, H. (1978). *Justice in America: Courts, Lawyers, and the Judicial Process,* 3rd ed. Boston: Little, Brown.

Johnson, B. D. (2005). Contextual disparities in guidelines departures: Courtroom social contexts, guidelines compliance, and extralegal disparities in criminal sentencing. *Criminology* 43:761–796.

Kramer, J. & Steffensmeier, D. (1993). Race and imprisonment decisions. *Sociological Quarterly* 34:357–376.

LaGrange, T. C. & Silverman, R. A. (1999). Low self-control and opportunity: Testing the general theory of crime as an explanation for gender differences in delinquency. *Criminology* 37:41–72.

Liu, X. & Kaplan, H. B. (1999). Explaining the gender difference in adolescent delinquent behavior: A longitudinal test of mediating mechanisms. *Criminology* 37:195–215.

Mauer, M. (1999). *Race to Incarcerate.* New York: The New York Press.

Miethe, T. D. & Moore, C. A. (1985). Socioeconomic disparities under determinate sentencing systems: A comparison of preguideline and postguideline practices in Minnesota. *Criminology* 23:337–363.

Mitchell, O. (2005). A meta-analysis of race and sentencing research: Explaining the inconsistencies. *Journal of Quantitative Criminology* 21:439–466.

Myers, M. S. & Talarico, S. (1987). *The Social Contexts of Criminal Sentencing.* New York: Springer-Verlag.

Nagel, S. S. (1962). Ethnic affiliations and judicial propensities. *Journal of Politics* 24:92–110.

Nobiling, T., Spohn, C., & DeLone, M. (1998). A tale of two counties: Unemployment and sentence severity. *Justice Quarterly* 15:401–427.

Overby, L. M., Brown, R. D., Smith, C. E., & Winkel, J. W. (2004). Justice in black and white: Race, perceptions of fairness, and diffuse support for the judicial system in a southern state. *Justice System Journal* 25:159–182.

Richardson, R. J. & Vines, K. N. (1970). *The Politics of Federal Courts.* Boston: Little, Brown and Company.

Roberts, D. E. (1993). Crime, race, and reproduction. *Tulane Law Review* 67:1945–1977.

Roberts, J. V. & Stalans, L. S. (1997). *Public Opinion, Crime, and Criminal Justice.* Boulder, CO: Westview Press.

Rottman, D. & Tomkins, A. J. (1999). Public trust and confidence in the courts: What public opinion surveys mean to judges. *Court Review* 36:24–31.

Russell, K. K. (1998). *The Color of Crime.* New York: New York University Press.

Savelsberg, J. J. (1992). Law that does not fit society: Sentencing guidelines as a neoclassical reaction to the dilemmas of substantivized law. *American Journal of Sociology* 97:1346–1381.

Spohn, C. (2000). Thirty years of sentencing reform: The quest for a racially neutral sentencing process [427–501], in *Policies, Processes, and Decisions of the Criminal Justice System*. Washington, DC: Department of Justice.

Spohn, C. & Holleran, D. (2000). Research note: The imprisonment penalty paid by young, unemployed black and Hispanic male offenders. *Criminology* 38:501–526.

Steffensmeier, D. & Demuth, S. (2001). Ethnicity and judges' sentencing decisions: Hispanic-black-white comparisons. *Criminology* 39:145–178.

Steffensmeier, D., Kramer, J., & Streifel, C. (1993). Gender and imprisonment decisions. *Criminology* 31:411–446.

Steffensmeier, D., Ulmer, J., & Kramer, J. (1998). The interaction of race, gender, and age in criminal sentencing: The punishment cost of being young, black, and male. *Criminology* 36:763–797.

Szykowny, R. (1994). No justice, no peace: An interview with Jerome Miller. *The Humanist,* 9–19 (January/February).

Tannenhaus, J. & Murphy, W. (1981). Patterns of public support for the Supreme Court. *Journal of Politics* 48:24–39.

Tonry, M. (1996). *Sentencing Matters*. New York: Oxford University Press.

Ulmer, J. T. & Johnson, B. (2004). Sentencing in context: A multilevel analysis. *Criminology* 42:137–177.

Ulmer, J. T. & Kramer, J. H. (1996). Court communities under sentencing guidelines: Dilemmas of formal rationality and sentencing disparity. *Criminology* 34:383–408.

Ulmer, S. S. (1973). Social background as an indicator to the votes of Supreme Court justices in criminal cases: 1947–1956 terms. *American Journal of Political Science* 17:622–630.

Warr, M. (1995). Poll trends: Public opinion on crime and punishment. *The Public Opinion Quarterly* 59:296–310.

Wenzel, J. P., Bowler, S., & Lanoue, D. L. (2003). The sources of public confidence in state courts—experience and institutions. *American Politics Research* 31:191–211.

Whitehead, J. T. (1998). "Good ol' boys" and the chair: Death penalty attitudes of policy makers in Tennessee. *Crime and Delinquency* 44:245–256.

Wicharaya, T. (1995). *Simple Theory, Hard Reality: The Impact of Sentencing Reforms on Court, Prisons, and Crime*. Albany, NY: State University of New York Press.

Wooldredge, J., Griffin, T., & Rauschenberg, F. (2005). (Un)anticipated effects of sentencing reform on the disparate treatment of defendants. *Law & Society Review* 39:835–873.

5

Contested Ground
Teaching Courts in the Twenty-first Century

ROBERT H. CHAIRES and SUSAN A. LENTZ

Introduction

The pomp and circumstance, fanfare and fireworks of a new millennium
have faded into the often deafening background noise of business—or crisis—as usual. In the twenty-first century the American court system is still
faced with sorting through all the dilemmas of the human condition, with
the added burden of deflecting increasing assaults on the independence of
the bench. As Alfred Carlton, president of the American Bar Association,
states, "We must defuse the escalating partisan battle over America's
courts" (cited in Madeira, 2003:21). This is a difficult charge, given that in
the twenty-first century the New Federalism shows strong indications of
exacerbating the centuries-old ideological divisions concerning the roles
and powers of federal and state governments. At the same time, as the War
on Terror evolves, judges and lawyers at all levels clash as redefinitions—
some terrifying to civil libertarians and minorities—of the Hobbesian balance of safety and security versus individual liberty emerge.

Writing nearly 20 years ago, Judge Edmund Spaeth (1985:11) stated: "To
describe the courts in this country is to describe Stephan Leacock's famous
rider, who hopped on his horse and rode madly off in all directions." This
comment, more than ever, remains true. For teachers and students of the
judicial process, it is more important than ever to approach American
courts as contested ground, as perhaps a horse that many interests attempt
to ride in all directions. This may not be a popular suggestion. After all,
judges are supposed to be neutral finders of a rational law, and the judiciary

Written especially for *Courts and Justice*.

is not supposed to be a political branch of government. However, as political and economic commentator George Will relates in *Newsweek* regarding the bitter acrimony in the Senate over President Bush's nominations for the federal courts: "More and more voters understand that judges are generally more important than elected officials" (Sept. 15, 2003:72). Quite simply, the courts, for better or worse, have become the default forum for virtually everything, from what happens in the bedroom to whether Microsoft is a de facto monopoly.

To examine this idea of contested ground and its implications, the roots of contested ground theory will be explored and applied to the courts. Next, we examine the mythology of courts that supports ideological division about the law, thus encouraging judges to be overt political actors—active players in making the courts contested ground. Finally, we explore some of the major issues facing the courts in the twenty-first century. These issues, in turn, suggest recommendations about understanding and teaching the courts as contested ground, and about adapting the courts classroom to enhance student ability to engage in critical thinking and reflection about courts in America.[1]

Ideology and the Courts as Contested Ground

The American court system is unique—but not because it utilizes a hybrid of common law and statute for decision making; many nations do. Nor is it unique in having a constitutional review power. Moreover, it is not unique because it has hierarchy and operates within a federalistic structure. Again, many nations do. Neither is it unique in involving both elected and appointed individuals as legal officials. While uncommon, several other nations do. For every attribute of the American court system (and there are many more), some nation, somewhere, has had that attribute in the past, uses it now, or ultimately has rejected it. Within the American system today is one characteristic that is largely unique: the civil jury trial, which actually dates back to ancient Athens (Guinther, 1988:2–8). Further, the civil trial is getting more attention in other nations. In Ontario, Canada, for example, a civil jury is available under some circumstances.

The true uniqueness of the American court system lies in its inclusion of so many characteristics, and the great divergence across America in how each aspect is understood and applied. In no other nation on earth do formal judges in an independent court system have such power at so many levels. No other nation relies upon a formal court system to resolve so many disputes, for so many people, on so many issues. And perhaps no other court system engenders so much criticism and critical acclaim, both at home and worldwide. All of this, of course, is why the courts are contested ground. Much of the history of the Anglo-American legal system has been about control of the courts, about limiting or expanding authority and jurisdiction, about whom the courts should serve, and how. Clearly, when the questions of whom and how occur, politics become involved—and when politics are involved, ideological conflict emerges.

A Twenty-first Century Issue

International law is the most rapidly expanding area in law schools. Besides the massive body of law developing in commerce, international criminal law is expanding. In July 1998, "The world community agreed by 120 votes that the Rome Statute for the International Criminal Court should be adopted" (Washburn, 1999:361). During this U.N. initiative, the United States played ambivalent roles that may have operated to exclude it from much of the negotiation and deliberative process. In a point, "The defeat by enormous majorities of the amendments offered by India and by the United States insured the passage of the Statute" (Washburn, 1999:371). Already, several nations have refused to extradite criminals to the United States for trial because prosecutors have declined to promise not to ask for the death penalty. Will American intransigence based on beliefs about the basic superiority of the American legal system decline? Why or why not?

Courts as Places of Ideological Conflict

Kliebard (1995) can be credited for the concept of "contested ground" that is exceptionally useful for understanding the courts. In many ways his *The Struggle for the American Curriculum* parallels the struggle to control the courts. Kliebard's work traces the rise and fall of various movements to "reform" American education. He describes the political and economic contexts—the ideological divides that shape educational reform. Not surprisingly, these ideological divides—for example, that education should reduce class conflict, that schools should support business needs, that decisions should be driven by scientific rationality—are much the same as those that drive reform movements in the judicial branch. Today, not much has changed, except that now the courts are intimately involved in the curriculum wars and in educational policy. Indeed, it could be said that by the end of the twentieth century the courts had become the "default forum" for individuals and groups who fail at the school-district level in their attempts to control educational policy—in everything from what textbooks should be used (or not used) to teacher conduct in the classroom. As a result, the ideological conflicts of the contested ground of education are being played out in the contested ground of the courts. This generates some significant issues for the courts educator. To appreciate this point, the concept of ideology as it applies here needs to be explored.

According to Apple (1990:20):

> Interpretations of the scope of ideology vary widely. The phenomena under it can be grouped into at least three categories: (1) quite specific rationalizations or justifications of the activities of particular and identifiable occupational groups (e.g., professional ideologies); (2) broader political programs and social movements; and (3) comprehensive world-views, outlooks, or what Berger and Luckman and others have called symbolic universes.

Apple's description is particularly useful for considering ideology and courts because, again, his context is education. He holds that curriculum is ideology because it involves choices about what knowledge is important. Quite similarly, trial and appellate courts are the places where decisions are made regarding what law and values should prevail. Consider that almost every year some state legislature enacts a law having to do with the teaching of Creationism or forbidding the teaching of evolution, or with some hybrid "equal time" requirement. Constitutional First and Tenth Amendment issues aside, the purpose of such laws is largely to use the classroom as a vehicle for inculcating one idea over another rather than for teaching students how to make their own choices. Quite similarly, when a judge prohibits a jury from hearing a "lesser evils defense" in an abortion clinic bombing ("I blew it up to save all the unborn children") or a "medical marijuana defense" in a drug possession prosecution, the intent is to ensure that the jury does not hear irrelevant information. For example, in *U.S. v. Rosenthal* (02-0531 N.D. of CA), a federal district court judge forbade the defendant from telling the jury that he had been officially appointed by the City of Oakland to grow medical marijuana under California's Proposition 215. The jury convicted the defendant under a federal criminal statute. On finding out the true story, however, the members became enraged, stating they would not have convicted under the circumstances. Indeed, California newspapers headlined the matter. These examples reflect Apple's third category of ideology, the adoption of a worldview. Thus, substantial parallels to Apple's concept of ideology in curriculum can be seen in the courts.

- Judges and lawyers subscribe to professional codes—the *Code of Judicial Conduct* and the *Cannons of Professional Responsibility*, respectively. These are ideologies in that they set forth the values of the profession. However, these codes are themselves contested ground and are changed or reinterpreted by various interest groups within and without the professions.

- Law itself—substantive, procedural, and evidentiary—is policy, a statement about what rights and duties will be enforced in a political jurisdiction. How easy, or difficult, it is to obtain a divorce, present grounds for a search warrant, bring a civil rights action against government, or file for bankruptcy, thus will represent the triumph of one ideological perspective over another.

- What happens in the courts is the creation of a "symbolic universe" (Berger and Luckman, cited in Apple, 1990:20). Indeed, individuals and groups may choose to avoid a formal court proceeding, or even recourse to the courts at all, because that universe is seen as hostile.

Complex legal issues aside, what occurs in individual courtrooms in any particular case can, and often does, vary greatly, as do appellate decisions from state to state and from federal circuit to federal circuit. Further, the law changes. The very nature of the American legal system encourages different litigants in similar circumstances to try again. Schools, including universities, are contested ground because they are places where conflict is important about the nature of knowledge as well as about how it will be taught. The courts are contested ground because they process, create, and legitimate ideological perspectives on: (1) actors and acted upon (i.e., judges, lawyers, criminals, victims, plaintiffs, and defendants); (2) institutions and movements, while being an institution and movement themselves; and (3) law, both in the symbolic (what and why) and practical (power) dimensions. Gabel and Feinman (1998) invoke an image of the courts as places constrained by ideology and the dominant social constructs generated by ideology. It is a view of court actors, judges, and lawyers, locked into a system they themselves cannot explain except by reference to normative models like politics and power. Arguably, teachers of courts may themselves become locked into normative models and explanations that reify a particular ideology into social fact. Consider, for example, how a course on the courts might differ if taught by a former prosecutor, an active ACLU attorney, or a Ph.D. in sociology.

To understand this point, it may be helpful to view the varying perspectives on the role(s) of the courts on a continuum rather than as an either/or division.

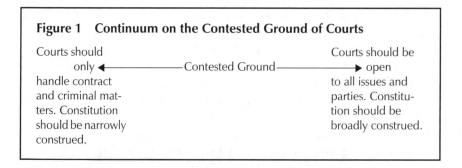

Figure 1   Continuum on the Contested Ground of Courts

Courts should only handle contract and criminal matters. Constitution should be narrowly construed. ◄——————Contested Ground——————► Courts should be open to all issues and parties. Constitution should be broadly construed.

As figure 1 indicates, subject-matter jurisdiction often reflects ideology about the role of courts. For many, the issue of subject matter is political; for others it is social and moral. Mensche (1998), in her history of mainstream legal thought, describes the evolution of American law in terms of what is private (outside governmental control) and public (subject to law). For example, for much of American history the family and the workplace were private domains, largely outside legal control. In this sense, the history of American legal evolution has been one of constant growth in the scope of what is public, hence subject to law. However, although the law might have changed, ideological conflict does not necessarily end. That family and workplace matters should be reclassified as private remains a constant thread of ideological conflict. Returning to the curriculum battles in the courts, for example, portrayal of the family in textbooks remains a hotly contested topic. Some groups battle ferociously, often in the courts, to ensure that nothing but images of traditional heterosexual nuclear families are seen in textbooks. Similarly, one has only to open a newspaper to see that worker rights remain a divisive issue.

Given Mensche's point, it is no wonder that individuals and groups vary greatly in their views concerning what the courts should do, at which level, to whom, and why. As the places where ideological conflict is played out, courts will always be contested ground—unless they are closed. As such, some view the courts as generating the conflict by existing as a forum for so many people and things. In this perspective the solution becomes simple: limit the forum. Others see the courts as the only practical place to resolve conflicts, particularly among parties with unequal resources, and for those groups who have been traditionally disenfranchised from the political process. The latter perspective operates to expand the forum.

As suggested in figure 1, the contested ground of expansion and contraction—what the courts should and should not do—has another dimension: beliefs about what the courts, and court actors, actually do and do not do. Belief, however, can become mythology, and myth is a potent force in contested ground.

A Twenty-first Century Issue

Much of American law in the nineteenth and twentieth centuries centered around images of a dominant white majority and politically weak, racial and ethnic minorities. It is generally agreed that somewhere between 2020 and 2050 there will cease to be any statistical majority racial or ethnic group in the United States. Will this make any difference in the contested ground of the courts? Will the faces of the judges of the future reflect the race and ethnicity of the population?

Myth and Manipulation in the Courts

In this context, myths can be considered as assumptions or perceptions, based on ideologies of what should or should not be, that drive actions or non-action. Reich (1987:14), for example, describes four continuing tales that shape popular thinking and political response in an endless cycle. These four—"rot at the top" (out-of-control big government and big business), "mob at the gates" (foreigners threatening our institutions), "triumphant individual" (entrepreneurs versus drones), and "benevolent community" (fixing the poor)—have endured throughout American history, but in each era they have been combined and conveyed in slightly different ways. Kappeler, Blumberg, and Potter (1996) similarly describe mythologies in criminal justice as unproven or unprovable assumptions and/or negligent, even deliberate, distortions of crime, violence, and safety that tend to polarize and demonize (see also Donziger, 1996, and in contrast Wilbanks, 1987).

While there can be little doubt that the courts are political actors in that they are forums in which political decisions are tested, they are also much more. What those additional roles are, or should be, is the substance of continuing debate, controversy, and accusation. The fear of many on the bench and the bar is not that the courts do things with political implications, but rather that the third branch of government may become just another majoritarian political institution. Edward Madiera (2003:21), chair of the ABA Commission on the 21st Century Judiciary, sees such concerns as a major issue for the commission: "The concept of the judiciary as a 'political' branch akin to the legislature and executive was anathema to our founding fathers but increasingly advocated in various states." The majority of state judges at all levels are elected in partisan or nonpartisan ways. However, most states have adopted the provision in the *Model Code of Judicial Conduct* that prohibits those running for judicial office from announcing how they might rule in a particular matter. In the past, this has operated largely to limit the "when I get in office I'll . . ." election rhetoric and to maintain at least a semblance of neutrality.

The decision in *Republican Party of Minnesota et al. v. Suzanne White, Chairperson, Minnesota Board of Judicial Standards et al.* (536 U.S. 765 [2002]) may remove the brakes on judicial election promises. Justice Scalia, writing for the majority in a deeply divided Supreme Court, held that the announcing clause of the *Code* was unconstitutional on First Amendment grounds. *Republican Party v. White* is a classic example of modern plurality decisions in arenas of extreme ideological conflict. There is a victor, but there are competing reasons for the victory. For example, Justice O'Connor concurred in the result but also held that electing judges *in itself* operated to undermine perceptions of an impartial judiciary. Justice Kennedy concurred on the grounds that any content-based restriction on speech must fail. Justice Stevens in his dissent stressed the same point that concerns Madiera: there is a *fundamental* difference between judicial elections and other elections. Three additional dissenting justices joined Stevens but added separately their own particular concerns.

Not only are the courts constantly embroiled in ideological debate, but they are also involved with mythology. For example, Reinarman and Duskin (1998) describe the drug war as an ideological construct, and Fishman (1998) describes the perceptions about the reality of crime waves as feeding from ideological roots. While all or many crime waves may be just myths, they are treated as real. Laws are passed, enforced, and litigated. Violators are acquitted, or found guilty by plea or trial and then punished. However, things are not quite so simple. Courts are contested ground in which myth and ideology are made real—for awhile. Not everyone follows or believes in a particular myth or ideology. To one person or another (or group), the courts will always be "good" or "bad" depending on how congruent the court's actions are with expectations shaped by ideology. Hence, a mythology about courts develops.

A Twenty-first Century Issue

For practical purposes, privacy is already dead; technology has rendered the concept physically moot. Federal 10th Circuit Judge Deanell Reece Tacha comments that "Perhaps nothing will affect the federal courts more than the explosion of the technological age and the specialization it spawns" (1999:21). Judge Tacha speaks about the enlightening side of technology. Some 75 years ago Justice Brandeis, dissenting in *Olmstead v. U.S.* (1928), however, expressed the dark side when he wrote, "The progress of science in furnishing the government with means of espionage is not likely to stop with wiretapping. Ways may someday be developed by which the government, without removing papers from secret drawers, can reproduce them in court. . . ." Today the private sector knows virtually everything about us, from what we read to the illnesses that may hide in our genes. Although for a while the government was prohibited from gathering such information, it could legally buy it from private sources. The effect of laws like the USA Patriot Act of 2002 is to put the government back in the business of legally knowing everything. There is no way to put the genie back in the bottle; electronic records are much too tempting. How might the courts fashion meaningful remedies for abuses of information?

Court Myths

Within the line of thought developed by Kappeler et al. (1996), there are both negative and positive myths (the term "myths and legends of criminal justice" was actually coined by Atkins and Pogrebin, 1978). "Good guy" myths survive and prosper because of "bad guy" myths. Still, while mythology in the criminal justice system is not simplistic, it is simple in comparison to the mythology of the court system, which has a much broader scope of actors, process, and subjects. Criminal justice is only one part of the court system, and while actors in the criminal justice system may view the courts as part of "their system," even collectively, they only deal with a relatively small part of it.

Court myths are no less subject to manipulation than are the political myths of Reich (1987) or criminal justice myths. In addition, the courts have a civil dimension that generates its own mythology. Arguably, the "litigation explosion" is another version of Reich's "entrepreneur tale." In the court version, the drones suck the blood of American corporations by frivolous litigation and plaintiffs' lawyers are the civil version of Kappeler et al.'s (1996) "bad guys" (see, for example, Olson, 1991; in contrast, Spence, 1989, both polemics). When ideology drives mythology, facts get lost, manipulated, or transformed. As Crossen (1994:19) relates, statistics have become a new battlefield of manipulation, of corrupted information, and "behind the explosion of corrupted information is, first, money." All this contributes to the courts as contested ground, out of which emerge decisions about which myth, which ideology, or which set of corrupted information will be legitimized.

Clearly, some interests more than others strongly depend on mythology and manipulation. Examination of the myths surrounding the judiciary in table 1 discloses that both negative and positive myths have become part of the "court mythology." Each myth has promoters, those who consciously or unconsciously support it and/or transmit it. Each myth also has manipulators, those who use the myth to obtain an end or effect. Manipulating myths is another way in which ideology is expressed, and in which the courts become the contested ground referenced in figure 1.

Table 1 is not intended to be exhaustive, nor can it be, but it does display one of the realities of positive and negative court mythology. Negative mythology generates more controversy and action than positive mythology does. It is axiomatic that active complainers are more visible and more often heard than those who, if not happy, are at least marginally satisfied. In large part, this is the nature of the public beast. In education, it is the same: it is easier to criticize teachers and systems than to praise them. Also consider that mythology is a form of education—bad education. Negative or positive, it is still mythology, and mythology discourages reflection on

Table 1   Court Myths

Positive Myths	Promoters	Manipulators	Effect
David and Goliath—Courts are places where the weak can win over the mighty if their cause is right and just.	"Feel good" movies and novels Optimists K–12 teachers	Plaintiffs' bar	Open courts (see figure 1)
Day in Court—Courts are places where the average person will find wise judges and fair juries who will listen to them.	Individual winners	Plaintiffs' bar	Open courts
Judges Are Wise and Fair—They are special people with vast knowledge and compassion.	Court television shows Bench Individual winners	Corporate winners	Decreased incentive for critical examination of judges and system
Negative Myths			
The Hired Gun—There exist attorneys who are so competent that they can win any case no matter what the facts and law are.	Cynical movies and novels News media Individual losers Corporate losers Criminal justice agencies	Defense bar Corporate losers Prosecutors Civil defense bar	Tort reform Criminal procedure reform Restrictions on contingency fees Closing court access Demonizing of criminal defense bar Changes in legal ethics standards
Just Another Bureaucracy—There is nothing special about the courts or judges. What they do could be better done in other forums.	Social science academics News media Pessimists	Politicians Proponents of ADR (alternative dispute resolution) Those who benefit from removing particular subject-matter jurisdiction	Emphasis on bureaucratic efficiency Diminishing status as coequal branch of government Proper lawmakers are always legislators Changes in legal education
Litigation Explosion—The courts are being overwhelmed by frivolous lawsuits pushed by greedy plaintiffs' lawyers.	Insurance industry Manufacturers	Insurance industry Manufacturers ADR proponents Defense bar Conservative media	Tort reform Closed courts Increased ADRs
Revolving Door Criminal Courts—Crime waves, weak laws, and liberal judges are making society unsafe.	Law enforcement News media Prosecutors	Politicians Conservative media	Reduction in judicial discretion Sentencing reform Increasing contraction of civil rights Racial disparity

the true state of affairs. Indeed, mythology tends to polarize ideas into simplistic frameworks. Thus, a major goal of any class on the courts must be to diminish the power of mythology by exposing it as such. This can be a painful process for both student and teacher, because it often calls for reflection on why we might *want* to believe something.

Mythology and Contested Ground

Court mythology persists for many reasons. As table 1 suggests, however, a primary reason is that a particular myth tends to support ideology about the overall role of government. For example, a litigation explosion myth can be explained within the ideology that government improves society by helping business interests, and that the courts as a branch of government should further that interest, not impede it—in particular, court resources should be expended on resolving interbusiness litigation rather than all those other things. Of course, other interests have different perspectives on what are important or not important matters for the courts to handle.

This points toward an overarching problem with the interactions of myth and ideology: they tend to focus on the immediate through the lens of crisis, on fixing the "here and now" at the cost of long-range planning or consideration of unintended consequences of "fixing" things. Even positive myths tend to discourage looking toward the future and analyzing the past; as the saying goes: "why fix things that aren't broken?" Well, one reason might be to avoid, or at least minimize, problems that have yet to occur. In fact, there is an entire field of study called long-range strategic planning that is used in many disciplines. Identification of such issues is why the ABA Commission on the 21st Century Judiciary was established. Whether such studies are ever used for anything is another story. However, the

A Twenty-first Century Issue

At the core of ideological divisions in the contested ground of the courts is whether the courts should be involved in social change at all. Rosenberg argues that the courts have little real power because they lack any substantial ability to enforce their decisions. However, the courts may have "an extrajudicial path of influence" that can serve as a "catalyst," but the "evidence is weak" (1993:228–229). There is much to suggest, for example, that police conduct is not largely affected by judicial decisions; they just learn better ways to justify the same conduct. Is the discourse on the importance of the courts, in Shakespeare's words, "much ado about nothing"? Will social evolution, or devolution, occur regardless of the presence of the courts?

absence of such study cannot help but support "business as usual." Further, the goal of long-range planning is not so much solving problems as it is limiting the number of directions that Leacock's aforementioned rider may irrationally take.

The Courts Classroom and Contested Ground

For students, especially undergraduates, issues of legal context like myth and manipulation are generally more important than "what the law is." Smith (1996), for example, argues that it would be better to teach criminal justice students a course on courts than a course on criminal procedure without context (in critical response, see Zalman, 1996). A teacher of a course in courts must assume that students are superimposing ideological assumptions over descriptive (mythological) statements about the courts. Students bring to the classroom important views and impressions about the real state of the world. While it cannot be assumed that students have any common idea about the who, what, and where of the actors—judges, lawyers, and juries—it also cannot be assumed that they come to the classroom as a blank slate. Students are likely to have had law courses before enrolling in a courts course, but the law course(s) may have been taught as if courts just processed cases based on legal arguments. For students who have had a system overview course, the presentation of the courts may have been even more simplistic. Structural descriptions of the courts showing the hierarchy and appellate routes through the state and federal system are simply inadequate to describe the roles of courts in American society.

How, then, does one strike a meaningful balance between treating students as blank slates or, at the other end of the continuum, filled with misinformation? O'Banion (1997:49), in *A Learning College for the 21st Century*, quotes from T. H. White's (1939:185–86) *The Once and Future King* the advice given by the Wizard Merlin to the young Arthur:

> The best thing for being sad . . . is to learn something. That is the only thing that never fails. You may grow old and trembling in your anatomies, you may lay awake at night listening to the disorder of your veins, you may miss your only love, you may see the world about you devastated by evil lunatics, or know your honor trampled in the sewer of baser minds. There is only one thing for it then—to learn. Learn why the world wags and what wags it. That is the only thing the mind can never exhaust, never alienate, never be tortured by, never fear or distrust, and never dream of regretting. Learning is the thing for you.

"Learn why the world wags and what wags it" speaks most directly to the issue of the contested ground of the courts, to the conflicting ideologies that may drive the future. It also speaks to a central theme in the curriculum and pedagogy of a course on the courts. "To do the courts" students need to learn, and teachers need to teach that there are many ways to wag the world. This suggests a means of striking a balance—you engage in discourse and reflection about "why."

The pedagogy of teaching courts involves interdependent considerations of description, critical analysis, and philosophic definition. In short, teaching courts must necessarily include imposing a multidimensional context on a system that is too often presented and perceived in unidimensional terms. Like other governmental organizations, the courts act and are acted upon. Unlike other government organizations, the courts are multitasked and empowered at a level without precedent short of Plato's theoretical philosopher-kings. Those tasks and that power make the courts evermore contested ground. That this is so places an obligation on teacher and student to examine continually and critically their own roles in creating or perpetuating the ideology and mythology of that contested ground.

A Twenty-first Century Issue

U.S. Third Circuit Court of Appeals Judge Richard Nygaard (1997:525) writing about courts in the 21st century, states:

> First, I view long-range plans much the same way as I do budgets—they are simply projections of where we want to be or believe we will be, and are written to provide some guidance for those in the pits who must prepare for the future but are not in on the policymaking that gets them there. Second, I believe that because the future, bound-up as it is in the progress of automation, thrusts planners and dreamers, as it must, into the realm of the theoretically-plausible and hopefully-possible, it requires that any long-range plan have an air or touch of science fiction about it. Hence, for me the ideal planner is a futurist—one whose head is planted firmly in the clouds and whose feet, while not on the ground, do nonetheless dangle fairly close to it.

Where are your feet and head? Better yet, where is your heart when it comes to the law?

Building the Model

If there are issues of myth and manipulation in the courts, then clearly one goal of a course on the courts is to reconcile what the courts do with what people *think* the courts do. This comparing of formal expectations with actual results can be called a positivistic/organization perspective of courts. If, as suggested, court actors—attorneys, judges, juries—modify the formal law and process in complex ways into informal patterns of law and process consistent with their ideologies, then this personal/ideological dimension should also be subjected to analysis. Finally, if the courts are more than the sum of their parts, if they serve a practical cultural role of being a legitimate place for the resolution of differences as well as a symbolic role of legitimizing ideology, then this legitimate/symbolic dimension is also a necessary part of the study of the courts. Each of these perspectives—the positivist/organization, the personal/ideological, and legitimate/symbolic—can be examined in the context of the differences between theory/ideal and practice/reality.

Placing a few of the current issues of the courts into this matrix generates a table that can be used as a platform from which to approach organized discourse on some of the major issues confronting the contested ground of the courts.

Of course what goes into each block of table 2 may, and should, change constantly. In addition, even though each point may not be subjected to inquiry, just cuing the student that a particular point is part of the contested ground of courts may be enough in itself to generate self-inquiry.

Table 2   Teaching/Learning Matrix for Courts

	Theory/Ideal	Practice/Reality
Positivist/ Organization	Formal structure Federalism	Courts as organizations Courts as subordinate, superior, and coordinate political actors
	Mixing of common and code law	Legal and political decision theories
	Legal education as training for profession and service	Legal education as training for hierarchy
Personal/ Ideological	Lawyers as advocates	Lawyers divided by status and legal subject matter
	The bar as a participatory democracy	The bar as an instrument of self-interest and restricting competition
	Judges as neutral	Judges as politicians in robes
	Judges as wise and learned	Vast variances in skills, knowledge, and temperament
Legitimate/ Symbolic	Courts as doing law and justice	Courts as instruments of social control and power
	Juries are important actors	Juries nullification as dangerous to vested interests
	Rational legal system Unified legal theory	Juries as mere pawns Law is a hodgepodge of morality, religion, compromise, and greed guised in rationality
	Equal Law	Law biased along gender and race lines

In looking at issues in both a descriptive and a critical manner and examining each in the context of myth and manipulation, the study of the courts becomes more dynamic. As curious as it may seem, the study and teaching of courts also become easier. Gradually, students begin to understand the ambivalence and contradictions of the court as a natural part of the process of meaningful evolution in systems and people. Perhaps most important, students begin to see themselves in their views of the courts. If, at the end of any courts course taught in any manner, students appreciate how different perspectives on opening and closing the courts affect the checks and balances of society and their own roles in imagining or creating those checks and balances, then curriculum and pedagogy have been successful.

Conclusion

The courts are conscious and unconscious political actors; the courts are processors and creators of law; the courts are a series of complex organizations that are in turn part of a greater complex organization; the courts are stages on which many dramas, and occasional comedies, of life and choice are played. The courts are both promoters of myth and makers of myth. The courts are many things to many people—that is why they are contested ground. That is why they will remain contested ground in the twenty-first century. The great and small issues of the past centuries have not disappeared. When we argue the meaning of Tenth Amendment sovereignty or the rights of immigrants, we employ the rhetoric of the eighteenth century. When we litigate zoning laws or the rights of workers, nineteenth-century discourse echoes in the courtroom. When we ask whether privacy and due process should outweigh national security, we "replay" the twentieth century.

However, things have changed. The world grows ever smaller and the technological interface ever larger. International law is no longer just about "over there," and there are growing consequences for American actions and reactions in a host of areas. In the twenty-first century the courts, because they are the default forums of America, cannot help but play a central role, if not *the* central role. It should be remembered, reflected upon, learned from, that one of the fastest growing areas of the United Nations and the World Community is courts.

Perhaps there is another message here: the words of Merlin to the young Arthur, "learning is the thing for you," may be good advice to judges, lawyers, and teachers of courts—lest we simply redo the future as the past.

Robert H. Chaires, JD, Ph.D. and Susan Lentz, JD, Ph.D. are on the faculty of Criminal Justice at the University of Nevada, Reno.

Endnote

1 Since this article is largely about teaching and learning about courts, substantial reference is made to critical education theory and practice, and to ideas about a curriculum (the knowledge) and pedagogy (the ways of teaching and learning). It is perhaps an irony that much of twentieth century's critical education theory grew out of nineteenth-century critical legal theory. Of course, they were one and the same more than two millennia ago in classical philosophy.

Bibliography

Apple, Michael W. (1990). *Ideology and Curriculum*, 2nd ed. New York: Routledge.

Atkins, Burton and Mark Pogrebin, eds. (1978). *The Invisible Justice System: Discretion and the Law*. Cincinnati: Anderson.

Crossen, Cynthia (1994). *Tainted Truth: The Manipulation of Fact in America*. New York: Simon and Schuster.

Donziger, Steven R. (1996). *The Real War on Crime*. New York: HarperPerennial.

Fishman, Mark (2006). "Crime Waves as Ideology," in G. W. Potter and V. E. Kappeler, eds., *Constructing Crime: Perspectives on Making News and Social Problems*, 2nd ed. Long Grove, IL: Waveland Press (pp. 42–58).

Gabel, Peter and Jay Feinman (1998). "Contract Law as Ideology," in D. Kairys, ed., *The Politics of Law*, 3rd ed. New York: Basic (pp. 497–510).

Guinther, John (1988). *The Jury in America*. New York: Facts on File Press (a research project of the Roscoe Pound Foundation).

Kappeler, Victor E. and Gary W. Potter (2005). *The Mythology of Crime and Criminal Justice*, 4th ed. Long Grove, IL: Waveland Press.

Kliebard, Herbert H. (1995). *The Struggle for the American Curriculum, 1983–1958*, 2nd ed. New York: Routledge.

Madiera, Edward W., Jr. (Spring, 2003). "The ABA Commission on the 21st Century Judiciary," *The Judges Journal*: 20–21.

Mensche, Elizabeth (1998). "The History of Mainstream Legal Thought," in D. Kairys, ed., *The Politics of Law*, 3rd ed. New York: Basic.

Nygaard, Richard L. (1997). "On Judging 2020—A Cybercourt Odyssey: A Look at the U.S. Courts in the 21st Century," *Ohio St. Law Journal*, Vol. 58: 528–532.

O'Banion, Terry (1997). *A Learning College for the 21st Century*. Phoenix, AZ: American Council on Education & Oryx Press.

Olson, Walter K. (1991). *The Litigation Explosion: What Happened When America Unleashed the Lawsuit*. New York: Truman Talley.

Reich, Robert B. (1987). *Tales of A New America*. New York: Times Books.

Reinarman, Craig and Ceres Duskin (2006). "Dominant Ideology and Drugs in the Media," in G. W. Potter and V. E. Kappeler, eds., *Constructing Crime: Perspectives on Making News and Social Problems*, 2nd ed. Long Grove, IL: Waveland Press (pp. 331–344).

Rosenberg, Gerald H. (1993). *The Hollow Hope: Can Courts Bring About Social Change*. Chicago: University of Chicago Press.

Smith, Christopher (1996). "Teaching the Irrelevance of Law on Criminal Procedure," *Journal of Criminal Justice Education* Vol. 7, No. 1: 45–58.

Spaeth, Edmund, Jr. (Summer, 1985). "Where is the High Court Heading?" *The Judges Journal*: 10–13, 47–49.

Spence, Gerry (1989). *With Justice For None*. New York: Penguin.

Tacha, Deanell Reece (1999). "The Federal Courts in the 21st Century." *Chapman Law Review* Vol. 2: 7–28.

Washburn, John (1999). "The Negotiation of the Rome Statute for the International Criminal Court and International Lawmaking," *Pace International Law Review* Vol. 11: 361–377.

Wilbanks, William (1987). *The Myth of a Racist Criminal Justice System*. Monterey, CA: Brooks/Cole.

Will, George (2003). "The Last Word: Dean and Big Differences." *Newsweek*, September 15: 72.

Zalman, Marvin (1996). "Reflections on Christopher Smith's Article 'Teaching the Irrelevance of Law on Criminal Procedure,'" *Journal of Criminal Justice Education* Vol. 7, No. 1: 59–63.

Questions to Consider

1. The authors describe historical and current conflicts between court officials (judges and lawyers) and ordinary citizens. What conflicts do they cite as examples? Can you think of any current examples in which there are attempts to limit the role of citizens in legal decision making?

2. Some have argued that the demands placed on courts to process cases have led many judges to assume a more "managerial role" in court proceedings. In such a role, judges actively negotiate with the parties about the course and outcome of litigation, seeking to cajole and perhaps pressure the parties to settle or plea bargain before the case goes to a jury trial. As much of this "case management" takes place in judicial chambers, off the record and out of the public eye, there is less and less public contact with the judicial process. In addition, there are fewer limitations on judicial power, as there is no requirement to provide written and reasoned opinions and no opportunity for appellate review. Are the administrative pressures cited by the authors again leading to court personnel slowly taking power away from juries and limiting public involvement in, and understanding of, court processes? If so, what might be done to reverse this trend?

3. Myths are assumptions about the nature of reality, and most of us readily recognize such myths. We may choose to believe some myths and disbelieve others. At this point, using the list of court myths cited by Chaires and Lentz, what myths do you believe to be true and which are not? Estimate the strength of each of your beliefs by listing any "facts" you may have to support that belief. At this point, what can you say about your list of facts in relation to your beliefs?

Section II
Decision Making in the Shadows
Little Understood Components and Processes in the Criminal Justice System

The three articles in this section highlight aspects of the court system that are seldom talked about, much less widely understood. Each article engages us with questions concerning the ability of the courts to provide justice for those who come before them, while contending with our increasing social demands for efficiency in government operations.

Christopher Smith outlines the operational flexibility benefits that magistrate judges provide to federal courts. But we also see a continuation of the problem noticed in the previous section, that of judges "forcing" litigants to forgo a jury trial, thereby obtaining their "consent" to have their issue heard before a magistrate judge. Problematically, such coercive actions remain unreviewable and even unnoticed by the public, as such actions are "cloaked in the impenetrable discretionary authority of judges."

Courts depend on our belief in their authority, and Smith's article provides rich insight into the role of, and perceived need for, authority by officials below the rank of full judge. Magistrate judges want lawyers to "jump" when instructed to do so and feel the need to be called by the higher status term "judge" rather than by the lower status term "magistrate." Notice also the recent growth in lesser judicial actors, such as magistrates and pro se law clerks, who are increasingly being given the ability to judge some aspect of a litigant's case.

Will there always be some conflict in perceived status among judicial actors? Is the responsibility that we would normally hold our public decision makers to becoming more and more diffuse as more people have a hand in the decision? Are we creating multiple and inaccessible levels of bureaucracy in the name of efficiency?

While many people know that plea bargaining serves as the operational foundation of our criminal court system, few will appreciate the complexity of this "guilty pleas industry" uncovered in Joseph Sanborn's article.

Our system of plea bargaining has been based on the need for more government efficiency. However, it has also created multiple unaddressed problems that have been blamed on a variety of factors, such as the creation of "too many citizen rights" or the tendency of judges to create overly complex rules for their own professional benefit. When we create a new social structure such as plea bargaining, we must be aware that such structures can create serious problems that also need to be addressed. Thus, in line with the larger questions of this book, one might ask to what extent a seemingly pragmatic attempt to solve the problem of case volume has created a longer term problem of increased executive-branch control of the courts. A bargain is only fair if it involves two equally situated parties. To what extent does the prosecutor have a natural advantage in the plea bargaining system? The United States sentences people to higher levels of incarceration than other nations. Is this outcome a product of judicial toughness or the structure of plea bargaining that invites overcharging by prosecutors?

Keith Wilmot's article develops the problem of hidden prosecutorial power on the federal level, which is problematic because the discretionary power of the prosecution is "unreviewed and unchecked." Most individuals outside the justice system are unaware of this power, although individual federal judges have often bitterly complained. Wilmot notes that, in addition to prosecutors gaining power relative to the judiciary, they are also increasingly able to circumvent the oversight of grand and petit juries. This concentration of power in the hands of the executive branch, at the expense of judicial and public control, is a trend noted throughout this text, and it once again raises the issue of who owns the courts.

6

From U.S. Magistrates to U.S. Magistrate Judges
Developments Affecting the Federal District Courts' Lower Tier of Judicial Officers

CHRISTOPHER E. SMITH

Congress created the office of U.S. magistrate in 1968 to provide additional case-processing resources for the federal district courts. In December 1990, the title for the office was changed to "U.S. magistrate judge" as part of the Judicial Improvements Act.[1] Full-time magistrate judges are appointed by district court judges for renewable eight-year terms and part-timers are appointed for renewable four-year terms.[2] Because they do not possess the attributes of Article III judges (i.e., presidential appointment, senate confirmation, and protected tenure), magistrate judges are considered "adjuncts" of the federal courts who perform tasks delegated by the district judges.

Initially, the magistrates' authority was primarily confined to the limited tasks performed by the old U.S. commissioners, lay judicial officers who handled warrants, arraignments, and petty offenses from 1793 until they were replaced by the newly-created magistrates after 1968.[3] Congress subsequently amended the Magistrates Act in 1976 and 1979 to authorize magistrates to assist district judges with a broad

Reprinted by permission of the American Judicature Society and the author from *Judicature*, vol. 75, no. 4 (Dec./Jan., 1992), pp. 210–215.

spectrum of tasks, including the supervision of complete civil trials with the consent of litigants.[4] After the 1979 Act, magistrates could perform virtually any task undertaken by district judges except for trying and sentencing felony defendants.[5] By June 1990, the 323 full-time magistrates and 153 part-time magistrates were such an integral component of the federal district courts that they were responsible for completing 450,565 tasks, including 4,220 civil and criminal evidentiary hearings, 45,201 civil pretrial conferences, and 1,008 complete civil trials.[6] Article III judges acknowledged that magistrates "contribute significantly to the administration of justice in the United States and are an integral part of the Federal judicial system"[7] by including the magistrates' interests in arguments presented to Congress concerning the need for higher salaries for judicial officers.[8]

Because these subordinate judicial officers were intended to be utilized flexibly according to the needs of each district court, the precise judicial roles performed by magistrate judges vary from district to district. For example, one 1985 study of magistrates' roles found that they could be classified as performing three model roles: "Additional Judge," supervising complete civil cases and otherwise sharing caseload responsibilities with district judges; "Team Player," handling motion hearings, conferences, and other tasks to prepare cases for trial before district judges; and "Specialist," primarily processing Social Security disability appeals and prisoner petitions for the district judges.[9] The specific mix of tasks assigned to magistrate judges within each district depends upon a variety of factors, including district judges' views on magistrate judges' proper judicial role and the nature of the caseload pressures.[10] Because the tasks performed by magistrate judges vary, their roles within each district court are susceptible to change as court reforms, changing caseload compositions, and other factors affect the demands placed upon federal courts and the district courts' case-processing capabilities. This article will discuss how recent developments affecting the federal courts are likely to shape the tasks and roles performed by the district courts' lower tier of judicial officers.

A New Title and Enhanced Status

The magistrate judges' original title, "magistrate," was a source of unhappiness for many of the lower tier judicial officers. District courts throughout the country received authorization to appoint magistrates in the early 1970s. Because neither district judges nor practicing attorneys knew how these new judicial officers, with their vaguely defined authority, ought to be regarded, many judges simply used magistrates as if they were merely permanent law clerks. Practicing

attorneys followed suit by failing to treat magistrates with the deference
and respect they would normally accord to a recognized judicial officer.[11]
As a result, many magistrates believed their effectiveness was hampered
because lawyers did not understand that they were indeed authoritative
judicial officers. For example, a lawyer interviewed for one study said
that "when a [district] judge tells you to do something, you jump. But
when a magistrate tells you to do something, well, you do it, but it's
not the same."[12]

"Magistrate" is a respected title in the British legal system, but in
the United States it is merely a generic term for judicial officer. Because
many state court systems employ the title "magistrate" for low-level
lay officials, practicing attorneys often confused the authoritative federal
judicial officers with the relatively inconsequential lay "justices of the
peace" who bear the title "magistrate" in many states. The potential
confusion that the title could cause was recognized when the new federal
judicial office was created and the Judicial Conference of the United
States subsequently discussed the issue in a report to Congress:

> Those who would prefer a change in title state that the term
> "magistrate" has traditionally referred to a low-level local official
> who performs a narrow range of functions in criminal cases, i.e.,
> a justice of the peace. They point out that this traditional association
> of the term is inaccurate when applied to the full-time United States
> magistrates. They also note that many state magistrates are not well
> regarded and some have been prosecuted for wrongdoing.[13]

The title "magistrate" contributed to many practical problems when
lawyers did not accord the subordinate judicial officers with appropriate
deference and respect. If lawyers do not "jump" when instructed to take
a specific action by a magistrate, then magistrates must waste time in
the aftermath of motion hearings and discovery conferences trying to
ensure that attorneys comply with the magistrates' orders. District judges
could always force compliance by reiterating the magistrates' orders,
but such redundant actions diminish the advantages for saving the
judicial system's resources that Congress sought to attain by making
magistrates authoritative judicial officers.[14] In addition, because
magistrates' authority to preside over civil trials depends upon the
consent of litigants,[15] the failure of attorneys to recognize magistrates'
status and authority as judicial officers can reduce the likelihood that
litigants will consent to magistrates' jurisdiction and thereby hinder the
implementation of this mechanism to reduce district judges' civil
caseload burdens. The magistrates' title may be an important component
of attorneys' willingness to recommend the consent trial option to their
clients:

> Some magistrates view the title "judge" not only as an entitlement
> [for themselves as authoritative federal judicial officers], but as a

functional necessity if they are to perform effectively when presiding over trials. . . . Many litigants may automatically prefer to have their cases heard by someone bearing the title of "judge." As a result, magistrates lose opportunities to gain visibility and build their reputations as judicial officers, and the potential flexibility and judicial economy of the magistrate system are diminished.[16]

In order to combat the confusion over magistrates' title, district judges in some districts addressed the magistrates as "judge" and instructed attorneys to do the same. This action reinforced the magistrates' status as judicial officers within those districts, but it exacerbated morale problems among magistrates in other districts who desired similar recognition but were forbidden by their supervising district judges from using the title "judge."[17]

As a result of the title change contained in the Judicial Improvements Act, the magistrate judges can expect to be more readily addressed as "judge." The new title and form of address will help educate attorneys and litigants about the magistrate judges' status as authoritative judicial officers within the federal courts. This should enhance the magistrate judges' contributions to effective case processing within the district courts by encouraging full cooperation and compliance from attorneys and by increasing the visibility and credibility of the litigants' option to consent to have civil cases tried before magistrate judges.

In 1979, when Congress considered the legislation that authorized magistrates to oversee consent trials, two members of Congress complained that "[f]rom the standpoint of appearance, procedure, and function, an impartial observer will not be able to tell the difference between a magistrate and an Article III judge."[18] In the context in which they raised this concern as part of the debate about the proper authority of non-Article III judicial officers, this was a significant issue to consider. But is this question as compelling today? Now that Congress has explicitly endorsed magistrate judges as "federal judicial officers,"[19] federal appellate court decisions have accepted the constitutionality of magistrates' authority,[20] and magistrates have supervised civil trials for more than a decade, does it matter whether an outside observer, be it a litigant or an attorney, knows the precise difference between a magistrate judge and an Article III district judge?

There may be legitimate, principled reasons to reopen the debate about the appropriate scope of non-Article III judges' authority.[21] However, because legislative and judicial policy makers have endorsed broad authority for magistrate judges, there is strong reason to give magistrate judges the title and status necessary for maximizing their contributions to the work of the district courts. Magistrate judges are different than Article III district judges in regard to their scope of authority and the delegation of tasks.[22] The title change contained in the Judicial

Improvements Act merely indicates that when magistrate judges serve as the presiding judicial officers for matters pending before the district courts, the litigants and attorneys should be made well aware that the magistrate judges are indeed authoritative judicial decision makers who are to be accorded appropriate deference and respect.

Consent Trial Authority

Recent court reform initiatives threatened the magistrates' status and authority within the federal courts. One of the recommendations made in 1989 by the Brookings Institution's task force on civil justice reform[23] was aimed directly at the broad exercise of authority by magistrates: "Procedural Recommendation II: Ensure in each district's plan that magistrates do not perform tasks best performed by the judiciary." The phrase "tasks best performed by the judiciary" seemed to imply that district judges rather than magistrates should preside over civil trials.

The task force report served as the basis for legislative proposals by Senator Joseph Biden, the chairman of the Senate Judiciary Committee. Biden's court reform bill, entitled "The Civil Justice Reform Act," contained, among other things, provisions requiring mandatory discovery-case management conferences and monitoring conferences for complex litigation that would both be "presided over by a judge and not a magistrate."[24] Such mandatory conferences would be designed to force district judges to become involved in case management for each civil case and would consequently reduce the likelihood that entire civil cases would be referred to magistrates by the consent of the litigants. In proposing his court reform legislation, Senator Biden made it quite clear that he did not think that magistrates could manage civil litigation effectively.[25]

Ultimately, Biden's "Civil Justice Reform" bill was scrapped in favor of "The Judicial Improvements Act of 1990," which was developed through negotiations between the Senate Judiciary Committee and the Judicial Conference of the United States.[26] In regard to authority of magistrates,[27] the legislation enacted by Congress followed the recommendation of the Federal Courts Study Committee's 1990 report to encourage more consent trials before magistrates. The Federal Courts Study Committee urged that "Congress . . . allow district judges and magistrates to remind the parties [in civil litigation] of the possibilities of consent to civil trials before magistrates."[28] The statutory change affecting magistrates' consent trial authority suited the interests of both district judges and magistrates by, respectively, maintaining district judges' discretion and autonomy with regard to case management[29] and encouraging the referral of more complete civil trials to the newly retitled magistrate judges.

The Judicial Improvements Act encourages civil consent trials by now permitting district judges and magistrate judges to inform litigants directly about their option of consenting to a trial before a magistrate judge: "[E]ither the district court judge or the magistrate may again advise the parties of the availability of the magistrate, but in so doing, shall also advise the parties that they are free to withhold consent without adverse substantive consequences."[30] The involvement of judicial officers in informing litigants about the consent option represents a significant change from previous statutory language that made clerks of court exclusively responsible for communications about the consent option and precluded any involvement by judges or magistrates.[31] When Congress officially authorized magistrates to preside over complete civil trials with the consent of litigants in 1979,[32] the statute precluded involvement by judicial officers and emphasized the voluntariness of litigants' consent in order to avoid the possibility that judicial officers might pressure litigants to consent."[33]

Magistrate judges in many districts should enjoy increased opportunities to oversee complete civil cases as a result of the statutory change. Some districts had failed to implement regular procedures for educating litigants and their attorneys about the consent option through notices from the clerk of court. Litigants often remained uninformed about their options because the court personnel with whom they came into the most frequent, direct contact through pretrial conferences and hearings, namely the district judges and magistrates, were forbidden from discussing the magistrates' consent authority.[34] Now judicial officers will be able to remind parties about the consent option throughout the stages of civil litigation. Under the previous system, some districts that had routinized the notice process informed litigants about the consent option only at the outset of litigation.[35] If litigants did not understand the scope of magistrates' authority, they would be reluctant to consider immediately consenting to an unfamiliar process under the authority of an unfamiliar judicial officer.[36] Because the parties may not recognize the desirability of consenting to a magistrate judge's jurisdiction for a firm and expedited trial date until after the initiation of discovery and pretrial conferences, the new procedure will provide the opportunity for useful reminders to litigants when judicial officers perceive that such a referral might be beneficial.

Pressure to Consent

Although the new procedure will increase the flexible utilization of magistrate judges and increase their status and authority in some districts, the involvement of judicial officers in informing litigants about the consent option also entails risks. The original statutory provision concerning notice to parties precluded the participation of judicial officers because they might coerce litigants into consenting. Congress was aware of the possibility, for example, that district judges might be "tempted to force disfavored cases into disposition before magistrates by intimations of lengthy delays manufactured in district court if the parties exercise their right to stay in that court."[37] Subsequent research revealed that this was a genuine risk that, in fact, came to fruition in some districts despite the statutory prohibition on communications from judicial officers to litigants concerning consent. A Federal Judicial Center study found that:

> There was a clear consensus among the [California lawyers] interviewed that when a judge raises the question of consent to a magistrate—for whatever reason—lawyers feel that they have little choice but to go along with the suggestion. Attorneys consistently reported feeling some pressure to consent, particularly in a "smaller" case; when interviewees were asked to describe the reasons for consent, the overriding one given was that the judge had suggested it.[38]

Another study found examples of district judges engaging in precisely the behavior that Congress feared, namely pressuring litigants to consent to the referral of disfavored cases to magistrates.[39]

Because the statutory revisions from the Judicial Improvements Act now invite judicial officers to communicate with litigants about the consent option, there are even greater risks that parties will be or will feel pressured to waive their right to have their case heard before an Article III judge. Such actions by judges are not likely to be challenged by attorneys: "Lawyers are not likely to admit publicly that they were weak in the face of improper conduct. They also [may] think twice about directly challenging the ethical conduct of a judge sitting in a court that provides a basis for their legal practice and livelihood."[40] Moreover, even if the issue of coercion is raised, it would be difficult to prove to an appellate court that a district judge had improper motives or undertook improper actions. Judges' coercive actions identified in one study "were essentially immune from external scrutiny because scheduling trial dates and refusing to grant continuances (two of the most frequently-manipulated mechanisms to pressure litigants) are part of a judge's prerogatives. Thus, the coercive actions were cloaked in the impenetrable discretionary authority of judges."[41] Because the new notice provision invites the participation of judicial officers, district judges and magistrate judges must become much more self-conscious about their own motives and the possible coercive consequences of their communications with litigants concerning the consent option.

Task Assignments

Current developments affecting the federal courts are certain to affect magistrate judges' task assignments in various districts, although it is uncertain precisely how those assignments will be affected. Although the changes affecting the subordinate judicial officers' title and consent trial authority should encourage increased references of complete civil cases to the magistrate judges, other factors may impede an increase in trials before magistrate judges.

The Judicial Improvements Act requires each district court to develop and implement a "civil justice expense and delay reduction plan."[42] In the course of examining mechanisms for effective case management and cost-effective discovery, districts may create new procedures that actually limit the exercise of magistrate judges' authority. For example, expense and delay reduction plans may make magistrate judges exclusively responsible for oversight of discovery, pretrial conferences, and other preliminary matters, thus formalizing the subordinate judicial officers' roles as "Trial Preparers" rather than as "Autonomous Judges" presiding over civil consent trials.[43] Because district judges exert significant control over the magistrates' roles through their authority to appoint and reappoint the subordinate judicial officers and through their power over the delegation of tasks,[44] Article III judges will continue to have substantial influence over the definition of magistrate judges' roles within each district court. If the judges within a district believe that magistrate judges should exercise limited authority, the expense and delay reduction plans are likely to reflect that preference.

The precise tasks assigned to magistrate judges within a district depend not only upon the district judges' conceptualizations of the proper role for their judicial subordinates, but also upon the caseload composition within the district.[45] If a magistrate judge works within a district containing large prisons, they may become "Specialists" in prisoner petitions. Similarly, in districts that receive especially large numbers of Social Security disability appeals, the magistrate judges' working lives may be absorbed by the process of reviewing administrative law judges' findings in such cases. Although some districts utilize alternative mechanisms (e.g., staff attorneys, pro se law clerks, district judges' law clerks) for processing prisoner and Social Security cases, these two particular categories of cases have a significant impact upon workloads of magistrate judges in many districts.[46]

How are the federal courts currently being affected by these categories of cases? In regard to Social Security disability appeals, the federal district courts have experienced a steady decline in such cases. Disability cases peaked in 1984 at 24,215[47] in the aftermath of the Reagan administration's attempt to remove summarily 336,000 beneficiaries from that Social Security program.[48] By contrast, in 1990 there were only 5,212 of such cases filed in the federal district courts.[49] Thus, unless a magistrate judge serves a district that is especially affected by disability cases, these Social Security cases are becoming less burdensome and therefore are having fewer limiting effects upon magistrate judges' availability for other tasks, such as consent trials.

In regard to prisoners' petitions, the burden upon the federal courts has continued to grow. There were only 29,303 prisoners' petitions filed in the district courts in 1982[50] but that number grew to 42,630 in 1990.[51] After handling only 11,578 prisoner matters in 1980, the magistrate judges' burden peaked at 27,002 in 1987 and then dropped back to a consistent plateau just below 21,000 in 1989 and 1990.[52] Because prisoners' filings in the federal courts have shown steady annual increases throughout the 1980s, the recent reduction in the magistrate judges' burden must indicate that district judges are employing alternative mechanisms for processing such cases, such as *pro se* clerks[53] or their own law clerks. Although the burden upon the magistrate judges generally has, for the moment, stabilized, the tremendous increases in the number of people imprisoned throughout the United States make it likely that the number of prisoners' petitions will increase as well. There were only 329,821 people in prison in 1980, but that number leaped to 771,213 in 1990 as the result of aggressive prosecutions and stiffer sentences for narcotics and other offenses.[54]

Although rising prison populations make it appear likely that magistrate judges will continue to have some portion of their working lives absorbed by prisoners' petitions, other developments may reduce the number of such petitions in the federal courts. The Supreme Court has taken the initiative to create new rules for habeas corpus petitions that have the effect of precluding multiple petitions, enforcing procedural bars, and otherwise limiting prisoners' access to the federal courts.[55] Other potential exclusionary mechanisms have been discussed in justices' opinions[56] and may be on the horizon for implementation in future decisions. In addition, President Bush and Congress are working on legislative proposals that would, if passed, place additional limitations upon prisoners' opportunities to file habeas corpus petitions in the federal courts.[57] Although habeas corpus petitions typically constitute only 25 to 30 percent of the prisoners' petitions filed in federal court, they have constituted 40 percent of the magistrate judges' prisoner tasks in recent years.[58] The current developments aimed at reducing the number of habeas corpus petitions may reduce the magistrate judges' burden or, alternatively, district judges may simply assign their judicial subordinates more prisoner civil rights cases, which typically comprise more than 60 percent of the prisoner filings.[59]

Effect of Felony Prosecutions

Magistrate judges' workload is being affected by the increase in federal felony prosecutions, especially for narcotics offenses. Increases in felony prosecutions tie up the district judges because "speedy trial" requirements make criminal cases move to the head of the docket queue. Because magistrate judges cannot conduct trials and sentence offenders in felony cases, an increase in felony prosecutions should make litigants more inclined to consent to civil trials before magistrate judges as district judges' time becomes increasingly absorbed by felony cases. By consenting to a trial before a magistrate judge, litigants in civil cases can obtain an early and firm trial date. They may also be able to choose which magistrate judge will preside over the trial if the district court's case-processing procedures utilize references to multiple available magistrate judges. Although the increases in felony prosecutions may lead to more civil case responsibilities for magistrate judges, the subordinate judicial officers also have their time absorbed in assisting the felony work of district judges; "Magistrates handled 313 percent more detention hearings in 1990 than in 1985, 111 percent more search warrants, 45 percent more preliminary examinations, 44 percent more arrest warrants, and 38 percent more arraignments."[60]

As with other developments affecting the federal courts, the magistrate judges' task assignments are affected by increases in criminal prosecutions, but it is not clear that such changes will necessarily lead to broader, more flexible utilization of the subordinate judicial officers. For example, although the magistrate judges' responsibilities for preliminary criminal matters increased in conjunction with the increasing criminal caseload in the district courts, the number of civil consent cases for magistrate judges was virtually the same in 1990 as it was in 1986 (4,958 to 4,960).[61] Although the increase in felony cases during the late 1980s did not consistently escalate the number of civil consent cases for magistrate judges, the new statutory notice provisions permitting judicial officers to inform and remind litigants about the consent option may generate such an increase in the future. The number of civil consent trials before magistrate judges is most likely to rise if district judges continue to be preoccupied with felony cases and if those judges evince a concomitant willingness to refer complete civil cases to their judicial subordinates.

Conclusion

Recent and ongoing developments in the federal courts will shape the status, authority, and workload of the U.S. magistrate judges. With their new title and increased opportunities to educate the bar about the breadth of their judicial authority, especially their ability to supervise civil consent trials, magistrate judges are poised to fulfill the potential that their supporters have envisioned for broad, flexible contributions to the case-processing responsibilities within each district court.

Although the subordinate judicial officers received a vote of confidence from Congress in the passage of the supportive Judicial Improvements Act instead of Senator Biden's limiting Civil Justice Reform bill, it remains to be seen whether the magistrate judges will be able to exercise the full range of judicial tasks authorized by statute and desired by many of the incumbent judicial officers themselves.[62] Because the precise tasks assigned to magistrate judges are still significantly influenced by the preferences of the district judges with whom they work and by the nature of their individual districts' caseloads, the recent efforts to enhance magistrate judges' status, authority, and usefulness within the federal courts may, in fact, have little effect upon the subordinate judicial officers' contributions to the court system. The Judicial Improvements Act and the federal courts' continuing docket pressures have set the stage for broader, more innovative use of magistrate judges, but the actual implementation of reforms is dependent on the district judges' willingness to delegate important responsibilities to their judicial subordinates.

Endnotes

1. References to the lower tier judicial officers concerning their status and authority prior to December 1990 will use the previous title ''magistrate'' rather than the new title ''magistrate judge.''
2. See Smith, ''Who Are the U.S. Magistrates?'' 71 *Judicature* 143 (1987); Smith, ''Merit Selection Committees and the Politics of Appointing United States Magistrates,'' 12 *Just. Sys. J.* 210 (1987).
3. See Spaniol, ''The Federal Magistrates Act: History and Development,'' 1974 *Ariz. L. Rev.* 566; Peterson, ''The Federal Magistrates Act: A New Dimension in the Implementation of Justice,'' 56 *Iowa L. Rev.* 62 (1970).
4. See McCabe, ''The Federal Magistrates Act of 1979,'' 16 *Harv. J. Legis.* 343 (1979).
5. See, e.g., *Gomez v. United States*, 109 S.Ct. 2237 (1989) (magistrates not authorized to supervise the selection of jurors in felony criminal cases).
6. Administrative Office of the U.S. Courts, *Annual Report of the Director of The Administrative Office of the U.S. Courts* 25 (1990). Because these figures are drawn from individual magistrate judges' reports concerning their own activities and the categories of activities are not precisely defined (e.g. different activities may be classified as separate ''civil pretrial conferences'' by different magistrate judges), case processing statistics provide only a rough picture of magistrate judges' responsibilities. Although the statistics from the Administrative Office cannot provide precise information on the magistrate judges' accomplishments, the figures demonstrate substantial contributions to the work of the district courts by the lower tier of judicial officers.

[7] Committee on the Judicial Branch of the Judicial Conference of the United States, *Simple Fairness: The Case for Equitable Compensation of the Nation's Judges* 81–82 (1988).

[8] See, Smith, "Federal Judicial Salaries: A Critical Appraisal," 62 *Temple L. Rev.*. 849 (1989).

[9] See Seron, *The Roles of Magistrates: Nine Case Studies* (Washington, D.C.: Federal Judicial Center, 1985); Seron, "Magistrates and the Work of the Federal Courts: A New Division of Labor," 69 *Judicature* 353 (1986).

[10] See Smith, *United States Magistrates in the Federal Courts: Subordinate Judges* 115–146 (New York: Praeger, 1990).

[11] Smith, "The Development of a Judicial Office: United States Magistrates and the Struggle for Status," 14 *J. Legal Prof.* 175, 184–185 (1989).

[12] Smith, supra n. 10, at 135.

[13] *The Federal Magistrates System: Report to the Congress by the Judicial Conference of the United States* 62 (1981).

[14] Many magistrates can cite examples of incidents in which the judicial officers wasted time reinforcing to attorneys the idea that magistrates are indeed authoritative federal judicial officers: "In some instances, it is very obvious to the magistrate that the attorney regards the magistrate as being of lesser importance. The magistrate may be forced to marshal resources in order to maintain his or her desired judicial role. For example, in a . . . case in which an attorney attempted to go over the magistrate's head to the judge in order to get a conference rescheduled, it was clear that the attorney never would have attempted such a maneuver if the district judge were presiding over the conference. After an attorney approached a judge about rescheduling, there would be nothing that the attorney could do but comply with the judge's orders. [In this] example, the magistrate hurried to contact the judge to ensure that the judge upheld the magistrate's decision. Thus the magistrate, because of the relatively new judicial office and uncertainty about [the] appropriate status and role for the magistrate position, must often actively seek to maintain proper behavior and respect on the part of attorneys." Smith, supra n. 10, at 195.

[15] "Upon the consent of the parties, a full-time United States magistrate or a part-time United States magistrate who serves as a full-time judicial officer may conduct any or all proceedings in a jury or nonjury civil matter and order entry of judgment in the case, when specially designated to exercise such jurisdiction by the district court or courts he serves." 28 U.S.C. sec. 636(c)(1).

[16] Smith, supra n. 11, at 181–182.

[17] Id. at 180–184.

[18] H.R. Rep. No. 1364, 95th Cong., 2d Sess. (1978) at 37 (statement of Reps. Drinan and Kindness).

[19] The "definition" section of the Judicial Improvements Act clearly endorsed the magistrate judges' status as judicial officers: "As used in this chapter the term 'judicial officer' means a United States district court judge or a *United States magistrate*" (emphasis supplied). 28 U.S.C. sec. 482 (1990).

[20] See, e.g., *Pacemaker Diagnostic Clinic of America, Inc. v. Instromedix, Inc.*, 725 F.2d 537 (9th Cir. 1984) (en banc), cert. denied, 469 U.S. 824 (1984).

[21] See Resnik, "The Mythic Meaning of Article III Courts," 56 *U. Colo. L. Rev.* 581 (1985).

[22] For example, district judges control the delegation of tasks to magistrate judges and, unless the parties have consented to a magistrate judge's authority, magistrate judges merely make recommendations to district judges concerning dispositive motions.

[23] See Litan, "Speeding Up Civil Justice," 73 *Judicature* 162 (1989).

[24] The relevant provisions proposed: "A requirement that . . . a mandatory discovery-case management conference, presided over by a judge and not a magistrate, be held in all cases within 45 days following the first responsive pleading" (S.2027, 101st

Cong., 2d Sess. sec. 471(b)(3) (1990)); and "[F]or cases assigned to the track designated for complex litigation, calendar a series of monitoring conferences, presided over by judge and not a magistrate, for the purpose of extending stipulations, refining the formulation of issues and focusing and pacing discovery" (Id. at sec. 471(b)(3)(I)).

25 Biden's statement introducing his court reform legislation expressed doubts about the magistrates' effectiveness: "The [pretrial] conference may lose some of its significance in the minds of the attorneys if presided over by a magistrate, since the unfortunate fact is that many attorneys seem to be far more willing to take frivolous positions before a magistrate. . . . [M]agistrates may themselves be more reluctant than judges to frame the contours of litigation, limit discovery, establish a date certain briefing schedule and address the full panoply of discovery case management conference issues." 136 Cong. Rec. S414 (daily ed. Jan. 25, 1990) (statement of Sen. Biden).

26 Some aspects of the negotiation process between the judiciary and Congress apparently angered members of the Senate Judiciary Committee: "The [Senate Judiciary] [C]ommittee complied with the request of the Judicial Conference to work with one body [i.e., a four-judge task force appointed by Chief Justice William Rehnquist], only to have the [Judicial] Conference seemingly defer to another body [i.e., the Conference's Committee on Judicial Improvements which rejected the negotiated legislative proposal]—which had no role whatsoever in the discussions and negotiations—at the point of decision. Such actions only serve to undermine the cooperative relationship between Congress and the judicial branch that our citizens rightly expect and deserve." S.416, 101st. Cong., 2d Sess. (1990) at 5.

27 To counteract Senator Biden's perception that magistrates are ineffective because lawyers do not respect their authority, district judges argued that magistrates can be very capable and authoritative, especially in districts in which judges permit them to perform a broad range of tasks: "[Magistrates] have informed me that it is a rare occasion indeed, that any attorney ever takes a frivolous position when appearing before them. If that should occur in some districts, I suspect that it is more of a reflection of how the magistrates are perceived by the Article III judges, and what duties or powers those judges have permitted the magistrates to perform. If that suspicion is true, one way to address the concerns of the [Brookings Institution's] Task Force is to leave the matter of who presides at the conference to the discretion of the district court adopting its plan." Enslen, *Prepared Statement of the Hon. Richard Enslen, U.S. District Court for the Western District of Michigan, presented in Testimony Before the Senate Judiciary Committee During Consideration of S.2027, The Civil Justice Reform Act of 1990* (Mar. 6, 1990) at 45.

28 *Report of the Federal Courts Study Committee* 79 (Apr. 2, 1990).

29 The district judges had argued to Congress that "the proposed diminution of the role of magistrates would hamper the proposed legislation's underlying purpose of improving case-processing efficiency." Robinson, *Prepared Statement of the Hon. Aubrey E. Robinson, Jr., Chief Judge, U.S. District Court of the District of Columbia, Presented in Testimony Before the Senate Judiciary Committee During Consideration of S.2027, The Civil Justice Reform Act of 1990* (Mar. 6, 1990) at 4.

30 28 U.S.C. sec. 636(c)(2) (1991).

31 "[T]he clerk of court shall, at the time the action is filed, notify the parties of their right to consent to the exercise of such jurisdiction. The decision of the parties shall he communicated to the clerk of court. Thereafter, neither the district judge nor the magistrate shall attempt to persuade or induce any party to consent to reference of any civil matter to a magistrate." 28 U.S.C. sec. 626(c)(2) (1982).

32 At least 36 district courts referred civil cases to magistrates for trial before Congress explicitly endorsed this practice with the 1979 Act. H.R. Rep. No. 1364, supra n. 18, at 4.

33 See Smith, "Assessing the Consequences of Judicial Innovation: U.S. Magistrates'

Trials and Related Tribulations," 23 *Wake Forest L. Rev.* 455, 474–476 (1988).

[34] See Smith, supra n. 10, at 85–87.

[35] One former magistrate described the old statutory notice provision as "unworkable on its face" because the notice was frequently attached to the summons and "such boilerplate is commonly ignored." Sinclair, *Practice Before Federal Magistrates* sec. 2303 (New York: Matthew Bender, 1987).

[36] In the districts in which magistrates were used as "Additional Judges," the practicing bar became familiar with the individual magistrates and knowledgeable about their authority. Thus there was greater willingness to consent. See Seron, *The Roles of Magistrates*, supra n. 9, at 38–39.

[37] H.R. Rep. No. 1364, supra n. 18, at 14.

[38] Seron, *The Roles of Magistrates*, supra n. 9, at 61–62.

[39] Smith, supra n. 10, at 103–104.

[40] Id. at 180.

[41] Id.

[42] 28 U.S.C. sec. 471 (1991).

[43] For a detailed typology of eight possible model roles for magistrates, see Smith, supra n. 10, at 127–132.

[44] Id. at 115–119; see Seron, "The Professional Project of Parajudges: The Case of the U.S. Magistrates," 22 *Law & Soc'y Rev.* 557 (1988).

[45] Smith, supra n. 10, at 140–141.

[46] See Seron, *The Roles of Magistrates*, supra, n. 9, at 83–92.

[47] .Administrative Office of the U.S. Courts, *Annual Report of the Director of the Administrative Office of the U.S. Courts* 180 (1986).

[48] See Mezey, *No Longer Disabled: The Federal Courts and the Politics of Social Security Disability* (New York: Greenwood, 1988).

[49] Administrative Office, supra n. 6, at 138.

[50] Administrative Office, supra n. 47, at 179.

[51] Administrative Office, supra n. 6, at 138.

[52] Id.

[53] See Zeigler & Hermann, "The Invisible Litigant: An Inside View of Pro Se Actions in the Federal Courts," 47 *N.Y.U. L. Rev.* 157 (1972).

[54] Cohen, "Prisoners in 1990," *Bureau of Justice Statistics Bulletin* 1 (May 1991). Increases in prisoner filings are not purely a function of increases in prison populations. See Thomas, Keeler & Harris, "Issues and Misconceptions in Prisoner Litigation: A Critical View," 24 *Criminology* 775 (1986).

[55] See, e.g., *McCleskey v. Zant*, 111 S.Ct. 2841 (1991) (failure to raise claim in initial habeas corpus petition in federal courts barred subsequent petition concerning claim); *Coleman v. Thompson*, 111 S.Ct. 2546 (1991) (procedural default under state court rules barred raising claim in subsequent federal court habeas corpus petition).

[56] In a concurring opinion in *Duckworth v. Eagan*, 109 S.Ct. 2875 (1989), Justice O'Connor argued that the Supreme Court should emulate its decision in *Stone v. Powell*, 428 U.S. 465 (1976), which precludes federal court consideration of habeas corpus "exclusionary rule" claims that have been previously raised in state courts, by similarly precluding federal court review of *Miranda* claims.

[57] See Diemer, "Blood for Blood: Senate Focuses upon Fighting Crime, *Cleveland Plain Dealer*, June 30, 1991, at 15–A.

[58] Administrative Office, supra n. 6, at 25, 140.

[59] Id.

[60] Id. at 24.

[61] Id. at 25.

[62] See Smith, supra n. 10, at 69–75, 182–187.

7

Pleading Guilty and Plea Bargaining
The Dynamics of Avoiding Trial in American Criminal Courts

JOSEPH B. SANBORN, JR.

Putting the Guilty Plea and Plea Bargaining into Context

Contrary to the ideals of the adversary process, the guilty plea is the norm and the trial is the exception in American criminal courts. This has been the case for nearly 150 years. Much of the credit for the avoidance of trial has been given to plea bargaining. For many, plea bargaining is a very controversial and unsatisfactory way in which to resolve a case. Some allege it is responsible for paradoxical results, such as innocent people falsely convicting themselves and criminals literally getting away with murder. Not surprisingly, controversy and confusion surround virtually every aspect of plea bargaining, ranging from its definition to its history, extent, and problems. This article attempts to resolve some of this controversy and confusion.

Defining Plea Bargaining

Simply agreeing on what plea bargaining *is* and *is not* is no simple task. For one thing, the term *plea bargaining* is relatively new. The phenomenon originally was called compromising or settling a criminal case (Miller, 1927; Polstein, 1962). Lesser pleas (Weintraub and Tough, 1942) and plea copping (Kuh, 1967) also were terms that were used to refer to plea bargaining. Finally, plea agreements (ABA, 1968) and even plea gambling (*Scott v.*

Written especially for *Courts and Justice*.

U.S., 1969) have been employed to capture what transpires in plea bargaining. All these titles, along with the more contemporary term of plea negotiation, attempt to portray the essence of plea bargaining. Probably no one title completely fits the situation, and all can be interpreted as having negative connotations (e.g., bargaining with criminals). Nonetheless, plea bargaining is the name that has stuck and is the one most likely to be recognized both in the literature and among the public.

Defining plea bargaining is no easier than deciding what to call it. It is possible for the definition to be both too narrow and too broad. For example, there are those who would define plea bargaining solely as an exchange between prosecutors and defense counsel (Note, 1970; Note, 1972; Segar, 1978). In fact, when Alaska purportedly abolished plea bargaining decades ago, only arrangements between opposing counsel were explicitly prohibited. This definition is too narrow in that defendants (and their counsel), in some locations at least, have negotiated a plea arrangement with the judge (Alschuler, 1976; Miller, McDonald, and Cramer, 1978). Plea bargaining has also been defined too narrowly, as when only sentence arrangements are reached (rather than negotiation over charges) (Miller et al., 1978) or when jail time is not involved (Jaspin, 1981).

At the other extreme, some would define plea bargaining as including any guilty plea offered by a defendant with a mere *expectation* of a reward or consideration (Neubauer, 2002). In other words, plea bargaining would occur with or without any overt bargaining, exchange, or arrangement between the parties. This definition is too broad in that it would mean that virtually all guilty pleas have to be the products of plea bargaining, which is far from true in many jurisdictions. As we will see, it is quite possible for a defendant to plead guilty without any deal or bargain and with nothing more than a mere hope that leniency will be granted. This is not plea bargaining, and the abolition of plea bargaining will not eliminate this nonnegotiated guilty plea. Even more problematic are definitions of plea bargaining that do not require guilty pleas. That is, even cases that are dismissed (or *nol prossed*) (McDonald, 1979; Miller et al., 1978) or diverted (McDonald, 1979) have been included within plea bargaining typologies. Similarly, sentencing "rewards" granted to defendants for requesting only a bench trial and for waiving the right to a jury trial also have been linked with plea bargaining (Alschuler, 1968; White, 1971). There are similarities between plea bargaining and these nonguilty plea situations, in which defendants may not be treated as harshly as the law permits because they have either offered some sort of service in exchange for the case being dismissed/diverted or have agreed not to exercise the full extent of their rights. Nevertheless, this is not the same as plea bargaining for one very simple reason. There is no guilty plea from the defendant and, in fact, there is a dismissal of charges when the case is either diverted or *nol prossed*, and there is a potential for acquittal when the accused opts for a bench trial. Without a guilty plea and a conviction, plea bargaining cannot exist.

Plea bargaining involves defendants pleading guilty or convicting themselves in *exchange* for some consideration from the state. The defendant may or may not be represented by counsel. A prosecutor usually represents the state, but it can't be ruled out that a judge arranged the "deal." The considerations offered the defendant typically involve a reduction in charge severity (or charge bargaining), a sentence agreement (or sentence bargaining), and/or elimination of other charges or cases (or dismissal bargaining). The first two considerations are *charge* and *sentence bargains*, respectively, which are the two types of plea bargains. The third consideration is *dismissal bargaining*, which is also referred to as *nol pros* bargaining (resulting from the prosecutor's discretion to dismiss or *nol pros* a case). As just stated, dismissal bargaining is not plea bargaining. Dismissal bargaining is often linked with plea bargaining, but it also frequently occurs independently without any conviction imposed against the defendant. For example, many first offenders are offered a chance to earn a case dismissal if they will agree to perform certain tasks, such as attending counseling, performing community service, or paying restitution. Even veteran offenders may be offered a dismissal of the charges against them if they will testify against more culpable and dangerous accomplices.

Although plea bargaining, by necessity, involves a guilty plea, not all guilty pleas involve negotiation or bargaining. That is, there are numerous types of guilty pleas tendered by defendants that are *not* the products of any explicit arrangement or understanding between the state and the accused. Despite this reality there is a tendency to assume that *all* guilty pleas have been secured through plea bargaining. This incorrect assumption ends up inflating estimates of the amount of plea bargaining occurring in many jurisdictions. To be sure, plea bargaining most likely accounts for most of the guilty pleas criminal courts accept in any given year. Nevertheless, it is important to remember that simply because there has been a guilty plea, this does not mean that a plea bargain has occurred.

Non-Negotiated Guilty Pleas

To acquire a better understanding of what plea bargaining entails, it is helpful to consider what plea bargaining is not. We have established that plea bargaining does not occur when the defendant pleads guilty without being given any specific promises. There are several of these non-negotiated guilty pleas defendants can enter in court. Probably the most prevalent is a plea that has never been given a specific identity as a guilty plea. Perhaps the terms that best describe this type of plea would be the *calculated* or *mercy* guilty plea. The calculated/mercy guilty plea is one in which the defendant pleads guilty with the anticipation that the judge will reward the plea with a less severe sentence. This plea could be entered even in serious cases that potentially could result in significant sentences. Judges might be prone to reward guilty pleas, in part, because defendants end up throwing themselves on the mercy of the court, and, in part, because defendants have saved the court significant time and resources by pleading guilty. It is possible that the defendant's reason for pleading guilty is simply thinking that the judge should more often than not reward putting oneself at the court's mercy. It is even more likely that the defense attorney calculates that the judge is likely to sentence those who plead guilty more leniently than those who are convicted by trial. Court data could disclose that sentences tend to be more severe when trials are involved. The calculated guilty plea comes dangerously close to resembling plea bargaining. In fact, one of the earliest treatises on plea bargaining referred to the calculated guilty plea as "implicit plea bargaining" (Newman, 1966). Nevertheless, the calculated guilty plea does not involve an agreement. If the judge elected to defy the "odds" by imposing the maximum sentence on the defendant, the latter would have no recourse to complain that the state had reneged on a deal or bargain. At most, the state merely would have violated the defendant's "expectations" or "calculations." For this reason, it is inappropriate to identify this guilty plea as a plea bargain (cf., Heumann, 2002).

Another non-negotiated guilty plea that could be fairly prevalent is the *straight* guilty plea. Like the calculated/mercy plea, the straight plea would be "on the nose," meaning the defendant would not attempt to secure a reduction in the severity or number of charges prior to pleading guilty. Unlike the calculated/mercy plea, however, the straight plea does not seek to influence the outcome of the prosecution via a sentence reduction. It can't be ruled out that in some cases, especially when the defendant is not represented by counsel, the guilty plea was offered in total ignorance of alternatives and consequences. In other words, some defendants simply may not know what they are doing when they plead guilty. This plea may be ill-advised and even unfair, but it will still be recorded as a straight guilty plea.

Assuming defendants know what they are doing, there could be a variety of motivations behind the straight guilty plea. It would most likely occur when the probable sentence is not severe. That is, the case should be destined for probation or perhaps minimum jail time, some or all of which the defendant already may have served in pretrial custody. For defendants who have committed only one or two nonserious crimes probation is a virtual guarantee. Since the sentence for these low-end offenders is relatively minimal, there is much less over which to negotiate and haggle (and to fear). Assuming they know this, it might make sense for these defendants to plead guilty simply to initiate the sentence, especially if the evidence against them is both legal and substantial and even more so if they have not been able to post bail and secure pretrial freedom. Defendants who are ineligible for the services of a public defender also could be tempted to plead guilty simply to avoid the costs of hiring an attorney to take the case to trial. Less common scenarios that could lead to a straight guilty plea are situations in which offenders charged with a particularly heinous crime, like child rape, would want to avoid the publicity attending trial, and situations in which offenders actually welcome incarceration and/or need to confess. However, it can't be ruled out that these individuals would try to trade for their guilty pleas rather than simply surrender their right to trial without any payback.

The *quick* guilty plea is yet another version of the non-negotiated guilty plea. Like the straight plea, this plea is much less likely when the sentence potential is significant. As the title implies, the quick guilty plea seeks a speedy resolution of the charges. At times it might behoove defendants to plead guilty when the state has thus far undercharged them. For example, if the charge is unauthorized use of an auto (a misdemeanor), defendants who actually have committed auto theft (a felony) might be tempted to enter a plea before the prosecutor learns that the charge should be higher than it is. Once the defendant is convicted via the guilty plea, double jeopardy would prevent any attempt to prosecute the defendant on the appropriate, higher charge. Assuming that sentencing can occur immediately, it might also benefit a defendant to plead guilty before the judge hears from the victim just how bad the crime really was.

Finally, the *slow* guilty plea is a non-negotiated guilty plea, but it will be recorded as a trial conviction. The slow guilty plea occurs when the defendant takes the stand and confesses to a crime less serious than the one charged (and perhaps committed). Here the accused hopes that a demonstration of "honesty" in admitting wrongdoing will convince the judge and/or the jury that the crime was truly not as serious as the prosecutor alleges. This is a huge gamble, since a conviction should be inevitable in light of the confession and the judge or jury might not accept this demonstration as sincere or accurate, choosing instead to convict on the higher charge.

There could be additional versions of non-negotiated pleas, but the point has been made that not all guilty pleas are the negotiated products of plea bargaining. In fact, a jurisdiction officially could prohibit plea bargaining and yet maintain a high rate of guilty pleas. When that is the case, chances are that an abundance of calculated/mercy guilty pleas are taking the place of plea bargains. It would be rare indeed for any major jurisdiction today not to be dependent on a high rate of guilty pleas.

Types of Plea Bargains

As mentioned earlier, negotiated guilty pleas result in either charge or sentence bargains. Charge bargains typically involve reducing charge severity and very often will be linked with the dismissal of other charges. Nonetheless, it would still seem appropriate to refer to a guilty plea as a charge bargain when the defendant pleads guilty "on the nose," without a charge reduction, in exchange for the dismissal of other charges. This could occur, for example, when the defendant pleads guilty to three burglaries (on the nose) in exchange for a dismissal of three other burglary charges. While the latter charges clearly were dismissal or *nol pros* bargains, the three convicted charges probably should be identified as charge bargains despite the lack of reduced charges. Similarly, a defendant's pleading guilty on the nose in exchange for a prosecutor's agreement not to seek an indictment via a three-strikes or habitual-offender statute would probably be best categorized as a charge bargain.

Sentence bargains are a little more complicated due to the possible variations. Guilty pleas can result in either complete or incomplete sentence bargains. A *complete sentence bargain* involves the defendant's agreeing with the prosecutor (or possibly the judge) that a particular sentence will follow the entry of a guilty plea. That is, an exact outcome is negotiated (e.g., five years incarceration) and assumes a contract-like status. Chances are that this outcome is less than what is theoretically possible according to the penal code. This "contract" is presented to the judge as a package. If the judge accepts the agreement, then the bargain is ratified, the court enters the conviction, and the agreed-upon sentence (or perhaps an acceptable, modified one) is imposed. If the judge cannot accept the agreement, then the defendant is allowed to withdraw the guilty plea. At that point, the prosecution and defense might try to work out another arrangement or perhaps will seek another judge. The one positive feature of the complete sentence bargain is the relative lack of surprises. Both sides know the specific terms, and the court either accepts or rejects the deal.

The *incomplete sentence bargain* is quite a different arrangement, however. The deal in this context typically commits the prosecutor to perform a certain task, but, importantly, the sentence's precise outcome is unknown. So, the prosecutor might agree to recommend a particular sentence *or* to remain silent at sentencing *or* not to oppose the defense attorney's sentencing request. As long as the prosecutor fulfills these terms, the bargain has been satisfied or completed. Missing here is any commitment or contract that a specific sentence must be imposed. In this respect, the incomplete sentence bargain is like the calculated/mercy guilty plea, since the sentence could be very different from what the defendant and defense counsel expect or want. Should this occur, there is no basis to appeal the sentence (assuming it is legal and is not a violation of judicial discretion) since the terms of the plea bargain have been fulfilled.

Historical Background of Plea Bargaining

Plea bargaining's controversial nature seems to have influenced estimates of its longevity. The assumption appears to be that the older plea bargaining is, the longer its heritage, and the more legitimacy it must have. This is false, of course. If plea bargaining is wrong or problematic, then it is so regardless of whether it is one year or one thousand years old. It could be argued that the older plea bargaining is, the longer the system has depended on it, and the less likely it is that plea bargaining can be eliminated. Advocates of plea bargaining suggest that it originated around the time of Cain and Abel or shortly thereafter (Newman, 1966; Wishingrad, 1974). Opponents of plea bargaining insist that the practice did not emerge until after the conclusion of the American Civil War (Alschuler, 1979a, 1979b; Friedman, 1979; Friedman and Percival, 1981; Haller, 1979). Both accounts are inaccurate. As is the often the case, the truth lies in between.

Plea bargaining can be traced back to twelfth-century England. There were two primary examples. The first, called *approvement,* involved a suspect charged with a felony, which at that time was a capital offense. Defendants who confessed to the crime, which amounted to a conviction, could avoid a death sentence by testifying against co-defendants who had assisted them in committing the offense. If the accomplice(s) were convicted due to this testimony, the life of the informant was spared, although this person forfeited all goods and lands and had to leave the country permanently. Any of these informants who were subsequently discovered in England could be killed without any legal consequences. If the informant failed to convince the jury of the accomplice's guilt, the informant was summarily executed. Obviously, this medieval plea bargain was more like plea gambling. Nevertheless, it had all the necessary features of plea bargaining: a guilty plea (or confession) that amounted to a self-conviction in exchange (hopefully) for a sentence concession from the state: exile in lieu of death. Approvement lasted until the mid-seventeenth century (Sanborn, 1986).

In thirteenth-century England, *abjuring the realm* (or *abjuration*) emerged. Abjuration involved a suspect who was able to reach a location that was considered a sanctuary. This safe haven allowed the accused a forty-day period during which to decide whether to go to trial or to confess the crime to a coroner. The former option virtually guaranteed conviction and death, especially if the accused had been chased to the place of sanctuary. The latter option meant that a conviction had occurred, and the defendant lost all goods and property and was forced to leave the country permanently. If this individual was ever found in England after the abjuration, summary execution was permitted. In abjuration all the necessary components of plea bargaining are present. The defendant was self-convicted via a confession and was granted a sentence reduction, from death to exile, in exchange. Abjuration lasted until the seventeenth century, when the concept of sanctuary was abolished (Sanborn, 1986).

Apart from state trials like those for treason, public prosecutors did not participate in regular criminal prosecutions in England until well into the nineteenth century. Victims or their representatives were responsible for prosecuting a criminal case (Fisher, 2003). Thus, the prosecutor, perhaps the most important mover for plea bargains, was absent from criminal court. This probably helps to explain why some research into eighteenth-century British criminal courts failed to discover plea bargaining occurring there (Feeley, 1997; Langbein, 1979). Nevertheless, research has disclosed convincing evidence of plea bargaining in at least one English criminal court during the latter half of the eighteenth century (Fisher, 2003).

The criminal court system in the United States does not appear to have become dependent on plea bargaining until the second half of the nine-teenth century. Tracing its history before the American Civil War is difficult and has just recently been initiated. Three studies have located plea bar-gaining in New York's (McConville and Mirsky, 1995) as well as in Boston's criminal courts in the first half of the nineteenth century (Ferdinand, 1992; Vogel, 1999), while another study of Middlesex County (MA) unearthed examples of plea bargaining in the late eighteenth century (Fisher, 2003). In fact, guilty pleas in Middlesex County outnumbered trials as early as the 1780s, or shortly after the founding of the country. One hundred years later the Middlesex County criminal court was dominated by plea bargaining (Fisher, 2003). It is interesting that guilty pleas toward the end of the Civil War accounted for more than 75% of the convictions in New York City, and by the end of the century this figure had risen to 85% (Moley, 1928). It is reasonable to infer that many, if not most, of these guilty pleas were the result of negotiation. It also appears that plea bargaining had become entrenched in the United States by the 1880s; one study has traced the ori-gin of plea bargaining in Alameda County, California, to this decade (Fried-man and Percival, 1981). Moreover, numerous appellate court cases at this time referred to prosecutors' obligations to honor the agreements they had made with defendants in securing their guilty pleas (Sanborn, 1986).

Despite the prevalence of guilty pleas in criminal courts by the close of the nineteenth century, plea bargaining appears to have remained one of the country's best-kept secrets until well into the twentieth century. It was not until the appearance of a couple of law review articles in the late 1920s (Miller, 1927; Moley, 1928) that plea bargaining first emerged from its jurid-ical closet. Amazingly, plea bargaining and the guilty-plea industry reen-tered the realm of the "unknown" until "rediscovered" and redisclosed in the mid-1950s (Comment, 1956; Newman, 1956). The U.S. Supreme Court did not address the validity of the calculated/mercy guilty plea (*Brady v. U.S.*, 1970) and the guilty plea bargain (*Santobello v. New York*, 1971) until the early 1970s. On both occasions the Supreme Court upheld the validity of these guilty pleas.

The Extent of Plea Bargaining

Confusion and exaggeration tend to create a false impression of how much plea bargaining there is in American criminal courts. It is still possible today to see estimates that *more than 90% of criminal cases are resolved by plea bargaining* (Gerber, 1998). This estimate is a distortion of reality. This estimate would mean that criminal courts have a 90% conviction rate. The closest this figure comes to telling the truth is that 90% of our convictions surely may be obtained via guilty pleas. That means that there would be 90 guilty pleas for every 10 trial convictions. That ratio could exist in many locations. This still does not mean that 90% of the convictions were plea bargains.

The problem with the distorted estimate is twofold. First, the estimate ignores the 30 to 45% of the caseload that prosecutors regularly *nol pros* or dismiss. Automatically, the number of dismissed charges tells us that convictions cannot occur in more than 60 to 70% of cases, and that assumes that all of the nondismissed cases result in conviction, which will not happen. Second, the estimate assumes that all the guilty pleas were negotiated. The proportion of guilty pleas resulting from negotiation will vary from one jurisdiction to another. In some locations, perhaps virtually all guilty pleas are bargained. It is possible, nevertheless, that in some locations very few of the guilty pleas were explicitly negotiated.

In the end it usually will be very difficult, if not impossible, to gauge the exact amount of plea bargaining in any criminal court. This is so because court data typically indicate the presence but not the character of a guilty plea. That is, we know when the defendant pleads guilty, but we tend not to know if the defendant tendered a negotiated or a non-negotiated guilty plea. Suffice it to say that in most major jurisdictions there should be a very high rate of guilty pleas, many of which were bargained.

Reasons for Criminal Court Dependency on Guilty Pleas

Why do so many cases result in guilty pleas, and most of them likely due to plea bargains? Two courthouse realities help facilitate the mass production of guilty pleas. First, *discretion* permits the resolution of cases via informal channels. That is, there is no requirement that charges be resolved only by trial. Instead, the courtroom workers have the discretion to negotiate rather than to litigate. Second, for the vast majority of defendants there is an *assumption of guilt* among all the courtroom workers. All court personnel, including defense attorneys, know or believe that very few of those accused of a crime are actually not guilty. Since most defendants are guilty anyway, there appears to be little need for trial; and since trial is neither mandated nor necessary, plea bargaining becomes an option. These courthouse realities explain how prosecutors, defense attorneys, and judges are authorized to pursue plea bargains and how generally they might rationalize doing so. Nevertheless, the motivations behind the guilty-plea industry run much deeper and are more complicated.

Systemic Reasons for Pleading Guilty in Criminal Court

The answer to the question posed above is that there are both systemic (or general) and case-specific reasons for the criminal court's dependency on plea bargaining. The general reasons are numerous, and at times controversial. The first reason typically cited to explain the abundance of guilty pleas is *case overload*. There are many behaviors that are criminal, and many individuals are arrested for committing these behaviors. Consequently, there are simply too many cases for the criminal court to process, especially through trial. Some argue that this is *the* reason for plea bargaining, but this is an exaggeration. Case overload can help explain a general pressure and inclination to negotiate. It can explain why prosecutors and some defense attorneys (particularly public defenders) lean almost automatically to dispose of a majority of their cases through guilty pleas. However, case overload cannot explain why any one case was negotiated or why so many defendants are willing to waive their right to trial. Moreover, one should expect a good deal of plea bargaining even in jurisdictions that are not swamped with cases. Nevertheless, the case overload problem hangs over the heads of prosecutors and public defenders (and judges) and certainly encourages both sides to prioritize their caseload and to decide which cases deserve or require trial versus those that can be resolved via negotiation. Prosecutors and public defenders understand that not every case can be brought to trial, and they will prioritize with that reality in mind.

Another general reason for the extent of guilty pleas is controversial, but it is undeniable and it complements the first reason. It concerns the nature and amount of rights that criminal defendants have. Simply put, some people believe that criminal defendants have been afforded so many rights that the courts cannot afford to implement them. The court procedure arguably is so good that we can't use it! The state then is forced to buy back (regarded by some as extorting) most of these rights from most defendants. Probably the most problematic right is the right to a jury trial, which is an administrative nightmare for the court. Any defendant who has committed a crime that *could result in six months incarceration* (meaning all felonies and many misdemeanors) is entitled to a jury trial. This is a considerable number of defendants. There is absolutely no way that all of these defendants could be offered a jury trial. Not only is a considerable amount of time spent in assembling a jury, but also the trial itself is complicated and lengthened by the jury's presence. Mistakes that can be tolerated when a judge is the sole fact finder can be completely unacceptable when a jury renders the verdict. Much of plea bargaining is about getting defendants to waive their right to a jury trial as well as their right to a bench trial. Complementing the too-many-rights proposition is the fact that rules of evidence and procedure have become more complex today compared to pre-Civil War times, which complicates and lengthens the trial (Langbein, 1978). Another related and bothersome feature is the ready availability of appeal. All trial convictions from criminal court are bound for appeal. Although the vast majority of these appeals are rejected by the appellate courts, the fact stands that all trial convictions, and especially those secured through jury trial, are vulnerable to reversal and that the appellate process requires considerable resources. Guilty pleas tend to offer the defendant a much more limited avenue of appeal, and it is possible for a plea bargain to include a defendant's agreement not to appeal the conviction.

Another controversial explanation for the number of guilty pleas is that defendants who exercise their right to trial are penalized for doing so. In other words, there are harsher sentences reserved for those convicted via trial than for those who plead guilty. This is where the extortion (referred to above) comes in. Prosecutors apparently have to offer some kind of reduction in charges and/or sentence to the defendant in order to secure a guilty plea. It is highly unlikely for most defendants to simply give up their right to trial without demanding some sort of payback. If defendants truly thought or were guaranteed that they would receive the same sentence regardless of whether they pled guilty or demanded trial, few would be expected to plead guilty. There would be nothing to gain from pleading guilty, and there would be nothing to lose by going to trial (for the vast majority of defendants). In order to reinforce the idea that one is better off by waiving rights and pleading guilty, there must be a perception, if not a reality, that defendants electing trial will be punished. Consequently, many defendants will plead guilty in exchange for the promised leniency and with some apprehension of being punished much more severely if they were bold enough to demand trial. It should be noted that some defendants who choose to plea bargain can end up worse off than they would have been if they had demanded a trial. This better-result-through-trial outcome obviously can occur when defendants are acquitted at trial, but it also can happen when they are convicted. In the latter situation a better sentence could occur due to the defendant's being convicted of fewer and/or lesser offenses and/or simply because the judge is not a harsh sentencer.

Two political scientists, Eisenstein and Jacob (1977), are credited with identifying another possible explanation for the abundance of guilty pleas.

This explanation involves the concept of the *courtroom work group*—consisting of the major courtroom workers (the judge, the prosecutor, and the defense attorney) and the relationships and interdependencies among them. These individuals rely on each other, working together for their own as well as the court's survival. Perpetual conflict, hostility, dishonesty, taking every case to trial, and even surprises cannot be tolerated if survival is the goal. Cooperation, the only acceptable means to achieve that end, means negotiating most cases instead of litigating, hence plea bargaining. Some cynics question whether individuals are being reasonable and doing justice, or whether there is a conspiracy (or cop-out) among work-group members not to do their job.

The final and bottom-line reason for the abundance of plea bargains is simple, albeit impossible to verify in all cases. *All parties stand to benefit* from pleading guilty via negotiation. The U.S. Supreme Court made specific reference to this "fact" when it noted that guilty pleas and plea bargaining "are important components of this country's criminal justice system. Properly administered, they can benefit all concerned" (*Blackledge v. Perry*, 1974: 71). This proposition is mostly a synthesis of the previous reasons. However, it needs to be noted that the failure of one of the major parties to perceive a benefit from plea bargaining, on a sustained basis could derail the assembly-line, guilty-plea process. Rather than note here how each party appears to benefit, the case-specific reasons to plea bargain that follow will detail the ways in which the participants gain from avoiding trial.

Case-Specific Reasons for Pleading Guilty in Criminal Court

For the courtroom work group, plea bargaining might constitute salvation from an otherwise impossible situation. For the defendant the motivation could be salvation from the death penalty. Prosecutors appreciate the certainty of conviction that a guilty plea represents. Trial guarantees nothing, even in cases where the evidence is overwhelming. Guilty pleas take the uncertainty (and some work) out of preparing cases for trial, and they compensate for uncooperative or unreliable witnesses; evidence problems due to illegal searches, seizures, and interrogations; constricting rules of evidence; and proof that, while substantial, may not be viewed by a judge or by all jurors as being beyond a reasonable doubt.

For concerned prosecutors, plea bargaining might spare victims and witnesses from having to recall and testify about traumatic events. Chances are that prosecutors have a particular sentence in mind, based on an estimate of what the case is worth (or the "going rate") in light of the accused's current charges and previous criminal record. It is also likely that the potential sentence following conviction on all charges would far exceed what the prosecutor expects or wants, which makes negotiation relevant and profitable. In this context, trial serves little or no purpose. Prosecutors typically can get all they want from plea bargaining and eliminate the prospect of not getting anything at all, which could happen if there is an acquittal. More importantly, prosecutors can secure returns from plea bargaining that would be unlikely or impossible if the case went to trial. For example, plea bargaining can be used to secure the defendant's cooperation in helping to convict co-defendants or other offenders involved in independent crimes. Plea bargaining also might provide the victim with a larger amount of restitution than that likely to be awarded by a judge following conviction. Finally, plea bargaining probably means the caseload will be processed a lot faster, with many more convictions than would occur via trial.

Defense attorneys frequently have their clients' lives in their hands. Plea bargaining can involve taking the death penalty off the table, guaranteeing that the defendant will not be sentenced to death. Even if death is not a possible sentence, many offenders face the prospect of lengthy incarceration that a charge and/or sentence bargain can greatly modify. To the extent that defense attorneys' reputations are gauged by their success in damage control or securing the best possible results for their clients, plea bargaining at times offers serious opportunities for counsel to arrange better outcomes. The potential of a trial penalty convinces the defense bar that trial should be reserved for cases that merit serious inquiry, like those defendants who insist on their innocence and those who face very serious sentences with or without negotiation. Reputation is secured by more than just outcomes. It is critical for defense attorneys (and for the other court actors as well) to maintain credibility among their fellow workers. If defense attorneys adamantly insist that every client they represent is categorically not guilty, their credibility could be damaged. For public defenders and for those assigned/appointed counsel who appear frequently in criminal court, caseload can be an issue. Plea bargaining can facilitate the resolution of cases for these lawyers, much like it does for prosecutors.

Judges also are prone to favor plea bargaining for caseload reasons. Having to conduct a trial for every defendant in an urban court most likely would create a significant backlog, if not an outright collapse of the court. In part, judges will be gauged by how well they move their docket. Judges who fail to resolve open cases more quickly could be assigned to less favorable posts. In addition, judges' reputations are determined by the frequency and nature of reversals of their bench and jury trial convictions. That is, the more a judge is reversed by the appellate courts, the more doubt is cast on a judge's ability to conduct a fair trial. Plea bargaining allows judges to escape most appellate scrutiny and resulting challenges to their commitment to justice (Fisher, 2003). Similarly, plea bargaining also removes from the judge the often difficult responsibility of determining witnesses' credibility, the guilt of the accused, and sometimes the extent of the punishment that should be imposed.

For the most part, defendants plea bargain because they believe that it will avoid the harsher outcome that is possible if their cases go to trial. Plea bargaining invariably should involve an offer for an outcome that is less severe than what is theoretically possible should the matter be litigated. Again, nothing is certain for defendants in trial situations. Even those not guilty or those with "good" cases cannot rely on vindication via trial. Judges and juries can get it wrong. Moreover, letting cases proceed to trial can expose allegations about defendants that they would prefer to remain undisclosed, whether accurate or not. Having victims and witnesses testify about what the defendant is supposed to have done can result in defendants looking much worse and as deserving more punishment than they would get following the mere recitation of facts offered when pleading guilty. For the minority of defendants who retain their own attorney, plea bargaining might be less expensive than the costs of taking the case to trial. For defendants in jail plea bargaining might mean an immediate release or quicker release from custody than would occur if a trial were needed.

Problems Associated with Plea Bargaining

As with many other aspects of plea bargaining, determining the problems that result from the court's dependency on the practice is controversial. Its very existence in the criminal court connotes an *unseemly bartering* for consideration and surrendering of rights. To be sure, plea bargaining has received more negative than positive press, and the general attitudes toward it among the public are probably unfavorable. Popularity cannot be the deciding factor in determining whether the practice should be allowed to exist, however. At the very least the public needs extensive education as to all the good and bad elements involved with plea bargaining before their attitudes should serve as a gauge for its survival.

Perhaps the easiest objection to deal with is the assertion that plea bargaining lets *guilty offenders avoid adequate punishment*. This may or may not be true in certain cases, but plea bargaining cannot be blamed for the court's pervasive failure to always punish adequately. Measures like the exclusionary rule, the protection against self-incrimination, judicial and jury nullification (where guilty defendants are wrongfully acquitted), *nol prossing* cases with or without bargaining, and structural bargaining (through which defendants are rewarded for demanding less of the criminal court than their entitlement) also contribute significantly to the system's leniently punishing criminals. Moreover, the presence of lenient sentencing judges in criminal court also opens the door for offenders to get away with certain crimes by receiving punishments that are substantially less severe than what the statutes provide. Ironically, plea bargaining will involve some defendants who would not have been punished at all, because their cases would have been dismissed or they would have been acquitted at trial. In addition, at least some would have been sentenced more leniently following a trial conviction. For this population plea bargaining actually secures greater punishment than would have happened otherwise.

Contention also surrounds criticisms that plea bargaining contributes to both the *cover-up of illegal searches and seizures* and *overcharging* by the prosecutor. It is possible that the trade between the defendant and the prosecutor could include a waiver of the former's right to file a motion to suppress to exclude the illegally seized items. Theoretically, the greater the potential for the evidence to be declared inadmissible, the greater the chance the defendant can secure a favorable deal from the prosecutor. To the extent that this trade-off occurs, illegally seized evidence can contribute to a conviction. Nevertheless, a good deal of plea bargaining will happen after a motion to suppress has been denied because the evidence was determined by a judge to have been legally acquired, and some jurisdictions (like New York) even allow a defendant to plea bargain while retaining a right to appeal adverse rulings on the motion to suppress.

Prosecutors may be encouraged to overcharge defendants in order to gain some leverage in plea bargaining. After all, to deal with the opposition it certainly makes sense for the prosecution to start with higher charges rather than lower ones. Interestingly, the U.S. Supreme Court has permitted prosecutors to seek an indictment on higher charges after a defendant refused to plea bargain on lesser charges, even though the prosecutor's decision to re-indict the accused was solely in reaction to the defendant's refusal to plead guilty (*Bordenkircher v. Hayes,* 1978). Nevertheless, a significant minority of the justices in that case felt the prosecutor's charging behavior was purely retaliatory or vindictive and was a due-process violation. These justices noted that had the prosecutor initially charged the defendant with the higher/highest possible charges, there would not have been any due-process claim in this plea-bargaining context. Thus, the potential message is clear that in order to avoid constitutional problems in the future, charging the highest feasible charge is probably the wisest course in many situations for the prosecutor.

Most importantly, however, overcharging is necessary and unavoidable. That is, overcharging must occur in the American criminal justice system for one very fundamental reason having nothing to do with plea bargaining: Once prosecution begins, charges against the accused cannot be raised. They can only be lowered by a judge's or jury's determination that the prosecution has failed to sustain the burden of proof required for the charges filed. Charges cannot be raised, however, because it would constitute a violation of the defendant's Sixth Amendment right to notice of the charges that are the basis of the accusation. Consequently, if the prosecutor discovers during trial that the accused actually has been undercharged, it is too late to compensate for this error. In short, even if plea bargaining were totally abolished, overcharging still would occur, unless the Sixth Amendment provision of notice of charges was abolished.

Another debatable but more serious contention is that plea bargaining results in the *innocent falsely convicting* themselves. When the plea-bargain offer substantially reduces the potential sentence, this problem becomes more pronounced and possible. For example, in *Bordenkircher v. Hayes* (1978) the difference between the plea bargain (five years in prison) and the potential sentence if convicted at trial (life imprisonment) was extreme (albeit the U.S. Supreme Court did not reverse the eventual life sentence in this case). The offer may be too good to turn down, even for the innocent. When this happens, plea bargaining appears intolerable—and perhaps it is. It is of little consolation that the innocent can be wrongfully convicted at trial as well. This concern certainly militates against permitting huge discrepancies between offered and potential sentences. Hopefully, the colloquy that must occur between the defendant and the judge when the former pleads guilty (see *Boykin v. Alabama*, 1969) should weed out at least some of these defendants who are prepared to wrongfully self-convict.

A far more pernicious, more prevalent, and more debated problem entails the *trial penalty* idea: If the defendant takes the court's time (by demanding trial), the court allegedly will take the defendant's time (by imposing a harsher and lengthier sentence on a trial conviction). Research is divided on this topic. While some studies have discovered what appears to be a trial penalty (Brereton and Casper, 1981–1982; Uhlman and Walker, 1980), other studies have failed to find this result (Eisenstein and Jacob, 1977; Rhodes, 1978). Considering all the nuances of the trial and sentencing process it can be difficult, if not impossible, to pinpoint whether an enhanced sentence following a trial conviction (compared to the plea-bargain offer) stems from permissible (e.g., discovery of new information concerning the accused during trial) or impermissible reasons (e.g., the judge openly acknowledging that the sentence is payback for the exercise of constitutional rights).

For example, in *Alabama v. Smith* (1989), the U.S. Supreme Court addressed a situation in which the defendant originally was sentenced to thirty years concurrently for a guilty plea to burglary and rape (a sodomy charge was *nol prossed*). Subsequently, the defendant appealed the sentence and won a reversal of the guilty-plea conviction. The defendant then went to trial before the same judge, who, after the jury convicted the offender on all three original charges, imposed two concurrent life sentences for the burglary and sodomy charges, accompanied by a consecutive sentence of 150 years for the rape charge. The Supreme Court determined that the enhanced sentence was legitimate because it was indeed based on the judge's explanation that he learned quite a bit more about the criminal incident due to the trial testimony and evidence that had not been disclosed via acceptance of the guilty plea. Inasmuch as this claim of a revelation of new evidence is likely to be available in many comparable situations, it should be rare for an appellate court to definitively find that a trial penalty has been exerted against a defendant solely due to an unwillingness to plea bargain.

For some observers it is possible to consider plea bargaining solely as a reward mechanism for those who surrender their right to trial; the U.S. Supreme Court portrayed plea bargaining in this manner, which enabled the Court to grant it legitimacy. To acknowledge that plea bargaining amounts to penalizing those who demand trial would have forced the Supreme Court to declare the practice unconstitutional. It is not constitutionally permissible to punish people for exercising their constitutional rights. Nevertheless, for other observers it is impossible to separate the rewarding of guilty pleas from the punishment of contesting guilt. If these two phenomena truly are inseparable, then the Supreme Court's conclusion is disingenuous at best.

A final, seemingly undeniable problem surrounding plea bargaining concerns the *role distortion* that results from the excessive amount of plea negotiation that occurs in criminal courts (Neubauer, 2002). Plea bargaining converts the prosecutor's role into that of an all-powerful, multifunctioning official. Due to the extent and significance of plea bargaining, prosecutors not only are responsible for their regular charging duties but also operate like jury and judge in convicting and sentencing offenders. Inasmuch as a guilty plea amounts to a conviction, and very often the sentence is arranged via the negotiation, the prosecutor has enormous, arguably disproportionate, influence and input into the charging, convicting, and sentencing functions. Judges, who appear to play a meaningful role only in the relatively few cases that proceed to trial, become little more than a rubber stamp in the typical plea bargain. Their ability to ensure that justice is done in all cases can be seriously compromised by an inability to scrutinize deals reached between prosecution and defense. Rather than focusing on vindicating their clients' rights, defense attorneys are sometimes forced to make literally life-or-death decisions in determining whether to take the case to trial or to a plea. Similarly, most defendants are not free simply to choose whether to exercise their constitutional rights. They know that there can be, and most likely will be, a very negative consequence for opting to take a losing case to trial. In short, plea bargaining, especially when there is so much of it, is not very compatible with the ideals of the adversary process.

Some Final Observations

The bottom line for plea bargaining in American criminal courts is that, although it is fraught with problems, some of which are potentially seri-

ous, it makes sense and is probably inevitable. Being rewarded for pleading guilty or acknowledging guilt makes sense, even when no remorse
accompanies the plea. Parents, teachers, and judges are all likely to
respond more leniently when an offender "fesses up." Not only is there an
absence of defiance in this situation, but also there is no need to spend
considerable time and effort to prove guilt. Even more critical at times is
that the confession or plea resolves doubt about criminal liability that a
trial may not. That this tendency to respond favorably to confessions of
guilt would be institutionalized into the plea-bargaining industry known
to rule criminal courts today is little more than a logical extension or evolution of a natural tendency.

Plea bargaining, or something like it, seems inevitable, given the amount
of crime and even the amount of rights enjoyed by criminal defendants in
this country. Simply put, there are probably too many criminals who have
too many rights for the full adversary process to have a chance to work. To
be sure, caseload pressure alone cannot explain plea bargaining. Nevertheless, there is no doubt whatsoever that the criminal courts could not survive the full exercise of defendants' rights. More importantly, full enforcement of the criminal law would also be impractical. There is room for
compromise. In American criminal courts that compromise has taken the
form of bargaining with offenders in a variety of contexts. To eliminate plea
bargaining there would have to be serious reforms both in the behaviors
that are considered crimes (e.g., decriminalizing prostitution and other
"victimless" crimes) and in the rights defendants have been afforded in the
criminal court, including even the appellate process. To some, these solutions could appear to be worse than the problem.

In the end, plea bargaining probably achieves "rough justice." That is,
most of those who plea bargain are guilty of the crimes with which they
are charged and to which they plead guilty. In addition, most offenders
likely receive sentences that are appropriate and close to what they
"deserve," given the seriousness of their crimes and their criminal records.
For many of these offenders trial is neither beneficial nor necessary, while
trials are reserved for those who have serious claims of being innocent
and/or who face significant punishment. In addition, most plea bargains
involve routine arrangements and relatively minimal sentences, not the
high stakes that make plea bargaining problematic.

Plea bargaining merits close scrutiny to ensure that innocent defendants
are not pressured into trading away their rights and to guarantee that prosecutors do not abuse their powers. Unless and until there are serious
reforms in both the penal code and criminal procedure, we certainly
should not expect plea bargaining or the predominance of the guilty plea
in the criminal court to wane.

References

Alschuler, A.W. (1968) "The Prosecutor's Role in Plea Bargaining." *University of Chicago Law Review*, 36:50.

Alschuler, A.W. (1976) "The Trial Judge's Role in Plea Bargaining, Part 1." *Columbia Law Review*, 76:1059.

Alschuler, A.W. (1979a) "Plea Bargaining and its History." *Columbia Law Review*, 79:1.

Alschuler, A.W. (1979b) "Plea Bargaining and its History." *Law and Society Review*: 12:211.

American Bar Association (ABA) (1968) *Standards Relating to Pleas of Guilty*. New York: American Bar Association/Institute of Judicial Administration.

Brereton, D. and J. Casper (1981–1982) "Does It Pay to Plead Guilty? Differential Sentencing and the Functioning of Criminal Courts." *Law and Society Review*: 16:45.

Comment (1956) "The Influence of the Defendant's Plea on Judicial Determination." *Yale Law Review*: 66:204.

Eisenstein, J. and H. Jacob (1977) *Felony Justice*. Boston: Little, Brown.

Feeley, M. M. (1997) "Legal Complexity and the Transformation of the Criminal Court Process: The Origins of Plea Bargaining." *Israel Law Review*, 31:183.

Ferdinand, T. (1992) *Boston's Lower Criminal Courts, 1814–1850*. Newark: University of Delaware Press.

Fisher, G. (2003) *Plea Bargaining's Triumph: A History of Plea Bargaining in America*. Stanford: Stanford University Press.

Friedman, L. M. (1979) "Plea Bargaining in Historical Perspective." *Law and Society Review*, 13:247.

Friedman, L. M. and R. Percival (1981) *The Roots of Justice*. Chapel Hill: University of North Carolina Press.

Gerber, R. J. (1998) "A Judicial View of Plea Bargaining." *Criminal Law Bulletin*, 34:16.

Haller, M. H. (1979) "Plea Bargaining: The Nineteenth Century Context." *Law and Society Review*, 13:273.

Heumann, M. (2002) "Plea Bargaining: Process and Outcome." *Criminal Law Bulletin*, 38:630.

Jaspin, E. (1981) "Back on the Street: How our Juvenile Justice System Fails." *Philadelphia Daily News*, September 21–25.

Kuh, R. H. (1967) "Plea Copping." *N.Y. County Lawyer's Association Bar Bulletin*, 24:160.

Langbein, J. H. (1978) "Torture and Plea Bargaining." *University of Chicago Law Review*, 46:3.

Langbein, J. H. (1979) "Understanding the Short History of Plea Bargaining." *Law and Society Review*, 13:261.

McConville, M. and C. L. Mirsky (1995) "The Rise of Guilty Pleas: New York, 1800–1865." *Journal of Law and Society*, 22:443.

McDonald, W. F. (1979) "From Plea Negotiation to Coercive Justice: Notes on the Specification of a Concept." *Law and Society Review*, 13:385.

Miller, J. (1927) "The Compromise of Criminal Cases." *Southern California Law Review*, 1:1.

Miller, H. S., W. McDonald, and J. A. Cramer (1978) *Plea Bargaining in the United States*. Washington, D.C.: U.S. Government Printing Office.

Moley, R. (1928) "The Vanishing Jury." *Southern California Law Review*, 2:97.

Neubauer, D. W. (2002) *America's Courts and the Criminal Justice System*, 7th ed. Belmont CA: Wadsworth.

Newman D. J. (1956) "Pleading Guilty for Considerations: A Study of Bargain Justice." *Journal of Criminal Law, Criminology, and Police Science*, 46:780.

Newman, D. J. (1966) *Conviction: The Determination of Guilt or Innocence Without Trial*. Boston: Little, Brown.

Note (1970) "The Unconstitutionality of Plea Bargaining." *Harvard Law Review*, 83:1387.

Note (1972) "Restructuring the Plea Bargain." *Yale Law Journal*, 81:286.

Polstein, R. (1962) "How to Settle a Criminal Case." *The Practical Lawyer*, 8:35.

Rhodes, W. (1978) *Plea Bargaining: Who Gains? Who Loses?* Washington, D.C.: Institute for Law and Social Research.

Sanborn, J. B. (1986) "A Historical Sketch of Plea Bargaining." *Justice Quarterly*, 3:111.

Segar, R. L. (1978) "Plea Bargaining Techniques." *American Jurisprudence Trials*, 25:69.

Uhlman, T. and D. Walker (1980) "'He Takes Some of My Time: I Take Some of His': An Analysis of Judicial Sentencing Patterns in Jury Cases." *Law and Society Review*, 14:323.

Vogel, M. E. (1999) "The Social Origins of Plea Bargaining: Conflict and the Law in the Process of State Formation, 1830–1860." *Law and Society Review*, 33:161.

Weintraub, R. G. and R. Tough (1942) "Lesser Pleas Considered." *Journal of Criminal Law and Criminology*, 32:506.

White, W. S. (1971) "A Proposal for Reform of the Plea Bargaining Process." *University of Pennsylvania Law Review*, 119:439.

Wishingrad, J. (1974) "The Plea Bargain in Historical Perspective." *Buffalo Law Review*, 23:499.

Cases Cited

Alabama v. Smith, 490 U.S. 794 (1989)
Blackledge v. Perry, 417 U.S. 21 (1974)
Bordenkircher v. Hayes, 434 U.S. 357 (1978)
Boykin v. Alabama, 395 U.S. 238 (1969)
Brady v. United States, 397 U.S. 742 (1970)
Santobello v. New York, 404 U.S. 257 (1971)
Scott v. United States, 419 F.2d 264 (D.C. Cir. 1969)

8

Prosecutorial Discretion under the Federal Sentencing Guidelines

KEITH A. WILMOT

Prior to passage of the Sentencing Reform Act of 1984, federal prosecutors possessed broad discretion to manipulate charges and to structure plea agreements (Schulhofer and Nagel, 1989: 238). Sentencing decisions made by the judge and subsequent decisions of the Parole Commission could temper the influence of prosecutorial discretion on sentence outcomes (Schulhofer and Nagel, 1989: 238–239). Therefore, in response to concerns about prosecutorial and judicial discretion concerns raised during the late 1960s and early 1970s, Congress chose to target reform efforts on disparities in the federal sentencing process (Tonry, 1996: 9–11). As a result of passage of the Crime Control Act of 1984 and the Sentencing Reform Act of 1984, Congress eliminated parole release discretion and dramatically curtailed judicial sentencing discretion (Tonry, 1996: 11). Prosecutorial discretion, however, remained virtually untouched (Schulhofer and Nagel, 1989: 238).

Judge Frank H. Easterbrook[1] (Nagel, Breyer, and McCarthy, 1989: 1834) noted, in a 1989 symposium entitled *Equality versus Discretion in Sentencing*, that prosecutorial discretion under the newly enacted federal sentencing guidelines assumed a more influential role:

> [A]lthough the amount of discretion vested in prosecutors and judges may have declined, the ratio has changed. That is, the prosecutor still has the same absolute power as before, while the district judge's power has been diminished. So the ratio of prosecutorial to district court power has changed, and that is a fundamental consequence. It may be

Written especially for *Courts and Justice*.

good or bad. I am not trying to say whether it is good or bad. It is something that has to be understood.

Because of the fact that prosecutorial discretion became greater *relative* to judicial discretion in criminal sentencing, prosecutors now exercise significant influence over criminal sentences in the federal system (Stith and Cabranes, 1998: 130). Whereas prosecutors have always had substantial discretion in charging and plea bargaining, under the Federal Sentencing Guidelines these decisions assume far greater significance for sentencing (Stith and Cabranes, 1998: 145). The prosecutor can influence a defendant's sentence through the following interrelated functions: (1) the charging decision; (2) the plea-bargaining process; (3) the presentence investigation report (PSI);[2] and (4) the sentencing hearing[3] (Parsons, 1994: 8). Another important area of influence is prosecutorial discretion in filing motions for downward departures based on substantial assistance to law enforcement authorities[4] (Stith and Cabranes, 1998: 130). These are crucial areas where the prosecutor can exert his/her influence on the sentencing process, which may lead to dissimilar treatment of similar offenders. More specifically,

> to the extent that the offense for which the defendant is convicted varies with the discretionary decisions of individual prosecutors and the same offense conduct does not always result in the same set of conviction charges, unwarranted disparity may be reintroduced into the federal criminal justice system.[5] (Nagel and Schulhofer, 1992: 502)

The Charging Decision under the Federal Sentencing Guidelines

The broad scope of most federal statutes allows the federal prosecutor the discretion to charge a course of criminal conduct under a variety of statutes that carry quite different sentencing outcomes (Standen, 1993: 1509). Essentially, the sentencing outcome is a result of the crime charged by the prosecutor, which in turn allows the prosecutor's charging decision to control plea bargaining (Standen, 1993: 1506). The fact that control of prosecutorial discretion lies within the executive branch and the Sentencing Commission is designated in the judicial branch makes attempts to control prosecutorial discretion in charging a very complex issue[6] (Nagel, 1990: 936). More precisely, there is nothing to prevent prosecutors from introducing unwarranted disparity by charging similar defendants differently, for reasons determined solely by the prosecutor (Zeno, 1991: 32).

According to a Senior Circuit Court Judge (Wilmot, 2002: 240), prosecutors have substantial discretion under the Federal Sentencing Guidelines:

> The prosecutor chooses whether to prosecute. He decides whether to plea bargain or not and he decides what the charge is going to be and he is the one that procures the evidence. The probation officers, who

prepare the pre-sentence reports, do not have the investigative ability, ordinarily, to do anything other than to get the version of the offense and the relevant conduct that is provided by the police, the prosecutor's office and the interview with the defendant or defendant's counsel. They do not have the resources to make an independent investigation. So in the final analysis, the prosecutor is the one who makes the decision. At least under the prior law, the prosecutor had, of course, the power to charge, but the sentencing power remained with the Court and the extent to which you are going to use relevant conduct in determining the sentence was up to the judge who is appointed by lifetime rather than the prosecutor who is a political appointee and whose responsibility it is to secure prosecutions and to secure the imprisonment of people who are found guilty.[7]

Furthermore, under a real offense system where the defendant is sentenced on the offense of conviction(s) *and* his/her relevant conduct (i.e., uncharged conduct, dismissed counts, and/or acquitted counts), the prosecutor can circumvent the role of both the grand jury and the petit jury (Parsons, 1994: 8; Lear, 1993: 1229–1236). Under real offense sentencing, the prosecutor is not required to subject *all* criminal conduct to grand jury review[8] or to evaluation by the petit jury during trial. In fact, the prosecutor has unchecked authority to present additional criminal conduct (i.e., relevant conduct) at the more informal sentencing hearing where proof of the evidence is considered under a "preponderance of the evidence" standard (Lear, 1993: 1229–1236).

For example, in the case of *United States v. Kikumura*,[9] the government indicted and convicted Kikumura for twelve passport and weapons violations. The prosecutor, at sentencing, introduced conduct that had not been presented at the grand jury hearing or at the trial; he proved these allegations using the weaker "preponderance of the evidence" standard. The sentencing judge departed upward from the guideline range for the offense of conviction after considering this unindicted and unconvicted conduct. As a result, the sentence for the offense of conviction, which fell within the guideline range of 27 to 33 months, was increased to 263 months.

As Lear states (1993: 1223), "the Guidelines render the grand and petit juries powerless to check such abuse should the need arise." Therefore, with a real offense sentencing system that takes advantage of unadjudicated conduct, the prosecutor, by not charging certain criminal behavior, can significantly influence other stages of the criminal justice process. In other words, the indictment does not always inform the defendant of the criminal activity that may be relevant for plea bargaining, trial, and sentencing purposes (Parsons, 1994: 8). Similarly, the prosecutor, by failing to introduce evidence, can significantly influence the defendant's charge by allowing a lesser charge to be filed. For example, as an Eighth Circuit Federal District Court judge states in an interview (Wilmot, 2002: 277):

Let's assume we have a drug quantity issue and, as you know, drug quantity drives the guideline sentence up dramatically. The probation officer has made a finding of five kilograms, the prosecutor wants, even at this stage [sentencing], after there's a plea that has been entered . . . the prosecutor can announce in chambers, "Well, we are not going forward." Keep in mind now the burden of proof at this stage is on the government to show the drug quantity even though the probation officer has made a calculation based on the discovery file. If the government lawyer says, "we are not going forward because we think this is a wonderful person now—he's cooperated, he's given us substantial assistance, he's pleaded guilty." I've seen that happen where the government says, "I am not putting on evidence as to drug quantity." If you don't put on evidence as to drug quantity or only put on some evidence as to drug quantity, that's all you can go on, particularly if there is a denial of some of the probation officer's report. You need some evidence. If the government puts on no evidence or only some of their evidence, they can at that stage control how much the guidelines impact on the defendant. Even though it is real offense conduct, if they don't prove up the offense and the defendant has put it in issue by saying, "I'm not stipulating to drug quantity or some other factors," that power remains in the hands of the prosecutor.[10]

Consequently, since the discretionary power of the prosecutor is unreviewed and unchecked, potential disparity may exist at the charging stage. Thus, the discretionary charging decision by the prosecutor may allow similar defendants to be charged differently for similar crimes, which can result in dissimilar sentence outcomes.

Plea Bargaining

Plea bargaining is critical to sentencing outcomes in the federal criminal courts. Approximately 90 percent of all convictions are the result of guilty pleas,[11] of which the vast majority are the result of plea agreements between the defense and prosecution (Stith and Cabranes, 1998: 130). Although prosecutorial practices vary from district to district and case to case in the federal system, the fundamental process of plea bargaining can be influenced by the prosecutor's discretion at various stages of the criminal justice system. These stages include: the preindictment stage, charge selection, the indictment stage, and substantial assistance motions (Parsons, 1994: 8–9; Stith and Cabranes, 1998: 130). For example, federal prosecutors have complete autonomy during plea bargaining at the preindictment stage since supervisory approval is not sought until the indictment is returned. Moreover, charges dismissed during the plea-bargaining process may be reintroduced as relevant conduct at the sentencing hearing. The discretionary decision by the federal prosecutor to file (or not to file) a substantial assistance motion also may be used as a bargaining tool in the plea-bargaining process, which can influence sentence outcomes (Parsons, 1994: 8–9; Stith and Cabranes: 130).

By providing general policy statements rather than explicit guidelines for plea negotiations, Congress recognized the delicate balance that must be achieved between the ideals of sentencing reform[12] and the practical realities of a system that must dispose of thousands of criminal cases every year (Wilkins, 1988: 187). To illustrate, Congress intended, as a primary purpose of sentencing reform, that there be equity among defendants with similar records convicted of similar criminal conduct (Wilkins, 1988: 187). There is, however, an inherent tension between equity and the primary goal of the defendant in plea bargaining—the goal of receiving a more lenient sentence (Wilkins, 1988: 187). As Stith and Cabranes (1998: 130) point out, "each guilty plea is in some sense unique; charging decisions and plea negotiations are, by their very nature, case-specific." Therefore, the parties who engage in plea bargaining obviously do not share the sentencing reformers' goal of reducing unwarranted sentence disparity (Yellen, 1993: 419). Thus, a defendant wants to be considered individually in order to receive a lighter sentence than a similarly situated offender (Yellen, 1993: 420) and, consequently, the defendant will enter a plea agreement only if properly induced (Parsons, 1994: 8).

In the final analysis, the U.S. Sentencing Commission (2000: 7) did not propose any major reforms of the plea-bargaining process. As Wilkins (1988: 188) states, "The potential of unanticipated problems that could undermine the effective administration of the system weighed heavily against a broad and sudden revamping of the plea negotiation process."

Therefore, the autonomous authority of federal prosecutors to charge and plea bargain under the federal sentencing guidelines adheres to the precedent in the Supreme Court decision *Bordenkircher v. Hayes*,[13] in which Justice Stewart's concurring opinion stated:

> In our system, so long as the prosecutor has probable cause to believe that the accused committed an offense defined by statute, the decision whether or not to prosecute, and what charge to file or bring before a grand jury, generally rests in his discretion. To hold that the prosecutor's desire to induce a guilty plea is an "unjustifiable standard," which, like race or religion, may play no part in his charging decision, would contradict the very premises that underlie the concept of plea bargaining itself. Moreover, a rigid constitutional rule that would prohibit a prosecutor from acting forthrightly in his dealings with the defense could only invite unhealthy subterfuge that would drive the practice of plea bargaining back into the shadows from which it has so recently emerged.

In sum, it is the unconstrained authority to charge and plea bargain by federal prosecutors, coupled with the principles of a real offense sentencing system and the defendant's relevant conduct, which play significant roles in sentencing for those defendants convicted of a federal crime.

Endnotes

[1] United States Court of Appeals for the Seventh Circuit; Senior Lecturer, University of Chicago.

[2] A personal interview with an Eighth Circuit Federal District Court Judge (July 2000) explained that "[Probation Officers] almost always refer to the discovery file in the presentence reports that I read. They almost universally refer to the discovery file with the government arriving at critical factors in their findings for drug quantity, that sort of thing" (Wilmot, 2002).

Additionally, an interview with a federal probation officer (August 2000) disclosed what information was obtained from the prosecutor. "Primarily, the information from the offense conduct is derived from the government's discovery file that we are allowed to peruse and write the offense conduct from. We also include any information that the defense counsel wants to add, like a defendants' version of the offense conduct. . . . The presentence report does recommend a sentence or a range to the judge. . . . We do recommend to the judge ideas about downward departures if we have some information or evidence to convey that possibly this is a departure issue that the parties might want to look at" (Wilmot, 2002).

[3] Sentencing factors shall be considered under the preponderance of the evidence standard (*McMillan v. Pennsylvania*, 477 U.S. 79 [1986]); as opposed to the constitutional requirement of proof beyond a reasonable doubt for proof of a statutory element of an offense (Stith and Cabranes, 1998: 151).

[4] Substantial assistance is a sentencing factor, but the judge may not exercise his or her discretion as to the extent of the downward departure unless he or she receives the prosecutor's motion requesting the court to depart downward (Stith and Cabranes, 1998: 76).

[5] For example, "defendants *convicted* of bank robbery under similar circumstances may all receive the same sentence (say, 41 months), but defendants who *commit* bank robbery under similar circumstances may receive different sentences (from probation to 41 months) if they are convicted of radically different offenses as a result of the plea bargaining process" (Nagel and Schulhofer, 1992: 502).

[6] The Sentencing Commission cannot dictate to a United States Attorney what counts to charge, since that is exclusively an executive decision. For example, if a federal prosecutor chose to circumvent the guidelines by charging a defendant arrested for distributing 500 grams of cocaine with a phone count (using telecommunications to commit a crime) (21 U.S.C. § 843(b) [1982])—resulting in less than one-fifth the sentence exposure—there is little the Commission can do about it (Nagel, 1990: 936). Also, see *United States v. Nixon*, 418 U.S. 683 (1974), which states that the decision to prosecute rests exclusively in the executive branch.

[7] Personal interview: May 2000.

[8] *United States v. Cox*, 342 F.2d 167 (5th Cir.) *cert. denied*, 381 U.S. 935 (1965), points out that neither the grand jury nor the judiciary may contravene the executive's decision not to indict. Also, Federal Rules of Criminal Procedure 7(a) authorizes prosecution only pursuant to indictment (or information if indictment is waived), thus eliminating the federal grand jury's right to proceed by presentment.

[9] 918 F.2d 1084 (3d Cir. 1990).

[10] Personal interview: May 2000.

[11] The percentage of convictions by guilty plea in the federal courts has risen from 87 percent in 1986 to 92 percent in 1995 (Stith and Cabranes, 1998: 130).

[12] Honesty, uniformity, and proportionality were the three objectives Congress sought to achieve in enacting the Sentencing Reform Act of 1984 (*Federal Sentencing Guidelines Manual*, 2000: 2).

[13] 434 U.S. 357 (1978).

References

Lear, Elizabeth T. 1993. "Is Conviction Irrelevant?" *UCLA Law Review* 40: 1179–1239.

Nagel, Ilene H. 1990. "Structuring Sentencing Discretion: The New Federal Sentencing Guidelines." *The Journal of Criminal Law & Criminology* 80: 883–943.

Nagel, Ilene H., Stephen Breyer, and Terence MacCarthy. 1989. "Equality Versus Discretion in Sentencing." *American Criminal Law Review* 26: 1813–1838.

Nagel, Ilene H., and Stephen J. Schulhofer. 1992. "A Tale of Three Cities: An Empirical Study of Charging and Bargaining Practices Under the Federal Sentencing Guidelines." *Southern California Law Review* 66: 501–566.

Parsons, Elizabeth A. 1994. "Shifting the Balance of Power: Prosecutorial Discretion under the Federal Sentencing Guidelines." *Valparaiso University Law Review* 29: 417–473.

Schulhofer, Stephen J., and Ilene H. Nagel. 1989. "Negotiated Pleas Under the Federal Sentencing Guidelines: The First Fifteen Months." *American Criminal Law Review* 27: 231–288.

Standen, Jeffrey. 1993. "Plea Bargaining in the Shadow of the Guidelines." *California Law Review* 81: 1471–1537.

Stith, Kate, and José A. Cabranes. 1998. *Fear of Judging Sentencing Guidelines in the Federal Courts.* Chicago: The University of Chicago Press.

Tonry, Michael. 1996. *Sentencing Matters.* New York: Oxford University Press.

U.S. Sentencing Commission. 2000. *Federal Sentencing Guidelines Manual.* West Publishing Company.

Wilkins, William W. Jr. 1988. "Plea Negotiations, Acceptance of Responsibility, Role of the Offender, and Departures: Policy Decisions in the Promulgation of Federal Sentencing Guidelines." *Wake Forest Law Review* 23: 181–202.

Wilmot, Keith A. 2002. *Prosecutorial Discretion and Real Offense Sentencing Under the Federal Sentencing Guidelines: An Analysis of Relevant Conduct.* Dissertation: The University of Nebraska at Omaha.

Yellen, David. 1993. "Illusion, Illogic, and Injustice: Real Offense Sentencing and the Federal Sentencing Guidelines." *Minnesota Law Review* 78: 403–427.

Zeno, Thomas E. 1991. "A Prosecutor's View of the Sentencing Guidelines." *Federal Probation* 4: 31–37.

Cases Cited

Bordenkircher v. Hayes, 434 U.S. 357 (1978)

McMillan v. Pennsylvania, 477 U.S. 79 (1986)

United States v. Cox, 342 F.2d 167 (5th Cir.) (1965)

United States v. Kikumura, 918 F.2d 1084 (3d Cir.) (1990)

United States v. Nixon, 418 U.S. 683 (1974)

Questions to Consider

1. Researchers have provided evidence that judges prefer to handle civil cases rather than criminal cases (most federal judges having come from corporate/business law backgrounds), but under federal law, judges must try criminal cases themselves and cannot shunt them to lower judicial officers. Note that as felony caseloads have increased, there has not been an increase in civil magistrate trials. Rather, magistrates have seen a dramatic increase in activity related to criminal trials, even though they may not be the ultimate trial judges. Are federal judges avoiding work on criminal trials? Why would they do this? Why would there be a rule that only a full federal judge can try a felony case? Is it appropriate for multiple judges to handle different segments of each criminal proceeding or are there potential problems with this approach? Should judges be told what cases they can try, or should the decision be left to each judge?

2. Numerous studies have indicated that people who regularly work in the court system (the repeat players) have a clear outcome advantage over those who only face the system one or two times (one-shot players). To what extent does the state have an innate advantage over those who are initially charged with a crime? To what extent do you think that our criminal procedural rules balance that potentially skewed bargaining system?

3. Congress took significant power away from federal judges when it created mandatory sentencing laws. This denial of judicial power (and to some extent jury power) gave significantly more power to the executive branch (prosecutors), who could then in effect determine the sentence through their unconstrained authority to charge and plea bargain. To what extent do you think that, for the sake of efficiency, prosecutors should hold this level of power? Is your answer affected by the fact that prosecutors, unlike judges, are not held accountable for their decisions?

4. It was argued in the last section that sentencing guidelines have the potential to offset what may be inappropriate public pressure on

judges. Does that potential help us to accept the resulting ability of prosecutors to pick the charge and thus pick the sentence? How does knowing that we elect the heads of most state level prosecution offices impact your assessment?

Section III
Limiting or Trusting Juries?

The preceding sections have raised the issue of public involvement in legal decision making, and with this issue comes many questions. Who has ultimate ownership of our nation's courts? Are the courts the exclusive domain of lawyers and judges, upon whom the public must rely to obtain needed services? What problems arise if we leave our court system to the total control of lawyers and judges? Does the public in effect subsidize the business of lawyers by paying the institutional overhead of courts? To what extent do citizens have a say in how their justice system operates?

One central method of public involvement in our system of justice is through the jury. Up to 12 people, selected from a larger group of community members, observe the trial process and make decisions about the many disputes generated by our society. There is probably not a more democratic institution in our society than the jury—citizens making day-to-day decisions about their community. For many years after this country was formed, it was understood that juries had more power than judges or lawyers. Their group decisions were seen as the best method of ensuring that justice was applied in individual cases. To do this, the jury was given the power to decide issues of fact, and the jury had the power and responsibility of making sure that the law provided for justice in the case before them. Slowly judges took away the jury's power to decide issues of law as well as some issues of fact. Given this historical pattern of decreasing jury power, one must ask just how healthy our democratic institution of the jury is, and what challenges it faces.

The articles in this section seek to provide some insight into these basic questions. Most of the historical and scientific evidence presented seems to indicate that the power and responsibility of juries has been, and is still, steadily eroding. In each article, we examine the current limits on jury decision making and the problems these limits create in achieving the goal of justice.

The first two articles highlight several limits that have been placed on jury decision making, raising the question of who ultimately controls court process. Steele and Thornburg focus on juror confusion caused by judicial instructions given in complex legal language and the reasons why judges fail to correct this confusion. This failure is particularly problematic because studies show that juries who receive plain English instructions are more likely to reach reliable verdicts. The authors argue that judges continue to use legalese, which causes juror confusion, because legal instructions are designed to appease appellate court judges rather than to enhance jury comprehension.

Saul Kassin next uses mock jury studies to argue that many lawyer trial tactics that unfairly affect the jury continue to be allowed by judges. These unfair tactics are allowed due to our deference to the adversary method, based on the assumption that the truth will emerge if opposing lawyers are given maximum freedom to promote each of their clients' self-interests. We might ask whether we promote falsity in the name of truth by allowing lawyers to manipulate the justice process. What do you think the chief goal of our court process should be? Is the process described in this article compatible with that goal?

Levine explores the process of jury sequestration and the historical reasons for keeping jurors shielded from publicity. Interestingly enough, however, the process of sequestering juries has other effects as well and may contribute to a group dynamic that fosters decision making even in cases of juror uncertainty.

Finally, in Scheflin and Van Dyke's article on jury nullification, we explore the range of appropriate jury power. Over the last 200 years, American judges have taken from the jury the ability to determine law. Is this simply an appropriate deference to judicial expertise, or can juries best "complete" or "perfect" the law given their joint perceptions of community justice? The stakes over who controls the court system are high, and the conflict between court professionals and juries is escalating. In 1998, the U.S. Court of Appeals for the 2nd Circuit ruled that judges could dismiss jurors who refuse to follow the law as defined by the judge. Similarly, in 1997, Colorado prosecutors obtained an obstruction of justice conviction against a juror who failed to reveal before trial that she had concerns with the underlying law in question.

This controversy reflects a much larger conflict over the goals of our society: are we to promote the rule of law, which is theoretically applied equally to everyone, by deferring to judicial expertise, or do we promote fairness and democracy by allowing a group of community citizens to decide by consensus what is just in each unique situation that is brought before them? The authors use empirical studies to argue that informing juries that they have the power to do justice seems to lead juries, in fact, to do just that.

9

Jury Instructions
A Persistent Failure to Communicate

WALTER W. STEELE, JR. and
ELIZABETH G. THORNBURG

Jury instructions play an essential role in the American judicial system, bridging the gap between the law, the evidence as presented in court, and the jury. Because jury instructions do play such a central role in any trial, one would expect jury instructions to be carefully drafted to maximize juror comprehension, but they are not. Research shows that most jurors do not understand their instructions,[1] and that the level of juror comprehension of instructions would improve dramatically if the instructions were rewritten with the jury in mind.

This article documents the existence of juror confusion and identifies the forces that lead to the continued use of incomprehensible instructions. It then suggests specific changes in the law and efforts that the organized bar and judiciary must make in order for understandable instructions to become the norm rather than the exception.

Documented Jury Confusion

Case Law

It is difficult to discover the extent to which jurors comprehend court instructions, because rules of evidence and procedure usually protect

Reprinted by permission of the American Judicature Society and the author from *Judicature*, vol. 74, no. 5 (Feb./March, 1991), pp. 249–254.

the mental processes of jurors from inquiry.[2] There are two lines of cases, however, that document jury misunderstanding: cases in which juries send judges notes during deliberations,[3] and cases from states that allow testimony about conversations among jurors during deliberations.[4] Both demonstrate the existence of juror confusion, and both demonstrate the courts' reluctance to correct the confusion.

The problems of confusion and judicial nonintervention are present in *Whited v. Powell*,[5] a Texas supreme court case. In *Whited*, a juror misunderstood the court's charge and misstated the law to another juror, who then changed his vote based on the misstatement. The supreme court characterized this as "express misconstruction of the court's charge," but refused to order a new trial.[6] The court noted that "it would be most unrealistic to expect that all members of the jury as ordinary laymen would thoroughly understand every portion of a complicated charge . . . Most of our jury verdicts would be of little value" if the misunderstanding of one or more jurors were grounds for new trial.[7] *Whited* is just one of many cases that demonstrate the judiciary's reluctance to require that instructions be comprehensible.[8] Apparently, the inclination of most courts is to let sleeping dogs lie rather than to undertake a campaign to improve the comprehensibility of jury instructions.[9]

Social Science Research

Social scientists have also proved that juries misunderstand instructions: there is an empirically demonstrable gap between what judges instruct and what juries understand.[10] Their studies reveal that a large percent of jurors fail to understand their instructions.[11] In fact, some studies showed that jurors who receive typical pattern instructions do not comprehend the issues better than jurors who receive *no instructions at all*.[12]

Fortunately, the social science studies also provide the basis for hope. Jurors who receive instructions rewritten into plain English are significantly more likely to reach a reliable verdict.[13] More important, researchers have identified the linguistic features of jury instructions that cause comprehension problems in jury instructions.[14] For example, constructions such as nominalizations,[15] phrases beginning with "as to," misplaced phrases, multiple negatives, and passive verbs confuse jurors; instructions rewritten to eliminate these constructions are significantly better understood.[16] In addition, instructions which are poorly organized or which use unnecessarily difficult vocabulary tend to confuse jurors. Using this information, lawyers and judges willing to make the effort can write comprehensible jury instructions, and appellate courts can test those instructions on appeal.[17]

Empirical Research

We decided to test some pattern jury instructions to see if jurors understood them. The subjects for our test were people called to jury service in Dallas County, Texas, who had not yet served on a jury. We selected five Texas pattern jury instructions for testing: (1) proximate cause; (2) new and independent cause; (3) negligence; (4) presumption of innocence; and (5) accomplice testimony.[18] These instructions present an even mix of short and long sentences, simple and difficult vocabulary, and straightforward and convoluted syntax.

We suspected that the instructions would confuse jurors for a number of reasons. Some of the pattern instructions were poorly organized; all of the instructions used difficult vocabulary; and some instructions were hard to understand due to their length. We rewrote the instructions, trying to eliminate these problems without changing the meaning of the instructions (see pages 116–118).

The next step was to test whether the rewritten instructions were more comprehensible than the pattern instructions. To do this we created four audio tapes. Each tape contained a recording of a "judge" reading each of the five instructions, some in pattern form and some in rewritten form. We then played one of the tapes for each juror. After each instruction, we stopped the tape and asked the juror to paraphrase the instruction.[19] Each juror heard and paraphrased all five instructions on the tape. We then analyzed the jurors' responses to see whether the jurors correctly paraphrased each legally significant element of the instructions.[20]

Results

The results of the experiment confirmed what other researchers had found: jurors' comprehension of the pattern instructions was low, and jurors understood the rewritten instructions better than the pattern instructions (see table 1).[21] For example, the jurors correctly paraphrased only 5.83 percent of the pattern instruction on "new and independent cause," but correctly paraphrased 29.67 percent of the rewritten instruction. Similarly, the jurors correctly paraphrased 19.49 percent of the pattern instruction on "negligence," but correctly paraphrased 35.28 percent of the rewritten instruction.[22]

The subjects' improved comprehension was dramatic. The overall gain in juror comprehension was 408 percent for the "new and independent cause" instruction, 112 percent for the "accomplice testimony" instruction, 81 percent for the "negligence" instruction, 60 percent for the "proximate cause" instruction, and 34 percent for the "presumption of innocence" instruction.

Table 1 Paraphrases of five pattern/rewritten instructions

	Percent legally incorrect	Percent of no paraphrase	Percent legally correct
New & independent cause			
pattern	1.67	92.50	5.83
rewritten	1.00	69.33	29.67
Accomplice testimony			
pattern	0.44	90.26	9.30
rewritten	1.07	79.17	19.76
Negligence			
pattern	1.54	78.97	19.49
rewritten	0.00	64.72	35.28
Proximate cause			
pattern	0.91	84.55	14.55
rewritten	0.77	75.90	23.33
Presumption of innocence			
pattern	3.86	78.77	17.37
rewritten	0.61	76.06	23.33

The percentage figures represent the percentage out of the total variables for each instruction. For example, if an instruction had ten variables (ten legally significant elements), and two of the ten were correctly paraphrased, the percentages would be 0% legally incorrect, 80% no paraphrase, and 20% legally correct. The results for multiple jurors were cumulated to get the results set out in the table. Note that the most frequent response by far was "no paraphrase." In other words, for the most part the jurors failed to comprehend large portions of the instruction, and thus were unable to paraphrase it.

Our experiment indicates that the jurors who participated failed to comprehend large portions of the instructions. This result should be of deep concern to both lawyers and judges, because jurors who do not understand their instructions may not render the verdict they intend or the verdict that they would render if they understood their instructions.[23]

This concern should be translated into action. We did successfully rewrite the instructions, and neither of us has any advanced training in English composition. We want practicing lawyers and judges to view our experiment as realistic and as a task within their reach. Jurors do not adequately understand instructions as currently drafted, but can understand significantly more when instructions are rewritten for clarity.

Can the System Change?

Although the research makes a convincing case for change to plain English in our jury instructions, overwhelming forces supporting the status quo may present an insurmountable obstacle. A number of factors make it difficult to bring about meaningful change in the way jury instructions are drafted. One set of factors arises from lawyer attitudes. Some lawyers and judges resist change, believing erroneously that jurors understand their instructions. Other lawyers believe that the confusion benefits their clients and, therefore, support the status quo rather than exert efforts to achieve greater clarity. Some lawyers and trial court judges are willing to change, but are afraid to do so because of the risk that the clearer instructions will be reversed by appellate courts because they are not the "pattern" instructions.

Lawyers and judges who do not resist change are still faced with some difficulties in rewriting jury instructions. Some are inherent in the nature of the law and cannot be eliminated. One inherent difficulty in writing jury instructions stems from the complexity of the law itself. Complicated concepts are more difficult to express clearly than simple ones. It is difficult to explain in a paragraph concepts that first-year law students spend months learning. Difficult, however, does not mean impossible.

The complexity of the law, and the difficulty of rewriting it, often stems from the subtleties of meaning acquired by legal terms of art and other legal language. This subtlety of meaning, however, "attaches as a function of usage, and not because of any inherent property of the word itself."[24] As lawyers speaking to each other use certain words, their knowledge of the underlying case law communicates something more to them than a simple dictionary definition of the word would show. This kind of extra communication, however, is restricted to members of the profession who understand the usage behind the word. It does not extend to lay people on juries. An explanation that would communicate a term of art to a jury with all its professional resonances, then, might need to be extremely long.[25]

A related roadblock to simplicity is the law's occasional vagueness. Some legal concepts are inherently general: "reasonable person"; "reasonable doubt"; "preponderance of the evidence"; "unconscionable." To redefine such concepts so that they can be standardized or quantified could have two unfortunate results. First, it might make the cost of litigation prohibitive by requiring quantifiable proof.[26] Second, greater specificity might rob the law of its flexibility and its ability to reflect community standards. Because of these problems, we do not propose a redefinition of such concepts to achieve greater clarity.

Other factors preventing change arise from the law surrounding instructions. Some of the rules of procedure governing the submission

Pattern and Rewritten Instructions

Pattern Charge

Proximate cause means that cause which, in a natural and continuous sequence, produces an event, and without which cause such event would not have occured; and in order to be a proximate cause, the act complained of must be such that a person using ordinary care would have foreseen that the event, or some similar event, might reasonably result therefrom. There may be more than one proximate cause of an event.

New and independent cause means the act of a separate and independent agency, not reasonably foreseeable, which destroys the causal connection, if any, between the act inquired about and the occurrence in question, and thereby becomes the immediate cause of the occurrence.

Negligence means failure to use ordinary care; that is to say, failure to do that which a person of ordinary prudence would have done under the same or similar circumstances, or doing that which a person of ordinary prudence would not have done under the same or similar circumstances.

Presumption of innocence All persons are presumed to be innocent and no person may be convicted of an offense unless each element of the offense is proved

Rewritten

An event often has many causes. In order to be a "proximate cause," three things must be true. First, the cause naturally and continuously led to the event. Second, the event would not have happened without the proximate cause. Third, a person using ordinary care would have foreseen that the proximate cause might reasonably lead to the event or to some similar event. There may be more than one proximate cause of an event.

Sometimes when a natural chain of events is set in motion, that chain is broken by a "new and independent cause." The law defines "new and independent cause" in its own particular way. To be a "new and independent cause" the cause must be all of the following:

First: The cause must, indeed, break a chain of events already set in motion so that it becomes the immediate cause of what happens.

Second: The cause must come from a source that is separate and independent from the defendant.

Third: The cause must be one that the defendant could not have foreseen using ordinary care.

A person can become negligent in two ways. The first way a person becomes negligent is by doing something that a person of ordinary care would not have done in the same situation or in a similar situation. The second way a person becomes negligent is by failing to do something that a person of ordinary care would have done in the same situation or in a similar situation.

My job as judge is to tell you about the laws that apply to this case. As jurors, you have two jobs.

First: In reaching your verdict you must

Pattern Charge

beyond a reasonable doubt. The fact that the defendant has been arrested, confined or indicted for, or otherwise charged with, the offense gives rise to no inference of guilt at his trial. In case you have a reasonable doubt as to defendant's guilt after considering all of the evidence before you, and these instructions, you will acquit him. You are the exclusive judges of the facts proved, and of the credibility of the witnesses and the weight to be given their testimony, but the law you shall receive in these written instructions, and you must be governed thereby.

Accomplice testimony An accomplice, as the term is here used, means anyone connected with the crime charges, as a party thereto and includes all persons who are connected with the crime, as such parties, by unlawful act or omission on their part transpiring either before or during the time of the commission of the offense. A person is criminally responsible as a party to an offense if the offense is committed by his own conduct, by the conduct of another for which he is criminally responsible, or by both. Mere presence alone, however, will not constitute one a party to an offense.

A person is criminally responsible for an

Rewritten

follow the laws that I am explaining to you; and

Second: You must decide what the facts are in this case. In other words, you must decide what happened.

To decide what the facts are you will have to decide how much of each witness's testimony you believe, and how much weight to give what is believed.

Our law states that anyone charged with a crime is presumed to be innocent unless the prosecution proves each part of the crime beyond a reasonable doubt. In deciding whether the prosecution has proved each part of the crime beyond a reasonable doubt, you must think about all of my instructions and about all of the evidence before you. After you have done this, if you have a reasonable doubt about the existence of any part of the crime you must find the defendant not guilty.

As part of the normal legal process, the defendant has been arrested, jailed, and charged, but these facts do not suggest that the defendant may be guilty, and you must not consider these facts as any evidence of the defendant's guilt.

This instruction is in two parts. First, I am going to tell you about the kind of witness known as an accomplice. The second part of the instruction will tell you when you can consider testimony from an accomplice.

To be an accomplice, a person must intend to help with the crime, and with that intention, a person must engage in one or more of the following activities by act or by omission either before or during the commission of the offense:

1. Solicit another person to commit the crime;
2. Encourage another person to commit the crime;

Pattern Charge	Rewritten
offense committed by the conduct of another if, acting with the intent to promote or asssist the commission of the offense, he solicits, encourages, directs, or aids or attempts to aid the other person to commit the offense. The term "conduct of another" means any act or omission and its accompanying mental state. A conviction cannot be had upon the testimony of an accomplice unless the jury first believes that the accomplice's evidence is true and that it shows that the defendant is guilty of the offense charged against him, and then you cannot convict the defendant upon said testimony unless the accomplice's testimony is corroborated by other evidence tending to connect the defendant with the offense charged, and the corroboration is not sufficient if it merely shows the commission of the offense, but it must tend to connect the defendant with its commission.	3. Direct another person to commit the crime; 4. Help another person to commit the crime; or 5. Try to help another person to commit the crime. Merely being at the scene of a crime does not make a person an accomplice. Now, when can you use testimony from an accomplice? You cannot use the testimony of an accomplice to convict the defendant unless: First, you believe that the accomplice's testimony is true. Second, you believe that the evidence from the accomplice shows that the defendant is guilty of the crime charged in this case. Third, there is some evidence *other than* the evidence from the accomplice which tends to connect *the defendant* with the commission of the crime. It is not enough that this other evidence shows that the crime was committed by *someone*. It must tend to show that the defendant committed the crime. Without all three things you must totally ignore the evidence from an accomplice.

of jury instructions hinder efforts at rewriting. Two notable examples are the rules prohibiting the judge from commenting on the evidence and the rules prohibiting the judge from informing the jury of the effect of its answers. Common law traditionally allowed the judge to aid the jury in comprehension of the instructions.[27] Unfortunately, this common law tradition has been abandoned in most states, although it still thrives in the federal system.[28] Pervasive as these rules may be, they make the instructions extremely awkward and difficult for the jurors to comprehend.

Another point of resistance arises because the drafting of jury instructions often gets a low priority in trial preparation. Because of time and financial constraints, many trial lawyers delay writing the instructions until the trial has started, anticipating that the case may settle on the courthouse steps or a plea bargain may be reached as the jury is impaneled. The inevitable result is a confused set of hastily prepared instructions.[29]

Finally, change is difficult because the instructions are proposed and drafted in a process driven by the adversary system. Each lawyer is primarily concerned with presenting instructions that benefit his or her client and is only secondarily concerned with improving the legal system as a whole by drafting clear instructions. Also, the ultimate decision on the form of instruction is made by the trial judge. Unfortunately, judges are the ones with the least to gain by using comprehensible but unorthodox instructions. Lawyers, at least, may be interested in rewriting instructions if they preceive that clarity benefits their clients. Trial court judges, however, lack that motivation and instead risk reversal by deviating by one word from the pattern instruction or the language of appellate opinions. The adversary system, then, tends to discourage lawyers from writing the clearest possible instructions and puts the ultimate control in the hands of the party with the least incentive to change.

Forces for Change

In order for the legal system to produce comprehensible instructions, three changes must occur. First, the law must be changed to create incentives for lawyers and judges to worry as much about comprehensibility as they do about technical correctness. Appellate courts could adopt a standard of clarity, judging the instructions by standards which have been developed by linguistic researchers in this field.[30] Second, changes must be made in the law governing the submission of jury instructions to eliminate requirements that hinder comprehension. Judges should be permitted to comment on the evidence and to inform the jury of the effect of their answers. Third, the movement to draft clear jury instructions must be taken out of the realm of the adversary system.

How would the process of change work, given adequate motivation? The models are found in the experience of the bench and bar in formulating codes of procedure and codes of evidence. Although the process is painful and costly, the American bench and bar have managed to come together in compromise to improve codes of trial procedure and codes of evidence. When these efforts are undertaken on a high plane, with a recognition of the need for improvement, and with a selfless willingness to make uncomfortable changes in the interest of justice, they have worked.

In fact, committees of lawyers and judges have created pattern jury instructions in a number of jurisdictions. Unfortunately, these committees have rarely managed to draft pattern instructions that are comprehensible to jurors. Because pattern instructions are drafted by committees of judges, lawyers, and law professors, concerns about legal accuracy and comparative advantage tend to outweigh concerns about clarity. Indeed, most of the social science research that has proved instructions to be unintelligible, including the research reported in this article, has been done using pattern instructions.

Two relatively minor changes in the techniques of the committees drafting pattern instructions would go a long way towards solving the problem. First, the emphasis of the lawyers and judges charged with the responsibility of drafting pattern jury instructions must change from one of stating the law in every minute detail to one of clearly stating the law so that jurors can understand it.[31] Second, the membership of such drafting committees must include lay persons. Lawyers and judges must realize that the education and experience that produce good lawyers and judges do not necessarily produce good writers of conventional prose. Further, the socialization of lawyers into legal discourse prevents them from "hearing" the instruction as jurors would. It may take a person without legal training to anticipate certain comprehension problems. Better yet, the proposed instructions could be empirically tested for juror comprehension, with problem areas rewritten and eliminated.[32] Such an effort could be undertaken by the courts or bar association of any state.[33]

The problem is clear: juror comprehension of instructions is pitifully low. Likewise, the general scheme of solutions is evident. Unfortunately, prospects for actual change appear dim. Real change would require all parties involved—trial and appellate courts, state bar committees, and the trial bar—to rise above their narrowly perceived self-interest and act instead in the interests of the judicial system as a whole.

Endnotes

[1] Lawyers and judges have suspected for some time that many jurors do not understand their instructions. See e.g. Cook, "Instructionese: Legalistic Lingo of Contrived Confusion," 7 *J. Mo. B.* 113 (1951); Head, "Confessions of a Juror," 44 *F.R.D.* 330 (1967); Hoffman & Brodley, "Jurors on Trial," 17 *Mo. L. Rev.* 235 (1952); Hunter, "Law in the Jury Room," 2 *Ohio St. L. J.* 1 (1935); Winslow, "The Instruction Ritual," 13 *Hastings L. J.* 456 (1962).

[2] See e.g., Fed R. Evid. 606(b), Tex. R. Evid. 606(b); Pope, "The Mental Operations of Jurors," 40 *Tex. L. Rev.* 849, 851–52 (1962).

[3] Meyer & Rosenberg, "Questions Juries Ask: Untapped Springs of Insight," 55 *Judicature* 105, 106 (1971).

[4] See, for example, the Texas cases *Compton v. Henrie*, 364 S.W.2d 179 (Tex. 1963) (one juror's repeated incorrect statement regarding "preponderance of the evidence"), and *Whited v. Powell*, 155 Tex. 210, 285 S.W.2d 364 (1956).

5 155 Tex. 210, 285 S.W.2d 364 (1956).

6 Id. at 215, 285 S.W.2d at 367.

7 Id. at 216, 285 S.W.2d at 368.

8 Case law shows that juries are often confused about instructions regarding: (1) the measure of damages [*Hoffman v. Deck Masters, Inc.*, 662 S.W.2d 438 (Tex. App. 1983) (jury miscalculation of damages due to misunderstanding of instructions would not justify retrial)]; (2) causation and the apportionment of negligence [*Kindle v. Armstrong Packing Co.* 103 S.W.2d 471, 473 (Tex Civ. App. 1937) (jury thought proximate cause meant whole cause; not ground for new trial)]; and (3) definitions of words such as "actual notice" [*Coakley v. Crow*, 457 S.W.2d 431, 435 (Tex. Civ. App. 1970), cert. denied, 402 U.S. 90 (1971))], "undue influence" [*Stephens County Museum, Inc. v. Swenson*, 517 S.W.2d 257, 259-60 (Tex. 1974)], "pledge" [*Martin v. U.S. Trust Co.*, 690 S.W.2d 300, 309 (Tex. App. 1985)], and "consent" [*Cortez v. Medical Protective Co.*, 560 S.W.2d 132, 135 (Tex. Civ. App. 1977)]. Such mmistaken notions lead to mistaken verdicts, yet courts refuse to grant new trials.

9 "Any attempt to rewrite the current approved jury instructions raises the fear that differences in interpretation will come to the surface and create disruption, while if you leave it in legalese everyone can nod and smile and believe whatever they want." Mathewson, "Verbatim," 15 *Student Lawyer* 6 (1986).

10 See e.g., Hastie, Penrod & Pennington, *Inside the Jury* (Cambridge: Harvard University Press, 1983); Charrow & Charrow, "Making Legal Language Understandable: A Psycholinguistic Study of Jury Instructions," 79 *Colum. L. Rev.* 601; Strawn & Buchanan, "Jury Confusion: A Threat to Justice," 59 *Judicature* 478 (1976); Strawn, Buchanan, Pryor & Taylor, "Reaching a Verdict, Step by Step," 60 *Judicature* 383 (1977); Elwork, Sales & Alfini, "Judicial Decision: In Ignorance of the Law or in Light of It?", 1 *Law & Hum. Behav.* 163, 173 (1970); Severance, Greene & Loftus, "Toward Criminal Jury Instructions that Jurors Can Understand," 75 *J. Crim. L. & Criminology* 198 (1984).

The American Bar Association has recently sponsored a study of jury comprehension in complex cases. The ABA researchers videotaped shadow juries composed of alternate jurors who had seen the same evidence and heard the same instructions as the actual juries hearing real cases in federal court. They found that jury instructions written in legalese were confusing and unclear. For example, the jurors in a criminal case were unable to define "beyond a reasonable doubt" despite an instruction on the burden of proof. 6 *BNA Civil Trial Manual* 116 (April 4, 1990).

11 For example, in one test jurors received detailed background information regarding a case, read a set of instructions, and took multiple choice retention and comprehension tests. The results showed that 86 percent of the criminal juries were unable to answer accurately questions concerning proof of guilt, and less than half of the civil juries were able to answer a question about proximate cause. Forston, supra n. 10, at 615.

12 Elwork, Sales & Alfini, *Making Jury Instructions Understandable* (Charlottesville, VA: Michie, 1982); Elwork, Sales & Alfini, "Judicial Decisions," supra n. 10, at 173. After seeing a personal injury trial on video tape, jurors were given either no instructions, pattern instructions, or rewritten instructions. Id.

13 Strawn, Buchanan, Pryor & Taylor, supra n. 10, at 387-88; Elwork, Alfini & Sales, "Toward Understandable Jury Instructions," 65 *Judicature* 432, 434-35 (1982).

14 Charrow, supra n. 10, at 1307-08.

15 A nominalization is a verb turned into a noun. Nominalizations are grammatical, but are difficult to understand because they do not communicate a scene that the juror can picture. For example: NOMINALIZATION: *Recovery* by Mr. Smith is predicated upon *circumvention* of the adultery statute. VERB: Mr. Smith can *recover* if he *circumvents* the adultery statute.

[16] Charrow, supra n. 10, at 1335-58. In the Charrows' experiment, for example, comprehension of instructions regarding agency increased 93 percent, comprehension of instructions about assumption of the risk increased 78 percent, and comprehension of an instruction about the use of evidence increased 52 percent, Id. at 1370 (Table 14).

[17] We suggest, for example, that any lawyer trying to write clear instructions should consult Elwork, Sales & Alfini, *Making Jury Instructions Understandable*, supra n. 12, at ch. 7. This book provides empirically supported, easy to follow advice for improving jury instructions.

[18] The civil instructions are from State Bar of Texas, 1 Texas Pattern Jury Charges (Supp. 1986). The criminal instructions are from McClung, *Jury Charges for Texas Criminal Procedure* (1987).

[19] This method of research is known as paraphrase testing. In a paraphrase task, the subject either listens to or reads some material and is then asked to explain it in his or her own words. The validity of paraphrase testing is supported by extensive psychological literature, and is based on the notion that a test subject will discuss (i.e. paraphrase) that which is understood and fail to discuss that which is not understood or is ignored. For a thorough discussion of paraphrase testing, see Charrow, supra n. 10, at 1309-11.

[20] For a full text of the pattern and rewritten instructions, the score sheets, and the statistical results, see Steele & Thornburg, "Jury Instructions: A Persistent Failure to Communicate," 67 *N.C.L. Rev.* 77, 88-94 and 110-119 (1988).

[21] An average of all five of the pattern instructions revealed that only 12.85 percent of the paraphrases were correct, as compared to 23.59 percent correct paraphrases from rewritten instructions, an impressive 91 percent gain in understanding.

[22] The comprehension figures, even for the rewritten instructions, are still quite low. Note, however, that these figures represent comprehension of instructions given in isolation. The subjects did not hear voir dire, opening statements, evidence, or closing arguments. It is likely that these parts of a trial also serve to increase their understanding of the instructions. Our purpose, however, was to test juror comprehension of instructions in and of themselves, so we did not provide them with these external clues to meaning.

[23] Social science researchers, for example, showed identical videotaped trials to juries, half using pattern instructions and half using rewritten instructions. They found a statistically significant difference in the verdicts reached by the two groups. See Elwork, Sales & Alfini, *Making Jury Instructions Understandable*, supra n. 12, at 174-76.

[24] Perlman, "Pattern Jury Instructions: The Application of Social Science Research," 65 *Neb. L. Rev.* 520, 536 n. 65 (1986).

[25] Id.

[26] Perlman notes, for example, that to change "substantial likelihood of confusion among consumers" to a quantified standard such as confusion of 65 percent of prospective customers would greatly increase the cost of trademark litigation. Id. at 538.

[27] See e.g., Walker, "Judicial Comment on the Evidence in Jury Trials," 15 *A.B.A.J.* 647 (1929).

[28] See *United States v. Block*, 755 F.2d 770, 775 (11th Cir. 1985).

[29] Farrell, "Communication in the Jury Room: Jury Instructions," 85 *W. Va. L. Rev.* 5, 21 (1982).

[30] Charrow, supra n. 10, at 1359-60.

[31] Pattern instructions have, in the past, tended to take their language from appellate opinions. But appellate opinions, while acceptable as intraprofessional communications, are not written for the purpose of explaining the law to lay persons. There are separate linguistic universes here: one for members of the bar, and one for the lay persons who serve on juries. When language written for one audience is directed instead to another, the resulting confusion should not be surprising.

32 These suggestions are so minor that one wonders why they have not already been adopted. Some have. In Pennsylvania, a subcommittee headed by two psycholinguists tested proposed pattern instructions for clarity. Nieland, *Pattern Jury Instructions: A Critical Look at a Modern Movement to Improve the Jury System* 25 (Chicago: American Judicature Society, 1979). Two law professors have written an exemplary set of instructions for the Alaska court system. Perlman & Saltzburg. *Alaska Pattern Civil Jury Instructions* (1981).

33 Other practices unrelated to the way in which instructions are written can affect the jury's ability to understand its job and follow the instructions. For example, studies have demonstrated that jurors who receive written copies of their instructions pay more attention to the instructions and reach more accurate results, yet only 16 jurisdictions currently allow the jury to take copies of the instructions into the jury room. Foston, supra n. 10, at 619. Also, some studies have indicated that jurors who are instructed in certain aspects of the law at the beginning as well as at the end of the trial are better able to evaluate evidence and understand their instructions. See e.g., Prettman, "Jury Instructions—First or Last," 46 *A.B.A.J.* 1066 *(1960)*.

10

The American Jury
Handicapped in the Pursuit of Justice

SAUL M. KASSIN

Whether it is true or not, the story is a favorite among students of trial advocacy: Clarence Darrow, smoking a cigar during the presentation of his opponent's case, stole the jury's attention by inserting a thin wire into the cigar and producing an ash that grew like magic with every puff.[1] In a more recent case involving personal injury in which the plaintiff had lost a leg, Melvin Belli carried into court a large L-shaped package wrapped in yellow butcher paper and tied with a white string, and placed it on counsel's table as a visible reminder. Then during his closing argument, Belli unwrapped the package, only to reveal a prosthesis.[2] These courtroom pranks as well as other, more common trial practices, are clever, entertaining, and perhaps even effective. But at what cost to the jury's pursuit of justice?

This article examines nonevidentiary social influences on the jury, influences that emanate from various trial practices and threaten to compromise a litigant's right to a fair trial. Broadly defined, there are two phases in the jury's decision-making task that are at risk. The first is the factfinding competence of *individual jurors*—that is, their ability to make accurate judgments of the evidence (e.g., by distinguishing among witnesses of varying credibility), and disregard information that is not in evidence (e.g., material received from the news media, voir

Reprinted by permission of the *Ohio State Law Journal* and the author from vol. 51 (1990), pp. 687–711.

dire questions, opening statements, closing arguments, and inadmissible testimony). The second phase of a jury's task is the deliberation of the *jury as a group*—that is, the process by which individual members contribute independently and equally to a joint outcome, exerting influence over each other through information and rational argument rather than heavy-handed social pressure.[3]

The following evaluation of juries is based on the results of controlled behavioral research, not on abstract legal theory, isolated case studies, or trial anecdotes. The reader should thus be mindful of both the strengths and weaknesses inherent in this approach. The most appropriate way to obtain a full and rich understanding of how juries function is to observe the decision-making process in action. Juries, however, deliberate in complete privacy, behind closed doors. Unable to observe or record actual jury deliberations, researchers have had to develop alternative, less direct strategies (e.g., analysis of court records in search of statistical relationships between various trial factors and jury verdicts; post-trial interviews with jurors, alternates, and other trial participants; jury simulation experiments). Most of the research reported in this paper was conducted within a mock jury paradigm.[4]

I. Factfinding Competence of Individual Jurors

As individual factfinders, jurors must competently process all evidence and instructions, disregard information that is not in evidence, and reconstruct disputed events by distinguishing among witnesses of varying credibility. We will see that the task is difficult, and that it is complicated even further by various questionable practices.

A. Jurors as Arbiters of Truth and Deception

Confronted with opposing sides and inevitably conflicting testimony, jurors must accept the testimony of some witnesses, and reject others. Toward this end, the courts instruct jurors to pay close attention not only to the content of the witness's testimony but to his or her demeanor while testifying. Indeed, many judges prohibit jurors from taking notes for fear that they will overlook informative nonverbal cues.[5]

Unfortunately, psychological research suggests that people perform at only slightly better than chance levels in evaluating truth and deception. Even individuals who make these judgments for a living (e.g., customs inspectors, law enforcement officers) are prone to error.[6] Based on a review of over thirty studies, Miron Zuckerman and others conclude that there is a mismatch between the nonverbal behaviors actually associated with deception and those cues used by perceivers.[7] People tend to focus on a speaker's face, for example, even though facial expressions are under conscious deceptive control.[8] At the same time, there is a tendency to overlook kinesic and paralinguistic cues, even though they are more revealing.[9] In short, there is reason to believe that jurors tune into the wrong channels of communication. Seduced by the silver tongue and the smiling face, they may fail to notice the restless body and the quivering voice.[10]

Human imperfections aside, the rules of evidence and trial procedure that guide the questioning of witnesses are intended to facilitate the jury's quest for the truth.[11] In theory, direct and cross examination should thus enhance the credibility of witnesses who are accurate and honest, while diminishing the credibility of those who are inaccurate or dishonest— in other words, it should heighten the jury's factfinding competence. There is no way to know how frequently the law's objectives are actually achieved. While much is written about effective questioning techniques, surprisingly little research has examined their prevalence or their impact on the jury.[12] One problem, however, seems evident. Even though trial attorneys are expected to adhere to rules of evidence and keep their trial strategies within the boundaries of ethical conduct,[13] they often bend the rules and stretch the boundaries.[14] Thus we ask, to what extent can the examination of witnesses be used to subvert a jury's quest for the truth?

There are several ethically questionable trial practices, or "dirty tricks," that could make it difficult for jurors to make sound credibility judgments. Coaching witnesses, leading their testimony in court, distracting the jury at critical moments in an opponent's case, making frivolous objections, and asking questions that invite the leakage of inadmissible evidence, are among the possibilities.[15] In this section, two such practices are evaluated: the presentation of deposition testimony, and the use of presumptuous cross-examination questions.

B. Deposition Testimony and the Surrogate Witness

As difficult as it is to evaluate witnesses by their demeanor, the task is needlessly complicated when jurors must make judgments of credibility without ever seeing the actual witness. Often, people who are scheduled to testify are not available to appear in court.[16] In order to secure the substance of what these prospective witnesses have to say, counsel may take a deposition and enter that deposition into the trial record.

The use of deposition testimony in lieu of the live witness raises an interesting procedural question: How is such testimony entered into the trial record? How is the information presented, and what effect does it have on the jury's ability to evaluate the witness? In most courts, depositions are transcribed and then read aloud from the witness stand by a clerk or by an individual appointed by the witness's attorney. Usually, the clerk reads the answers, while the attorney reads the questions; sometimes, the attorney reads the entire script.

As one might expect, the practice of using what I call "surrogate witnesses" in an adversarial context paves the way for abuse. In one case, for example, I observed pretrial auditions of more than thirty professional actors and actresses who were called to play the roles of various absent witnesses who had been deposed. The actors all read the transcripts flawlessly. What distinguished those who were hired from those who were not was their ability to project through subtle nonverbal behaviors—crossing legs, rolling eyes, smiling, or sighing at a critical moment—specific impressions of the witnesses they were supposed to represent.[17]

It should not be permissible to use surrogates in this manner. Indeed, deposition readers should not unduly emphasize any words or engage in suggestive conduct. Nevertheless, many litigators appreciate the potential for gain in this procedure. For example, one trial advocate advises that "whoever is playing the part of the witness on the stand will, most assuredly, be identified with that witness. True, he is nothing more than an actor, but human beings tend to associate a voice with a person; so be certain that the 'actor' projects a favourable image."[18] It is even suggested that when faced with a witness with undesirable characteristics, the "imaginative" lawyer should consider taking a deposition and then replacing that witness with an attractive surrogate.[19] Research on the social psychology of persuasion offers little guidance. It is clear that audiences are influenced by the *source* of a communication,[20] but do characteristics of the *messenger* have the same effect? Is it truly possible to alter the impact of a deposition and mislead the jury by manipulating the surrogate's demeanor?

To test this hypothesis, I conducted the following mock jury experiment.[21] Eighty-eight subjects read a summary of a case in which the plaintiff sought damages from a security company because he had been harassed and then shot by one of its guards. The defense claimed the plaintiff was drunk and had inadvertently shot himself in a scuffle with their guard. There were no eyewitnesses to the shooting, and the physical evidence was ambiguous. For all practical purposes, a jury's verdict would thus hinge on the relative credibility of opposing witnesses, the plaintiff and the guard. After reading a summary of the case, subjects watched a carefully staged videotape of the plaintiff's testimony. An actor was hired to play this critical witness in two contrasting roles. In one tape, he was attentive, polite, cooperative, and unhesitating in his response to questions; in the other, he read the same testimony, but was impolite, often annoyed, cautious and fumbling in his style. The actor read exactly the same transcript in both conditions, varying only his tone of voice, facial expressions, and body language.

Since a witness's demeanor is considered relevant, one would expect that even though subjects heard the same testimony read by the same actor, those who viewed the positive-demeanor witness would prove more favorable to the plaintiff than those who viewed the negative-demeanor witness. This expectation was confirmed. Subjects rated the positive witness as more likeable, sincere, and trustworthy, and his testimony as more believable, accurate, and persuasive. Seventy-two percent of those in the positive-demeanor group voted for the plaintiff, compared to only twenty-two percent in the negative-demeanor group. But what if subjects were told—both before and after watching the tape— that they were not seeing the actual witness, but an individual assigned to read the witness's deposition? Since the demeanor of a surrogate is not relevant to judging the credibility of a witness, and since the two tapes were identical in verbal content, jurors should not be affected by what they saw. But they were. Even though subjects were aware that they were merely watching a clerk reading from a transcript, those who watched the positive- rather than negative-demeanor tape rated the witness and the testimony itself as more credible, and were more likely to return a verdict for the plaintiff—sixty-one percent to thirty-three percent.

As noted earlier, deposition readers are not supposed to embellish their performances. But can judges necessarily detect the subtle nuances and manipulations of a professional actor? People are often not conscious of the nonverbal cues that guide their impressions. Moreover, what about *nonbehavioral* sources of bias such as the deposition reader's physical appearance? Persuasion researchers have found that communicators who are attractive elicit a greater change in attitudes and behavior than those who are not.[22] To examine whether jurors are likewise influenced by the physical appearance of a surrogate, I conducted an experiment similar to the one just described.[23] Mock jurors read about a criminal conspiracy case, and then listened to an audiotape of the testimony of a female witness accompanied by a series of slides taken in a courtroom. All subjects heard the same tape, but viewed slides of either an attractive or unattractive woman who was believed to be either the witness or a deposition reader.[24] Paralleling the results of the first study, perceptions of the witness's credibility were affected not only by the physical attractiveness of the witness, but by the surrogate's appearance as well.

Taken together, these studies suggest that jurors may be unable to separate a witness and his or her testimony from the messenger who delivers it. Thus, it seems that jurors—despite their best efforts to make sound credibility judgments—may be seriously misled by the behavior and appearance of those who read depositions. The solution to this problem is clear, and easily implemented: videotaped depositions. Since the opportunity for mischief is inherent in the mere substitution of one individual for another, videotape should be used to preserve the witness's demeanor for the record without introducing additional extraneous information. Jurors would then watch these tapes on a monitor stationed in the courtroom.[25]

C. Presumptuous Cross-Examination Questions and the Power of Conjecture

The opportunity to confront opposing witnesses through cross-examination is an essential device for safeguarding the accuracy and completeness of testimonial evidence. What impact does cross-examination have on the jury's ability to reconstruct the truth about an event? What are the dangers? Ideally, cross-examination should enhance a jury's factfinding competence by increasing the credibility of witnesses who are accurate and honest relative to those who are not. To be sure, cross-examination is an indispensable device. Many a mistaken and deceptive witness has no doubt fallen from the stand, exposed, scarred, and discredited from the battle of cross-examination. But cross-examination can also be used to exert an influence over the jury in a way that subverts its quest for truth.

Asking questions provides more than simply a mechanism for eliciting answers. Leading questions in particular may impart information to a listener through imagery, implication, and conjecture.[26] Carefully chosen words can obscure and even alter people's impressions, as when tax increases are called "revenue enhancements," and the strategic defense initiative is referred to as "star wars." Consider the following exchange between an attorney and the defendant in an illegal abortion case:

> Q: You didn't tell us, Doctor, whether you determined that the *baby* was alive or dead, did you Doctor?
>
> A: The *fetus* had no signs of life.[27]

In this example, the witness resisted the lawyer's imagery. Often, however, answers can be shaped by how a question is worded. In a classic experiment on eyewitness testimony, for example, Elizabeth Loftus and John Palmer had subjects watch films of an automobile collision. Those who were subsequently asked, "About how fast were the cars going when they *smashed* into each other?" estimated an average speed of forty-one miles per hour; those who were asked "About how fast were the cars going when they *hit* each other?" estimated an average of only thirty-four mph.[28] In fact, the wording of this critical question had a lasting effect on subjects' memories of the event. When asked one week later whether they could recall broken glass at the scene of the accident (there was none), only fourteen percent of those previously asked the hit question said they did, compared to thirty-two percent of those who had been asked the smash question. Once the seed of misinformation was planted, it took on a life of its own.

Even when a question does not mislead its respondent, it may still mislead the jury. When a question implies something that is never explicitly stated, for example, the listener may confuse what is said with what is only implied. Cognitive studies of pragmatic implications reveal that such confusion is common. In one study, mock jurors listened to an excerpt of testimony and indicated whether certain statements were true or false. After hearing the statement, "I ran up to the burglar alarm," for example, most subjects recalled that the witness had said, "I *rang* the burglar alarm." Apparently, people process information between the lines and assume they heard what was only implied.[29]

Due to the nearly unrestricted use of leading questions, cross-examination provides additional opportunity to influence jurors through questions that are designed to impart misleading information to the jury. In *Trial Ethics*, Underwood and Fortune note that "one of the most common abuses of cross-examination takes the form of a question implying a serious charge against the witness, for which counsel has little or no proof. All too often, trial attorneys ask such questions for the sole purpose of wafting unwarranted innuendo into the jury box."[30] When lawyers ask questions that suggest their own answers, are jurors influenced by the information implied by those questions? Is cross-examination by innuendo an effective device?

Research in non-legal settings tentatively suggests an affirmative answer. For example, William Swann and his colleagues examined the effects of hearing an interview in which the questioner implies that the respondent has certain personal characteristics.[31] They had subjects listen to question-and-answer sessions in which the interviewer probed for evidence of either extroverted behavior (e.g., "What do you do when you want to liven things up at a party?") or introverted behavior (e.g., "Have you ever felt left out of some social group?"). One-third of the subjects heard only the questions, one-third heard only the answers, and one-third heard both sides of the interview. When subjects heard only the questions, they inferred that the respondent had the traits sought by the interviewer (i.e., they assumed that the interviewer knew enough to ask extroverts about parties and introverts about difficult social situations). Suggestive questions thus serve as proof by conjecture.

In the context of a trial, of course, jurors hear not only the questions asked but the answers they elicit. It stands to reason that under the circumstances, conjectural evidence may be buried under the weight of the witness's testimony. Yet those subjects in the Swann study who—

like jurors—heard both sides of the interview, were also misled. Consider the implications. The respondents in these experimental interviews did not actually possess the implied traits, so it seems odd that their answers did not override the effects of the interviewers' questions. In fact, however, the result makes sense. Limited to answering specific questions, respondents provided evidence to confirm the interviewers' conjecture. Subjects who heard the full interview were thus left with false impressions shaped by the questions. As Swann and his colleagues put it, "once respondents' answers 'let the cat out of the bag,' observers saw no reason to concern themselves with how the bag was opened."[32]

In light of these provocative findings, it is important to examine the effects of presumptuous cross-examination questions in legal proceedings in which jurors have the benefit of knowing the context of the questions (e.g., the adversarial relationship between the cross-examiner and witness) and hearing the responses they evoke (e.g., the witness's admission or vehement denial of the implication, or an objection from the witness's attorney).

In a recent study, 105 mock jurors were randomly assigned to one of seven groups.[33] All subjects read a transcript of a rape trial in which the defense argued that the victim was mistaken in her identification. Some subjects read a version of the case in which the cross-examiner asked a presumptuous derogatory question of the victim (i.e., "Isn't it true that you have accused men of rape before?" followed by "Isn't it true that, four years ago, you called the police claiming that you had been raped?"); others read a version in which such questions were asked of an expert for the defense (i.e., "Isn't it true that your work is poorly regarded by your colleagues?" followed by "Hasn't your work been sharply criticized in the past?"). Within each version, the cross-examiner's questions were met with one of three reactions: an admission ("yes," "yes it is [has]"), a flat denial ("no," "no it isn't [hasn't]"), or an objection by the witness's attorney, after which the question was withdrawn before the witness had a chance to respond. An additional group of subjects read a transcript that did not contain any presumptuous questions.

Our results provided strong but qualified support for the hypothesis that negative presumptuous questions would diminish a witness's credibility. When the recipient of the question was the victim, the question did not significantly diminish her credibility. In fact, except when the question elicited an admission, female subjects—who are generally less sympathetic to the defense in this case than males— disparaged the defense lawyer who conducted the cross-examination. When the recipient of the presumptuous question was an expert, however, the technique of cross-examination by innuendo proved highly effective. When the expert's professional reputation was called into question—even though the charge was not corroborated by other evidence—subjects lowered their ratings of his credibility as a witness (i.e., he was perceived as less competent, believable, and persuasive). Indeed, among female subjects, subjective estimates of guilt were elevated in all the innuendo groups, a result that reflects the diminished impact of the defense expert. These effects were obtained regardless of whether the presumptuous question had elicited a denial, an objection, or an admission. It is particularly interesting that this effect was obtained even though many of our subjects reported that they did not actually *believe* the derogatory implications concerning the expert. In short, even when the expert denied the charge, even when his attorney objected to the question, and even though many subjects in both situations did not accept as true the cross-examiner's presumption, the witness became "damaged goods" as soon as the reputation question was raised.

Why were our mock jurors so influenced by uncorroborated presumptions? There are at least two possible explanations. First, research in communication suggests that when people hear a speaker offer a premise in conversation, they naturally assume that he or she has an evidentiary basis for that premise.[34] Within the context of a trial, it is conceivable that jurors—naive about the dirty tricks of cross-examination—adhere to a similar implicit rule. In other words, jurors may assume that a lawyer who implies something about an expert's reputation must have information to support that premise, and treat it though it were a foregone conclusion. A second possible reason for the impact of presumptuous questions is that after all the evidence in a case has been presented, jurors may be unable to separate in memory the information communicated within the questions from those contained within the answers. Studies indicate that people often remember the contents of a message but forget the source,[35] and that people often cannot discriminate among the possible sources of their current knowledge.[36] This kind of confusion is particularly likely to occur when the different sources of information are distant in time and equally plausible—as when jurors must recall after days, weeks, or months of testimony, whether a particular belief was derived from a lawyer's questions or a witness's answers.

From a practical standpoint, this study suggests that the use of presumptuous questions is a dirty trick that can be used to distort juror evaluations of witness credibility. As cross-examiners regularly employ such tactics, judges should be aware of the dangers and make a serious effort to control them. According to Rule 3.4(e) of the American Bar Association 1981 Rules of Professional Conduct, counsel "shall not allude to any matter that the lawyer does not reasonably believe is relevant or that will not be supported by admissible evidence." In practice, however, many judges demand only a "good faith belief" in the truthfulness of the assertions contained in cross-examination questions.[37]

Two approaches can be taken to the problem. Since witnesses have an opportunity to deny false assertions, and since lawyers have an opportunity to object or "set the record straight" on redirect examination, one approach is to allow cross-examiners a good deal of latitude, and trust the self-corrective mechanisms already in place. Our study suggests, however, that both a witness's denials and an attorney's objections may fall on deaf ears. In the case of our expert, subjects lowered their ratings of his credibility even when he flatly denied the charge and even when his attorney won a favorable ruling on an objection. In fact, these strategies may well backfire. People are suspicious of others who are forced to proclaim their innocence too vociferously.[38] Likewise, research indicates instructions to disregard objectionable material are often ineffective, perhaps even counterproductive.[39]

Rather than taking a hands-off policy, our results lead me to believe that judges should intervene to control presumptuous leading questions. As a matter of judicial discretion in trial management, judges may admonish counsel who insert false premises into their questions.[40] Perhaps cautionary instructions to the jury would prove effective. If jurors are moved by conjecture because they follow the implicit rule of conversational logic that speakers have an evidentiary basis for their premises, then perhaps jurors should be forewarned about the use of dirty tricks. Recall that Swann's experiment had subjects listen to an interviewer ask questions that presumed the respondent to be introverted or extraverted. Hearing the questions, subjects inferred that the interviewee possessed the implied traits. When they were told, however, that the interviewer's questions were chosen at random (i.e., without a reason), subjects did not make the inference. Thus, it may be similarly effective to caution jurors that the premises contained within questions are not evidence, and alert them to possible abuses.

To summarize, psychological research indicates that suggestive examination questions can mislead a jury in two ways. First, the questions themselves can misinform others through the power of conjecture. Second, suggestive questions can actually produce support for that conjecture by shaping the witness's testimony. If counsel wants to portray a witness as greedy, lazy, neurotic, introverted, or extraverted, he or she can do so by asking a series of biasing questions. Since a witness can tell a story only in response to specific inquiries, it is not impossible to get that witness to provide the necessary evidence. Redirect examination offers a possible safety valve, and to some extent its rehabilitative potential is self-evident. It is important to note, however, that first impressions often resist change despite subsequent contradictory information,[41] and that neither denial nor judicial admonishment is likely to have fully curative effects.

D. Nonevidentiary Temptations

As part of their factfinding role, jurors are instructed to recognize and disregard nonevidentiary sources of information—much of which is revealed within the courtroom (e.g., voir dire questions, inadmissible testimony, opening statements, closing arguments). Can human decisionmakers maintain separate files in memory for evidence and nonevidence? And can they delete the latter from awareness upon instruction to do so?

In a series of experiments on "reality monitoring," Marcia Johnson and her colleagues have found that people are often unable to recall the sources of their knowledge.[42] Under certain circumstances people remember the *content* of a message, while forgetting the *source*. People are especially vulnerable to confusion when the possible sources of information are equally plausible—as when jurors must recall after a trial presentation whether their beliefs are based on what was said by the lawyers or witnesses, or whether they are the product of their own self-generated inferences. In the end, it means that jurors may erroneously attribute their own versions of reality, or counsel's version, to reality itself.

Research on the effects of opening statements illustrates the possible consequences of source confusion in the courtroom. In a series of mock jury experiments, Lawrence Wrightsman and others consistently found that strong opening statements are persuasive—even when they are not subsequently borne out by the evidence.[43] In one study, for example, subjects read one of three versions of an auto theft trial. In one version, defense counsel promised in his opening statement that he would provide evidence of an alibi, evidence that was never forthcoming. In contrast to subjects to whom the claim was never made, those who received the empty promise were more likely to vote for the defendant's acquittal. The strategy failed only in the third version of the trial, where the prosecutor reminded the jury in his closing argument of the discrepancy between what was promised and what was proved.[44] Absent reminder, jurors may simply lack the necessary awareness of the sources of their trial beliefs.

Additional problems arise when jurors are exposed to inadmissible testimony, prompted by an attorney's question and subsequently stricken from the record. It should come as no surprise that jurors are often influenced by this leakage of nonevidentiary information. In one study, for example, mock jurors read a transcript of an armed robbery and murder trial. When the only available evidence was weak and circumstantial, not a single juror voted guilty. In a second version of the case that also contained a recording of a suspicious telephone conversation between the defendant and a bookmaker, and in which the judge ruled the tape admissible, the conviction rate increased to twenty-six percent. In a third version of the case in which the judge ruled the wiretapped conversation inadmissible and admonished to disregard the tape, the conviction rate increased even further, to thirty-five percent.[45] Additional research has shown that when the judge embellishes his or her ruling by admonishing jurors at length, they become even more likely to use the forbidden information.[46]

Judicial admonishment may well backfire for a variety of reasons. First, it draws an unusual amount of attention to the information in controversy, increasing its salience relative to the evidence. Indeed, the psychology of instructions-to-disregard parallels recent studies on the paradoxical effects of thought suppression. For example, Daniel Wegner and his colleagues found that when people were told to actively suppress thoughts of a white bear, that novel image intruded upon consciousness with remarkable frequency.[47] A second problem is that instructions to disregard are a form of censorship, a restriction on the juror's decisionmaking freedom. Again, research in other contexts indicates consistently that people react against prohibitions of this sort in order to assert their right to consider all possible information.[48] A third reason why instructions-to-disregard may be counterproductive is that jurors do not share the law's "due process" model of what constitutes a fair trial, the assumption that a verdict is just if procedural fairness is achieved. Ask jurors what they seek, and most will cite outcome accuracy as the main objective (i.e., "to make the *right* decision"). Thus, it is notable that jurors seem most likely to succumb to the temptation to use inadmissible evidence when that evidence exonerates the criminal defendant.[49]

Sometimes inadmissible evidence is properly introduced via the "limited admissibility rule" which permits the presentation of evidence for one purpose, but not another.[50] In such cases, the judge admits the evidence, restricts its proper scope, and instructs the jury accordingly (e.g.. when a defendant's criminal record is admitted for its bearing on the issue of credibility, not guilt). Can jurors compartmentalize evidence in this manner, using it to draw one inference, but not another? This rule is one of the paradoxes of evidence law, and is viewed by many as a lesson in futility. One survey revealed that ninety-eight percent of the lawyers and forty-three percent of the judges questioned believed jurors could not comply with this instruction.[51] They are probably right. Mock jurors who learn that a defendant has a criminal record and are limited in their use of that evidence are more likely to vote for conviction even though their judgments of the defendant's credibility are unaffected by that information.[52] Likewise, mock juries spend a good deal of time discussing a defendant's record—not for what it implies about credibility, but for what it suggests about criminal predispositions.[53]

E. Voices from an Empty Chair

In one trial, a defendant accused of armed robbery claims he was drinking in a bar at the time, but does not bring in alibi witnesses who were supposed to have been with him. In another trial, a party involved in a traffic accident fails to call to the witness stand a friend or relative who was a passenger during the collision. Cases such as these pose a dilemma: When a prospective favorable witness does not take the stand, should opposing counsel be permitted in closing argument to cite that witness's absence as proof of his or her adverse testimony? Should the judge invite jurors to draw negative inferences from that missing witness?

The courts are divided on how they manage this situation. Nearly a century ago, in *Graves v. United States*, the United States Supreme Court introduced what has come to be known as the missing witness rule, or empty chair doctrine. The rule states that "if a party has it peculiarly within his power to produce witnesses whose testimony would elucidate the transaction, the fact that he does not do it creates the presumption that the testimony, if produced, would be unfavorable."[54] In operational terms, this rule enables lawyers to comment on a witness's absence in closing arguments and judges to suggest possible adverse inferences to the jury. The reasons for this doctrine are straightforward.[55] The courts assume that litigants who fail to call knowledgeable witnesses are concealing evidence and should be pressured to come forward with that evidence. In addition, it is argued that jurors on their own will draw adverse inferences from the absence of an expected witness. Stephen Saltzburg, for example, suggested that once jurors are presented with a theory about a case, they naturally come to expect certain kinds of supporting proof and are likely to make adverse inferences about any party that fails to satisfy these expectations. Carrying this analysis one step further, Saltzburg argued that judges should take juror expectations and inferences into account before ruling to exclude evidence considered relevant but prejudicial.[56]

The empty chair doctrine has been criticized on at least three grounds. First, it is said to be unfair to draw adverse inferences from missing evidence because there are many other possible reasons for a witness's failure to appear in court.[57] Second, constitutional issues arise in cases where an expected witness does not testify on behalf of a criminal defendant, whose own silence is protected by the fifth amendment.[58]

A third criticism of the empty chair rule is that it sends a confusing mixed signal to jurors about their role as factfinders. Although jurors are admonished time and again to base their judgments only on evidence produced in court, the missing witness instruction may encourage them to speculate on other matters not in evidence.[59]

On their own, do jurors make adverse inferences concerning absent witnesses? What are the effects of empty chair comments? Indirectly, psychological research suggests an "it depends" answer to these empirical questions. When a prospective witness is central to a case and, hence, conspicuously absent, juries are likely to speculate, even without prompting. This suggestion is based on studies indicating that people are biased against criminal defendants who remain silent, even when they are specifically admonished not to draw negative inferences.[60] In contrast, when a witness is not clearly essential to a case, juries are not likely to be influenced by his or her absence. This suggestion is based on studies on the "feature-positive effect," the finding that humans are relatively insensitive to events that do *not* occur.[61]

To examine more directly the effects of missing witnesses on legal decision-making, my students and I conducted the following mock jury study.[62] Upon arrival in a mock courtroom, fifty subjects—participating in small groups—read one of four versions of an insanity murder trial in which either a central witness (the defendant's close friend) or a peripheral witness (a co-worker of the defendant) was absent,[63] and in which the judge and opposing counsel either did or did not suggest an adverse inference.[64] Opinions of the case were assessed both before and after subjects deliberated.

The results of this experiment were generally consistent with the predictions derived from other research. Three findings in particular are noteworthy. First, all subjects were aware of the witness's absence, but when asked if they needed additional information, far more subjects in the comment than no-comment condition expressed a need for testimony from that witness. Second, there was an effect on case-related opinions: among subjects who read the missing-central transcript, empty chair comments increased the likelihood of conviction and enhanced their evaluations of the prosecuting attorney. In the missing-peripheral condition, however, the same empty chair comments decreased the likelihood of conviction and diminished subjects' evaluations of the prosecuting attorney. Third, subjects in the comment condition, after deliberating, were somewhat more likely than those in the no-comment condition to express a desire for testimony from the defendant (who did not testify). This latter result suggests the possibility that jurors who read the empty chair comments had discussed the defendant's failure to testify during their deliberations.

Is the missing witness inference "natural," an argument made by proponents of the empty chair doctrine? No, the inference is not as natural as it may seem. Subjects in the no-comment group knew that the prospective central or peripheral witness had not testified, but they did not hold the defendant responsible unless prompted to do so by the judge and opposing counsel. To be sure, all subjects recognized that the missing witness was absent, but only those in the comment condition were moved by his absence. Should empty chair comments, then, be permitted? Our study does not provide a clear answer to this second question. For trial attorneys, there are potential costs and benefits associated with empty chair comments, depending on the status of the witness in question. Lawyers who comment on a missing-central witness may draw the jury's attention to a gap in the opponent's case, reap the benefits of the inferences likely to be drawn, and elicit the perception that they themselves are competent. On the other hand, attorneys who drag a missing-peripheral witness into evidence risk alienating the jury by making what appears to be an implausible argument, and eliciting the perception that they themselves are desperate, if not incompetent. Our results thus support the conclusion that the empty chair doctrine cannot easily be used for unfair strategic purposes, without regard for the extent to which the jury already expects testimony from that witness.

II. The Jury Deliberation Process

It is often said that the distinctive power of the jury is that it functions as a group. Indeed, although the jury meets in complete privacy, the courts have articulated a clear vision of how juries should deliberate to a verdict. Basically, there are three components to this ideal.

The first component is one of independence and equality. No juror's vote counts for more than any other juror's vote. A twelve-person jury should thus consist of twelve independent and equal individuals, each contributing his or her own personal opinion to the final outcome. Unlike other task-oriented groups, the jury's role is ideally structured to promote equal participation. The cardinal rule of jury decisionmaking is that verdicts be based only on the evidence introduced in open court. By limiting the task as such, jurors are discouraged from basing their arguments on private or outside sources of knowledge. The courts try to foster this ideal in a number of ways. For example, jurors are told to refrain from discussing the trial until they deliberate, thus ensuring that each juror develops his or her own unique perspective on the case, uncontaminated by others' views. In addition, the courts often exclude from service people who are expected to exert a disproportionate amount of influence over other jurors (such as lawyers or others who have expertise in trial-relevant matters).

The second component of an ideal deliberation is an openness to informational influence. Inside the jury room, members have a duty to share information, exchange points of view, and debate the evidence. This deliberation requirement means that jurors should maintain an open mind and withhold their judgment until "an impartial consideration of the evidence with his fellow jurors."[65] It also means that consensus should be achieved through rational, persuasive argument. As the Supreme Court put it almost a century ago, "[t]he very object of the jury system is to secure unanimity by a comparison of views, and by arguments among the jurors themselves. . . . It cannot be that each juror should go to the jury-room with a blind determination that the verdict shall represent his opinion of the case at that moment; or, that he should close his ears to the arguments of men who are equally honest and intelligent as himself."[66]

The third ideal of deliberation follows from the second. Although juries should strive for a consensus of opinion, that goal should not be achieved through heavy-handed social pressure. Obviously, those who dissent from the majority should not be beaten, bullied, or harangued into surrendering their convictions for the purpose of returning a verdict. The reason is simple: if jurors comply with the majority to avoid rejection or terminate an unpleasant experience, then their final vote might not reflect their true beliefs. In the Supreme Court's words, "the verdict must be the verdict of each individual juror, and not a mere acquiescence in the conclusion of his fellows. . . ."[67]

As in other decisionmaking groups, juries reach a verdict through two processes—informational and normative.[68] Through informational social influence, individuals conform because they are genuinely persuaded by majority opinion; through normative influence, individuals comply in order to avoid the unpleasant consequences of social pressure. Indeed, groups often reject, ridicule, and punish individuals who frustrate a common goal by taking a deviant position.[69] The importance of both processes has been well documented in recent conformity research,[70] and in jury research as well.[71] As Kalven and Zeisel noted in *The American Jury*, the deliberation process "is an interesting combination of rational persuasion, sheer social pressure, and the psychological mechanism by which individual perceptions undergo change when exposed to group discussion."[72]

Although jury verdicts should follow a vigorous exchange of information and a minimum of normative pressure, the delicate balance between these competing forces can be altered by various aspects of a jury's task.[73] For example, normative influences are heightened in groups that decide on questions of values rather than facts,[74] and in groups that take frequent public ballots.[75] In addition, recent research implicates two procedural factors that may compromise the integrity of jury deliberations: (1) the dynamite charge, and (2) the acceptance of nonunanimous verdicts.

A. The Dynamite Charge

Recently, I received a phone call from a criminal lawyer whose client had been convicted on six counts of tax fraud. After two days of testimony, arguments, and instructions, the twelve-person jury spent three days deliberating. On the second day of deliberation, the jury informed the judge that it was at an impasse on some counts. The jurors were reconvened, but then on the third day said they were hopelessly deadlocked on all counts, with no verdict in sight. At that point, the judge issued à special instruction, one that is designed to prod hung juries toward a verdict. Twenty minutes later, as if a spell had been cast, the jury reached unanimous guilty verdicts on all counts.

The instruction that preceded the jury's decision was modeled after the *Allen* charge, first used in Massachusetts,[76] and approved by the United States Supreme Court in *Allen v. United States.*[77] Used to blast deadlocked juries into a verdict, this supplemental instruction is believed to be so effective that it is commonly known as the "dynamite charge."[78] For judges confronted with the prospect of a hung jury, this instruction can be used to avert a mistrial by imploring jurors to reexamine their own views and to seriously consider each other's arguments with a disposition to be convinced. In addition, it may state that "if much the larger number were for conviction, a dissenting juror should consider whether his doubt was a reasonable one which made no impression on the minds of so many men, equally honest, equally intelligent with himself."[79]

Trial anecdotes suggest that the dynamite charge is effective. Those who believe the effect is desirable argue that it encourages all jurors to reevaluate their positions and that, after all, those who are in the voting minority are typically obstinate holdouts who should "properly be warned against stubbornness and self-assertion."[80] Opponents, however, fear that legitimate dissenters, "struggling to maintain their position in a protracted debate in the jury room, are led into the courtroom and, before their peers, specifically requested by the judge to reconsider their position.[81] The charge places the sanction of the court behind the views of the majority, whatever they may be. . . ."[82]

The dynamite charge has its share of proponents and critics. In 1968, the American Bar Association opposed this instruction on the grounds that it coerces the deadlocked jury into reaching a verdict and places inordinate amounts of pressure on those in the minority.[83] The dynamite charge has been prohibited or restricted in certain state and federal courts.[84] In 1988, however, the United States Supreme Court ruled that the dynamite charge is not necessarily coercive, and reaffirmed its use on a routine basis.[85]

Although the dynamite charge has stirred controversy for many years, and although the Supreme Court has now upheld its use, until recently no empirical studies had examined its impact on the jury's deliberation process. Thus, my colleagues and I sought to test the hypothesis that the dynamite charge upsets the delicate balance of social influence forces, causing those in the majority to exert increasing amounts of normative rather than informational pressure, and causing those in the minority to change their votes.[86]

In order to test this hypothesis in a controlled setting, we contrived an artificial experimental situation in which lone subjects "deliberated" by voting and passing notes. Overall, seventy-two individual subjects read about a criminal tax case, thinking they would participate on a mock jury. In fact, subjects were taken to a cubicle and told they would communicate with three others in different rooms by passing notes. These so-called deliberations were structured by discrete rounds. After reading the case summary, subjects wrote down a verdict and a brief explanation. They signaled the experimenter over an intercom. The experimenter collected the subject's note, supposedly collected other subject's notes, photocopied them, and distributed the copies to each subject. After reading the other notes, subjects began a second round of deliberation voting, writing an explanation, signaling the experimenter and receiving written feedback from three fictitious peers. Subjects were instructed that this procedure would be reiterated until the group reached unanimity. In fact, unless subjects changed their votes, the session was terminated after seven rounds. At that point, a questionnaire was administered and subjects were debriefed.

Six sets of notes—three guilty, three not guilty—were written and photocopied.[87] All subjects received three notes at a time. Those assigned to the majority received two randomly selected sets of notes that agreed with their guilty or not guilty verdicts, and one set that did not. In contrast, subjects assigned to the minority received three randomly selected sets of notes that all disagreed with their verdicts. By the end of the first round, subjects thus found themselves in either the majority or minority faction of a three-to-one split. Unless subjects changed their vote, these divisions persisted.[88] After the third round, half the subjects were reminded that since verdicts had to be unanimous, they would continue to "deliberate."[89] For the other half, the experimenter—acting as judge—delivered an instruction patterned after the *Allen* charge.

Three results were consistent with the hypothesis that the dynamite charge is effective because of normative pressure on those in the voting minority. First, among subjects caught in a deadlocked jury (i.e., who remained committed to their initial votes after the third round), those in the minority changed their verdicts more often than those in the majority after receiving the dynamite charge, but not in the no-instruction control group. Second, minority subjects who heard the dynamite charge reported feeling heightened pressure from the judge—more than in the majority and minority-no-instruction groups.[90] Third, compared to all other subjects, those in the majority who received the dynamite charge exhibited in their notes diminishing amounts of informational influence strategies (e.g., citing facts or laws relevant to the case), coupled with a significant increase in normative social pressure (e.g., derogating those who disagreed, refusing to yield) immediately following the judge's instruction. Clearly, the dynamite charge tipped in an undesirable direction the balance of forces operating on our subjects, subjectively empowering the voting majority relative to the minority.

Taken as a whole, our results call into question the use of the dynamite charge as a means of eliciting verdicts from deadlocked juries. This study should be considered tentative, however, with regard to its generalizability to real trials. To systematically test the impact of the dynamite charge on the votes, perceptions, and behaviors of individual jurors, we contrived an artificial situation in which lone subjects "deliberated" by passing notes.[91] It remains to be seen whether the same results would emerge within live, interacting groups of jurors. It also remains to be seen whether alternative forms of instruction yield better results (i.e., verdicts from deadlocked juries through informational rather than normative influence).[92]

B. Less-Than-Unanimous Verdicts

The problem with the dynamite charge is that it may produce verdicts in which the jury's unanimity is more apparent than real. However, even the appearance of unanimity is often not necessary. In a pair of 1972 decisions, the United States Supreme Court ruled that states may allow juries to return verdicts without having to secure agreement from all members.[93] Finding neither a legal nor historical basis for the unanimity tradition, the Court concluded that, as a practical matter, juries function similarly under unanimous and nonunanimous decision rules. Writing for the *Johnson* majority, Justice White argued that majority jurors would maintain an open mind and continue to deliberate in good faith even after the requisite majority is reached.[94] In dissent, Justice Douglas argued that once a requisite majority is reached, majority jurors will become closed-minded, and vigorous debate would give way to "polite and academic conversation."[95]

Are unanimous and nonunanimous juries equivalent in the extent to which they achieve the ideals of deliberation? Several studies have addressed the question, and the results converge on the same answer: the differences are substantial. In one study, Charlan Nemeth had several hundred students at the University of Virginia read about a murder trial and indicate whether they believed the defendant to be guilty or not guilty.[96] Three weeks later, these students participated in six-person mock juries constructed to split four to two in their initial vote, favoring either conviction or acquittal. The groups were given two hours to reach a decision. Half were instructed to return a unanimous verdict, the other half needed only a two-thirds majority. Compared to those driven toward unanimity, majority-rule juries took less time to settle on a decision (many of these groups, in fact, concluded their deliberations without a single change in vote). When subjects were given an opportunity to evaluate the quality of their deliberations, those who had participated in majority juries were less satisfied, less certain of their verdicts, and less influenced by others' arguments.

In a more extensive study, Reid Hastie and his colleagues recruited over 800 people from jury pools in Massachusetts.[97] After a brief voir dire, these subjects were randomly assigned to participate in sixty-nine twelve-person mock juries, all of whom watched a videotape of a reenacted murder trial. An approximately equal number of juries were instructed to reach a verdict by either a twelve to zero, a ten to two, or an eight to four margin. Based on objective analyses of the deliberations as well as jurors' own subjective reports, the results were striking. Compared to unanimous juries, those that deliberated under a more relaxed rule spent less time discussing the case and more time voting. After reaching their required quorum, these groups usually rejected the hold-outs, terminated discussion, and returned a verdict within just a few minutes. Needless to say, those who participated in majority juries viewed their peers as relatively closed-minded, felt less informed about the case and less confident about the final verdict. Hastie and his colleagues also observed that many of the majority jurors were quite combative during their deliberations, as "larger factions in majority rule juries adopt a more forceful, bullying, persuasive style because their members realize that it is not necessary to respond to all opposition arguments when their goal is to achieve a faction size of only eight or ten members."[98]

C. Summary Policies that Compromise the Deliberation Process

In nineteenth century England, juries that were unable to achieve unanimity "were locked up in a cart, without meat, drink, fire, or candle, and followed the judge from town to town. Only their verdict could secure their release."[99] American juries were similarly subverted. Judges used to urge deadlocked juries to resolve their disagreements through such coercive measures as the denial of food and drink, excessive deliberation hours, and the threat of confinement. Today, the strategies may differ, but the objective is the same. The dynamite charge and the relaxation of a unanimous verdict requirement are driven by a contempt for the hung jury and the costs incurred by a mistrial. Proponents of these policies seem to base their opinions on the assumption that a jury becomes deadlocked because of one obstinate holdout, the chronic anti-conformist. Opponents, on the other hand, base their views on the belief that juries are hung as a genuine response to close, difficult cases in which the evidence allows for well-reasoned disagreement and does not compel a particular verdict. To be sure, not all deadlocked juries are created equal, and anecdotes can be found to support either position. Kalven and Zeisel's research, however, suggests that hung juries occur in only about five percent of all criminal jury trials, and do so especially in close cases in which the minority consists of a group rather than one member—a finding that lends support to the latter, more rational image.[100]

Neither the dynamite charge nor suspension of the unanimity requirement have desirable effects on the quality of the jury's decisionmaking apparatus. Used to implore the deadlocked jury to return a verdict, the dynamite charge may well encourage members of the voting majority to exert increasing amounts of normative pressure without added informational influence, thus intimidating members of a voting minority into compliance. The net result, of course, is an illusion of unanimity. Even worse is the outright acceptance of nonunanimous verdicts. This policy weakens and inhibits dissenting jurors, breeds closed-mindedness, impairs the quality of discussion, and leaves many jurors unsatisfied with the final verdict. And yet, without a potent and vocal dissent based on legitimate differences of opinion, the jury is reduced to a mere collection of individuals, losing its strength as a vital decisionmaking group.

III. Conclusions

The American trial jury is a truly unique institution. In the words of Kalven and Zeisel, "[i]t recruits a group of twelve laymen, chosen at random from the widest population; it convenes them for the purpose of the particular trial; it entrusts them with great official powers of decision; it permits them to carry on deliberations in secret and to report their final judgment without giving reasons for it; and, after their momentary service to the state has been completed, it orders them to disband and return to private life."[101]

This article rests on a conviction that juries should not be evaluated by case studies, autobiographical accounts, and news stories, but by hard empirical research designed to answer concrete, behavioral questions. With that objective in mind, trial practices that influence the decisionmaking process were examined for their effects on both individual jurors and the jury as a group.

Jurors are expected to base their opinions on an accurate appraisal of evidence to the exclusion of nonevidentiary sources of information. Thus, trials are structured by an elaborate network of rules to focus jurors on the evidence, to facilitate their search for the truth, and to insulate them from various social influences. Research on how jurors assess the credibility of witnesses, and their ability or willingness to resist the lure of certain kinds of extraneous information, gives rise to the conclusion that there is much room for improvement. To begin with, jurors are supposed to distinguish among witnesses of varying credibility, an often difficult task. Yet that task is more complicated than is necessary. To be sure, the occasional intrusion into the trial record of inadmissible testimony and objectionable arguments is an inevitable fact of life in an adversarial system. But too often, American courts compound the problem by permitting counsel to (1) use surrogates to present deposition testimony for absentee witnesses, leaving the jury to disentangle the appearance and demeanor of the messenger from the message and its original source; (2) impart information through conjecture and innuendo, leaving jurors to assume the truth of uncorroborated matters and confuse in memory the sources of their knowledge; and (3) invite jurors to draw adverse inferences from missing witnesses, leading them to create evidence from the absence of evidence, and sending a confusing mixed signal concerning speculation and the boundaries of their fact-finding role.

Turning to the jury as a group, it is perhaps the greatest asset of the jury that a group of independent citizens, strangers to one another, are placed behind closed doors and directed to reach a common decision. Bringing a diversity of perspectives to bear on the task, these jurors share information, clash in their values and argue over competing interpretations. Remarkably, out of this conflict, ninety-five percent of all juries succeed in returning a verdict. Intolerant of lengthy deliberations and the five percent of juries that declare themselves hung, however, the courts have sanctioned procedures and structural changes in the jury that widen the gap between the ideals and realities of deliberation. One example is the *Allen* instruction, otherwise known as the dynamite charge. Used to implore the deadlocked jury to return a verdict, research suggests it may tip in an undesirable direction the balance of informational and normative forces operating within the jury, further empowering the voting majority relative to the minority, and intimidating the latter into compliance. A second example is provided by the United States Supreme Court's decisions to uphold the right of states to relax the jury's unanimity requirement. Indeed, research clearly indicates that a less-than-unanimous decision rule weakens dissent, breeds closed-mindedness, impairs the quality of discussion, and leaves many jurors unsatisfied with the final verdict.

In light of recent research on human decisionmaking and behavior, consciousness should be raised in American courtrooms about common trial practices and procedures that lead individual jurors and the groups to which they belong to exhibit less-than-ideal performance. Prescriptions for how juries should function are clear. In reality, however, the American jury is too often handicapped in the pursuit of justice.

Endnotes

[1] McElhaney, "Dealing with Dirty Tricks," 7 Litigation 45, 46 (1981).

[2] M. Belli, Melvin Belli: My Life on Trial 107-9 (1976).

[3] Allen v. United States, 164 U.S. 492, 501 (1986).

[4] The mock jury paradigm involves simulating trials in the form of transcripts, audiotapes, or videotapes, and recruiting subjects to act as jurors. This method has two advantages. First, it enables researchers to secure control over events that take place in the "courtroom" and design controlled experiments that can establish causal relationships between specific trial characteristics and jury verdicts. Second, it offers a good deal of flexibility, enabling researchers to manipulate variables that cannot be touched in real cases (e.g., evidence, arguments, trial procedures, judge's instructions, the composition of the jury) and obtain measures of behavior that are otherwise too intrusive (e.g., mid-trial opinions, attention, comprehension, and recall; physiological arousal; videotaped deliberations). In short, trial simulations enable us to observe not only the outcome but the process of jury decisionmaking. A more extensive discussion of this technique appears in Bray & Kerr, "Methodological Considerations in the Study of the Psychology of the Courtroom," The Psychology of the Courtroom 287, 296-98 (1982). For a description of practical applications, see Kassin, "Mock Jury Trials," 7 Trial Dipl. J. 26 (1984).

As with other indirect methods of inquiry, the mock jury paradigm is not without its shortcomings. In exchange for a highly controlled environment, the approach suffers from the problem of external validity (i.e. generalizability to real trials). As a general rule, generalizability is enhanced by research conditions that approximate the real event. Still, legitimate empirical questions can be raised. For more detailed critiques, see Dillehay & Neitzel, "Constructing a Science of Jury Behavior," Review of Personality and Social Psychology 246 (1980); Ebbesen & Konecni, "On the External Validity of Decision-Making Research: What do we Know about Decisions in the Real World?" Cognitive Processes in Choice and Decision Behavior (1980).

[5] For a review of arguments against notetaking, see S. Kassin & L. Wrightsman, The American Jury on Trial: Psychological Perspectives 128 (1988).

[6] DePaulo & Pfeifer, "On-the-Job Experience and Skill at Detecting Deception," 16 J. Applied Soc. Psychology 249, 261-62 (1986); Kraut & Poe, "Behavioral Roots of Person

Perception: The Deception Judgments of Customs Inspectors and Laymen," 39 *J. Personality & Soc. Psychology* 784, 788 (1980).

[7] Zuckerman, DePaulo & Rosenthal, "Verbal and Nonverbal Communication of Deception," 14 *Advances in Experimental Soc. Psychology* 1, 38-40 (1981).

[8] Deceivers often wear false smiles to mask their real feelings; see Ekman, Friesen & O'Sullivan, "Smiles When Lying," 54 *J. Personality & Soc. Psychology* 414, 415 (1988).

[9] Deception is often accompanied by fidgety movements of the hands and feet, and restless shifts in posture. When people lie, especially when they are highly motivated to do so, there is also a rise in their voice pitch and an increased number of speech hesitations. See DePaulo, Lanier & Davis, "Detecting the Deceit of the Motivated Liar," 45 *J. Personality & Soc. Psychology* 1096 (1983); see also, Streeter, Krauss, Geller, Olson & Apple, "Pitch Changes During Attempted Deception," 35 *J. Personality & Soc. Psychology* 345, 348-49 (1977).

[10] People sometimes become more accurate in their judgments of truth and deception when they are too busy to attend closely to what a speaker says. See Gilbert & Krull, "Seeing Less and Knowing More: The Benefits of Perceptual Ignorance," 54 *J. Personality & Soc. Psychology* 193, 201 (1988). Although distracting jurors from the content of a witness's testimony is a ludicrous idea, it is possible that credibility judgments would be improved by a more specific demeanor instruction, one that redirects attention toward cues that are more diagnostic than facial expressions. Research suggests, for example, that when people are encouraged to pay more attention to the voice than to the face, they make more accurate judgments of truth and deception. See DePaulo, Lassiter & Stone, "Attentional Determinants of Success at Detecting Deception and Truth," 8 *Personality & Soc. Psychology Bull.* 273, 277 (1982). Liars are also betrayed by movements of the lower body, so jurors could be instructed to consider these cues as well. Ironically, however, the witness's body is often hidden from view—by the witness stand.

[11] E. Cleary, *McCormick on Evidence* § 5 (2d ed. 1972).

[12] For a review of this literature, see Loftus & Goodman, "Questioning Witnesses," *The Psychology of Evidence and Trial Proc.* 253 (1985).

[13] *Model Rules of Professional Conduct* Rule 3.4 (1983).

[14] See generally R. Underwood & W. Fortune, *Trial Ethics* (1988); Underwood, "Adversary Ethics: More Dirty Tricks," 6 *Am. J. Trial Advoc.* 265 (1982).

[15] McElhaney, supra note 1, at 45-48; Underwood, supra note 14, at 269-89.

[16] The death of a prospective witness is an obvious problem. Those who live beyond a certain distance from the courthouse, or who are sick, handicapped, out of the country, or in prison, may also be excused. See *Fed. R. Civ. P.* 32(a)(3).

[17] See generally, Kassin, supra note 4, at 27.

[18] A. Morrill, *Trial Diplomacy* 52 (1972). Conversely, it is advisable to present the testimony of witnesses who are "singularly impressive" live rather than via deposition. See R. Keeton, *Trial Tactics and Methods* 18 (1973).

[19] A. Morrill, supra note 18, at 52.

[20] For a recent review of this literature see R. Petty & J. Cacioppo, *Communication and Persuasion* 204-9 (1986).

[21] Kassin, "Deposition Testimony and the Surrogate Witness: Evidences for a 'Messenger Effect' in Persuasion," 9 *Personality & Soc. Psychology Bull.* 281, 283-84 (1983).

[22] E.g., Chaiken, "Communicator Physical Attractiveness and Persuasion," 37 *J. Personality & Soc. Psychology* 1387, 1395 (1979); see also Pallak, "Salience of a Communicator's Physical Attractiveness and Persuasion: A Heuristic versus Systematic Processing Interpretation," 2 *Soc. Cognition* 158, 168 (1983).

[23] Kassin, "Deposition Testimony and the Surrogate Witness: Further Evidence for a 'Messenger Effect' in Persuasion," Unpublished data (1990).

[24] Attractiveness was determined through pretesting.

[25] See, e.g., McCrystal, "Videotape Trials: Relief for Our Congested Courts," 49 *Den. U.L. Rev.* 463, 465-66 (1973); see also Kornblum, "Videotape in Civil Cases," 24 *Hastings L.J.* 9, 23-26 (1972).

[26] See Conley, O'Barr & Lind, "The Power of Language: Presentational Style in the Courtroom," 6 *Duke L.J.* 1375, 1386-89 (1978).

[27] Danet, "'Baby' or 'Fetus'?: Language and the Construction of Reality in a Manslaughter Trial," 32 *Semiotica* 187, 206 (1980).

[28] When other verbs were substituted for these, estimates varied considerably, e.g., "collided" yielded 39 mph; "contacted" yielded 32 mph. See Loftus & Palmer, "Reconstruction of Automobile Destruction: An Example of the Interaction Between Language and Memory," 13 *J. Verbal Learning & Verbal Behav.* 585, 586 (1974).

[29] See Harris & Monaco, "Psychology of Pragmatic Implication: Information Processing Between the Lines," 107 *J. Experimental Psychology: General* 1, 6-9 (1978); see also Johnson, Bransford, & Solomon, "Memory for Tacit Implications of Sentences," 98 *J. Experimental Psychology* 203 (1973).

[30] R. Underwood & W. Fortune, supra note 14, at 346.

[31] Swann, Giuliano & Wegner, "Where Leading Questions Can Lead: The Power of Conjecture in Social Interaction," 42 *J. Personality & Soc. Psychology* 1025, 1034 (1982); see also Wegner, Wenclaff, Kerker & Beattie, "Incrimination Through Innuendo: Can Media Questions Become Public Answers?," 40 *J. Personality & Soc. Psychology* 822, 830-32 (1981).

[32] Swann, Giuliano & Wegner, supra note 31, at 1033. This effect is so powerful that it even influences the self-perceptions of the respondents themselves. After being interviewed, they took personality tests in which they were asked to describe themselves on various dimensions. Those who had answered questions about introverted or extroverted behaviors later rated themselves as such on the questionnaires.

[33] Kassin, Williams & Saunders, "Dirty Tricks of Cross Examination: The Influence of Conjectural Evidence on the Jury," 14 *Law and Human Behavior* 373 (1990).

[34] Grice, "Logic in Conversation," 3 *Syntax and Semantics* 41, 44 (1975); Hopper, "The Taken-For-Granted," 7 *Human Communication Research* 195, 198 (1981).

[35] Kelman & Hovland, "'Reinstatement' of the Communicator in Delayed Measurement of Opinion Change," 48 *J. Abnormal & Soc. Psychology* 327, 332-35 (1953); Pratkanis, Greenwald, Leippe & Baumgardner, "In Search of Reliable Persuasion Effects: III. The Sleeper Effect is Dead. Long Live the Sleeper Effect," 54 *J. Personality & Soc. Psychology* 203, 205 (1988).

[36] Johnson, "Discrimination the Origin of Information," *Delusional Beliefs: Interdisciplinary Perspectives* (Otmanns & Maher eds. 1987); Johnson & Raye, "Reality Monitoring," 88 *Psychological Rev.* 67, 82 (1981).

[37] *U.S. v. Brown*, 519 F.2d 1368 (6th Cir. 1975).

[38] Shaffer, "The Defendant's Testimony," *The Psychology of Evidence and Trial Procedure* (Kassin & Wrightsman eds. 1985); Yandell, "Those Who Protest Too Much are Seen as Guilty," 5 *Personality & Soc. Psychology Bull.* 44, 47 (1979).

[39] Carretta & Moreland, "The Direct and Indirect Effects of Inadmissible Evidence," 13 *J. Applied Soc. Psychology* 291, 291-93 (1983); Sue, Smith & Caldwell, "Effects of Inadmissible Evidence on the Decisions of Simulated Jurors: A Moral Dilemma," 3 *J. Applied Soc. Psychology* 345, 351-53 (1973); Wolf & Montgomery, "Effects of Inadmissible Evidence and level of Judicial Admonishment to Disregard on the Judgments of Mock Jurors," 7 *J. Applied Soc. Psychology* 205, 216-18 (1977).

[40] In some cases, the courts have even sustained the right of an opposing party to call a cross-examiner to the witness stand to inquire into the "good faith basis" for a specific

line of questions. See *United States v. Cardarella,* 570 F.2d 264, 268 (8th Cir. 1978); *United States v. Pugliese,* 153 F.2d 497,498-99 (2d Cir. 1945).

41 See, e.g., Asch, "Forming Impressions of Personality," 41 *J. Abnormal & Soc. Psychology* 258, 288-90 (1946); Darley & Gross, "A Hypothesis-Confirming Bias in Labeling Effects," 44 *J. Personality & Soc. Psychology* 20, 21-22 (1983); Greenwald, Pratkanis, Leippe & Baumgardner, "Under What Conditions Does Theory Obstruct Research Progress?", 93 *Psychological Rev.* 216, 227 (1986); Hamilton & Zanna, "Context Effects in Impression Formation: Changes in Connotative Meaning," 29 *J. Personality & Soc. Psychology* 649, 652-54 (1974); Hayden & Mischel, "Maintaining Trait Consistency in the Resolution of Behavioral Inconsistency. The Wolf in Sheep's Clothing?" 44 *J. Personality* 109, 129-31 (1976); E. Jones & G. Goethals, *Order Effects in Impression Formation: Attribution Context and the Nature of the Entity,* 42-43 (1971); Kruglanski & Freund, "The Freezing and Unfreezing of Lay Inferences: Effects on Impressional Primacy, Ethnic Stereotyping, and Numerical Anchoring," 19 *J. Experimental Soc. Psychology* 448, 461-65 (1983); Lord, Ross & Lepper, "Biased Assimilation and Attitude Polarization: The Effects of Prior Theories on Subsequently Considered Evidence," 37 *J. Personality & Soc. Psychology* 2098, 2108 (1979).

42 See, e.g., Johnson, Bransford & Solomon, "Memory for Tacit Implications of Sentences," 98 *J. Experimental Psychology* 203, 204 (1973); Johnson & Raye, supra note 36, at 81-82.

43 Pyszczynski & Wrightsman, "The Effects of Opening Statements on Mock Jurors' Verdicts in a Simulated Criminal Trial," 11 *J. Applied Soc. Psychology* 301, 309-10 (1981); Wells, Wrightsman & Meine, "The Timing of the Defense Opening Statement: Don't Wait Until the Evidence Is In," 15 *J. Applied Soc. Psychology* 758, 769 (1985).

44 Pyszczynski, Greenberg, Mack & Wrightsman, "Opening Statements in a Jury Trial: The Effect of Promising More Than the Evidence Can Show," 11 *J. Applied Soc. Psychology* 434, 442 (1981).

45 Sue, Smith & Caldwell, supra note 39, at 350-51; see also Caretta & Moreland, supra note 39, at 305-6.

46 Wolf & Montgomery, supra note 39, at 216.

47 Wegner, Schneider, Carter & White, "Paradoxical Effects of Thought Suppression," 53 *J. Personality & Soc. Psychology* 5, 8-9 (1987).

48 This explanation is based on Brehm's 1966 theory of psychological reactance. See S. Brehm & J. Brehm, *Psychological Reactance: A Theory of Freedom and Control* 3-7 (1981); see also Worchel, Arnold & Baker, "The Effect of Censorship on Attitude Change; The Influence of Censor and Communicator Characteristics," 5 *J. Applied Soc. Psychology* 227, 237 (1975) (for relevant empirical support).

49 Thompson, Fong & Rosenhan, "Inadmissible Evidence and Juror Verdicts," 40 *J. Personality & Soc. Psychology* 453, 460 (1981).

50 *Fed. R. Evid.* 404(a)(3).

51 Note, "To take the Stand or Not to Take the Stand: The Dilemma of the Defendant with a Criminal Record," 4 *Colum. J. L. & Soc. Probs.* 215, 218 (1968).

52 Wissler & Saks, "On the Inefficacy of Limiting Instructions: When Jurors Use Prior Conviction Evidence to Decide on Guilt," 9 *L. & Hum. Behav.* 37, 47 (1985).

53 See Shaffer, supra note 38, at 145. The inherent prejudice of this rule is indicated by the finding that mock jurors told of a defendant's criminal record view the remaining evidence as more damaging than those who are uninformed. See Hans & Doob, "Section 12 of the Canada Evidence Act and the Deliberations of Simulated Juries," 18 *Crim. L.Q.* 235, 244-46 (1975).

54 *Graves v. United States,* 150 U.S. 118, 121 (1893).

55 E. Cleary, *McCormick on Evidence* § 272 (3d ed. 1984); J. Chadbourn, *Wigmore's Evidence,* § 286 (3d ed. 1970).

[56] Saltzburg, "A Special Aspect of Relevance: Countering Negative Inferences Associated with the Absence of Evidence," 66 *Calif. L. Rev.* 1011, 1012 (1978).

[57] For example, a litigant may choose to protect family members and friends from the stress of cross-examination, or may fear that a witness will lack credibility. See Stier, "Revisiting the Missing Witness Inference: Quieting the Loud Voice from the Empty Chair," 44 *Md. L. Rev.* 137, 144–45 (1985).

[58] In *Griffin v. California*, the United States Supreme Court ruled that neither judges nor prosecuting attorneys may comment on a defendant's failure to take the witness stand. 380 U.S. 609, 615 (1965). Indeed, judges may instruct jurors not to draw adverse inferences from a defendant's silence. *Lakeside v. Oregon*, 435 U.S. 333, 340–41 (1978). Questions are thus raised about whether the fifth amendment is compromised by comments concerning absent witnesses other than the defendant. See McDonald, "Drawing an Inference from the Failure to Produce a Knowledgeable Witness: Evidentiary and Constitutional Consideration," 61 *Calif. L. Rev.* 1422, 1423–26 (1973); see also Tanford, "An Introduction to Trial Law," 51 *Mo. L. Rev.* 623, 680–81 (1986).

[59] S. Kassin & L. Wrightsman, supra note 5, at 113.

[60] Shaffer & Case, "On the Decision Not to Testify in One's Own Behalf: Effects of Withheld Evidence, Defendant's Sexual Preferences, and Juror Dogmatism on Juridic Decisions," 42 *J. Personality & Soc. Psychology* 335, 344 (1982).

[61] Fazio, Sherman & Herr, "The Feature-Positive Effect in the Self-Perception Process: Does Not Doing Matter as Much as Doing?," 42 *J. Personality & Soc. Psychology* 404, 409–10 (1982); Newman, Wolff & Hearst, "The Feature-Positive Effect in Adult Human Subjects," 6 *J. Experimental Psychology: Hum. Learning & Memory* 630, 647–48 (1980).

[62] Webster, King & Kassin, "Voices from an Empty Chair: The Missing Witness Inference and the Jury," *Law and Human Behavior* (in press).

[63] Id. To establish juror expectations for a missing witness, defense counsel's opening statement included mention of the fact that the defendant had talked about his emotional difficulties to a close friend and to a co-worker. In the missing-central version of the case, the close friend did not testify. In the missing-peripheral version, the co-worker did not testify. All versions of the transcript thus contained the same information, varying only in the present and absent sources of that information.

[64] In the *no-comment* condition, neither the prosecutor nor the judge made reference to the missing witness. In the *comment* condition, the prosecutor argued in closing, "I put it to you, ladies and gentlemen—where is Mr. Steven Marshall (John Mills)? Is it possible that Mr. Marshall (Mills) would not have corroborated the misinformed opinion of the psychiatrists? I think it is. Members of the jury, if your best friend (co-worker) were in this kind of trouble, wouldn't you want to be here to help him? I think, in weighing the evidence, you will come to the conclusion that I have." Id.

Also in the comment condition, the judge's charge to the jury included the following instruction, approved for use in federal courts: "If, according to appropriate procedures, the court is shown that a witness is available to one of the parties alone, and the anticipated testimony of the witness would elucidate some material issue, and the party who fails to produce the witness offers no explanation, then the factfinder may be permitted, but is not required, to infer that the testimony would have been unfavorable to the party who failed to call the witness." See I. Devitt & C. Blackmar, *Fed. Jury Prac. and Instructions*, § 17.19 (3d ed. 1977); see also Fed. Judicial Ctr. Comm. to Study Crim. Jury Instructions, *Pattern Crim. Jury Instructions* 49 (1982) (for alternative language).

[65] American Bar Association Project on Minimum Standards for Criminal Justice (1968), Standards Relating to Trial by Jury, Section 5.4. Open-mindedness is such an important aspect of deliberation that if a juror dies before a verdict is announced, the jury cannot

return a verdict even if all the remaining jurors swear that the deceased had agreed with their decision. The reasoning behind this rule is that "[t]he jurors individually and collectively have the right to change their minds prior to the reception of the verdict. . . ." E. DeVitt & C. Blackmar, *Fed. Jury Pract. and Instructions*, § 5.23 (3d ed. 1977).

66 *Allen v. United States*, 164 U.S. 492, 501-2 (1896).

67 Id. at 501.

68 Asch, "Studies of Independence and Conformity: A Minority of One Against a Unanimous Majority," 70 *Psychological Monographs*, Whole No. 416 (1956); Deutsch & Gerard, "A Study of Normative and Informational Social Influence Upon Individual Judgment," 51 *J. Abnormal & Soc. Psychology* 629 (1955).

69 See, eg., Schacter, "Deviation, Rejection, and Communication," 46 *J. Abnormal & Soc. Psychology* 190 (1951); for a review see Levine, "Reaction to Opinion Deviance in Small Groups," *Psychology of Group Influence* (P. Paulus ed. 1980).

70 See, e.g., Campbell & Fairey, "Informational and Normative Routes to Conformity: The Effect of Faction Size as a Function of Norm Extremity and Attention to the Stimulus," 57 *J. Personality & Soc. Psychology* 457, 458 (1989).

71 See, e.g., Kaplan & Miller, "Group Discussion and Judgment," *Basic Group Processes* 65 (P. Paulus ed. 1983); Kaplan & Miller, "Group Decision-Making and Normative Versus Information Influence: Effects of Type of Issue and Assigned Decision Rule," 53 *J. Personality & Soc. Psychology* 306 (1987); Stasser, Kerr & Bray, "The Social Psychology of Jury Deliberations," *Psychology of the Courtroom* 221 (Kerr & Bray eds. 1982).

72 H. Kalven & H. Zeisel, *The American Jury* 489 (1966).

73 There are important reasons to protect individual jurors from normative influences that elicit mere public compliance. First, justice is undermined when a jury renders a verdict not supported even by its membership (e.g., criminal defendants should not be convicted by juries internally plagued by a reasonable doubt). Second, unanimous votes produced by normative influences may undermine perceptions of justice among those who serve on juries.

74 Kaplan & Miller, supra note 71, at 311.

75 Hawkins, "Interaction Rates of Jurors Aligned in Factions," 27 *Am. Soc. Rev.* 689 (1962) (public vote in jury deliberation).

76 *Commonwealth v. Tuey*, 62 Mass. 1 (1851).

77 164 U.S. 492 (1896).

78 It has also been called the "shotgun" instruction, the "third degree" instruction, the "nitroglycerin" charge, the "hammer" instruction, and the "hanging" instruction. See Marcus, "The *Allen* Instruction in Criminal Cases: Is the Dynamite Charge About to be Permanently Defused?" 43 *Mo. L. Rev.* 613, 615 (1978).

79 *Allen*, 164 U.S. at 501. The full text of the charge reads as follows:

That in a large proportion of cases absolute certainty could not be expected; that although the verdict must be the verdict of each individual juror, and not a mere acquiescence in the conclusion of his fellows, yet they should examine the question submitted with candor and with a proper regard and deference to the opinions of each other; that it was their duty to decide the case if they could conscientiously do so; that they should listen, with a disposition to be convinced, to each other's arguments; that, if much the larger number were for conviction, a dissenting juror should consider whether his doubt was a reasonable one which made no impression upon the minds of so many men, equally honest, equally intelligent with himself. If, upon the other hand, the majority was for acquittal, the minority ought to ask themselves whether they might not reasonably doubt the correctness of a judgment which was not concurred in by the majority.

Id.

[80] *People v. Randall,* 9 N.Y.2d. 413, 214 N.Y.S.2d 417, 174 N.E.2d 507 (1961) (quoting *People v. Faber,* 199 N.Y. 256, 260–61.

[81] Id. at 850, 139 Cal. Rptr. at 869, 566 P.2d at 1005 (quoting *United States v. Bailey,* 468 F.2d 652, 662 (5th Cir. 1972)).

[82] *People v. Gainer,* 19 Cal.3d 835, 850, 139 Cal. Rptr. 861, 869, 566 P.2d 997, 1005 (1977).

[83] American Bar Association Project on Minimum Standards for Criminal Justice, Standards Relating to Trial by Jury, Standards 5.4 (1968).

[84] See Jensen, "After *Lowenfield:* The *Allen* Charge in the Ninth Circuit," 19 *Golden Gate U.L. Rev.* 75, 85 (1989); Marcus, supra note 78, at 617; Notes and Comments, "On Instructing Deadlocked Juries," 78 *Yale L.J.* 100, 103–6 (1968).

[85] *Lowenfield v. Phelps,* 484 U.S. 231 (1988).

[86] Kassin, Smith & Tulloch, "The Dynamite Charge: Effects on the Perceptions and Deliberation Behavior of Mock Jurors," 14 *Law and Human Behavior* 537 (1990).

[87] Each set consisted of six notes written in the same handwriting.

[88] As one might expect, several members of the minority capitulated; in these instances, the session was terminated and questionnaires administered.

[89] This no-instruction control procedure was designed to resemble what often happens when jurors are deadlocked and the judge directs them to return for further discussion.

[90] It is interesting that even though all subjects received the same deliberation notes, those in the minority-dynamite group imagined they were under greater pressure from the other jurors.

[91] Further research is clearly needed. One approach would be to conduct field experiments on real cases in which deadlocked juries are randomly assigned to receive either the *Allen* charge or a control instruction. Because random assignment of real juries is not feasible, however, a more realistic approach is to conduct a large-scale laboratory study involving interacting mock jurors.

[92] The American Bar Association, for example, offered an alternative charge, one which emphasizes jurors' duty to consult with one another without singling out those in the minority. The instruction reads:

> It is your duty, as jurors, to consult with one another and to deliberate with a view to reaching an agreement, if you can do so without violence to individual judgment. Each of you must decide the case for yourself, but do so only after an impartial consideration of the evidence with your fellow jurors. In the course of your deliberations, do not hesitate to reexamine your views and change your opinion if convinced it is erroneous. But do not surrender your honest conviction as to the weight or effect of evidence solely because of the opinion of your fellow jurors, or for the mere purpose of returning a verdict.

See American Bar Association Project on Minimum Standards for Criminal Justice, Standards Relating to Trial by Jury, Standard 5.4 (1968).

[93] *Apodaca v. Oregon,* 406 U.S. 404 (1972) (the Court upheld convictions by votes of 11 to 1 and 10 to 2); *Johnson v. Louisiana,* 406 U.S 356 (1972). Current practices are varied. The federal courts still require unanimous verdicts, but a handful of states permit non-unanimous verdicts in criminal trials, and over 30 states allow these verdicts in civil actions.

[94] We have no grounds for believing that majority jurors, aware of their responsibility and power over the liberty of the defendant, would simply refuse to listen to arguments presented to them in favor of acquittal, terminate discussion, and render a verdict. On the contrary it is far more likely that a juror presenting reasoned argument in favor of acquittal would either have his arguments answered or would carry enough other jurors with him to prevent conviction.

Johnson, 406 U.S. at 361.

95 [N]onunanimous juries need not debate and deliberate as fully as must unanimous juries. As soon as the requisite majority is attained, further consideration is not required either by Oregon or by Louisiana even though the dissident jurors, might, if given the chance, be able to convince the majority. . . . It is said that there is no evidence that majority jurors will refuse to listen to dissenters whose votes are unneeded for conviction. Yet human experience teaches that polite and academic conversation is no substitute for the earnest and robust argument necessary to reach unanimity.
Id. at 388–89.

96 Nemeth, "Interactions Between Jurors as a Function of Majority vs. Unanimity Decision Rules," 7 *J. Applied Soc. Psychology* 38, 42–43 (1977).

97 R. Hastie, S. Penrod & N. Pennington, *Inside the Jury* 45 (1983).

98 Id. at 112.

99 *Walker v. United States*, 342 F.2d 22, 28 (5th Cir. 1965).

100 H. Kalven & H. Zeisel, supra note 72, at 453.

101 H. Kalven & He. Zeisel, supra note 72, at 3.

11

The Impact of Sequestration on Juries

JAMES P. LEVINE

Wander into the Holiday Inn on New York City's Staten Island most any evening and you will encounter a rather puzzling sight. At either end of one or more corridors armed law enforcement officials will be on guard, poised to jump into action should one of the doors on the floor open. The visitor observing this scene might well proceed with trepidation, imagining that the room of a criminal suspect or fugitive is under surveillance. In fact, what is taking place is the routine monitoring of a sequestered jury.

Jury sequestration refers to the physical isolation of the jury from the rest of society. It is the opposite of what is technically called "separation of the jury," the condition that exists when jurors are permitted to go their separate ways when court is not in session. Sequestration can take place at two points in the judicial process, during the trial itself (a rare phenomenon) or during deliberations. Its primary purpose is to shield jurors from biasing outside influences that might vitiate the integrity of the trial and deprive defendants of their right to verdicts based on law and evidence. It is thus seen as an instrument to further due process of law.

When sequestration is ordered, jurors are kept together as a group and forbidden to have significant contact with anyone but each other. Access to the media is denied or strictly limited: exposure to trial coverage is prevented; newspapers are banned or censored; television viewing is off limits or highly restricted. Jurors are cut off from family, friends, and

Reprinted with permission from *Judicature*, Vol. 79, No. 5, March–April 1996, pp. 266–272.

neighbors; they become a world unto themselves. They are confined to the courtroom or the juryroom during working hours, and they are required to eat and sleep in special quarters. Court officers keep track of their every activity, sometimes even following them into bathrooms. Sex is normally off-limits, physical activity is severely constrained, and solitude is all but impossible.

Jurors can be held in contempt of court and are subject to fines and imprisonment if they depart from court-imposed restrictions. Says University of Texas law school professor Michael Tigar, an opponent of sequestration: "There are prison systems that provide more privileges than some sequestered jurors receive."[1] It is no exaggeration to call sequestered juries prisoners of the court.

Much attention has recently been focused on sequestrations during the trial itself. There have been celebrated cases featuring long periods of isolation, such as the eight-and-one-half month Charles Manson case in the 1970s, the second Rodney King case, which lasted 57 days, and the O.J. Simpson case, which went on for 266 days—setting the record for sequestration. While such lengthy confinements are rare, it is more common for juries to be sequestered for several nights during deliberations. Until New York State changed its law in June 1995, *all* criminal juries in that state had to be sequestered while they were deliberating and even now sequestration is mandatory in cases of serious felonies. In other cases New York now follows the more flexible policy of the federal court system and the other 49 states where judges have the discretion to keep the jury apart from the community during the entire trial or during deliberations.

This article assesses some of the impacts of sequestration on jury decision making, a topic that has received little scholarly analysis. This may to some extent be due to the infrequency of sequestration outside New York, but it also reflects the paucity of solid information about how sequestration works in practice. Mock jury research, which has been so helpful in learning about a wide range of influences on jurors, has not been used, in part because of the impracticality of isolating and confining subjects as part of an experiment.

In assessing sequestration we are by default forced to rely on theoretical speculation about human behavior, a smattering of tangentially related empirical data, and insights garnered from reportage. Because this is no substitute for systematic evaluation done in a methodologically rigorous fashion, the following analysis suffers from over-reliance on anecdotes and an insufficient grounding in rigorous studies. It is in truth a collection of hypotheses and a consideration of their plausibility rather than a definitive demonstration of how sequestration works in practice. But it does subject a controversial judicial practice to the spotlight of systematic analysis and raises issues that have received insufficient scrutiny: Does sequestration make jury decision makers fairer and more rational, or does it put undue pressures on jurors that undermine their capacity for objectivity? Does it prompt the jury to concentrate on the evidence by fending off improper external influences, or does it trigger counterproductive psychological and social dynamics that debase the decision-making process? Is it a protection for defendants, as originally anticipated, or does it ironically function to promote convictions? Are the benefits worth the costs? Does sequestration further the ideals of justice?

Shielding the Jury

The historic rationale for sequestering juries was to insulate them from the insidious invasions of the press and the pressures of the community. Preventing communications from sources other than fellow jurors was supposed to focus attention on the evidence introduced at the trial and the instructions of judges, the only material that was to be the basis of verdicts.

The media in particular are thought to be a contaminating source of prejudice. News coverage is ubiquitous and even an innocuous radio program of music and weather can burst forth with commentary about a trial in progress. Newspaper headlines dramatize the latest information or rumors about cases, and the most obedient jurors trying to follow judges' orders that they not follow the case might lay their eyes on such potentially biasing words in print.

There is much controversy about the effectiveness of sequestering juries in warding off publicity. In certain notorious cases the press is saturated with prejudicial pre-trial commentary, in which case sequestration during either the trial or deliberations may be too late to do any good. Any number of mock jury experiments have shown that pre-trial publicity increases convictions, the judges' admonitions to disregard such publicity notwithstanding.[2] A thorough review of this research prompted jury expert Norbert Kerr to conclude that "intense pretrial publicity can adversely affect . . . jury verdicts" and to doubt the effectiveness of common remedies.[3]

Another intrusion from which jurors are spared by sequestration is community opinion. Frightful cases entailing violence often create public fervor for convictions that can result in a rush to judgement. Where the defendant is the subject of public scorn there can be pressures to convict. Less frequently, those on trial who engender sympathy can receive public support.

Since jurors' identities are part of the public record except in the rare instances when anonymous juries are used, any number of individuals who happen to cross paths with jurors are in a position to offer their views and influence the verdict. Going home when court is out of session can entail encounters with merchants, neighbors, family, and other acquaintances who may be all too eager to volunteer opinions.

When jurors are permitted to commingle with the community, judges warn them to avoid any exposure to discussion of the trial. But such instructions may well fall on deaf ears, as jurors thirst to find out more about the case than they heard in court. The most conscientious of jurors may inadvertently find themselves at the center of discussions about the case, whether at the local bar or in the family living room. Telling jurors to shut themselves off to normal communications and to tune out all trial-related discourse may well be in vain.

Even in the absence of propaganda or pressure, sequestration may shield jurors from distractions that interfere with their concentration on the case. Being limited to dreary hotel rooms and meaningless banter during group meals may sharpen their wits when it comes to jury room exchanges. While going home provides all kinds of creature comforts and may be an outlet for relieving pent-up stress, it can also confront jurors with the woes and worries that beset everyone—overdue bills, leaking roofs, truant children, marital problems, and the like. Carrying these problems back to the court may well subject jurors to fits of daydreaming and self-absorption when they are supposed to be attending to discussions about the case.

Some trial procedures intended to protect defendants' rights are difficult to carry out in practice, such as the rule of *Batson v. Kentucky* prohibiting the use of peremptory challenges to exclude people from juries because of their race.[4] But it is a relatively straightforward task to quarantine jurors physically. While stories are told of jurors smuggling newspapers, unblocking their telephones,[5] watching banned television programs,[6] and sneaking out of their hotel rooms,[7] such breaches of sequestration are hopefully uncommon. Sequestration thus seems quite effective in screening out potentially biasing publicity, and it may at times contribute to more objective fact-finding.

Fostering Juror Intimacy

Being thrown together in close quarters engenders closer relations among jurors. While even non-sequestered juries often develop close attachments as a result of socializing with one another for days on end, the cutting off of contact from the outside world occasioned by sequestration can intensify the bonding process. Jurors have referred to themselves as having become a family, warmly recounting after trials are over how close they had become even in the face of acute differences of opinion about the evidence.[8]

How might such camaraderie impact deliberations? First, becoming emotionally connected with each other might well incline jurors to listen to competing arguments. Communications tend to be more positive when one has a personal relationship with someone else than when people confront one another as anonymous functionaries. Relatively few juries are unanimous at the outset of deliberations;[9] some degree of persuasion is normally necessary to achieve the unanimity that most jurisdictions still require. Positive personal feelings may well be one ingredient impelling jurors to open themselves up to other perspectives.

A second consequence of juror bonding may be to enable people to overcome barriers to communication based on differences in background. Juryroom tensions based on race, ethnicity, or class that may accentuate prejudicial responses to defendants or victims may be defused when jurors get to know each other. Social psychology evidence demonstrates that gaining information about specific individuals who are part of a stereotyped group diminishes reliance on stereotypes.[10] Moreover, personal contact with members of a disliked group produces positive attitudes toward such individuals if not to the entire group.[11]

By its very nature sequestration generates potentially beneficial contact among people who have little in common and who might share mutual disdain for one another. Jurors cloistered together tend to talk to each other about the petty details and diversions of life. They also wind up commiserating with each other about the travails of their jury experience, lamenting everything from lawyer monotones to hard juror chairs to inadequate ventilation. What they find is greater rapport than they might have expected. Jurors from different worlds who by force of their sequestered circumstance wind up spending hours idly talking with one another may well hear each other more when the focus turns to the case at hand.

There can, of course, be a deleterious consequence of being brought together in close quarters against one's will. Cliques can emerge, sometimes based on background factors such as race or ethnicity, which can reduce inter-group contact; there are reports that the O. J. Simpson jury was so plagued.[12] Even in the absence of such clustering, one can develop animosities toward co-jurors that obstruct effective deliberations. Thus, one of the jurors in the Joel Steinberg murder case dealing with the death from child abuse of his six-year-old illegally adopted girl later chastised some of his co-jurors in no uncertain terms: "Hate is too strong a word, but I have no desire to run into them again."[13]

The intimacy foisted onto jurors by sequestration can thus be a two-edged sword, a means of bringing juries together as a concerted decision-making team or a source of aggravation that serves to promote greater discord. Social psychological theories are of limited use in determining which way the sword most commonly strikes, as an aid or a hindrance to rational deliberation.

Compounding Stress

Jury experience is inherently trying. Not only do jurors have their personal lives disrupted, but they are often required to deal with gruesome factual details, emotionally charged testimony, incomprehensible legal jargon, unpleasant disagreements with co-jurors, and agonizing decisions. Considerable research has now demonstrated the ubiquity of juror stress.[14]

The length and complexity of modern trials can take its toll. The aggravation they experience, normally held within, surfaced during a libel case in White Plains, New York, which had run four months and showed no signs of reaching a conclusion. A contingent of the despairing jury demanded a meeting with the judge where they exploded in anger. So distraught were the jurors that the judge declared a mistrial and dismissed the jury.[15]

Cases entailing violence are especially distressing for the jury. Jurors hearing the case of serial sex killer Jeffrey Dahmer, after listening to weeks of very graphic descriptions of dismemberment, mutilation, and sex with corpses, later revealed the toll the trial had taken on them. Said one juror: "I think that there are fourteen other victims in this case and that is the fourteen jurors. They have been through some traumatic times . . . I am beginning to think there is no such thing as normal after this."[16] While the Dahmer case was horrifying in the extreme, even less upsetting cases can afflict the psyches of jurors.

Sequestration surely compounds this stress. Not a single former juror who contacted New York State's Jury Project created in 1993 by Chief Judge Judith Kaye had good things to say about it.[17]

Studies have shown that persons forced to co-exist with strangers in conditions of isolation against their will sometimes become frustrated, angry, and aggressive.[18] What is true of those like disaster victims confined to close quarters with people they do not know is surely true of some sequestered jurors: they can become disoriented and distressed. Thus, one juror sequestered during the Reginald Denny beating case emerging from the Los Angeles riots that took place after the Rodney King verdict was reported to have suffered a breakdown. He was kept on the jury despite having been witnessed running up and down the corridor of the hotel where the jurors were staying, shouting: "I can't take it any more."[19]

Juror Retaliation

Jurors who resent the experience of sequestration and are disturbed by it may vent their wrath on one of the trial adversaries. The physical and psychological discomfort of having one's life disrupted may be attributed to the accused, who is blamed for having caused the entire unpleasant situation. To avenge the ordeal of sequestration, the juror comes down hard on the persons thought to have been responsible for triggering it—even if the defendants are in fact innocent. One study comparing sequestered and unsequestered New York juries showed that the former produced 16 percent more convictions than the latter, although there were insufficient controls for case differences in the research to provide confidence in the findings.[20] Jurors may also take out their anger on the prosecution. Since it is the state that initiates the entire trial process, it is the state who deserves to be punished.

Juror Capitulation

Jurors can cope with stress in another way that is adverse to the ideal of justice. Those unduly upset by their ordeal may capitulate to the will of the majority in hopes of speeding up a verdict. In the classic movie *Twelve Angry Men*, one of the jurors switches his vote from guilty to not guilty to hasten a verdict, because he did not want to waste the tickets he had to a night baseball game. While such flippancy is probably rare, any number of real jurors have confessed how desperately they wanted to get out.

The tension of juryroom conflict can itself erode a juror's fortitude. Many a juror has spoken of the anguish they experienced simply by being part of a minority holding out against dominant sentiment. A juror who believed John Hinckley guilty of attempting to murder President Ronald Reagan but who eventually submitted to fellow jurors who thought him not guilty by reason of insanity minced no words: "I changed because of the pressure. I had the shakes all day. I had to get out of there."[21]

Feelings of intimidation experienced by dissidents on the jury may well be intensified by the pangs of sequestration. It is bad enough to be isolated in a minority position within the jury; it is worse to have no escape. As another member of the Steinberg jury put it: "Until you've been sequestered, you can't imagine how horrible it is. It makes you feel powerless and helpless."[22]

The irritation if not downright hostility of those in the majority against dissenters can become a nagging undercurrent during the hours spent away from the jury room. Even idle chitchat and exchange of pleasantries can become unnerving when the atmosphere is fraught with tension. The agony of being "odd person out," the stubborn one or two or three jurors holding up a verdict, may be heightened by the omnipresence of one's adversaries. When your antagonists are constantly "in your face," it may be hard for beleaguered jurors to resist the temptation to yield to their point of view. We know from previous field and experimental research that majorities within juries tend to prevail,[23] and sequestration may reinforce such majoritarian pressure. Thus, one reason why two jurors who initially voted to convict O.J. Simpson reversed themselves after less than four hours of discussion might have been the desire to end their "captivity" and resume their normal lives. Unanimous verdicts so achieved, rather than representing the triumph of the majority's persuasiveness, may be the flawed results of a terribly stressful decision-making context.

Short of making complete about faces, jurors who are fed up may agree to compromise verdicts.[24] Jury deliberations in the "Chicago Seven" cases arising out of the clash between antiwar protesters and police during the 1968 Democratic National Convention ended in just such fashion. After five days of anguish, the sequestered jury acquitted all of the defendants of conspiracy; they convicted five of inciting a riot; and they absolved two completely. The juror who engineered the deal later said that the negotiated verdict was reached "although a majority of jurors felt all the defendants guilty on both counts—and three jurors felt all of them were innocent."[25] This groping for middle ground has also been observed in mock jury research.[26]

Juror Obstinacy

An opposite effect of experiencing the isolation of sequestration, equally pernicious, is juror stubbornness. The constant presence of one's adversaries may be perceived by some jurors as a challenge to their willpower, and holding out becomes an act of face-saving defiance as much as an assertion of confidence in one's point of view. The intimidating effects of sequestration can thus engender closed-mindedness, creating a siege mentality that stymies productive deliberations.

On the other hand, judges tell of unsequestered juries who quickly resolve their apparent deadlocks after getting "a good night's sleep."[27] The support system provided by those at home can provide an outlet for stress and a reinforcement of ego that permits jurors to open their minds to the arguments of peers. Replacing intensely charged juror interactions with intervals of normal routines and relationships can take the edge off of the taxing psychodynamics of the jury room. Avoiding sequestration can thus prevent needlessly hung juries.

Influence of Court Officers

It has been suggested that sequestration can improperly favor the prosecution due to the continuous interaction between jurors and court officers, who are generally perceived to be affiliated with the law enforcement system. Bailiffs, marshals, court-employed bus drivers and the like are sometimes the sequestered jurors' sole contact with the outside world. Those guarding the jurors are often sworn peace officers who carry guns, hardly to be distinguished from police. The association that develops between such personnel and the jury can foster a connection that compromises the neutrality of the jurors.

This can happen in two ways. First, court personnel may pass along their own predispositions, which are more likely than not oriented toward conviction. It was in recognition of this biasing effect that the Supreme Court of Nebraska overturned a murder conviction rendered by sequestered jurors who had played black jack with the local sheriff who dropped in on them in the course of supervising the sequestration.[28]

A second even more subtle biasing impact can paradoxically occur when court officers are acting most professionally. The American Bar Association's Committee on Jury Standards stipulates that procedures should be put into place so that "the inconvenience and discomfort of the sequestered jurors is minimized."[29] Jurors who are treated well in furtherance of this policy may develop a certain fondness towards their keepers—a peculiar manifestation of the "Stockholm syndrome," the surprising tendency of some kidnapping victims to become attached to their abductors. Jurors who feel positive toward court officers may generalize such good will to other law enforcement officials.

Dissuading Service

Fear of sequestration is one reason some people try to avoid jury service. Worries about being pent up with strangers in an unfamiliar environment for an unspecified period of time may be one factor accounting for the fact that only about two out of every five people called for jury service actually come to court.[30] Those receiving notices in the mail often simply disregard them, knowing full well that there will probably be no follow-up and certainly no drastic consequences.

Those who do show up will commonly allege all kinds of problems that would ensue from being sequestered to justify getting excused—medical conditions, young children in need of supervision, elderly parents in need of assistance, and the like. For example, 95 percent of the pool of 4,482 people contacted as possible jurors in the second trial of the police officers who beat Rodney King said sequestration would create prohibitive hardships.[31]

Among those precluded from serving by the risk of sequestration are the physically disabled who require special assistance and members of religious groups whose beliefs would be compromised if they could not go home on weekends. Court personnel have reported that many women have asked to be excused from serving on juries due to nighttime child care duties.[32] This obstacle to jury service may actually put the practice of sequestration in legal jeopardy in that the right of women to fair representation on juries is now constitutionally protected.[33]

What part sequestration plays in decisions to avoid jury duty is anyone's guess. It may well be a minor element, but to the extent that people are creatures of routine, the threat of abrupt and unpredictable changes in one's daily regimen posed by sequestration may be decisive. It is one thing to come to court every day, engaging in what may actually be a welcome diversion from the tedium of work or school or retired life; it is another thing to put oneself at the mercy of the court after hours.

Sequestration, then, can have pernicious impacts *prior to* its imposition. Court administrators, in attempts to make jury duty less onerous, have been coming up with various strategies to encourage more cooperativeness from citizens—from one day/one trial to cleaner bathrooms in the courthouse. But perhaps one of the least palatable aspects of jury service is being removed from one's home and family as a ward of the court. This facet of jury service, while a relatively rare occurrence, may well be scary enough to deter some from serving at all and an impediment to attempts to further democratize the jury system.

Costs of Sequestration

Sequestration is expensive. New York's former policy of requiring it in all criminal cases cost about $4 million annually. Each of the 1,400 juries sequestered in the year ending April 30, 1994 cost the state an average of $2,816 per night: $709 for lodging; $208 for meals; and $1,899 for court officers' overtime.[34] Sequestering the O.J. Simpson jury cost about $1 million.

Although these expenditures are a tiny fraction of the total criminal justice budget, opportunity costs are at stake: the money could be spent otherwise. Thus, abolishing mandatory sequestration in New York freed up funds which will help defray the cost of recent legislation raising jurors' compensation from the paltry $15 a day paid through the end of 1996 to $27.50 in 1997 and $40 in 1998. Since low juror pay is a significant deterrent to jury service, such re-allocation broadens the pool of jurors and presumably creates more representative panels.

Learning More

Jury research is now a veritable cottage industry. Social scientists study the effects of virtually every imaginable factor on juries: race, gender, and class of defendants; social demography of the jurors themselves; type of crime; different kinds of evidence and testimony; public attitudes toward crime and criminals; size of jury; unanimous versus non-unanimous decision rules; and so forth.[35] Practitioners serving as consultants have used a potpourri of investigative methods to study jury selection and claim to know a great deal about the relationships between jurors' backgrounds and their decision-making proclivities.[36] Yet an issue of considerable moment for both the integrity of the judicial process and the welfare of jurors has escaped systematic scrutiny; we remain relatively uninformed about the effects of sequestration.

State legislatures have over the years grappled with the issue of sequestration as they fashion and refashion their rules of criminal procedure. Trial judges must determine which cases warrant the drastic step of sequestration, and appellate courts often have to decide whether verdicts rendered in the absence of sequestration violated constitutional rights.[37] Yet these policy makers and legal authorities must act in an empirical vacuum, resting decisions on vague cogitations about the impact of trial publicity and the nature of the deliberative process. This situation needs correcting: we need to learn more about how the jury actually functions when it is quarantined from the community.

A number of research strategies could prove fruitful. It might be possible to sequester mock juries experimentally if subjects were permitted to terminate their participation on demand. A more feasible approach would be to interview ex-jurors about their experiences under sequestration, just as the Capital Jury Project has quite poignantly captured the sentiments of former jurors in capital cases who were eager to talk about the life-or-death decisions they made.[38]

In the aftermath of New York's abolition of mandatory sequestration in many cases, there is a golden opportunity to do a "before-and-after" study: the viewpoints and the verdicts of jurors sequestered before the law took effect can be compared with the behavior of subsequent juries allowed to go home during deliberations. A number of useful questions could be posed and answered: Do conviction rates go up? Are there more hung juries? Do juries reach verdicts more quickly? Do more prospective jurors show up in court? Are jurors more satisfied with their experiences?

The Pursuit of Justice

The negative impacts of sequestration normally appear to outweigh its virtues. Its potential for unnerving and even infuriating jurors is apparent, offsetting whatever advantages it may have in shielding jurors from prejudicial publicity and the distractions of personal life. Its effect on the quality of deliberations is also problematic: while it may bond some juries it may fracture others. It may foster a too-cozy relationship between jurors and court officers; and it is surely a deterrent to jury service.

On balance, sequestration seems to undermine the pursuit of justice. Both the personal well-being of jurors and the public interest in quality decision making seem best served by keeping the jury free unless there is substantial reason to do otherwise. Sequestration should be used quite selectively, reserved for cases that promise to receive frenzied, inescapable media saturation.

This condemnation of sequestration is expressed with some uneasiness. Cost-benefit analysis is always a problematic and subjective endeavor, belying precision. Assessing whether sequestration comes at too high a price in both money and human costs involves the making of personal value judgments. Is sequestration worth it if it spares a single innocent defendant from a wrongful verdict? Would curtailing press coverage as the British do be a less harmful means of providing a fair trial? How much stress and strain on jurors is *too* much stress and strain? Social science cannot answer these questions, but it can provide better measurement of the costs and benefits of sequestration.

Endnotes

1 Quoted in Hansen, Sequestration Little Used, Little Liked, 81 *ABA* J. 16, 17 (October 1995).

2 Kramer, Kerr, and Carroll, Pretrial Publicity, Judicial Remedies, and Jury Bias, 14 *Law and Hum. Behav.* 409 (1990); Otto, Penrod, and Dexter, The Biasing Impact of Pretrial Publicity on Juror Judgments, 18 *Law and Hum. Behav.* 453 (1994).

3 Kerr, The Effect of Pretrial Publicity on Jurors, 78 *Judicature* 120 (1994).

4 476 U.S. 79 (1986).

5 A sequestered New York juror deciding the case of a teen-ager on trial for the murder of his parents made an illicit phone call during which he was told about a news conference held by detectives who said that even the defendant's sister thought him guilty—information that was conveyed to other jurors. Glaberson, Compulsory Jury Seclusion: New York Benefit or Waste? *N.Y. Times*, July 5, 1991, at A1.

6 A case has been reported of a jury that rigged a coat hanger into a television antenna to watch forbidden programs. Letter from G. Thomas Munsterman of the National Center for State Courts (Arlington, Virginia), March 14, 1995.

[7] In one New York case, court officers captured a juror who was observed at night using bed sheets to escape from his second story hotel window. *People v. Convers*, 189 A.D. 2d. 607 (1993).

[8] Yarrow, Jury Renders Mixed Verdict in Attica Case. *N.Y. Times*, February 5, 1992 at B4.

[9] Kalven and Zeisel, *The American Jury* 488 (1966).

[10] Locksley. Hepburn, and Ortiz. Social Stereotypes and Judgments of Individuals: An Instance of the Base-Rate Fallacy. 18 *J. Res. and Dev. in Educ.* 23 (1982).

[11] Cook. Interpersonal and Attitudinal Outcomes in Cooperating Interracial Groups. 12 *J. Res. and Dev. in Educ.* 97 (1978).

[12] Margolick, Excused Juror Tells Judge That Racial Hatred Permeates and Divides Simpson Panel, *N.Y. Times*, April 14. 1995, at A13.

[13] Polsky, Trials and Tribulations, *N.Y. Newsday*. February 1. 1995, at B4.

[14] Hafemeister and Ventis. Juror Stress: What Burden Have We Placed on Our Juries? 1992 *St. Ct. J.* 35 (1992); Hafemeister. Legal Report: Juror Stress, 8 *Violence and Victims* 177 (1993); Hafemeister and Ventis. Juror Stress: Sources and Implications, 1994 *Trial* 68 (1994).

[15] Hernandez, Westchester Trial Illustrates the Burdens of Jury Services, *N.Y. Times*, December 19, 1994, at A1.

[16] Quoted in Hafemeister and Ventis. Juror Stress: What Burden . . . ., supra n. 14, at 35, 37–38.

[17] New York State Office of Court Administration, *The Jury Project: Report to the Chief Judge of the State of New York* 114 (1994).

[18] Schulman and Winick. Some Aspects of Sequestration in Jury Trials: Does It Aid the Defense or the Prosecution? 18 *IJA Rep.* 1 (1985).

[19] Hamilton. Denny Beating Trial Judge Releases Juror Transcripts: Record Reveals Behavior before Removing 2, Retaining 1, *Washington Post*, October 15, 1993, at A2.

[20] Winick and Smith. Past-Trial Sequestered Juries Tilt Toward Guilty Verdicts. *N.Y. Law Journal*. December 12. 1986. at 1.

[21] Jurors Assert That Pressure Forced Them to Alter Votes, *N.Y. Times*, June 23, 1982, at B6.

[22] Polsky. supra n. 13. at B5.

[23] Kalven and Zeisel. supra n. 9. at 488; Stasser. Opinion Change During Group Discussion. 3 *Personalty and Soc. Psychology Bull.* 252 (1977); Tanford and Penrod, Jury Deliberations: Discussion Content and Influence Processes in Jury Decision Making, 16 *Applied Soc. Psychology* 16 (1986).

[24] Levine. Jury Room Politics, 16 *Trial L. Q.* 21 (1984).

[25] Richards, Juror for Chicago 7 Convinced Panel Reached Proper Verdict. *The Oregonian*. March 1. 1970, at 1.

[26] Hastie, Penrod, and Pennington, *Inside the Jury* 60 (1992): Greene, On Juries and Damage Awards: The Process of Decisionmaking. 52 *Law and Contemp. Prob.* 241 (1989).

[27] Letter from G. Thomas Munsterman. March 14, 1995.

[28] *Simants v. State*, 202 Neb. 828, 277 N.W. 2d. 217 (1979).

[29] American Bar Association. Judicial Administration Division, Committee on Jury Standards, *Standards Relating to Juror Use and Management* 173 (1993).

[30] Levine. *Juries and Politics* 44 (1992).

[31] Jury Pool Small for Beating Trial. *N.Y. Times*, January 5, 1993, at A8.

[32] New York State Office of Court Administration, supra n. 17, at 115.

[33] *J.E.B. v. Alabama* ex rel. T.B.. 114 S.Ct. 1419 (1994).

[34] New York State Office of Court Administration, supra n. 17, at 133.

[35] For a compilation of much of this research, see Kassin and Wrightsman. *The American Jury on Trial: Psychological Perspectives* (1988) and Frederick. *The Psychology of the American Jury* (1987).

36 Fukurai, Butler, and Booth, *Race and the Jury: Racial Disenfranchisement and the Search for Justice* (1993); Abramson, *We, the Jury: the Jury System and the Ideal of Democracy* 143–176 (1994).

37 *United States v. Carter*, 602 F.2d 799 (1979); *West Virginia v. Young*, 173 W. Va. 1, 311 S.E.2d 118 (1983); *Livingston v. Florida*, 438 So. 2d 235 (1984); *Minnesota v. Sanders* 376 N.W.2d 196 (1985).

38 Bowers and Vandiver, *The Capital Jury Project* (1991).

12

Merciful Juries
The Resilience of Jury Nullification

ALAN W. SCHEFLIN and JON M. VAN DYKE

The power of a jury to soften the harsh commands of the law and return a verdict that corresponds to the community's sense of moral justice has long been recognized.[1] Widely disputed, however, is whether jurors should be told they have this authority. Proponents have seen a right to a jury nullification instruction as an inalienable part of the heritage of democracy,[2] whereas opponents have argued that it is tantamount to anarchy.[3] Although in the past judges did instruct jurors about their role,[4] and judges in Maryland and Indiana still do,[5] most courts now refuse to explain honestly to jurors that they have the ultimate power to decide whether it is appropriate to apply the law to the facts presented to them.[6]

This judicial lack of candor has been periodically challenged; during the past few years a persistent grass roots movement has developed to promote the notion that our juries should be fully informed of their powers. Information about jury nullification has been spreading to an increasingly larger group of citizens and potential jurors. This movement serves to illustrate the resilience of the "jury nullification" concept and its link to fundamental notions of democracy.

This article discusses this new populist movement, analyzes some recent court decisions, reports some of the significant developments related to jury nullification during the past decade, and concludes that

Reprinted by permission of the *Washington and Lee Law Review* and the authors from vol. 48, no. 1 (winter, 1991), pp. 165–183.

our judicial system would be better served if judges instructed jurors of their true powers.[7]

What's in a Name?

Persuaders have long been aware of the significance of what something is called. For example, when President Ronald Reagan wanted financial and other support for the "Contras" who were fighting the Sandanista government in Nicaragua, he found it advisable to rename them "freedom fighters," which had a patriotic and positive tone, rather than "Contras," a term with negative connotations. Similarly, people who believe abortion is immoral have stopped calling themselves "anti-abortionists," opting instead for the more positive "pro-lifers."

Jury nullification debate similarly has been hampered by semantics. The term "jury nullification" is widely used by commentators and will also be used here by the authors, but it is not a term that accurately describes what is being advocated. The jury power at issue here is not a power to "nullify" statutes or precedents in order to create or substitute a new version of the law.[8] Instead, it is a power to "complete" or "perfect" the law by permitting the jury to exercise that one last touch of mercy where it may not be appropriate and just to apply the literal law to the actual facts.

According to Professor George Fletcher, the term "jury nullification"

> is unfortunate and misleading, because it suggests that when the jury votes its conscience, it is always engaged in an act of disrespect toward the law. The acquittal, supposedly, nullifies the law. In place of the law, it is said, the jury interposes its own moral judgment or political preferences.[9]

Fletcher rejects the view that jury nullification is an affront to the rule of law, and he provides a healthier and more accurate image:

> [T]he function of the jury as the ultimate authority on the law [is] not to "nullify" the instructions of the judge, but to complete the law, when necessary, by recognizing principles of justification that go beyond the written law. It would be better if we abandoned the phrase "jury nullification" and spoke instead of the jury's function in these cases of completing and perfecting the positive law recognized by the courts and the legislature.[10]

If "jury nullification" originally had been call "jury mercy," some of the emotional opposition might not have developed. Fletcher is correct to observe that this opposition has been based on a sense that when juries "nullify" they are acting *extra*-legally, outside the bounds of law. Under this view, the act of "nullification" appears to stand in opposition to the law.

Fletcher's perspective is more cordial. Jury nullification is not *extra-legal*; quite the opposite. Nullification is an integral part of the law itself, serving the unique and vital function of smoothing the friction between law and justice, and between the people and their laws. Nullification then becomes a tolerable, and occasionally beneficial, side-effect of the power to return general verdicts of acquittal not subject to judicial review. Take, for illustrative purposes, the case of Leroy Reed.

"Inside the Jury Room": *Wisconsin v. Leroy Reed* [11]

Leroy Reed, a sincere but dull-witted convict on parole, was arrested by his parole officer for illegal possession of a weapon. Reed enjoyed the television detective program "The Equalizer" and thought he might like to become a private investigator himself. Off went letters to mail-order detective companies for brochures, books, and courses. Some of the information he received stated he would need a gun. Reed obediently bought one, not fully realizing that he was violating a condition of his parole. No one in the courtroom doubted that Reed was only vaguely aware of what was going on and that he had not caused harm, was not likely to cause harm, and certainly did not have any intent to cause harm or violate rules. Punishing him would be like rebuking a five-year-old for not knowing algebra. Under the technical wording of the law, however, Reed was guilty. His defense lawyer pleaded for a jury nullification instruction, but the trial judge called it "an invitation to anarchy."

Once in the jury room, it was clear that the jurors were unanimous about two things: that Reed was guilty under the law, but morally was innocent. The just thing to do would be to acquit him. But the jurors had been told they had to follow the letter of the law. What should they do? During the spirited two-hour debate, some jurors argued that their oath required them to convict even though it meant doing an injustice. Others argued that they must follow what their consciences told them was the right thing to do in this case.

Both sides, however, seemed upset that the law had left them in this predicament. In the end, the conscience arguments converted the last remaining holdout. When he reluctantly retreated from his belief that the jury had no moral leeway, a verdict was reached.

Leroy Reed was acquitted. Some jurors went home having less respect for the legal system than when they had first reported for jury duty. Imagine how much worse they would have felt upon learning that an honest jury nullification instruction could have solved their dilemma and made them proud and respectful of the legal process. Other jurors, however, when finally told about jury nullification, did not condemn the failure to receive the instruction.[12]

The doctrine of jury nullification strikes a resonant chord in the community. Professors Hans and Vidmar report on the results of a 1979 Canadian survey "where people were asked whether jurors should be instructed that they are entitled to follow their own conscience instead of strictly applying the law if it will produce a just result."[13] The survey showed that

> over three-quarters of the respondents said yes. Furthermore, people who had actually served on a jury were even more supportive; 93% of them endorsed the idea of giving these instructions. (On the other hand, Canadian judges were overwhelmingly opposed: Fewer than five percent agreed that jurors should receive such instructions.)[14]

Despite its popular appeal, judges in the United States, like their Canadian counterparts, are not kind to arguments for nullification.

Judicial Decisions

The decisions concerning jury nullification during the past decade have been relatively predictable, with most courts acting defensively and negatively when litigants have requested a jury nullification instruction.[15] The nullification doctrine is raised by defendants with some regularity in cases of tax protests,[16] abortion protests,[17] antinuclear protests,[18] and euthanasia,[19] but it usually meets an icy judicial reception.

One particularly illuminating example is *State v. Ragland*,[20] decided by the New Jersey Supreme Court in 1986. The defendant, a prior convicted felon, was charged with four separate crimes all stemming from the same incident—(1) conspiracy to commit armed robbery, (2) unlawful possession of a weapon, (3) unlawful possession of a weapon without a permit, and (4) possession of a weapon by a convicted felon. The trial court severed the last charge "to avoid the inevitable prejudice in the trial of the other charges that would be caused by introducing defendant's prior felony conviction, an essential element in the severed charge."[21]

After the jurors found the defendant guilty of the first three charges, the trial judge gave the jury the following instruction and asked them to give their verdict on the fourth charge:

> If you find that the defendant, Gregory Ragland, was previously convicted for the crime of robbery and that he was in possession of a sawed-off shotgun, *as you have indicated* . . . then you *must* find him guilty as charged by this Court.[22]

The defendant appealed on the ground that this instruction took from the jurors their right to reach an independent verdict and, indeed, constituted a "directed verdict" from the judge.

All seven justices on the New Jersey court agreed that the above instruction was improper because the instruction included the "as you have indicated" phrase. The court reasoned that the use of this phrase denied the jury the power to evaluate the evidence anew to determine whether the prosecutor had proved beyond a reasonable doubt that the defendant had violated the fourth charge.

The justices divided sharply, however, on whether the use of the word "must" in this charge was proper, with four concluding that it was and three arguing that it was not. The three judges in the minority argued that the use of language such as "must" should be discontinued "because of its potential to be interpreted in a manner that compromises jury independence and blurs the accepted dichotomy between judge and jury."[23]

The majority opinion of Chief Justice Wilentz acknowledged that precedents are divided on this issue,[24] but argued in strongly emotional language that "must" is an appropriate word to use because New Jersey juries do not have a "'right' to announce a verdict of acquittal despite its determination of guilt."[25] Chief Justice Wilentz argued that no evidence exists that jury nullification serves society well,[26] that an instruction to jurors about their power "would confuse any conscientious citizen"[27] and produce "total arbitrariness"[28] and "cynicism,"[29] and that a system that included a jury nullification instruction would be "almost ludicrous."[30]

Although *Ragland* remains the judicial norm, a decision that strikes a dramatically different tone is *Stevenson v. State*,[31] in which the Maryland Court of Appeals reaffirmed the constitutionality of Article 23 of the Maryland Declaration of Rights, which states that:

> In the trial of all criminal cases, the Jury shall be the Judges of Law,
> as well as of fact, except that the Court may pass upon the sufficiency
> of the evidence to sustain a conviction.[32]

The majority's decision in this case also helps explain how this provision is to be interpreted and applied.

Dorothy Lou Stevenson was convicted by a jury of murdering her husband by pouring gasoline on him while he slept and then igniting the gas with a match. At the beginning of the trial, the trial judge explained to the jurors the unique constitutional role that juries play in Maryland and, pursuant to Article 23, informed them that:

> Under the Constitution of Maryland, [you are] the judge of the law
> as well as of the facts. Therefore, anything which I may say about

the law, including any instructions which I may give you, is merely
advisory and you are not in any way bound by it.[33]

After the evidence was presented, the judge did not again make such
a statement, but instead gave instructions on the issues of law and
"couched all of his remarks in mandatory language."[34] Mrs. Stevenson
argued that the preliminary instruction violated her right to due process
under the Fourteenth Amendment of the United States Constitution and
specifically infringed upon her privilege against self-incrimination, the
presumption of innocence, and the requirement of proof beyond a
reasonable doubt.[35]

The majority opinion rejected these arguments and reaffirmed the
propriety of issuing the preliminary instruction under Article 23. It also
clarified exactly what the jury's power includes and thus responds to the
fears expressed by Chief Justice Wilentz in New Jersey. The Maryland
jury's role under Article 23 "is confined 'to *resolv[ing] conflicting interpretations of the law [of the crime]* and to decid[ing] whether th[at] law
should be applied in dubious factual situations,' *and nothing more.*"[36]

The Maryland jury's responsibility thus is to determine whether it is
equitable and just to apply the law defining a crime to the facts presented
to it. The jury has no role in determining whether evidence should be
admitted, whether witnesses are competent to testify, whether the court
has jurisdiction, or whether the statutes are constitutional.[37] In summary,
the Maryland Court of Appeals stated:

> Implicit in the decisions of this Court limiting the jury's judicial role
> to the "law of the crime" is a recognition that all other legal issues
> are for the judge alone to decide.
>
> Because of this division of the law-judging function between judge
> and jury, it is incumbent upon a trial judge to carefully delineate
> for the jury the following dichotomy: (i) that the jury, under Article
> 23, is the final arbiter of disputes as to the substantive "law of the
> crime," as well as the "legal effect of the evidence," and that any
> comments by the judge concerning these matters are advisory only;
> and (ii) that, by virtue of this same constitutional provision, all other
> aspects of law (e.g., the burden of proof, the requirement of
> unanimity, the validity of a statute) are beyond the jury's pale, and
> that the judge's comments on these matters are binding upon that
> body. In other words, the jury should not be informed that all of the
> court's instructions are merely advisory; rather only that portion of
> the charge addressed to the former areas of "law" may be regarded
> as nonbinding by it, and it is only these aspects of the "law" which
> counsel may dispute in their respective arguments to the jury. On
> the other hand, the jury should be informed that the judge's charge
> with regard to any other legal matter is binding and may not be
> disregarded by it.[38]

In 1981, the Maryland Court of Appeals addressed this matter once again and said that the jury's role in evaluating the law of the crime was limited to those instances where the law is unclear or in dispute: "[I]n those circumstances where there is no dispute nor a sound basis for a dispute as to the law of the crime, the court's instructions are binding on the jury and counsel as well."[39]

A subsequent case that illustrates the leeway still given to a jury in Maryland is *Mack v. State.*[40] The defendant in *Mack* was charged with assault and battery and use of a handgun in the commission of a crime of violence. The trial court instructed the jurors that they had to find the defendant guilty of a crime of violence (assault and battery) in order to find him guilty of the second crime, which required a violent crime as a prerequisite. The trial judge also informed the jury that this instruction was binding.[41] Nonetheless, the jury found the defendant not guilty on the first charge and guilty on the second. When the defendant challenged this decision as inconsistent with the "binding" instructions, the trial judge ruled "that the jury's verdict was 'in all probability, a compromise verdict' that could stand."[42] The Court of Appeals accepted this illogical result as within the jury's power and affirmed the verdict.

An Empirical Study

The general judicial hostility to nullification ignores the popular sentiment for the doctrine and does not seem to be influenced by the data suggesting that a nullification instruction would not spawn "runaway" juries.

It is extremely difficult to develop definitive studies that illustrate how a jury nullification instruction affects a jury's deliberation, but Professor Irwin A. Horowitz of the University of Toledo Department of Psychology attempted such a study recently.[43] Professor Horowitz sought to study "whether the jury functioned differently if it was given nullification instructions; whether the impact of such instructions depended on the precise form in which they were given; and whether their impact also depended on the type of case in which they were given."[44]

Horowitz assembled forty-five six-person juries, drawing names from the official jury pool used in Toledo, Ohio.[45] He then chose three different factual situations and asked fifteen of the juries to evaluate each of three situations presented with professionally-acted audio tapes and slides. The cases involved (1) the murder of a grocer during a robbery attempt, (2) the killing of a pedestrian by a drunk college student driving in a foggy night, and (3) the "mercy" killing of a terminally ill and suffering cancer patient by a sympathetic nurse who had the consent of the patient and her family.

The fifteen juries were in turn broken into groups of five and each group was given one of three jury instructions: (a) a standard instruction taken from the Ohio Pattern Juror Instructions, which does not make any reference to nullification; (b) the Maryland Instruction, which contains nullification language;[46] and (c) what Professor Horowitz characterizes as a "radical" nullification instruction, taken from one of the present authors' earlier articles.[47] The result was that all fifteen of the juries convicted the alleged murderer of the grocer despite the three different instructions they received, but variations occurred in their evaluations of the other two fact situations. Two of the five juries that received the "standard" and "Maryland" instructions acquitted the drunk college student but *none* of those receiving the "radical" instruction reached a verdict of acquittal. And in the "mercy" killing case, one of the five "standard" juries acquitted the nurse, two of the "Maryland" juries acquitted, and *four* of the "radical" juries acquitted.[48]

Although the sample Horowitz used is small and more work clearly is required, this study does show that juries told that they have power are more likely to exercise it and to reach results that—at least in these cases—appear to be more just and equitable.[49]

From the Judicial to the Political Arena

The controversy over the propriety of a jury nullification instruction lay dormant for most of this century until resurrected in the 1960s as part of the defense strategy in anti-Vietnam War demonstration trials.[50] As mentioned above, it did not meet with a warm judicial reception, and most judges still refuse to instruct juries honestly about their nullification power. Such refusal in the 1960s did not significantly undermine the legitimacy of the judiciary because few people knew about nullification. This is no longer true in the 1990s. The jury nullification movement is more active now than at any previous period. Journalists have noted that juries have appeared to invoke their nullification power in many prominent recent cases.[51] More significantly, frustration with the judicial system, and in particular the perception that judges are dishonest with juries, has caused proponents of jury nullification to seek satisfaction from two more hospitable forums—voters and legislators.

Voters and Legislators

Debate about jury nullification raises fundamental, and unanswered, questions about sovereignty in a constitutional democracy. It was therefore natural that nullification proponents would seek out the two major forums for lawmaking, the popular vote and legislation.

In the summer of 1989, Larry Dodge, a Montana businessman, joined with his friend Don Doig to found the Fully Informed Jury Association (FIJA). This "national nonprofit nonpartisan group [is] dedicated to jurors being fully informed of their rights."[52] Within eighteen months, the organization had jury rights lobbyists in thirty-five states.[53]

FIJA sponsored the first Bill of Jury Rights Conference in November 1990. The purpose of the gathering was to plan strategy to lobby legislators to enact "fully informed jury" statutes, and to urge voters to pass initiatives, referenda, or constitutional amendments to protect the heritage of the jury's right of nullification.[54] The Conference concluded with a ceremony at the federal courthouse to kickoff a national Jury Rights Campaign.

Because public sentiment supports jury nullification,[55] FIJA's appeal spans the political and social spectrum:

> Conservatives and constitutionalists, liberals and progressives, libertarians, populists, greens, gun owners, peace groups, taxpayer rights groups, home schoolers, alternative medicine practitioners, drug decriminalization groups, criminal trial lawyers, seat belt and helmet law activists, environmentalists, women's groups, anti-nuclear groups, ethnic minorities, . . . and judges (yes, some judges are sympathetic).[56]

As of January 1991, FIJA had successfully persuaded legislators to introduce bills in the state legislatures of Alaska, Arizona, Georgia, Louisiana, Massachusetts, New York, Oklahoma, Tennessee, and Wyoming.[57]

These bills differ widely in language. One of the more interesting options is the Massachusetts bill, introduced by Senator Robert L. Hedlund,[58] which seeks to soften the confrontation between the legislature and the judiciary. Senator Hedlund has strong feelings about its importance: "I see this bill as supporting one of the two pillars of freedom—the right to a fully informed jury. The other pillar is the right to vote."[59] If passed, the bill will amend the handbook all potential trial jurors receive and would add a new segment to the video presentation they watch. Senator Hedlund's bill states:

> In informing the jurors of the nature and extent of their duties and responsibilities . . . the handbook shall inform the jurors that in all cases they have the historical, constitutional, and natural right to judge not only the liability, guilt, or innocence of the defendant(s) under the law as charged, but to exercise their conscience in doing so and that, if they determine according to their conscience that the law as charged by the judge is unjust or wrongly applied to the defendant(s), it is their obligation, right, and duty to judge according to their conscience.

By its wording, the bill would apply both to civil and criminal jury trials. Application of jury nullification in civil cases is less pressing an issue because the judge always maintains the authority to alter or reject the verdict. Thus, a jury that votes its conscience can be judicially reversed. Discussions of jury nullification in the context of civil cases thus tend to be rare.[60]

Senator Hedlund's bill contains one great virtue and one great vice. Its virtue is that it attempts to avoid a direct confrontation with judges and therefore does not order them to instruct juries about their nullification power. The jurors will receive accurate information from their handbook, and judges will not be compelled to give it to them.[61]

The one great vice in the bill is that it makes a statement of jury power that is far too broad. Under its terms, for example, a jury could *convict* on the basis of conscience if the jurors feel the law is too soft or lenient. The bill needs to be amended to remove that impression. Language must be added to convey to the jury that it may exercise its conscience or "mercy" power only for leniency. No defendant may be judged by a standard harsher than the law on the books. *Ex post facto* convictions are unacceptable.

Another illustration of the breadth of the bill's language is to be found in the sentence that permits jurors to exercise conscience if the law as charged by the judge "is unjust or wrongly applied" to the defendant(s). It would be better to say that jurors, in the exercise of their consciences, "may acquit the defendant if the application of the law, as given by the judge, would result in an unjust conviction."

Having jurors speculate on the "justness" of a law is to distract them from their central task of applying the facts to the law in that particular case. If a law is unjust, its application in any case is unjust, and voters, legislators, or judges should remove it from the books. Juries do not have this power. Their power is limited to refusing to apply the law in the single case presented to them, and then only when following the technical mandate of the law would offend the community's sense of justice.

Senator Hedlund's bill undoubtedly will undergo language changes as it moves through the legislative process. In rewritten form, it may serve as a model for laws that truly make our nation a "government of the people, by the people and for the people."[62]

Legislation has not been the only path to jury nullification law reform. FIJA has been busy circulating petitions for ballot initiatives in many states, including Arkansas, California, Colorado, Florida, Idaho, Montana, Utah, and Washington. In some of these states, amendments to the state constitutions are sought. By the end of 1991, FIJA hopes to have electoral campaigns in all fifty states.

One of the most elaborate jury nullification provisions appeared as an initiative to amend the Oregon Constitution:[63]

> It is the natural right of every citizen of the state of Oregon, when serving on a criminal-trial jury, to judge both the law and the facts pertaining to the case before the jury, in order to determine whether justice will be served by applying the law to the defendant. It is mandatory that all jurors be informed of this right. Before the jury hears a case, and again before jury deliberation begins, the court shall inform the jurors of their rights in these words: "As jurors, your first responsibility is to decide whether the prosecution has proven beyond reasonable doubt every element of the criminal charge. If you decide that the prosecution has proven beyond reasonable doubt every element of the criminal charge but that you cannot in good conscience support a guilty verdict, you are not required to do so. To reach a verdict which you believe is just, each of you has the right to consider to what extent the defendant's actions have actually caused harm or otherwise violated your sense of right and wrong. If you believe justice requires it, you may also judge both the merits of the law under which the defendant has been charged and the wisdom of applying that law to the defendant. Accordingly, for each charge against the defendant, even if review of the evidence strictly in terms of the law would indicate a guilty verdict, you have the right to find the defendant not guilty. The court cautions that with the exercise of this right comes the full moral responsibility for the verdict you bring in." As part of their oath, the jurors shall affirm that they understand the information concerning their rights which this section requires the court to give them, and that no party to the trial may be prevented from encouraging jurors to exercise this right. For the jurors to be so informed is declared to be part of the defendant's fundamental right to trial by jury, and failure to conduct any criminal trial in accordance with this section shall not constitute harmless error, and shall be grounds for a mistrial. No potential juror may be disqualified from serving on a jury because he or she expresses willingness to judge the law or its application, or to vote according to his or her conscience.

As the Oregon Supreme Court succinctly stated, this initiative, if adopted, "would enshrine in the Oregon Constitution the concept of 'jury nullification.'"[64] The Court expressed hostility toward the initiative,[65] but did not strike it down.

Juridical Dishonesty

Essential to the success of the grass roots jury nullification movement is publicity. People need to be informed about the right to fully informed juries. Jury nullification makes news in most major criminal trials where a clash of values attracts public attention. Articles about jury nullification now appear in newspapers and magazines with great frequency. When the Public Broadcast System (PBS) aired "Inside the Jury Room," an estimated twenty-five million viewers saw the program.[66] Jury nullification is getting more press coverage than ever before. Millions of people are learning what the judges refuse to tell them.

Contacting Potential Jurors

Press coverage has the advantage of reaching many people, but it does so at a time in their lives when the jury nullification issue is not very pressing. For potential jurors, however, information about jury nullification may have a more direct impact on the juror's deliberations.

On January 25, 1990, the *San Diego Reader* published a three-quarter page advertisement[67] with the following headline:

ATTENTION JURORS & FUTURE JURORS
You Can Legally Acquit Anti-Abortion
"Trespassers" Even If They're "Guilty"

The advertisement began by saying "[s]uppose you're on the jury in the trial of pro-life 'rescuers' who blocked the entrances to an abortion facility. The judge will probably tell you it makes no difference whether you agree with their actions. . . . He's Not Telling the Truth." The text went on to praise a Philadelphia jury that had used its "common-law right to 'nullify'" a trespass law.

The timing of the appearance of the advertisement was well planned. Trials were beginning for Operation Rescue defendants accused of trespass and other offenses at the site of a medical clinic. That the advertisement was designed to influence jury verdicts cannot be in doubt. Indeed, the publisher of *The Reader* was one of the defendants and his lawyer told the press that he was aware the advertisement would be run.[68]

Three weeks before the San Diego advertisement appeared, leaflets were distributed outside the courthouse in El Cajon, California. The demonstrators stopped when warned by the marshal that they could be arrested for felony jury-tampering. To combat the information being handed out, judges gave jurors special instructions to disregard the leaflets.

California was not the first location where such leaflets appeared. Operation Rescue adherents in Jackson, Mississippi, distributed leaflets urging jurors to "nullify every rule or 'law' that is not in accordance with the principles of Natural, God-given, Common, or Constitutional Law."[69]

Many of these leaflets present a distorted and incorrect discussion of nullification. Potential jurors who read them may taint the deliberations of actual juries with misinformation. Only an accurate jury nullification instruction from the judge can eliminate this problem.

In fact, many of the pamphlets and leaflets go further than presenting misinformation. They suggest or hint that potential jurors should deceive judges.

Should Jurors Be Honest with Judges?

Sir Walter Scott wrote the much quoted phrase, "Oh! what a tangled web we weave [w]hen first we practise to deceive!"[70] Proponents of jury nullification have written about the lack of candor involved when the judge fails to tell the jury about nullification. This dishonesty now has spawned a more virulent deception in the reverse direction: jurors lying to judges.

In 1988, the authors received a four-page pamphlet entitled "The Informed Juror." Written by Paul deParrie and sponsored by an Oregon group called Advocates for Life, the pamphlet gives a very brief description of nullification before calling on conservatives, "especially Christians," to refrain from showing during voir dire that they have strong feelings about abortion. The pamphlet's author advises:

> During jury selection it may be wise to refrain from elaborating on answers to questions asked by attorneys. Any appearance of being educated, involved or opinionated may be sufficient cause to be rejected, thus being removed from the opportunity to be a watchman for abuses by the executive and judicial departments of government. This does not mean that you would be untruthful in answering questions. Simply keep your answers brief if you would like to improve your chances of serving on a jury.

Not all anti-abortion activists have been content with silence or brevity. For some, outright deception appears justified. One such illustration surfaced in San Diego where a published advertisement stopped just short of advocating lying.[71] Noting that "before you even get on the jury, they may ask you whether you know about your right to 'nullify,'" the advertisement then offered a suggested response:

> *Don't believe a word they say. . . .*
> *Here's How to Do It*
>   It's easy. The most important rule is, *don't let the judge and prosecutor know that you know about this right.*
>   It is unjust and illegal for them to deny you this right. So, if you have to, it's perfectly all right for you to make a "mental reservation."

> Give them the same answer you would have given if you were
> hiding fugitive slaves in 1850 and the 'slave catchers' asked if you
> had runaways in your attic. Or if you were hiding Jews from the Nazis
> in Germany.

This recommendation for "pious dishonesty" was then followed by
two other suggestions:

> The second rule is, *educate the other jurors* about jury nullification
> and, if possible, persuade them to vote "not guilty."
>   The third rule is *stick to your guns.* Don't let other jurors make
> you change your position.

Millions of potential jurors may be exposed to similar advertisements,
leaflets, or pamphlets. That means that countless juries may contain
members who have concealed their awareness of nullification, who hold
seriously incorrect views about it, and who intend to "educate" the other
jurors to rebuff laws they do not like.

When jury nullification was a judicial secret, it was easier to refuse
to give jury nullification instructions.[72] Such refusal today, however,
may seriously compromise the justice of our jury verdicts.

Should Judges Be Honest with Jurors?

What should the judge do about the fact that jurors may know something
about nullification, accurate or not? Suppose, for example, we have a
panel of potential jurors in a criminal case that has attracted media
attention. Some of these jurors have seen literature about a right to nullify
laws. What they read contained many errors. The defense lawyer or
prosecutor may request to ask questions about nullification on voir dire.
Should the lawyers be allowed to voir dire about nullification? If not,
these jurors will contaminate the jury deliberations. If so, information
about nullification will be made public. The judge may decide to give
an antinullification instruction, but this, of course, will reinforce what
the literature said would happen and would not correct any errors about
the doctrine.

Judicial failure to give honest and correct instructions on nullification
may thus directly contribute to contamination of jury deliberations. It
is a sad irony that while judges continue to refuse to give accurate jury
nullification instructions, they in fact are creating the anarchy they seek
to avoid.

Conclusion

The renewed grass roots interest in a "fully informed jury" reinforces
our earlier views that judges should give jurors an accurate and honest

instruction about the jury's role and power. The instruction should state that the judge must properly make rulings on procedural matters and will be guiding the trial so that all constitutional protections are provided to the litigants. The instruction should also say that the jury does not have the power to create new statutes or evaluate the constitutionality of the statutes before them. The jury should be encouraged to pay respectful attention to the acts of the legislature which, after all, reflect the democratic wishes of the community's majority. But the jurors should also be told that their function is to represent the community in this trial and that their ultimate responsibility is to determine the facts that occurred and to evaluate whether applying the law to these facts will produce, in the eyes of the community, a just and equitable verdict.

This type of honest instruction would reinforce our nation's commitment to a government where the people are sovereign, and it would serve to bring the people and their laws together in closer harmony.

Endnotes

[1] See, e.g., *Lessard v. State*, 719 P.2d 227, 231 (Wyo. 1986) (citing numerous other cases).

The topic of "jury nullification" has been discussed in detail by the authors in their previous writings: J. Van Dyke, *Jury Selection Procedures: Our Uncertain Commitment to Representative Panels* 225–51 (1977); Scheflin & Van Dyke, "Jury Nullification: The Contours of a Controversy," 43:4 *Law & Contemp. Prob.* 51 (1980); Scheflin, "Jury Nullification: The Right to Say No," 45 *So. Cal. L. Rev.* 168 (1972); Van Dyke, "The Jury as a Political Institution," 16 *Cath. Law.* 224 (1970); Van Dyke, 3 *The Center Mag.* 17 (No. 2, March-April 1970).

[2] Among those advocating giving jurors an honest instruction about their powers, in addition to the authors in the articles cited supra in note 1 are: Timko, "Jury Nullification Thru the Initiative Process," in *Jury Nullification* Vol. 1 (1987); Becker, "Jury Nullification: Can A Jury Be Trusted?," 16 *Trial* 41 (Oct. 1980); Freeman, "Why Not A Jury Nullification Statute Here Too?," 131 *New L.J.* 304 (March 19, 1981); Kaufman, "The Right of Self Representation and the Power of Jury Nullification," 28 *Case W. Res. L. Rev.* 269 (1978); Kunstler, "Jury Nullification in Conscience Cases," 10 *Va. J. Int'l L.* 71 (1969); McCall, "Sentencing By Death Qualified Juries and the Right to Jury Nullification," 22 *Harv. J. on Legis.* 289 (1985); Osterman, "Should Jurors Be Told They Can Refuse To Enforce The Law?: Law Must Respect Consciences," 72 *A.B.A.J.* 36 (March 1986); Sax, "Conscience and Anarchy: The Prosecution of War Resisters," 57 *Yale Rev.* 481 (1968); Schultz, "Will 'Jury Nullification' Save Ollie North?," 11 *Legal Times* 18 (March 6, 1989); Note, "Jury Nullification and Jury-Control Procedures," 65 *N.Y.U.L. Rev.* 825 (1990); Note, "Laws That Are Made to Be Broken: Adjusting for Anticipated Noncompliance," 75 *Mich. L. Rev.* 687 (1977); Note, "The Jury's Role Under the Indiana Constitution," 52 *Indiana L.J.* 793 (1977); Note, "Toward Principles of Jury Equity," 83 *Yale L.J.* 1023 (1974); Note, "Jury Nullification: The Forgotten Right," 7 *New Eng. L. Rev.* 105 (1971).

Articles discussing jury nullification or the "dispensing power" of juries which provide support for nullification but do not reach an explicit conclusion on whether an instruction should be given include: Barkan, "Jury Nullification in Political Trials," 31 *Soc. Prob.* 28 (Oct. 1983); Howe, "Juries As Judges of Criminal Law," 52 *Harv. L. Rev.* 582 (1939); Jacobsohn, "A Right to Disagree: Judge, Juries, and the Administration of Criminal Justice in Maryland," 1976 *Wash. U. L. Q.* 571; Kamins, "Jury Nullification—A Rarity in Criminal-Law Practice," 194 *N.Y.L.J.* 1 (Aug. 20, 1985); Levine, "The Legislative Role of Juries," 1984 *A.B.F. Res. J.* 605; Myers, "Rule Departures and Making Law: Juries and Their Verdicts," 13 *Law & Soc. Rev.* 781 (1979); Pacelle, "Sanctuary Jurors' Dilemma: Law or Justice?," 8 *Am. Law.* 95 (Sept. 1986).

3 Recent works arguing that such an instruction should not be given to the jurors include: M. Kadish & S. Kadish, *Discretion to Disobey: A Study of Lawful Departures from Legal Rules* (1973); Allen, "Editorial: Nihilism at Santa Barbara," 57 *A.B.A.J.* 999 (Oct. 1971); Christie, "Lawful Departures from Legal Rules: 'Jury Nullification' and Legitimated Disobedience," 62 *Cal. L. Rev.* 1289 (1974); Goldsmith, "Jury Nullification and the Rule of Law," 17 *The Colo. Law.* 2151 (1988); Kadish & Kadish, "On Justified Rule Departures by Officials," 59 *Cal. L. Rev.* 905 (1971); Marshall, "Should Jurors Be Told They Can Refuse To Enforce The Law?: Jurors Must Respect The Law," 72 *A.B.A.J.* 36 (March 1986); McBride, "The Jury is Not a Political Institution," 11 *Judge's J.* 37 (April 1972); Scott, "Jury Nullification: An Historical Perspective on a Modern Debate," 91 *W. Va. L. Rev.* 389 (1989); Simson, "Jury Nullification in the American System: A Skeptical View," 54 *Tex. L. Rev.* 488 (1976); Tavris, "The Law of An Unwritten Law: A Common Sense View of Jury Nullification," 11 *West St. L. Rev.* 97 (Fall 1983); Note, "Jury Nullification in Historical Perspective: Massachusetts as a Case Study," 12 *Suffolk U.L. Rev.* 968 (1978); Comment, "Jury Nullification and the Pro Se Defense: The Impact of *Dougherty v. United States*," 21 *U. Kan. L. Rev.* 47 (1972).

4 See Scheflin & Van Dyke, supra note 1, at 56–63.

5 Id. at 79–85.

6 Id. at 59–68.

7 We will not revisit the major arguments rejecting or supporting nullification. These may be found in our prior work, see supra note 1, and in the work of others, see supra notes 2 and 3. Nor will we discuss two evolving questions: the application of jury nullification in civil trials, and the expansion of jury powers to influence the admission of evidence. Our focus in this article is on the emerging politics of the nullification debate as it shifts from the courthouse to the statehouse and ballot box.

8 Some opponents of jury nullification have argued that juries will have the power to "ignore" or "disregard the law," or to return a verdict that may "fly in the face of both the evidence and the law." Indeed, the more radical proponents like jury nullification for just this reason. But this rhetoric does nullification a disservice. Lawless "Rambo" juries have no place in the legal system; the supremacy of the rule of law is essential in a constitutional democracy. Juries should not act as quasilegislators deciding which laws to eliminate or revise.

9 G. Fletcher, *A Crime of Self-Defense: Bernhard Goetz and the Law on Trial* 155 (1988). The quote continues: "There are some who defend this residual power in juries as the highest expression of democracy and community control over the machinery of the state, and others who decry the same power as an invitation to anarchy." Id.

10 Id.

11 The story of Leroy Reed is told in a remarkable television documentary where, for the first time, television cameras were allowed to film an actual jury deliberating to verdict. "Inside the Jury Room" (1986) was a segment of the PBS show "Frontline." The film was written and produced by Alan M. Levin and Stephen J. Herzberg.

12 Law Professor Stephen J. Herzberg, co-producer of "Inside The Jury Room," met with the jurors immediately after the trial. He explained jury nullification to them and said

that they did have the right to return an acquittal. It was a highly emotional session. Many of the jurors were crying. Herzberg, "Inside the Jury Room," presented at the Bill of Jury Rights Conference, St. Louis, Missouri (No. 10, 1990). The authors wish to thank Franklin M. Nugent for an audiotape of Professor Herzberg's talk. The authors also wish to thank Professor Herzberg for supplying us with additional information about the case and with a videotape of his postverdict discussions with the jurors and the judge.

A case in which the failure to give a nullification instruction may have produced a conviction is reported in Pacelle, supra note 2, at 95. According to Pacelle, many of the jurors are still suffering from their experience.

[13] V. Hans & N. Vidmar, *Judging the Jury* 158 (1986), (citing Doob, "Public's View of Criminal Jury Trial," and Doob, "Canadian Trial Judges' View of the Criminal Jury Trial," in *Law Reform Commission of Canada Studies on the Jury* (1979)).

[14] V. Hans & N. Vidmar, supra note 13, at 158.

[15] See, e.g., *Medley v. Commonwealth*, 704 S.W.2d 190 (Ky. 1985); *People v. St. Cyr*, 341 N.W.2d 533 (Mich. App. 1983); *State v. Perkins*, 353 N.W.2d 557 (Minn. 1984); *State v. Maloney*, 490 A.2d 772 (N.H. 1985); *State v. Champa*, 494 A.2d 102 (R.I. 1985).

[16] See generally *United States v. Krzyske*, 836 F.2d 1013 (6th Cir. 1988); *United States v. Wiley*, 503 F.2d 106 (8th Cir. 1974).

In *United States v. Ogle*, 613 F.2d 233, 236 (10th Cir. 1980), Ogle, a tax protester, was convicted of trying to influence potential jurors by supplying them with a "Handbook for Jurors." The Handbook contained an inaccurate description of jury nullification ("it is unnecessary for jurors to follow the law of the land where they conceive of the law being contrary to their concepts of morals").

[17] See, e.g., *United States v. Anderson*, 716 F.2d 446 (7th Cir. 1983).

[18] See, e.g., *State v. Champa*, 494 A.2d 102 (R.I. 1985).

[19] See S. Kassin & L. Wrightsman, *The American Jury On Trial: Psychological Perspectives* 157–58 (1988). Kassin and Wrightsman describe two euthanasia cases. In the first, the jury acquitted. In the second, the jury convicted because, as one juror explained, "We had no choice. The law does not allow for sympathy." Id. at 158.

In their book *Judging the Jury*, supra note 13, professors Hans and Vidmar observe that euthanasia cases demonstrate the unique value served by jury nullification. In these cases, "the legal authorities feel compelled to bring charges, but they rely on the jury's sense of fairness to acquit the defendant." Id. at 158.

[20] 105 N.J. 189, 519 A.2d 1361 (1986).

[21] *State v. Ragland*, 105 N.J. 189, 192, 519 A.2d 1361, 1362 (1986).

[22] Id. (emphasis added).

[23] Id. at 220, 519 A.2d at 1377 (Handler, J., concurring in part and dissenting in part). The dissenting judges did not, however, advocate giving a jury nullification instruction. Id. at 221, 519 A.2d at 1378.

[24] Id. at 198–99, 519 A.2d at 1365–66. One decision subsequent to *Ragland* that strikes a very different tone and criticizes a trial judge for confining a jury too narrowly is *Cheek v. United States*, 59 U.S.L.W. 4049 (1991). The jury indicated that it felt constrained by "the narrow and hard expression" of the law as given by the judge, id. at 4051 n.6, and the United States Supreme Court agreed that the instruction was too strict, reversing and remanding for a new trial.

[25] Id. at 204, 519 A.2d at 1369.

[26] Id. at 206, 519 A.2d at 1370.

[27] Id. at 208, 519 A.2d at 1371.

[28] Id. at 210, 519 A.2d at 1372.

[29] Id. at 209, 519 A.2d at 1371.

[30] Id. at 210, 519 A.2d at 1372.

11 289 Md. 167, 423 A.2d 558 (1980). The majority opinion was written by Judge Digges
for himself and three other judges. Judges Eldridge and Davidson dissented, arguing
that Article 23 of the Maryland Declaration of Rights violates the 14th Amendment
of the United States Constitution. Id. at 194, 423 A.2d at 572. Judge Cole also dissented
with regard to the specific manner in which the instructions were given in this case,
reserving the question of the status of Article 23 under the United States Constitution.
Id. at 204, 423 A.2d at 577.

12 *Md. Const. Declaration of Rights* art. 23.

13 *Stevenson v. State,* 289 Md. 167, 171, 423 A.2d 558, 560 (1980).

14 Id. at 171, 423 A.2d at 561.

15 Id. at 188, 423 A.2d at 569.

16 Id. at 179, 423 A.2d at 564 (emphasis in original) (quoting from *Dillon v. State,* 277
Md. 571, 581, 357 A.2d 360, 367 (1976) (emphasis in original)).

17 Id. at 178, 423 A.2d at 564.

18 Id. at 179-80, 423 A.2d at 565.

19 *Montgomery v. State,* 292 Md. 84, 89, 437 A.2d 654, 657 (1981). In *Allnutt v. State,*
the Maryland Court of Special Appeals noted that:
> Instances of dispute of the law of the crime are an endangered species rapidly
> approaching extinction. Once an appellate court has ruled on the "law of the
> crime," the matter then becomes settled law, and thereafter the jury is no longer
> the judge of the law with respect to that particular matter. Consequently, disputes
> of the law of the crime will decrease in number with each successive appellate
> ruling.

59 Md. App. 694, 703, 478 A.2d 321, 325 (1984).

40 300 Md. 583, 479 A.2d 1344 (1984).

41 *Mack v. State,* 300 Md. 583, 600, 479 A.2d 1344, 1352 (1984).

42 Id.

43 See Horowitz, "The Effect of Jury Nullification Instruction on Verdicts & Jury
Functioning in Criminal Trials," 9 *Law & Hum. Behav.* 25 (1985); Horowitz, "Jury
Nullification: The Impact of Judicial Instructions, Arguments, and Challenges on Jury
Decision Making," 12 *Law & Hum. Behav.* 439 (1988).

44 V. Hans & N. Vidmar, supra note 13, at 159 (describing studies of Professor Irvin
Horowitz). The quote ends "The answer he got was yes to all three questions." Id.

45 All 170 participants had previously served as jurors in Ohio courts. Horowitz (1985),
supra note 43, at 30.

46 The instruction used by Professor Horowitz was as follows:
> Members of the Jury, this is a criminal case and under the Constitution and laws
> of the State of Maryland in a criminal case the jury are the judges of law as well
> as the facts in the case. So that whatever I tell you about the law while it is intended
> to be helpful to you in reaching a just and proper verdict in the case, it is not
> binding upon you as members of the jury and you may accept or reject it. And
> you may apply the law as you apprehend it to be in the case.

Horowitz (1985), supra note 43, at 29 (quoting Scheflin & Van Dyke, supra note 1,
at 83, quoting *Wyley v. Warden,* 372 F.2d 742, 743 n.1 (4th Cir. 1967)).

47 The instruction is taken from Van Dyke (1970), supra note 1. Jurors were told the
following:
> 1. "Although they are a public body bound to give respectful attention to the
>   laws, they have the final authority to decide whether or not to apply a given
>   law to the acts of the defendant on trial before them";
> 2. That "they represent (the community) and that it is appropriate to bring into
>   their deliberations the feelings of the community and their own feelings based
>   on conscience";

    3. And, jurors were told that despite their respect for the law, "nothing would
      bar them from acquitting the defendant if they feel that the law, as applied to
      the fact situation before them, would produce an inequitable or unjust result."
Horowitz (1985), supra note 43, at 30–31.

[48] Horowitz, supra note 43, at 32.

[49] Kassin & Wrightsman identify two potential problems arising from the Horowitz study. First, "jury nullification is like a door that can swing both ways. Just as it can license jurors to acquit the guilty, it is argued, it can enable them to convict those who are innocent." S. Kassin & L. Wrightsman, supra note 19, at 161. Carefully worded jury instructions should all but eliminate this possibility. Even if such a conviction occurred, it could be reversed. Jury convictions, unlike jury acquittals, are not final.

    The second concern is that when the jury nullification instruction is made explicit, jurors will become "diverted from the external to the internal, from the evidence onto their sentiments." Id. at 161. It seems more likely to us that jurors will deal more openly and honestly with their sentiments, but would not be "diverted" from their initial task of finding the true facts.

[50] Credit goes to Professor Sax for rekindling the flame of jury nullification. See Sax, supra note 2.

[51] Among the recent highly publicized trials where jury nullification appears to have played a role are those of Mayor Marion Barry of Washington, D.C., for drug use, Oliver L. North for his role in the Iran-Contra Affair, and Bernhard Goetz for his assault in a New York City subway.

    After Mayor Barry's jury returned a conviction for a relatively minor charge and acquittals on the other counts, the trial judge Thomas Penfield Jackson spoke at Harvard Law School and expressed his dismay that the jurors had failed to return more convictions even though the evidence was "overwhelming" on at least a dozen counts. Bruce Fein then wrote a column chastising Judge Jackson for his "acid carping at jurors for nullifying the law." Fein, "Judge, Jury . . . and the Sixth," *Wash. Times*, Nov. 8, 1990, at G3. Judge Jackson had said:

    The jury is not a minidemocracy or a minilegislature. They are not to go back
    and do right as they see fit. That's anarchy. They are supposed to follow the law.

Commentator Fein responded by saying:

    Jury nullification in a particular case is no more a legislative repeal of a criminal
    law, or anarchy, than are the commonplace decisions of prosecutors to resist
    prosecutions where the crime is deemed inconsequential or mitigated by special
    circumstances.

Id.; see also Thompson, "Sifting the Pool; Juror Questionnaires Explore Drug Addiction, Prejudice," *Wash. Post*, June 5, 1990, at A1.

    The jury in Oliver North's trial similarly returned a verdict that indicated sympathy with the accused, convicting him on only three of the twelve charges against him. Georgetown University Law Professor Paul F. Rothstein analyzed the trial by saying: "It's jury nullification. . . . The instructions on aiding and abetting left [the jurors] little choice, but I think they sort of vaguely felt in their minds that his superiors ordered it and he was in a bind. . . .'" Strasser, "Jury in North's Trial Settled on the Concrete; Abstractions Rejected," *Nat'l L.J.*, May 15, 1989, at 9; see also Schultz, supra note 2.

    Regarding the Goetz case and jury nullification, see G. Fletcher, supra note 9; Pinsley, "Goetz Appeal Explores Jury Nullification Issue," *Manhattan Lawyer*, Nov. 1, 1988, at 11; April 5, 1987, sec. 4, at 6, col. 1.

[52] *Fully Informed Jury Association, Media Handout* 2 (Oct. 30, 1990).

[53] Adler, "Courtroom Putsch?," *Wall St. J.*, Jan. 4, 1991, at A1, col. 1.

[54] FIJA has many other jury reform proposals besides the nullification issue. Discussion of them is beyond the scope of this article.

[55] See sources cited supra note 13.

[56] *The FIJActivist* 1 (Special Outreach Issue, 1990).

[57] Some of these bills, such as the ones in Arizona and Wyoming, have been defeated. Others remain to be debated.

[58] The authors would like to thank David J. Shagoury, aide to Senator Hedlund, for helpful discussions about jury nullification.

[59] Telephone interview with Massachusetts Senator Robert L. Hedlund (January 28, 1991). The authors would like to thank Senator Hedlund for providing us with additional information about his bill.

[60] See *Zenith Radio Corp. v. Matsushita Electric Indus. Co., Ltd.*, 478 F. Supp. 889 (E.D. Pa. 1979); V. Hans & N. Vidmar, supra note 13, at 160–63; Scheflin & Van Dyke, supra note 1, at 69–71.

[61] With this silver lining, however, comes a dark cloud. If judges do not give nullification instructions, or, worse yet, give a strong statement that jurors must follow the judge's instructions, jurors may rightly become confused about their role. Some judicial cooperation inevitably will be necessary.

[62] A. Lincoln, Address at Gettysburg (Nov. 19, 1863).

[63] Oregon's Constitution presently recognizes a right of jury power. Article I section 16 provides "In all criminal cases whatever, the jury shall have the right to determine the law, and the facts under the direction of the court as to the law, and the right of new trial, as in civil cases." *Ore. Const.* art. I, § 16.

[64] *Fauvre v. Roberts*, 309 Ore. 691, 694, 791 P.2d 128, 130 (1990).

[65] The Court ruled against proponents of the initiative who were challenging the wording of the description of the provision in the Attorney General's certification of the ballot title. Id. at 696, 791 P.2d at 132.

[66] Herzberg, supra note 12.

[67] At the bottom right of the advertisement there is a small box, labelled "ATTENTION LAWYERS," which contains a reference to our article in 43:4 *Law & Contemp. Prob.* 52 (1980). Neither of us was contacted before this reference was used. Statements in the advertisement are in direct contradiction to our position. We categorically and emphatically do not endorse jurors lying to judges nor do we endorse telling jurors to disbelieve everything they hear from judges.

[68] See Jackson, "DA's Office Decries 'Jury Nullification' Ad," *San Diego Union*, Jan. 26, 1990, at B1.

[69] The authors thank Jerry Mitchell, reporter for the Jackson, Mississippi *Clarion-Ledger*, for sending us the leaflet. This particular leaflet was sponsored by the Christian Action Group of Jackson, Mississippi.

[70] Sir Walter Scott, "Marmion," Canto VI, Stanza 17, in *Complete Poetical Works* 145 (1900).

[71] See supra text at note 65.

[72] Larry Dodge has reported a case from New York in which one of the jurors began to explain jury nullification to the others, but they sent a note to the judge about him. The judge permitted him to continue to deliberate after telling him to "keep his politics out of the case and apply the law as given." The juror agreed, went back to the deliberations, and hung the jury. He was later threatened with perjury and contempt charges, but they were never brought. Dodge, "A Complete History of the Power Rights and Duties of the Jury System," a talk delivered at the State of the Nation Conference, sponsored by the Texas Liberty Association (July 7, 1990).

Questions to Consider

1. In the Steele and Thornburg article about confusing jury instructions, what institutional interests prevent change? Some argue that trial court judges are merely following legal rules, but who makes these rules?

2. The issue of lawyers trying to manipulate the jury often becomes a matter of public discussion when celebrity criminal trials are broadcast by the media. There are usually two poles of argument. Some argue that we must let lawyers do what they want because "if they were your lawyers, wouldn't you want them to have the freedom to help you?" Others argue that the judge must prevent lawyers from using misleading tactics because jurors, throughout the whole process of the trial, may not be able to distinguish between such tactics and facts. Kassin points out that our current system of giving lawyers the ability to confuse while encouraging jury ignorance creates problems. Consider a third option: give the jury as much information as possible and trust in the joint common sense of 12 people. (Note that in criminal trials, all the jurors have to agree.) This option would include giving juries information on the potentially manipulative language of lawyers. What do you think would be the merits or demerits of such a system? Why haven't judges or lawyers accepted this third option? What, if any, shift in courtroom power would occur if this were put into effect?

3. What purposes are served by jury sequestration? Does this procedure really insulate juries from prejudicial publicity? Why or why not? What other mechanisms might courts use other than jury sequestration to achieve the same goals?

4. Our society has created many institutional systems in an attempt to meet our community needs, but invariably people try to play that system to their own personal advantage. For example, Scheflin and Van Dyke point out how some groups in society have tried to play the jury system by getting jurors with predetermined conclusions on specific cases. Does "playing the system," whether the system is a tax system, a welfare system, or a justice system, create pressures to destroy that

system even though it attempts to provide some level of justice for all? How do we retain a relatively good system in the face of those trying to abuse the system?

5. Scheflin and Van Dyke argue that judicial failure to inform jurors that they have the power to nullify a law only makes things worse. Do you agree or disagree? Why?

Section IV
Problems for the Judiciary

Courts, like all public institutions, face ongoing administrative problems. This section explores one of the most compelling and complex questions confronting court operation: who ultimately makes the decisions? To understand why this question is so complex, one must understand that courts are inherently political institutions, with judges and other members of the legal profession trying to maintain their independence from outside control.

David Orrick first looks at the growing societal trend to professionalize the administration of public institutions. The need for efficiency and competence, given limited resources, puts pressure on professional groups, such as doctors with hospitals and lawyers with courts, to yield some of their traditional power to others specifically trained to manage these complex institutions. While there is a valid need for professional independence, professional competence does not necessarily translate into administrative competence. The lack of competence leaves ordinary people to cope with disorganized and ineffective courts. The problem of improving disorganized courts is inhibited not only by the desire of judges to retain the reins of power, but also by the political nature of courts. For example, Orrick points out that political patronage rather than competence is often the basis for appointing court administrators, and that local authorities continue to battle with state authorities over control of court processes.

Taking a somewhat different tack in understanding court administration, Frances Bernat looks at how judges as a group, or perhaps more specifically the chief judges in any system of judges, look to manage the flow of cases through their system by manipulating the complex system of legal rules. This article looks very closely at one example in Arizona where the U.S. Supreme Court invalidated a state rule that took power away from juries in deciding issues related to Arizona's death penalty. It is both interesting and daunting to watch state courts seek to contain the broad implications of a Supreme Court ruling on their local discretionary decision making.

Elliot Slotnick continues the discussion of judicial independence by looking at how we choose our judges. If we want judges to be less political, we need to give them some measure of independence, yet in a democratic society we need to make our officials accountable. The tension between these needs is reflected in the various ways judges are chosen and retained. Slotnick points out that the tension between accountability and independence is currently out of balance. The concept of democratic accountability is unfortunately considered more as potential rather than made into reality.

The next article in section IV continues the theme of politics and power by addressing the pressing societal issues of race and diversity. Courts are part of our social fabric, and they do not escape from the problems faced by other institutions. Barbara Graham looks at the racial composition of judges in this country, and follows through with a primary question related to diversity: should our judges, to whom we give power over crucial issues in our lives, reflect who we are as a society? How good is that reflection, and how might we make the image more clear? Graham explains some of the structural problems inhibiting diversity in our judiciary, such as the fact that the pool of lawyers from which judges are chosen contains relatively few minorities. Interestingly, while politics may keep some minorities from being elected, the political perspective of state governors makes a major difference in whether minorities get appointed to the bench. Once minorities have their foot in the door, they, as other such appointees, are almost universally retained by the electorate.

Finally, we turn to a comprehensive analysis of the ways courts function by looking through the lens of wrongful convictions. Marvin Zalman provides a sobering analysis that starts with the probable fact that we wrongfully incarcerate approximately 3,500 to 7,400 innocent people each year in this country. Is this a sign that we have some major structural problems with our court system or is it simply an acceptable side effect of an imperfect human institution? If the latter, how many wrongful incarcerations would be OK? Is the fact that the poor, who account for over 80 percent of those prosecuted, are more likely to be both rightly and wrongly incarcerated and receive longer sentences in both situations a social justice problem? Similarly, if it is true, as the studies suggest, that prosecutorial misconduct was present in almost half of the convictions where the accused were later exonerated by DNA analysis, might we be giving prosecutors too much unchecked power? Zalman proposes some alternative models for how we might restructure our court process that are well worth our consideration.

13

Court Administration in the United States
The Ongoing Problems

DAVID ORRICK

This is a revision of a monograph originally prepared in the late 1980s. The need for updating stems in large part from the support for all branches of government provided by the constant developments in computers and in everything connected with them, from the Internet to software that is increasing in its user-friendly interface. Unfortunately, in other areas, the original concerns remain, and may, in some respects, have grown even more problematic.

In any review of the system by which justice is delivered in the United States at the beginning of the twenty-first century, the concept of "court administration" continues to play an important role. That review should begin with the publication of the President's Commission on Law Enforcement and Administration of Justice in 1967.[1] In that extraordinary document, specific reference was made for the need for improved administration in the courts, pursuant to the theme of the whole Report:

> States should provide for clear administrative responsibility within courts and should ensure that professional court administrators are available to assist the Judges in their management functions.[2]

The Report went on immediately to provide a useful working definition of the contribution a court administrator can make to the efficient operation of the courts:

Revised from an article reprinted by permission of the author from the *Anglo-American Law Review*, vol. 19 (Jan/March 1990), pp. 36–54.

(administrative officers can) aid the judiciary by collecting judicial statistics, managing fiscal affairs, supervising court personnel and performing duties in connection with the assignment of Judges and scheduling of cases.[3]

The passage of 40 years since that statement provides a more than civilized distance in time to review the extent to which this recommendation has been followed, and to offer some explanation for the failure, if any, to reach that goal. Unfortunately, it continues to be the premise of this paper that those goals have not been met, and that under the current and foreseeable circumstances, the problems in reaching them will be neither easily nor quickly solved.

For the courts' colleagues in the criminal justice system, the police and correctional agencies, the significance in this presidential report lies in its terrible stimuli, the specific trauma of the assassination of President Kennedy, and the general, miserable deterioration in human relations experienced in American cities during the 1960s, reflected in both the type and amount of crime, drug abuse, and riots that were taking place. These problems for those other parts of the criminal justice system, developing at the same time as an unprecedented expansion in criminal defendants' rights and the rights of access to the courts by poor people, have led to unprecedented stress on all components of the justice system, including the courts. Until the 1960s, America's courts were able to stumble along in an inefficient, poorly administered way. Since the 1960s, the need for well-administered courts, to handle an ever-increasing workload of more difficult cases, has been obvious to all.

It would be improper to begin by suggesting that the United States' concerns for court administration only began in the 1967 Report. The recommendations for improved court administration provided there should more properly be considered as part of what is at least the second, perhaps even the third, generation of high visibility efforts at such improvements. It is generally accepted that the original stimulus to recognize the need for efficient administrative practices in the courts came as far back as 1906, with Roscoe Pound's speech to the American Bar Association (ABA).[4] It was not until the mid-1930s, however, that the ABA really made any major efforts to come up with recommendations for improvement in this area. After this original sloth, the ABA must be given much credit, to this day, for its ongoing contributions, as most recently reflected in its Model State Judicial Article,[5] and comprehensive *Standards*.[6]

In the actual terms of concerns for administration being translated into positions with administrative duties, it is generally acknowledged[7] that the states of Ohio (1923), California (1926), and North Dakota (1927) were the first to do something. North Dakota's place in this early group is particularly interesting: even now, it is still one of the United States' most sparsely settled units, with the very generous ratio of one trial judge for every 3,430 people. It would not be the first American state court system one would think of when considering the possibilities of the usual administrative stress on the courts caused by high population numbers and the general problems government faces in America's heavily metropolitan states. North Dakota's numbers, for example, compare with the ratio in California, whose coastal area most certainly is heavily metropolitan, of one judge for every 17,634.[8]

More recently, New Jersey, under the leadership of the legendary Chief Justice Vanderbilt, is usually acknowledged as producing the first statewide administrative office in 1948. At the local level, the first trial court administrative office was established in the Los Angeles Superior Court— that forum of Sergeant Joe Friday and Dragnet fame—in 1957.[9]

Even prior to the production of the 1967 President's Commission Report, 25 of the states had established statewide court administrative offices.[10] In the 40 years since, all the rest of the states have established some sort of statewide function to deal with these administrative concerns, with jurisdictionwide offices in the District of Columbia, Guam, and Puerto Rico as well. The incumbents of these offices together form the Conference of Court Administrators (COSCA), which began life in the mid-1950s as the National Conference of Court Administrative Officers (NCCAO).

National organizations for trial court administrators have existed for some time: the original National Association for Court Administration (NACA) merged with the National Association of Trial Court Administrators (NATCA) to become the National Association of Court Managers (NACM) in the early 1980s. Organizations such as these are able to interact nicely with groups such as the Conference of Chief Justices (CCJ) and the various groups representing the interests of the states' trial Judges. The very existence of these groups is a positive sign.

Yet in some states there is still sufficient wariness about the credibility and authority of an administrator per se in the court system that the incumbent holds a judge's title and rank, perhaps on the feeling that one judge will only listen to another judge, whatever the topic. New York calls its equivalent to other states' State Court Administrator "Chief Administrative Judge." In New York's neighbouring state, Connecticut, is another of the United States' oldest and most established state court systems, where the State Court Administrator also holds judicial rank.

Because of details like this, there is still much substance to the general feeling in the 1967 Report's observation: "In many . . . states (having such an office) the functions of this office are limited, and its potential has not yet been realized."[11]

This observation could even be shared with those offices that have been created since 1967. In Vermont, for example, the State Court Administrator's office, created in 1968, has had to contend all along in its trial court of general jurisdiction with lay Judges, whose position there seems sacrosanct. The anachronistic assignment system for the lawyer Judges on that court dates back to the circuit riding days of Chief Justice John Marshall: it seems equally sacrosanct. This is a specific example; in the remainder of this paper we suggest some general reasons why that potential has not been realized.

The Court Administrator and the Judicial Role

To the extent to which the professional literature is a barometer of the concerns in the (academic) field, the need for court administrators has long been part of conventional wisdom. One searches in vain for monographs with titles that suggest otherwise. Yet it is possible that a properly conducted research exercise might raise the possibility that there is still some doubt among the Judges as to this need. It is the basic justification for the court administrator's position that he can relieve the Judge of many of the routine tasks that go along with the management of any agency, inside or outside the justice system.

Ideally, this frees up the Judge to concentrate on providing justice in the individual case, resolving the specific dispute between the litigants, or determining the guilt or innocence of the defendant to the criminal charge—the "micro" sense of justice, to steal the shorthand of Malthus' dismal science—while allowing the administrator to provide justice in the broader, "macro" sense by keeping the court running at its most efficient on an overall, day-by-day basis.

When the Judge and administrator can work together in close harmony, the Judge's adjudicative skills, ultimately what he is being paid uniquely to provide, can be exercised to the fullest in a *sequence* of individual cases.

Reality suggests otherwise. In many states, the judge continues to be an elected official, at both the trial and appellate levels. This can even include the Chief Justice himself of the Supreme Court, or its terminological equivalent. (Is it reflective of the problems courts face that there is not even agreement among the states on the title of that court of last resort?) It has been one of the provocative, but time-honoured traditions of the American governmental process that "to the winner go the spoils."[12] In many elective positions in America, the successful candidate, whether or not in the judiciary, has several positions that are his to fill under the general power of patronage.[13] The newly elected Judge can "bring on his own team," to include such close assistants as private secretaries, law clerks, court officers, etc.

It does not necessarily follow that these team members are in any way qualified to hold the positions to which they are appointed. In the usual way of things, they are people who have been (financial) supporters or campaign workers for the Judge during his election campaign, people to whom the Judge is returning a favour. It does follow that such a court system is subject to interruption in the experience level of people holding important, if sometimes low visibility, jobs. A Judge's private secretary, who organizes his calendar, and his law clerk, who does his legal research, can have a lot to do with the pace with which he delivers his findings of fact, for example. Almost accidentally, perhaps, Aikman's recent work[14] includes several charming, if disturbing, anecdotes about the relationship of Judge to Administrator, and the latter's job security under differing selection processes for the former. These are part of the idiosyncratic charm of Aikman's work. They probably would not be accepted by the publishing protocols for texts in police science and correctional administration. In Aikman's case, they are a precious resource, reflective of his decades of experience in front-line court administration. They would also be valuable fuel for a doctoral student looking for a thesis topic. Many of Aikman's comments can be examined empirically, in the best traditions of social science's continuing obsession with empiricism.

In some instances, this susceptibility to change may affect the Chief Court Administrator for the state himself, a very high visibility position. In the controversial and hard-fought election for Chief Justice in Ohio in November 1986, the incumbent was defeated for reelection. That defeat also led to a change in State Court Administrators, to nobody's surprise, since the incumbent Administrator was correctly perceived to be very personally associated with the defeated Chief Justice.

The spoils system is totally contrary to the English tradition of governmental support jobs—the Civil Service, in the crudest embrace of that term, being protected from such change. It is not the purpose here to discuss the advantages and disadvantages of the spoils system. Rather, we emphasize the effect it can have on the experience level of those involved in administrative matters in the court. Decisions from the bench get made in the individual case, regardless of who the decision-maker is and the turnover in Judges. But great value is lost to the ongoing process of administration when the incumbent administrator's position is tied too strongly to that of the Judge, so that if the Judge goes, the administrator, and all the *in loco* experience he has gained, goes too. As long as judicial positions continue to be elective, and the feeling persists that patronage is still an appropriate part of the judicial scenario, there is no easy end in sight to this problem.

Job Qualifications and Experience

There are not likely to be many formal job qualifications in situations where the administrator position is a patronage appointment for the

Judge. The person who took over the State Court Administrator's position in Ohio in November 1986 had no prior experience as a court administrator at any level.[15]

But even in states with appointive Judges, and the possibly stronger sense of continuity in administrative matters that this may allow, the issue of the experience and the qualifications the court administrator brings to his job is still an open book. An assertive judiciary could go a long way to curing this by imposing its own standards. But it would be hard for the Judges to impose strict criteria on formal educational and experience attainments. In many of the individual United States, the Judges themselves have no formal job credentials other than having been admitted to the state bar for a period of time. Their own context is no guide for them, nor can they look to outside bodies such as universities for assistance in establishing job credentials for their administrators.

In large part because of the stimuli provided by the 1967 President's Commission, the number of degree programmes in "criminal justice"—approximately the same area of study that Europe knows as "criminology"—has exploded since 1967. They now number well over 600. Inside that number, there may be no more than 10 to 15 programmes emphasizing court administration matters through major programmes or actual degrees.[16] At the Master's level, three academic institutions, the University of Southern California, American University, and the University of Denver, offered a Master's Degree in Judicial Administration. None of these programmes exist any longer in their original form. In the best traditions of American private education, the University of Denver's programme has switched to preparing people to become law firm administrators as well as Court Administrators, with the former the predominant group of students. Given the difference in salaries between the public and private sector, this may be no great surprise. American University still shows some interest in Court Administration, as shown by its work with the Bureau of Justice Assistance on a Judicial Leadership Forum held in December 2004.[17]

Compared to the almost limitless opportunities he would have to pursue a career in police or correctional administration, where a programme is available in each of the 50 states, with most states having such a programme in one of the state-funded colleges or universities, the would-be court administrator has few choices. In a land 3,000 miles from coast to coast, he may have to go a long way from home to pursue the court choice. Attending a programme in some state other than his own ensures much larger tuition and travel costs. This possibility of great expense may well mean that some capable would-be court administrators have not been able to read for a degree for financial reasons. This is another problem with no easy end in sight.

The explanations for this lack of programmes quickly become circular. The earliest consequence of the presentation of the 1967 Report was legislation, the Omnibus Crime Control and Safe Streets Act of 1968.[18] Among other things, this statute led to financial assistance being given to universities in developing criminal justice programmes: perhaps at least as importantly, financial assistance was also offered to students pursuing careers in criminal justice, who wanted to take university-level courses, and/or read for a degree in that field.

One of the most provocative statements in the whole 1967 Report opened the Courts Chapter: "the criminal court is the central, crucial institution in the criminal justice system . . ."[19] but it did not lead, via the 1968 Safe Streets Act, to the development of a lot of degree courses or programmes emphasizing court administration. This paper is not the appropriate forum to grumble too long about those missed opportunities. What can and must be done is to emphasize the impact of this lack of an educational infrastructure on the position of court administrators in the United States.

As a direct result of this lack of educational underpinning to the field of court administration, there is no generally accepted *academic,* i.e., university degree based credential for entry to a position in the field in court administration, in the same way, for example, that the Master's degree in Social Work (MSW) was accepted for so long as the probation officer's union card. There is now some healthy challenge to the MSW from the development of Master's level programmes in criminal justice. That competition has been healthy, even to the point that it may have produced an embarras de richesse. It has certainly helped to lead to a reexamination of the direction for probation, with a heightened awareness of its place as a sanction.[20] Court administration has no such luxury available to it.

The closest the nation has to an accrediting body for court administrators is the Institute for Court Management (ICM), now an arm of the National Center for State Courts (NCSC). The ICM offers a variety of courses, unquestionably of great relevance for the court administrator-to-be, which can eventually lead to the credential of "Fellow."

In something of a catch-22 situation, these courses are usually aimed at people already in administrative positions: in something approaching academic incest, it was common for incumbent senior members of the NCSC's own staff to become ICM fellows. Moreover, ICM, whilst independent in its days in Denver, was not a degree granting institution, and is unlikely ever to become so, unless it can be formally associated with an accredited university. While in Denver, the University of Denver would have been the obvious choice. Now, with the NCSC's headquarters physically on the campus of the Law School at William and Mary College, the affiliation choice is equally obvious. But it has not happened, and is not likely to. Until then, the world of court administration must be grateful for William and Mary's hospitality. It would for that reason not attract someone interested in receiving a "relevant" college degree to use in his career. Nor, unfortunately, may the noncredit certificate program that Michigan State University, pre-eminent in its contributions to police science and to traffic matters, is developing in conjunction with NACM.[21] If only MSU would get into the courts' waters with both of its large Spartan feet!

It would be wrong, even by implication, to lay blame for the lack of development of courses and degree programmes in court administration at the feet of those energetic souls who developed the field of criminal justice as a whole into the thriving component of academe that it represents today. The lack of courses and programmes in court administration is simply a mysterious absence in face of the important contribution that the field of public administration as a whole has made to American academe. Courses in public administration are a vital part of the skeleta of degree programmes in politics (sometimes called political science or government in American university nomenclature). As Hays and Graham argue, in their *Handbook of Court Administration*,[22] court administration is "simply a specialized form of public administration."[23]

It cannot be easily explained why courses in court administration did not develop as a natural part of courses on public administration and other parts of politics curricula, when courses in constitutional law, the Supreme Court, and judicial theory are time-honoured areas of study. That is for another time, and the analysis of the politics of curriculum development. There certainly did not need to be those terrible stimuli provided by the social upheaval of the 1960s, which led to programmes in criminal justice being developed, for programmes in court administration to have developed at universities.

Over the years, the best "court-watchers" in academe that were able to explain appellate court voting patterns at the drop of a notepad—these days, the personal computer—have been the researchers in politics faculties.[24] This contact refutes the argument that is occasionally made, suggesting that courses in court administration have not developed because non-legally trained scholars are intimidated by the court environment. It makes the failure of academe to be more interested in matters of court administration all the more of a mystery, again with no obvious resolution in sight.

Management Skills

As a direct result of the general lack of qualifications for the court administrator positions, it is not surprising to find that the most sophisticated management techniques, whether or not dependent on the use of the most up-to-date technology, are not being used in America's courts. It is not to criticize the incumbent court administrator to note this, when the explanation is probably that most of these incumbents have never received any formal management training. In far too many of America's courts, even highly cost-effective personal computers are still not being used for much of the humdrum repetitive accounting and word processing work the courts must perform. One would not, could not, expect to see them in operation if the administrator himself is unaware of their capabilities. The lack of up-to-date equipment in a court may be more apparent to the casual visitor than the lack of up-to-date management techniques, but both absences reduce the highest efficiency of the courts.

At its worst, this lack of use of top management skills can cost the government, and vicariously, the individual taxpayer, large sums of money. One of the characteristics about courts that is so easily overlooked is their responsibility as money handlers. Without any of the hoopla attached to a bank, an extraordinary amount of money is taken in by the average court in America on a routine, continuing daily basis.

The combination of court filing fees, court costs, and fines is in addition to the comparatively staggering amount of money that the court now handles in its more recently developed role as broker in enforcing child support payments against the obligated parent, which itself adds up to millions of dollars. In many instances, because of a lack of sophisticated money-management skills in the court administrator's office, this money, which could have been placed in (short-term) interest-bearing accounts from which the government would profit, sits around idly in a current account. These are the harsh consequences of a lack of skills. It may be hard to measure the impact of unskilled administrators not being able to produce maximum efficiency from their judicial and nonjudicial staff. A lack of dollars is very easily measured.

Now, at the beginning of the twenty-first century, untrained court administrators face the challenge of persuading their judges and/or politicians of the value of accepting credit and debit cards in payment for court fees and fines, when that is the reality of the world of purchases and bill payments. That which has made life so simple for the retail community has not yet been fully embraced by the courts.

Upsetting the Apple Cart

Reference has been made above to the influence of the President's Commission, via its own literature, and more importantly, the legislation it spawned, on the administration of justice. Notwithstanding its view of the centrality of the criminal court to the criminal justice process, the basic theme of the Commission's legacy has been crime control. In that respect, the title of the enabling act speaks volumes in its reference to "safe streets."

One of the immediate results of the Safe Streets Act was the creation of a federal funding agency, the Law Enforcement Assistance Agency (LEAA), which served for many years as a conduit for federal funds to the states' criminal justice systems. That this money was necessarily provided via the conduit of an executive branch agency was an ongoing source of irritation to the courts, in a problem distinctive, if not unique, to the United States with their dedication to maintaining the separation of (governmental) powers.

The reality of the delivery of LEAA funds was that the courts perceived themselves as having to deal with executive agencies, invariably attached to the governor's office in the individual states, to receive these moneys, in competition with other executive agencies, the police, and corrections. In comparative terms, the courts did not receive as much from the LEAA coffers as seemed appropriate to their role as one-third of the criminal justice system, in the crude breakdown of "Police, Courts and Corrections." And even inside that breakdown, much of the money technically identified for the courts' use was spent on prosecutorial and other matters:

> expenditures for "purely courts" . . . include(d) "alternatives to institu-
> tionalization," "community-based detention," "pretrial detention,"
> "investigating units," "youth services," "probation programs," and
> other non-court functions.[25]

Even though it was "raided" by these other recipients, the pot of money received by the courts in absolute terms from the federal government through LEAA was quite substantial. During the existence of LEAA, approximately $256 million from LEAA discretionary funds, and approximately $344 million from LEAA formula funds (the former block grants), were allocated for state court improvements.[26] But still, by comparison with what the other components received, it did not seem like much. For the courts, this was the worst of both worlds: comparatively an inadequate amount of money, provided through an awkward funding mechanism.

The courts' interaction with LEAA through the state's funding agencies was at best an unhappy marriage. This is not to imply that an infusion of money is a complete solution to the courts' administrative problems and planning capabilities. Rather, we suggest that many energetic people in the state court systems were needlessly distracted by the mechanisms by which the money was provided, and spent more of that energy on changing those mechanisms than in improving the courts.

These complaints were heard. By the mid-1970s, the Crime Control Act of 1976 had led to the creation of separate state judicial planning committees. The Conference of Chief Justices created a Task Force on a State Court Improvement Act in 1978, largely because those planning concepts introduced in the 1976 legislation had not seemed to work. That action led, in

1984, to the creation of the State Justice Institute (SJI) as a direct federal mechanism to fund state courts with federal money. The Act specifies that the recipients, either by grant or contract, of the SJI's funds would be:

> "state and local courts and their agencies" and "national non-profit organizations controlled by, operating in conjunction with, and serving the judicial branches of state governments."[27]

With the establishment of the State Justice Institute, the gauntlet was thrown more squarely at the courts' feet to make those improvements in court administration, unencumbered by influence from the other branches of government as to the use of that money.

Later, in 1993, in a somewhat entrepreneurial development that has been seen elsewhere in the field, former employees of the NCSC created the Justice Management Institute (JMI). Together with the State Justice Institute, JMI has made valuable contributions, especially in the fields of case-flow management and records management.

It would be nice to be able to say that the establishment of these three significant organizations, NCSC, SJI, and JMI, has solved the states' courts' needs for supplementary funds to improve the field of court administration. A different conclusion must be drawn. At first glance, it may seem a matter for a dinner-table conversation why the SJI and the NCSC are needed side-by-side when their basic missions seem so similar. When a commitment by Chief Justices as a genre to the improvement in their own states' courts is an unwritten part of their job description, it would be churlish to criticize them for their success in getting the 1978 State Court Improvement Act to lead to the delivery of the SJI in "only" six years. The current Chairman and Vice-Chairman of the Board of Directors of SJI, as of November 2007, are both retired Chief Justices from state courts.

The mission of SJI has included serving as an information clearinghouse across the board for the state courts, establishing resource centers with a practical emphasis, allowing work-shop approaches for exposure to new technologies and courthouse methods. SJI's mission also included support for convening significant meetings, up to the national level, to assist in the application of new developments in court work. In addition, SJI provides for the delivery of state-to-state "technical assistance," specifically focused at a particular jurisdiction's distinctive challenges. These duties have often duplicated services already being provided, with considerable conceptual success, by the NCSC.

The NCSC is largely a self-funded resource by the state courts, for them to use as needed. There is a certain, quasi-constitutional elegance to this design. It is surely an example of the Tenth Amendment in action—*the powers not delegated to the United States by the Constitution . . . are reserved to the States respectively.* Like the Council on State Governments, the NCSC has shown that the states can work together fairly well. This structure can itself explain why the NCSC has itself seen some lean times, when state budgets have, from time to time, not easily allowed expenditures on the external help that NCSC can provide, given that NCSC's help has mostly been provided on a project-by-project basis.

With the same seductiveness that attached to the LEAA, the SJI has provided federal funds to state courts not previously available. The reality of SJI has been, of course, that it has been forever subject to the whimsy of Congress for its ongoing funding. With the SJI, a distinct measure of federal fiscal influence, much more targeted to the states' courts than the LEAA funds ever were, has been incorporated into the "improvements" formula.

But, if the (federal) lord giveth, the Lord (can) taketh away. So, by as early as FY 2002, Congress' Appropriations Bill, with a sunset budget, called for the demise of SJI by September 30, 2003, the end of the federal fiscal year. "Saving SJI" became the states' courts' version of *Saving Private Ryan*. Both exercises, albeit successful, generated casualties.

That fiscal leverage has become even more distinct. Use of outside money by public agencies to support attendance at conferences and meetings has always carried with it the potential of the "junket" abuse of support funds. SJI's scholarship funding can no longer be used to pay for state court personnel to attend annual conferences, for example. By FY 2006, Congress required cash matches for its SJI grants. Hitherto, SJI had frequently used soft matches, that notorious form of money laundering that made it to the major leagues with LEAA. The response has been enlightening. In FY 2005, requests for SJI funding included only $392,892 as cash match. For FY 2007 applications, that match amount had grown to $3.66 million.[28] The states are collectively riding a tiger, and are clearly not yet prepared to jump off. There has, at least in the courts, been some progress from the wretched fiscal excess of LEAA in its heyday, with the federal government dispensing "goodies" to state law enforcement agencies who could only have dreamed of the receipt of such largess without that external funding source. Sadly, the concept of Homeland Security has taken us back to those days for law enforcement.

Then, as now, the courts, in their comparative innocence, were free of sucking on such federal udders. It would be wrong to say that the SJI is not needed, although the token budget (the U.S. House approved $4.64 million and the U.S. Senate even less, $3.5 million for FY 2008[29]) is a fiscal insult in view of the courts' overall needs. As an example: Vermont, whose courts' needs for support in languages other than English are much smaller than many more heterogeneous states, received a grant from SJI to improve court interpreter services at SJI's final FY 2007 Board of Directors' meeting.[30] This is the sort of issue that should be addressed at the national level, involving such organisations as the Modern Language Association and the American Bar Association with their enormous collateral resources.

SJI will remain an important conduit for support to state courts. Clearly, its annual budget needs to be increased to make its role even more valuable. Even without such fiscal improvement, SJI will continue to be of assistance to NCSC, often relying on the latter for its own support of the states' courts.

Jurisdictional Variety

In documenting the history of the creation of court administrative offices earlier, proper distinction was made between the establishment of the first statewide office and the first local office. As local courts expand in size, it is most appropriate to have local administrative offices established. The sheer size of many of the American states makes it hard for a central office in the state capital to effectively administer the local courts spread round the jurisdiction. It makes great good sense if the statewide office can thus have the link of the local administrative office, when it is the same state-wide law that is being processed through all the different locations.

Yet, in a matter not unrelated to the ongoing influence of an elective judiciary, the problem exists of the local court administrator serving two masters—his local (chief) trial Judge, and the state court administrator in the state capital. With this influence of local tradition, it is not hard to see why there are some states, such as Illinois—where the local influence is still so strong that even justices of the State Supreme Court are elected on a regional basis—in which the influence of the statewide administrator is by no means as great as it could be. This is that unreached potential to which the President's Commission referred. The disturbing point is that the potential will remain as unattainable for the foreseeable future.

Funding Source Variety

One of the key explanations for the ongoing local influence on the courts, even in the face of a long-established statewide administrative office, is the influence of the funding source, a dependency that can range from paper clips to new buildings. The majority of courts in the United States continue to be funded locally, typically at the county level. This invariably means that administrative improvements that the statewide administrator and his local trial court colleague want to make have to be funded locally. Both may want computers to be installed to assist in coordinating court statistics across the state, and for the myriad repetitive tasks for which the machines are preeminently suited. But without their ability to sell the idea to the local legislators, the idea will go a-wasting. Again, the role of the local Judge cannot be ignored. In an elective situation, he may not want to alienate the local political power base to which he undoubtedly owes much assistance in his own election by looking greedy, by making his own court too "fancy." He may well have run an election campaign based on frugal efficiency in the court system, totally in conflict with the legitimate needs of both the local and statewide court administrators.

Adequacy of the Physical Plant

The role of bricks and mortar in the orderly administration of justice cannot be downplayed. The great majority of America's courthouses were built in the nineteenth century. They are a wonderful living monument to the architectural and popular attitudes toward government of that century:

> A committee from Pike County, Illinois visited the court house at Clinton, Missouri [and] reported to its own constituents that ". . . after you have gone through [it] leaves you feeling you are sorry you entered. . . . It gives you a mean opinion of the people of the County." There was widespread sentiment, then, that the beauty sometimes and the size often of the local dispensary of justice was in fact a mirror of the aspirations and character of the county which it served.[31]

They are proof of the preparedness of the taxpayers to invest hardearned dollars in visual proof of the role of the court in society. The typical American county courthouse dominates the older part of the county seat's skyline in much the same way as the church or cathedral influences the landscape of English municipal life. This is proper in a society that does not espouse an established religion, where the courthouse plays much the same role as the church in England. It is the courthouse to which one goes in the United States to look for birth records at the local level: it was at the Appomattox courthouse that the Civil War surrender took place.

Unfortunately, these courthouses must now be damned with much faint praise. Although many of them are architectural masterpieces, they are by and large unsuited to the way in which justice is "dispensed" today. These are courthouses where the courtroom dominates the building, and where there are proportionately few support offices: in the 1890s, there was little need for them. The typical mid-nineteenth century courthouse in America was an extravagant building. In many instances, the courthouse at the time of its construction was the most expensive government building in the county. Unfortunately, this extravagance often took the form of sheer size and splendour, and not in office space, which may have been excessive at the time of construction, but into which the court could have moved as its needs changed.

The roll of time has made many of America's courthouses into architectural white elephants. Because of the methods of construction, often they cannot easily be adapted to suit the modern needs of multiple support offices with separate needs. On top of this, there is the relentless increase in the number of records to be stored. Needs may change, but records just continue to build up. In fact, as many American historians have discovered, the county courthouse in America is a veritable gold mine of information. In the continuing absence of university programmes in court administration, for the foreseeable future the only university types likely to go near courthouses will be the historians, dealing ad hoc with these precious records, however well-managed.

When it is the instinct, if not the very definition of the law, to preserve, the not infrequent problem one sees in the American courthouse is of an information repository bursting at the seams. It should not be the court administrator's job, at the local or even the state level, to be an archivist. All too often, he has to be.

In short, many of America's courthouses need to be rebuilt, or extensively renovated. The latter option is not always available to the court's leadership because of the construction of the building. So, even in that situation where the court administrator has been able to persuade the county commissioners to provide him with the computer support, for example, that he so badly needs to keep up with all those records he keeps accumulating, he may then turn round and find he is in a building totally unsuited both electrically[32] and environmentally to the sensitive requirements of high technology. The temperature and humidity levels that must be contended with during the summer in many of the American states are beastly. The observation that court folks in the late 1800s, in the days before central air-conditioning, were wise enough not to hold court in high summer is no solution to those who must sweat through the year-round exercise represented by modern court processing demands.

What is equally clear is that the court administrator who would strive for a new courthouse, in order to take fullest advantage of modern management skills and technology, does not have the support for government expenditures that the court system enjoyed in the late 1800s. The fiscal reality of the early twenty-first century is one of taxpayer revolts, tax caps, limitations on government spending in the states, etc. Nor is this to suggest that the typical modern court administrator is as concerned with the grandeur of the building as court-related people seemed to be in the later 1800s. Even the hard-nosed attitude of producing a functional building will be hard to translate into bricks and mortar, when government expenditures are proportionately so limited. It would also be difficult to sell the county electorate and legislature on the need for some characterless modern "office building" to replace that magnificent structure on the corner of America's equivalent of High Street and Church Street.

The Rays of Hope

The above cannot be pictured as too happy an image of the constraints on effective court administration in the United States: more than once, pessimism has been expressed in this paper over the likelihood of the problem-causing conditions being changed. In some instances, the problems are not even distinctively American in nature. Courts all over the Western world are faced by such problems as increasing caseloads and a build-up of records. But by injecting some optimism into the view of the future, certain developments and characteristics of the court administration scene should be listed as possible aids in alleviating the problems.

The Role of Organizations

Roscoe Pound's rallying cry was delivered at the annual meeting of the ABA. We repeat here the compliment, that after its sloth in not reacting to Pound's goads earlier, the ABA has consistently been at the forefront in recommending improvements in court administration, and, for that matter, in the whole of the criminal justice system. The maturation of the professional organizations representing the interests of both statewide and local court administrators has helped those involved in the field to have a better sense of their own identity, a crucial detail in the absence of official credentialing bodies and some other sense of fraternity. COSCA now has routine and useful dialogues with CCJ, itself no less valuable as a linking device for the Chief Justices in the individual states, and is able to speak on behalf of the state courts with a national voice. The two organizations are even smart enough to hold their annual meetings back-to-back to enhance the fluidity of that dialogue.

The National Association of Court Managers (NACM), with over 2,500 members, but needing many more for its help to be fully appreciated, will continue to provide a valuable service given its emphasis on trial court administration and its valuable publication, *The Court Manager.*

Major Independent Meetings

In recent years, important publicity has been given to the problems of court administration through several meetings held in their own right, and not just as component parts of annual meetings of such organizations as the American Society of Criminology, the Academy of Criminal Justice Sciences, or the American Society of Public Administration. The number of papers presented on court administration there has always been miserably low. The independent meetings include the aptly titled reprise of the title of Pound's speech, "The National Conference on the Causes of Popular Dissatisfaction with the Administration of Justice" (affectionately known as the "Pound Conference"). This was held in 1976, and spawned local versions in many of the individual states in that same year. There have also been the First (1971) and Second (1978) National Conferences on the Judiciary, the latter of which (both were held in Williamsburg, Virginia) also served as the opening ceremony of the headquarters of the newly moved NCSC. Later, in 1988, the NCSC hosted the most important conference held to date on the issue of technology in the courts.[33]

LEAA and Its Progeny

For all the controversy that has been attached to LEAA and the comparative amount of help that it gave to the courts, that help was substantial in absolute terms. Whatever the "procedural" problems, LEAA was the direct or indirect stimulus for many major developments in the courts. It must be hoped that the SJI, designed as the "courts-only" federal support agency, will be able to make progress from that original awkward stimulus through delivery mechanisms the courts find more acceptable.

Publications

In addition to the *Standards* published by the ABA, another important reference document was produced with LEAA support—the findings of the National Advisory Commission on Criminal Justice Standards and Goals.[34] These national standards provide a useful comparison with, and, in most instances, a supporting view for the ABA's proposals. Although the number of texts and ordinary reference material—such stuff as the routine products of university-based textbook writers—for court administration is minuscule in comparison to the amount of such material available for the other components of the criminal justice system, some important work has been done. One example is the Gallases' text, *Managing the Courts*,[35] which has been argued as providing the first comprehensive definition of court administration.[36]

There are also now referred journals, such as the *Justice System Journal*, beginning in 1975, published by the ICM, and the *Judge's Journal*, from the ABA, both emphasizing matters concerning the courts. These are more recent publications coming along to help out *Judicature*, for so long the only worker in the vineyard. All these are in addition to the coverage routinely given to court-related matters in the main *ABA Journal*. When so much comment, hardly positive, has been made about the lack of university involvement in court administration, it may be noted that the American Judicature Society, with its long-running *Judicature* magazine, has moved from Chicago, and is now associated with Drake University in Des Moines, Iowa.

For its part, NACM produces *The Court Manager* on a quarterly basis, with practical assistance to court administrators alongside articles meeting the ordinary standards of university-sourced monographs. What remains absent is a substantial literature involving court matters in the major criminal justice journals that do not claim to be police- or corrections-specific.

By way of a "footnote," to the matter of publications, it may be noted that the basic textbooks on courts, serving those universities who do bother to offer at least an introductory class on the courts, are now in long number editions. That is testimony to their quality and staying power. As an example: David Neubauer's *America's Courts and the Criminal Justice System*, published by Thomson Wadsworth, the behemoth publishing group, recently went to its ninth edition. It is better than most, but like all its "competition," it lacks much content on court administration. In well over 400 pages, Neubauer has less than one page on court administration!

Independent Technological Developments

Notwithstanding the possibly disparaging comments made above about the level of managerial skills displayed by the largely untrained court administrators, there have been independent technological developments, as discussed so fully back at the Denver conference, that have allowed court administrators to succeed despite their own limitations in their workplace. It is as if those three legs of the tripod—word processing,[37] the database, and spreadsheets[38]—on which the enormous success of the personal computer (the PC) has been built, were specially designed for the courts. This is immediately useful assistance available to even the smallest courts.

With the constant improvements in the software that is the modern computer's raison d'etre, today's major word processing programmes allow the trial judge to prepare his findings of fact by himself, in legible typescript, rather than iffy handwriting. Word processing has even turned many appellate judges into more productive opinion-writers, when delays in preparing drafts for review are minimized.

To their credit, the courts were aware early of the value of word processing. There is a certain irony to the states' early use of word processing provided by Wang. For its time, the Wang software was very good, and their products were put to good use by the courts. Unfortunately, Wang was one of those manufacturers collected in the thinning out of the competition, as they underestimated the perceived value of personal computer development. The IBM PC came along, and when Mr. Gates was able to persuade

IBM of the value of his DOS operating system to make them work, the ignition switch was fired on the remorseless juggernaut of the MS-DOS based operating system. This has culminated in the latest version of Microsoft Office, in its Word word processing component being thrust on the courts. Even WordPerfect, the mature word processing product before Word was even born, and well-suited to legal needs, has suffered from the marketing power of the Microsoft Office suite being incorrectly perceived by courts as working better with the Windows operating system.

For all his genius, An Wang, after whom his eponymous product was named, did not anticipate the development of the personal computer, and the sense of personal control it gave the individual at each desk. He was not alone. Ask the folks at Digital.

In an exquisite irony, in the year 2007, almost every computer in any size or category of courthouse is now part of a network. From the perspective of the individual data enterer—some of whom were the young assistant court clerks back in the mid-1980s, who are now approaching retirement—his or her keyboard might as well be the dumb terminal of the late 1970s. Part of a network, the ability to store material to the CPU at that desk sitting alongside that keyboard was lacking. In one sense, the wheel has come full circle. It does come in handy to be able to save material to that local CPU, but that happens less and less as the network becomes even better.

Even more so than ever, it is essential that the computer support people, or if you must, the "Information Technology" folks, have an awareness of the unique needs faced in the courts. As a result of the lack of ability of computer network professionals to have learned about the distinctive needs of the courts before starting to work in that environment (because of that wholesale absence of courses in college on court administration), they often lack that awareness. They learn as they go along, taught by administrators who also lack that college preparation. Well-meaning errors get compounded that way. As Aikman notes, at the local government level, trial courts often piggy-back on computers systems originally designed for hospitals.[39]

The development of the spreadsheet has been of enormous help to the courts. There is nothing more tedious than the manual assembly of those statistical data that are essential for the good management of case flow (dealing with the cases in board), and an awareness of the consequences of caseload (the cases entering and leaving the system). Unfortunately, there is no national standard in spreadsheet design. This is the sort of thing that could easily be done at the universities, if there was more investment in court administration majors. So, there is extraordinary variance in what information is easily available from one state to another.

The development of "the computer" has also allowed the ability to handle information that would have been unthinkable in the past. Even if there are no national standards, calendaring software is useful. It allows the scheduling of cases to be done efficiently. A skill that required the experience of a veteran court worker is now gone.

The development of the Internet, and the World Wide Web, has also been of enormous value to the courts. In the past, depending on the size and workload of the court, one or more full-time workers might be needed to handle information inquiries from the public as to the scheduling of case activities such as motions hearing, trials, arraignments, and so forth. Now, Joe and Joan Public use the telephone, or more likely, some form of even higher speed electronic access, to find such information out for themselves. There may be no single aspect of computer development more useful to the courts than this.

Now, electronic filing is de rigueur in certain court contexts. In another of his wonderful anecdotes, Aikman notes a conversation with Norman Meyer, the Clerk of the U.S. Bankruptcy Court for the U.S. District of New Mexico, where the latter estimates that 90% of the filings in that court are electronic.[40] This is a bittersweet follow-up to this author's receipt of an award for his proposal, albeit with the added temptation of a fee discount, for electronic filing, as presented at that National Center Technology Conference back in 1988!

Typically, today's citizen can find the court's calendar, or even simply learn about its workload, from a link on the court's Web site. Unfortunately, the problem is the unacceptable variety in the quality of Web sites, at both the state and local (trial court) level. Some are very good, others are awful. No claim is made that it was a world-class research experiment, but this author's students, in a standard, introductory level course on the courts, quickly came to this conclusion from a required class presentation where they were required to show a state court's home page. To suggest that Web sites maintained by (state) police and correctional agencies may not be much better is not the point here, since those sites do not need to be as user-friendly to citizens seeking public information about the day-by-day activity of the agency and their interaction with it.

In a similar vein, the Internet allows court fees and fines to be paid online. As long as this concept is properly supported, it relieves the courts of the enormous responsibility of being daily money-handlers at a volume that would make a corner-store owner proud. To use this online feature to its fullest may logically require a preparedness of the courts to accept credit and debit card payment methods. Immediately the question is raised, should the courts, or the government unit of which it is part, be prepared to accept that fee, typically a few percentage points, on the total amount that is the bank's incentive to offer credit cards. The bird in the hand, a credit card payment, is worth 94% of the one in the bush. While this is no different a question from whether one should be able to use a credit card to pay for a driver's license at the Department of Motor Vehicles, the lack of debate—the stuff of university life—is reflective of the lack of guidance being offered to court administrators.

At both the local and higher levels, advances in technology have already allowed the court administrator to ignore somewhat the problem of a building ill-suited to some technological upgrades. Ironically, in the smaller courts, some of those problems identified with the first computer revolution, that generated by affordable mainframes, have never been faced, as those courts moved straight into the second revolution in computers, the rise of the (networked) PC and desktop publishing, developments of great value to courts. PCs are less much demanding of controlled humidity environments than mainframe computers supported by "dumb" terminals. The development of wireless networks has been an even greater godsend, at much less cost than the mere networking of a courthouse with a wired system. Those old buildings from the nineteenth century are not always amenable to walls being ripped apart and being rewired with an aesthetically pleasing result. Wireless networks should also make the courthouses more lawyer-friendly, as the advocates remain able to stay in touch with their offices while waiting for their hearings to begin.

Similar advances have been made in video technology, with systems now available for the video recording of depositions, and for the taping of courtroom activity to serve as the verbatim transcript of proceedings. While video transcripts are by their nature available immediately, they can reduce to nothing the court administrator's concerns about getting the court stenographer's unique code converted into ordinary written form with that promptness demanded by the appellate process in the United States.

The Role of Key Individuals

In many respects, court administration now is where criminal justice administration was in general in the 1950s and 1960s as to the influence of a comparative handful of key figures. In an unusual family heritage, Geoff Gallas carried on the concerns of his parents, displayed in their seminal *Managing the Courts*,[41] through his doctoral research, ongoing authorship of scholarly monographs, and his position as former Director of Research at the National Center for State Courts. Ernest Friesen, coauthor with the elder Gallases of *Managing the Courts*, had served as the head of the Administrative Office of the U.S. Courts before going on to be the original Director of the Institute for Court Management and Law School Dean. He continues to be among the most productive authors and spokesmen on court management issues.

Edward McConnell, former President of the National Center for State Courts, came to that position after 20 years service as the State Court

Administrator for New Jersey, beginning with the challenging early years of that office in 1953. At that point, it was serving as the research laboratory for all the wonderful ideas of Chief Justice Vanderbilt, one of the true pioneers in court administration among the ranks of the Judges. One of the key points in the intellectual and moral leadership of court administration concerns in the United States came with the retirement of Mr. McConnell, whose grasp of the NCSC's helm was synchronous with that body's national reputation on court matters. While his mantle as leader of the NCSC has passed on, no one can bring to the position the eminence in the field that McConnell has developed. Court watchers in America may find out just how much the field in general, and the NCSC in particular, owes to McConnell.[42]

In a rather delightful irony, one of the great forces since 1969 in pushing the concerns of the state courts—Chief Justice Vanderbilt's trenches, where the common man's lawsuits and criminal troubles are dealt with, as opposed to those matters of national concern and high finance that concern America's federal courts—was the former Chief Justice of the United States, Warren Burger, *ex officio* the top federal judicial officer in the country. Properly honoured as the Honorary Chairman of the National Center for State Courts, Burger had successfully invested a lot of his enormous political capital in getting the NCSC successfully resettled to its headquarters in Williamsburg.

In the twenty-five years since this piece was originally written, the NCSC's headquarters have remained unquestionably the most anachronistically modern architecture in that restored colonial town. Williamsburg is less than 200 miles from the nation's seat of power in Washington, DC, hence the NCSC is so much closer and more visible to those in Washington than it had been when it was based in Denver. Without sounding too cynical, it is reasonable to assume that those involved with the Law School at the College of William and Mary, one of America's oldest and most prestigious colleges, will remain quite happy to be landlords to (they own that modern anachronism!) and associated with a rather new organization when it was so vigorously supported by the nation's Chief Justice. Burger was almost alone in seeing the need for a support agency for the states' courts and to offer a similar assistance to them as could be provided to the federal courts by the Administrative Office of the U.S. Courts, established back in 1939,[43] and its "daughter," the Federal Judicial Center.

In comparison to England, where the voluntary movement of Judges off the bench to other careers is frowned upon, as if the resignation is a violation of a lifetime nonrevocable trust, such voluntary movement is a common occurrence in the United States. At times, the move is to another area of public service related to the law. It was U.S. Senator Heflin, erstwhile Chief Justice of Alabama, who was the main sponsor of the bill that became the State Justice Institute Act.

It is interesting, albeit disturbing, to see that Aikman, in 2007,[44] came up with the same list of key players, including Chief Justice/Senator Heflin, that we identified in the late 1980s, and that few other charismatic leaders in court administration have developed in the meantime.

Similarly, one of the most productive authors on court matters was Professor Leflar, who had once served as Associate Justice of the Arkansas Supreme Court. There were also many lively septuagenarians, such as ex-Chief Justice Trainor of California, forced to retire by mandatory retirement ages in the individual states, who have been able to continue to pass on their intellectual energy to young law students at law schools not bound by such mandates. Unfortunately, America's court administrators do not come from its law schools. Still, it is good to know that at least some of its future lawyers are being sensitized to the administrative difficulties faced by the courts.

That key individuals can have such an impact is a reflection of the small size of the field of court administration. As valuable as the contribution of the people mentioned above and the others of whom space precludes a mention here has been, it must be tempered by the bittersweet observation that the field of those interested in court administration matters is small—too small, particularly in the academic community.

Unlike the ordinary tradition, where the ideas of the great scholars at the universities can be handed down via their students, the absence of a sufficient number of major academic institutional bases for the field of court administration means that the ideas and spirit of the pioneers will not be as easily handed down to the next generation, when those pioneers are working in the courts. In that respect, nothing has changed since the late 1980s.

In a different scenario, McConnell would have retired as the Warren Burger Chair of Judicial Administration at the College of William and Mary. His disciple, both in New Jersey and at the NCSC, Sam Conti, would be Professor of Court Administration at the University of Illinois (one of America's many superb state-funded universities with no degree in court administration), instead of having served as the State Court Administrator in that state, a role where his extraordinary instructional skills can hardly be used.

The National Center for State Courts and Other Organizations

In addition to the comments above about the federal SJI, reference has been made above on several occasions to the NCSC, which now includes the ICM. In many respects, particularly in the absence of a decent scholarly base, the single most optimistic contribution to addressing ongoing concerns in court administration in the individual states is the ongoing vigour of the NCSC. This is notwithstanding the creation of the SJI in 1984.

Established in 1971, with some financial support from that same LEAA with which the courts had such difficulty working, and as a direct result of the First National Conference on the Judiciary in 1971, the NCSC was originally based in Denver, along with the ICM, which had been founded the previous year. ICM, still based in Denver, has since merged with the NCSC, and is essentially its educational and training arm. The articles of incorporation explain the NCSC's perception of its own role:

> to conduct research projects on courts and court-related topics in order to identify needs and provide both short and long-term solutions to state court problems;
>
> to conduct education and training programs, seminars and conferences;
>
> to serve as a technical assistance resource for the transfer and adaptation of improvement in court standards, operations, management and technology; and
>
> to serve as a clearinghouse through which members of the courts community and others interested in courts can exchange information and encourage improvement in court administration, practices and procedures.[45]

The range of services offered by the NCSC has grown perhaps even further than its founders envisaged. It collates annual statistics about courts activity. These include the salary data that all state judges and their administrators find so useful in going to bat before their state legislators to ask for pay raises! The FBI and their UCR have nothing to compare with the sizzle on that steak! Unfortunately, there are few professors and their students out there taking advantage of these precious data.

The NCSC continues to fill a special role as the Secretariat for many of the court-related organizations in the country, assisting in the production of their documents and the provision of services to their constituents and members. Only a few states, such as California, predictably, perhaps, have the domestic resources to do much of their own research and development. Many reports, some quite esoteric to outsiders, are completed each year by the NCSC. Their titles attest to the concerns expressed by the courts—inasmuch as the great majority of their reports are written in direct response to a request by the host court—and to the NCSC's consistency. The NCSC's best work rivals in quality any work that a university-based research team could produce, but it is an oasis in the desert. Its *Caseflow Management: The Heart of Court Management in the New Millennium*,[46] now in its third printing, remains the "bible" for state court administrators at both the trial and appellate level.

The NCSC was a vigorous user of LEAA funds during their availability. Now, after the creation of the SJI, it has already become a major recipient of funds from that agency. The funding base of the NCSC is the combination of SJI and other federal money, with charges (the equivalent of a membership fee) assessed against the states on a population *per capita* basis. This is together with the funds provided in the contracts entered into between the NCSC and the states on the individual projects, and the receipt of generous contributions from dedicated people in the legal and lay communities committed to supporting it.

Now the most visible organization assisting the state courts in their administrative and management concerns, the NCSC can probably attribute its ongoing success to its continuing ability to meet the goals stated in its articles of incorporation. The wording of the legislation creating the SJI suggests that the NCSC's role as the most visible agency assisting the state courts will gain added security in the years to come through the funding it will receive from the SJI.

However, the impression should not be gained that the NCSC is the only agency assisting the state courts in their administrative concerns. The American Judicature Society (AJS) was founded in 1913 with a structure that incorporates representatives from each of the states regardless of size, in much the same way as the U.S. Senate. It continues to assist the courts, but seems to have taken something of a back seat since the development of the NCSC. Like ICM's *Justice System Journal* and NACM's *The Court Manager*, AJS's eponymous *Judicature* journal serves as a valuable provider of written material related to the courts.

Other groups that have provided valuable assistance on court related matters over the years include the American Academy of Judicial Education, the National Association of State Judicial Educators, and the National Judicial College. For a long time, the Institute for Judicial Administration, at New York University, was the only university-based research organization interested in court matters.

Finally, in a development illustrative of the "American way," more generalized organizations, the "think-tanks" such as the RAND Corporation, are showing more and more interest in the courts, providing healthy competition for the NCSC, the AJS, and other nonprofit groups in those many situations where a court wanting to have work done for it must engage the competitive bid process and reward the resulting contract via the legendary RFP.

Conclusion

Although the problems faced by the courts in America's states are large, not easily solved, and in some instances (e.g., the variety of funding sources and jurisdictions) uniquely American, the dedication of those working in courts, and the support the courts can theoretically receive, gives some confidence that the courts will be able to continue to address and master the most serious of these problems as they arise. The technological support available from the world of computers will continue to be of great help, but only if it can be guided by those familiar with the courts' needs. That guidance is still lacking.

Notes

1 President's Commission on Law Enforcement and Administration of Justice, *The Challenge of Crime in a Free Society* (hereafter, The Report), Washington, DC: U.S. Government Printing Office, 1967.

2 Ibid. at p. 156.

3 Ibid.

4 "The Causes of Popular Dissatisfaction with the Administration of Justice," as originally reprinted in 20 *J. Am. Jud. Soc'y*, 178 (1937). Like Gilbert and Sullivan librettos, its title and content have proven to be disturbingly timeless.

5 This was incorporated into the President's Commission task report, *The Courts*, at pp. 92–95.

6 Including *Standards Relating to Court Organization* (1974); *Standards Relating to Trial Courts* (1976); *Standards Relating to Appellate Courts* (1976); all published in Chicago.

7 See e.g. Ernest C. Friesen, Jr., Gallas, Edward C., and Gallas, Nesta M., *Managing the Courts*, Indianapolis, IN: Bobbs Merrill, 1971 at pp. 16–17.

8 Adapted from Appendix E and Figure J in State Court Caseload Statistics: *Annual Report, 1984*, Williamsburg, VA: National Center for State Courts.

9 Friesen et al., op cit. supra at pp. 239–270.

10 U.S. Bureau of Justice, Bureau of Justice Statistics, *State Court Organization*, 1980.

11 The Report at p. 156.

12 See generally Raymond J. Wolfinger, "Why Political Machines Have Not Withered Away and Other Revisionist Thoughts," *Journal of Politics*, 34 (May 1972), 265–398.

13 It is estimated, for example, that the elective District Attorney in Cook County, Illinois, which includes Chicago, and which is the United States' largest single court jurisdiction, has nearly 400 such patronage positions at his disposal.

14 Alexander Aikman, *The Art and Practice of Court Administration*, vol. 128, in the CRC Press series on Public Administration and Public Policy, Taylor and Francis Group, Boca Raton, 2007.

15 Aikman, op. cit. in Chapter 7, "On Being a Court Administrator," passim.

16 Charles P. Nemeth, *Directory of Criminal Justice Education*, Cincinnati: Anderson Publishing Co., 1986.

17 Final Report, Bureau of Justice Assistance and American University, Washington, DC, 2005.

18 42 U.S.C. Sec. 3701 (Pub. L. 90–351).

19 The Report at p. 125.

20 Harry E. Allen and Clifford E. Simonsen, *An Introduction to Corrections*, New York: Macmillan, 5th edition, 1989, at p. 718.

21 Aikman, op. cit. at p. 33.

22 Vol. no. 49 in CRC Press's same series on Public Administration and Public Policy. No other volume, other than Aikman's, out of the 128 deals with court administration matters!

23 As repeated in Aikman, op. cit. at p. 151.

24 Scholars such as Glendon Schubert and Sheldon Goldman, for example, have based excellent careers on their analyses for judicial behaviour.

25 See *Twentieth Century Fund Task Force on the Law Enforcement Assistance Administration, Law Enforcement: The Federal Role*. New York: McGraw-Hill, 1976, at p. 108.

26 U.S. Senate Committee on the Judiciary, Senate Report No. 98–480. U.S. Code Congressional and Administrative News, 5728, 5738 (1984).

27 42 U.S.C. Sec. 10705(b)(1)(A) & (B).

28 www.statejustice.org, E-SJI News, "The Voice of the State Justice Institute," vol. 17, No. 10, at p. 1.

29 E-SJI News, vol. 17, No. 12, November 2007, at p. 1.

30 E-SJI News, vol. 17, No. 10, September 2007, at p. 1.

31 Paul Reardon, "The Origins and Impact of the County Court System," in Richard Pare (ed.), *Courthouse*, New York: Horizon Press, 1978, at p. 27. This is an excellent illustrated appraisal of America's courthouses from an architectural standpoint, producing a document that has justly received high praise in the photographic press.

32 It is not at all hard, for example, to find a county courthouse whose electrical service capacity is less than the typical American single family house of today.

33 National Conference on Court Technology, April 24–27, 1988, Denver, Colorado.

34 *Courts volume*. Washington, DC: U.S. Government Printing Office, 1973.

35 op. cit. supra at endnote 7.

36 James Maddex, "Major Developments in Court Administration since 1967," paper delivered at the annual meeting of the Academy of Criminal Justice Sciences, Orlando, Florida, March 1986, at p. 10. This is one of several instances where we share Maddex's somewhat optimistic view of the courts' future.

37 See the favourable review of the WordPerfect word processing software in Donna Baron, "Verdict on WordPerfect," *American Bar Association Journal*, vol. 73, May 1987, at pp. 106–107. The original version of this article, with its need for legally oriented footnotes, was itself composed, in 1990, with that same WordPerfect software, by this author, the world's most incompetent typist. I was an independent confirmation of the value of this kind of help. Now, as a sign of the times, this revision is being composed with Microsoft Word, for reasons we explain immediately following.

38 See e.g. David P. Anderson, "Spreadsheet Software: Making the Microcomputer Work for the Court Administrator," *Justice System Journal*, vol. 10, No. 2 (1985).

39 Aikman, op. cit., at fn 87, p. 287.

40 Aikman, op. cit. at chapter 9, fn 6, p. 251.

41 op. cit. supra at endnote 7.

42 In the summer of 1990, (Mark) Zaffarano wrote a profile of McConnell in *The Court Manager*, the sort of piece, of course, that might not have appeared in an "ordinary" scholarly journal aimed at a university audience.

43 42 U.S.C. Sec. 3701 et seq. If there has been little emphasis on the concerns of administration of justice in America's federal courts in this paper, it is largely because of the general observation that in comparative terms, the same enormity of problems simply does not exist in the nation's federal courts.

44 op. cit at pp. 26–28.

45 Reprinted in the National Center for State Courts, *1983 Annual Report*. Williamsburg, VA: NCSC, 1983, at p. 7.

46 Steelman, David C., with John Goerdt and James E. McMillan, Williamsburg, VA: NCSC, 2004.

14

*Ring*ing in Arizona
Did the U.S. Supreme Court's Decision in *Ring v. Arizona* Adversely Impact the State High Court's Workload?

FRANCES P. BERNAT

Introduction

Capital punishment is the most serious form of punishment that a state can impose on an offender. It has been the subject of debate and concern from ancient times until the present. Each state has the power to determine if it will utilize capital punishment and, if so, the process under which a death sentence can be imposed (Brandenburg, 2007). In recent years, challenges to capital punishment laws have focused on the role that judges and juries play in the determination of who should be sentenced to death.[1] While national legal analysis has tended to focus on the U.S. Supreme Court, the impact of the high court's decisions is felt at the local level. States may have to rewrite their laws and state courts may have to relitigate capital punishment decisions when the Court finds state law to be unconstitutional. Arizona is one such state. It had to rewrite its state capital punishment statute and reconsider state court judgments in light of the U.S. Supreme Court's decision in *Ring v. Arizona* (2002).

State Law Prior to *Ring*

Prior to 2002, after a jury in Arizona determined that a person was guilty of first degree murder, the trial judge alone determined if aggravating factors warranted a death sentence. Arizona's state statute had been presumed valid

Written especially for *Courts and Justice*.

since its enactment in the 1970s (Gerber, 2004[2]). In *Walton v. Arizona* (1990), the Court held that Arizona's death penalty statute was constitutional even though a trial judge alone determined whether or not to impose the death penalty. The *Walton* decision ostensibly empowered a judge to impose a more severe sentence than one associated with a jury verdict's determination of guilt. All this changed when the Court reversed itself in 2002.

Ten years after *Walton*, in *Apprendi v. New Jersey* (2000), the U.S. Supreme Court held that a trial judge could not impose a sentence that exceeded the maximum the offender would have received in light of the facts determined by the jury verdict. The *Apprendi* decision formed the basis for reconsideration of the Arizona death penalty statute. In *Ring v. Arizona* (2002), the Court was asked to reconsider its *Walton* holding in light of *Apprendi*. In a 7–2 decision the *Ring* Court reconciled the incongruity between *Walton* and *Apprendi* by overturning *Walton*. According to the *Ring* Court, because Arizona's capital punishment statute enabled judges to impose death without a jury determination of aggravating circumstances, the Arizona statute violated the Sixth Amendment's right to trial by jury as articulated in *Apprendi*.

Justice O'Connor wrote a dissent that was joined by Chief Justice Rehnquist. She believed that the Court majority's decision was a mistake. She argued that rather than overrule *Walton*, the Court should have overruled *Apprendi*. Justice O'Connor was concerned that the *Ring* decision would encumber the courts with numerous appeals. She noted that due to *Apprendi* the number of criminal appeals to the Court increased 77 percent in 2001. She worried that the state and federal court system would be flooded with appeals. In this regard, the *Ring* Court's majority decision did not determine if "harmless error" occurred and remanded the case to the state court to make that determination.

This chapter attempts to ascertain the impact of *Ring* on the State of Arizona and its caseload. Death penalty cases handed down between April 3, 2003 and August 15, 2006, for a total of 37 cases, are discussed.[3] The starting date for the cases used in this chapter was selected because it was the date when the Arizona Supreme Court ruled on the remanded *Ring* case[4] (*Arizona v. Ring, et seq.*, commonly referred to as *Ring* III).

Capital Punishment and the Need for a Jury Determination

The U.S. Supreme Court held in *Ring v. Arizona* that death penalty sentencing decisions require attention to the basic principles of the Sixth Amendment. The idea that "death is different" has been articulated in cases since *Furman v. Georgia* (1972) and requires courts to be more exacting in their death penalty reviews than in noncapital cases (Barsanti, 2004; Vollum,

Table 1   Post-*Ring* Arizona Supreme Court Death Penalty Cases, 2003–2006

Right to Trial by Jury	McGregor	Ryan	Berch	Jones	Hurwitz	Bales	*Retired**
AZ v. Ring III (2003)	**Def.**	Def.	Def.	Con/Dis			Con/Dis
AZ v. Grell (2003)	Def.	Def.	**Def.**	Def.			Def.
AZ v. Harrod (2003)	**Def.**	Def.	Def.	Con/Dis			
AZ v. Hoskins (2003)	**Def.**	Def.	Def.	Con/Dis			
AZ v. Pandeli (2003)	**Def.**	Def.	Def.	Con/Dis			
AZ v. Rutledge I (2003)	Def.	**Def.**	Def.	Def.			Def.
AZ v. Lehr (2003)	Def.	**Def.**	Def.	Con/Dis			
AZ v. Tucker (2003)	Def.	**Def.**	Def.	Con/Dis			Def.
AZ v. Finch (2003)	Def.	Def.	**Def.**	Con/Dis			
AZ v. Phillips (2003)	Def.	Def.	**Def.**	Con/Dis			
AZ v. Canez (2003)	Def.	Def.	**Def.**	Con/Dis			
AZ v. Jones (2003)	Def.	**Def.**	Def.	Con/Dis			
AZ v. Prince (2003)	**Def.**	Def.	Def.	Con/Dis	No part		
AZ v. Ring (2003)	**Def.**	Def.	Def.	Con/Dis	No part		
AZ v. Cropper (2003)	**Def.**	Def.	Def.	Con/Dis	No part		
AZ v. Prasertphong (2003)	Def.	**Def.**	Def.	Con/Dis	No part		
AZ v. Rutledge I (2003)	Def.	**Def.**	Def.	Con/Dis	No part		
AZ v. Nordstrom (2003)	Def.	**Def.**	Def.	Con/Dis	No part		
AZ v. Sansing (2003)	**Def.**	Def.	Def.	Dissent	No part		
AZ v. Montano (2003)	**Def.**	Def.	Def.	Con/Dis			
AZ v. Dann (2003)	Def.	Def.	**Def.**	Con/Dis			
AZ v. Davolt (2004)	Def.	Def.	Def.	**Def.**	Recused		Def.
AZ v. Armstrong (2004)	Def.	Def.	**Def.**	Con/Dis			
AZ v. Moody (2004)	Def.	Def.	**Def.**	Con/Dis	Recused		Def.
AZ v. Murdaugh (2004)	Def.	**Def.**	Con/Dis	Def.			Def.
AZ v. Carreon (2005)	**State**	State	State	State	State		
AZ v. Anderson (2005)	State	State	State	State	**State**		
AZ v. Roseberry (2005)	State	State	**State**	State	State		
AZ v. Henderson (2005)	**Def.**	Def.	Def.		Def. Concur		Def.
AZ v. Lamar (2005)	**Def.**	Def.	Def.	Def.			Def.
AZ v. Glassel (2005)	State	**State**	State	State*	State		
AZ v. Gomez (2005)	Def.	Def.	Def.		**Def.**	Def.	
AZ v. Ellison (2006)	State	State	State		State	**State**	
AZ v. Hampton (2006)	State	State	State		**State**	State	

* Designates a retired justice or a judge who joined the court on the case.
Bold designates the justice who wrote the court majority opinion.
Def. indicates that the justice sided with the defendant.
State indicates that the justice sided with the State to affirm the verdict/death sentence.
Con/Dis indicates that the justice concurred in the result to overturn the verdict, but dissented as to the constitutional basis for the decision.

Del Carmen, & Longmire, 2004). Prior to *Ring*, state laws differed in the fact-finding process required in capital cases. While most capital punishment states reserved this decision to the jury, five states left the sentencing decision to the judge alone (Arizona, Colorado, Idaho, Montana, and Nebraska). Four states (Alabama, Delaware, Florida, and Indiana) provided for a jury recommendation ("advisory verdict") but enabled the judge to make the sentencing determination.

In *Ring*, the statutory scheme used in Arizona was held unconstitutional. According to the Court majority in *Ring*, "The right to trial by jury guaranteed by the Sixth Amendment would be senselessly diminished if it encompassed the factfinding necessary to increase a defendant's sentence by two years, but not the factfinding necessary to put him to death. We hold that the Sixth Amendment applies to both" (p. 609). Thus, the *Apprendi* holding that a jury is the entity that must determine any fact that would extend a defendant's term of imprisonment must also apply in capital cases. This reasoning was consistent with another capital punishment case decided by the U.S. Supreme Court in 2002, *Kelly v. South Carolina*, in which the Court determined that a jury is entitled to have information about a capital defendant's parole eligibility (Vollum et al., 2004). The foundation of the Sixth Amendment is not limited to a determination of guilt, it includes all the essential elements of capital crimes with which defendants are charged and sentenced. In short, jury deliberations matter in both determinations of whether a person is guilty of a crime and in determinations of whether a person should be sentenced to death.

Because Arizona's capital sentencing law was unconstitutional, the Arizona state legislature immediately rewrote its statutory law to comply with *Ring* (Gerber, 2004). The new Arizona statute removes the judge from determining the specific facts for or against the imposition of a death sentence (see Arizona Revised Statutes, section 13-703). It requires a jury to determine the absence and presence of mitigating and aggravating factors.

States, like Arizona, that did not utilize a jury to determine whether to impose a capital sentence had to revise their capital punishment laws. States that enabled a jury to recommend a sentence, advisory verdicts, may also have a constitutional defect under *Ring* if judges are able to disregard the jury process (Challis, 2003; Laffey, 2003). Consequently, Colorado, Idaho, Montana, and Nebraska immediately rewrote their death penalty laws (Peterson, 2003). States with laws akin to Arizona, likewise, modified their laws to comport with *Ring*. After *Ring*, then, all states with similar laws to Arizona and those with laws that could empower a judge to disregard jury pronouncements about mitigating and aggravating factors changed their death penalty statutes.

Changing state death penalty statutes was only one responsibility of the states following *Ring*. States also had to determine how to handle existing capital defendants' claims and determine if the death sentence could be imposed in light of *Ring*. Like Justice O'Connor, Scott and Gerbasi (2003, p. 109) worried that *Ring* would impact "nearly 800 death sentences in nine states and may require resentencing of hundreds of inmates." In the states directly affected by *Ring* (Arizona, Colorado, Idaho, Montana, and Nebraska) 168 death penalty decisions were subject to being overturned (BBC News, 2002; Laffey, 2003).

In Arizona, its supreme court had to consider the impact of *Ring* on its capital cases that were *previously* decided and on cases *in process* under the old law. An important issue was whether *Ring* could be applied retroactively to capital defendants who were already serving a death sentence under an unconstitutional law (Barsanti, 2004; Manemeit, 2005).

Ring III

In *Ring* III, the Arizona Supreme Court consolidated for appeal 31 capital punishment cases that had been pending in order to respond to the U.S. Supreme Court's *Ring* holding and remand. Certainly, the *Ring* decision created what Heytens (2006) calls a *"transitional moment"*—a period of time in which new rules that were not in effect when lower courts issued their holdings are announced. These new rules require lower courts to reconsider convictions and sentences of defendants. These transitional moments can affect the public's view of the legal system. The Arizona Supreme Court's review of the consolidated cases recognized the importance of this transitional moment. Their ultimate holding placed great deference to federalism and their duty to uphold the supremacy of constitutional (state and federal) law.

The Arizona Supreme Court first focused on the general constitutional parameters that impacted the death penalty cases. After reviewing the history of Arizona's capital punishment laws, the Arizona Supreme Court determined that the capital defendants whose appeals were not finalized could be resentenced under Arizona's new capital sentencing law. The Arizona Supreme Court ruled that an *ex post facto* violation would not occur because a *substantive change* to the definition of the crime under which the defendants were convicted did not occur. Rather, the Arizona Supreme Court held that the new law provided for a *procedural change*; a jury rather than a judge will determine if the death penalty is to be imposed. This distinction is crucial because if the change was considered substantive, then the state would be barred from relitigating the defendant's conviction if the sentences were overturned. Procedural changes to a law do not prohibit a state from retrying or resentencing a defendant. Additionally, the Arizona Supreme Court determined that double jeopardy did not bar resentencing because the capital defendants had been put on notice that they could receive a sentence of death and such a penalty had been imposed at their first trial. The consolidated cases were not ones in which defendants were given life imprisonment and who might now face a sentence of death.

The Arizona Supreme Court also reviewed the degree to which the unconstitutional statute provided a procedural process that tainted the defendants' trials from beginning to end. Such a taint would create a procedural error violating fundamental fairness. The Arizona Supreme Court held that since the procedural error only pertained to the sentencing phase, a structural error did not exist. It was on this last point that two justices dissented. In an opinion by retired Justice Feldman, the justice opined that the error was structural and therefore would require all the death penalty sentences to be overturned. He argued that constitutional law mandates immediate reversals so that the court would not have to speculate about what a nonexistent jury would have found to be harmless error. Justice Feldman concurred that the sentences should be overturned but dissented as to the court majority's finding that the error was not structural.

Ring and Harmful Error Analysis by the Arizona Supreme Court

The court majority in *Ring* III determined that they needed to review the consolidated cases to discover if the death sentence, itself, was "tainted" by the unconstitutional process. As required by the U.S. Supreme Court's decision in *Ring*, the Arizona Supreme Court had to determine if the trial judge's determination that the death penalty should be imposed was "harmless error" beyond a reasonable doubt. If the error was harmless, then the trial courts' verdicts and death sentences would be upheld.

For several cases pending appeal, the resentencing request was based on a judicial finding that the defendant was a recidivist. Under state law, a finding that a defendant was a recidivist was an aggravating factor that only a judge could find since such matters were not presented to a jury deliberating whether to find a defendant guilty of a capital crime. The Arizona Supreme Court held that no error occurred because the legislature permitted judges to enhance a sentence upon a judicial finding that the defendant was a recidivist. The Arizona Supreme Court then considered if the Arizona State Constitution nonetheless required a jury to find that a defendant was a recidivist beyond a reasonable doubt. The Arizona Supreme Court held that the state constitution provided the same right to a trial by jury as found in the Sixth Amendment. The Arizona court held that the state constitution also imposes a duty on the state's high court to make sure that justice is done. If any errors occurring at trial are harmless then the court should uphold the verdict but, if any errors are harmful then they affect the integrity of a verdict and the case must be remanded for retrial.

Critical to whether the defendants in the consolidated cases should have their cases retried is whether *Ring* required the Arizona Supreme Court to remand the cases because a jury did not find aggravating factors warranting the imposition of the death sentence. The Arizona Supreme Court sought to determine if a jury verdict of guilt for murder in the first degree *implicitly* denotes a jury finding that an aggravating factor exists. In this regard, some defendants were given the death penalty because the trial judge had found an aggravating factor, such as the homicide was committed for financial gain; multiple homicides had been committed; or the victim was less than 15 or older than 70 years of age.

In reviewing these cases, the Arizona Supreme Court held that if it is evident that the jury had considered the aggravating factor in determining the guilt of the defendant, then the sentence could stand. However, if the jury determination on the factor was not evident, then the error was not harmless under *Ring* and the defendant must be resentenced. The Arizona Supreme Court determined, for example, that in a felony murder case where a person is convicted of both robbery and murder, the aggravating factor that the murder was committed for financial gain was not implicit within a jury verdict and resentencing was required. If the defendant was found guilty of multiple homicides and the sentencing judge used the multiple homicides as the aggravating factor, harmless error occurred and resentencing was not required because it was clear that the aggravating factor was used to find the defendant guilty of multiple killings. Similarly, if a victim's age was the aggravating factor, and a jury found the defendant guilty of an age-related offense or the defendant stipulated to the age of the victim, then the sentencing error was harmless.

The Arizona Supreme Court's review of the consolidated cases was compounded by factors that might have been proven at trial. The Arizona Supreme Court was asked to consider whether a defendant's concession to an aggravating factor, or failure to challenge one or more aggravating factors, was harmless error. If the defendant had conceded the existence of an aggravating factor, then only if a jury would have beyond a reasonable doubt imposed the death sentence would the judge's decision to sentence the defendant to death be harmless error. If the Arizona Supreme Court could not determine what the jury would have decided, then the case had to be remanded for resentencing. Similarly, when a defendant failed to challenge a factor but the state had met its burden of proving the factor beyond a reasonable doubt, the death sentence would stand. If, however, the state did not establish beyond a reasonable doubt the existence of an aggravating factor, then the case must be remanded for resentencing. The

Arizona Supreme Court now had its work cut out for itself, it had to review the consolidated cases, and cases coming up on review where a death sentence was imposed, under the now unconstitutional state statute to determine if harmful or harmless error occurred at the defendant's trial.

The ruling in *Ring* III distinguishes the need for a jury to find the statutory elements of the offense from the determination by a judge that a sentence be proportionate to the crime (a Sixth Amendment versus an Eighth Amendment analysis). The Arizona Supreme Court held that when the jury did not have the opportunity to find the aggravating factor beyond a reasonable doubt when it found a person guilty of murder in the first degree, then the case needed to be remanded for resentencing. If, however, a case has stipulated factors or the existence of the aggravating factors was so overwhelming that a jury would have found them to exist without mitigation, the death sentence imposed under the old law constituted harmless error and would stand.

The Arizona Supreme Court then held that separate decisions would be rendered for each death penalty case. The Arizona Supreme Court stated that it needed to apply the principles in *Ring* III in order to determine whether a reasonable jury could have found the existence of aggravating factors that would warrant the imposition of death and whether they would have found the lack of a mitigating factor that would necessitate sentencing leniency.

Post-*Ring* Arizona Supreme Court Cases

The impact of Supreme Court decisions like *Ring* impact court caseloads. Kader et al. (2005) in their review of the Arizona Supreme Court's 2003–2004 civil and criminal law decisions found that the court heard 18 criminal law sanction cases out of a total of 21 criminal law appeals; of these, 12 involved capital punishment. Considering its 27 civil law opinions, Kader et al. (2005) found that the Arizona court was very stable, issuing unanimous opinions 95 percent of the time. In its criminal law caseload, however, only 11 of the 21 cases were unanimous. Kader determined that the Arizona Supreme Court issued a reversal of a lower court opinion 60 percent of the time (counting both civil and criminal law cases). When considering Arizona's capital punishment reversal rates, however, Gerber (2004) found that the state has amongst the highest appellate reversal rates in the nation. Gerber found that

> 79% of (Arizona's) death sentences eventually fall on appeal, including 49.1% in the first direct appeal, less success than a flip of a coin. In Pima County the reversal rate is 71%; in Maricopa County it is 84%. In this state's two largest counties, appellate courts throw out more than

seven in ten death sentences for trial court errors. . . . Since 1973, fifty-seven of Arizona's retried capital defendants have received life sentences, twelve have received a term of years, six have been resentenced to time served, and a surprising seven have been acquitted. In total, 82% of Arizona's retried capital defendants have won sentences less than death. Of the 228 persons sentenced to death in Arizona since 1973, 49% had their sentences or convictions reversed at least once. (pp. 366–367)

Subsequent to *Ring* III, the Arizona court overturned almost all of the consolidated cases on the basis that harmful error had occurred (see *Arizona v. Canez, Cropper, Dann, Finch, Harrod, Hoskins, Jones, Lamar, Lehr, Montano, Moody, Murdaugh, Nordstrom, Pandeli, Phillips, Prasertphong, Prince, Ring* IV, *Rutledge* II, *Tucker,* and *Sansing*). Chief Justice Jones, who had joined in Justice Feldman's concurrence and dissent in *Ring* III, argued that resentencing should occur because a Sixth Amendment error existed and that the defect under the old law was structural. In his view, the harmless error analysis should not have been completed; rather all these defendants should have had their cases immediately remanded for resentencing.

In one case, the Arizona Supreme Court remanded *Arizona v. Grell* (2003) for resentencing but did so on different grounds than a Sixth Amendment harmful error basis. In *Grell,* the Arizona Supreme Court determined that under the Eighth Amendment the trial court needed to determine if the defendant was mentally retarded; a fact that would prohibit the imposition of a death sentence.

In nine capital punishment cases decided between January 2005 and October 2006, the Arizona Supreme Court affirmed the capital sentences of six defendants (see *Arizona v. Anderson, Carreon, Ellison, Glassel, Hampton,* and *Roseberry*). In these six cases, the Arizona Supreme Court determined that the jury's determination that the death sentence be imposed was not in error. Because a jury had voted to impose the death sentence, and any of the defendant's proffered mitigation factors were not sufficient to result in leniency, the death sentence was sustained.

In three cases, the Arizona Supreme Court found in favor of the defendants and overturned their death sentences. In *Arizona v. Henderson* (2005), the trial judge had determined the existence of aggravating and mitigating factors. In light of *Ring* III, the Arizona Supreme Court determined that harmful error occurred. Newly appointed Justice Hurwitz (who had argued the case for the capital defendants before the U.S. Supreme Court in *Ring*) argued that the sentencing scheme was unconstitutional on the same grounds as Justices Feldman and Jones in *Ring* III. He would have placed the burden on the state in capital appeals to show harmless error rather than on the defendant to show harmful error. Nonetheless, the Arizona Supreme Court's opinion in *Henderson* did not require a remand to the lower court because by the time of the appeal's conclusion the defendant had been released from prison and completed his community supervision. In remanding another case for resentencing, *Arizona v. Lamar* (2005), the Arizona Supreme Court determined that the defendant was entitled to have a jury, not the judge, determine the existence of aggravating factors warranting a death sentence. In *Arizona v. Gomez* (2005), the Arizona court found the trial court's decision to have the defendant wear shackles, even if not clearly visible, when no security concerns were evident, during the sentencing phase before the jury constituted reversible error. The defendant's capital sentence violated his due process rights and was vacated.

Discussion and Conclusion

In Arizona, the Arizona Supreme Court is mandated to hear all appeals from sentences imposing the death penalty. If the Arizona Supreme Court had in *Ring* III determined as a preliminary matter that Justices Feldman and Jones were correct—that the Sixth Amendment required resentencing of all the death sentences imposed under Arizona's old law—then the court would not have heard rearguments and could have immediately sent the cases back to the trial courts for reconsideration. As it is, the Arizona Supreme Court remanded for resentencing all of the cases where it found a Sixth Amendment trial by jury error. Although the Arizona Supreme Court expended considerable time and effort on these appeals it was fruitful because the court clarified its philosophical view of federal and state constitutional law. In addition, the Arizona Supreme Court, in exercising its power of judicial review in these cases, reaffirmed the role of the court in interpreting law and demanding fundamental fairness.

Because most of the cases decided in 2005 and 2006 resulted in an affirmation of the jury's verdict imposing death, it is unlikely that any further litigation stemming from the old Arizona capital punishment statute's failure to ensure a defendant's right to trial by jury will contribute to the court's workload. It remains to be seen what other arguments, like the issue of mental retardation raised in *Gomez*, may be raised to challenge and overturn death sentences in the state. The Arizona Supreme Court, at present, is satisfied that the new law is constitutional and enforceable.

As a final note, the defendant in *Ring* was sentenced to life imprisonment on July 18, 2007 (Associated Press, 2007). According to the Associated Press (2007), four defendants, including Ring himself, stipulated to life sentences. One of the *Ring* III defendants received a 25-year sentence after pleading guilty to a lesser offense, five defendants received a death sentence after a retrial, five defendants received life sentences after a retrial, and ten cases are still pending disposition (Associated Press, 2007). One defendant not directly affected by *Ring*, Robert Comer, was executed in 2007. After all his appeals were exhausted in 2000, he refused to retain his lawyers and did not wish to continue any further litigation that challenged his sentence (Palmer, 2007).

Notes

[1] Because a defendant is someone who has not been convicted of a crime, the Sixth Amendment applies because it governs the trial process. The Eighth Amendment, most commonly associated with death penalty analysis, applies when convicted offenders challenge it as being cruel and unusual punishment.

[2] Rudolph J. Gerber was one of the persons who wrote the capital punishment law in the 1970s, ironically he notes that he asked Sandra Day O'Connor about what type of law he should help write and she replied, "Draft a death penalty we can live with" (Gerber, 2004, p. 364).

[3] A total of 37 cases were found through a WESTLAW search conducted on October 2, 2006.

[4] In *Ring* III, the state high court was asked to correct the constitutional error found by the U.S. Supreme Court in *Ring*.

References

Apprendi v. New Jersey, 530 U.S. 466 (2000).
Arizona v. Anderson, 111 P.3d 369 (2005).
Arizona v. Armstrong, 93 P.3d 1076 (2004).
Arizona v. Canez, 74 P.3d 932 (2003).
Arizona v. Carreon, 107 P.3d 900 (2005).
Arizona v. Cropper, 76 P.3d 424 (2003).
Arizona v. Dann, 79 P.3d 58 (2003).
Arizona v. Davolt, 84 P.3d 456 (2004).
Arizona v. Ellison, 140 P.3d 899 (2006).
Arizona v. Finch, 68 P.3d 123 (2003).
Arizona v. Glassel, 116 P.3d 1193 (2005).
Arizona v. Gomez, 123 P.3d 1131 (2005).
Arizona v. Grell, 66 P.3d 1234 (2003).
Arizona v. Hampton, 140 P.3d 950 (2006).
Arizona v. Harrod, 65 P.3d 948 (2003).
Arizona v. Henderson, 115 P.3d 601 (2005).
Arizona v. Hoskins, 65 P.3d 953 (2003).
Arizona v. Jones, 72 P.3d 1264 (2003).
Arizona v. Lamar, 115 P.3d 611 (2005).
Arizona v. Lehr, 201 Ariz. 509 (2002).
Arizona v. Montano, 77 P.3d 1246 (2003).
Arizona v. Moody, 94 P.3d 1119 (2004).

Arizona v. Murdaugh, 97 P.3d 844 (2004).

Arizona v. Pandeli, 65 P.3d 950 (2003).

Arizona v. Phillips, 67 P.3d 1228 (2003).

Arizona v. Prasertphong, 76 P.3d 438 (2003).

Arizona v. Prince, 75 P.3d 114 (2003).

Arizona v. Ring et seq. (*Ring* III), 65 P.3d 915 (2003).

Arizona v. Ring (*Ring* IV), 76 P.3d 421 (2003).

Arizona v. Roseberry, 111 P.3d 402 (2005).

Arizona v. Rutledge (*Rutledge* I), 66 P.3d 50 (2003).

Arizona v. Rutledge (*Rutledge* II), 77 P.3d 40 (2003).

Arizona v. Sansing, 77 P.3d 30 (2003).

Arizona v. Tucker, 68 P.3d 110 (2003).

Associated Press State & Local Wire. (2007). Convicted Murderer at Center of Landmark Ruling Sentenced. July 18, 2007. Accessed at http://www.lexisnexis.com.ezproxy1.lib.asu.edu/us/1nacademic/frame.do?tokenKey=rsh-2...   on September 14, 2007.

Barsanti, J. E. (2004). *Ring v. Arizona*: The Sixth and Eighth Amendments Collide: Out of the Wreckage Emerges a Constitutional Safeguard for Capital Defendants. *Pepperdine Law Review* 31: 519–573.

BBC News. (2002). U.S. Court Overturns Death Sentences. Monday, June 24, 2002. Accessed at http://www.ccadp.org/timring-landmark.htm on September 14, 2007.

Brandenburg, E. (2007). Casenote: *Kansas v. Marsh*: A Thumb on the Scale of Death? *Mercer Law Review* 58: 1447–1461.

Challis, J. M. (2003). Note: I'm Sorry Your Honor, You Will Not Decide My Fate Today: The Role of Judges in the Imposition of the Death Penalty: A Note on *Ring v. Arizona*. *Saint Louis University Public Law Review* 22: 521–557.

Furman v. Georgia, 408 U.S. 238 (1972).

Gerber, R. J. (2004). Symposium: Capital Concerns: The Death Penalty in America: Survival Mechanisms: How America Keeps the Death Penalty Alive. *Stanford Law and Policy Review* 15: 363–379.

Heytens, T. J. (2006). Managing Transitional Moments in Criminal Cases. *The Yale Law Journal* 115: 922–996.

Kader, D. et al. (2005). The Supreme Court of Arizona: Its 2003–2004 Decisions. *Arizona State Law Journal* 37: 17–157.

Kelly v. South Carolina, 534 U.S. 246 (2002).

Laffey, C. (2003). Note: The Death Penalty and the Sixth Amendment: How Will the System Look After *Ring v. Arizona*. *St. John's Law Review* 77: 371–399.

Manemeit, C. (2005). Note & Casenote: *Summerlin v. Stewart*: Did the Ninth Circuit Actually Get This One Right? *QLR* 23: 1289–1329.

Palmer, C. (2007). Robert Comer Gets Death Wish, Other Arizona Executions Pending. *Arizona Capital Times*, May 25, 2007. Accessed at http://lexisnexis.com.ezproxy1.lib.asu.edu/us/1nacademic/delivery/PrintDoc.do?filesS...

Peterson, K. (2003). States Struggle with Death Penalty Process. Accessed at http://www.stateline.org/live/printable/story?contentId=15190 on September 14, 2007.

Ring v. Arizona, 536 U.S. 584 (2002).

Scott, C. L. & Gerbasi, J. B. (2003). *Ring v. Arizona*: Who Decides Death? *Journal of the American Academy of Psychiatry and the Law* 31: 106–109.

Vollum, S., Del Carmen, R. V., & Longmire, D. R. (2004). Should Jurors be Informed about Parole Eligibility in Death Penalty Cases? An Analysis of *Kelly v. South Carolina*. *The Prison Journal* 84: 395–410.

Walton v. Arizona, 497 U.S. 639 (1990).

15

Review Essay on Judicial Recruitment and Selection

ELLIOT E. SLOTNICK

Introduction

Research in the area of the recruitment and selection of judges for state and federal tribunals has historically occupied a home near the center of the concerns of judicial politics scholars, legal practitioners, and nonprofessional analysts and observers of American judicial systems. As noted by Dubois, "It is fairly certain that no single subject has consumed as many pages in law reviews and law-related publications over the past 50 years as the subject of judicial selection" (1986a:31). (For a representative annotated bibliography see Chinn and Berlsson [1980].) Underlying this concern is the premise stated by Peltason (1955:29) that "the decision as to who will make the decisions affects what decisions will be made." The scene in which discussion unfolds is set by the premise that courts occupy a unique position in the American political system for, while "ours is a government of laws and not men," the judiciary, nevertheless (and, perhaps, ironically) clearly plays a major policymaking role. A great deal has been written about judicial recruitment and selection, but it has been argued that much allegedly social scientific scholarship has been of a rather polemical nature, with authors joining a debate aimed at deciding which method

Reprinted by permission of the *Justice System Journal* from vol. 13, no. 1 (1988), pp. 109–124.

of judicial selection is "best" and most suited to bringing about an often inadequately articulated, but clearly preferred result. The focal point for such writing is often the balance that a particular selection mechanism strikes between the values of accountability of American judges, arguably maximized in electorally-based selection systems, and judicial independence and expertise, arguably best served by appointive selection systems (see Dubois, 1986a).

Skeptical analysts have, however, questioned the relevance of research seeking the answer to the largely normative question of which judicial selection system is "best," and have asked whether examination of judicial selection is an important enterprise at all—raising the possibility "that selection procedures are formalities with little impact on types of judges selected or upon the quality of judicial decision . . ." (Flango and Ducat, 1979:25). Happily, the eclectic research conducted during the past several years on judicial recruitment amply demonstrates the value of this area of inquiry.

Researchers continue to address the question of the "best" selection method, yet they often state their motivating assumptions, goals, and axes-to-grind at the outset, and examine fundamental issues empirically. In addition, research on judicial recruitment mechanisms is pursued for reasons other than the supposition that alternative systems produce judges with particular characteristics who, as judges, will favor certain decisional outcomes. Even if scholars were convinced that different decisional propensities did not flow from alternative selection procedures, judicial selection processes would constitute an important research focus. Critical issues of democratic theory, including questions relating to what political forces exercise control over recruitment processes and could structure their rewards, would remain. To the extent that the concepts of representation, access, and participation remain important constructs in democratic theory, and to the degree that elite recruitment, campaigns and elections, executive/legislative relationships, etc. remain concerns of broad interest to students of politics, studying judicial treatment and selection remains of compelling importance.

In this article I shall attempt to review the contributions to our knowledge about judicial recruitment and selection at the state level with primary focus on research published since 1983. Unprecedented attention has been focused on all facets of judicial recruitment in recent years for several complementary reasons. At the federal level, Presidents Carter and Reagan enjoyed unique opportunities to remake the lower federal bench by filling large numbers of newly created judgeships. Increased attention has been placed on recruitment to the U.S. Supreme Court, reflecting the resignations of Chief Justice Burger and Justice Powell, the promotion of William Rehnquist, the appointment of

Antonin Scalia, and the nominations Robert Bork, Douglas Ginsburg, and Anthony Kennedy.

Attention to state judicial recruitment has been less subject to the ebbs and flows associated with such contextual events, largely because the coexistence of disparate state procedures has always invited comparative empirical research, and because the state judicial recruitment arena has always been a hotbed of reform-oriented writing and activity. Inasmuch as changes in state selection procedures could be accomplished through processes less demanding than altering the federal constitution, increased attention has been focused on those mechanisms. Increasingly, interests seeking to utilize courts to pursue their policy goals have found state tribunals a congenial route to policy success, thus helping to politicize state selection processes and make them more competitive.

State Judicial Selection Research

The staple of state judicial selection research has been judicial elections, perhaps best represented by the broad based writing of Dubois, whose pathbreaking analysis (1980) address citizens' levels of electoral interest, knowledge, participation, and the determinants of voting choice. The study also focused on the extent of electoral competition, the implications of incumbency, and the role of interests such as bar associations. The research shed light on numerous issues about which little systematic was known and, understandably, helped to generate a great deal of research that refined and extended our understanding.

Hall (1984) provided a temporal expansion of our scholarly gaze with an historical analysis of the relationship of judicial elections to the value of democratic accountability in four states (California, Ohio, Tennessee, and Texas). Hall's analysis initially demonstrated that between 1846 and 1912 every new state entering the union adopted partisan elections as mechanisms for reinforcing judicial professionalism and accountability. As governmental bureaucracies expanded, desires for legal professionalism no longer seemed best served by the simple following of the democratic will. Indeed, judicial accountability became intimately linked with professionalism, and subsequent reform of selection procedures gravitated first towards nonpartisan balloting and, ultimately, merit selection procedures.

By examining turnout rates and roll-off figures (turnout for a judicial election compared to turnout for the major statewide partisan office) for judicial elections in his four-state sample between 1850 and 1920, Hall was able to assess comparatively the implications of such devices as the Australian ballot, nonpartisan elections, and separation of judicial from other elections. Hall's analysis also supplied historical context for the advantages of judicial incumbency, while demonstrating that there are explicable reasons when incumbency fails, such as a judge's failure to stay within "prevailing majoritarian norms on major public issues" (1984:363), a finding that rings true when applied to contemporary judicial electoral settings.

Despite incumbents' occasional losses, Hall concluded, "Democratic accountability was usually a potential rather than a real threat" (1984:368) in the four states studied. Existing accountability tended to be party oriented, and only under highly controversial circumstances did it extend to curbing judges as individuals. Moreover, democratic accountability declined as the mode of judicial selection moved further from direct partisan election, creating a scenario where "judicial elections became the tail on the electoral kite . . . and the public lost its best means of regulating judicial policy making" (1984:369).

Hall, of necessity, relied heavily on aggregate electoral data supplemented by documentation of contextual political concerns. Aggregate voting data remains the central focus for most studies of contemporary judicial elections (see Atkins et al., 1984; Baum, 1983; Dubois, 1984; Scheb, 1983), but analysts have also relied on sample survey techniques to produce greater understanding of individual voting decisions in the judicial electorate (see, e.g., Griffin and Koran, 1983; Lovrich and Sheldon, 1983 and 1985; Sheldon and Lovrich, 1983). Unfortunately, the substantial costs of such analyses have tended to limit their scope and breadth.

Dubois' effort (1984) to examine voting cues in 123 contested nonpartisan primary and subsequent runoff elections for California's major trial courts between 1976 and 1980 utilized more sophisticated analytic techniques than did previous research. Employing a multivariate model that included numerous potential voting cues such as incumbency, occupational ballot labels, ethnicity of a candidate's surname, campaign spending levels, and newspaper and bar association endorsements, Dubois had much success in post-dicting election results.

Dubois' research confirmed the importance of voting cues in nonpartisan elections where shorthand guides may be critical for voters acting with limited information. More broadly, it indicated a gradual rise in judicial electoral competition, slight chinks in the armor of judicial incumbency, and a shift in the nature of judicial campaigning which, tied to a rapid rise in election costs, has helped create greater public clamor for judicial accountability. Such trends collectively attest to the increased visibility of, and public interest in, judicial elections, while also raising questions and concerns for future research. How do judicial elections compare to other low visibility electoral contests, and how does incumbency fare as compared to alternative electoral arenas? If incumbency is no longer as potent as it used to be, why is this so?

What will the rise in electoral competition auger for the nature of judicial campaigns, their cost, and their ability to attract candidates?

Dubois' findings also clearly differentiated between primary and runoff elections and between those in small counties and those in metropolitan areas. Incumbency, one of the most powerful factors in primary elections, appeared to be a hindrance in runoff campaigns, while several factors seemingly unimportant in primaries, such as higher campaign spending, information in voter pamphlets, and/or candidacy endorsements, were far better predictors of runoff election results. Ballot cues were dominant in explaining Los Angeles County results, but were insignificant for understanding results in small and medium-sized counties, while in small counties the impact of campaign spending was clearly greater than in Los Angeles. These findings attest to the complexity of judicial elections and the necessity of narrowly focused research which attempts to understand the diversity of such elections.

Such efforts isolating critical variables in narrow research settings are well represented by the recent work of Baum (1983), Atkins et al. (1984), and Scheb (1983). Baum's research provided an in-depth examination of the electoral fate of incumbents—previously elected judges seeking re-election—and appointed judges seeking election on one set of lower courts in Ohio from 1962 through 1980, with attention to the size and urbanism of judicial constituencies and the implications for voting outcomes of partisan balance and electoral tides. Baum's findings confirmed, for the most part, past research and conventional wisdom. A scant 8 percent of primary or general election campaigns by incumbents resulted in defeat, and only 13 percent of new judges were recruited through the competitive electoral route. Rather, paths to judicial office followed gubernatorial appointment or election to open seats. Baum's findings clearly have implications for the debate over the form that judicial elections should take, for although "Common Pleas elections are more dangerous for incumbents than are retention elections under merit selection systems, . . . the similarities are more striking than the differences" (1983:429). The "competitiveness" of contested elections may, in fact, closely resemble noncontested retention ballots. In full agreement with Dubois, Baum cautions against drawing too many conclusions from limited research contexts. Underlining the differences between Common Pleas and Supreme Court elections in Ohio, Baum asserts, for example, that "a particular system may vary in its working not only among states but within them—between higher and lower courts, between urban and rural counties. . . . The certainty of many commentators' conclusions about judicial election seems unjustified in light of the uncertainties that remain" (1983:430).

In light of these uncertainties, focused analyses which isolate interesting electoral variables are clearly warranted. In an important addition to the literature offering counterpoint to most studies which suggest that judicial elections do not provide voters with salient cues that generate electoral interest and participation, Atkins, DeZee, and Eckert (1984) focused on the significance of racial cues in 1976 Florida Supreme Court races, only one of which contained a black candidate. Race made a clear difference in a landmark election in which the first black statewide candidate was successful in a southern state since Reconstruction: in predominantly black precincts, there were higher voter participation rates and support levels for the black candidate than were evidenced for the victorious candidates in the other Supreme Court races decided in the same election. More broadly, the study demonstrated that elections historically of low salience can, under important contextual circumstances, generate increased voter mobilization. The low saliency of judicial elections appears to be tied only partially to the invisibility of the office and/or its perceived unimportance. Analysts must make a more concerted effort to isolate additional factors which render such elections more salient affairs.

In a related study illuminating another facet of judicial elections, Griffin and Koran (1983) examined retention election processes. Their analysis of two Wyoming Supreme Court retention elections was based on a survey of respondents' voting behavior, levels of information, and specific reasons for voting decisions, and thus was subject to the generic problems of perceptual recall associated with this mode of analysis. There was great symmetry in respondents' answers across the two elections, clearly suggesting that voters were not differentiating between their two retention ballots. One of the interesting findings was that low levels of information were related to nonvoting or failure to recall one's vote, yet among those voting, some information increased one's propensity to vote "yes" on retention while a great deal of information was related to a greater likelihood of voting "no." This finding is somewhat analogous to that from earlier studies of public opinion about the U.S. Supreme Court (e.g., Kessel, 1966)—that to know the court was not, necessarily, to love it, with the most critical evaluations coming from among the most knowledgeable.

The larger picture that emerges from the Griffin and Koran study is that retention elections are prototypical landslides attributable to a lack of information, particularly unfavorable information, which would induce a voter to defeat an incumbent with a "no" vote. Because negative voting was not anti-institutional in character, but associated with unfavorable information about the judge, the authors view the retention election process as one fostering only limited accountability: judges may be held accountable if questionable behavior becomes public, yet their retention is assured in the absence of such negative information.

The broadest-based study of retention elections was recently published by Hall and Aspin (1987). Eschewing the strategy of examining a single retention election or retention elections in a single state, Hall and Aspin empirically examined all such elections in each of 10 states between 1964 and 1984. The analysis provides historical context and examines the most frequent criticisms of retention elections, including the charges that they insulate judges from popular control, create life-tenured judges, lack voting cues, are issueless, and are met by low voter turnout.

Hall and Aspin found a mean affirmative vote of 77.2 percent in retention elections and an affirmative vote below 60 percent less than 3 percent of the time. Only 22 retention elections (1.2%) resulted in defeat, with 10 such occurrences in Illinois. In 9 of these 10 instances the incumbent received more than 50 percent, but less than the 60 percent affirmative vote uniquely required under Illinois law. The average rolloff rate across all retention elections was a robust 36.2 percent. The analysis confirmed that voters did not differentiate significantly among judges, while also noting that the rare defeat of a judge did not tend to affect the affirmative votes for other candidates appearing on the same retention ballot. Defeats did not follow gradual erosion of support for a judge, but occurred instead somewhat precipitously often in one's first retention bid. While the mean affirmative vote has appeared to decline over time, the authors positively link retention voting to temporal patterns of public trust in government.

Mention should also be made of research examining efforts by the organized bar to assess candidacies in retention elections. Griffin and Murdock (1985) utilized data from the 1978, 1980, and 1982 Wyoming State Bar Judicial Polls to determine how attorneys' perceptions of personal and judicial attributes related to whether a judge's retention was favored. Interestingly, the factors correlating most highly in linking attorneys' evaluations with their retention recommendations were attributes over which the judges did have some control, including their fairmindedness and deliberateness in reaching decisions, their openmindedness and impartiality, and their courteousness towards litigants, witnesses, and lawyers. In a related, methodologically-oriented study concerned with the potential problem of bias in judicial evaluation surveys, Koebel (1983) concluded that when carefully designed and administered, no systematic biases necessarily existed in bar evaluation polls. The impact of such polls, however, may be another matter, as revealed by Scheb's assessment (1983) of the 1978, 1980, and 1982 Florida Advisory Preference Polls on appellate judges, where none of 54 incumbents were denied retention. The aggregate correlation found between bar poll results and voter support was negligible, leading to the conclusion that idiosyncratic factors such as ballot design and voter ignorance of retention election procedures were more helpful for understanding retention majorities than the bar's advisory input.

Focus on individual electoral behavior in the context of contested primary and general judicial elections emerges as the major concern of Sheldon and Lovrich whose studies (Lovrich and Sheldon, 1983, 1985; Sheldon and Lovrich, 1983) examined, albeit somewhat differently, registered voters' responses to surveys regarding elections in Oregon and Washington. They explored voter knowledge and voting behavior while also addressing the complex question of how different recruitment systems influenced electoral behavior and voter attitudes towards the tenuous balance between accountability and independence that lies at the heart of popular concern with judicial elections.

While not necessarily so characterized in that light by the authors, the picture they draw of the judicial electorate's lack of knowledge is not a very encouraging one, with only a slight majority able to identify more correct than incorrect candidate names from a proffered list (Sheldon and Lovrich, 1983). Over two-thirds of the voters admitted to being unable to name both candidates in a contested race (Lovrich and Sheldon, 1985), over one-third admitted to having no information at all about the judicial election, and a plurality of voters claimed some, but not enough information. It is striking that nearly half of those claiming to have no information actually voted and that fewer than one in five actual voters felt that they had enough information on which to base their vote (Sheldon and Lovrich, 1983). As one might expect, participation increased among those who perceived themselves as more knowledgeable, and voters across all knowledge levels supported nonpartisan judicial elections. Apparently such an electoral process, unencumbered by partisan mediation, was perceived by the voters as assuring the most direct judicial accountability.

The most interesting facet of the Lovrich and Sheldon studies is their exploration of public attitudes on the appropriate balance between judgeship accountability, and judicial independence. The most highly informed voters (based on candidate knowledge) were the least favorably disposed towards the most widely held model of accountability whereby judges are expected to act as "delegates" and strictly follow the public will. Rather, these relatively informed voters favored a more equal balance between independence and accountability and, indeed, they were the least critical of the "trustee" model of adjudication, whereby judges act most independently on behalf of the public and not simply through their mandate. Those with lower levels of knowledge were most favorably disposed to a view of elections as "sanctions," whereby judges acting independent on the electorate's desires could be removed. Based on their data the authors concluded that successful efforts to educate the public would have beneficial consequences by producing public support of a significant degree of judicial independence, a goal they clearly favor (Lovrich and Sheldon, 1983:250).

These preferences were also supported by Lovrich and Sheldon's analysis of the relationship between the "articulation" of an electoral system—that is, the number of actors involved in the initiation, screening, and affirmation of candidates—and the voters' preferred model of judicial elections. Highly articulated electoral settings coincided with greater electoral participation, varied information sources, and a greater likelihood of informed voting. Voters in such settings adopted "a position most in line with a balance between democratic accountability and judicial independence." They resembled "a responsible electorate which comes to the polls relatively well informed to cast ballots, and reflect an appreciation of the special character of judicial elections" (Lovrich and Sheldon, 1985:290–291).

Throughout their research Sheldon and Lovrich cast their findings in a reform mold, asserting that nonpartisan elections can aid in maintaining an appropriate balance between judicial accountability and judicial independence as long as voters are knowledgeable. The onus for ensuring such a system is seen to lie with candidates and legal professionals who have inadequately met their responsibility to supply the information to the electorate that the authors claim they want (Sheldon and Lovrich, 1983:245). Such research has taken important first steps in going beyond simple analysis of voting results to a richer examination of the perceptions of the judicial electorate. The work is clearly suggestive of important questions at the nexus of the judicial process and democratic theory. How can candidates effectively establish name recognition and offer useful and more information to the electorate in a manner consistent with the unique constraints of judicial elections? How does the problem of the "ignorant" judicial voter compare with other electoral settings? How could policymakers frame electoral settings so as to minimize the possibility that the "unknowledgeable" will decide electoral outcomes? Would such engineering be justified? Similarly, how could policymakers ensure a highly articulated selection system? Most broadly, the research resuscitates the timeless normative questions of what role should courts play in a democratic polity and, further, what role could or should judges play in fostering that role.

Sheldon and Lovrich are, perhaps, too optimistic about the level of accountability implicit in contemporary judicial elections given the thrust of their data. Interestingly, Dubois is even more sanguine and argues that such elections should be assessed by "their ability to allow voters to control the general direction and broad boundaries of public policy. . ." (1986a:41–42), not voters' specific knowledge of candidates and their issue stances. Further, Dubois argues, there are inherent tradeoffs and, at times, mutually inconsistent objectives and goals in alternative selection mechanisms which analysts must deal with more realistically and with greater sophistication.

Another facet of the judicial electoral process to which attention has been turned is campaign financing (Dubois, 1986b; Dubois, 1986c; Nicholson and Weiss, 1986). Dubois' broad-scaled analysis of judicial campaign spending examines the generic questions of the overall costs of such campaigns and the difficulties such costs can create for candidates. Useful comparisons are drawn between the costs of judicial campaigns and the contesting of other low visibility elections. Dubois examined over 400 candidates competing in 153 contested nonpartisan primary and runoff elections for seats on the major California trial court between 1976 and 1982. Given the dearth of research in this area, Dubois' limited objectives of describing overall spending levels and identifying "factors that drive those costs upward and . . . affect candidates' attitudes and expectations" about how much money they will need are understandable and warranted (1986c:267). Dubois showed that significant increases in the absolute cost of judicial elections occurred between 1976 and 1978, but electoral costs remained relatively constant since 1976 in real dollar terms and have actually gone down when one controls for inflation. Campaign spending does not increase proportionately with constituency size suggesting, perhaps, that activists' fundraising efforts in such elections cannot keep pace with the growth of a mass electorate. "Open" races lacking incumbents—with a greater amount of competition—cost more than races contested by incumbents. Average spending by candidates, however, is approximately 25 percent higher in races with incumbents, predominantly because of the incumbent candidates' spending.

In a conclusion which runs somewhat counter to emerging conventional wisdom, Dubois asserts that, viewed from the systemic level, "judicial election costs are neither extraordinarily high nor caught in an inexorable upward spiral" (1986c:281). Indeed, the amount of money spent appears to be so minimal as to raise serious questions about the relative ability of judicial candidates to "compete" in the electoral marketplace with higher spending candidates seeking more visible offices. Thus, Dubois questions "whether a sufficient amount of money is being spent on judicial elections to help voters make intelligent choices among competing candidates" (1986c:283). However, despite the relatively small amounts of money involved, judicial candidates operate under numerous constraints which can make even the minimal expenditures at stake seem quite formidable to the individual contestant, with the constraints perhaps such "as to limit judicial candidacies only to the wealthy" (1986c:283).

Researching contributions rather than expenditures, Dubois examined the conflict of interests that might arise when candidates rely on contributors, particularly lawyers, for their solvency (1986b). Viewing 1980 elections, Dubois challenged, in part, emerging conventional wisdoms about judicial campaign financing. The data revealed that lawyers, although the largest source of funds, contributed under 40 percent of the total and made relatively small contributions. The vast amount of borrowed money for these campaigns was derived from candidates and/or their families. Dubois concluded that "the contributor base for judicial elections is actually quite varied, with well more than half of all the dollars contributed in larger amounts originating with groups and individuals who are outside the legal community" (1986b:12). While the dominance of personal financing may dispel allegations of undue influence by contributors on judges, concerns about access to judicial office on an equitable basis are clearly exacerbated. Indeed, in research on funding of election to Cook County Circuit Courts in 1984 which produced similar results, Nicholson and Weiss (1986) are clearly unhappy about the implications of their findings. They note that heavy reliance on personal funding disadvantages potential candidates of modest means, while the stockpiling of large sums of money by the financially strongest candidates can add an aura of impropriety to the electoral setting. They conclude, "The problems inherent in the funding of judicial elections may be one more reason for seriously considering . . . alternative selection methods" (Nicholson and Weiss, 1986:25).

The studies of judicial campaign finance raise numerous questions including that of the object of campaign expenditures. Do candidates attempt to develop judicial campaign issues or, alternatively, are they simply seeking name recognition? What kinds of issues are pressed? How do expenditures in such campaigns compare with those in other low-cost elections and how might this relate to the unique constraints of judicial campaign competition? What do judicial campaign contributors want for their participation? Are they more altruistic than donors in other electoral settings? How does the pattern of personal versus third party financing compare to other electoral settings? Most broadly, do the concerns about the representativeness of an elective judiciary, the role of incumbency and money in competition, and the sources of campaign funding suggest that the option of public financing needs to be considered in an electoral arena rarely suggested as fertile ground for that reform movement?

While much analysis has focused on judicial electoral processes, there has been little examination of alternative methods of state judicial selection, particularly gubernatorial appointment. Such appointment processes are often analogous to federal judicial recruitment and researchers can adopt approaches resembling work on federal judicial selection as exemplified by Dubois' "State Trial Court Appointments: Does the Governor Make A Difference?" (1985). The analysis examined 658 appointments by three governors between 1959 and 1977 to

California's major trial court. In addition to providing a comparison of the appointee's demographic, educational, career, and political characteristics, sitting judges were surveyed about the processes through which they were appointed.

The data clearly revealed that different gubernatorial administrations open up distinct paths to the bench, like Slotnick's finding (1984a) that different paths to federal judgeships characterize appointees in a single administration on racial and gender lines. Partisan political activity was one factor distinguishing the three governors' selection processes, which led to distinct ideological results as well. While Governor Reagan's Judicial Selection Advisory Boards appeared to remove the governor somewhat from the selection process, partisan ideology remained facilitated through prior staff screening. Appointees' perceptions also varied across administrations, with Reagan's most likely to view support by the bar and business leaders as critical, while Governor "Pat" Brown's designates felt that support of local political leaders and personal friendship with the governor was a key to their success (Dubois, 1985:23–24).

Although Dubois demonstrated politicization of gubernatorial appointment processes across administrations, it is noteworthy that "characteristics related to professional preparation and experience did not vary much by governor" (Dubois, 1985:28). Indeed, as research on the federal level has suggested (see Slotnick, 1983b), "quality" of the judicial branch in an absolute sense may not be affected by alternative selection processes as much as such processes help to determine whose definitions of judicial merit will prevail. Thus, white males appointed by President Carter to the federal bench had higher incomes, were older, enjoyed more years at bar, were admitted to practice before higher level tribunals, were more likely to be private practitioners in traditional legal practices, and were more likely to receive higher ABA ratings than their "nontraditional" (female and/or nonwhite) counterparts (Slotnick, 1984b). The paths to federal judgeships for nontraditional appointees were more likely to emerge from the academy (for women) or from other judgeships (for nonwhites) than for white males. Most importantly, Slotnick's analysis suggested that, "while differences abounded among the candidates . . . , they did not . . . underline the inherent superiority of . . . the white male nominees." Rather, differences between the career paths of white male and nontraditional appointees reflected "the different socio, economic, and political roles played in the aggregate by the groups to which nontraditional candidates belong . . . and the opportunities available to members of these groups" (1984b:388).

Much comparative research across presidential administrations (Goldman, 1965, 1972, 1981, 1985, 1987; Fowler, 1983, 1984) offers further testimony to the relationship between the values of the appointing authority and the characteristics of an administration's nominees. Thus, Fowler argued that President Carter's ''merit'' appointment process was a mechanism for broadening participation and accomplishing affirmative action, while the centralized Reagan approach best furthered his ideological goals (1983). Indeed, formal judicial selection mechanisms may not be central to understanding the outcomes of appointment processes. Such formal processes may be highly visible ''and an easy target for the reformer's criticisms,'' yet they may also serve as smoke-screens ''tending to obscure from the analyst's view the most important concerns for understanding recruitment outcomes'' (Slotnick, 1984a:237–238). The lessons learned from research at the federal level were reflected in Dubois' findings and his conclusion in California that ''the two parties draw their support from different social classes and have distinct commitments to particular ethnic and sexual groups,'' which is ''reflected in the different demographic mix of judges appointed under each governor'' (1985:28). These case studies, as well as work on the federal level, demonstrate the need for systematic analyses of executive management style, party organization, and other variables which might affect recruitment outcomes.

Concluding Thoughts

An examination of judicial selection literature published during the past several years reveals that this is an area in which a great deal of wide-ranging scholarly activity is taking place at both the federal and state judiciary levels. Clearly, from the perspective of the academic social sciences, while many research approaches and diverse methodologies have been utilized by analysts to examine judicial recruitment concerns, this is not an area where great theoretical advances of broad interest and applicability are likely to be made. Studies have tended to take place in limited research contexts where analysts have viewed the trees but not the forest. Research approaches have often been idiosyncratic and many case studies have been accompanied with little synthesis and integration of knowledge. In part, this may reflect a healthy situation in which judicial selection research and commentary is undertaken from many quarters, and ''any discussion of the subject must include diverse viewpoints and recognize the potential contributions to be found in the alternative perspectives brought . . . by practicing attorneys, judges, academic researchers, public office holders, journalists, and members of the public'' (Dubois, 1986a:31). Scholars are raising numerous interesting and important questions about the processes which exist for the recruitment of judges, and they are receiving answers which have greatly expanded our substantive understanding of judicial selection while also providing the grist for the mill of future research.

Often, the findings of the studies discussed throughout this essay have had significant policy implications for actors participating in judicial selection processes in some capacity. Thus, for example, studies of judicial elections have made it clear that the dearth of information about candidates and races is a major roadblock to such elections playing their intended role in a democratic polity. We have also learned that institutional arrangements may affect voter turnout more than information and knowledge. Clearly, the research in this area is suggestive of directions that reforms of judicial campaigns can take as well as of strategic alterations that might be made by judgeship candidates contesting those elections. At the federal level, analysts have underscored the complexity of judicial selection behavior, while documenting that reforms in processes, per se, may not be directly translatable into alternations in judicial behavior. At bottom, our discussion has also demonstrated that there are numerous questions which have not been addressed or about which much remains unsaid.

Little research has attempted to bridge the gap between state and federal selection arenas. Thus, for example, while research has documented systemic differences among federal judges at different levels of the bench (Slotnick, 1983a), it might be instructive to compare and contrast judges across state and federal benches. Such a linkage could lead to a broadened assessment and understanding of the strengths, weaknesses, capabilities, and unique roles of judiciaries operative at diverse governmental levels. More broadly, analysts of judicial recruitment have failed to incorporate their research with studies of elite recruitment in other political contexts. This is particularly telling with regard to understanding the emergence of individuals from underrepresented groups, particularly minorities and women, to governmental positions.

In addition, it should be stressed that studies of judicial selection have implications which go well beyond the primary concern of who gets chosen to fill judgeship vacancies. Rather, research in this area has clear implications for a broader understanding of elite recruitment, elections and voting behavior, political participation, political campaigns, executive-legislative relations and, ultimately, questions about the very nature of representative democracy and the requirements of democratic theory.

Fortuitous circumstances such as the large numbers of vacant judgeships at the federal level and contested judgeships in the state judiciaries have surely given an impetus and momentum to research in this area. The breadth and scope of the studies discussed throughout this essay clearly suggest that the area will continue to be a productive and provocative one for research scholars in the years ahead.

References

Atkins, Burton, Mathew DeZee, and William Eckert (1984) "State Supreme Court Elections: The Significance of Racial Cues," 12 *American Politics Quarterly* 211.

Baum, Lawrence (1983) "The Electoral Fate of Incumbent Judges in the Ohio Court of Common Pleas," 66 *Judicature* 420.

Chinn, Nancy and Larry Berkson (1980) *Literature on Judicial Selection*. Chicago: American Judicature Society.

DuBois, Philip (1980) *From Ballot to Bench: Judicial Elections and the Quest for Accountability*. Austin: University of Texas Press.

_____ (1984) "Voting Cues in Nonpartisan Trial Court Elections: A Multivariate Assessment," 18 *Law & Society Review* 395.

_____ (1985) "State Trial Court Appointments: Does the Governor Make a Difference?" 69 *Judicature* 20.

_____ (1986a) "Accountability, Independence, and the Selection of State Judges: The Role of Popular Judicial Elections," 40 *Southwestern Law Journal* 31.

_____ (1986b) "Financing Trial Court Elections: Who Contributes to California Judicial Campaigns?" 70 *Judicature* 8.

_____ (1986c) "Penny For Your Thoughts? Campaign Spending in California Trial Court Elections, 1976–1982," 38 *Western Political Quarterly* 265.

Flango, Victor and Craig Ducat (1979) "What Difference Does Method of Judicial Selection Make?" 5 *The Justice System Journal* 25.

Fowler, W. Gary (1983) "A Comparison of Initial Recommendation Procedures: Judicial Selection Under Reagan and Carter," 1 *Yale Law and Policy Review* 299.

_____ (1984) "Judicial Selection Under Reagan and Carter: A Comparison of Their Initial Recommendation Procedures," 67 *Judicature* 265.

Goldman, Sheldon (1965) "Characteristics of Eisenhower and Kennedy Appointees to the Lower Federal Courts," 18 *Western Political Quarterly* 755.

_____ (1972) "Johnson and Nixon Appointees to the Federal Lower Courts," 34 *Journal of Politics* 934.

_____ (1981) "Carter's Judicial Appointments: A Lasting Legacy," 64 *Judicature* 344.

_____ (1985) "Reorganizing the Judiciary: The First Term Appointments," 68 *Judicature* 313.

_____ (1987) "Reagan's Second Term Judicial Appointments: The Battle at Midway," 70 *Judicature* 324.

Griffin, Kenyon and Michael Horan (1983) "Patterns of Voting Behavior in Judicial Retention Elections for Supreme Court Justices in Wyoming," 67 *Judicature* 68.

Griffin, Kenyon and Margaret Maier Murdock (1985) "Practicing Attorneys and Judicial Retention Decisions: Judging the Judges in Wyoming," 69 *Judicature* 37.

Hall, Kermit (1984) "Progressive Reform and the Decline of Democratic Accountabilty: The Popular Election of State Supreme Court Judges, 1850–1920," 2 *American Bar Foundation Research Journal* 345.

Hall, William and Larry Aspin (1987) "What Twenty Years of Judicial Retention Elections Have Told Us," 70 *Judicature* 340.

Kessel, John (1966) "Public Perceptions of the Supreme Court," 10 *Midwest Journal of Political Science* 167.

Koebel, C. Theodore (1983) "The Problem of Bias in Judicial Evaluation Surveys," 67 *Judicature* 224.

Lovrich, Nicholas, Jr. and Charles Sheldon (1983) "Voters in Contested, Non-Partisan Judicial Elections: A Responsible Electorate or a Problematic Public," 36 *Western Political Quarterly* 241.

_____ (1985) "Assessing Judicial Elections: Effects upon the Electorate of High and Low Articulation Systems," 38 *Western Political Quarterly* 276.

Nicholson, Marlene and Bradley Weiss (1986) "Funding Judicial Campaigns in the Circuit Court of Cook County," 70, *Judicature* 17.

Peltason, Jack (1955) *Federal Courts in the Political Process.* New York: Random House.

Scheb, John II (1983) "Is Anyone Listening? Assessing Bar Influence in Merit Retention Elections in Florida," 67 *Judicature* 112.

Sheldon, Charles and Nicholas Lovrich, Jr. (1983) "Knowledge and Judicial Voting: The Oregon and Washington Experience," 67 *Judicature* 234.

Slotnick, Elliot (1983a) "Federal Trial and Appellate Judges: How Do They Differ?" 36 *Western Political Quarterly* 570.

_____ (1983b) "Lowering the Bench or Raising It Higher?: Affirmative Action and Judicial Selection During the Carter Administration," 1 *Yale Law and Policy Review* 270.

_____ (1984a) "Judicial Selection Systems and Nomination Outcomes: Does the Process Make a Difference?" 12 *American Politics Quarterly* 225.

_____ (1984b) "The Paths to the Federal Bench: Gender, Race, and Judicial Recruitment Variation," 67 *Judicature* 370.

16

Judicial Recruitment and Racial Diversity on State Courts
An Overview

BARBARA LUCK GRAHAM

The informal and formal processes of determining who becomes a judge evoke intense interest and debate among various groups that seek to influence the nature, character and policy outcomes of our nation's courts. Political parties, bar associations, political elites, and interest groups (business, union, environmental, or civil rights organizations, etc.) struggle to participate and influence the processes of judicial recruitment and selection at the national and state level with the desired goal of shaping judicial policy outcomes favorable to their interests. The political struggle over judicial recruitment and selection also raises the issue of diversity on the bench whereby members of racial and ethnic minority groups and women seek representatives of their groups to serve on courts in order to insure that they have a voice in judicial decision-making. Viewed in this context, judicial recruitment is an important area of study because it speaks to the broader theoretical issue of minority group elite recruitment and representation in the judicial arena.

The issue of racial diversity on courts is one that has been given uneven scholarly attention in the literature on judicial recruitment.[1] On one hand, considerable attention has been paid to minority group representation at the federal court level. For example, conventional wisdom

Reprinted by permission of the American Judicature Society and the author from *Judicature*, vol. 74, no. 1 (June/July 1990), pp. 28–34.

now posits that representational criteria such as race, gender, and religious factors figure prominently for nomination to the U.S. Supreme Court and the lower federal courts.[2] To be sure, the determination of how much weight will be attached to representational factors varies among presidents and is usually dependent upon partisan and ideological considerations. Yet the literature seems to suggest that there is an expectation that diversity on the federal bench will continue to be an issue as long as the federal courts are accorded special status in our dual legal system.

Only recently, however, has similar attention been given to minority judicial recruitment at the state level. Recognizing the importance of state courts in the administration of justice and that most minority citizens are likely to come into contact with state, not federal courts, minority groups are now focusing on the extent to which state judicial systems provide opportunities to serve on the bench. Minority group efforts to penetrate access to the state bench become more problematic when we consider the existence of 50 state court systems accompanied with varied formal and informal judicial recruitment and selection processes to fill vacant seats on these courts. Whether states become and remain committed to a diverse bench will be a major challenge for minority groups and women in the 1990s.

An examination of the literature on judicial recruitment and black representation on the state bench reveals that additional research is necessary to address the important questions raised in this area. This study seeks to fill a major gap in the literature in its examination of minority judicial recruitment at the state level. The purpose of this article is to examine characteristics of judicial recruitment as it pertains to racial diversity on the state bench. It focuses on four major areas of concern. First, data are examined which explore the extent to which blacks are represented on state courts at all levels of the judicial hierarchy. Next, it looks at the structural and contextual explanations of black underrepresentation on state courts. Third, it examines two remedies for correcting the problem of black underrepresentation on the state bench. Finally, it considers the consequences and implications of the lack of racial diversity on the state bench for the administration of justice.

The research population under investigation is the universe of black judges presiding over state courts of general and limited jurisdiction in the United States. The data source for identifying black judges comes from a list of black judges in the United States compiled by the Joint Center for Political Studies (JCPS) and the Judicial Council of the National Bar Association.[3] This roster includes names, addresses and indication of the court presided over by the judge as of July 1986. Attempts were made to verify the existence of the judges on the specified courts and to determine how they initially obtained their seats for the highest general jurisdiction and special jurisdiction courts (civil or criminal) in the states. These data collection efforts involved gathering information from state court clerks and administrators,[4] court biographical directories,[5] state reporters and state official manuals. As a result, this study analyzes data on 714 state court judges covering 41 states for 1986.

Several major developments compel a reexamination of how characteristics of judicial recruitment affect racial diversity on the state bench. Greater attention to the policymaking activities of state courts raises the issue of whether women and minorities will have the opportunity to influence outcomes at all levels of the state judiciary. This development comes at a time when the U.S. Supreme Court and the lower federal judiciary are becoming increasingly conservative on issues of civil liberties and civil rights. The importance of this research is also underscored in light of several states' reexamination of their methods of selecting state judges. A contemporary assessment of black representation on state courts is expected to reveal additional insights into the problem of minority judicial recruitment at the state level.

Are Blacks Underrepresented?

The few empirical studies that analyze black judicial recruitment largely draw upon a data base in the early 1970s; a period in which there were extremely small numbers of black judges on state courts.[6] In 1972, Cook noted that one of the major research problems that occurs in an examination of black representation in the judiciary was identifying and locating black judges on state courts.[7] In order to assess the factors that affect black judicial recruitment, it is first necessary to offer a recent profile of black representation on state courts. In this section, two major issues are addressed. First, data are presented which show the nationwide distribution of black judges on state courts by level of court. In analyzing these data, I attempt to address the substantive question of whether blacks are actually underrepresented on state courts.

The JCPS publication identified 714 black judges presiding over state courts of general and limited jurisdiction and included a listing of quasi-judicial officials as of July 1986.[8] These data were coded and classified according to the distribution of black judges on the state bench by level of court and are presented in table 1. The number of seats on states' major appellate and trial courts are also included. As of 1986, we find that 41 states had black representation on their major and minor courts. Specifically, the data in table 1 reveal that nine states; Alaska, Hawaii, Maine, Montana, New Hampshire, North Dakota, South Dakota, Vermont and Wyoming, lacked black representation on their state courts. One might argue that opportunities for recruitment would be increased or limited depending on the size of the black population in the state. If the percentage of the black voting age population in the state is used as a measure of black population size,[9] we find that among the nine states listed above, seven had a black voting age population of less than one-half of 1 percent. Contrastingly, Idaho and Utah, states with less than one-half of 1 percent black voting age population, had black representation on their state courts.

Table 1   Distribution of black judges on state bench by level of court, 1986

State	State supreme court	Intermediate appellate court	General trial court	Total major courts	Limited juris. courts	Total all
Alabama	1 (9)	— (8)	4 (124)	5	14	19
Arizona	— (5)	— (18)	1 (101)	1	1	2
Arkansas	— (7)	— (6)	— (62)	0	2	2
California	1 (7)	4 (77)	29 (724)	34	54	88
Colorado	— (7)	— (10)	3 (107)	3	2	5
Connecticut	— (7)	— (9)	7 (139)	7	—	7
Delaware	— (5)	•	1 (13)	1	4	5
Florida	1 (7)	1 (46)	7 (362)	9	7	16
Georgia	— (7)	1 (9)	4 (131)	5	15	20
Idaho	— (5)	— (3)	1 (33)	1	—	1
Illinois	— (7)	3 (34)	42 (780)	45	—	45
Indiana	— (5)	— (12)	2 (206)	2	3	5
Iowa	— (9)	— (6)	1 (153)	1	—	1
Kansas	— (7)	1 (10)	2 (215)	3	—	3
Kentucky	— (7)	— (14)	2 (91)	2	—	2
Louisiana	— (7)	1 (48)	5 (192)	6	27	33
Maryland	1 (7)	1 (13)	11 (109)	13	10	23
Massachusetts	— (7)	1 (10)	4 (61)	5	12	17
Michigan	1 (7)	2 (18)	22 (196)	25	44	69
Minnesota	— (7)	— (12)	4 (224)	4	—	4
Mississippi	1 (9)	•	1 (79)	2	31	33
Missouri	— (7)	1 (32)	6 (303)	7	4	11
Nebraska	— (7)	•	— (48)	0	1	1
Nevada	— (5)	•	2 (35)	2	—	2
New Jersey	— (7)	1 (28)	11 (321)	12	21	33
New Mexico	— (5)	— (7)	— (59)	0	1	1
New York	1 (7)	3 (47)	24 (484)	28	35	63
North Carolina	1 (7)	2 (12)	1 (72)	4	14	18
Ohio	— (7)	2 (53)	6 (330)	8	19	27
Oklahoma	— (12)**	— (12)	1 (143)	1	2	3
Oregon	— (7)	— (10)	1 (85)	1	1	2
Pennsylvania	1 (7)	1 (24)	24 (330)	26	10	36
Rhode Island	— (5)	•	— (19)	0	1	1
South Carolina	1 (5)	1 (6)	1 (31)	3	51	54
Tennessee	— (5)	— (21)	8 (125)	8	3	11
Texas	— (18)**	1 (80)	6 (374)	7	27	34
Utah	— (5)	— (7)	— (29)	0	1	1
Virginia	1 (7)	1 (10)	2 (122)	4	2	6
Washington	— (9)	— (16)	3 (133)	3	1	4
West Virginia	— (5)	•	2 (60)	2	1	3
Wisconsin	— (7)	— (13)	3 (197)	3	—	3
Total	11 (289)	28 (741)	254 (7402)	293 (8432)	421	714

( ) Number of seats on state courts. See Council of State Governments. The Book of the States, 1988-89 Edition. (Lexington, KY) 157-160 for a complete description of how these figures were derived.
— No black judges on court.
• Court does not exist in state.
** Includes state supreme court and court of criminal appeals seats.

Table 1 also demonstrates that 41 percent (N = 293) of the black judges identified by the JCPS roster were classified as general jurisdiction judges and 59 percent (N = 421) were either limited jurisdiction judges or quasi-judicial officials. This finding indicates that black judges are more likely to be found on limited jurisdiction courts such as municipal courts, small claims courts, family courts or justice of the peace courts. It is likely that limited jurisdiction courts serve as important access routes for black judgeships in the state judiciary and subsequently advancing through judicial hierarchy.[10] An examination of biographical data on black judges serving on general jurisdiction courts indicates that many of them served on limited jurisdiction courts prior to their 1986 positions.

The fact that most black judges in the state judiciary are located on limited jurisdiction courts also suggests that they currently have limited opportunities to participate in judicial policymaking at the trial and appellate levels. The data presented in table 1 show that 87 percent (N = 254) of the black judges preside over trial courts of general jurisdiction and 13 percent (N = 39) preside over intermediate appellate courts and state supreme courts. General jurisdiction courts address a wide range of issues on matters such as criminal offenses, personal injury actions, divorce cases and the overall important policymaking function of allocating resources (in terms of gains and losses) that affect millions of individuals. Moreover, issues of discrimination in a variety of contexts are frequently before state courts; thus minority judges may be able to bring additional sensitivity and insight in dealing with these issues. Without greater numbers of black judges at the major trial and appellate levels, one can argue that the black community is deprived of the minority perspective on legal matter's and the development of the law at the state level.

The judicial recruitment literature also indicates the importance of region as a contextual factor in contributing to our understanding of the distribution of judicial selection systems throughout the country. An overview of the distribution of the five major selection systems indicates the nonrandom tendency of states to choose one selection system over another. For example, we find that elective systems (partisan and nonpartisan) dominate among southern states, merit systems are most often found in the midwest and western regions, and gubernatorial appointment systems are primarily found in the northeast. A breakdown of table 1 by region indicates that the north central states have the highest number of general jurisdiction black judges (N = 88), followed by the northeast (N = 70), south (N = 56) and the west (N = 40).[11] These findings are somewhat striking given that 15 states make up the south as defined in this study and that the south has the highest black voting age population and the highest percentage of black elected officials compared to other regions of the country. This finding illustrates a wide disparity in regional distributions of general jurisdiction black judges. In contrast, the south leads the other regions for limited jurisdiction judges (N = 210), followed by the northeast (N = 79), north central (N = 71) and the west (N = 61). Region, then, is a useful contextual variable when examining recruitment patterns of blacks to the state bench.

Have black attorneys made progress in obtaining seats on state courts? The American Judicature Society reported in 1973 that slightly more than 1 percent of judges on the state bench were black.[12] The trends presented in table 2 indicate that progress has been made for obtaining general jurisdiction seats over time. What is significant about the figures presented in table 2 is that a large percentage of black judges (46 percent) for which data were available obtained their seats since 1980. If this trend continues, one can speculate that black attorneys will continue to make progress in obtaining seats on the state bench in the 1990s.

Against this background, are blacks underrepresented in the state judiciary? Of course, representation can be defined in several ways such as symbolic, substantive, and proportional.[13] Symbolic representation is exemplified by the presence of judges by identifiable members of their race or gender. Smith and Crockett have shown how black judges provide symbolic pride, inspiration and serve as a symbol of law and justice for members of their group.[14] Once on the bench, it is argued that black judges provide substantive representation by deciding cases in a manner which reduces the vestiges of racism in the legal system.[15] Empirical studies have shown that once on the bench, black judicial decisionmaking increases equality of treatment among defendants.[16]

Table 2   Year general jurisdiction judges initially obtained seats*

Year	N	%
1957-1969	14	6%
1970-1974	40	17%
1975-1979	72	31%
1980-1986	109	46%
Total	235	100%

*The year the judge initially reached the bench could not be determined for 58 judges.

The most prevalent definition of representation found in the judicial recruitment literature is proportional representation; that is, the proportion of black judges should reflect the same proportion of blacks in the general population. Indeed, if this definition is used, unquestionably blacks are underrepresented on the state bench. Yet, using proportional representation as the yardstick is problematic since for a large majority of seats on state courts, only licensed attorneys are eligible to serve as judges. From another perspective then, an argument can be raised that the black attorney population is the most relevant population to measure against the proportion of black judges on the state bench.

Recent figures indicate that black judges make up approximately 3.8 percent of all the full- and part-time seats on the state bench.[17] Similarly, black attorneys constitute approximately 3 percent of the legal profession. Tentatively, one could conclude from these figures that black judges are not underrepresented on the state bench since the proportion of judges on the state bench are roughly equal to the number of attorneys. On the other hand, we should consider the point that black attorneys are grossly underrepresented in the legal profession; figures indicate that there are about 25,000 black attorneys out of a total pool of 750,000.[18] From this perspective, using the proportion of black attorneys as the population to measure against is misleading for it does not take into account the small pool of available black attorneys to serve on the bench. In the following section, I will consider the utility of this contextual factor in explaining black representation on the state bench.

Explaining a Homogeneous Bench

What explains black underrepresentation on the state bench? The judicial recruitment and selection literature advances two dominant approaches in accounting for the lack of racial diversity on the state bench: structural and contextual explanations. The theoretical underpinnings of the empirical research that highlights structural characteristics of judicial recruitment and selection are generally linked to elite recruitment in other political contexts. This view suggests that structural and systemic forces in the political environment affect the extent to which underrepresented groups gain access to positions at all levels of government. For example, the political participation literature has demonstrated that barriers to voting (e.g., vote dilution techniques and registration requirements) have enhanced black nonvoting and engenders the inability of black citizens to choose representatives of their choice. Drawing on this literature, studies have sought to determine whether judicial selection mechanisms are central to our understanding of recruitment outcomes for minority groups.

Contextual explanations have also emerged in explaining the paucity of black judges on the state bench. This approach suggests that other factors besides judicial selection affect the extent to which blacks will be represented on the state bench. The contextual variable that has received the most attention in the literature is the availability of black attorneys to serve on the state bench. The expectation is that the lack of black attorneys correlates with the lack of black judges on the bench. State statutory qualifications are likely to affect the size of the pool of available attorneys from which judges are selected. The primary ones include age, residency requirements, and legal qualifications such as being a member of the state bar or having practiced law for a certain period of time. These requirements[19] vary among the states, but because of the lack of nationwide data on black attorneys by state, it is difficult to assess the impact of these qualifications or the extent to which they affect the numbers of black attorneys to serve on the state bench.

Three early studies offer some insights on the effects of judicial selection and black representation on the state bench. Cook found that in southern courts, electoral systems did not produce black judges on major courts but a large majority of blacks served on rural courts of limited jurisdiction where in many instances a law degree was not a necessary qualification.[20] Her examination of black representation on northern courts revealed that nonpartisan elections were more favorable in enhancing black representation on state courts, partisan elections were least favorable and that gubernatorial appointment tended to produce idiosyncratic results. In her study, Cook also demonstrated that the very low percentage of black lawyers correlated with the lack of black judges on both northern and southern courts, but this variable did not account entirely for the small number of black judges.

Smith examined black judicial attitudes toward recruitment and selection based on an early 1970s survey of 185 state and federal judges.[21] His study indicated that while 55 percent of the judgeships were listed as elective, 77 percent of the black jurists surveyed were appointed to the bench. His analysis also demonstrated that judicial elections tended to be less influential in the recruitment of black judges. Black voters, according to Smith, were less influential in getting blacks to judicial office than professional standing, political party and friendship.

A 1973 American Judicature Society study revealed that black judges constituted approximately 1.3 percent of the judiciary.[22] Despite the argument that black attorneys stand a better chance of acquiring judgeships through the elective rather than the appointive process, the study showed that most black jurists surveyed attained their positions through some form of appointment. The study found that the prime reason for the small proportion of black judges was the small number of black lawyers available to serve on the bench.

Recent attempts to address the question of whether different methods of judicial selection result in different degrees of access to the bench depending on such factors as gender and race include a 1985 study published by the Fund for Modern Courts.[23] In a nationwide survey, the study demonstrated that the success of women and minorities in achieving judicial office depends on methods of selection—that a higher percentage of women and minorities attained more judicial positions through appointment than an elective process.

When statistical controls were employed, Dubois found only minor differences between elective and appointive systems for female and nonwhite judges recruited to sit on the California trial court bench.[24] He attributed this finding to the underrepresentation of women and nonwhites in the legal profession. Utilizing the Fund for Modern Courts data, Alozie directly addressed the question of whether methods of formal judicial selection account for the differential distribution of black judges on state judiciaries.[25] He found that the percentage of black lawyers in the state was the most significant factor in explaining the degree of variation of black judges in the state, not formal methods of judicial selection.

In another study, Graham addressed the question of whether formal and informal methods of judicial selection predict the likelihood of a black or white attorney serving as a trial judge.[26] In an examination of individual level data collected on 3,823 black and white trial court judges in 36 states, Graham found that formal structures made little difference in black representation because black judges who were formally elected were actually appointed to the bench. Moreover, the study showed that informal methods to the bench, that is, actual routes, were significant. Specifically, gubernatorial appointment and legislative appointment systems seemed to increase black representation on the state trial bench. Overall, the study provided support for the contention that structural arrangements of state judicial selection are significant in accounting for black underrepresentation on the state bench.

A closer examination of these competing approaches in explaining black underrepresentation on the state might reveal that scholars have viewed the trees but not the forest in addressing this problem. The research that suggests that blacks will increase their judgeships by increasing the proportion of black lawyers does not adequately consider the extent to which structural forces in the political and legal environments not only affect the proportion of black judges, but also the availability of black attorneys. Walton's observation is noteworthy here, for he argues that "by barring blacks from the voting booths, the bar rosters and associations, law schools, and full participation in the political arena, states have determined to a great extent the parameters of the black judiciary."[27] Focusing on contextual factors alone does little to expand our substantive understanding of how state judicial recruitment affects outcomes for minority participants. What this literature does reveal is that we are only beginning to make advances in our understanding of the impact of structural characteristics of judicial recruitment for minority representation on state courts.

Patterns of Accession

For descriptive purposes, the data presented in table 1 were reexamined within the context of how black judges reach the state bench by the states' formal designation and by actual routes. The judicial selection literature identifies five major formal routes to the state bench: gubernatorial appointment, Missouri Plan, legislative appointment, partisan election and nonpartisan election. As Berkson pointed out, almost no two states are alike in the methods used to select their judges and few states employ the same method for choosing judges at all levels of the state judiciary.[28] Table 3 presents the patterns of accession to the state bench by formal and actual routes for the general jurisdiction judges.

Table 3   How black judges reach the bench: formal and actual routes, 1986

Selection system	Formal route[1]	%	Actual route	%
Gubernatorial appointment	18	6.1	18	6.2
Missouri Plan	39	13.3	36[2]	12.4
Legislative appointment	14	4.8	12[3]	4.1
Partisan election	106	36.2	50	17.2
Nonpartisan election	97	33.1	24	8.2
Circuit court appointment	19	6.5	19	6.5
Supreme court appointment	—	—	14	4.8
Vacancy	—	—	113	38.8
Court reorganization/consolidation	—	—	5	1.7
Total	293	100.0	291[4]	99.9

— not applicable

1. In some states, different formal selection systems may be used for trial and appellate courts. The figures for the formal designation category were derived by first calculating the total for trial and appellate courts separately and then collapsing both totals into one category. The coding for the formal routes is: appellate courts 1×gubernatorial appointment (CA), 2×Missouri Plan (FL, KS, MD, MA, MO, NY), 3×legislative appointment (SC, VA), 4×partisan election (AL, IL, MS, NC, PA, TX) and 5×nonpartisan election (GA, LA, MI, OH); trial courts 1×gubernatorial appointment (NJ, NC [special judges of superior courts in NC are appointed by governor]); 2×Missouri Plan (AZ, CO, DE, IA, MD, MA, MO, IN). 3×legislative appointment (CT, SC, VA); 4×partisan election (AL, IL, IN, KS, MS, NY, PA, TN, TX, WV); 5×nonpartisan election (CA, FL, GA, ID, KY, LA, MI, MN, NV, OH, OK, OR, WA, WI) and 6×circuit court appointment (IL-associate circuit court judges).

2. Excludes 3 judges who initially reached the bench through court reorganization.

3. Excludes 2 gubernatorial appointments in filling vacancies in Virginia and South Carolina.

4. The author was unable to identify how 1 Ohio judge and 1 Louisiana judge reached the bench.

An examination of the formal route category shows that most black general jurisdiction judges preside over courts in states which formally use partisan and nonpartisan elections.[29] This was not an unexpected finding since 25 of the 36 states with black representation on their major courts formally use elective systems for all or some of their judgeships. When the actual routes to the major state court bench were determined, the figures presented in table 3 indicate the prevalence of interim appointments in formal selection systems, primarily partisan and non-partisan systems. With the exception of Illinois and Louisiana, all states with elective systems examined in this study permit the governor to fill vacancies occurring between elections. Most of the black judges in elective systems initially obtained their seats by gubernatorial appointment. Moreover, vacancy appointments were more common in nonpartisan systems than partisan systems. These findings are compatible with prior research which indicates that in elective systems, a considerable proportion of judges initially reach the bench by executive appointment.[30]

The data presented in table 3 are significant in that they demonstrate the importance of the politics of the appointing governor in determining the extent to which minorities will occupy seats on our nation's state courts, despite the formal method used to select judges. Glick observed that "governors usually pick individuals who have been involved in state politics and whose past activity either has been of personal benefit, or has benefited a political party or political allies."[31] He also acknowledged that governors make symbolic appointments to these positions in their attempt to satisfy several constituencies. This analysis suggests that greater attention to the appointment politics of governors might reveal important insights for understanding minority recruitment outcomes.

Remedies

What can be done to remedy the problem of the lack of racial diversity on the state bench? The two remedies discussed here seek to address the broad problem of a racially homogeneous state bench. The first remedy involves the development of affirmative action policies to overcome past inequities in judicial recruitment and selection. Such efforts could be successfully implemented among appointive systems of judicial selection, including the filling of vacancies in elective systems. Since representational criteria are generally among the host of other factors in determining recruitment outcomes, affirmative action goals are clearly consistent with attracting legally qualified minority candidates to the state bench. President Carter's innovations on the federal level in the creation of merit panels among the states serves as a model.[32] Carter's appointments of minorities and women to the federal bench during his single term in office was a dramatic departure from the appointment practices of previous presidential administrations.[33] In addition, various groups (civil rights organizations, women's groups, bar associations) will have to play a greater role in state judicial recruitment and selection in order to realize the goals of a diverse state bench.

Elective systems have structural components not found in appointive systems that are likely to affect the chances of minorities in obtaining seats on the state bench in greater numbers. Several states use at-large or multi-member boundaries as the geographic basis for electing judges.[34] Lawsuits have been filed by minorities challenging the use of at-large and multimember districts in state judicial elections because they have not been successful at the polls.[35] Lower federal court decisions have responded to black voters' claims by expanding the concept of minority vote dilution to judicial elections.[36] The Fifth and Sixth Circuit Courts of Appeals have subsequently applied Sections 2 and 5 of the Voting Rights Act of 1965 as amended to judicial elections.[37] In response to these decisions, several jurisdictions must redraw their judicial districts in order to insure that black voters will have the opportunity to elect judicial candidates of their choice. The immediate effect of these decisions will be felt in the south where much of the litigation originated. Consequently, judicial redistricting is expected to be successful in bringing minorities to the bench in those areas where there [is] a heavy concentration of minorities.[38]

Conclusion

The purpose of this article was to present an overview of the characteristics of judicial recruitment and selection as they contribute to our understanding of black representation on the state bench. Viewed in this context, this research has important implications about the ongoing debate with respect to who gets chosen to fill judgeships on the state bench. This study revealed that although black attorneys have made significant gains on the state bench since the 1970s, black underrepresentation still remains a problem. An examination of the literature that attempted to explain the problem demonstrates the need for systematic analyses of structural variables which might affect minority recruitment outcomes. It was also suggested that the application of affirmative action criteria and judicial redistricting were expected to enhance minority representation at the state level. This article has clear implications about the direction future research should take in addressing the problem of a racially homogeneous state bench. Slotnick has argued that analyses of judicial recruitment have failed to take into account studies of elite recruitment in other political contexts.[39] Since this research suggests that minority representation is as important in the state judiciary as it is in other branches of government, perhaps future research should consider the extent to which institutional arrangements, political participation and elite behavior reveal insights about judicial recruitment and selection.

Endnotes

[1] For an overview and annotated bibliography of this extensive literature, see Chinn and Berkson, *Literature on Judicial Selection* (Chicago: American Judicature Society, 1980); Slotnick, "Review Essay on Judicial Recruitment and Selection," 13 *Just. Sys. J.* 109 (1988).

2 See, for example, Abraham, *The Judicial Process* (New York: Oxford University Press, 5th ed., 1986).

3 See Joint Center for Political Studies, *Black Judges in the United States* (Washington, D.C.: 1986).

4 The author would like to thank the state court clerks and administrators for their assistance in the collection of the data.

5 Two directories are: *The American Bench: Judges of the Nation* (Sacramento: Reginald Bishop Foster & Associates, Inc., 3rd ed., 1985/86); *California Courts and Judges* (San Francisco Law Book Service Co., 4th ed., 1985).

6 See Cook, "Black Representation in the Third Branch," 1 *Black L. J.* 260 (1972); Smith, *Race Versus Robe* (Port Washington, NY: Associated Faculty Press, 1983); American Judicature Society, "The Black Judge in America: A Statistical Profile," 57 *Judicature* 18 (1973). But see Alozie, "Black Representation on State Judiciaries," 69 *Soc. Sci. Q.* 979 (1988).

7 Cook, supra n. 6 at 261.

8 "Quasi-judicial officials are defined as officers required to investigate facts, hold hearings, and recommend official actions on the basis of those facts." See Joint Center for Political Studies, supra n. 3 at 11.

9 See Joint Center for Political Studies, "Black Elected Officials: A National Roster" (Washington, D.C., 16th ed., 1987).

10 See Smith, supra n. 6; Ryan et al., *American Trial Judges: Their Work Styles and Performance* (New York: Free Press, 1980).

11 The geographic divisions used in this study are compatible with those found in JCPS, *Black Elected Officials*, supra n. 9. They are south = MD, WV, VA, KY, NC, SC, TN, GA, MS, AL, FL, TX, LA, OK, AK, DE; northeast = PA, NJ, NY, CT, MA, RI; north central = OH, IL, IN, WI, MO, MI, MN, IA, KS; WEST = CA, OR, WA, ID, AZ, CO, NM, UT, NV.

12 American Judicature Society, supra n. 6, at 18.

13 See Pitkin, ed., *Representation* (New York: Atherton Press, 1969).

14 Smith, supra n. 6; Crockett, "Judicial Selection and the Black Experience," 58 *Judicature* 438 (1971).

15 See Crockett, "Racism in the Courts," 20 *J. of Pub. L.* 685 (1970).

16 See, for example, Welch, Combs and Gruhl, "Do Black Judges Make a Difference?", 32 *Am. J. of Pol. Sci.* 126 (1988).

17 Fund for Modern Courts, *The Success of Women and Minorities in Achieving Judicial Office: The Selection Process* 13 (New York: 1985).

18 These figures were supplied by the National Bar Association, Washington, D.C., January 22, 1990.

19 See National Center for State Courts, *State Court Organization*, 1987 (Williamsburg, VA: 1988) for a listing of state trial and appellate court qualifications to serve on the bench.

20 Cook, supra n. 6.

21 Smith, supra n. 6.

22 American Judicature Society, supra n. 6.

23 Fund for Modern Courts, supra n. 17.

24 Dubois, "The Influence of Selection System on the Characteristics of a Trial Court Bench: The Case of California," 8 *Just. Sys. J.* 59 (1983).

25 Alozie, supra n. 6.

26 Graham, "Do Judicial Selection Systems Matter? A Study of Black Representation on State Courts," forthcoming. *Am. Pol. Q.* (1990).

27 Walton, *Invisible Politics* 224 (Albany: SUNY Press, 1985).

[28] Berkson, "Judicial Selection in the United States: A Special Report," 64 *Judicature* 179 (1980).

[29] Data were not collected on the limited jurisdiction judges in this study because of the difficulty in obtaining biographical data for these judges and the fact that judicial selection mechanisms vary considerably among these judgeships and they frequently do not conform to the five major methods of judicial selection discussed in this article. See Berkson, supra n. 28.

[30] See Herndon, "Appointment as a Means of Initial Accession to Elective State Courts of Last Resort," 38 *N. Dak. L. Rev.* 60 (1962); Atkins and Glick, "Formal Judicial Recruitment and State Supreme Court Decisions," 2 *Am. Pol. Q.* 427 (1974); Dubois, *From Ballot to Bench* (Houston: University of Texas Press, 1980).

[31] Glick, *Courts, Politics, and Justice* 89 (New York: McGraw-Hill, 2nd ed., 1988).

[32] See, for example Goldman, "Should There Be Affirmative Action for the Judiciary?," 62 *Judicature* 488 (1979); Slotnick, "The U.S. Circuit Judge Nominating Commission," 1 *L. & Policy Q.* 465 (1979); Slotnick, "Federal Appellate Judge Selection During the Carter Administration: Recruitment Changes and Unanswered Questions," 6 *Just. Sys. J.* 283 (1981).

[33] See Goldman, "Reagan's Judicial Legacy: Completing the Puzzle and Summing Up," 72 *Judicature* 318 (1989) for a comparative analysis.

[34] See National Center for State Courts, supra n. 19.

[35] See American Judicature Society, "The Voting Rights Act and Judicial Elections: An Update on Current Litigation," 73 *Judicature* 74 (1989).

[36] See Davidson, ed., *Minority Vote Dilution* (Washington, D.C.: Howard University Press, 1984) for a discussion of this concept. See also *Voter Information Project, Inc. v. City of Baton Rouge*, 612 F.2d 208 (5th Cir. 1980).

[37] See *Haith v. Martin*, 618 F.Supp. 410 (E.D.N.C. 1985) aff'd 477 U.S. 901(1986); *Mallory v. Eyrich*, 839 F.2d 275 (6th Cir. 1988); *Chisom v. Edwards* 839 F.2d 1056 (5th Cir. 1988), cert. denied, *Roemer v. Chisom* 109 S.Ct. 390 (1988).

[38] For example, the first election after judicial redistricting in Mississippi produced two black winners in contested judicial elections—the first in the history of Mississippi elections. See Canerdy, "Black Candidates Appear to Do Poorly in Judicial Races," *The Clarion-Ledger*, June 21, 1989, at 1, col. 1. See also McDuff, "The Voting Rights Act and Judicial Elections Litigation: The Plaintiffs' Perspective," 73 *Judicature* 82 (1989).

[39] Slotnick, supra n. 1.

17

Courts and the Challenges of Wrongful Convictions

MARVIN ZALMAN

The Growth and Scope of Actual Innocence as a Policy Issue

Americans who pay attention to the news have grown accustomed over the last decade to reading stories about people freed from prison for crimes they did not commit. In the early 1990s, these stories were highly unusual and deeply unsettling. They no longer seem unusual, but they remain deeply unsettling. Wrongful conviction, defined as the convictions of people who are factually innocent, has become a policy issue. Horror stories of people "buried alive" in prison for other people's crimes were known before 1990 but were treated as the inevitable failings of a human system (Yant, 1991). In fact, common law–adversary system trial procedures have long reflected anxiety about wrongful convictions, as have constitutional rights that the Supreme Court required the states to follow during the "due process revolution" of the 1960s (Graham, 1970). Jurists and lawyers could proudly point to the presumption of innocence, proof beyond a reasonable doubt, availability of defense counsel, an impartial jury, the ability to cross-examine prosecution witnesses, and many other rights as procedural shields against erroneous criminal verdicts.

After 1990 something happened that changed complacent, if contested, views about the accuracy of American trials. That something was the introduction of DNA testing as a police investigation tool. Forensic serology had advanced by 1990 in its ability to match a suspect's blood with a limited proportion of individuals, but properly conducted DNA testing raised the probability of a match between a biological sample and a suspect's DNA to

Written especially for *Courts and Justice*.

293

near certainty. Conversely, a DNA nonmatch absolutely excludes a suspect (Saferstein, 2004: 328–405). As the number of exonerations grew, it became apparent that unlike past exonerations, which depended on factors that were open to dispute, DNA exonerations provided absolute proof of innocence (Borchard, 1932; Lassers, 1973).

This realization set the ground for the problem-perception stage of wrongful conviction public policy development. That is, a problem becomes a public policy issue when enough people perceive it not simply as a private woe that nature or cruel circumstance inflicted on them or imposed on others, but as a public concern that is amenable to government intervention and reform (Jones, 1984: 38–50). The normal policy trajectory from problem perception to the formulation and implementation of policies typically begins with aggregation, whereby groups of people organize to seek governmental redress and favorable public policies. These interest group demands are channeled through lobbying activity to reach political elites capable of formulating and enacting policies favoring those groups. This is the "agenda setting" stage (Cobb and Elder, 1972; Zalman, 2005: 173). The policy process does not always follow this neat script. Sometimes, instead of a significant *number* of people creating pressure to elevate an issue to the agenda setting stage, a significant *person* with the influence to do so moves an issue to a position of policy prominence.

No mass movement advocating for the wrongly convicted existed in the early 1990s. Several factors, however, advanced wrongful conviction as a policy issue. One was a remarkable body of psychological research conducted after 1970 that examined misidentification and suggested procedures for reducing lineup error rates (Doyle, 2005; Cutler and Penrod, 1995; Loftus, 1979). In New York two enterprising public defenders and law school clinical professors, Barry Scheck and Peter Neufeld, started the first law school clinic innocence project that pursued cases of inmates who claimed they were innocent (Scheck et al., 2003). Documentary film makers produced powerful accounts of wrongful convictions that stirred national attention (Bikel, 2000; Morris, 1988; Siegel, 1997). And news stories published more and more inherently dramatic stories of DNA exonerations (Warden, 2003; Zalman, 2007).

Janet Reno, who was attorney general of the United States from 1993 to 2001, read these stories and was in a position to do something about them. As the former Dade County chief prosecutor, she was appointed in 1989 as a special prosecutor to examine an especially sordid miscarriage of justice that put James Richardson on Florida's death row for poisoning his children. This wrongful conviction involved gross prosecutorial misconduct that framed an innocent man. Prosecutors failed to turn over exculpatory evidence to the defense and kept important witnesses off the stand. They relied on a jailhouse snitch who lied about Richardson making an in-jail confession and rewarded him with probation for an attempted murder conviction. Reno recommended that Richardson be released (Doyle, 2005: 122–3; Radelet et al., 1992: 197–213). As attorney general, Janet Reno's curiosity and sense of justice were piqued by news accounts of DNA exonerations, and she directed Jeremy Travis, then director of the National Institute of Justice, to probe the matter (Travis, 1998). This led the NIJ to fund a study that published a persuasive and much quoted report, *Convicted by Juries, Exonerated by Science* (Connors et al., 1996). Soon after the Justice Department sponsored a task force of police, prosecutors, and psychologists who published initial standards for error-reducing lineup procedures (Doyle, 2005: 169–87; Technical Working Group, 1999).

As the Justice Department was exploring wrongful convictions, Scheck and Neufeld's Innocence Project at Cardozo Law School was uncovering an unsettling number of convictions against innocent people. They sensed that these exonerations were at the tip of a wrongful conviction iceberg. With journalist Jim Dwyer they wrote a book that not only recounted their cases with power and pathos, but organized the book to focus on the range of reasons why miscarriages of justice occur (Scheck et al., 2003). This came shortly after Hugo Bedau and Michael Radelet expanded a seminal and influential law review article on errors in capital cases into a more popular book, which also raised doubts about the accuracy of criminal convictions among the wider public (Bedau and Radelet, 1987; Radelet et al., 1992). Scheck, Neufeld, and Dwyer's popular book, first published in 2000, helped to raise public awareness of wrongful convictions and to shape a public policy approach. This approach basically involves breaking the topic of wrongful conviction into a list of specific "causes." There is something artificial about this because every miscarriage of justice involves multiple causes, but the approach focuses energies of reformers toward specific and attainable policies and programs.

In a relatively short period of time wrongful conviction was on the criminal justice *systemic agenda*, meaning "all issues that are commonly perceived by members of the political community as meriting public attention and as involving matters within the legitimate jurisdiction of existing governmental authority" (Cobb and Elder, 1972: 5). Indeed, wrongful conviction issues have moved onto the *institutional*, or *governmental*, *agenda* in that they have "widespread attention, a shared concern that some type of action is required, and a recognition that the matter is appropriate for the jurisdiction of a government unit" (Marion and Oliver, 2006: 82). For example, the tremendous resistance by many prosecutors to DNA testing by inmates claiming innocence in the 1990s led to calls for reform (Medwed, 2004). As a result, after four years of legislative maneuvering, Congress passed the *Innocence Protection Act* as a watered-down part of the 2004 *Justice for All Act,* which provides standards and funding for DNA testing of potential exonerees (Leahy, 2004a, 2004b; Weich, 2005). Because state legislation allowing for DNA testing of prisoners was a requirement of the act, at least thirty-eight states and the District of Columbia have passed "innocence statutes." These allow special appeals by prisoners with DNA-based claims who have exhausted appellate remedies (Jones, 2005: 1249; Zacharias, 2005: 193–95). The *Justice for All Act* also raised the level of compensation for individuals wrongly convicted in federal court from $5,000 to $50,000 per year of wrongful incarceration (Kleinert, 2006: 506). Notice, however, that these legislative reforms deal with only one or two aspects of the larger problem of wrongful conviction: the lack of resources for and resistance to postconviction DNA testing and the low level of compensation for exonerees.

Just to list the discrete issues typically associated with wrongful conviction as causes or as problems gives some idea of the vast range and complexity of the issue: mistaken eyewitness identification and suggestive police behavior during identifications; false confessions; police and prosecutorial negligence and tunnel vision; police and prosecutorial perjury and misfeasance; perjury by perpetrators, witnesses, and jailhouse snitches; forensic science issues of "junk science," perjury by forensic examiners, and substandard laboratories; ineffective assistance of defense counsel because of incompetence, overwork, or lack of resources; racial or class biases that overtly or subtly influence decisions; the psychological effects of wrongful conviction and treatments; and the establishment of state innocence commissions (see Giannelli and Raeder, 2006; Leo, 2005: 203–7; Mays and Ruddell, 2008: 187–209; Scheck et al., 2003; Zalman, 2005: 176–8). Each of these issues has generated a substantial scholarly literature and for each one a number of reform policies have been advocated. At the present time many discrete reform efforts are under way.

A big public problem that affects many people will generally be treated as a more urgent policy issue. Because no records are kept on exonerations, and because an acquittal does not necessarily mean that a defendant is factually innocent, it is impossible to know the precise number of actual innocence convictions. Some have argued that the 200 DNA exonerations proven by the spring of 2007, or even twice that number if non-DNA exonerations are added, is a minute portion of the one million or so felony convictions meted out every year in the United States (Gross et al., 2005: 527–29; Innocence Project, n.d.; Marquis, 2005: 521). Other data, based on surveys of criminal justice professionals who are best informed about miscarriages of justice, suggest that there are approximately 5,000 to 10,000 felony convictions of innocent defendants every year, with about 2,000 to 4,000 sent to prison. This is an estimate, not a count or a firm figure. It is based on three surveys of state judges, prosecutors, police chiefs and sheriffs, and defense attorneys. The first, conducted in Ohio in the early 1980s, has been widely cited (Huff et al., 1986). Two recent replications, one in Ohio by Robert Ramsey and James Frank (2007), and the second, a Michigan replication of Ramsey and Frank (2007), provide remarkably similar estimates: that approximately .5 of 1 to 1 percent of all felony convictions are imposed on innocent defendants.

> The BJS reported 1,051,000 state felony convictions and sentences in 2002, a jail sentence rate of 28%, and a prison sentence rate of 41% (DuRose and Langan, 2004). A wrongful conviction prevalence rate of ½% would result in 5,255 innocent persons convicted, and of those, 1,471 wrongly jailed and 2,154 wrongly imprisoned. For a 1% incidence rate the comparable figures are 10,510 wrongly convicted, 2,943 wrongly jailed, and 4,309 wrongly imprisoned. (Zalman et al., 2008: 94–95)

These estimates and the considered judgment of those who have given sustained attention to the issue of wrongful convictions is "that many defendants who are not on this list [of exonerees], no doubt thousands, have been falsely convicted of serious crimes but have not been exonerated" (Gross et al., 2005: 527). This suggests that wrongful convictions may pose a major challenge to the courts.

A Challenge to the Criminal Justice System

Wrongful convictions cast doubt on the accuracy of the criminal justice system generally but whether they systemically challenge the courts is open to question. While every wrongful conviction is a failure of justice (Forst, 2004), most wrongful convictions are caused by errors or poor procedures by police and forensic investigators, and most of the proposed reforms challenge these agencies. In contrast, recommended changes in court policies and procedures are relatively modest and cannot be deemed a serious challenge to the judiciary. The adequate compensation of the wrongly convicted, for example, is primarily a matter of legislative reform (Bernhard, 2004), even if the agency most likely to administer individual compensation requests is a court of claims (Judiciary and Judicial Procedure, 2006; Stashenko, 2007). Major reforms designed to reduce eyewitness identification error involve changes to police lineup procedures like placing only one suspect in a lineup, ensuring that suspects not stand out, cautioning witnesses that the suspect may not be in the lineup, double-blind lineup administration, and sequential lineup administration—all of which require police agencies to overcome resistance and implement novel approaches (Fisher, forthcoming; Wells, 2006). A judicial reform like the greater acceptance of eyewitness expert testimony plays a smaller role and is conceptually and operationally a reform that courts can take in stride (Higgins and Skinner, 2003).

Similarly, most recommendations to reduce the number of false confessions focus on police interrogation methods. These include videotaping entire interrogation sessions and limiting the interrogation of teenagers and mentally vulnerable persons (Drizin and Colgan, 2001; Blair, 2005). Other reforms, like capping the length of interrogations and prohibiting police lies and subtle promises to suspects, are likely to encounter substantial police resistance (White, 1997: 135–55). Most changes are likely to be made administratively by police departments or through legislation, although two state supreme courts have required videotaping (*Stephen v. State*, 1985; *State v. Scales*, 1994) and another authorized jury instructions to weigh confessions "with great caution and care" where the interrogation was not taped (*Commonwealth v. DiGiambattista*, 2004: 533–4). Allowing expert witnesses to testify in court about false confessions is helpful but not as central as changes in police procedures (Davis and Leo, 2006). Likewise, dealing with "jailhouse snitches" who claim to hear the confessions of fellow inmates requires changes in police and prosecution procedures. Canadian policies resulting from high-profile wrongful convictions based on snitch testimony requires police and prosecutors to make a collective and high-level decision whether to use a snitch's statement after a thorough review of the facts of the case, the reliability of the witness, and the truthfulness of the proposed evidence (Kaufman Commission, 1998: recommendations 36–69; Sophonow Commission, 2000: 193–201). Scheck et al. (2003: 355–6) recommend that courts should presume jailhouse snitches to be unreliable. A rule that judges should warn jurors to be especially vigilant in evaluating snitch testimony does not pose major challenges to the judiciary.

The courts' comparatively modest roles in these wrongful conviction reforms do not call for monumental or expensive changes, nor do they pose challenges to the essential judicial function. In sum, growing awareness that convicting the innocent is not a minute or a transient issue has led activists, scholars, and officials to focus on discrete processes and lists of piecemeal fixes that generally lay outside the courts. These proposed reforms do not constitute a fundamental challenge to, or require massive or expensive changes in, the judicial process.

Challenges to the Judicial Process: Prosecutors and Defense Attorneys

Two standard wrongful conviction "causes" that more fundamentally challenge the judicial process are the "ineffective assistance of counsel" and "prosecutorial misconduct" (see Giannelli and Raeder, 2006: 79–91, 99–107). These concerns are critical to the adversary trial, which is characterized by a neutral and passive fact finder (judge or jury), a highly structured forensic (legal) process, and the gathering and presentation of evidence by the parties (adversaries) (Landsman, 1984). The central precept of the adversary trial is that the "clash of proofs" by the adversaries will result in a resolution of disputes in a manner acceptable to the parties and to society. Because lawyers are the chief actors in a common law trial, an incorrect result may occur if the "sides" are unbalanced by talent, resources, or power. "Essential guarantees of the Bill of Rights may be disregarded because counsel failed to assert them, and juries may be deprived of critical facts needed to make reliable determinations of guilt or punishment. The result is a process that lacks fairness and integrity" (Bright, 1994: 1837). The problems are real. A recent American Bar Association (ABA) report characterized the state of indigent defense as in crisis (ABA, 2004: iv, 8–20). Wide-ranging and comprehensive investigative journalism has identified many cases of prosecutors' wrongs, suggesting that they occur with predictable regularity in perhaps one out of every six felony prosecutions (Armstrong and Possley, 1999; Tulsky, 2006a; Weinberg et al., 2003).

Concern about prosecutorial unfairness and the weaknesses of defense counsel have concerned the judiciary for a long time. Major twentieth century Supreme Court cases advanced trial fairness by guaranteeing lawyers to defendants in felony, misdemeanor, and juvenile cases and on first appeals (*Gideon v. Wainwright*, 1963; *Argersinger v. Hamlin*, 1972; *In re Gault*, 1967; *Douglas v. California*, 1963). The Court also held that defendants' due process and fair trial rights are violated by prosecutors knowingly introducing perjured or misleading testimony (*Alcorta v. Texas*, 1957; *Mooney v. Holohan*, 1935), or allowing witnesses to lie about receiving benefits for testifying (*Napue v. Illinois*, 1959). Despite these advances, the Court has been criticized for creating weak standards for what constitutes ineffective assistance of counsel (*Strickland v. Washington*, 1984) and ruling that the negligent failure by the police to preserve evidence of guilt (in a case where the defendant was later exonerated by DNA) is not a due process violation (*Arizona v. Youngblood*, 1988). A major advance in fairness— requiring prosecutors to divulge exculpatory information to the defense— was later watered down (*Brady v. Maryland*, 1963; *United States v. Agurs*, 1976; *United States v. Bagley*, 1985).

Although Supreme Court cases play an important part in advancing or limiting rights, appellate case law alone does not provide the resources by which rights are implemented. To establish fair trials *in fact*, legislatures play critical roles with appropriate legislation and adequately funding the criminal justice system. And, in the final instance, it requires competence and professionalism by the prosecutors, defense lawyers, and trial judges who manage and adjudicate cases to ensure a high quality and fair justice system. It also requires that these system actors be willing to advocate and implement policy changes within the scope of their authority, to keep up with the challenges to a workable and fair system of justice.

By these political criteria the justice system gets a mixed report card. There is a broad consensus that the rule of law ideal, although under pressure, is usually met in practice and that most system participants are honest and competent (Allen, 1996; Walker, 1998). Even while attorneys strive to win cases, they play by known rules of a trial system that is usually fair (Eisenstein et al., 1988). But closer inspection displays many problems, including a worrisome level of prosecution excessiveness in some jurisdictions (Humes, 1999), high levels of recurrent prosecutorial misconduct (Gershman, 2002), and a chronic and woeful underfunding of criminal defense (ABA, 2004; Backus and Marcus, 2006).

The Crisis in Indigent Defense

The crisis in indigent defense affects the entire adversary system because "poor people account for more than 80% of individuals prosecuted. These criminal defendants plead guilty approximately 90% of the time. In those cases, more than half the lawyers entered pleas for their clients without spending any significant time on the cases, without interviewing witnesses or filing motions. Sometimes they barely spoke with their clients" (Backus and Marcus, 2006: 1034, footnotes omitted). These assertions are backed up by a substantial volume of research, including many comprehensive reports completed since 2000 by state court systems or expert groups. For example, they have declared the entire systems of indigent defense in Georgia, Virginia, Louisiana, Pennsylvania, and North Dakota to be inadequate to meet the constitutional requirements of effective assistance of counsel (Backus and Marcus, 2006: 1035–6). An ABA report concluded that a national crisis existed based on extensive testimony of leading lawyers, jurists, and scholars in twenty-two states. This does not mean that all defense lawyers, public defenders, and assigned counsel are ineffective, or that all defenders' systems are entirely inadequate. Case studies of pubic defenders' offices in Chicago and New York City show defenders providing effective lawyering under enormous pressures, with what appears to be adequate if not lavish resources (Davis, 2007; Feige, 2006). Indeed, one empirical study shows that public defenders and private attorneys win an equal percentage of acquittals in the few cases that go to trial (Hoffman et al., 2005: 239). Nevertheless, when this study examined the overall effectiveness between private lawyers and public defenders, clients of public defenders received longer incarceration sentences, even when taking into account the seriousness of the charges and the number of motions filed (Hoffman et al., 2005).

The problem of underfunded indigent defense was decried in many law review articles in the 1990s, and the problem was especially acute in the representation of defendants facing the death penalty (Bright, 1994). Although a few states have taken steps to guarantee effective defense counsel in capital cases, in general the financial squeeze has grown worse. In the 1970s state and local funding for indigent defendants rose sevenfold and then doubled between 1978 and 1990. But in this time, the indigency rate rose from about half of all defendants to 80 percent in 1992, leading to a decrease in spending per indigent defendant in constant dollars (Hoffman et al., 2005: 225–6).

As a result of underfunding and/or excessive caseloads, there is widespread evidence that many lawyers, who would be competent under reasonable conditions, are not adhering to recognized national professional standards of criminal defense. Too many defenders or assigned counsel do not keep abreast of the criminal law in their jurisdiction, allow delay to occur, do not work diligently to secure their clients' pretrial release, do not meet with clients at any length to get relevant facts about the case, do not adequately prepare their cases through prompt investigation, do not avoid conflicts of interest, do not challenge illegally seized evidence, do not adequately prepare for trial or explore sentencing alternatives, and more (ABA, 2004: 15–16). What too many defense attorneys become are "meet 'em and plead 'em lawyers" (ABA, 2004: 16).

Although not provable with scientific certainty, the gross underfunding of indigent defense likely results in injustices, including wrongful convictions, excessive prison sentences, and death sentences for prisoners more deserving of life terms. Furthermore, convicting factually guilty defendants represented by incompetent lawyers, who might have lost good legal defenses as a result, is unjust in a system dedicated to the rule of law.

The chronic underfunding of indigent defense, which pits poor and often minority defendants against the (usually) adequately funded prosecution, threatens the deeply held ideals of due process, a fair trial, and equal justice before the law (*Griffin v. Illinois*, 1956). These ideals have deep historical roots and were so important to the political liberty on which the United States was founded that they were enshrined in the Constitution and Bill of Rights. This means that such rights cannot be eliminated by ordinary legislation, as has happened in times of crisis.

The question is how to reconcile these highly cherished ideals with a perceived inability to pay for them or when they conflict with entrenched institutional practices. The political economy of the United States is the most individualistic and capitalistic of the Western democracies, and the least supportive of the well-being of poor and working-class people (Janoski, 1998), which extends to criminal defense. Further, providing an adequate indigent criminal defense can be seen as incompatible with the efficient and effective operation of the criminal courts. The highly regarded federal judge Richard Posner, a leading scholar of the generally conservative law and economics movement, comments:

> I can confirm from my own experience as a judge that criminal defendants are generally poorly represented. But if we are to be hardheaded we must recognize that this may not be an entirely bad thing. The lawyers who represent indigent criminal defendants seem to be good enough to reduce the probability of convicting an innocent person to a very low level. If they were much better, either many guilty people would be acquitted or society would have to devote much greater resources to the prosecution of criminal cases. A bare-bones system for defense of indigent criminal defendants may be optimal. (quoted in Smith, 2001: 356 n. 10)

Posner probably reflects the views of most legislators and judges who fund and manage the judiciary, even while they wish to have a fair system. Knowledge that a substantial, if unknown, number of wrongful convictions result from underfunded indigent defense has increased the challenge to the judicial system, but whether a solution will be forthcoming is not clear.

Prosecutorial Power and Misconduct

Prosecutorial misconduct has been closely linked to wrongful convictions. It was identified in 45 percent of the first 130 DNA exonerations (Scheck et al., 2003: 365). Investigative reporters have found a large number of cases of abuse, some of it blatant. A *Chicago Tribune* national survey of homicide cases decided between 1963 and 1999 identified "at least 381 defendants [who] have had a . . . conviction thrown out because prosecutors concealed evidence suggesting innocence or presented evidence they knew to be false. Of all the ways that prosecutors can cheat, those two are considered the worst by the courts. And that number represents only a fraction of how often such cheating occurs" (Armstrong and Possley, 1999). In one New York case prosecutors obtained a conviction against two African American brothers by concealing an eyewitness account by the victim's brother that asserted the killers were white. A broader survey by the Center for Public Integrity disclosed 2,012 cases of prosecutorial misconduct out of 11,452 legal appeals based on such charges (Weinberg et al., 2003). A recent investigative study of appeals from trials in San Jose (discussed in detail below) disclosed 100 instances of serious prosecutorial misconduct in 727 cases (Tulsky, 2006a). A standard legal text that is updated annually displays an unremitting series of appellate cases on all manners of errors by prosecutors (Gershman, 2002; see Davis, 2007: 123–41).

In addition to concealing evidence or presenting false evidence, prosecutors distort the truth by attacking the defendant's character, creating prejudicial innuendo, or by suggesting that reliance on constitutional rights is evidence of guilt. Although the Supreme Court has spoken clearly about these issues, a stream of appeals shows that prosecutors continue to utilize such unfair and truth-distorting tactics. As for the fundamental rule of *Brady v. Maryland* (1963) that prosecutors must disclose exculpatory evidence to defendants in a timely fashion, this duty "has been interpreted by the courts more narrowly than its ethical counterpart" (Gershman, 2001: 328). Thus, only admissible evidence need be turned over; for example, the Supreme Court upheld a prosecutor who did not disclose polygraph evidence that key prosecution witnesses lied (*Wood v. Bartholomew*, 1995). In addition, prosecutors are in a unique position to help the truth in a case emerge, for example, by immunizing defense witnesses who have potentially material testimony to offer (Gershman, 2001: 334). This, however, is not a legal obligation and is entirely within the prosecutor's discretion.

There is broad agreement among scholars about the factors that generate misconduct. Prosecutors are the most powerful actors in the criminal process and hold virtually unaccountable power over whom to prosecute and for which crimes, and whether to plea bargain. Prosecutors' powers are so ingrained that they cannot recognize their magnitude, especially when they make legal decisions in good faith. "Prosecutors become so accustomed to the arbitrary exercise of their power and discretion at the charging stage that they, at best, honestly believe they are making evenhanded decisions, and, at worst, engage in willful blindness" (Davis, 2007: 39). Because of these enormous powers, and because "the line between legal prosecutorial behavior and illegal prosecutorial misconduct is a thin one," it is not surprising that a number of prosecutors engage in misconduct believing that there is nothing wrong with their actions (125–26).

Finally, prosecutors accused of misconduct are rarely sanctioned. Cases of elected prosecutors being voted out of office for excessive actions are extremely rare. Disbarment and prosecution occur only when cases of misconduct draw an unusual amount of publicity, forcing authorities to act. In 1999 three Illinois prosecutors were put on trial for perjury and other counts for persisting in reprosecuting three men and sending them to the death chamber for a murder when the identity of the actual killer was known. They were acquitted. The trial was said to be "virtually unparalleled in the history of American jurisprudence" (Possley and Armstrong, 1999). There have been only one or two disbarments for prosecutorial misconduct and one happened because a stubborn prosecutor refused to agree to a lesser sanction (Toobin, 2005; Weinberg et al., 2003: 80). The disbarment proceeding against the North Carolina prosecutor in the Duke lacrosse rape case was probably driven less by the level of misconduct, although it was substantial, than by the media frenzy the case generated (Parker, 2007).

One expert explained that bar association committees do not impose sanctions on prosecutors because of deference to the executive branch, and because of the mistaken belief that chief prosecutors or judges perform this task (Yaroshefsky, 2004). In fact there is evidence that prosecutors who have engaged in misconduct are often promoted or become judges (Armstrong and Possley, 1999; Tulsky, 2006a).

Several overlapping theoretical models have been developed to explain prosecutorial conduct. Legal analysis, for example, posits two models of prosecution: the minister of justice model and the neutral prosecutor model. In the minister of justice model, a prosecutor must be personally convinced that a defendant is guilty before going forward with a case and this imposes obligations to carefully probe the facts of a case that may exculpate a defendant. The neutral prosecutor model, in contrast, does not hold that it is "the prosecutor's function to make a personal evaluation of the truth; it is the jury's function" (Gershman, 2001: 310). Under the latter view, "When the issue stands in equipoise in his own mind, when he is honestly unable to judge where the truth of the matter lies, I see no flaw in the conduct of the prosecutor who fairly lays the matter before the judge or jury" (Uviller, 1973: 1159). Although the minister of justice model is the "high road" that is often found in the rhetoric about the prosecutor's role, in reality, the neutral prosecutor model is more often at work, and is driven by and merges with a psychological model of prosecutor behavior. "Other accounts blame misconduct on prosecutors' 'score-keeping mentality' or conviction psychology that compels them to win at all costs. This mentality stems from institutional, professional, and political pressures to win convictions" (Schoenfeld, 2005: 252, citation omitted).

A more explicitly psychological model is the "tunnel vision" theory. This posits that "prosecutors ultimately seek justice, and because most defendants are guilty, prosecutors feel compelled to sidestep problems that could sacrifice a guilty verdict." This focus and the "cognitive process of applying stereotypes to cases" has led prosecutors to allow witnesses to lie about their background, discount conflicting information, or "neglect evidence that is contrary to their version of events" (Schoenfeld, 2005: 252; see Findley and Scott, 2006).

Although the tunnel vision theory acknowledges that this perspective is reinforced by institutional pressures (Findley and Scott, 2006: 322–33), Schoenfeld (2005) has generated a more explicitly institutional theory grounded in the sociology of trust relationships. In this view, prosecutors act as agents for the public, but such trust relationships are "inherently unbalanced" for three reasons. First, agents hold a monopoly of information. Second, they have the power to control the well-being of their principals because of their delegated powers and discretion. Finally, the role of agent is ambiguous, creating tension between acting on behalf of the principal and acting for their own interests. This ambiguity creates the space in which violations of the trust relationship can occur (254–56). Schoenfeld's violated trust theory draws on the data and concepts of other theories.

Whichever theory works the best, the reality is that most prosecutors are ethical and manage their difficult responsibilities within the canons of professional responsibility (Delsohn, 2003), however, prosecutorial misconduct is sufficiently common to create a challenge to the legitimacy of the judicial process that is made worse by the links between it and wrongful convictions.

Are Judges Part of the Problem?

The standard script of what causes wrongful convictions does not include errors by trial or appellate judges. It may be that other causes are easier to detect. When exonerations follow jury trials it is natural to ask why the jury failed to see the weaknesses in the case. The jury may have been misled by a mistaken eyewitness or a false confession. The defense attorney may have been inadequate in failing to puncture this kind of error. Research has shown that eyewitness testimony and confessions have powerful effects on juries, making it difficult for them to evaluate other exculpatory evidence (Kassin and Gudjonsson, 2004: 56–8). With such obvious causes it is more difficult to parse trial transcripts to see whether poor rulings by judges contribute to failures of justice that increase the likelihood that innocent defendants will be convicted.

A rare journalistic study systematically examined the work of trial and appellate judges (as well as of prosecutors and defense attorneys) (Tulsky, 2006a). Unlike typical investigative journalism that looks for problem cases and ignores professional conduct, this series examined what social scientists call a "universe" of cases. Tulsky and a panel of legal experts examined virtually every appeal taken from jury trial convictions in San Jose (Santa Clara County) to California's Sixth District Court of Appeal. The panel included former judges and prosecutors and recognized national experts in criminal justice. They read the appellate decision and the trial transcript in every case. In addition, Tulsky interviewed the participants in some of the cases. By conducting a systematic review, the *San Jose Mercury News* series could show the proportion of cases in which errors occurred.

The findings are disturbing. Overall, the series found "questionable conduct" by prosecutors, lawyers, and judges in 261 out of 727 felony convictions that had been appealed. The 36 percent "error rate" included cases in which questionable conduct was committed by one or more of the system's actors. In 167 cases, or 21.8 percent of the total cases, a trial judge engaged in questionable conduct. When judges acted in biased ways, it was almost always in favor of the prosecution (Tulsky, 2006b).

- "In more than 50 of the 727 cases reviewed by the *Mercury News*, judges allowed prosecutors to introduce questionable—and often improper—evidence."

- "In nearly 50 other cases, defense attorneys were restricted from introducing their own evidence, rulings that often raised concerns from appellate justices or independent experts."

- "In 48 cases, judges failed to give the jury appropriate guidance on the law—in ways that either bolstered the prosecution's view of the case or undermined the defense's contentions."

- In 10 cases . . . judges made explicit remarks or took actions in the presence of the jury that suggested their bias against the defendant" (Tulsky, 2006b).

There were several reasons for this state of affairs, including a social culture in which judges and prosecutors were very close and defense attorneys were excluded. The professional orientation of judges was shaped by the fact that more "than a third of the county's 79 judges spent the bulk of their careers in the district attorney's office." Political pressure, in which judges perceived to be "soft on crime" can be removed from office, was another inducement for pro-prosecution rulings. The series reminded readers that in the mid-1980s two California supreme court justices were removed from office in a retention election by voters angered that they had not supported the death penalty in many of their rulings. The message that has stayed with judges is that they can lose their office if they rule in favor of defendants.

Added to this is the relative invisibility of judicial discretion, because judges' errors are almost never revealed in the news media. The public fails to understand the many ways in which judges' rulings can shape the fairness of a trial and possibly affect its outcome.

> No role is more crucial than the judges' handling of issues of evidence. They determine what evidence can be admitted, and what evidence should be excluded. And they preside over decisions on what evidence the defense can see through the discovery process. Those decisions are especially important when it comes to gang and juvenile cases, where the law limits defense access and the judge must decide whether to grant it.
>
> Often in such cases, defense attorneys are left wondering whether evidence they could not see would have helped them. Only rarely do they learn the answer. (Tulsky, 2006b)

In one case a judge told the lawyers that he would examine confidential juvenile records to determine whether they contained questionable identification evidence. The judge later assured the parties that the record did not contain such evidence; the defendant was found guilty and received a sentence of 62 years to life for car jacking. Appellate judges discovered that no such juvenile record existed; when they more closely reviewed the record, they found that questionable identification did taint the case, and ordered a retrial. The judge's lies are shocking because his actions might never have come to light were it not for the extra inquisitiveness of the appellate court. What is just as disturbing is that the reversal was not the kind of serious legal error that causes much concern within legal circles and almost never becomes a matter of public concern.

To make matters worse, the series indicated that the appellate court was not effective in suppressing trial court errors. The bottom line about the Sixth District Court of Appeal is that "the court often goes to great lengths to preserve guilty verdicts." The panel of experts, after "examining the court's reasoning in each case . . . found that it routinely avoids commenting on troubling courtroom behavior, explains the problems away or says they do not matter." Tulsky (2006c) pointed out that state courts of appeals are almost always the last appeal for most cases, thus making the work and style of these courts critically important to defendants and to the tenor of local justice. Santa Clara University law professor Gerald Uelmen found that the Sixth District Court of Appeal was "more tolerant of errors" than other California district courts of appeal because it was created to relieve the workload of other appellate courts in 1982. Its first set of judges were appointed by "tough on crime" Governor George Deukmejian (Tulsky, 2006c).

It is worth noting that the panel found most of the appellate courts' rulings proper, including hundreds of cases in which defendants' claims of error were rejected, as well as the "small number of cases in which the court was troubled enough by the errors to grant some relief." That said, the panel of experts found "nearly 250 incidents of questionable conduct to which the court employed methods that minimized or dismissed the concerns." These included more than 100 cases where the experts felt the court was wrong in finding errors to be harmless. Examples of faulty legal reasoning or instances of highly implausible logic were found. For example, the court upheld a trial judge who excluded the violent history of a wife in a spouse assault case (she broke the jaw of a subsequent husband), by arguing that the defendant "must have been really threatening if he scared so tough a woman" (Tulsky, 2006c).

The article suggested that short of reversing cases, an appellate court can shape the tone of justice in lower courts by the strength of its language in addressing excessive or inappropriate behavior by lawyers or judges or by publishing such opinions. It found that the "6th District tends to avoid both steps." For example, in nine cases in which prosecutors diminished the importance of the reasonable doubt standard with trivializing examples, the appellate court disapproved in mild language (Tulsky, 2006c).

Political scientists and legal scholars who study appellate courts examine the overall results of court decisions and pay close attention to the written opinions of supreme courts. They rarely explore the large number of unwritten appeals by intermediate appellate courts that have become very common. Scholars rarely have the resources to examine the mundane ways in which appellate decisions fall short of the mark in ensuring that judges and lawyers act in accordance with accepted legal norms. Although Tulsky's investigative journalism was not motivated entirely by a concern about wrongful conviction, a small number of actual innocence cases were uncovered by the series. Trial and appellate court errors do not necessarily mean that miscarriages of justice result. Yet, negligent or misguided lawyering and judging cast serious doubt on the accuracy of trials and these errors "increase the small chance of wrongful convictions" (Tulsky, 2006d). With this realization, the challenge of wrongful conviction to the fairness, accuracy, and legitimacy of the courts begins to come into complete focus.

The Ultimate Challenge of Wrongful Conviction

The "adversary" criminal jury trial originated in England and spread to the United States and other countries that had been English colonies (so-called "common law" countries). Most other countries employ the "inquisitorial" trial model that developed in continental European countries (so-called "civil law" or "Roman law" countries). The relative merits of these systems have been debated for centuries. The debate as to which system is "best" is in some ways a sterile one. The jury trial and the adversary trial (it is possible to have an adversary trial system without juries) are constitutionality embedded in American legal culture. Indeed, comparative law scholars note that legal "transplants" are often rejected because adopters fail to understand that a legal procedure is dependent on a web of practices and expectations that are part of the way that lawyers and judges operate (Damaška, 1997).

Nevertheless, a number of writers have recently expressed the "heretical notion that the adversary system may no longer be the best way for our legal system to deal with all the matters that come within its purview" (Menkel-Meadow, 1996). Menkel-Meadow is concerned that the complexities of civil cases are not captured by the binary yes-no decision generated by the adversary trial and that the adversary trial itself distorts the truth because it "leaves out important information, simplifies complexity and obfuscates where it should clarify" (49). Indeed, there is a consensus among scholars that the search for the truth is far more central to the modern inquisitorial trial than it is to the adversary trial (Pizzi, 1999). "Criminal trials serve a broad range of important societal functions that are unrelated to the accuracy of the determinations of guilt or innocence" (Givelber, 1997: 1364). They can require "that the government publicly account for its actions" and shed light on illegal or inappropriate police procedures. Public trials provide litigants a forum "for criticizing government actions with which they disagree" and "criminal trials provide the legal crucible for forging interpretations of constitutional rights. These values are served by the guilty as well as the innocent going to trial" (1364). The difference in emphasis is captured by this arresting quotation:

> In the end, a statement made by an eminent comparative law scholar, after long and careful study, is instructive: he said that if he were innocent, he would prefer to be tried by a civil law court, but that if he were guilty, he would prefer to be tried by a common law court. This is, in effect, a judgment that criminal proceedings in the civil law world are more likely to distinguish accurately between the guilty and the innocent. (quoted in Givelber, 1997: 1317)

This dramatic challenge has generated a few proposals for coming to grips with the strong perception that the adversary trial is failing at a fundamental task (but not *the* fundamental task) in our system—of separating the guilty from the innocent. An expert on evidence law has provided an intriguing sketch for a modified jury trial procedure. D. Michael Risinger (2004) suggests that there are two kinds of criminal trials. One kind, common in homicide cases, is where there is no question that the defendant committed the act. In such a case, the role of the jury is to ascertain the defendant's state of mind. This in effect requires "the resolution of . . . complex, no-one-right-answer, normatively charged judgments about what was going on in his head" (1299). Risinger allows, somewhat uncomfortably, that lawyers' emotional appeals, or the "story theory of lawyering" (Schrager, 1999), is inevitable and may be permissible up to a point in trials dominated by multivalent issues (such as inferring a state of mind from the known facts). In this kind of trial the defense lawyer and the prosecutor will engage in storytelling techniques designed to reach jurors on an emotional level, using what Risinger (2004) calls "heartstrings and gore" lawyering.

But there is a second kind of trial where the identity of the perpetrator is in question. Risinger (2004) calls these cases of "brute fact innocence" (1298). In trials that involve questions of actual innocence, "heartstrings and gore" lawyering, or the techniques by which lawyers can distort the truth (Gershman, 2002), can produce miscarriages of justice. "[B]inary fact determinations of the nontechnical type are the kinds of decisions where ordinary juries can most often be led to miscarry by adversary excess, especially in the context of high profile and highly dramatic cases" (Risinger,

2004: 1309). Risinger proposes a "mechanism that matches procedures to cases depending on the nature of the issues actually in play in the case, with current procedures for cases turning on normative assessment and special new procedures for cases turning on specific and specifiable issues of fact" (1307). He does not lay out a detailed procedure but a quick sketch, so to speak.

> The defendant would be required to isolate the one (or perhaps two) binary exterior ultimate facts that underlie his claim of innocence. All other elements of the case would be conceded by binding judicial admission, a circumstance to be explained to the jury in the most unambiguous fashion after alternative proposals for the explanatory charge have been made by the defense and the prosecution. Thereafter, in the actual trial, all proffers of evidence by both sides would have to be found "usably" relevant to the factual issues as limited. Prosecution use of expert testimony would be closely screened for reliability, and the court would be prevented from excluding, on the ground of "invasion of the province of the jury," any defense-proffered expert evidence on the weaknesses of eyewitness identification, false confessions, the commonness of false testimony by jailhouse snitches, and the weaknesses of any expert evidence proffered by the prosecution. Closing arguments would be expected to stick closely to the factual issues raised in the application. The cross-sectional jury would be retained, together with the finality rule for acquittals. Convictions would be reviewable not merely on the basis of sufficiency, but also on the issue of whether they were "unsafe." (1311–12, footnotes omitted)

Risinger wishes his tentative proposal be treated as a preliminary idea, given the "law of unintended consequences," and be discussed by scholars and lawyers' committees before any such change be implemented. His bold idea, however, is a sign that trial experts have begun to confront the challenges that wrongful convictions pose to the courts.

Another suggestion is that defendants be afforded a limited right to have a judge order the state's investigators to conduct discrete tests designed to ascertain the truth (Zalman, forthcoming). In the French trial system, the court has the primary obligation to generate trial facts and this is done through judicially directed police investigations. This is diametrically opposed to the "party presentation" of evidence that is characteristic of the adversary system. A French procedure that could advance the accuracy of police investigations when defendants claim to be innocent is that a defendant has the right to request of the investigating magistrate that further investigations be carried out (McKillop, 1997: 539–40), and when confronted with experts' reports "to ask for a 'counter-expertise' or a 'complementary expertise'" within ten days (538). A defendant's request that police conduct an investigation along specific lines strikes at the heart of the adversary process. The defendant is supposed to do his own investigation. Yet, for an indigent defendant, or any defendant who is confronted with an issue for which the prosecution is uniquely positioned to investigate, the matter carries some logic. One could imagine a statutorily created practice that allows a defense motion to the court to consider, and order where reasonable preconditions have been met, a specific investigation on the part of the police to obtain exculpatory evidence or to clarify evidence that is questionable.

By analogy, something like this is beginning to happen in regard to DNA testing. For a decade after the initiation of DNA testing in criminal cases a large number of prosecutors fought bitterly to prevent convicted defendants from getting access to DNA samples to prove their innocence, while happily using DNA to prove guilt (Medwed, 2004). This attitude, which flies in the face of basic fairness, has exposed the worst aspects of the culture of prosecutorial overzealousness. It is now, slowly, beginning to change as the Innocence Protection Act has provided the impetus for forcing states to allow prisoners to request DNA tests, a concrete example of the power of the wrongful conviction challenge to the justice system.

Finally, it is worth noting that North Carolina was the first state in the nation to create an Innocence Inquiry Commission modeled after a similar commission in England (Jonsson, 2006). This procedure allows the commission to investigate petitions by prisoners claiming actual innocence, and to petition an appellate court to order a new trial if the commission believes there is a basis for the prisoner's claim. It is too early to know whether this system will prove workable and effective in identifying and exonerating the wrongly convicted. What the effort does show is that the challenge of wrongful convictions has provided the impetus for some radical rethinking of the judicial process. If estimates of thousands of wrongful convictions a year are close to being accurate, this fact will soon undermine the faith of the public in the courts. This challenge is real and is present, and will require a fundamental evaluation of the role and functioning of criminal courts.

References

Allen, Francis A. (1996). *The Habits of Legality: Criminal Justice and the Rule of Law* (New York: Oxford University Press, 1996).

American Bar Association (2004). *Gideon's Broken Promise: America's Continuing Quest for Equal Justice: A Report on the American Bar Association's Hearings on the Right to Counsel in Criminal Proceedings* (Chicago: American Bar Association), available at http://www.abanet.org/legalservices/sclaid/defender/brokenpromise/fullreport.pdf (last accessed, June 9, 2007).

Armstrong, Ken and Maurice Possley (1999). "Trial & Error. How Prosecutors Sacrifice Justice to Win." *Chicago Tribune* [Five Part Series, January 10–14, 1999], available at   http://www.chicagotribune.com/news/nationworld/chi-dptrialerror-special, 1,1581428.special (last accessed, June 2, 2007).

Backus, Mary Sue and Paul Marcus (2006). "The Right to Counsel in Criminal Cases, A National Crisis." *Hastings Law Journal* 57:1031–1130.

Bedau, Hugo Adam and Michael L. Radelet (1987). "Miscarriages of Justice in Potentially Capital Cases." *Stanford Law Review* 40:21–120.

Bernhard, Adele (2004). "Justice Still Fails: A Review of Recent Efforts to Compensate Individuals Who Have Been Unjustly Convicted and Later Exonerated." *Drake Law Review* 52:703–38.

Bikel, Ofra (exec. dir.) (2000, January 11). *Frontline: The Case for Innocence* (PBS Video).

Blair, J. P. (2005). "A Test of the Unusual False Confession Perspective: Using Cases of Proven False Confession." *Criminal Law Bulletin* 41(2):127–44.

Borchard, Edwin M. (1932). *Convicting the Innocent: Errors of Criminal Justice* (New Haven: Yale University Press).

Bright, Stephen B. (1994). "Counsel for the Poor: The Death Sentence Not for the Worst Crime but for the Worst Lawyer." *Yale Law Journal* 103:1835–83.

Cobb, Roger W. and Charles D. Elder (1972). *Participation in American Politics: The Dynamics of Agenda-Building* (Baltimore: Johns Hopkins University Press).

Connors, Edward, Thomas Lundregan, Neal Miller, and Tom McEwan (1996, June). *Convicted by Juries, Exonerated by Science: Case Studies in the Use of DNA Evidence to Establish Innocence After Trial* (National Institute of Justice, NCJ 161258).

Cutler, Brian L. and Steven D. Penrod (1995). *Mistaken Identification: The Eyewitness, Psychology, and the Law* (New York: Cambridge University Press).

Damaška, Mirjan (1997). "The Uncertain Fate of Evidentiary Transplants: Anglo-American and Continental Experiments." *American Journal of Comparative Law* 45:839–52.

Davis, Deborah and Richard Leo (2006). "Strategies for Preventing False Confessions and Their Consequences." In Mark R. Kebbell and Graham M. Davies, eds., *Practical Psychology for Forensic Investigations and Prosecutions*, pp. 121–49 (Chichester, England: John Wiley & Sons).

Davis, Kevin (2007). *Defending the Damned: Inside Chicago's Cook County Public Defender's Office* (New York: Atria Books).

Delsohn, Gary (2003). *The Prosecutors—Kidnap, Rape, Murder, Justice: One Year Behind the Scenes in a Big-City DA's Office* (New York: Plume).

Doyle, James M. (2005). *True Witness: Cops, Courts, Science, and the Battle Against Misidentification* (New York: Palgrave Macmillan).

Drizin, Steven A. and Beth A. Colgan (2001). "Let the Cameras Roll: Mandatory Videotaping of Interrogations Is the Solution to Illinois' Problem of False Confessions." *Loyola University of Chicago Law Journal* 32:337–424.

Eisenstein, James, Roy B. Flemming, and Peter F. Nardulli (1988). *The Contours of Justice: Communities and Their Courts* (Boston: Little, Brown).

Feige, David (2006). *Indefensible: One Lawyer's Journey into the Inferno of American Justice* (New York: Little, Brown).

Findley, Keith A. & Michael S. Scott (2006). "The Multiple Dimensions of Tunnel Vision in Criminal Cases." *Wisconsin Law Review* 2006:291–397.

Fisher, Stanley Z. (forthcoming). "Eyewitness Identification Reform in Massachusetts." *Massachusetts Law Review.*

Forst, Brian (2004). *Errors of Justice: Nature, Sources, and Remedies* (Cambridge: Cambridge University Press).

Gershman, Bennett L. (2001). "The Prosecutor's Duty To Truth." *Georgetown Journal of Legal Ethics* 14:309–54.

Gershman, Bennett (2002). *Prosecutorial Misconduct,* Second Edition (St. Paul, MN: West) [annual updates].

Giannelli, Paul and Myrna Raeder (eds.) (2006). *Achieving Justice: Freeing the Innocent, Convicting the Guilty.* (Report of the ABA Criminal Justice Section's Ad Hoc Committee to Ensure the Integrity of the Criminal Process. Washington, DC: American Bar Association.)

Givelber, Daniel (1997). "Meaningless Acquittals, Meaningful Convictions: Do We Reliably Acquit the Innocent?" *Rutgers Law Review* 49:1317–96.

Graham, Fred P. (1970). *The Due Process Revolution: The Warren Court's Impact on Criminal Law* (New York: Hayden Book).

Gross, Samuel R., Kristen Jacoby, Daniel J. Matheson, Nicholas Montgomery, and Sujata Patil (2005). "Exonerations in the United States, 1989 Through 2003." *Journal of Criminal Law & Criminology* 95(2):523–60.

Higgins, Edmund S. and Bruce S. Skinner (2003). "Establishing the Relevance of Expert Testimony Regarding Eyewitness Identification: Comparing Forty Recent Cases with the Psychological Studies." *Northern Kentucky Law Review* 30:471–86.

Hoffman, Morris B., Paul H. Rubin, and Joanna M. Shepherd (2005). "An Empirical Study of Public Defender Effectiveness: Self-Selection by the 'Marginally Indigent.'" *Ohio State Journal of Criminal Law* 3:223–55.

Huff, C. Ronald, Arye Rattner, and Edward Sagarin (1986). "Guilty Until Proved Innocent." *Crime & Delinquency* 32:518–44.

Humes, Edward (1999). *Mean Justice* (New York: Simon & Schuster).

Innocence Project (n.d.). Accessible at http://www.innocenceproject.org/.

Janoski, Thomas (1998). *Citizenship and Civil Society: A Framework of Rights and Obligations in Liberal, Traditional, and Social Democratic Regimes* (Cambridge, UK; New York: Cambridge University Press).

Jones, Charles O. (1984). *An Introduction to the Study of Public Policy,* Third Edition (Belmont, CA: Wadsworth).

Jones, Cynthia E. (2005). "Evidence Destroyed, Innocence Lost: The Preservation of Biological Evidence under Innocence Protection Statutes." *American Criminal Law Review* 42:1239–70.

Jonsson, Patrik (2006, August 10). "North Carolina Creates a New Route to Exoneration." *Christian Science Monitor.*

Judiciary and Judicial Procedure, 28 U.S.C. § 2513 (2006).

Kassin, Saul M. and Gisli H. Gudjonsson (2004). "The Psychology of Confessions: A Review of the Literature and Issues." *Psychological Science in the Public Interest* 5(2):33–67.

Kaufman Commission (1998). Proceedings Involving Guy Paul Morin (Ontario Ministry of the Attorney General), available at http://www.attorneygeneral.jus.gov.on.ca/english/about/pubs/morin/.

Kleinert, Michael E. (2006). "Note: Improving the Quality of Justice: The Innocence Protection Act of 2004 Ensures Post-conviction DNA Testing, Better Legal Representation, and Increased Compensation For the Wrongfully Imprisoned." *Brandeis Law Journal* 44:491–508.

Landsman, Stephen (1984). *The Adversary System: A Description and Defense* (Washington, DC: American Enterprise Institute for Public Policy Research).

Lassers, Willard J. (1973). *Scapegoat Justice: Lloyd Miller and the Failure of the American Legal System* (Bloomington: Indiana University Press).

Leahy, Patrick (2004a, October 9). Statement of Senator Patrick Leahy—The Justice for All Act of 2004. Retrieved February 23, 2006, from http://leahy.senate.gov/press/200410/100904B.html.

Leahy, Patrick (2004b). Justice for All Act of 2004: Section-by-section Analysis. Retrieved February 23, 2006, from http://leahy.senate.gov/press/200410/100904E.html.

Leo, Richard A. (2005). "Rethinking the Study of Miscarriages of Justice: Developing a Criminology of Wrongful Conviction." *Journal of Contemporary Criminal Justice* 21(3):201–23.

Loftus, Elizabeth (1979). *Eyewitness Testimony* (Cambridge, MA: Harvard University Press).

Marion, Nancy E. and Wilard M. Oliver (2006). *The Public Policy of Crime and Criminal Justice* (Upper Saddle River, NJ: Prentice-Hall).

Marquis, Joshua (2005). "The Myth of Innocence." *Journal of Criminal Law & Criminology* 95(2):501–21.

Mays, G. Larry and Rick Ruddell (2008). *Making Sense of Criminal Justice: Policies and Practices* (New York: Oxford University Press).

McKillop, Bron (1997). "Anatomy of a French Murder Case." *American Journal of Comparative Law* 45:527–83.

Medwed, Daniel S. (2004). "The Zeal Deal: Prosecutorial Resistance to Post-conviction Claims of Innocence." *Boston University Law Review* 84:125–83.

Menkel-Meadow, Carrie (1996). "The Trouble with the Adversary System in a Postmodern, Multicultural World." *William & Mary Law Review*, 38:5–44.

Morris, Errol (dir.) (1988, August 25). *Thin Blue Line* (Documentary Film).

Parker, Laura (2007, June 11). "Trial This Week for Prosecutor in Duke Case; Mike Nifong to Face Ethics Charges." *USA Today.*

Pizzi, William T. (1999). *Trials Without Truth: Why Our System of Criminal Trials Has Become an Expensive Failure and What We Need to Do to Rebuild It* (New York: New York University Press).

Possley, Maurice and Ken Armstrong (1999, January 12). "Prosecution on Trial in DuPage." *Chicago Tribune.*

Radelet, Michael L., Hugo Adam Bedau, and Constance E. Putnam (1992). *In Spite of Innocence* (Boston: Northeastern University Press).

Ramsey, Robert J. and James Frank (2007). "Wrongful Conviction: Perspectives of Criminal Justice Professionals Regarding the Frequency of Wrongful Conviction and the Extent of System Errors." *Crime & Delinquency* 53(3):436–70.

Risinger, D. Michael (2004). "Unsafe Verdicts: The Need for Reformed Standards for the Trial and Review of Factual Innocence Claims." *Houston Law Review* 41:1281–1336.

Saferstein, Richard (2004). *Criminalistics: An Introduction to Forensic Science*, Eighth Edition (Upper Saddle River, NJ: Prentice Hall).

Scheck, Barry, Peter Neufeld, and Jim Dwyer (2003). *Actual Innocence: When Justice Goes Wrong and How to Make It Right* (New York: Penguin/New American Library; originally published in 2000 by Doubleday with the subtitle: *Five Days to Execution, and Other Dispatches From the Wrongly Convicted*).

Schoenfeld, Heather (2005). "Violated Trust: Conceptualizing Prosecutorial Misconduct." *Journal of Contemporary Criminal Justice* 21(3):250–71.

Schrager, Sam (1999). *The Trial Lawyer's Art* (Philadelphia: Temple University Press).

Siegel, Jane (exec. dir.) (1997, February 25). *Frontline: What Jennifer Saw* (PBS Video).

Smith, Abbe (2001). "Can You Be a Good Person and a Good Prosecutor?" *Georgetown Journal of Legal Ethics* 14:355–400.

Sophonow Commission (2000). The Inquiry Regarding Thomas Sophonow (Manitoba Department of Justice), available at http://www.gov.mb.ca/justice/publications/sophonow/index.html?/index.html.

Stashenko, Joel (2007, May 16). "Bill Aims for Quicker Resolution of Claims in DNA Exonerations." *New York Law Journal* (LegalTrac, Thomson Gale).

Technical Working Group for Eyewitness Evidence (1999). *Eyewitness Evidence: A Guide for Law Enforcement* (National Institute of Justice, NCJ 178204).

Toobin, Jeffrey (2005, January 17). "Annals of Law: Killer Instincts: A Prosecutor Manipulates a Death-row Case." *New Yorker*, pp. 54–63.

Travis, Jeremy (1998, March 18). "Proceedings: National Commission on the Future of DNA Evidence" (National Institute of Justice), available at http://www.ojp.usdoj.gov/nij/topics/forensics/dna/commission/frstmtg.htm.

Tulsky, Fredric (2006a, January 23). "Tainted Trials, Stolen Justice: Part Two: Prosecutors over the Line." *San Jose Mercury News* [Five Part Series, January 22–26, 2006], available at http://www.mercurynews.com/taintedtrials (last accessed, June 2, 2007).

Tulsky, Fredric (2006b, January 25). "How Judges Favor the Prosecution." *San Jose Mercury News*.

Tulsky, Fredric (2006c, January 26). "Last Chance, Little Help." *San Jose Mercury News*.

Tulsky, Fredric (2006d, August 17). "Conviction Overturned After *Mercury News* Investigation." *San Jose Mercury News*.

Uviller, H. Richard (1973). "The Virtuous Prosecutor in Quest of an Ethical Standard: Guidance From the ABA." *Michigan Law Review* 71:1145–68.

Walker, Samuel (1998). *The Rights Revolution: Rights and Community in Modern America* (New York: Oxford University Press).

Warden, Rob (2003). "The Revolutionary Role of Journalism in Identifying and Rectifying Wrongful Convictions." *UMKC Law Review* 70:803.

Weich, Ronald (2005, March). "The Innocence Protection Act of 2004: A Small Step Forward and a Framework for Larger Reforms." *The Champion* 29:28–31.

Weinberg, Steve, Neil Gordon, and Brooke Williams (2003). *Harmful Error: Investigating America's Local Prosecutors* (Washington, DC: Center for Public Integrity).

Wells, Gary L. (2006). "Eyewitness Identification: Systemic Reform." *Wisconsin Law Review* 2006:615–43.

White, Welsh S. (1997). "False Confessions and the Constitution: Safeguards Against Untrustworthy Confessions." *Harvard Civil Rights-Civil Liberties Law Review* 32:105–57.

Yant, Martin (1991). *Presumed Guilty: When Innocent People are Wrongly Convicted* (Buffalo: Prometheus Books).

Yaroshefsky, Ellen (2004). "It Is Time to Take Prosecution Discipline Seriously." *University of the District of Columbia Law Review* 8:275–99.

Zacharias, Fred C. (2005). "The Role of Prosecutors in Serving Justice After Convictions." *Vanderbilt Law Review* 58:171–239.

Zalman, Marvin (2005). "Cautionary Notes on Commission Recommendations: A Public Policy Approach to Wrongful Convictions." *Criminal Law Bulletin* 41(2):169–94.

Zalman, Marvin (2007, March). "Journalism as Research: Fredric Tulsky's Series on A Flawed Adversary System (Tainted Trials, Stolen Justice) in the *San Jose Mercury News*, January 2006." A paper presented at the annual meeting of the Academy of Criminal Justice Sciences, Seattle, WA.

Zalman, Marvin (forthcoming). "Notes on the 'Adversary System' and Wrongful Convictions." In C. Ronald Huff and Martin Kilias, eds., *Wrongful Conviction: International Perspectives on Miscarriages of Justice* (Philadelphia: Temple University Press).

Zalman, Marvin, Brad Smith, and Angie Kiger (2008). "Officials' Estimates of the Incidence of 'Actual Innocence' Convictions." *Justice Quarterly* 25(1):72–100.

Law Cases Cited

Alcorta v. Texas, 355 U.S. 28 (1957).
Argersinger v. Hamlin, 407 U.S. 25 (1972).
Arizona v. Youngblood, 488 U.S. 51 (1988).
Brady v. Maryland, 373 U.S. 83 (1963).
Commonwealth v. DiGiambattista, 813 N.E. 2d 516 (Mass, 2004).
Douglas v, California, 372 U.S. 353 (1963).
Gault, In re, 387 U.S. 1 (1967).
Gideon v. Wainwright, 372 U.S. 335 (1963).
Griffin v. Illinois, 351 U.S. 12 (1956).
Mooney v. Holohan, 294 U.S. 103 (1935).
Napue v. Illinois, 360 U.S. 264 (1959).
State v. Scales, 518 N.W.2d 587 (Minn. 1994).
Stephen v. State, 711 P.2d 1156 (Alaska 1985).
Strickland v. Washington, 466 U.S. 668 (1984).
United States v. Agurs, 427 U.S. 97 (1976).
United States v. Bagley, 473 U.S. 667 (1985).
Wood v. Bartholomew, 516 U.S. 1 (1995).

Questions to Consider

1. Have you ever considered the career option of being a court administrator? What challenges must one confront in order to become such a professional? What do you think are some of the major issues a court administrator must deal with in his or her job?

2. Slotnick recounts studies that show that the more citizens know about courts, the more likely they are to be critical of them. How might court officials benefit by keeping their activities low profile? As you learn more about courts, how do you feel about courts?

3. Some studies indicate that increasing a person's knowledge about the social role of courts leads to higher support for judicial independence. If court officials really seek to address their problems and publicize these efforts, how might they gain more power and prestige in the long term?

4. How would you go about choosing judges for your community? How would you ensure that they are "just" judges?

5. How would having a diverse judiciary affect the decisions made in our court system? Is it important to look at the collective as well as individual decisions of such judges? If our courts reflect who we are, how does our society benefit?

6. If you were in a courtroom and witnessed obvious gender or racial bias against another by a court professional, how would you feel? Would you feel differently if you were the person being discriminated against? Given the level of bias evidenced by the readings, how do you think this affects people's perceptions of the courts?

7. Zalman points out that the misconduct by prosecutors is rarely sanctioned by judges. Perhaps, as some argue, this is because most criminal court judges have been prosecutors in the past. Additionally, potential disciplinary entities like judges and bar associations, which might sanction misconduct, tend to defer to the necessity claims of the executive branch. Later in this text, some argue that, in the name of necessity, the executive is increasingly taking control of the courts at the

expense of the citizenry. What changes do you think might help curtail what may be an inherent problem of abuse of power by the powerful?

8. Zalman proposes some possible changes: one looks to change the procedures in each case depending on the nature of that case's issues and the other incorporates a more European system that would give more power of investigation to indigent defendants. What are the pros and cons with these suggestions?

Section V
Politics in the Decision-Making Process

It has often been claimed that law is politics. In the context of courts, this would mean that decisions made by our court systems are made politically. For our purposes, we will define decisions made politically as decisions that are substantially influenced by factors outside of the immediate facts in controversy. Thus, political legal decisions would be those influenced by negative factors such as racial bias or by positive factors such as understanding cultural differences. The results of such politically influenced decisions, therefore, may be less just or more just than if one strictly followed a legal rule.

Some legalists argue that legal decisions are not political because legal decision makers are simply following the law. The following five articles in this section argue that this nonpolitical perspective is a naive picture of the legal process. Whether the actors are judges, prosecutors, defense lawyers, juries, or even those who choose judges under a "merit" system, the following articles point to numerous political components in their decision making.

An even more important lesson from these articles is that all decision makers have perspectives that they bring to new issues. This "outside" perspective can bring wisdom as well as prejudice. The challenge for our criminal justice system is to devise methods to harness this wisdom while limiting the prejudice.

In the first article, Bennett Gershman explains why prosecutors act unfairly and why the justice system fails to stop such unfair practices. He argues that prosecutors often act unfairly because such tactics "work"; they know that juries often act politically by considering information (even illegal and prejudicial statements) that has been presented by prosecutors. Little is done to correct this situation because the governing rules, such as the harmless error doctrine, are very vague and subjective. Such vagueness allows judicial values to become more prominent, leading to inconsistent decisions. Further, even if prosecutors are found to have acted unfairly, there are few, if any, sanctions. Once again we see the need to confront the dilemma of power; how do we give needed discretionary independence to court officials yet effectively control abuses of that power?

The articles by Rodney Uphoff and Alissa Worden reflect similar problems with defense attorneys. Uphoff updates a classic 1967 study by Abraham Blumberg, who argued that defense attorneys were co-opted by the legal system to serve its organizational ends. Uphoff finds more variety in defense functions but still uncovers multiple ways in which outside forces, such as economic realities, court procedures, and methods of delivering legal services, affect the decisions defense attorneys make in representing their clients.

Alissa Worden compares defense attorney delivery systems in her focus on the growing method of private contracting. While this system seems like it would be more efficient, she points to the many pitfalls, such as price fixing and monopoly practices, which debilitate logical and efficient decision making.

Mary Dodge and her colleagues explore alternatives to the traditional belief that we must eliminate all politics from our legal system. They use the "three strikes" laws in California to show that, while most judges do not allow jurors to be told that defendants face mandatory severe sanctions for minor felony charges, jurors still act politically by often refusing to convict when three-strikes punishment for relatively minor offenses is a possibility. They argue instead that not trusting juries engenders this kind of haphazard response, and that we need to give jurors all the facts as well as some voice in sentencing. A *Decision Quest/National Law Journal* poll in October 1998 found that three out of four Americans eligible to serve on a jury say they would act on their own beliefs of right and wrong regardless of legal instructions from a judge. Clearly juries are as potentially political as judges and prosecutors, and efforts at control are really battles over levels of control and dominance. Also in question is our underlying trust in democracy and in ourselves.

David Keys explores how court professionals create their own norms and categories for case disposition. While we often use the term "plea bargaining," it is usually the prosecutors who set the terms of the agreement. There seems to be many factors that influence the creation of these categories, and as other studies have shown, these norms may vary significantly from one geographical area to another. A significant factor, only partially stated in this article, is the potential role of a jury verdict in this decision. Such a decision is more unpredictable for both the prosecutor and defense attorney. One might thus ask what the issues of control and uncertainty play in this process of avoidance. If we cannot avoid some level of political influence on the process, is it better to have a single decision maker or a group decision maker?

18

Why Prosecutors Misbehave

BENNETT L. GERSHMAN

The duties of the prosecuting attorney were well-stated in the classic opinion of Justice Sutherland fifty years ago.[1] The interest of the prosecutor, he wrote, "is not that he is in a peculiar and very definite sense the servant of the law, the twofold aim of which is that guilt shall not escape or innocence suffer. He may prosecute with earnestness and vigor—indeed, he should do so. But, while he may strike hard blows, he is not at liberty to strike foul ones."[2]

Despite this admonition, prosecutors continue to strike "foul blows," perpetuating a disease which began long before Justice Sutherland's oft-quoted opinion. Indeed, instances of prosecutorial misconduct were reported at least as far back as 1897[3] and as recently as the latest volume of the *Supreme Court Reporter.*[4] The span between these cases is replete with innumerable instances of improper conduct of the prosecutor, much of which defies belief.

One of the leading examples of outrageous conduct by a prosecutor is *Miller v. Pate,*[5] where the prosecutor concealed from the jury in a murder case the fact that a pair of undershorts with red stains on it, a crucial piece of evidence, were stained not by blood, but by paint. Equally startling is *United States v. Perry,*[6] where the prosecutor, in his summation, commented on the fact that the "defendants and their counsel are completely unable to explain away their guilt."[7] Similarly,

Reprinted by permission of West Group from the *Criminal Law Bulletin*, Vol. 22, No. 2 (March/April 1986), pp. 131–143. Copyright © 1986 by West Group, 610 Opperman Drive, St. Paul, MN 55164. All rights reserved.

[in] *Dubose v. State*,[8] the prosecutor argued to the jury: "Now, not one sentence, not one scintilla of evidence, not one word in any way did this defendant or these attorneys challenge the credibility of the complaining witness."[9] At a time when it should be clear that constitutional and ethical standards prevent prosecutors from behaving this way,[10] we ought to question why prosecutors so frequently engage in such conduct.

Much of the above misconduct occurs in a courtroom. The terms "courtroom" or "forensic misconduct" have never been precisely defined. One commentator describes courtroom misconduct as those "types of misconduct which involve efforts to influence the jury through various sorts of inadmissible evidence."[11] Another commentator suggests that forensic misconduct "may be generally defined as any activity by the prosecutor which tends to divert the jury from making its determination of guilt or innocence by weighing the legally admitted evidence in the manner prescribed by law."[12] For purposes of this analysis, the latter definition applies, as it encompasses a broader array of behavior which can be classed as misconduct. As will be seen, prosecutorial misconduct can occur even without the use of inadmissible evidence.

This article will address two aspects of the problem of courtroom misconduct. First, it will discuss why prosecutors engage in courtroom misconduct, and then why our present system offers little incentive to a prosecutor to change his behavior.

Why Misconduct Occurs?

Intuition tells us that the reason so much courtroom misconduct by the prosecutor[13] occurs is quite simple: it works. From my experience as a prosecutor for ten years, I would hypothesize that most prosecutors deny that misconduct is helpful in winning a case. Indeed, there is a strong philosophical argument that prosecutorial misconduct corrupts the judicial system, thereby robbing it of its legitimacy. In this regard, one would probably be hard pressed to find a prosecutor who would even mention that he would consider the thought of some form of misconduct.

Nonetheless, all of this talk is merely academic, because as we know, if only from the thousands of cases in the reports, courtroom misconduct does occur. If the prosecutor did not believe it would be effective to stretch his argument to the ethical limit, and then risk going beyond that ethical limit, he would not take the risk.

Intuition aside, however, several studies have shown the importance of oral advocacy in the courtroom, as well as the effect produced by such conduct. For example, the student of trial advocacy often is told of the importance of the opening statement. Prosecutors would undoubtedly agree that the opening statement is indeed crucial. In a University of Kansas study,[14] the importance of the opening statement was confirmed. From this study, the authors concluded that, in the course of any given trial,[15] the jurors were affected most by the first strong presentation which they saw. This finding leads to the conclusion that if a prosecutor were to present a particularly strong opening argument, the jury would favor the prosecution throughout the trial. Alternatively, if the prosecutor were to provide a weak opening statement, followed by a strong opening statement by the defense, then, according to the authors, the jury would favor the defense during the trial. It thus becomes evident that the prosecutor will be best served by making the strongest opening argument possible, thereby assisting the jury in gaining a better insight into what they are about to hear and see. The opportunity for the prosecutor to influence the jury at this point in the trial is considerable, and virtually all prosecutors would probably attempt to use this opportunity to their advantage, even if the circumstances do not call for lengthy or dramatic opening remarks[16]

An additional aspect of the prosecutor's power over the jury is suggested in a University of North Carolina study.[17] This study found that the more arguments counsel raises with respect to the different substantive arguments offered, the more the jury will believe in that party's case. Moreover, this study found that there is not necessarily a correlation between the amount of objective information in the communication and the persuasiveness of the presentation.

For the trial attorney, then, this study clearly points to the advantage of raising as many issues as possible at trial. For the prosecutor, the two studies taken together would dictate an "action packed" opening statement, containing as many arguments that can be mustered, even those which might be irrelevant or unnecessary to convince the jury of the defendant's guilt. The second study would also dictate the same strategy for the closing argument. Consequently, a prosecutor who, through use of these techniques, attempts to assure that the jury knows his case may, despite violating ethical standards to seek justice,[18] be "rewarded" with a guilty verdict. Thus, one begins to perceive the incentive that leads the prosecutor to misbehave in the courtroom.[19]

Similar incentives can be seen with respect to the complex problem of controlling evidence to which the jury may have access. It is common knowledge that, in the course of any trial, statements frequently are made by the attorneys or witnesses, despite the fact that these statements may not be admissible as evidence. Following such a statement, the trial judge may, at the request of opposing counsel, instruct the jury to disregard what they have heard. Most trial lawyers, if they are candid, will agree that it is virtually impossible for jurors realistically to disregard these inadmissible statements. Studies here again demonstrate that our intuition is correct, and that this evidence often is considered by jurors in reaching a verdict.

For example, an interesting study conducted at the University of Washington[20] tested the effects of inadmissible evidence on the decisions of jurors. The authors of the test designed a variety of scenarios whereby some jurors heard about an incriminating piece of evidence while other jurors did not. The study found that the effect of the inadmissible evidence was directly correlated to the strength of the prosecutor's case. The authors of the study reported that when the prosecutor presented a weak case, the inadmissible evidence did, in fact, prejudice the jurors. Furthermore, the judge's admonition to the jurors to disregard certain evidence did not have the same effect as when the evidence had not been mentioned at all. It had a prejudicial impact anyway.

However, the study also indicated that when there was a strong prosecution case, the inadmissible evidence had little, if any, effect.[21] Nonetheless, the most significant conclusion from the study is that inadmissible evidence had its most prejudicial impact when there was little other evidence on which the jury could base a decision. In this situation, "the controversial evidence becomes quite salient in the jurors' minds."[22]

Finally, with respect to inadmissible evidence and stricken testimony, even if one were to reject all of the studies discussed, it is still clear that although "stricken testimony may tend to be rejected in open discussion, it does have an impact, perhaps even an unconscious one, on the individual juror's judgment."[23] As with previously discussed points, this factor—the unconscious effect of stricken testimony or evidence— will generally not be lost on the prosecutor who is in tune with the psychology of the jury.

The applicability of these studies to this analysis, then, is quite clear. Faced with a difficult case in which there may be a problem of proof, a prosecutor might be tempted to sway the jury by adverting to a matter which might be highly prejudicial. In this connection, another study[24] has suggested that the jury will more likely consider inadmissible evidence that favors the defendant rather than inadmissible evidence that favors conviction.[25]

Despite this factor of "defense favoritism," it is again evident that a prosecutor may find it rewarding to misconduct himself in the courtroom. Of course, a prosecutor who adopts the unethical norm and improperly allows jurors to hear inadmissible proof runs the risk of jeopardizing any resulting conviction. In a situation where the prosecutor feels there is a weak case, however, a subsequent reversal is not a particularly effective sanction when a conviction might have been difficult to achieve in the first place. Consequently, an unethical courtroom "trick" can be a very attractive idea to the prosecutor who feels he must win.[26] Additionally, there is always the possibility of another conviction even after an appellate reversal. Indeed, while a large number of cases are dismissed following remand by an appellate court, nearly one half of reversals still result in some type of conviction.[27] Therefore, a prosecutor can still succeed in obtaining a conviction even after his misconduct led to a reversal.

An additional problem in the area of prosecutor-jury interaction is the prosecutor's prestige; since the prosecutor represents the "government," jurors are more likely to believe him.[28] Put simply, prosecutors "are the good guys of the legal system,"[29] and because they have such glamour, they often may be tempted to use this advantage in an unethical manner. This presents a problem for the prosecutor in that the "average citizen may often forgive, yea urge prosecutors on in ethical indiscretions, for the end, convictions of criminals certainly justifies in the public eye any means necessary."[30] Consequently, unless the prosecutor is a person of high integrity and is able to uphold the highest moral standards, the problem of courtroom misconduct will inevitably be tolerated by the public.

Moreover, when considering the problems facing the prosecutor, one also must consider the tremendous stress under which the prosecutor labors on a daily basis. Besides the stressful conditions faced by the ordinary courtroom litigator,[31] prosecuting attorneys, particularly those in large metropolitan areas, are faced with huge and very demanding case loads. As a result of case volume and time demands, prosecutors may not be able to take advantage of opportunities to relax and recover from the constant onslaught their emotions face every day in the courtroom.[32]

Under these highly stressful conditions, it is understandable that a prosecutor occasionally may find it difficult to face these everyday pressures and to resist temptations to behave unethically. It is not unreasonable to suggest that the conditions under which the prosecutor works can have a profound effect on his attempt to maintain high moral and ethical standards. Having established this hypothesis, one can see yet another reason why courtroom misconduct may occur.

Why Misconduct Continues?

Having demonstrated that courtroom misconduct may, in many instances, be highly effective, the question arises as to why such practices continue in our judicial system. A number of reasons may account for this phenomenon. Perhaps the most significant reason for the continued presence of prosecutorial misconduct is the harmless error doctrine.

Under this doctrine, an appellate court can affirm a conviction despite the presence of serious misconduct during the trial. As Justice Traynor once stated, the "practical objective of tests of harmless error is to conserve judicial resources by enabling appellate courts to cleanse the judicial process of prejudicial error without becoming mired in harmless error."[33]

Although the definition advanced by Justice Traynor portrays the harmless error doctrine as having a most desirable consequence, this desirability is undermined when the prosecutor is able to misconduct himself without fear of sanction. Additionally, since every case is different, what constitutes harmless error in one case may be reversible error in another. Consequently, harmless error determinations do not offer any significant precedents by which prosecutors can judge the status of their behavior.

By way of illustration, consider two cases in which the prosecutor implicitly told the jury of his personal belief in the defendant's guilt. In one case, the prosecutor stated, "I have never tried a case where the evidence was so clear and convincing."[34] In the other case, the prosecutor told the jury that he did not try cases unless he was sure of them.[35] In the first case the conviction was affirmed, while in the second case the conviction was reversed. Interestingly, the court in the first case affirmed the conviction despite its belief that the "prosecutor's remarks were totally out of order."[36] Accordingly, despite making comments which were "totally out of order," the prosecutor did not suffer any penalty.

Contrasting these two cases presents clear evidence of what is perhaps the worst derivative effect of the harmless error rule. The problem is that the stronger the prosecutor's case, the more misconduct he can commit without being reversed. Indeed, in the *Shields* case, the court stated that "the guilt of the defendant was clearly established not only beyond a reasonable doubt, but well beyond any conceivable doubt."[37] For purposes of our analysis, it is clear that by deciding as they do, courts often provide little discouragement to a prosecutor who believes, and rightly so, that he does not have to be as careful about his conduct when he has a strong case. The relation of this factor to the amount of courtroom misconduct cannot be ignored.

Neither can one ignore the essential absurdity of a harmless error determination. In order to apply the harmless error rule, appellate judges attempt to evaluate how various evidentiary items or instances of prosecutorial misconduct may have affected the jury's verdict. Although it may be relatively simple in some cases to determine whether improper conduct during a trial was harmless, there are many instances when such an analysis cannot properly be made, but nevertheless is made. For example, consider the situation when an appellate court is divided on whether or not a given error was harmless. In *United States v. Antonelli Fireworks Co.*,[38] two judges (including Judge Learned Hand) believed that the prosecutor's error was harmless. Yet, Judge Frank, the third judge sitting in the case, completely disagreed, writing a scathing dissent nearly three times the length of the majority opinion. One wonders how harmless error can be fairly applied when there is such a significant difference of opinion among highly respected members of a court as to the extent of harmfulness of trial errors. Perhaps even more interesting is the Supreme Court's reversal of the Court of Appeals for the Second Circuit's unanimous finding of harmless error in *United States v. Berger*.[39] As noted, *Berger* now represents the classic statement of the scope of the prosecutor's duties. Yet, in his majority opinion for the Second Circuit, Judge Learned Hand found the prosecutor's misconduct harmless.

The implications of these contradictory decisions are significant, for they demonstrate the utter failure of appellate courts to provide incentives for the prosecutor to control his behavior. If misconduct can be excused even when reasonable judges differ as to the extent of harm caused by such misbehavior, then very little guidance is given to a prosecutor to assist him in determining the propriety of his actions. Clearly, without such guidance, the potential for misconduct significantly increases.

The *Shields* case presents yet another factor which suggests why the prosecutor has only a limited incentive to avoid misconduct. In *Shields*, the court refused to review certain "potentially inflammatory statements" made by the prosecutor because of the failure of the defense to object.[40] Although this approach has not been uniformly applied by all courts, the implications of this technique to reject a defendant's claim are considerable. Most important, it encourages prosecutors to make remarks that they know are objectionable in the hope that defense counsel will not object. This situation recalls the previous discussion which dealt with the effect of inadmissible evidence on jurors. Defense counsel here is in a difficult predicament. If he does not object, he ordinarily waives any appealable issue in the event of conviction. If he does object, he highlights to the jury the fact that the prosecutor has just done something which, some jurors may feel, is so damaging to the defendant that the defense does not want it brought out.

The dilemma of the defense attorney in this situation is confirmed by a Duke University study.[41] In that study, jurors learned of various pieces of evidence which were ruled inadmissible. The study found that when the judge admonished the jury to disregard the evidence, the bias created by that evidence was not significantly reduced.[42] Consequently, when a prejudicial remark is made by the prosecutor, defense counsel must act carefully to avoid damaging his client's case. In short, the prosecutor has yet another weapon, in this instance an arguably unfair aspect of the appellate process, which requires preservation of an appealable issue.[43]

A final point when analyzing why prosecutorial misconduct persists is the unavailability or inadequacy of penalties visited upon the prosecutor personally in the event of misconduct. Punishment in our legal system comes in varying degrees. An appellate court can punish a prosecutor by simply cautioning him not to act in the same manner again, reversing his case, or, in some cases, identifying by name the prosecutor who misconducted himself.[44] Even these punishments, however, may not be sufficient to dissuade prosecutors from acting improperly. One noteworthy case[45] describes a prosecutor who appeared before the appellate court on a misconduct issue for the third time, each instance in a different case.

Perhaps the ultimate reason for the ineffectiveness of the judicial system in curbing prosecutorial misconduct is that prosecutors are not personally liable for their misconduct. In *Imbler v. Pachtman*,[46] the Supreme Court held that "in initiating a prosecution and in presenting the state's case, the prosecutor is immune from a civil suit for damages under Section 1983."[47] Furthermore, prosecutors have absolute, rather than a more limited, qualified, immunity. Thus, during the course of a trial, the prosecutor is absolutely shielded from any civil liability which might arise due to his misconduct, even if that misconduct was performed with malice.

There is clearly a need for some level of immunity to be accorded all government officials. Without such immunity much of what is normally done by officials in authority might not be performed out of fear that their practices are later deemed harmful or improper. Granting prosecutors a certain level of immunity is reasonable. Allowing prosecutors to be completely shielded from civil liability in the event of misconduct, however, provides no deterrent to courtroom misconduct.

Conclusion

This analysis was undertaken to determine why the issue of misconduct seems so prevalent in the criminal trial. For the prosecutor, the temptation to cross over the allowable ethical limit must often be irresistible because of the distinct advantages that such misconduct creates in assisting the prosecutor to win his case by effectively influencing the jury. Most prosecutors must inevitably be subject to this temptation. It takes a constant effort on the part of every prosecutor to maintain the high moral standards which are necessary to avoid such temptations.

Despite the frequent occurrences of courtroom misconduct, appellate courts have not provided significant incentives, to the prosecutor to avoid misconduct. It is not until the courts decide to take a stricter, more consistent approach to this problem, that inroads will be made in the effort to end it. One solution might be to impose civil liability on the prosecutor who misconducts himself with malice. Although this will not solve the problem, it might be a step in the right direction.

Endnotes

1 Berger v. *United States*, 295 U.S. 78 (1935)
2 Id. at 88.
3 See *Dunlop v. United States*, 165 U.S. 486 (1897) where the prosecutor in an obscenity case, argued to the jury, "I do not believe that there are twelve men that could be gathered by the venire of this court . . . , except where they were bought and perjured in advance, whose verdict I would not be willing to take. . . ." Id. at 498. Following this remark, defense council objected and the court held that statement to be improper.
4 See *Caldwell v. Mississippi*, 105 S. Ct. 2633 (1985) (improper argument to capital sentencing jury); *United States v. Young*, 105 S. Ct. 1038 (1985) (improper argument but not plain error).
5 386 U.S. 1 (1967). In this case, the Supreme Court overturned the defendant's conviction after the Court of Appeals for the Seventh Circuit had upheld it. The Court noted that the prosecutor "deliberately misrepresented the truth," and that such behavior would not be tolerated under the Fourteenth Amendment. Id. at 67.
6 643 F.2d 38 (2d Cir. 1981).
7 Id. at 51.
8 531 S.W.2d 330 (Texas 1975).
9 Id. at 331. The court noted that the argument was clearly a comment on the failure of the defendant to testify at trial.
10 See *Griffin v. California*, 380 U.S. 609 (1965), where the Supreme Court applied the Fifth Amendment to the states under the Fourteenth Amendment.
11 Alschuler, "Courtroom Misconduct by Prosecutors and Trial Judges," 50 *Tex. L. Rev.* 627, 633 (1972).
12 Note, "The Nature and Function of Forensic Misconduct in the Prosecution of a Criminal Case," 54 *Col. L. Rev.* 946, 949 (1954).
13 Of course, there is also a significant amount of defense misconduct which takes place. In this respect, for an interesting article which takes a different approach than this article, see Kamm, "The Case for the Prosecutor," 13 *U. Tol. L. Rev.* 331 (1982), where the author notes that "courts carefully nurture the defendant's rights while cavalierly ignoring the rights of the people."
14 Pyszczynski, "The Effects of Opening Statement on Mock Jurors' Verdicts in a Simulated Criminal Trial," 11 *J. Applied Soc. Psychology* 301 (1981).
15 All of the cited studies include within the report a caveat about the value of the study when applied to a "real world" case. Nonetheless, they are still worthwhile for the purpose of this analysis.
16 In some jurisdictions, attorneys may often use the voir dire to accomplish the goal of early influence of the jury.
17 Calder, "The Relation of Cognitive and Memorial Processes to Persuasion in a Simulated Jury Trial," 4 *J. Applied Soc. Psychology* 62 (1974).

[18] See *Model Code of Professional Responsibility* EC 7-13 (1980) ("The duty of the prosecutor is to seek justice.").

[19] Of course, this may apply to other attorneys as well.

[20] Sue, "The Effects of Inadmissible Evidence on the Decisions of Simulated Jurors—A Moral Dilemma," 3 *J. Applied Soc. Psychology* 345 (1973).

[21] Perhaps lending validity to application of the harmless error doctrine, which will be discussed later in this article.

[22] Sue, note 20 supra, at 351.

[23] Hastie, *Inside the Jury* 232 (1983).

[24] Thompson, "Inadmissible Evidence and Juror Verdicts," 40 *J. Personality & Soc. Psychology* 453 (1981).

[25] The author did note that the defendant in the test case was very sympathetic and that the results may have been different with a less sympathetic defendant.

[26] Of course, this begs the question: "Is there a prosecutor who would take a case to trial and then feel that he didn't have to win?" It is hoped that, in such a situation, trial would never be an option. Rather, one would hope for an early dismissal of the charges.

[27] Roper, "Does Procedural Due Process Make a Difference?" 65 *Judicature* 136 (1981). This article suggests that the rate of nearly 50 percent of acquittals following reversal is proof that due process is a viable means for legitimatizing the judiciary. While this is true, the fact remains that there is still a 50 percent conviction rate after reversal, thereby giving many prosecutors a second chance to convict after their original misconduct.

[28] See *People v. McCoy*, 220 N.W.2d 456 (Mich. 1974), where the prosecutor, in attempting to bolster his case, told the jury that "the Detroit Police Department, the detectives in the Homicide Bureau, these detectives you see in court today, and myself from the prosecutor's office, we don't bring cases unless we're sure, unless we're positive." Id. at 460.

[29] Emmons, "Morality and Ethics—A Prosecutor's View," *Advanced Criminal Trial Tactics* 393-407 (P.L.I. 1977).

[30] Id.

[31] For an interesting article on the topic, see Zimmerman, "Stress and the Trial Lawyer," 9 *Litigation* 4, 37-42 (1983).

[32] For example, the Zimmerman article suggests time off from work and "celebration" with family and friends in order to effectively induce relaxation.

[33] R. Traynor, *The Riddle of Harmless Error* 81 (1970).

[34] *People v. Shields*, 58 A.D.2d 94, 96 (N.Y.), aff'd, 46 N.Y.2d 764 (1977).

[35] *People v. McCoy*, 220 N.W.2d 456 (Mich. 1974).

[36] *Shields*, 58 A.D.2d at 97.

[37] Id. at 99.

[38] 155 F.2d 631 (2d Cir. 1946).

[39] 73 F.2d 278 (1934), rev'd, 295 U.S. 78 (1935).

[40] *Shields*, 58 A.D.2d at 97.

[41] Wolf, "Effects of Inadmissible Evidence and Level of Judicial Admonishment to Disregard on the Judgments of Mock Jurors," 7 *J. Applied Soc. Psychology* 205 (1977).

[42] Additionally of note is the fact that if the judge rules the evidence and did not admonish the jury, then the biasing effect of the evidence was eliminated. The authors of the study concluded that by being told not to consider certain evidence, the jurors felt a loss of freedom and that in order to retain their freedom, they considered it anyway. The psychological term for this effect is called reactance.

43 Of course, this does not mean that appeals should always be allowed, even in the absence of an appealable issue. Rather, one should confine the availability of these appeals to the narrow circumstances discussed.

44 See *United v. Burse*, 531 F.2d 1151 (2d Cir. 1976), where the Court named the prosecutor in the body of its opinion.

45 *United States v. Drummond*, 481 F.2d 62 (2d Cir. 1973).

46 424 U.S. 409 (1976).

47 Id. at 431. 42 U.S.C. § 1983 authorizes civil actions against state officials who violate civil rights "under color of state law."

19

The Criminal Defense Lawyer
Zealous Advocate, Double Agent, or Beleaguered Dealer?

RODNEY J. UPHOFF

In theory, the criminal defense lawyer is called to be a zealous advocate vigorously representing those persons accused by the state of violating the law.[1] As the champion of the accused, the criminal defense lawyer plays an essential role in the adversary system by challenging the prosecutions' efforts to secure a conviction.[2] Defense counsel's responsibility is to probe and test the state's evidence fo ensure that the accused is convicted only if the prosecution can muster sufficient evidence to prove the defendant's guilt beyond a reasonable doubt.[3] Moreover, it is counsel's duty to defend the accused zealously, even if counsel knows the defendant is guilty.[4]

In principle, therefore, a criminal defense lawyer, through counsel's legitimate efforts, may actually frustrate the search for the truth. Indeed, defense counsel may be ethically required to do so.[5] Defense counsel's zealous representation of a client is not, of course, without bounds. As an officer of the court, a defense lawyer's advocacy is constrained by various ethical rules.[6] Nevertheless, although disagreement exists as to how far a criminal defense lawyer may go on behalf of a client in certain tough ethical situations,[7] there is little question that defense counsel is required to be an able, devoted defender standing with the accused in an adversarial struggle with the state.[8]

However, is defense counsel, in practice, really a zealous advocate striving to provide a vigorous defense to the accused? Or is defense counsel too often a "double agent" merely seeking to persuade the client to accept a plea bargain, which is designed primarily to redound to the benefit of the lawyer and the criminal justice system?[9] Is there, in fact, a significant gap between the theoretical role of defense counsel and the actual practices of most criminal defense lawyers? To answer these questions, the first section of this article explores the observations made by Abraham Blumberg in 1967 that led him to conclude that defense lawyers were co-opted by the criminal justice system to serve organizational ends rather than their clients' interests.[10] The second section examines the behavior of defense lawyers in three counties to ascertain whether Blumberg's portrayal of defense counsel as double agent indeed is accurate. After discussing a number of important systemic variables that adversely affect the behavior and zeal of criminal defense lawyers, the second section concludes that "beleaguered dealer" more aptly describes the role of defense counsel in these counties. Finally, the third section considers the extent to which strengthening the system for the delivery of indigent defense services will enhance zealous advocacy and improve the quality of representation provided to most criminal defendants.

Defense Lawyer as "Double Agent"

In his oft-cited article "The Practice of Law as Confidence Game: Organization Co-optation of a Profession," Abraham Blumberg turned his attention to the question of whether the traditional legal conception of the role of a criminal defense lawyer actually squared with social reality.[11] Blumberg correctly noted that the traditional view was based on the notion of a criminal case as an adversary, combative proceeding in which defense counsel zealously defended the accused. In fact, Blumberg stated, few cases actually are decided by trial.[12] Rather, the vast majority of cases are resolved by the plea-bargaining process, a process dictated by the organizational structure of criminal courts.[13] This court organization has its own set of goals and discipline, which in turn impose certain demands and conditions of practice on the actors in the system, including defense counsel.[14] As a result of organizational pressure, defense lawyers abandon their ethical commitment to their clients and instead "help the accused redefine his situation and restructure his perceptions concomitant with a plea of guilty."[15]

According to Blumberg, the formal and informal relations of all of the various actors in the criminal justice system were more important than the needs of any client.[16] Hence, in order to ensure continued positive relations and to cope with an intolerably large number of cases, these actors were bound together in "an organized system of complicity."[17] Blumberg described a variety of different systemic practices and institutional evasions that serve to pressure the accused to plead guilty while permitting the system to maintain an outward commitment to due process.[18] Defense lawyers were key players in the successful operation of the system. Owing their primary allegiance to the system, defense lawyers, whether public defenders or retained counsel, were concerned largely with strategies designed to manipulate clients into pleading guilty.[19]

Blumberg focused much of his attention on the efforts of criminal defense lawyers to "con" their clients.[20] To pull off this con, the criminal defense lawyer had to collect a fee, convince the client to accept a guilty plea, and still terminate the litigation as quickly as possible." Counsel was a double agent because she pretended to help the client when, in fact, her main objective was to limit the scope and duration of the client's case, not to do battle.[22] Thus, defense counsel utilized her unique role in the organization to persuade or cajole the client to accept a result—a plea bargain—that served the interests of the organization and the lawyer above those of the client.[23]

But do Blumberg's damning observations about criminal defense lawyers really reflect the reality of the contemporary criminal justice system? To address this question, this article examines the practices of criminal defense lawyers in three counties: Milwaukee County, Wis., Dane County, Wis., and Cleveland County, Okla.[24] There is no methodological significance to the selection of these three counties. They were selected simply because the author has been a participant observer in each.[25] As with Blumberg's article, no empirical data supports the author's observations about the behavior of criminal defense lawyers in these counties. Nonetheless, the picture of the criminal defense bar portrayed in this article is quite similar to that painted by others looking at defense lawyers in other criminal justice systems.[26]

Defense Lawyer as Beleaguered Dealer: Observations of Lawyers at Work

Blumberg presented a very cynical, negative picture of criminal defense lawyers and of their relationships with their clients. With broad strokes, Blumberg painted the portrait of the criminal defense lawyer as a manipulative con artist who succumbs to the pressures of making a living in a closed community by "duping" clients to enter pleas that benefit the system more than the clients.[27] Although it is true, as it was in 1967, when Blumberg's article appeared, that the vast majority of clients in Milwaukee, Dane, and Cleveland Counties plead guilty instead of going to trial.[28] Nevertheless, it does not follow that the large number of guilty pleas is simply the product of defense lawyer double-dealing. Rather, numerous factors, including some of the systemic pressures described by Blumberg, affect a defendant's plea decision and the behavior of a criminal defense lawyer. Indeed, the varied conduct of defense lawyers in these three counties confirms that Blumberg's premise that court organization dictates defense counsel's role, that of double agent, is suspect.

Admittedly, many of Blumberg's observations about certain systemic pressures and practices accurately reflect similar aspects of the criminal justice systems in Milwaukee, Dane, and Cleveland Counties. In all three counties, private defense lawyers almost always want their fees in advance and routinely look to the client's family and friends to contribute to the client's defense.[29] Certainly, there are lawyers in each county who prey on the ignorance or anxieties of their clients and their clients' families to increase their fees and to enhance the collection of those fees.[30] At times, court personnel, prosecutors, or judges will aid defense counsel's efforts to collect a fee, and this assistance may subsequently be used to pressure defense counsel.[31] And there are lawyers who manipulate their clients by lying to them about the complexity of the case, the working of the system, or the dangers of going to trial in order to maximize the lawyer's financial return on a particular case.[32] There are, therefore, lawyers in each county who fit Blumberg's double agent profile.

Simply to characterize all criminal defense lawyers as double agents, however, grossly distorts the overall picture of the criminal defense bar in these counties. Not all defense lawyers "ultimately are concerned with strategies which tend to lead to a plea."[33] Nor is it true that "it is the rational, impersonal elements involving economics of time, labor, expense and a superior commitment of the defense counsel to these rationalistic values of maximum production of court organization that prevail, in his relationship with a client."[34] If Blumberg's image of defense counsel is entirely accurate, what explains those cases that do go to trial: stubborn clients, bad salesmanship by the lawyers, ideological zealots, or desire to deflect "outside" scrutiny?[35] Blumberg's analysis offers no explanation.

Unquestionably, however, each county has a number of criminal defense lawyers, especially public defenders in Dane and Milwaukee Counties, who are committed professionally and ideologically to obtaining the best possible results for their clients.[36] Although heavy case loads affect the ability of public defenders—and, in some instances, their willingness and enthusiasm—to go to trial, most public defenders in Milwaukee and Dane Counties bargain as aggressively as possible on behalf of their clients. These public defenders, in turn, usually advise their clients of the available, albeit often quite limited, options, in an honest, unbiased manner.

Moreover, in each county there are private lawyers specializing in criminal cases who can and will aggressively defend those clients with the economic resources to pay for a zealous defense. Instead of seeking to limit the litigation, some lawyers file numerous motions in an effort to wear down the prosecution and achieve a favorable outcome for their clients.[37] Finally, there are lawyers in each county who have zealously defended their clients at great personal sacrifice. Dedication, commitment to principle, and personal values, not financial gain, drive some criminal defense lawyers.[38]

Blumberg posited that criminal defense lawyers function as double agents because conning the client into a quick plea ensured that a case would be profitable and enabled counsel to serve the ends of a complicitous, closed system.[39] Yet, if court structure and organization dictate defense counsel's role, why is it that not all defense lawyers in Milwaukee, Dane, and Cleveland Counties behave alike? Why do only some criminal defense lawyers in these counties succumb to personal or systemic pressure and function as double agents while others do not? Why is it that some defense lawyers in these counties conduct vigorous defenses and others put up only a staged or token resistance?

There is no single explanation for why criminal defense lawyers play their role so differently. Nor is there a simple answer as to why some public defenders and private lawyers operate some of the time as double agents.[40] A public defender may be lazy, inexperienced, incompetent, overwhelmed, burned out, focused on a particularly difficult and time-consuming case, subject to personal problems, or distracted by a combination of such factors.[41] Private lawyers must not only cope with these factors but also try to earn a living. Only infrequently does a criminal defense lawyer command a fee commensurate with the time it takes to investigate and defend a criminal case fully and competently. Simply put, most people accused of a crime cannot afford to pay for effective assistance of counsel.[42] Most low-income defendants who do not qualify for public defenders in Wisconsin or for court-appointed counsel in Cleveland County cannot obtain adequate legal representation.[43] It is these defendants in all three counties who face the real prospect of being represented by double agents. Although, at times, a defendant will be advised by defense counsel that the meager retainer paid will only cover a negotiated plea, too often the accused neither understands nor ever learns of the real limits of counsel's representation. Unhappily, it may not be until the client insists on a trial that the defense lawyer's limited zeal becomes obvious.[44]

Often, however, it is not defense counsel's lack of zeal but the defendant's lack of money that dictates counsel's actions. Often a defendant who wishes to hire a lawyer can only raise a minimal retainer. Once retained, the lawyer may prod and push the prosecutor for a dismissal or a favorable plea bargain, but if the prosecutor refuses, the client is often left with an unhappy choice: Accept the negotiated deal or go to trial. Even if the lawyer wants to fight the charge and is willing to go to trial for an additional $1,500, the client rarely chooses to do so. The economic realities of the system, not counsel's lack of zeal, frequently pressure the defendant to accept a plea.[45]

In Milwaukee, Dane, and Cleveland Counties, there also are some defense lawyers who are afraid of trying cases, view trials personally as losing ventures, or do not want to alienate a judge or prosecutor by refusing a settlement. These lawyers are not really responding to economic forces or case load pressure but to personal needs or psychological limitations that interfere with their ability to perform in accordance with their professional responsibilities.[46] For many defense lawyers, however, the spirit is willing, but the resources are lacking.

What is clear, then, is that most criminal defense lawyers in Milwaukee, Dane, and Cleveland Counties cannot be characterized simply as double agents. Systemic pressures and organizational obligations certainly influence but do not dictate the behavior of the criminal defense lawyer. As with many of his observations, Blumberg's generalizations about defense lawyers as double agents simply sweep too broadly.[47]

Are most defense lawyers, then, zealous advocates? If so, why is it that the vast majority of cases end in guilty pleas?[48] Blumberg's focus on the role played by defense lawyers in producing guilty pleas underplays the fact that a defendant's decision to plead guilty is shaped by a variety of individual factors and systemic features.[49] For many defendants, the plea decision has little to do with the zeal or even the availability of defense counsel. Rather, a significant number of defendants simply want to plead guilty. Some defendants plead guilty because they really are willing to accept responsibility for their actions. Others want to end the matter quickly and see a guilty plea as the fastest way out of a bothersome predicament. Still other defendants engage in their own simple cost-benefit analysis and conclude that fighting the charge is not worth the time, money, or risk.[50] For some defendants, then, the decision to plead guilty does not depend on the availability or actions of defense counsel.

Nonetheless, for other defendants, various systemic factors, including the availability, cost, and quality of counsel, profoundly influence the plea-bargaining process and, ultimately, the plea decision.[51] A comparison of the features and the culture of the criminal justice system in Milwaukee, Dane, and Cleveland Counties reveals many striking similarities in the plea-bargaining process. However, that comparison also reveals significant differences in the delivery of indigent defense services, local bail practices, and the workings of the local prosecutor's office. These systemic variations not only have an impact on the plea-bargaining process in each county, but also affect the general zeal of the local defense bar.

The most significant systemic feature distinguishing Cleveland County from the two Wisconsin counties is the absence of a public-defender system in Cleveland County. Rather, Cleveland County uses an assigned-counsel system to provide representation to indigent defendants.[52] An indigent defendant in Cleveland County obtains representation, therefore, only if the court chooses to appoint counsel. Only those defendants able to retain counsel are represented at their initial appearance. Defendants unable to make bail generally must wait at least three weeks before the court will act on their application for court-appointed counsel.[53] Those defendants who bail out or have a bond posted for them are presumed to be able to afford counsel.[54] Hence, no lawyer is appointed until the defendant appears before the court and demonstrates an inability to hire counsel. Even then, the defendant is generally denied appointed counsel, told to make additional efforts to secure retained counsel, and threatened with bail revocation if counsel is not obtained. Defendants have had their bail revoked and been forced to return to jail in order to secure appointed counsel.

Felony defendants who remain in jail for at least three weeks are usually deemed indigent, and counsel is appointed. Appointments are made by the local judges from a list of all of the lawyers in the county who practice criminal law.[55] Appointed lawyers in Cleveland County are not paid on an hourly basis. Rather, defense lawyers are paid at a fixed rate of $250 for a misdemeanor case and $500 for a felony.[56] Except in a capital case, therefore, a lawyer will not be compensated more than $500 regardless of the amount of time devoted to a case. Any appointed lawyer wishing an investigator or expert assistance must apply to the judge. Judicial approval of such litigation expenses, however, is very rare.[57]

Milwaukee and Dane Counties have local public-defender offices that are part of a statewide program.[58] Public-defender staff attorneys are state employees with salaries and benefits comparable to those provided to the lawyers in the Wisconsin Attorney General's Office.[59] These staff lawyers answer to the lawyer who directs their office, not to the local judges. Moreover, indigency determinations are made not by the judges but by the local public defender's office. Hence, any person charged with a crime will obtain representation as long as that person meets the eligibility standards set by statute.[60] The public defender's office then assigns the indigent defendant a staff attorney or a private lawyer from a list maintained by the local office. Some clients secure representation even prior to charges being issued.[61]

Although public defenders represent the majority of indigent defendants in Milwaukee and Dane Counties, private lawyers in each county defend roughly 25 percent of the clients served by the public-defender program.[62] Private lawyers presently are paid $45 per hour for in-court time and $35 per hour for out-of-court work with no specified limit on the number of hours to be spent on a case.[63] The bills generated by private lawyers handling assigned cases are paid by the public-defender program. In addition, private lawyers can also obtain funds for investigative and expert services from the local office.[64] Finally, the Milwaukee and Dane County offices have their own investigative staff, some access to social workers, and the ability to fund expert services. Even though the Wisconsin public-defender program definitely needs increased funding, the funding problem is not at the same crisis level experienced by Cleveland County and numerous other jurisdictions.[65]

Many indigent defendants in Milwaukee and Dane Counties are in custody at the time of their initial appearance, but, unlike in Cleveland County, defendants usually are represented by counsel at that court appearance. Not only does defense counsel's early intervention allow him to argue about bail but it enhances counsel's ability to mount an effective defense. Finally, in stark contrast with the judicial reluctance to appoint assigned counsel in Cleveland County, judges in Milwaukee and Dane Counties actively encourage defendants to seek legal assistance from the public defender's office. As a result, many more defendants come to court with a lawyer in these Wisconsin counties than in Cleveland County. Thus, the system's structure for delivering indigent defense services encourages representation in Milwaukee and Dane Counties while discouraging it in Cleveland County. Unrepresented defendants in Cleveland County have little ability to do more than just accept whatever plea bargain is offered to them.[66] Easy access to free defense services or the imposition of barriers to obtaining such representation substantially affects the plea-bargaining process and the actors involved in that process.

A second significant systemic difference between Cleveland County and the two Wisconsin counties is Cleveland County's more limited use of personal recognizance bonds and its heavy reliance on bail bondsmen. When a person is arrested, that person's family and friends generally make every effort to post bail. Unable to raise sufficient funds on their own, many people in Cleveland County turn to a bail bondsman to obtain the needed bond. Money paid to a bail bondsman, however, is no longer available to secure counsel, pay fines, or satisfy court costs. For many defendants and their families, the lack of additional funds compels them either to forgo defense counsel or hire counsel at a bargain price. Unfortunately, it is defense counsel retained for an inadequate fee who is least likely to act as a zealous advocate and most likely to function as a double agent.[67]

In addition, those defendants who do not secure a bond prior to their initial court appearance rarely are represented at that initial appearance. Without counsel to make a bail argument on their behalf, fewer defendants in Cleveland County are released on their own recognizance than in Milwaukee or Dane County. Continued incarceration increases the pressure on defendants to use a bail bondsman or plead guilty to obtain their release. In Cleveland County, defendants unable to make bail at times are provided counsel solely to facilitate the entry of a guilty plea. At other times, defendants will languish in jail for periods well beyond the normal sentence meted out for a particular charge simply because counsel is never appointed and the matter is not brought to the attention of the judge or prosecutor. When the case finally surfaces, the defendant is allowed to plead guilty for time served.[68]

Although, infrequently, a defendant unable to post low bail in Milwaukee or Dane County will be held for an inordinate length before the case is located and resolved, the system generally operates to avoid such cases. Indeed, the Wisconsin bail provisions specifically "are designed to see that a maximum number of persons are released prior to trial with a minimum of financial burden upon them."[69] A sizable number of persons arrested for a misdemeanor are given a citation and released.[70] If the person is detained and the accused's family or friends cannot post the necessary cash bail, the defendant will remain incarcerated until the initial court appearance. Fortunately, most defendants have an initial court appearance within twenty-four hours of their arrest. Moreover, most defendants in Milwaukee and Dane Counties are represented at the initial appearance, usually by a public defender. Counsel's bail arguments regularly lead either to a recognizance bond or a reduction in the amount of bail.[71]

Some defendants in Milwaukee and Dane Counties fail to make bail and are subject, therefore, to some of the same pressure experienced by detainees in Cleveland County. Nevertheless, these defendants at least have had a lawyer assigned to them who now is working on their behalf. For the unrepresented defendant in Cleveland County, the pressure is much greater.[72]

Finally, for those defendants in Milwaukee or Dane Counties who do post cash bail, that money will be returned to the person posting it unless the defendant fails to appear for a court appearance. Sometimes a defendant can retain counsel by offering the lawyer a lien on this bail money. Often the bail money can be used to pay a fine, restitution, or court costs. In short, a comparison of Milwaukee, Dane, and Cleveland Counties demonstrates that the bail practices in a given community have a considerable impact on the plea decisions of many defendants in that community.[73]

The operation of the district attorney's office in Milwaukee, Dane, and Cleveland Counties represents the third significant systemic feature affecting defendants' plea decisions and the behavior of criminal defense lawyers in these three counties. There are many similarities in the attitude of the staff and in the workings of the three offices,[74] but there also are some significant differences. With over ninety attorneys, the size of the Milwaukee office allows for more specialization and more overall expertise. Nevertheless, the volume of cases handled by the system and each prosecutor, the number of courts, and the greater time it takes for cases to work through the system increase the opportunity for defense counsel in Milwaukee to "shop" for a better plea bargain, to leverage defense strengths to the defendant's advantage, and to resist prosecutorial pressure to "play ball."

In contrast to Milwaukee's large staff, Dane County has twenty-six prosecutors and Cleveland County nine. Operating in smaller, more closed courthouse communities than in Milwaukee County, the prosecutors in Dane and Cleveland Counties tend to be more cohesive and communicative about defense lawyers and their practices. Because they know most defense lawyers very well, Dane and Cleveland County prosecutors have an edge over their Milwaukee counterparts.

Although news travels faster in the courthouse communities of Dane and Cleveland Counties, the systemic pace is slower than in Milwaukee County. Thus, prosecutors in Dane and Cleveland Counties seemingly have more time to spend on minor charges and are less willing either to divert cases from the system or dismiss them once they are filed.[75] This reluctance to divert or dismiss charges in part reflects the fact that Dane and Cleveland Counties rely on a deputy district attorney to issue virtually all charges.[76] Accordingly, once charges have been issued, most assistant district attorneys are very hesitant to dismiss a case. This is so even though the initial charging decision rested primarily on the deputy's review of police reports with little opportunity to evaluate the strengths or weaknesses of the case or the existence of any mitigating factors. This is particularly so in Cleveland County because the office relies on law student interns to handle almost the entire misdemeanor case load.[77] The interns' limited discretion makes it difficult to negotiate the dismissal of any issued charge or to secure a significant reduction in the standard offer for a particular offense.

In Milwaukee County, however, charges generally are issued following a charging conference in which one of the prosecutors on duty that week meets with the complainant, police officers, witnesses, and, at times, the defendant and defense counsel, before deciding what, if any, charges to file.[78] Although the charging system used in Milwaukee County involves an enormous front-loading of prosecutorial resources, the system produces better-informed and more accurate charging decisions. This charging process also eliminates many weak or unsubstantiated cases that otherwise would clog the system.

There are several lessons to be learned in studying the systems in Milwaukee, Dane, and Cleveland Counties. First, variations in significant systemic features influence the behavior of a system's defense lawyers. In Cleveland County, for example, the system for appointing counsel works to discourage defendants from actually obtaining counsel. Defendants are pressured to waive their rights and plead guilty without the assistance of counsel. In other cases, the delay in appointing a lawyer or the system's bail practices pressure the defendant simply to "get it over with." Once a lawyer finally is appointed, the client may instruct the attorney simply to obtain the best plea bargain possible.[79] The defense lawyer may be very willing to challenge the state's case and even argue with the defendant about the shortsightedness of a guilty plea.[80] Nonetheless, if the client persists in wanting a plea bargain, defense counsel may be left simply securing the best deal possible, even though counsel believes a conviction is unjust and a guilty verdict unlikely.

Second, a criminal justice system driven by plea bargaining exerts substantial pressure on a criminal defendant not to go to trial. Defendants face considerable moral, psychological, physical,[81] and economic pressure to plead guilty. Many defendants confess and few suppression motions are granted, so that most defendants battle tough odds should they choose to go to trial. Even if the evidence is less than overwhelming, a defendant may be reluctant to risk trial because of numerous prior convictions, the fear of judicial retaliation for going to trial, or the amount of pretrial incarceration to be endured before a trial will occur. Above all, the prosecutor usually has a wide range of bargaining threats— charging additional offenses, adding sentence enhancers, and including a charge with a mandatory minimum sentence, to name a few—that also deter defendants from turning down proposed deals.[82]

Although most defendants want to plea bargain, they often are not satisfied with the deals they receive. Yet, few defendants actually want to go to trial. For criminal defense lawyers, then, much of their time is spent negotiating a deal against an adversary who generally can dictate the terms. Under such circumstances, defense counsel is not a double agent but a beleaguered dealer negotiating from a position of weakness. It is not defense counsel's profit motive but the structure of the system that primarily influences the decision of many defendants to accept a plea bargain.

Third, because so many defendants are unable to afford counsel, the local structure for delivering indigent defense services largely determines the overall quality of representation provided to criminal defendants in a particular community. Thus, the existence of a reasonably well-funded public-defender program in Milwaukee and Dane Counties explains in large part why more defendants in these counties receive competent, zealous representation than in Cleveland County. As full-time criminal practitioners, the Wisconsin public defenders are better trained and have more resources than the appointed lawyers in Cleveland County. It is not surprising, then, that these public defenders generally pursue more aggressive defense tactics.[83] Moreover, by filing motions, taking cases to trial, and disseminating information to private lawyers who do not specialize in criminal law, the public defenders encourage and educate other defense lawyers to be more zealous. In addition, retained counsel in these two counties tend to be more aggressive, knowing that they will not be singled out by the prosecutor's office and retaliated against for taking cases to trial. Finally, not only do appointed lawyers in Wisconsin have access to experts and investigative assistance but they also receive adequate compensation without imposed limits. Private lawyers appointed to represent indigent defendants in Wisconsin, therefore, are provided with a financial incentive to prepare adequately and to take cases to trial.[84]

On the other hand, the appointed-counsel system in Cleveland County, based on a fixed flat-compensation scheme, serves to encourage the very behavior by defense counsel condemned by Blumberg.[85] A defense lawyer earns a modest or, at times, even a decent fee if the client enters a quick plea. There is, however, an economic disincentive to investigate, to research, or, above all, to take a case to trial. A lawyer who chooses to spend time, energy, and money in the defense of a case does so at his own expense. In Cleveland County, as in other jurisdictions around the country, not enough lawyers are willing to make that personal sacrifice.[86] Defense counsel may not be a con but feels pressure to strike a deal. Frequently, appointed counsel enters the negotiation process without much leverage. In fact, the prosecutors in Cleveland County know full well the economic realities confronting appointed counsel.

Nonetheless, it is not just profit motive or financial pressure that causes some criminal defense lawyers to be less than zealous. Heavy case loads create time pressure and stress that can overwhelm even the best-intentioned, most competent defense lawyer.[87] Certainly there are some public defenders in Milwaukee and Dane Counties who respond to case load pressures by cajoling, threatening, or manipulating their clients into pleading guilty.[88] Like private lawyers who accept an insufficient retainer and then force a plea bargain on an unwitting client, some public defenders will oversell the advantages of a plea bargain, conduct an inadequate investigation, or fail to prepare properly for trial, thereby coercing guilty pleas from reluctant defendants.

Most public defenders in Milwaukee and Dane Counties, however, do not respond to heavy case loads by operating as double agents. Rather, they attempt to cope with their heavy case loads by allocating their time and limited investigative resources in the best possible way.[89] Consequently, some cases are not adequately researched or investigated. Some defendants, therefore, receive better representation at the expense of others. Moreover, overworked public defenders have less time to spend with their clients and this hampers their ability to develop trusting, meaningful attorney-client relationships.[90] Absent a good attorney-client relationship, the defendant is even more susceptible to buckle under the pressure to plead guilty.

Despite serious time pressure and heavy case loads, the public defenders in Milwaukee and Dane Counties, for the most part, bargain effectively for many of their clients. They know the system well and thus are able to evaluate the worth of a proposed plea bargain and the merits of taking a case to trial.[91] In addition, faced with their own case load pressures and the knowledge that these public defenders generally have the capacity and willingness to fight if an acceptable deal is not struck, the prosecutors in these counties have some incentive to bargain reasonably. Unlike appointed counsel in Cleveland County, defenders of the indigent in Wisconsin, albeit beleaguered, pose a credible threat.

But as their resources become increasingly strained, overburdened public defenders in Milwaukee and Dane Counties are more vulnerable to prosecutorial pressure and less able to use tactics, such as filing a well-briefed motion, that apply pressure on the prosecutor.[92] In short, the final lesson to be learned from examining these three counties is that even the lawyers in a well-structured indigent defense system will find it difficult to act aggressively without adequate time and resources. Large case loads exert added pressure on public defenders to obtain acceptable plea bargains for most of their clients. There is that subtle but constant pressure when negotiating numerous cases not to push a prosecutor too hard in one case so that counsel will obtain favorable consideration in other cases.[93] And there is real pressure to avoid antagonizing prosecutors because of the tremendous discretion they have to reward or punish defendants in the plea bargain process. Faced with these pressures, the overworked public defender may produce the same results as the underpaid private lawyer: "plea bargains too easily accepted by one-shot clients on the advice of lawyers trying, either out of self-interest or for the good of their clients as a class, to maintain good personal relations with the judges and prosecutors with whom they must regularly work.''[84]

Defense Lawyer as Effective Advocate: Structuring the System to Enhance Zeal

Criminal defense lawyers in Milwaukee and Dane Counties appear to defend their clients more zealously and effectively than lawyers in Cleveland County primarily because of the superior resources allotted to the representation of indigent defendants in Wisconsin. Simply put, zealousness comes with a price tag. Until society is prepared to increase the resources allocated to the defense of persons accused of crimes, few defendants will receive effective zealous assistance of counsel.

Because most criminal defendants are indigent, improving the delivery of indigent defense services in a local system constitutes the best means of enhancing the overall quality of representation in that system. Moreover, improving the indigent defense system in a community heightens the zeal and effectiveness of the private defense bar. This improvement, however, cannot be attained simply by sleight of hand or minor structural tinkering. In most jurisdictions, substantial resources are needed to correct serious shortcomings in the delivery of indigent defense services.[95] In light of the keen competition for dollars in austere state budgets and the incessant clamor for a war on crime, the prospects for major funding increases for defense services are dim. And yet, increased funding is imperative if the crisis in the delivery of indigent defense services occurring in many counties across the United States is to be adequately addressed.[96]

Assuming, therefore, that some additional funds are made available for indigent defense services, how must the system be structured for delivering those services to ensure that more defendants are provided a zealous defense? Again, there is no simple answer. It is clear, however, that if the system truly is to enhance zeal and effective advocacy, it must lessen defense counsel's vulnerability to the pressures inherent in the plea-bargain-driven criminal justice system.[97]

An adequately funded, independent, ''mixed'' statewide program of salaried public defenders and assigned private counsel represents the indigent defense system least susceptible to these insidious pressures.[98] First, a mixed system is desirable because it blends experienced, well-trained criminal law specialists together with private lawyers who may bring fresh, creative approaches to systemic problems as a result of their civil experience. In addition, a strong assigned-counsel component of the program ensures that the local defense bar will continue to play an active role in criminal defense litigation. If the private bar lacks an investment in the indigent defense program, the organized bar may not rally enthusiastically behind the program. Without the vigorous support of the bar, the public-defender program will have difficulty garnering legislative votes for needed funding.[99] Finally, the continued involvement of private lawyers in the criminal justice system lessens the institutionalization of criminal defense work with its concomitant dangers.[100]

Next, this mixed public-defender program must be structured to insulate defense counsel from direct economic pressure. Counsel should not have to curry favor with the judiciary to be appointed to cases or face economic retaliation for not settling or defending a case as a judge sees fit. The program must control the hiring and firing of its staff lawyers as well as the selection of appointed counsel. Neither the judiciary nor any local government entity should control the salaries or compensation paid to indigent defenders.[101] Economic control includes the real threat of interference with counsel's representation.[102] Defense counsel's independence must be respected and encouraged.

So, also, assigned counsel must be adequately compensated. Flat, fixed fees, especially with low maximum limits, discourage lawyers from being effective advocates. Instead, lawyers are rewarded for resolving cases as quickly as possible without an adequate inquiry into the merits of the case. Any contract or assigned-counsel system relying on a fixed-fee method of compensation builds into the system an economic disincentive to take cases to trial.[103] This does not mean that many cases should or would be tried even under this proposed public-defender system. Indeed, the systemic pressures that already coerce many defendants into pleading guilty will continue to force most defendants to accept plea bargains. But the indigent defense system should not add to that pressure. Rather, the system must be structured to facilitate access to counsel. As in the Wisconsin public-defender system, defendants must get representation early with as few procedural hurdles as possible.[104]

Early representation is meaningless, however, unless defense counsel has ready access to the resources needed to mount a vigorous defense. Adequate support staff and investigative resources are crucial if effective representation is to be provided.[105] Care must be taken to ensure that assigned counsel as well as staff lawyers have sufficient access to investigators and expert services. Moreover, adequate training must be provided for public-defender staff lawyers, and low-cost continuing education programs must be developed for assigned counsel.[106] A lawyer cannot practice criminal law competently without keeping current on changes in substantive law and criminal procedure.[107]

In addition, this public-defender system must provide reasonable salaries with manageable case loads. Excessive case loads create undue pressure to settle, not to try jury trials. The public defender's compensation package must be designed to reward effective, aggressive lawyering, not to encourage the mere processing of a set number of cases. Adequate performance measures together with merit raise incentives[108] improve the likelihood that public defenders will act zealously.[109]

A statewide public-defender program must secure adequate funding if it is to provide competent defense services. Given the budget pressures confronting virtually every state legislature, however, even an adequately funded program will still face tough choices on allocating funds.[110] The history of the Wisconsin public-defender program since 1977 suggests that it is extremely difficult to balance reasonably high salaries, excellent benefits, good working conditions, and strong support and litigation services with reasonable case loads.[111] In striking an appropriate balance, program administrators must bear in mind that together with the lawyer actually handling a case, they are responsible for the quality of representation ultimately provided.[112] Administrators and legislators also must remember that requiring public defenders to handle too many cases invariably results in deficient representation.

The top priority for a public-defender program, therefore, must be to keep case loads at a level that allows staff attorneys to perform in accordance with the standards of a competent criminal defense lawyer.[113] This means, in part, developing a mechanism to divert cases to assigned counsel when case loads get too heavy. In addition, this means giving public defenders sufficient time to interview their clients, to investigate, to research, and to prepare adequately for negotiations, trials, and sentencings.[114]

There is no cost-free method for generating more time. Faced with the challenge of keeping case loads light while providing quality representation to an increasing number of clients, the program may have to use a salary structure that is unlikely to produce career public defenders. Thus, it may be necessary to keep salaries fairly low and hire more new law school graduates, thereby creating more positions but with fewer cases per attorney. Staff lawyers would earn less money but have improved working conditions, less stress, and more job satisfaction.[115] Any loss of expertise due to increased lawyer turnover would arguably be offset by the increased zeal of the larger staff and the greater use of senior staff lawyers as supervisors.[116]

Moreover, some additional time may be created by providing staff lawyers with better litigation support. It may be desirable to spend more money on investigators or paralegals, who could assume many of the tasks that are often inefficiently handled by lawyers. Finally, difficult and complex cases often strain the resources of a small public-defender office. One advantage of a statewide program would be the central administration's ability to shift resources or use special units to defend selected cases efficiently and effectively.[117]

Yet, even though improving the indigent defense system in a community would affect the quality of representation afforded many defendants, a significant number of low-income defendants would remain largely unaffected. The working poor, many making only minimum wage, do not qualify under existing indigency standards for an indigent defender.[118] Unable to afford to hire a zealous advocate, the low-income defendant is forced to take whatever bargain the prosecutor proffers.

The prospects for improving the representation of these defendants are particularly bleak. It may be that a percentage of low-income defendants could qualify as partially indigent and, therefore, for a small retainer, receive the same representation provided to other defendants by the public-defender program.[119] Expanding the number of indigent clients served by the program, however, increases case load pressure and decreases the time available to provide zealous representation to others in the program. In light of the substantial financial needs already facing most jurisdictions, expansion of the program to cover more low-income people is highly unlikely.[120]

There are limits, then, to the extent to which dramatic change can occur in the criminal justice system. Undoubtedly, improving indigent services will lead to greater zeal and more effective lawyering. And yet, even though the overall zeal of the defense bar may increase, the nature of the plea-bargaining process and the system itself substantially limit a dramatic difference in the role of the criminal defense lawyer. That is because in most cases, the defendant, the case itself and the system substantially limit the options available to the defendant and to counsel.

Given the pressure that the prosecutor and the system bring to bear on criminal defendants, even zealous defense lawyers generally will be beleaguered dealers. If negotiations fail, however, the zealous advocate must have the will and ability to fight on behalf of a client. Unless we give defense lawyers the necessary resources and incentives to challenge the state, our adversary system indeed will drift further toward the co-optative system Blumberg described.

Endnotes

[1] "The basic duty defense counsel owes to the administration of justice and as an officer of the court is to serve as the accused's counselor and advocate with courage and devotion, and to render effective, quality representation." ABA, *Standards for Criminal Justice* Standard 4-1.2(b) (3d ed. 1991). The ethics codes enshrine the principle of zealous partisanship. See, e.g., *Model Code of Professional Responsibility* DR 7-101, EC 7-1, EC 7-4, EC 7-19 (1981); *Model Rules of Professional Conduct* Preamble (1983). As Charles Wolfram observes, "[T]he American lawyer's professional model is that of zeal: a lawyer is expected to devote energy, intelligence, skill and personal

commitment to the single goal of furthering the clients' interests as those are ultimately defined by the client." C. Wolfram, *Modern Legal Ethics* 585 (1986). Moreover, numerous cases trumpet the lawyer's obligation to be a vigorous defender. See, e.g., *Von Moltke v. Gillies*, 332 U.S. 708, 725-726 (1948) (the right to counsel demands undivided allegiance and service devoted solely to the interests of the client).

[2] As Justice Powell has noted:

> In our system a defense lawyer characteristically opposes the designated representative of the State. The system assumes that adversarial testimony will ultimately advance the public interest in truth and fairness. But it posits that a defense lawyer best serves the public not by acting on behalf of the State or in concert with it but rather by advancing "the undivided interests of his client."

Polk County v. Dodson, 454 U.S. 312, 318-319 (1981). For an excellent summary of the basic principles of the U.S. adversary system of criminal justice, see W. LaFave & J. Israel, *Criminal Procedure* 24-32 (1985).

[3] Justice White eloquently summarized the role of the criminal defense lawyer:

> But defense counsel has no comparable obligation to ascertain or present the truth. Our system assigns him a different mission . . . . Defense counsel need present nothing, even if he knows what the truth is. He need not furnish any witnesses to the police, or reveal any confidences of his client, or furnish any other information to help the prosecution's case. If he can confuse a witness, even a truthful one, or make him appear at a disadvantage, unsure or indecisive, that will be his normal course. Our interest in not convicting the innocent permits counsel to put the State to its proof, to put the State's case in the worst possible light, regardless of what he thinks or knows to be the truth. Undoubtedly there are some limits which defense counsel must observe, but more often than not, defense counsel will cross-examine a prosecution witness, and impeach him if he can, even if he thinks the witness is telling the truth, just as he will attempt to destroy a witness who he thinks is lying. In this respect, as part of our modified adversary system and as part of the duty imposed on the most honorable defense counsel, we countenance or require conduct which in many instances has little, if any, relation to the search for truth.

United States v. Wade, 388 U.S. 218, 256-258 (1967) (White, J., dissenting in part and concurring in part).

[4] Id. See also C. Wolfram, note 1 supra, at 586-587.

[5] "The procedural and legal system are supposedly designed to produce results based on just laws fairly applied on the basis of accurate facts; but a lawyer's objective within that system is to achieve a result favorable to the lawyer's client, possibly despite justice, the law, and the facts." C. Wolfram, note 1 supra, at 585. Because defense counsel must be a zealous partisan, counsel's efforts may well interfere with the search for the truth. M. Freedman, *Understanding Lawyers' Ethics* 161-171 (1990); A. Amsterdam, *Trial Manual for the Defense of Criminal Cases* 2-327 (1984); C. Wolfram, note 1 supra, at 588-589, 641, 650-651. Even commentators critical of the legal profession's commitment to the principles of partisanship and nonaccountability generally recognize that the criminal defense lawyer must pursue the defendant's interests even at the expense of an accurate outcome. D. Luban, *Lawyers and Justice: An Ethical Study* 58-63 (1988).

[6] As Chief Justice Burger noted in *Nix v. Whiteside*, 475 U.S. 157 (1986), the lawyer's "overarching duty" to advocate and advance the client's interests is limited by the lawyer's "equally solemn" responsibilities and duties as an officer of the court. Id. at 166-168. In certain situations, ethical provisions require defense counsel to take action or to disclose information adverse to the interests of the client. See J. Burkoff, *Criminal Defense Ethics* ch. 6 (1986). Nonetheless, there is considerable disagreement regarding the extent to which defense counsel's advocacy must be tempered by his

duties as an officer of the court. Compare Chief Justice Burger's view in Nix v. Whiteside, supra, at 157, 168 (emphasizing defense counsel's role as an officer of the court) with that of Justice Brennan in Jones v. Barnes, 463 U.S. 745, 761-762 (1983) (Brennan, J., dissenting) (stressing that counsel must function as an advocate as opposed to a friend of the court). See also Justice White in United States v. Wade, note 3 supra, at 218, 257-258 (White, J., dissenting in part and concurring in part) (defense lawyer's mission is not to ascertain or present the truth); Justice Black in Von Moltke v. Gillies, note 1 supra, at 708, 725-726 (right to counsel demands undivided allegiance and service devoted solely to the interests of the client); Justice Powell in Polk County v. Dodson, note 2 supra, at 312, 318 (defense counsel best serves the public by advancing the individual interests of the accused); Commission on Professional Responsibility of Roscoe Pound-Am Trial Lawyers Found., The American Lawyer's Code of Conduct preamble (1982) ("It is clear that the lawyer for a private party is and should be an officer of the court only in the sense of serving a court as a zealous, partisan advocate of one side of the case before it, and in the sense of having been licensed by a court to play that very role.").

[7] Even after Nix v. Whiteside, note 6 supra, at 157, for example, there is a continuing controversy as to how the criminal defense lawyer should respond when counsel knows or suspects that the client is going to testify falsely. Lefstein, "Client Perjury in Criminal Cases: Still in Search of an Answer," 1 Geo. J. Legal Ethics 521 (1988). For a discussion of various resolutions to the perjury issue, see M. Freedman, note 5 supra, at 109-141.

[8] As Justice Powell observed:

> [T]he duty of the lawyer, subject to his role as an "officer of the court," is to further the interests of his clients by all lawful means, even when these interests are in conflict with the interests of the United States or of a State. But his representation involves no conflict of interest in the invidious sense. Rather, it casts the lawyer in his honored and traditional role as an authorized but independent agent acting to vindicate the legal rights of a client, whoever it may be.

In re Griffiths, 413 U.S. 717, 724 n.14 (1973).

To vindicate the rights of an accused, a lawyer must be an effective as well as loyal advocate. Polk County v. Dodson, note 2 supra, at 312, 322. At a minimum, therefore, a criminal defendant is guaranteed the right to "reasonably effective assistance of counsel." Strickland v. Washington, 466 U.S. 668, 687 (1984). The line between ineffective and adequate assistance of counsel is difficult to draw. See Mounts, "The Right to Counsel and the Indigent Defense System." 14 N.Y.U. Rev. L. & Soc. Change 221-241 (1986). Yet, unquestionably, defense counsel ethically bound to provide competent, timely, and informed representation. See Model Rules of Professional Conduct Rule 1.1, 1.3, 1.4 and commentary (1983) Model Code of Professional Responsibility DR 6-101, DR 7-101 (1981); ABA, note 1 supra, Standard 4-1.3.

[9] See Blumberg, "The Practice of Law as Confidence Game: Organizational Co-optation of a Profession," 1 Law & Soc'y Rev. 15, 28-31 (1967) (describing criminal defense lawyers as double agents because they serve organizational ends while appearing to help their clients).

[10] Id. at 15-39. See also M. Heumann, Plea Bargaining 80 (1978) (concluding that defense lawyers ultimately succumb to the culture of the court system, a culture that rewards cooperation and sanctions a formal adversarial approach).

[11] Blumberg, note 9 supra, at 18. Blumberg's work continues to be cited regularly. See, e.g., D. Luban, note 5 supra, at 60-61; Schneyer, "Sympathy for the Hired Gun," 41 J. L. Educ. 11, 23-24 (1991).

[12] Blumberg indicated that usually over 90 percent of criminal convictions followed a negotiated guilty plea. Blumberg, note 9 supra, at 18.

¹³ Intolerably large case loads must be disposed of by a court system lacking sufficient resources. As a result, "the principals, lawyer and assistant district attorney, rely upon one another's cooperation for their continued professional existence, and so the bargaining between them tends usually to be 'reasonable' rather than fierce." Id. at 22–23.

¹⁴ Id. at 19.

¹⁵ Id. at 20.

¹⁶ Blumberg reasoned:

Accused persons come and go in the court system schema, but the structure and its occupational incumbents remain to carry on their respective career, occupational and organizational enterprises. The individual stridencies, tensions, and conflicts a given accused person's case may present to all the participants are overcome because the formal and informal relations of all the groups in the court setting require it. The probability of continued future relations and interaction must be preserved at all cost.

Id.

¹⁷ Id. at 22.

¹⁸ Id. at 22–23.

¹⁹ Id. at 23. See also Sudnow, "Normal Crimes: Sociological Features of the Penal Code in the Public Defender's Office," 12 *Soc. Probs.* 255–277 (1965) (public defenders are mere functionaries primarily concerned with quickly disposing of cases).

²⁰ Blumberg detailed at length the nature of this "confidence game," in which the criminal defense lawyer manipulated the client into accepting a guilty plea that the client was "conned" into believing was the desirable fruit of counsel's vigorous efforts on the client's behalf. Blumberg, note 9 supra, at 24–31.

²¹ Id. at 27.

²² Id. at 28–29.

²³ Blumberg expressed this conclusion in the following language:

[T]he lawyer's role as agent-mediator may be seen, as unique in that he is in effect a double agent. Although, as "officer of the court" he mediates between the court organization and the defendant, his roles with respect to each are rent by conflicts of interest. Too often these must be resolved in favor of the organization which provides him with the means for his professional existence. Consequently, in order to reduce the strains and conflicts imposed in what is ultimately an over-demanding role obligation for him, the lawyer engages in the lawyer-client "confidence game" so as to structure more favorably an otherwise onerous role system.

Id. at 38.

²⁴ Milwaukee County is a large urban county of 959,275 people, most of whom live in the city of Milwaukee. Dane County's population of 367,085 is concentrated in Madison, the capital of Wisconsin. Like Dane, Cleveland County is a moderate-size county of 174,253 people. Norman, the home of the University of Oklahoma, is the largest city in Cleveland County.

²⁵ The author practiced law in Milwaukee from 1978 to 1984 as a public defender and in a private firm from 1988 to 1990. He directed a clinical program at the University of Wisconsin in Dane County from 1984 to 1988. The students in this program defended indigent clients charged with misdemeanor offenses. Since joining the faculty at the University of Oklahoma College of Law in 1990, he has supervised law students handling criminal cases in the Cleveland County courts. His comments, therefore, are based on his own observations as a participant in each system as well as discussions with and observations of third-year law students working in these three systems. He also interviewed criminal defense lawyers, prosecutors, and judges in each county.

Similarly, Blumberg's article was "based upon observations made by the writer during many years of legal practice in the criminal courts of a large metropolitan area.'' Blumberg, note 9 supra, at 18.

[26] See, e.g., L. McIntyre, *The Public Defender* (1987); J. Casper, *Criminal Courts: The Defendant's Perspective* (1978); Coyle, Strasser & Lovelle, "Fatal Defense," *Natl L.J.* June 11, 1990, at 30; Alschuler, "The Defense Attorney's Role in Plea Bargaining," 84 *Yale L.J.* 1179 (1975); Skolnick, "Social Control in the Adversary System," 11 *J. Conflict Resolution* 52 (1967); R. Herman, E. Single & I. Boston, *Counsel for the Poor* (1977); Arthur Young & Co., *Seattle-King County Public Defender Association Evaluation Project: Final Report* (1975).

Moreover, many of the author's observations about the representation provided by assistant public defenders in Milwaukee and Dane Counties mirror those of the Spangenberg Group, a nationally recognized consulting firm offering technical assistance and research concerning indigent defense systems. See Spangenberg Group, *Caseload/Workload Study for the State Public Defender of Wisconsin, Final Report* (1990).

[27] Blumberg, note 9 supra, at 18–38.

[28] It is difficult to obtain exact figures on the percentage of cases actually tried in each jurisdiction. In Cleveland County, 38 cases were tried in 1989 and 29 in 1990. In comparison, 5,724 criminal cases were disposed of by guilty pleas in Cleveland County in 1989 and 5,029 in 1990. In Dane County, 165 cases were decided by trial in 1989 and 141 in 1990. This compares with 5,095 cases disposed of by guilty pleas in Dane County in 1989 and 6,184 in 1990. The Director of State Courts Office for Wisconsin does not maintain statistics on the manner in which cases were disposed of in Milwaukee County. The statistics maintained by the Milwaukee County Clerk of Courts Office reflect that in 1989 there were 428 criminal jury trials out of 14,756 cases that either were pleaded out or dismissed. In 1990, there were 461 criminal jury trials held in Milwaukee County while 16,029 cases were pleaded out or dismissed.

[29] These observations are borne out not only by the author's experiences and conversations with defense lawyers but also by clients unable to raise sufficient funds to retain or keep private counsel, who subsequently looked to the public-defender office or the author's clinical program for assistance.

[30] For a similar observation, see Alschuler, note 26 supra, at 1190–1194.

[31] Id. at 1195. See also M. Mayer, *The Lawyers* 161–162 (1967) (reporting that the courts commonly grant postponements to private lawyers to aid them in collecting fees). Judicial willingness to tolerate numerous continuances is not surprising given the willingness of many of these lawyers to contribute to judicial reelection campaigns.

[32] Unfortunately, it is not only defense lawyers who sometimes lie to their clients. Others have observed that both civil and criminal lawyers lie to their clients for reasons of self-interest. See Lerman, "Lying to Clients," 138 *U. Pa. L. Rev.* 659 (1990); Hellman, "The Effects of Law Office Work on the Formation of Law Students' Professional Values: Observation, Explanation, Optimization," 4 *Geo. J. Legal Ethics* 537 (1991); Alschuler, note 26 supra, at 1194–1198.

[33] Blumberg, note 9 supra, at 23.

[34] Id.

[35] According to Blumberg, the criminal justice system shrouds itself in secrecy to avoid close scrutiny, which would reveal the complicitous nature of the system. Id. at 22. See also A. Dershowitz, *The Best Defense* (1982).

[36] In their study of the Wisconsin public-defender program, the Spangenberg Group was particularly impressed with the quality and dedication of the public defenders in the Milwaukee office. See Spangenberg Group, note 26 supra, at 39. For a similar positive reaction to the lawyers in the Cook County public defender office, see McIntyre, note 26 supra, at 172–173.

[37] Good criminal defense lawyers frequently use an aggressive motion practice to further their clients' interests. *The Champion*, a monthly magazine put out by the National Association of Criminal Defense Lawyers, regularly contains articles urging defense lawyers to file a variety of different motions. See, e.g., Hingson, "State Constitutions and the Criminal Defense Lawyer: A Necessary Virtue," 14 *The Champion* 6 (Dec. 1990); Preiser & Swisher, "Aggressive Defense of White Collar Clients," 15 *The Champion* 6 (June 1991).

[38] Not all lawyers are willing to make a financial sacrifice like that of Connecticut lawyer Chester Fairlie, who ruined his private practice and exhausted his own savings by spending over 650 hours to defend an accused murderer. See ABA & National Legal Aid & Defender Ass'n, *Gideon Undone: The Crisis in Indigent Defense Funding* 11, 14–15 (1982).

Nonetheless, there are numerous examples in all three counties of lawyers who have unselfishly made personal and financial sacrifices on behalf of their clients. See also Spangenberg, "Why We Are Not Defending the Poor Properly," 1 *Crim. Just.* 48 (1986) (noting that despite many problems, many public defenders and private lawyers were dedicated to providing quality representation to indigent defendants).

[39] Blumberg, note 9 supra, at 28.

[40] Indeed, as Ted Schneyer suggests, there are many forces and pressures at work that discourage zealousness and tempt the criminal defense lawyer to be an indifferent advocate. Schneyer, note 11 supra, at 23–24. See also Alschuler, note 26 supra, at 1180 (nature of plea-bargaining system necessarily tempts lawyers to make decisions not really in their clients' interest).

[41] A number of commentators complain that public defenders provide perfunctory representation. See, e.g., Sudnow, note 19 supra. Many have linked the public defender's cooperative approach to defending their clients to the defender's deferential attitude toward the judiciary. See M. Levin, *Urban Politics and the Criminal Court* (1977); Dimock, "The Public Defender: A Step Towards a Police State," 42 *A.B.A.J.* 219–221 (1965); C. Silverman, *Criminal Violence, Criminal Justice* (1978); G. Robin, *Introduction to the Criminal Justice System* (1984). More commonly, inadequate representation by public defenders has been traced to excessive case loads and underfunded programs. See, e.g., Klein, "The Emperor Gideon Has No Clothes: The Empty Promise of the Constitutional Right to Effective Assistance of Counsel," 13 *Hastings Const. L.Q.* 625, 661–662 (1986). Other commentators as well as numerous empirical studies suggest, however, that defendants represented by public defenders fare no worse than those represented by retained private counsel. See, e.g., J. Casper, note 26 supra; Herman, Single & Boston, note 26 supra; L. McIntyre, note 26 supra. Nonetheless, these commentators report that public-defender clients often mistrust their lawyers and believe they receive inadequate representation. See also note 90 infra and accompanying text.

[42] As overhead costs and inflation drive legal costs up, few defendants are able to raise sufficient money to pay a significant retainer. Even fewer are able to afford the cost of the investigator or expert needed to mount an effective defense.

[43] The problem is particularly acute in Cleveland County because the judges apply such a low indigency standard that few defendants qualify for court-appointed counsel. See notes 52–57, 60 infra and accompanying text.

[44] On numerous occasions, defendants would come to the Milwaukee public-defender office seeking assistance after their lawyer successfully withdrew from a case. The lawyer would have claimed irreconcilable differences as the basis for the motion to withdraw. In reality, however, it was the defendant's insistence on a trial and counsel's unwillingness to go to trial for the meager retainer the defendant could scrape up that prompted the motion to withdraw.

⁴⁵ Alschuler, note 26 supra, at 1203.

⁴⁶ Trial work is often incredibly stressful. Stress, fear, and personal convenience shape the behavior of some lawyers and influence the recommendations made to their clients. See L. McIntyre, note 26 supra, at 150–151. Moreover, given the uncertainty of predicting trials, the cautious nature of most lawyers, and the fear of a severe sentence after a guilty verdict, even well-intentioned lawyers may present clients with their options in a manner that influences them to plead guilty rather than go to trial. See Alschuler, note 26 supra, at 1205–1206.

⁴⁷ For a similar conclusion based on her study of the Cook County public defender, see L. McIntyre, note 26 supra, at 47–48.

⁴⁸ Although statistics vary from jurisdiction to jurisdiction, most studies indicate that over 90 percent of the convictions in the state courts are the result of guilty pleas. See Bureau of Justice Statistics, U.S. Dep't of Justice, *Bulletin: Felony Sentences in the State Courts, 1988*, at 6 (1990). Undoubtedly, the percentage of misdemeanor cases disposed of by a guilty plea is even higher. See Smith, "Forgotten in the Courts," 2 *Crim. Just.* 14, 17 (1987). In Milwaukee County, for example, out of 38,202 misdemeanor cases disposed of during 1986, there were only 114 trials. See G. Barczak, *Milwaukee County Circuit Court Annual Report* (1986).

⁴⁹ To Alschuler, the whole plea-bargaining system is structured to coerce guilty pleas and thereby to deprive defendants of their right to trial. See Alschuler, note 26 supra, at 1199–1206, 1306–1314.

⁵⁰ The author shares Malcolm Feeley's observation that most defendants are concerned primarily with resolving their cases quickly with a minimal expenditure of time and money. See generally M. Feeley, *The Process Is the Punishment: Handling Cases in a Lower Criminal Court* (1979). Indeed, one of the most common observations of the clinical students both at the University of Wisconsin and the Oklahoma College of Law is that so many defendants are uninterested in their own cases. Often, the students were frustrated by clients' indifference and decision to just get the matter over with despite the weakness of the state's case.

⁵¹ Numerous variables affect the working of a criminal justice system. The local crime rate, funding for the different systemic actors, effectiveness of the local police, arrest policies, economic health of the local community, and availability of social services and treatment programs are among the many factors contributing to the number of cases in the system and the manner in which these cases will be handled. Also, events and decisions at the state and national level influence the local system. For example, statewide prison overcrowding and parole release policies may influence local plea-bargaining practices and sentencing decisions. Or federal funding for the war on drugs may mean an additional position in the district attorney's office, allowing for more aggressive prosecution of defendants charged with drug offenses.

⁵² There are four primary systems for the delivery of defense services to indigent defendants:

1. A public-defender program, in which full-time or part-time salaried staff attorneys handle cases as part of a public or private nonprofit agency;

2. An assigned-counsel system, in which the court appoints a private attorney from a list of available attorneys to handle a particular case;

3. A contract system, in which an individual attorney, a group of attorneys, or a bar association agrees to provide defense services for a fixed amount; and

4. A mixed system, in which both salaried and public defenders and assigned counsel represent a significant number of indigent defendants.

See N. Lefstein, *Criminal Defense Services for the Poor* 7–8 (1982); Bureau of Justice Statistics, U.S. Dep't of Justice, *Special Report, Criminal Defense Systems—A National Survey* 3 (1984).

As of 1988, sixty-eight of Oklahoma's seventy-seven counties used the assigned counsel method. Oklahoma's two largest counties had public defender agencies, and seven counties used a contract system. See Spangenberg Group, *Oklahoma Indigent Defense Systems Study Final Report* 9-10 (1988).

[53] Prior to July 1991, however, defendants who appeared at their initial arraignment without counsel were to be informed of their right to counsel and assigned a lawyer if they were financially unable to employ counsel. Okla. Stat. tit. 22, § 464 (Supp. 1985).

[54] This practice is inconsistent with *McGraw v. State*, 476 P.2d 370 (Okla. Crim. App. 1970), in which the court held that the fact that defendant was free on bond did not preclude a finding that he lacked the financial ability to retain counsel. As the court noted, "[I]t is understandable that an accused with limited resources might use them to pay for a bond to secure his freedom rather than paying a lawyer's fee." Id. at 373. It appears that the problem of denying counsel to persons who make bail may be widespread in Oklahoma. See Spangenberg Group, note 52 supra, at 50-51. It also is not uncommon for judges around the country to view the defendant's ability to post bond as a significant factor in determining indigency. See National Legal Aid & Defender Ass'n, *The Other Face of Justice: A Report of the National Defender Survey* 60-61 (1973). According to Alschuler, Texas trial judges apply the same "unfair and unrealistic" test: Anyone who can make bond is not indigent. See Alschuler, note 26 supra, at 1257 no. 214. But see ABA, note 1 supra, Standard 5-6.1 ("counsel should not be denied because of a person's ability to pay part of the cost of representation, because friends or relatives have resources to retain counsel, or because bond has been or can be posted.").

[55] The judges insist that any lawyer with any criminal experience who practiced in Cleveland County take several criminal appointments each year. Given the minimal compensation available for handling these cases, many lawyers consider these cases a financial burden. The burden becomes very onerous in serious felony or capital cases. See *State v. Lynch*, 796 P.2d 1150 (Okla. 1990) (holding that Oklahoma's statutory scheme for compensating lawyers appointed to represent indigent defendants provides an unreasonable, arbitrary rate of compensation).

[56] Prior to July 1, 1991, the maximum fees by statute that an appointed Oklahoma lawyer could receive were as follows: Title 22, Section 1271 of the Oklahoma Statutes provided that compensation should be "reasonable and just" but should not exceed $500 per case, regardless of the severity of the charges; Title 22, Section 464 of the Oklahoma Statutes provided that fees for services rendered until the defendant is discharged or bound over after a preliminary hearing were not to exceed $100; Title 22, Section 701.4 of the Oklahoma Statutes provided for "reasonable and just" compensation in capital cases with a maximum of $200 for services prior to a preliminary hearing, $500 for the preliminary hearing, and $2,500 for services from the time a defendant is bound over through final disposition in trial court.

For administrative ease, Cleveland County judges for years have simply awarded lawyers the set amount of $250 for a misdemeanor and $500 for a felony, regardless of the actual time spent. The judges assume that most lawyers in most cases put in a sufficient number of hours of work that it is unlikely that any lawyer will reap a significant financial windfall from handling these cases. The judges recognize, however, that in some cases, especially ones that go to trial, lawyers are grossly undercompensated.

In *State v. Lynch*, note 55 supra, at 1164, the Oklahoma Supreme Court recognized the inadequacies of Oklahoma's statutory scheme and set up guidelines for compensating appointed counsel based on the hourly rate of prosecutors and the public defenders in Oklahoma's two largest counties. It held off implementing these guidelines in noncapital cases until August 24, 1992 to give the legislature an opportunity to address the problem.

In response to *Lynch*, the Oklahoma legislature passed the Indigent Defense Act, Okla. Stat. tit. 22, § 1355 (Supp. 1990). Pursuant to this statute, each judicial district is to develop its own system for delivering indigent defense services. This legislation is still being implemented, and its effects on Cleveland County have yet to be felt.

[57] Throughout Oklahoma, courts seldom approve requests for investigators, forensic testing, or experts. See Spangenberg Group, note 52 supra, at 46–48. Lack of access to investigative assistance or expert services is a common weakness of many indigent defense systems, especially assigned counsel or contract systems. See Mounts & Wilson, "Systems for Providing Indigent Defense: An Introduction," 14 *N.Y.U. Rev. L. & Soc. Change* 193, 199 n.33 (1986); Coyle, Strasser & Lavelle, note 26 supra, at 30; Smith, note 48 supra, at 17.

[58] In 1977, the Wisconsin legislature created the Office of the State Public Defender, an independent agency under the direction of the Public Defender Board. Wis. Stat. § 15.78 (1989). The governor, with the advice and consent of the Senate, appoints the nine members of the board, who, in turn, select the state public defender. The state public defender supervises the operation of the program, which is divided into two divisions: appellate and trial. As of September 1990, there were 258 staff attorneys located in 37 offices throughout Wisconsin and approximately 1,400 private lawyers certified to accept appointment cases. See Office of the State Pub. Defender, 1989–91 *Biennial Report* (1991). The Milwaukee trial office had 46 staff lawyers compared with 18 in the Dane County office.

[59] In most jurisdictions, salaries of public defenders lag behind those of their prosecutorial counterparts. In Wisconsin, however, public defenders as state employees generally earned more during the past decade than most assistant district attorneys with comparable experience. This lack of salary parity led the Wisconsin District Attorneys Association to push for legislation that created state funding for the operation of all local district attorney offices and made assistant district attorneys state rather than county employees. See Wis. Stat. Ann. § 978.001–978.14 (West 1991).

[60] Wis. Stat. § 977.07(2) (1989) provides:

If the person's assets, less reasonable and necessary living expenses, are not sufficient to cover the anticipated cost of effective representation when the length and complexity of the anticipated proceedings are taken fully into account, the person shall be determined to be indigent in full or in part. The determination of the ability of the person to contribute to the cost of legal services shall be based upon specific written standards relating to income, assets and the anticipated cost of representation.

The specific written standards are set forth by administrative rule. See Wis. Admin. Code § S.P.D. 3.01 (1990).

In Cleveland County, on the other hand, judges determine the defendant's right to appointed counsel based on their subjective assessment of the defendant's indigency. The judges use the pauper's affidavit set forth in Okla. Ct. Crim. App. R. 1.14 to obtain information, but no guidelines exist as to how that information is to be analyzed. Accordingly, there is considerable variance in indigency determinations. This problem is not unique to Cleveland County. See Spangenberg Group, note 52 supra, at 49–51. For an extended discussion of the need to develop specific eligibility criteria that compares liquid assets with the anticipated cost of counsel, including litigation expenses, and the merits of removing the eligibility determination from judicial control, see National Study Comm'n on Defense Servs. *Guidelines for Legal Defense Systems in the United States* 72–96 (1976).

[61] Section 969.06 of the Wisconsin Statutes, read in conjunction with Section 977.05(b) of the Wisconsin Statutes, provides for representation of an indigent "as soon as

practicable after a person has been detained or arrested.'' In practice, however, the public defender's office represents eligible persons seeking assistance even before any arrest or detention. For a discussion of the importance of early representation, see ABA, note 1 supra, Standard 5-5.1 and commentary (2d ed. 1980); National Study Comm'n on Defense Servs., note 60 supra, at 48–71.

⁶² In his last report to Governor Thompson and the Wisconsin legislature, State Public Defender Nicholas Chiarkas noted that the public-defender trial staff was now handling 62.3 percent of all indigent cases statewide, with the remainder handled by assigned private lawyers. See Office of State Pub. Defender, note 58 supra, at 5–6. Since 1977, staff lawyers in the Milwaukee and Dane County offices generally have defended about 75 percent of the program's clients in each county.

⁶³ As of December 1, 1992, the rate will be $50 per hour for in-court work and $40 for other work. Id. at 15.

⁶⁴ Private lawyers must seek prior approval from the local public-defender office before hiring an expert or investigator. See Wis. Admin. Code § S.P.D. 2.12 (1990).

⁶⁵ For a discussion of the Wisconsin funding needs, see Spangenberg Group, note 26 supra, at 28–49. Clearly, there are other jurisdictions, including Cleveland County, where the funding shortfalls are much worse. See, e.g., Coyle, Strasser & Lavelle, note 26 supra, at 30–44; Special Comm. on Criminal Justice in Free Soc'y, Criminal Justice Section, *Criminal Justice in Crisis* (1988). For a discussion of the serious funding crisis in Oklahoma, see Spangenberg Group, note 52 supra, at 30–46.

As Spangenberg noted in the fall of 1989, ''[T]he problem has grown substantially worse for most indigent defense systems since 1986. With a few exceptions, indigent defense delivery in the country once again has reached a crisis stage.'' Spangenberg, ''We Are Still Not Defending the Poor Properly,'' 4 *Crim. Just.* 11 (1989). Norman Lefstein detailed the extent of the national crisis in his study done at the behest of The American Bar Association. See N. Lefstein, note 52 supra. For other accounts of the continuing crisis in the delivery of indigent defense services in this country, see Spangenberg, note 38 supra, at 13–15, 48; Murphy, ''Indigent Defense and the U.S. War on Drugs,'' 6 *Crim. Just.* 14, 14–20 (1991); Monahan, ''Who Is Trying to Kill the Sixth Amendment,'' 6 *Crim. Just.* 24, 24–28, 51–52 (1991).

⁶⁶ Some unrepresented defendants do obtain better plea bargains by negotiating their own deals. Like Alschuler, this author has observed some sympathetic prosecutors make offers to unrepresented defendants that went well below the norm given the person's record and the charge. See Alschuler, note 26 supra, at 1274–1278. If the unrepresented defendant wants to contest the charge or the prosecutor's initial offer is harsh, however, the defendant has little leverage or ability to obtain the desired result.

⁶⁷ Many commentators have decried the inadequate representation provided by poorly paid courthouse ''regulars'' or ''pleaders,'' who turn over cases as quickly as possible to maximize their profits. See, e. g., Bazelon, ''The Defective Assistance of Counsel,'' 42 *U. Cin. L. Rev.* 1, 8–11 (1973); Alschuler, note 26 supra, at 1182–1186.

⁶⁸ After the arraignment, the next court appearance in Cleveland County is referred to as the call docket. At the call docket, each defendant must announce whether he wants a jury trial, court trial, or date to plead guilty. Call dockets are held roughly six weeks apart. At the call docket on November 19, 1991, it was ''discovered'' that seven misdemeanor defendants had each been incarcerated for almost six weeks because of their inability to post minimal bond. Each was charged with public intoxication in violation of Title 37, Section 8 of the Oklahoma Statutes (1990), which carries a maximum jail sentence of thirty days. The usual disposition for this offense is a small fine, some community service, or a weekend in jail. Upon learning that these defendants were still incarcerated—the jail was checked when the defendants did not appear in

person at the call docket—the cases were set for disposition. Each defendant pleaded guilty for time served.

This problem is, of course, not unique to Cleveland County. For a brief look at the problems with "forgotten" detainees in the Baltimore city jail, see Presser, "Lost and Found," *A.B.A.J.*, Nov. 1991, at 42.

[69] Wis. Stat. Ann. § 969.03 comment L. 1969, ch. 225 (West 1985). Sections 969.02 and 969.03 of the Wisconsin Statutes spell out the procedures for releasing persons charged with misdemeanors and felonies. Although surety bonds by individuals or corporate sureties are still permitted, such bonds are rarely used.

[70] See Wis. Stat. § 968.085 (1989).

[71] Moreover, in Milwaukee County there is a nonprofit social service agency, the Wisconsin Correctional Service, which runs various programs for the Milwaukee court system. These programs further facilitate the pretrial release of a number of defendants, especially those with drug, alcohol, or mental health problems, who would otherwise remain incarcerated. Success on a release program enhances a defendant's chance to obtain a favorable outcome. Dane County has some similar programs, but they are not as structured or as extensive as those of Milwaukee County. Cleveland County does not have any agency involved in a pretrial release program.

[72] The pressure on indigent defendants is compounded by the policy of the Cleveland County sheriff not to permit pretrial detainees any visitors except for a lawyer for their first seven days in jail.

[73] For an article making the same point based on a study of the pretrial detention practices in Houston, Texas, see Wheeler & Wheeler, "Reflections on Legal Representation of the Economically Disadvantaged: Beyond Assembly Line Justice," 26 *Crime & Delinq.* 319 (1982). See also H. Zeisel, *The Limits of Law Enforcement* 47–49 (1982) (discussing the inequities of a bail system that exerts undue pressure on incarcerated defendants to plead guilty).

[74] None of the offices adheres to a policy of no plea bargaining. Presumably, a major policy decision such as this would have a substantial impact on the behavior of defendants and their lawyers. See Spangenberg, note 65 supra, at 12 (policies of limited or no plea bargaining have great impact on indigent defense resources).

[75] Although assistant district attorneys in all three counties complained of heavy case loads and serious time pressures, the prosecutors in Milwaukee County seemingly labored under heavier work loads. As a result, the Milwaukee prosecutors were more responsive when defense counsel demonstrated the weakness of the state's case. Prosecutors in both Dane and Cleveland Counties routinely filed and then more aggressively pursued cases that either would not have been issued or would have been quickly dismissed in Milwaukee County.

[76] Dane County has two deputy district attorneys, while Cleveland County has one. In both counties, the district attorney is also involved in charging decisions in certain cases. Additionally, in Cleveland County, all drug charges are filed by one assistant district attorney and all child molestation cases by another. Occasionally, the deputy district attorney will speak to the complainant, other witnesses, the arresting officers, or the suspect in making a charging decision. Charges usually are issued, however, based on a review of the police reports and the suspect's criminal record.

[77] The law student interns are authorized to practice pursuant to Okla. Sup. Ct. R. 2. Although the intern program is designed to give the students "real-world" experience under the supervision of an experienced lawyer, the students are all supervised by one prosecutor who rarely appears with them in court. The interns generally seek advice from their supervisor, however, before reducing or dismissing a charge.

[78] This charging conference procedure is used in all felony and serious misdemeanor

cases. All other misdemeanor charges are filed based on the prosecutor's review of police reports and rap sheets.

[79] Generally, a lawyer should not even begin plea negotiations without the consent of the client. See ABA, note 1 supra, Standard 4-6.1(b) (2d ed. 1980). In the latest edition of *Standards for Criminal Justice*, Standard 4-6.1(b) has been modified by the deletion of the phrase "although ordinarily the client's consent to engage in such discussions should be obtained in advance." Because the commentary to this standard has yet to be published, the rationale for this change is unclear. Nevertheless, because a lawyer may find it necessary to discuss information revealed by the client while plea bargaining, counsel generally should secure the client's permission before negotiating with the prosecutor. Compare *Model Code of Professional Responsibility* DR 4-101(B), DR 4-101(C) (1981) with *Model Rules of Professional Conduct* Rule 1.6(1983).

[80] Because the defendant ultimately controls the decision whether to plead guilty or to go to trial, defense counsel should present the available options as clearly and as objectively as possible. See *Jones v. Barnes*, note 6 supra, at 745, 751; *Model Rules of Professional Conduct* Rule 1.2 (1983); ABA, note 1 supra, Standard 5.2(a). Even when the defendant is anxious just to plead guilty to get the matter over with, counsel must ensure that the defendant is cognizant of the consequences of a guilty plea. This is particularly so when representing young defendants, who often do not recognize the potential impact of a criminal conviction on their employment opportunities, eligibility for military service, or insurance rates. Like Feeley, this author has frequently seen public defenders or clinical law students attempt to dissuade defendants who are anxious to get their cases over quickly from pleading guilty. See M. Feeley, note 50 supra, at 222. See also ABA, note 1 supra, Standard 4-4.1 (defense counsel's duty to investigate exists regardless of defendant's admission of guilt or stated desire to plead guilty).

[81] Unquestionably, the deplorable conditions in many county jails, including the real risk of physical harm to pretrial detainees, spur some defendants to plead guilty. For a brief look at some of the hardships endured by pretrial detainees, see *Wallace v. Kern* 371 F. Supp. 1384 (E.D.N.Y. 1974), rev'd., 499 F.2d 1345 (2d Cir. 1974).

[82] There is little question to anyone familiar with the criminal justice system that the prosecutor wields extraordinary power, and has enormous discretion. See ABA, note 1 supra, Standard 3-1.1, at 3–7 (2d ed. 1979). For a summary of the scope of the prosecutor's discretion, see W. LaFave & J. Israel, note 2 supra, at 559–594. Moreover, the "give and take" of plea bargaining gives the prosecutor considerable leverage to coerce a guilty plea. See *Bordenkircher v. Hayes*, 434 U.S. 357 (1978) (not improper for prosecutor to carry out threat to prosecute defendant as a habitual offender because of defendant's unwillingness to plead to underlying felony).

[83] Not all public defenders have a reputation for providing aggressive, zealous representation. See Klein, note 41 supra, at 657–663. For a thorough and damning account of the abysmal quality of representation provided to indigents in New York by both assigned counsel and the Legal Aid Society, see McConville & Mirsky, "Criminal Defense of the Poor in New York City," 15 *Rev. of L. & Soc. Change* 581 (1986-1987). See also Sudnow, note 19 supra. Most of the criticism leveled against public defenders, however, springs from underfunded, overloaded programs that provide substandard representation. Adequately funded programs tend to get high marks for the quality of representation delivered to the program's clients. See, e.g., U.S. Dep't of Justice, *An Exemplary Project: The D.C. Public Defender Service* (1975); Arthur Young & Co., note 26 supra.

[84] Arguably, reasonable rates paid by the Wisconsin public-defender program provide a financial incentive for lawyers to spend unnecessary time defending a case, turn down reasonable plea offers, or go to trial on hopeless cases. Admittedly, some lawyers

may overwork a case. While at the Milwaukee public-defender office, the author reviewed a private lawyer's voucher that included twenty-five hours for time spent calling every Brown in the Milwaukee phone book trying unsuccessfully to make initial contact with his newly assigned client. The public-defender program would selectively cut bills such as the one submitted in Brown's case. Although this power is used sparingly, it does discourage abuse. See Wis. Stat. § 977.08(4) (1989) (Public Defender Board reviews decisions of the state public defender regarding payment of private lawyer vouchers). Finally, the client makes the ultimate decision on pleading guilty or going to trial. The client's reluctance to go to trial, fear of an increased sentence, and interest in a quick resolution generally will override the desire of an overzealous assigned lawyer looking to make some extra money by "milking" an appointed case.

[85] See *State v. McKenny*, 582 P.2d 573, 577 (Wash. 1978) (compensation scheme unrelated to work actually performed creates "an economic disincentive against satisfactory representation"); ABA, note 1 supra, Standard 5-2.4, at 5–33 (2d. ed. 1979) (flat payment rates should be discouraged because the inevitable result is lawyers doing only what is minimally necessary to qualify for flat payment). For a chilling study of the inadequate representation provided to many capital defendants in several Southern states using an assigned-counsel method, see Coyle et al., note 26 supra, at 30–44. A number of courts have struck down statutory schemes for compensating assigned counsel with low maximum awards on the ground that as administered, such systems unfairly and arbitrarily compelled some lawyers to shoulder a heavy financial burden that properly should be borne by the state. See, e.g., *State v. Lynch*, note 55 supra, at 1150; *State v. Smith*, 242 Kan. 336, 747 P.2d 816 (1987).

Nevertheless, it is evident that in many jurisdictions, the compensation provided to appointed lawyers in an assigned-counsel system still is woefully inadequate. Unfortunately, too often these assigned lawyers also provide woeful representation. See N. Lefstein, note 52 supra at 17–24; McConville & Mirsky, note 83 supra at 899–901: Smith, note 48 supra, at 17; Herman, Single & Boston, note 26 supra, at 161.

[86] See Mounts & Wilson, note 57 supra, at 194; N. Lefstein, note 52 supra, at 19–20. For personal accounts of private lawyers laboring under financial pressure to induce clients to plead guilty and not go to trial, see ABA & National Legal Aid & Defender Ass'n, note 38 supra, at 10–11, 14–15. As Dean Paul Carrington observed, "while there will be admirable exceptions of lawyers laboring to do what few will ever know or care about, a system that desires zealous advocacy on the whole will have to reward it." Carrington, "The Right to Zealous Counsel," 1979 *Duke L.J.* 1291, 1294. See also Spangenberg Group, note 52 supra, at 37–46 (commending Oklahoma lawyers for continuing to take indigent appointments despite inadequate compensation but noting that experienced lawyers increasingly were opting out of such appointments).

[87] "No attorney, no matter how skilled, trained, and committed, can provide competent representation under working conditions which do not allow such skill, training, and commitment to be practiced." Mounts, note 8 supra, at 221. See also ABA, note 1 supra, Standard 5-4.3, at 5–48 (2d ed. 1979); ABA & National Legal Aid & Defender Ass'n, note 38 supra, at 5.

[88] For a summary of the adverse effects of an excessive case load on a public defender's ability to prepare, investigate, research, and consult with clients, see Klein, note 41 supra, at 662–675.

[89] In his recent report, Spangenberg praised the Wisconsin public defenders for their dedication and quality. Yet, he concluded that an increasing number of the public defenders' clients were suffering because the lawyers were laboring under the strain of an excessive case load and work load. See Spangenberg Group, note 26 supra, at 32–49.

[90] See Mounts, "Public Defender Programs, Professional Responsibility and Competent

Representation,'' 1982 *Wis. L. Rev.* 473, 486. As many commentators have noted, defendants often mistrust their lawyer, especially when counsel is appointed, not retained. See *Jones v. Barnes*, note 6 supra, at 745, 761 (Brennan, J., dissenting); Herman, Single & Boston, note 26 supra, at 153. For a detailed count of the reasons clients mistrust their lawyers, especially public defenders, See J. Casper, note 26 supra; L. McIntyre, note 26 supra, at 62–73.

[91] Like any experienced criminal practitioner, most public defenders can assess realistically the value of a proffered plea bargain because they know the prosecutor's standard offers and the judge's sentencing proclivities. See Alschuler, note 26 supra, 1229–1230.

[92] See Spangenberg Group, note 26 supra, at 34.

[93] "Defense counsel should not seek concessions favorable to one client by any agreement which is detrimental to the legitimate interests of a client in another case." ABA, note 1 supra, Standard 4-6.2(d). Although public defenders probably do not often explicitly "trade off" one client to secure a favorable deal for another, the give-and-take process involved in bargaining numerous cases with a handful of prosecutors invariably works to the advantage of some clients and the disadvantage of others. For a brief look at this troublesome and, perhaps, unresolvable problem, see Alschuler, note 26 supra, at 1210–1224.

[94] Schneyer, note 11 supra, at 24 (emphasis in the original). See also Alschuler, note 26 supra, at 1254–1255; Klein, note 41 supra, at 669–673.

[95] See note 65 supra.

[96] As Mounts and Wilson point out, there are many political factors contributing to this serious underfunding of defense services. Mounts & Wilson, note 57 supra, at 200–201. Because increased spending for defense services is so politically unpopular, the litigation model may well be one of the most effective means of securing additional funding. See Wilson, "Litigative Approaches to Enforcing the Right to Effective Assistance of Counsel in Criminal Cases," 14 *N.Y.U. Rev. L. & Soc. Change* 203 (1986). In Oklahoma, for example, it was not until the Supreme Court of Oklahoma forced the legislature's hand by adopting its own statewide compensation scheme for court-appointed counsel in *State v. Lynch*, note 55 supra, at 1150, that the Oklahoma legislature finally passed a measure creating the Indigent Defense Act. See note 56 supra.

[97] Alschuler argues that the intolerable nature of the plea-bargaining system is such that all defense lawyers are "subject to bureaucratic pressures and conflicts of interest" that can only be avoided by "restructur[ing] our criminal justice system to eliminate the overwhelming importance of the defendant's choice of plea." Alschuler, note 26 supra, at 1313. He calls, therefore, for the abolition of the plea-bargaining system and sufficient resources to pay for the added costs of more trials. Id. at 1180, 1314.

While the author of this article concurs with many of Alschuler's observations, especially his descriptions of the destructive impact of plea bargaining on the attorney-client relationship, the author does not agree that the abolition of plea-bargaining is either feasible or desirable. Given the existing crisis in the criminal justice system at all levels, with only a small percentage of cases going to trial, the resources needed to adequately fund this restructured system would be staggering. Moreover, the working poor and many middle-class defendants would be unable to afford aggressive advocacy under this restructured system. In a system devoid of plea-bargaining, these defendants may face far harsher dispositions. It is more desirable, therefore, to expand and adequately fund defense services and, thus, permit defense lawyers to function as effective adversaries of the state. See also Mounts, note 90 supra, at 488 (suggesting that budgetary problems are the primary stumbling block to a public defender's ability to provide quality representation).

[98] In a mixed system, both staff public defenders and assigned private lawyers represent a "substantial number" of indigent clients. N. Lefstein, note 52 supra. at 8. For an excellent summary of the advantages of a mixed system, see ABA, note 1 supra, Standard 5–1.2 and commentary (2d. ed. 1979). See also National Study Comm'n on Defense Servs. note 60 supra, at 124–136 (recommending mixed defender and assigned-counsel system, with each handling a substantial share of cases) 144–180 (recommending a state defender office to organize, coordinate, and monitor the delivery of defense services throughout each state).

[99] See Spangenberg, note 38 supra, at 15; National Study Comm'n on Defense Servs., note 60 supra, at 134–135. In Wisconsin, the support of the state bar has been instrumental in enabling the Wisconsin public-defender program to avert financial crisis. See Gimbel, "The Public Defenders' Changing Image," Wis. B. Bull., Sept. 1985, at 9, 10.

[100] Echoing earlier observations by Alschuler, Spangenberg noted that a substantial diminution of the role of the private bar in the criminal system raised the specter of a system dominated by institutional lawyers too comfortable and too cooperative to protect their clients' rights. See Spangenberg, note 38 supra, at 14–15; Alschuler, note 26 supra, at 1210–1222. For an extended look at the dangers of an institutional defender program primarily committed to the cost-efficient processing of defendants, see McConville & Mirsky, note 83 supra, at 582–695.

[101] The ethics codes clearly require a defense lawyer to exercise independent judgment on behalf of a client without allowing an employer or administrator to direct or regulate counsel's advocacy. See Model Code of Professional Responsibility DR 5–107(B) (1981); Model Rules of Professional Conduct Rule 5.4(c) (1983). See also Polk County v. Dodson, note 2 supra, at 312, 321–322 (concluding that the state must respect the professional independence of the individual public defender, who, in turn, must make case decisions free from administrative control). There is little question that assistant public defenders and appointed counsel are unlikely to feel free to engage in legitimate but judicially unpopular defense tactics if they are economically dependent on the judiciary. See National Study Comm'n on Defense Servs., note 60 supra, at 218–221; ABA, note 1 supra, Standards 5–1.3, 5–3.1 and commentary (2d. ed. 1979).

Similarly, a county's interest in obtaining defense services at the lowest possible cost cannot be permitted to compromise defense counsel's independence and the quality of representation provided by counsel. See State v. Smith, 140 Ariz. 355, 681 P.2d 1374 (1984).

[102] To guarantee the professional independence of the defender program, most commentators urge the creation of a board that sets general policies for the operation of the program but is removed from the day-to-day operation of the program and precluded from interfering in any cases. See ABA, note 1 supra, Standards 5–1.3, 5–1.6, 5–2.4; National Study Comm'n on Defense Servs., note 60 supra, at 224–231.

[103] "Since a primary objective of the payment system should be to encourage vigorous defense representation, flat payment rates should be discouraged. The inevitable effect of such rates is to discourage lawyers from doing more than what is minimally necessary to qualify for the flat payment." ABA, note 1 supra, Standard 5–2.4, at 5–33 (2d. ed 1979). See also notes 85–86 supra and accompanying text. For an unduly optimistic view of the contract system, see Spears, "Contract Counsel: Different Way to Defend the Poor," 6 Crim. Just. 24–31 (1991) (arguing that quality criteria in the initial bidding process, prior approval by the funding agency of any change in the lawyers in the contracting firm, and a noncause termination clause in the contract ensures quality representation by the contracting firm). Most commentators, however, believe that the contract system provides an economic incentive to turn over cases quickly without regard for quality representation. See, e.g., National Study Comm'n on Defense Servs.,

note 60 supra, at 169-170: Wilson, *Contract Bid Programs: A Threat to Quality Indigent Defense Services* (Mar. 1982,) (unpublished report for National Legal Aid and Defender Association). See also *State v. Smith*, note 101 supra (finding that contract system in Mohave County based on flat payment for one-fourth of county's total case load militated against inadequate representation by overburdened defense counsel).

[104] See notes 61-66 supra and accompanying text.

[105] As a national study has concluded:

> Quality representation is not only related to the compensation of counsel. It also depends upon the availability of supporting services and facilities as these are not only vital to the presentation of the defense's case, they are often required to disprove the prosecution's case. Since the state already has the police to conduct investigations and supply expert testimony, assigned counsel would be forced to operate under a distinct disadvantage without the availability of necessary supporting services and facilities. This is an inequity which no system of justice should tolerate.

National Study Comm'n on Defense Servs., note 60 supra, at 272. See also ABA, note 1 supra, Standard 5-1.4.

Although it is evident that defense counsel can seldom function effectively without adequate support, it is abundantly clear that support services are virtually nonexistent or badly underfunded in most jurisdictions. See N. Lefstein, note 52 supra, app. at F-1-F-68. Even though the Wisconsin public-defender program is better funded than most, it is seriously deficient in investigative and support services. See Spangenberg Group, note 26 supra, at 33, 43-44.

[106] See ABA, note 1 supra, Standard 5-1.5.

[107] "The practice of criminal law has become highly specialized in recent years, and only lawyers experienced in trial practice, with an interest in and knowledge of criminal law and procedure, can properly be expected to serve as assigned counsel." ABA, note 1 supra, Standard 5-2.2, at 5-27 (2d ed. 1979). Many courts and commentators have noted the increased complexity of handling a criminal case. See, e.g., *State v. Smith*, note 85 supra, N. Lefstein, note 52 supra, at 18; National Study Comm'n on Defense Servs., note 60 supra, at 433-439.

[108] My experience as the chief staff attorney of the Milwaukee office confirms that to encourage zeal and productivity, merit raises are essential. See also Carrington, note 86 supra, at 1305-1307 (arguing for bonus system for staff attorneys to inspire zeal together with the right to fire one's appointed lawyer); National Study Comm'n on Defense Servs., note 60 supra, at 454-458.

[109] Developing adequate performance measures poses a serious problem for any public defender administrator or board. There are national case load standards, but they are only a crude starting point for assessing the adequacy of a staff lawyer's performance. Local case load standards must be tailored to reflect local variations such as the prosecutor's charging system, local plea-bargaining practices, and court congestion. For a detailed look at one approach to developing case load standards weighted to reflect various local factors, see Spangenberg Group, note 26 supra, at 16-93.

Setting reasonable case load standards, however, only solves part of the problem. A public defender may meet case load requirements and handle a prescribed number of cases but provide poor representation. An effort must be made to ensure that aggressive, competent lawyering is rewarded and that quality representation is not sacrificed at the altar of case load statistics. Supervision and evaluation by experienced senior lawyers constitutes the best mechanism for ensuring quality representation. See National Study Comm'n on Defense Servs., note 60 supra, at 440-441.

[110] Given the demonstrated inability of local government to fund indigent defense services adequately, the author assumes that this proposed program is state funded and administered as an independent state agency. For the advantages of this approach,

see National Study Comm'n on Defense Servs., note 60 supra, at 242–258.

[111] See Spangenberg Group, note 26 supra, at 1–15. For additional background on the often heated political battles over the budget for the Wisconsin public defender program, see Phelps, "Dust Settles After Legislative Battle," *Wis. B. Bull.*, Sept. 1985, at 20–23; Phelps, "Mounting Stress on Wisconsin's Justice System," *Wis. B. Bull.*, Mar. 1987, at 32.

[112] Program administrators who are lawyers are bound to ensure that the lawyers in their program are not violating the rules of professional conduct. *Model Rules of Professional Conduct* Rule 5.1 (1983). If the supervising lawyers know that their lawyers are handling so many cases that they are neglecting the rights of their clients, these supervisors as well as the staff lawyers are in violation of their ethical responsibilities. For a further discussion of the ethical problems confronting supervisors and staff lawyers grappling with excessive case loads, see Klein, "Legal Malpractice, Professional Discipline, and Representation of the Indigent," 61 *Temp. L.Q.* 1171 (1988); Mounts, note 90 supra, at 473.

[113] See note 109 supra.

[114] Public defenders also must recognize the importance of spending more time talking with their clients about their cases and then devote the necessary time. See, e.g., Wilkerson, "Public Defenders as Their Clients See Them," 1 *Am. J. Crim. L.* 141, 142 (1972) (most widely shared grievance among public-defender clients is lack of contact with or visits from their lawyer). Absent increased and improved communications, public defenders will not be able to overcome the mistrust most clients feel toward their assigned lawyers. See, e.g., J. Casper, note 26 supra. at 36 (lack of time spent with clients is a significant factor contributing to the poor image of public defenders).

[115] Keeping salaries low is not a desirable solution. but it is preferable to making do with inadequate support services or excessive case loads, both of which compromise the quality of defense services. The issue in part turns on whether good lawyers could still be attracted to and retained by the program if salaries were not comparable to those in the prosecutor's office as recommended by the National Study Commission. See National Study Comm'n on Defense Servs., note 60 supra, at 278–284. Given the poor job market, the increased number of clinical students anxious to get into defender programs, and the attractiveness of a public-defender job for lawyers looking for litigation experience, attracting good candidates is unlikely to be a problem. A loan forgiveness program for students going to a public defender's office or doing other public service work would encourage even more quality graduates to apply for public-defender positions.

Although it is possible that a lower salary structure will lead to increased turnover, the job market and enhanced job satisfaction may counter that trend. Moreover, it is clear that many lawyers do public-defender work for reasons other than money. See L. McIntyre, note 26 supra, at 80–84, 89. Finally, it is not clear that higher turnover and loss of experience necessarily results in lower-quality representation. That depends on the extent of the turnover, the quality of the training programs, and the zeal and quality of the new recruits.

[116] For a discussion of the importance of monitoring training and supervision, see National Study Comm'n on Defense Servs., note 60 supra, at 434–447.

[117] Not only does a statewide program best serve the goal of quality representation, it "offers the most efficient and flexible means of allocating available resources." National Study Comm'n on Defense Servs., note 60 supra, at 175.

[118] Even using the Wisconsin indigency test, which is more generous than the standardless determinations made in Cleveland County and many other jurisdictions, see note 59 supra, many people on small fixed incomes do not qualify for public-defender

representation. Realistically, however, a person receiving a monthly Social Security benefit cannot hire counsel. Unfortunately, public-defender administrators facing case load increases on top of existing crushing case loads are not inclined to argue for a loosening of indigency standards. In fact, the Wisconsin public-defender office continues to use outdated figures as to the anticipated cost of retaining counsel by applying their indigency test to hold dawn their case load. See Wis. Admin. Code § S.P.D. 3.02(1). See also *State v. Dean*, 163 Wis. 2d 503, 471 N.W.2d 310 (Wis. Ct. App. 1991) (Wis. Admin. Code § S.P.D. 3.02 use $300 for cost of hiring lawyer in criminal traffic case when evidence suggests real cost is $500 to $1,000). The use of outdated figures works to deny counsel to low-income persons who really cannot afford representation. As a result, some low-income defendants are challenging the public defender's denial of counsel. In *State v. Dean*, the Wisconsin Court of Appeals held that the trial court should have exercised its inherent power to appoint counsel despite the indigency determination of the public defender. Most needy defendants, however, do not challenge the public defender's denial of counsel but simply go without counsel.

[119] Such an approach was recommended by the National Study Commission in its 1976 report on defense services. See National Study Comm'n on Defense Servs., note 60 supra, at 104–122.

[120] Indeed, it already appears that overtaxed indigent defense systems are being asked to handle more indigent cases each year, thus exacerbating existing case load problems. See Spangenberg Group, note 26 supra, at 4. Budgetary pressures are likely to produce a tightening of indigency standards rather than an expansion of coverage to include the working poor. In fact, the drive toward a tightening of eligibility requirements is already under way in many states. See Spangenberg. note 38 supra, at 48. The problem, of course, is that people squeezed out of the indigent defense system usually are left with two bad alternatives: pro se representation or hiring a cheap lawyer.

Some public-defender programs have urged decriminalization as a means to retard case load growth and the spiraling costs both of the public-defender program and the criminal justice system as a whole. See Phelps, "Mounting Stress on Wisconsin's Justice System," *Wis. B. Bull.*, Mar. 1987, at 33–34. As Nicholas Chiarkas noted in his agency's annual report, the public defender's office achieved several major goals with the enactment of the latest Wisconsin biennial budget: Various misdemeanor offenses were decriminalized and the line between misdemeanor and felony property offenses was raised from $500 to $1,000. See Office of State Pub. Defender, note 58 supra, at 7, 9. While these legislative changes are desirable from the standpoint of many defendants, the result will be the greater use of civil forfeiture actions where no right to counsel exists.

20

Privatizing Due Process
Issues in the Comparison of Assigned Counsel, Public Defender, and Contracted Indigent Defense Systems

ALISSA POLLITZ WORDEN

Since 1963, when the U.S. Supreme Court declared that indigent defendants are entitled to counsel in felony prosecutions, the task of providing representation for the poor has taken on increasing significance and complexity. In recognizing the "widespread belief that lawyers in criminal courts are necessities, not luxuries," (*Gideon v. Wainwright*, 372 U.S. 335, 1963), the Court acknowledged the transformation of criminal courts from the relatively simple tribunals of the nineteenth century into today's complicated procedural mazes of strategy and negotiation. More importantly, rejecting the convenient but improbable assumption that as officers of the court in an adversarial system prosecutors and judges adequately protect defendants' interests, the Court attempted to correct the imbalance of power between prosecutors and the accused by ensuring that all defendants be afforded the opportunity for expert advocacy.

This guarantee has been the subject of controversy, however, as the Court has expanded the right to counsel to cover many misdemeanor and some juvenile proceedings, increasing the burden on state and local governments to supply representation to the poor. This responsibility

Reprinted by permission of the *Justice System Journal* from vol. 14, no. 3 and vol. 15, no. 1 (1991), pp. 390–418.

cost taxpayers almost one billion dollars in 1986 (Criminal Defense for the Poor, 1988)—a burden that is highest in communities with greatest need and fewest resources, those with high crime rates and large poverty populations. Careful implementation of the Court's policy, therefore, is important for practical and fiscal reasons. But designing and operating effective programs for providing representation is important from a due process perspective as well. Justice in an adversarial system depends in large measure on the balance of skill and experience between opposing counsel; and court-appointed counsel is the rule rather than the exception in most felony proceedings.[1] The quality of representation afforded indigents, therefore, not only affects defendants' experiences in the criminal justice system, but also cumulatively determines the character of justice itself.

However, although there has been much debate over the best way to provide counsel for the poor, evaluation studies have been inconclusive and sometimes unsystematic. In particular, there have been few studies of contracting with private attorneys for indigent defense, an increasingly popular alternative to assigned counsel and public defender programs. This article attempts to offer a more stable foundation for empirical research by drawing upon theories of privatization to provide a framework for analyzing the potential comparative benefits and drawbacks of contracting.

A second and related purpose of this article is to explore conceptual and methodological issues associated with evaluative research on indigent defense and to derive recommendations for future research from these explorations.[2] Evaluation studies comparing publicly paid counsel with privately retained attorneys have found little evidence that the quality of representation differs significantly across program types. However, these studies seldom examine more than two or three courts and hence are of limited generalizability (particularly insofar as they do not permit comparison of features within program types) and very few studies include contract systems. Furthermore, there is little agreement on how to best measure program effectiveness and efficiency. The steady increase in contracting prompts a reconsideration of ways of evaluating programs offering counsel for the poor.

The Right to Counsel and the Contracting Innovation

Although the right to counsel for indigents was not constitutionally guaranteed in state felony courts until 1963, in some jurisdictions a tradition of representation for the poor had already existed for decades. The two dominant forms of providing counsel from these traditions developed (McConville and Mirsky, 1989; McIntyre, 1987).[3] The most common means of providing representation for the poor is the assigned counsel system, used in 52 percent of all counties. Assigned counsel systems distribute the burden of indigent representation among members of the private bar through case-by-case assignment by judges or magistrates. For decades this service was formally or informally provided *pro bono* in many jurisdictions, but today virtually all assigned counsel jurisdictions reimburse attorneys for indigent representation with either state or county funds. The public defender system, which had its origins in rapidly growing urban areas at the turn of the century, is now in use in 37 percent of all counties, including many of the most heavily populated urban areas (Criminal Defense for the Poor, 1988). Public defender systems are comprised of centrally staffed and administered offices, whose salaried attorneys represent all or most defendants deemed indigent.

Recently a small but growing number of jurisdictions began to contract with private practitioners or firms to provide this service. The administration of contract systems varies considerably, but in its simplest and perhaps most common form, contracting involves bidding by private attorneys and law firms for representation of all criminal defendants found indigent during the term of the contract, in return for a fixed payment. The use of contracting for indigent defense, as for other state and local services, has grown considerably over the past decade, and there is reason to believe it will become a more rather than less popular option for implementing the Supreme Court's mandate.[4]

While the best means of providing counsel for the poor has been a matter of debate within the bar and among academics for many years, contracting has become the object of political and professional controversy. The American Bar Association and the National Legal Aid and Defender Association have both debated the merits of this increasingly popular alternative to traditional programs (Lefstein, 1982; Moran, 1982), and several national studies of indigent defense have recently been completed (Criminal Defense for the Poor, 1988; Spangenberg et al., 1986a; Spangenberg et al., 1986b). Concerns about the quality and accountability of contract programs have been added to a longstanding agenda of issues including the competing merits of state and county administration and funding, the relative effectiveness of public defender and assigned counsel programs, and the feasibility of continued local bar involvement in criminal defense during an era of increasing professional specialization. The growing popularity of contracting as an alternative to traditional programs has rekindled professional and academic interest in understanding and evaluating alternative means of representing the poor.

The Premises of Privatization

The concept of privatization encompasses a variety of arrangements by which government responsibility for a function is shifted in whole or in part to the private sector. In the United States, privatization typically involves a change in the production rather than in the provision of a service or product: while government continues to *provide* a service or product by arranging for its production—by ensuring that specified members of society in fact receive the service or product—responsibility for *production* is turned over to the private sector (Kolderie, 1986; Morgan and England, 1988)[5] The most common form of privatization in this country is contracting, whereby government retains responsibility for defining the service to be offered and the population to be served, as well as for selecting producers of that service, and arranges through written contract with private individuals or firms for the actual production of the service.

Privatization in general, and contracting in particular, have become increasingly popular means of performing public functions at the state and local level in the wake of diminishing federal support for subnational government, increasing agitation for taxpayer relief, and a consequent drive to cut unnecessary programs and reduce the costs of mandated functions (Donahue, 1989; Poole and Fixler, 1987).[6] In some cases privatization has been adopted as a corrective to perceived public management problems. In corrections, for example, privatization has been endorsed as a solution to a host of administrative problems, including overcrowding, failure of rehabilitation programs, and the rising costs of liability for inmate and employee safety (Robbins, 1986). Moreover, privatization, especially contracting, is seen as a means of imposing some predictability and stability on program costs, an especially important concern in local governments that are unprepared to absorb unexpected budget overruns (Houlden and Balkin, 1985b). More generally, the use of private entrepreneurs has been seen as a promising alternative to the pathologies of bureaucracies—organizational and procedural rigidity, excessive regulation, self-protective civil service systems, and the absence of internal and external incentives to operate innovatively and efficiently (Savas, 1987).

Proponents argue that contracting produces three important and related improvements in service production.[7] First, contracted service production is thought to be more efficient than public production because competition for contracts motivates all would-be producers to bid at a price that represents minimum production costs and profit; in contrast, public agencies have few incentives to conserve resources. Second, privatization is thought to induce more flexibility in production compared with rule-bound public agencies, contractors are better situated to take advantage of economies of scale and production innovations, staying competitive by simultaneously improving service quality and minimizing costs. Third, under some conditions private producers are exempt from regulations that govern public agencies, and therefore may expeditiously secure resources and bypass costly reporting and accounting procedures (Salamon, 1989).

Of course, since the assigned counsel and public defender alternatives do not neatly correspond to classic bureaucratic organization, the virtues of flexibility, minimal regulation, and efficiency may not exclusively characterize contractual service provision of indigent defense. Assigned counsel systems are typically quite decentralized, and may be flexible, innovative, and efficient.[8] Public defender offices more closely approximate bureaucracies in that they are vulnerable to rigidity and routinization (Sudnow, 1965). However, public defender offices differ from classic bureaucracies insofar as they are only loosely hierarchical and are staffed by attorneys who, unlike many other public servants, are socialized to see themselves as autonomous professionals. Furthermore, despite negative images and reports of client distrust (e.g., Casper, 1972), some public defender offices are characterized by strong advocacy cultures (McIntyre, 1987; Bohne, 1978; Eisenstein and Jacob, 1977: Ch. 6).

The extent to which improvements over traditional public service provision are actually realized in the privatization of any particular function is a matter for empirical analysis, not mere speculation, and many agree that there has been far too little empirical research supporting these claims. Even the most committed advocates of privatization concede that it is not an appropriate alternative to public production for all services (Savas, 1987), although there exists some disagreement about the conditions that favor privatization. Chamberlin and Jackson suggest that privatization is appropriate

> . . . when purchases are frequent, information is abundant, the costs
> of a bad decision are small, externalities are minimal, and
> competition is the norm. . . . At the other extreme . . . where
> externalities and collective interests abound, natural monopolies are
> dominant, distributional goals are important, or debate and
> experience will alter preferences, then governmental determinations
> of service levels and public provision should continue. (1987: 604)

In other words, when there exists (1) ongoing competition among producers, (2) the opportunity for informed and repeated choices among producers, and (3) consensus on the specific characteristics and benefits of the service, contracting is an acceptable and often desirable substitute for public production. To what extent do these conditions hold for the market of indigent defense services?[9]

Characteristics of the Market: Competition

The bars of many jurisdictions include enough attorneys to generate competition for indigent defense contracts, but in some small communities there may be only a few attorneys specializing in criminal defense, and of these only a handful willing to combine their civil practices with a substantial number of criminal cases. Because criminal law is not a lucrative subspecialty and defense work is more psychologically and emotionally taxing than many other fields, meaningful competition for indigent defense contracts may exist only in jurisdictions whose bars are sufficiently diverse and specialized to generate competition among general practitioners and criminal defense specialists (see Meeker et al., 1989). Paradoxically, contracting appears to be most appealing in jurisdictions with few lawyers willing or able to handle poverty cases and too few cases to justify a public defender office. Not surprisingly, contracting has been adopted most widely in western states with small and scattered populations (Criminal Defense for the Poor, 1988), perhaps in part because the political culture of western states is more receptive to entrusting public functions to the private market (Donahue, 1989; Poole and Fixler, 1987).

Characteristics of Selection Process

The appropriateness of the contract alternative for indigent defense also hinges on characteristics of the producer selection process: specifically, the degree of rationality with which a choice can be made and, if the selecting agent is not also the consumer or beneficiary of the product, the closeness of communication between decision makers and actual consumers regarding product quality. Of course, the ideal conditions for rational selection involve full information about the likely quality and costs of services offered by each bidder; consequently, in the absence of reliable predictions about quality, the process of decision making is presumably improved by the opportunity to review (or repeat) the decision process frequently.[10]

The policy environment for indigent defense departs from these conditions in several ways, largely because attorney performance is difficult to evaluate and because there is little communication between implementors and consumers regarding service quality. In the first place, except at the point of contract renewal, policy implementors (typically county commissioners and judges) can make only prospective judgments about the quality of bidders' work. While the quality of an attorney's performance in private practice can be evaluated indirectly and informally by reputation and observation, these evaluations are usually based on work performed by the attorney under a set of economic incentives quite different from those prevailing under a contract arrangement.[11]

Even if implementors were capable of overseeing and evaluating contract attorneys, they would find little consensus among professionals regarding the differences between exemplary, acceptable, and marginally adequate representation. While in some policy areas the work of would-be contractors can be readily evaluated by informed experts following established professional standards (the work of civil engineers, for example), even the Supreme Court agrees that evaluating the quality of counsel is difficult, and it has generally avoided the issue in claims of defective assistance of counsel (see *United States vs. Cronic*, 104 Supreme Court 2039 (1984) and *Strickland vs. Washington*, 104 Supreme Court 2052 (1984)). Moreover, implementors' ideas about desirable characteristics may conflict. Contracts for indigent defense are made by elected commissioners, often with the advice of local trial judges and sometimes even prosecutors. Commissioners may be primarily concerned with minimizing expenditures, judges may prefer attorneys who will heed the court's crowded calendars, and prosecutors may lobby for contractors with whom they can build comfortable working relationships. Moreover, the constituents represented by these actors, although probably generally indifferent or ignorant, may agree that they do not want to pay for zealous defense of accused criminals.

Those for whom the quality of counsel is most important, of course, have no voice in the selection process. While in some policy areas beneficiaries of contracted services are able to express their satisfaction or dismay with services, such as garbage collection or the provision of school lunches, the consumers of indigent defense have little voice in selecting or assessing the representation they receive in criminal court. Policy officials' fiscal concerns are effectively balanced by consumer reactions when consumers are also taxpayers and voters; a county commission that tries to save money by contracting with inexperienced or incompetent garbage collectors, for example, will soon learn of its mistake. But implementors feel little political pressure to award bids for representing accused criminals to the attorney or firm offering the highest quality service at a reasonable price, and accused criminals, especially poor ones, do not constitute an important segment of most office-holders' constituencies.[12]

Finally, while frequent evaluation and review of contractors' performance may be desirable in theory, one of the often cited drawbacks of contracting is that it introduces the possibility of service interruption and discontinuity as contracts are renegotiated or awarded to new producers (Morgan and England, 1988). From the point of view of funding authorities, contracts for indigent defense can be made no more frequently than once a year; indeed, given the backlogs in many criminal courts and the complex and prolonged nature of criminal defense work, there are sound ethical and professional reasons for preferring multi-year contracts to single-year agreements. However, long-term agreements may compromise the efficiency and cost effectiveness of contracting by reducing lawyers' incentives to process cases quickly.

Characteristics of the Product: The Defense Attorney's Role

Contracting may be desirable when there is little ambiguity about the nature of the service to be contracted, but professionals do not always concur on the proper role of the criminal defense attorney. Some see the defense lawyer as little more than a check against prosecutorial exploitation in the plea bargaining process (see McConville and Mirsky, 1989);[13] others point out that defense counsel's failure to assume more vigorous roles is a flaw in what should be a more adversarial system (Alschuler, 1975). At a minimum, defense lawyers are professionally obligated to safeguard basic due process rights; therefore, counsel may be expected to not only render advice but also consider all reasonable legal defenses for their clients.

Others argue further that lawyers defending the poor should not only effectively represent individual clients, but should also pursue thorough litigation policy reforms that would benefit the poor as a class, sometimes noting that other public officials in the courts, including prosecutors and attorneys general, are expected to initiate or pursue policy change through litigation (Carlin et al., 1966; Sykes, 1969; Bohne, 1978).[14] Some advocate the establishment of public defender offices for this purpose, reasoning that an institutionalized "repeat player" free of competing obligations is better able to protect the specific and general interests of indigents accused of crime (see Houlden and Balkin, 1985b; National Advisory Commission on Criminal Justice Standards and Goals, 1973). Clearly these alternative roles demand different amounts of time, skill, effort, and perhaps idealism in the provision of legal representation. Therefore, evaluating the quality, or effectiveness, of contract programs is complicated by the lack of agreement on exactly what kinds of services participating lawyers should provide.

Contracting may be less than ideal for functions that incorporate social objectives other than specific products or services, since such objectives (which may have few vocal constituents) may be sacrificed to visible and politically popular goals such as minimizing public expenditures (Chamberlin and Jackson, 1987). Morgan and England point out that the cost savings that may be possible through contracting must be balanced against other, less tangible values: "Efficiency remains a laudable goal,

but not to the exclusion of other equally fundamental principles—
constitutional protections, equity, citizenship, and community"
(1988:986). Some argue that contracting of functions such as corrections
represents a threat to civil rights because unlike government agents,
contractors performing government functions are not clearly bound to
constitutional restrictions on state actions toward individuals (Sullivan,
1987). Of course, because canons of ethics guide the actions of attorneys
regardless of the financial terms of their relationship, there is no *prima
facie* reason to presume that contract systems for indigent defense are
any more or less protective of constitutional rights than any other
arrangement, including representation of fee-paying clients.[15] Moreover,
contracting, in theory at least, should present no threat to the equity
of program administration provided that clear definitions of eligibility
are established and overseen by government.

A more subtle trade off is suggested by what Morgan and England call
the "second face" of privatization: the diminished conception of
community responsibility for public functions that accompanies
delegation of public functions to private organizations (1988). While
Morgan and England focus on supplementing more than on substituting
public producers with private ones (as exemplified in the trend toward
employment of private security companies to accomplish ends that are
in fact the formal responsibility of public law enforcement), their general
argument regarding the value of maintaining some functions as public
or collective responsibilities may apply to indigent defense. The relevant
public, in this case, is the bar rather than the general citizenry. Contract
systems relieve private attorneys of what would otherwise be their
periodic ethical obligation to represent the poor. As a profession, the
bar seeks responsibility for its own regulation and quality control; but
the concentration of indigent defense work in the offices of only one
or a handful of attorneys reduces the bar's involvement in, and hence
commitment to, monitoring this work. That this concern is real rather
than merely rhetorical is evidenced by the task forces and commissions
created at national and state levels to study the contracting option and
to develop guidelines and regulations governing its use.[16]

In sum, the premises of privatization are not altogether consistent with
the function of criminal representation of the poor, although it must be
remembered that some of the potential problems with contracting might
be identified just as readily with assigned counsel or public defender
programs. The following section addresses some of the specific pitfalls
of privatization as they apply to indigent defense contracts, with a view
toward developing a research agenda that would not only examine the
claims of contracting advocates, but would also specify the conditions
under which contracting is most compatible with the needs of the poor
and the ethics of the legal profession. In particular, the following section

discusses, first, the need to carefully evaluate claims that contracting is inherently more efficient than other forms of service production, and second, the difficulties of maintaining the accountability of contract attorneys.

The Promises and Pitfalls of Privatization

The Efficiency Assumption. There have been few studies that model the decision to privatize at the local level, but those that exist unsurprisingly reveal that policy makers are most likely to privatize under conditions of fiscal strain (see Ferris, 1987; Worden and Worden, 1989).[17] This suggests that privatization may result from public officials' concern with program efficiency (Morgan and England, 1988; Dunleavy, 1986; Wilson, 1988). Contracting potentially offers a superior means of reducing and capping the costs of indigent defense. The costs of traditional assigned counsel systems can be only imperfectly predicted, since caseloads fluctuate, lawyers vary in the time they are willing to spend on indigent defendants, and in small jurisdictions one or two major felony cases can dramatically increase annual program costs. Public defender systems operate like any other government agency: they typically submit budget requests for annual allocations based on estimates of their workload over the upcoming year. However, because contract systems often provide for lump sum payments in return for representation of all or a specified proportion of indigent defendants, in theory they permit officials to precisely predict program costs even without knowing what the year's caseload will bring.

But there is reason to question whether contracting lives up to its promise of efficiency. The efficiency of contracting may be compromised by price-fixing and collusion among apparent competitors, as well as by the inadvertent creation of private monopolies as losing bidders drift out of the market of potential suppliers leaving providers dependent upon the original contractor (Morgan and England, 1988; McEntee, 1985; Kolderie, 1986). There is little danger of this occurring when the market of suppliers includes a large number of approximately equivalent bidders who will continue to conduct private business if they fail to receive government contracts. When the government is the major or sole purchaser of the service in question, however, the successful bidder may have little or no competition when the contract comes up for renewal.

In some jurisdictions these problematic conditions may obtain for criminal defense work. In most courts at least half, and sometimes virtually all, felony defendants are found eligible for court-appointed counsel.[18] As more lawyers choose to specialize rather than maintain general practices, fewer attorneys will be interested in (or capable of) sustaining criminal practices to serve the small number of non-indigent criminal defendants who seek counsel. Informal agreements among bidders is also more likely when few wish to compete for the contract; and just as fees for privately retained counsel are established by local norms, expectations about the going rate for advising the indigent may be established over several bidding cycles. Therefore, although competitive bidding may in fact reduce service production costs, the conditions that permit competition do not exist (or cannot be sustained) in all jurisdictions.

Discerning whether or not contracting represents an *improvement* in program efficiency is also complicated by the difficulty of accurately estimating comparability and program costs. Across jurisdictions or within jurisdictions where only a portion of indigent defense work is contracted, the comparability between cases represented by the contractor and cases represented by assigned counsel or public defenders must be assessed, lest the work for which costs are compared in fact represent systematically different degrees of difficulty or seriousness.[19] Moreover, reported expenditures for different program types may underestimate the true costs of functions turned over to the private sector (Kolderie, 1986; McEntee, 1985). The costs of administrative oversight, record-keeping, client screening, and program monitoring are seldom included in estimates of assigned counsel or contract program costs because in many jurisdictions these functions are performed by regular court staff or are not performed at all (Houlden and Balkin, 1985b), although they are included in the program budgets of public defender programs.

Maintaining Accountability and Program Monitoring

Contracting also raises potential problems of accountability (Moe, 1987). As James Gentry points out,

> A particular sort of market failure occurs when the purchaser of a good is unable to observe its consumption. In such a case, the purchaser cannot accurately gauge the quantity and quality of the good delivered. The supplier may therefore provide to the consumer less than was purchased and retain the residual without fearing sanctions from the unwitting buyer. (1986:356)

In the case of indigent defense, consumption of the good delivered is not only difficult to observe—it is largely concealed by the lawyer-client privilege. Moreover, the lines of accountability between policy implementors and service producers is quite attenuated. After all, county (and state) officials are the involuntary implementors of an indigent defense policy promulgated by the Supreme Court, and as such their motivation to ensure effective implementation of indigent defense may be shaped by concerns other than a commitment to the policy itself (Johnson and Canon, 1984).

As is the case with many policies designed to benefit the poor, few community leaders advocate greater expenditures for better representation of indigent criminal defendants. Indeed, one might reasonably hypothesize that even those community organizations that monitor the effectiveness and equity of programs designed to benefit the poor invest few resources in lobbying for better provision of legal assistance to accused criminals. Therefore, efficiency (defined as minimum cost per case) may be pursued at the expense of quality or comprehensiveness of service.

The problem of maintaining accountability (ensuring the delivery of an acceptable level of service) is further complicated by the difficulty of monitoring attorney performance. The danger in contracting indigent defense, of course, is that having secured the contract, attorneys may invest minimal effort in indigent clients in order to maximize time invested in fee-paying clients. A possible solution to this problem is careful structuring of provider incentives in the contract-writing stage (Sullivan, 1987; Donahue, 1989). Separate budget lines could be established for attorney fees and associated investigative expenses, to encourage more assiduous investment in pretrial preparation. Attorneys could be required to demonstrate a commitment to (and experience in) criminal defense work prior to seeking the contract, and secondary defense systems could be established to accommodate cases with multiple defendants. Maximum caseloads could be established to allow bidders to more accurately estimate their expected costs. Agreements could be struck only with attorneys who establish non-profit organizations. However, many and probably most contracts for indigent defense contain no such provisions. Contracts typically do not reimburse attorneys in proportion to their actual investment in cases, but instead specify a lump sum for a certain number of cases, a term during which the attorney is responsible for all defendants found indigent, or a fixed amount per case.

Of course, carefully structured contracts may raise the costs of representation above that generated by a simple lump-sum low-bid process, and they potentially pose some of the same difficulties generated by assigned counsel systems (for instance, caps on caseloads require counties to provide for the possibility that these caps will be exceeded, and that additional resources will be needed to accommodate the overflow). However, these conditions do permit an indirect form of accountability, by structuring the bidding decisions of participating attorneys and, further, by minimizing the disincentives to provide careful and effective representation.

Toward a Systematic Evaluation of Alternatives

Despite its significance for defendants and for the bar (or perhaps because of it) debate over alternative means of representing the poor has sometimes been shaped by ideology and self interest. Advocates of privatization as well as policy implementors often merely assume the relative efficiency of contracting, questioning neither the actual prospects for cost savings nor the fate of equally important goals, such as program effectiveness and equity, under a contract arrangement. On the other hand, members of the bar may view contracting, as they have sometimes viewed public defenders, as a threat to private practice, particularly in urban areas where some attorneys build substantial practices on court assignments (McConville and Mirsky, 1989; Blumberg, 1967).

While indigent defense is not a policy problem for which contracting is indisputably a superior alternative, that is not to say that a carefully structured contract program would not provide equal or better representation (at reasonable cost) in many communities now served by other program forms. There is, at any rate, little doubt that a growing number of jurisdictions will experiment with this alternative, rendering further research on the actual operation of these programs imperative. Despite the large number of studies conducted over the past three decades, we still cannot conclude with certainty that either the public defender or the assigned counsel programs are superior; so few studies have examined contract programs that their claimed benefits and drawbacks must be considered speculative rather than known. The final section of this article considers some of the conceptual and methodological issues confronting researchers working in this area and offers some specific suggestions for future analyses.

Measurement Issues: Efficiency, Effectiveness, and Equity

Some of the issues associated with measuring program efficiency or cost effectiveness have already been discussed. For example, researchers should be careful to include all relevant costs for any program, and should ensure that programs under comparison are in fact responsible for similar types of work. Moreover, because efficiency is typically measured as cost per case (e.g., Grier, 1971; Spangenberg, 1986b), care should be taken to ensure that the number of cases processed accurately reflects the number of defendants eligible for representation in each jurisdiction studied. Anecdotal evidence suggests that eligibility for free counsel is sometimes determined by the amount of money left in program budgets rather than by actual need for the service; while on the other hand, assigned counsel programs that appear extremely efficient may in fact be programs that exhaust their budgets before the end of the fiscal year and rely thereafter on the *pro bono* representation of private counsel.

Extant studies illustrate the importance of careful attention to differences within as well as across program types. Public defender programs appear to be less expensive per case than assigned counsel systems (Grier, 1971; Cohen et al., 1983; Singer and Lynch, 1983). While some of the few studies that compare contract with assigned counsel or public defender programs find no differences in costs per case (Worden and Worden, 1989; Lefstein, 1982), other studies have found that the efficiency of contract systems depends on program characteristics. Houlden and Balkin found, for example, that contract attorneys operated more efficiently than did assigned counsel on a per-case basis, but that was because the former spend much less time with indigent clients. The two programs' costs per attorney hour were almost identical (1985b). (Of course, an alternative conception of efficiency could explain this finding: perhaps contract attorneys' expertise and experience in criminal law, and their familiarity with other criminal court actors, permits them to handle cases more expeditiously than assigned counsel, who may seldom practice criminal law outside of court appointments.) A study of programs operating in Michigan counties found that while overall contract programs' costs per case were little different from those of other program types, whether or not contracts were competitively bid made a very important difference in costs. Competitively bid contracts were much less expensive and non-bid programs much more expensive than either assigned counsel or public defender programs (Worden, 1990).

Evaluating program effectiveness or quality has proven even more problematic than assessing program costs. Evaluation requires not only the establishment of a baseline for comparison but also determination of appropriate measures of attorney performance. The comparative studies of indigent defense programs that have appeared in academic journals over the past twenty years represent a range of judgments about the proper baseline for evaluation of program quality. Many studies draw direct comparisons between attorneys handling indigent cases (whether as private counsel assigned by the court, or as public defenders) and privately retained counsel (e.g., Gitelman, 1971; Stover and Eckart, 1975; Wheeler and Wheeler, 1980), while others simply compare alternative means of representing indigents (e.g., Clarke and Kurtz, 1983; Grier, 1971; Benjamin and Pedeleski, 1969). Still others, perhaps by virtue of access to more diverse jurisdictions, attempt comparisons of more than one indigent defense program with privately retained counsel (Flemming, 1986; Houlden and Balkin, 1985a; 1985b; Hermann, et al., 1977; Levine, 1975; Casper 1972; Taylor et al., 1972). While some suggest that it is not altogether reasonable to compare indigent defense programs with the representation provided by the private bar (Houlden and Balkin, 1985b), in fact most such comparisons reveal only slight differences in performance measures. As a baseline for evaluation, the performance of privately retained attorneys may provide an ethically sound starting point; after all, it is difficult to make a normative or ethical argument that accepts or condones representation of a significantly different caliber for fee-paying and indigent defendants. So perhaps research should be directed toward discerning the nature and extent of differences between the representation provided to the poor and that provided to fee-paying clients.

An alternative, of course, is to formulate standards independent of empirically established reference points. Cavender, for example, focused his comparison of private attorneys and public defenders on the American Bar Association's standards regarding effective representation at sentencing (1987). These standards state specific responsibilities for defense attorneys, including the explanation of sentencing alternatives, discussion of rehabilitative sentencing, and review of pre-sentence investigations and recommendations (American Bar Association, 1971). As guidelines for effective representation are further developed at both the national and state levels (and particularly as guidelines for contract systems are articulated), these standards might be used as practical operationalizations of effective counsel.

Regardless of the nature of their comparisons, most researchers have focused on one or more of three overlapping conceptualizations of effectiveness of counsel: process measures, outcome measures, or attorney-client relationship measures. Process measures assess the number of formal opportunities taken by an attorney to defend his or her client's case, as well as the investment of effort made in developing the case. They include, for example, the frequency of appearances, number of motions filed, and number of days taken to dispose of cases (Luskin and Luskin, 1987; Flemming, 1986; Houlden and Balkin, 1985a; 1985b), as well as the time spent on investigation and research (Lefstein, 1982; Levine, 1975). In the few studies that have employed these measures only small differences have emerged among program and attorney types, (Luskin and Luskin, 1987; Houlden and Balkin, 1985a; 1985b; Levine, 1975), although there is suggestive evidence that contract attorneys invest less effort in formal pre-trial proceedings (Flemming, 1986) and in investigation (Lefstein, 1982).

These measures must be used with caution. While some are no doubt valid indicators of effective representation (e.g., effort invested in investigation and research) others may not be. For example, despite constitutional guarantees of speedy trial, lengthy delays between arrest and final disposition may be in a defendant's best interests if such delays in fact represent strategic efforts to weaken a prosecutor's case;[20] while in some courts, under some circumstances, insisting on preliminary hearings may be a misguided violation of local norms.

Outcome measures assess performance in terms of dispositions and sentences, and include mode of disposition (guilty plea or trial), frequency of dismissals, and frequency of acquittals, as well as measures of sentence severity. While some early studies found that attorney type was related to differences in dispositions and sentences (Benjamin and Pedeleski, 1969; Summer, 1969; Gitelman, 1981; Cohen et al., 1983), most studies that control for defendant and case characteristics have uncovered few differences between privately retained attorneys and public defenders (Sterling, 1983; Nardulli, 1986; Stover and Eckart, 1975; Wheeler and Wheeler, 1980; Flemming, 1986; Taylor, et al., 1972). Some studies suggest, however, that public defenders secure more dismissals than assigned counsel, but that their clients suffer more severe sentences (Clarke and Kurtz, 1983; Cohen et al., 1983). There are too few studies of contract systems to permit generalization about their relative effectiveness (see Houlden and Balkin, 1985b).[21]

Dispositional characteristics appeal to researchers because they are readily available in public records. However, some of these variables, such as acquittal rate, vary little across jurisdictions. Furthermore, outcomes reflect numerous contextual influences which must be controlled to isolate the effects, if any, of type of counsel. For example, variation in guilty plea rates across clients in different programs may tell us more about prosecutors' policies than about defense lawyers' skills (Flemming, 1990). Sentence severity may reflect attorney effectiveness only under some conditions where, for example, sentence negotiation is not constrained by sentencing guidelines or probation officers' recommendations. Thus these measures should be employed with caution and only in studies of sufficient scope to ensure that contextual variables are controlled.

More generally, these measures tend to presume that the quality of counsel rests largely in the ability to get clients off—through acquittal or lenient sentencing—but a broader view of advocacy embraces activities designed to preserve or establish a place for clients in their communities. Additional potentially useful measures would include the frequency with which attorneys secure constructive and rehabilitative outcomes such as diversion and first offender treatment, or, in less serious cases, the frequency with which attorneys propose restitution as a means of restoring defendant-victim relationships.

Attorney-client relationship variables include some of the measures used by Cavender (1987), such as attorneys' explanation of sentencing alternatives and time spent with clients (Levine, 1975; Stover and Eckart, 1975), as well as client perceptions of attorney competence (Casper, 1972; Hermann et al., 1977). Although they have been few in number, studies of defendant attitudes suggest that clients of publicly paid attorneys, particularly of public defenders, are less trustful, cooperative, and deferential than are clients of privately retained lawyers (Casper, 1972; Hermann et al., 1977; and see Flemming, 1986; but see also Atkins and Boyle, 1976). Given that indigent defendants are of course represented by publicly rather than privately *paid* counsel, the important research and policy questions are first, whether or not this distrust compromises effective representation, and second, whether some indigent defense programs engender better client-attorney relationships than others. For example, Casper's finding that indigent defendants were less trusting of public defenders than of counsel employed in a private non-profit (albeit publicly funded) office suggests that the more attenuated the apparent relationship between court authorities and counsel, the more confidence clients feel in their lawyers' independence (19___). If this observation is generalizable, with all other things being equal, contract programs may engender more satisfied clients than traditional public defender offices.

Future research should be directed toward two goals in developing measures of effectiveness of counsel. First, research should explore the relationships among the measures already in use in order to determine whether there exist patterns or clusters of behaviors that define the boundaries between effective and ineffective counsel. Extant studies typically compare alternative program types across several of the variables mentioned above, but fail to examine the possibility that correlations among these measures might permit the building of scales and indices that constitute more sensitive gauges of effectiveness.[22]

Second, for the purpose of comparing program types (and in particular, for the purpose of comparing variations on the contract system), institutional or programmatic characteristics should be employed as indirect indicators of effectiveness. Some such characteristics are informal; for example, it has long been conventional wisdom that some of the strengths of public defender programs are the informal socialization and training that new attorneys receive in such offices, and the pooled experience and resources that can be brought to each new case (McIntyre, 1987; Hermann et al., 1975). Institutional subcultures of this sort may develop in contracting attorneys' offices as well (see Eisenstein et al., 1987). On the other hand, much has been written about the institutional defects of centralized programs that process defendants in an assembly-line fashion (Gilboy and Schmidt, 1979; Gilboy, 1981), and the dangers of organizational cooptation by powerful judges and prosecutors (Sudnow, 1965; but see Battle, 1973). Other indicators of institutional effectiveness are formal and may even appear in contracts themselves. For example, contracts (as well as assigned counsel and public defender systems) that set aside part of program budgets for investigatory expenses, training, or secondary systems (to handle conflict cases or overloads) increase incentives to conduct thorough defenses, but programs lacking such features create incentives to provide minimal defense. Examination of these institutional characteristics might better illuminate dimensions of effectiveness that are overlooked in individual level studies of attorney performance.

These issues speak indirectly to a final normative concern, program equity. Indigent defense programs are equitable to the extent that they offer services of similar quality to defendants who are similarly situated financially. Very little research has been conducted on variation in eligibility guidelines across jurisdictions (for one example, see Spangenberg et al., 1986b). Some of this work relies on statutory definitions that may have little operational meaning. Research is needed on formal and informal means of determining eligibility, and on their comparability across jurisdictions within states. Furthermore, equitable programs must provide representation of equivalent quality to co-defendants, an increasingly common problem as narcotics offenses assume a larger share of the criminal justice system's caseload. Viewed from another angle, indigent defense systems are equitable to the extent that they provide approximately equal compensation to attorneys charged with representing the poor. Because representing the poor is an ethical obligation that often takes time away from attorneys' private practices, fairness requires that this burden be distributed evenly among members of the legal profession.

Research Design Issues

Studies of indigent defense systems have been handicapped by a variety of data collection and methodological problems that may account in part for the difficulty of drawing conclusions from these studies. The problem of comparability across jurisdictions, especially when those jurisdictions are in different states, plagues all criminal court research. Indigent defense programs that are not state organized and administered may be organized by county or circuit, or may include multiple circuits, and counties may opt to use different program forms for misdemeanor and felony courts.

Moreover, information about locally administered indigent defense programs is seldom available in central locations such as state archives or even state bar associations. The result of this fragmentation of information is that multi-jurisdictional studies—studies that permit not only comparison of two or three programs, but also the rigorous testing of hypotheses about the consequences of variation in program form— are very difficult to execute in many states. Case study comparisons have generated interesting and important hypotheses about how (and to some extent, why) programs differ, but more extensive studies are needed to test these predictions. In particular, studies that examine differences between types of contracts, different ways of organizing public defender offices, and varying degrees of centralization in assigned counsel systems may tell us a great deal about the best ways to design these programs (e.g., Houlden and Balkin, 1985b).

Furthermore, as previously noted many studies, even those that rely upon coded data from case records, fail to control for important defendant and case attributes, despite evidence from many courts that factors such as bail status, offense seriousness, and prior record—factors that may be correlated with defendants' socioeconomic status—are strong predictors of outcomes (Spohn et al., 1981). Failure to control for these factors may produce a distorted picture of the differences between various indigent defense programs and privately retained counsel.

Finally, studies that have commendably sought to assess variation in soft but significant measures of effectiveness such as attorney-client relationships have relied more heavily on the attorney than on the client (e.g., Levine, 1975; Cavender, 1987), while some studies of client evaluations suffer from sample selection bias, insofar as only convicted defendants are interviewed (e.g., Atkins and Boyle, 1976). Defendants' reports may prove more reliable indicators or actual practices than formal rules or even attorneys' recollections, so future research should not only incorporate measures of defendant perceptions when possible, but should also seek validation of attorneys' self-reports by eliciting evaluations of specific instances of performance from their colleagues, from prosecutors, and from the bench.

Conclusions

This article begins and ends with the modest objective of stimulating reconsideration of the ways in which we evaluate indigent defense in trial courts. As contracting becomes an increasingly common but controversial means of representing the poor accused of crimes, a systematic consideration of the premises and problems of contracting, as well as a thoughtful reconsideration of traditional assigned counsel and public defender systems, is in order. One might reasonably conclude from this discussion that no system is inherently preferable to all others, but rather, that some program features may be desirable accompaniments to one or more program types. Moreover, it is sensible to assume that some means of providing representation are better suited for some types of jurisdictions than for others; for example, a full-time public defender office is ill-suited for a sparsely populated and isolated rural county, while assigned counsel systems may be an inadequate option in communities with few criminal defense practitioners.

One need not conclude, as some have, that contracting is an inherently flawed means of ensuring that the poor are represented in criminal court; indeed, under some conditions contracting may produce higher quality representation than do other systems. However, policy makers' interest in the contracting alternative is motivated by efficiency concerns rather than by the professional standards of bench and bar, and contracting tends to shift responsibility and accountability for effective indigent representation away from the legal profession into the hands of a few private practitioners. The chief danger in the move toward contracting, then, is that efficiency considerations will assume overriding importance in the eyes of elected officials who must design and fund local indigent defense programs and that consequently effectiveness and equity will be sacrificed. The traditional refuge of defendants deprived of adequate counsel is the appellate process, and some state courts have expressed willingness to scrutinize the operations and incentives inherent in simple contract systems (e.g., *Smith v. State of Arizona*, 140 Arizona 355, 1984). But the appellate process should serve only as an occasional check on the errors of policy makers, not as an intrusive corrective. Policy implementors and the legal profession, as well as indigent defendants, are best served by careful consideration of the potential and limitations of alternative means of representation, and by choices based on judgment balanced by efficiency and due process values.

Endnotes

[1] Estimates of felony indigency rates vary considerably, from a low of about 48 percent (Spangenberg et al., 1986) and rising rapidly (Criminal Defense for the Poor, 1988) to 60 percent (Moran, 1982; Gilboy, 1981), to 90 percent in some Michigan counties (Worden, 1990).

[2] The focus of this article is on programs that are primarily county-administered and county-funded; a host of other issues attend programs that are centrally administered and funded, although many of the issues raised in this article are germane to arguments for and against centralization of program administration.

[3] Although the U.S. Supreme Court has stated unambiguously that states must provide counsel to indigents accused of crimes (*Gideon v. Wainwright*, 372 U.S. 335; *Argersinger v. Hamlin*, 407 U.S. 25, 1972), the Court has not specified how such services are to be provided, nor what constitutes indigency for purposes of receiving free counsel; consequently, states have devised various systems and rules for organizing and funding indigent defense programs. In most states indigent defense at the trial

court level is statutorily delegated to county governments. In 33 states indigent defense services are organized wholly or partly at the county or judicial circuit level, and in 24 states funding for indigent defense programs is derived completely or primarily from county rather than state budgets (Criminal Defense for the Poor, 1988).

4   In 1982 fewer than 7 percent of all counties had contract programs; by 1986 over 11 percent did (Criminal Defense for the Poor, 1988). It is important to note that jurisdictions employing public defenders are disproportionately urban, and hence a majority of indigent criminal defendants in the U.S. are in fact represented by public defenders rather than assigned counsel or contract attorneys.

5   The distinction between provision and production has been a source of confusion among critics and advocates of privatization. Kolderie distinguishes between these two functions: a service is "publicly or socially provided (a) where the decision whether to have it (and the decisions about who shall have it and how much of it) is a political decision, (b) when government arranges for the recipients not to have to pay directly for the service themselves, and (c) when the government selects the producer that will service them" (1986:286). Although referring to legal representation as something produced by attorneys is an awkward twist on conventional usage of the term, for the sake of consistency with the privatization literature this distinction will be adopted here.

6   The shift toward privatization may have also been accelerated by the increasing reliance at the city and county level on professional managers, whose training and orientation sensitize them to efficiency issues, and who may also be more up-to-date on innovative ways of providing services than local elected officials (Morgan, 1979).

7   Some advocates of privatization also argue that privatizing is good for its own sake: these ideological arguments are premised on the notion that less government is better. Often, however, these arguments are applicable to a more complete form of privatization than contracting, viz., to turning over to the private sector both decisions about provision AND production of the service (see Savas, 1987); indeed, outside the United States privatization usually refers to public divestiture of functions that in this country have always been private, such as health care. Because indigent defense is a constitutionally mandated service, this perspective is not relevant to this discussion.

8   In a sense, of course, the assigned counsel systems operating in most counties represent an extremely decentralized form of privatization. However, assigned counsel systems are seldom formally limited to a specified subset of the bar (although informally they sometimes are), and an attorney's commitment to representing indigents in criminal matters is ethically and historically grounded more in professional obligations than in financial or business exchanges between the court and members of the bar (McIntyre, 1987). Public defender systems, at least as they operate in most counties, represent pure public production of indigent representation. Only contract systems represent privatization in the conventional sense.

9   The following section sets aside, for the moment, the question of whether contracting is better or worse than existing alternatives, evaluating it from the theoretical perspective on optimal and inappropriate conditions for contracting. Subsequent sections consider the ways in which contracting might or might not be superior to assigned counsel and public defender systems, and suggest ways of evaluating the quality of these alternatives.

10 An alternative to contracting that gives service production consumers more responsibility for producer selection is the voucher system. Voucher systems depend for their success on the ability of consumers or beneficiaries to make informed and thoughtful choices among producers; she who chooses the producer (usually from among a group of pre-approved individuals or firms) will also directly enjoy or suffer the consequences of her decision, and she is therefore motivated to make the best and

perhaps the most economical selection. Consumer choices about some products, such as food, are made frequently, and from among producers whose relative attractions can be readily assessed; for such products or services some form of privatization (such as food stamps) is quite appropriate (Savas, 1987). However, although voucher systems have been suggested for use in indigent criminal defense (Casper, 1972), and have been used to a limited extent by the Legal Services Corporation for the representation of poor people in civil cases, the assumption of informed consumer choice may not hold for legal representation as well as it does for some other services and products (Meeker et al., 1989).

11 The most common fee arrangement among attorneys is an hourly charge, secured by a retainer. Contract systems typically do not reimburse attorneys in proportion to their actual investment in cases, but instead pay a lump sum for a specified number of cases, or a specified term during which the attorney is responsible for all defendants found indigent, or a fixed amount per case (Spangenberg et al., 1986; Worden, 1990). Clearly the economic incentives produced by these arrangements differ from those characterizing conventional fee agreements.

12 This phenomenon was documented in a study of Kalamazoo, Michigan's experiences with contract attorneys; the original attorney group was found to be too enthusiastic in defense of the poor, and failed to cooperate to a satisfactory degree with judges and prosecutors. The contract was subsequently awarded to a more amenable group of lawyers at the urging of the local bench (Eisenstein et al., 1987: Chapter 6).

13 This viewpoint was recently expressed by the director of California's public defender office, who in rejecting the role of a strong due process advocate characterized his office as the loyal opposition (Panel Urges Abolition, 1988).

14 The argument that poverty lawyers should handle not only routine litigation but impact litigation as well was an important justification for the founding of the predecessor to the Legal Services Corporation during the Johnson administration. The fate of the Corporation over the past ten years illustrates the controversial nature of such reform-oriented programs.

15 Indeed, there is some reason to suspect that attorneys in private practice, be they assigned counsel or on retainer, are more protective of their clients' interests at the expense of victims than are public defenders, who may identify more strongly with the court (see Ford and Regoli, 1990).

16 Concern about the importance of the private bar's role in indigent defense at the local level was expressed even prior to *Gideon*; almost thirty years ago an article in the *Stanford Law Review* recommended that local bars play an active role in providing lists of qualified attorneys, supervising their performance, monitoring the funding process to ensure adequate allocations, establishing referral services for the marginally indigent, and providing training and resources to young lawyers interested in taking appointments ("Representation of Indigents in California," 1961; see also Grier, 1971). An active role was also endorsed by the National Advisory Commission on Criminal Justice Standards and Goals (1973). More recently McConville and Mirskey documented the New York City bar's efforts to improve the quality of appointed representation in response to claims of inadequate counsel (1989); Gilboy illustrates the political conflict that may emerge when local bars attempt to actively participate in the appointment process in the face of judges' preferences for particular lawyers (1981). It is also true, of course, that bar association activity sometimes reflects professional self-interest and a desire to monopolize and manage the availability of legal services, and to restrict the legal activities of groups that do not share lawyers' interests (see Kessler, 1986).

17 While in some cases political resistance to privatization may affect this choice (in the form of public employee union objections; see Ferris, 1987), indigent defense is of

little interest to constituent groups. One might expect to find, however, that the bar takes an interest in the choice to switch from an assigned counsel to a contract system (Worden and Worden, 1989).

[18] It is important to note in this connection that appointment rates may be only weakly correlated with actual indigency rates, since judges and administrators employ widely differing standards of indigency (Lefstein, 1982).

[19] Casper, for example, attributed defendants' preferences for a non-profit legal aid agency over public defenders to a distrust of the latter; but the lighter caseloads of the former might partially account for the better relationships they developed with defendants (1972; see also Levine, 1975; Meeker et al., 1989).

[20] However, for a privately retained attorney delay may be an attempt to ensure that fees are paid before the case is resolved and the client disappears or is incarcerated (Blumberg, 1967). Furthermore, lengthy disposition time may be more or less valuable to a defendant depending on pretrial detention status. A defendant free on bond can maintain social, family, and perhaps work commitments and thus endure fewer hardships as a result of delayed disposition. However, recent research finds little difference in case processing times for publicly paid and privately retained attorneys (Luskin and Luskin, 1987; Flemming et al., 1987); and another study concluded that local legal cultures is the most important determinant of case processing time (Church, 1978). Given the significance of bail status as a predictor of case outcome (Spohn, et al., 1981), a more important measure of effective representation might be attorneys' success in obtaining reasonable bail. An additional important (but often overlooked) procedural factor, one that varies considerably across systems, is the amount of time elapsed between arrest and attorney appointment; defendants deprived of an advocate for several days after arrest may feel overwhelmed by the authority of law enforcement officers and prosecutors.

[21] Further evidence that lawyers make little difference in sentencing is found in sentencing studies that control for attorney type (Talarico, 1979; Uhlman and Walker, 1979; Willison, 1984; but see Spohn et al., 1981).

[22] For example, Casper examined the relationship between defendants' assessments of the fairness of their treatment and dispositional characteristics; and there exists an intriguing body of theoretical research on the dimensions of perceived fairness in court proceedings which could be fruitfully applied to policy problems. (See Casper, 1978; Thibaut and Walker, 1975; Tyler, 1984; Tyler, 1987; Casper et al., 1988; and especially Landis and Goodstein, 1987.)

References

Alschuler, Albert W. (1975) "The Defense Attorney's Role in Plea Bargaining," *Yale Law Journal* 1179.

American Bar Association Project on Standards for Criminal Justice (1971) *Standards Relating to the Prosecuting Function and the Defense Function.* New York: American Bar Association.

Atkins, Burton and E. Boyle (1976) "Prisoner Satisfaction with Defense Counsel," 12 *Criminal Law Bulletin* 427.

Battle, Jackson L. (1973) "Comparison of Public Defenders' and Private Attorneys' Relationships with the Prosecution in the City of Denver," 50 *Denver Law Journal* 101.

Benjamin, Roger W. and Theodore B. Pedeleski (1969) "The Minnesota Public Defender System and the Criminal Law Process," 4 *Law and Society Review* 279.

Blumberg, Abraham (1967) "The Practice of Law as a Confidence Game: Organizational Cooptation of a Profession," 1 *Law and Society Review* 15.

Bohne, Brenda Hart (1978) "The Public Defender as Policy Maker," 62 *Judicature* 176.

Carlin, Jerome E., Jan Howard and Sheldon L. Messenger (1966) "Civil Justice and the Poor: Issues for Sociological Research," 1 *Law and Society Review* 9.

Casper, Jonathan D. (1972) *American Criminal Justice; The Defendant's Perspective.* Englewood Cliffs, NJ: Prentice-Hall.

_____ (1978) "Having Their Day in Court: Defendant Evaluations of the Fairness of Their Treatment," 12 *Law and Society Review* 237.

Casper, Jonathan D., Tom R. Tyler, and Bonnie Fisher (1988) "Procedural Justice in Felony Cases," 22 *Law and Society Review* 483.

Cavender, Gray, Barbara Cable Nienstedt, and Ronald S. Everett (1987) "Effectiveness of Counsel: An Empirical Analysis," 10 *Journal of Crime and Justice* 195.

Chamberlin, John R. and John E. Jackson (1987) "Privatization as Institutional Choice," 6 *Journal of Policy Analysis and Management* 586.

Church, Thomas W., Jr. (1978) *Justice Delayed: The Pace of Litigation in Urban Trial Courts.* Williamsburg, VA: National Center for State Courts.

Clarke, Stevens and G. Kurtz (1983) "The Importance of Interim Decision to Felony Trial Court Dispositions," 74 *Journal of Criminal Law and Criminology* 476.

Cohen, Larry J., Patricia P. Semple, and Robert E. Crew, Jr. (1983) "Assigned Counsel versus the Public Defender: A Comparison of Relative Benefits," in William F. McDonald, editor, *The Defense Counsel.* Beverly Hills: Sage.

Criminal Defense for the Poor 1986 (1988) Washington, DC: Department of Justice, Bureau of Justice Statistics.

Donahue, John D. (1989) *The Privatization Decision.* New York: Basic Books.

Dunleavy, Patrick (1986) "Explaining the Privatization Boom: Public Choice versus Radical Approaches," 64 *Public Administration Review* 13.

Eisenstein, James, Roy B. Flemming, and Peter F. Nardulli (1987) *The Contours of Justice.* Boston: Little-Brown.

Eisenstein, James and Herbert Jacob (1977) *Felony Justice,* Boston: Little-Brown.

Ferris, James M. (1987) "The Decision to Contract Out: An Empirical Analysis," 22 *Urban Affairs Quarterly* 289.

Flemming, Roy B. (1986) "Client Games: Defense Attorney Perspectives on Their Relations with Criminal Clients," 1986 *American Bar Foundation Research Journal* 253.

_____. (1990) "The Political Styles and Organizational Strategies of American Prosecutors: Examples from Nine Courthouse Communities," 12 *Law and Policy* 25.

Flemming, Roy B., Peter Nardulli, and James Eisenstein (1987) "The Timing of Justice in Felony Trial Courts," 9 *Law and Policy* 179.

Ford, David A. and Mary Jean Regoli (1990) "The Effectiveness and Impacts of Defense Counsel in Cases of Wife Battery." Paper presented at the Law and Society Association annual meeting, Berkeley.

Gentry, James Theodore (1986) "The Panopticon Revisited: The Problem of Monitoring Private Prisons," 96 *Yale Law Journal* 353.

Gilboy, Janet (1981) "The Social Organization of Legal Services to Indigent Defendants," 1981 *American Bar Foundation Research Journal* 1023.

Gilboy, Janet A. and John R. Schmidt (1979) "Replacing Lawyers: A Case Study of the Sequential Representation of Criminal Defendants," 70 *Journal of Criminal Law and Criminology* 1.

Gitelman, Morton (1971) "The Relative Importance of Appointed and Retained Counsel in Arkansas Felony Cases—An Empirical Study," 24 *Arkansas Law Review* 442.

Grier, Richard (1971) "Analysis and Comparison of Assigned Counsel and Public Defender Systems," 49 *North Carolina Law Review* 705.

Hermann, Robert, Eric Single, and John Boston (1977) *Counsel for the Poor: Criminal Defense in Urban America* Lexington, MA: Lexington.

Houlden, Pauline and Steven Balkin (1985a) "Costs and Quality of Indigent Defense: Ad Hoc vs. Coordinated Assignment of the Private Bar Within a Mixed System," 10 *Justice System Journal* 159.

_____ (1985b) "Quality and Cost Comparisons of Private Bar Indigent Defense Systems: Contract vs. Ordered Assigned Counsel," 76 *Journal of Criminal Law and Criminology* 176.

Johnson, Charles A. and Bradley C. Canon (1984) *Judicial Policies: Implementation and Impact.* Washington: CQ Press.

Kessler, Mark (1986) "The Politics of Legal Representation: The Influence of Local Politics on the Behavior of Poverty Lawyers," 8 *Law and Policy* 149.

Kolderie, Ted (1986) "The Two Different Concepts of Privatization," 46 *Public Administration Review* 285.

Landis, Jean M. and Lynne Goodstein (1987) "When Is Justice Fair? An Integrated Approach to the Outcome Versus Procedure Debate," 1986 *American Bar Foundation Research Journal* 675.

Lefstein, Norman (1982) *Criminal Defense Services for the Poor.* Chicago: American Bar Association Standing Committee on Legal Aid and Indigent Defense.

Levine, James P. (1975) "The Impact of 'Gideon': The Performance of Public and Private Criminal Defense Lawyers," 8 *Polity* 215.

Luskin, Mary Lee and Robert C. Luskin (1987) "Case Processing Times in Three Courts," 9 *Law and Policy* 207.

McConville, Michael and Chester A. Mirsky (1989) *Criminal Defense of the Poor in New York City.* New York: Center for Research in Crime and Justice, New York University School of Law.

McEntee, Gerald W. (1985) "City Services: Can Free Enterprise Outperform the Public Sector?" 55 *Business and Society Review* 43.

McIntyre, Lisa J. (1987) *The Public Defender: The Practice of Law in the Shadows of Repute.* Chicago: University of Chicago Press.

Meeker, James W., John Dombrink and Beth Quinn (1989) "Competitive Bidding of Legal Services for the Poor: An Analysis of the Scientific Evidence," paper presented at the 1989 meeting of the Law and Society Association, Madison.

Moe, Ronald C. (1987) "Exploring the Limits of Privatization," 47 *Public Administration Review* 453.

Moran, Thomas, ed. (1982) *Gideon Undone: Crisis in Indigent Defense Funding.* Chicago: American Bar Association and the National Legal Aid and Defender Association.

Morgan, David R. (1979) *Managing Urban America.* North Scituate, MA: Duxbury.

Morgan, David R. and Robert E. England (1988) "The Two Faces of Privatization," 48 *Public Administration Review* 979.

Nardulli, Peter F. (1986) "'Insider Justice': Defense Attorneys and the Handling of Felony Cases," 77 *Journal of Criminal Law and Criminology* 379.

National Advisory Commission on Criminal Justice Standards and Goals (1973) *The Courts.* Washington: U.S. Government Printing Office.

"Panel Urges Abolition of California Defender's Office" (1988) 19 *Criminal Justice Newsletter* 5.

Poole, Robert W. Jr. and Philip E. Fixler, Jr. (1987) "Privatization of Public-Sector Services in Practice: Experience and Potential," 6 *Journal of Policy Analysis and Management.*

"Representation of Indigents in California—A Field Study of the Public Defender and Assigned Counsel Systems" (1961) 13 *Stanford Law Review* 522.

Robbins, Ira P. (1986) "Privatization of Corrections: Defining the Issues," 69 *Judicature* 324.

Salamon, Lester M. et al. (1989) *Privatization: The Challenge to Public Management.* Washington: National Academy of Public Administration.

Savas, E. S. (1987) *Privatization: The Key to Better Government.* Chatham: Chatham House.

Singer, Shelvin and Elizabeth Lynch (1983) "Indigent Defense Systems: Characteristics and Costs," in William F. McDonald, editor, *The Defense Counsel.* Beverly Hills: Sage.

Spangenberg, Robert L., Beverly Lee, Michael Battaglia, Patricia Smith, and A. David Davis (1986a) *National Criminal Defense Systems Study.* Washington: U.S. Department of Justice.

Spangenberg, Robert L., Richard L. Wilson, Patricia A. Smith, and Beverly N. W. Lee (1986b) *Containing the Costs of Indigent Defense Programs: Eligibility Screening and Cost Recovery Procedures.* Washington: U.S. Department of Justice.

Spohn, Cassia, John Gruhl, and Susan Welch (1981-82) "The Effect of Race on Sentencing: A Reexamination of an Unsettled Question," 16 *Law and Society Review* 71.

Sterling, Joyce (1983) "Retained Counsel Versus the Public Defender: The Impact of Type of Counsel on Charge Bargaining," in William F. McDonald, editor. *The Defense Counsel.* Beverly Hills: Sage.

Stover, Robert V. and Dennis R. Eckart (1975) "A Systematic Comparison of Public Defenders and Private Attorneys," 3 *American Journal of Criminal Law* 265.

Sudnow, David (1965) "Normal Crimes: Sociological Features of the Penal Code in a Public Defender Office," 12 *Social Problems* 255.

Sullivan, Harold J. (1987) "Privatization of Public Services: A Growing Threat to Constitutional Rights," 47 *Public Administration Review* 461.

Summer, Marvin R. (1969) "Defending the Poor: The Assigned Counsel System in Milwaukee County," 1969 *Wisconsin Law Review* 525.

Sykes, Gresham M. (1969) "Legal Needs of the Poor in the City of Denver," 4 *Law and Society Review* 255.

Talarico, Suzette M. (1979) "Judicial Decisions and Sanction Patterns in Criminal Justice," 70 *Journal of Criminal Law and Criminology* 117.

Taylor, Jean C., Thomas P. Stanley, Barbara J. DeFlorio and Lynne N. Seekamp (1972) "An Analysis of Defense Counsel in the Processing of Felony Defendants in San Diego, California," 49 *Denver Law Journal* 233.

Thibaut, John and Laurens Walker (1975) *Procedural Justice: A Psychological Analysis.* Hillside, NJ: Lawrence Earlbaum.

Tyler, Tom R. (1984) "The Role of Perceived Injustice in Defendants' Evaluations of Their Courtroom Experience," 18 *Law and Society Review* 51.

_____ (1987) "Conditions Leading to Value-Expression Effects in Judgements of Procedural Justice: A Test of Four Models," 52 *Journal of Personality and Social Psychology* 333.

Uhlman, Thomas and Darlene Walker (1979) "A Plea Is No Bargain: The Impact of Case Disposition on Sentencing," 60 *Social Science Quarterly* 218.

Wheeler, Gerald R. and Carol L. Wheeler (1980) "Reflections on Legal Representation of the Economically Disadvantaged: Beyond Assembly Line Justice," 26 *Crime and Delinquency* 319.

Willison, David (1984) "The Effects of Counsel on the Severity of Criminal Sentences," 9 *Justice System Journal* 87.

Wilson, L. A., II (1988) "Rescuing Politics from the Economists: Privatizing the Public Sector," in Richard C. Hula, editor, *Market-Based Public Policy.* New York: St. Martin's Press.

Worden, Alissa Pollitz (1990) "Counsel for the Poor: An Evaluation of Contracting for Indigent Defense," paper presented at the annual meeting of the Law and Society Association, Berkeley.

Worden, Alissa Pollitz and Robert E. Worden (1989) "Local Politics and the Provision of Indigent Defense Counsel," 11 *Law and Policy* 401.

21

Calling a Strike a Ball
Jury Nullification and "Three Strikes" Cases

MARY DODGE, JOHN C. HARRIS, and ALISON BURKE

In 1994, the California "Three Strikes and You're Out" ballot initiative received overwhelming public endorsement. The hue and cry over clogged courtrooms and overloaded corrections facilities hardly squelched the fervor for harsher punishment. Few people, however, predicted the discrepancies between public opinion and juror reactions to defendants who committed what appeared to be minor crimes and who now face 25 years to life in prison. Increasing juror dissatisfaction, hung juries, and nullification cases suggest that the controversy over the three-strikes initiative extends beyond the predicted impact as jurors have balked at the severe consequences for some defendants.

California's three-strikes law, unlike those of other states, provides that a defendant with a history of "serious" or "violent" conviction is subject to the law's sentencing provisions regardless of the nature of the current felony. It includes a second-strike provision specifying that a person convicted of any felony with one prior conviction of a "serious" or "violent" offense can be sentenced to twice the term of punishment that would otherwise apply. The most draconian provisions, however, are reserved for a convicted felon with two "strike priors" who can receive three times the punishment that would otherwise apply or 25 years to life in prison, whichever is greater [CA Penal Code §667; §1170.12; §1192.7(c); §667.5(c)]. While judges have the authority to dismiss prior allegations (*People v. Superior Court of San Diego ex rel. Romero*, 1996), that power does not appear to be

Written especially for *Courts and Justice*.

used frequently and varies according to jurisdiction (Legislative Analyst's Office, 1999; Males & Macallair, 1999; Zimring, Hawkins, & Kamin, 2001).

The controversy over jury verdicts and sentencing developed as a seemingly large number of offenders were incarcerated for nonviolent crimes. Shichor and Sechrest (1996) note that 70 percent of all defendants charged as second- and third-strikers are currently facing nonserious, nonviolent criminal charges. According to the Legislative Analyst Office (1997), less than one-fourth of second-strikers were sentenced to prison for a violent or serious offense; the most common second-strike offenses are possession of a controlled substance, petty theft with a prior theft, and second degree burglary. Less than half of third-strikers were admitted to prison for nonserious, nonviolent offenses. The most common third-strike offenses are robbery and first degree burglary, followed by possession of a controlled substance and second degree burglary. The California Department of Corrections (2003) reports that there were over 7,000 third-strikers and 31,000 second-strikers incarcerated at the end of June 2003. Table 1 shows the number of third- and second-strike inmates serving sentences for lower-level property crimes, drug crimes, and miscellaneous offenses.

Table 1   Incarceration and Strike Offense

Offense Category	Third Strikers	Second Strikers
Petty Theft w/ Prior*	349	1926
Receiving Stolen Property	169	719
Vehicle Theft	225	1137
Forgery/Fraud	62	598
Controlled Substance Related	564	3695
Controlled Substance Possession	665	4238
Marijuana Related	34	315
Possession of a Weapon	385	1488
Driving Under the Influence	42	333

* "Wobbler" offenses can be punished as misdemeanors or felonies at the discretion of the prosecutor.
Source: Department of Corrections State of California (August 2003).

When the three-strikes law was passed the public favored harsh punishment. Recent trends, however, have undermined punitive efforts that result in excessive and harsh punishment. In stark contrast to previous legislation, in 2000 California voters overwhelmingly approved Proposition 36 that mandates treatment for nonviolent drug offenders and earmarks $120 million for rehabilitation efforts. Additionally, individual jurors are questioning the applicability of the three-strikes law to certain nonviolent offenders. Researchers have found that global public response to crime policy differs significantly from specific situational attitudes; punitive global attitudes are diminished under specific situations (Applegate et al., 1996). The research also showed that respondents favored a discretionary application of three-strikes laws when an offender committed a nonviolent crime or posed little physical threat to society. These findings are similar to investigations of mandatory sentencing, which suggest that community standards tend to be less punitive than existing law and that the public views long-term incarceration as an inadequate solution to crime (Blumstein & Cohen, 1980; Miller, Rossi, & Simpson, 1991; Samuel & Moulds, 1986).

The legitimacy of the three-strikes law and appropriateness of punishment have been questioned in cases involving nonviolent and seemingly nonserious offenses. The California law has been subjected to harsh criticisms (Marder, 2002). Some of these criticisms have come from unexpected sources. Ninth U.S. Circuit Court of Appeals Judge Harry Pregerson has voiced his opposition to the law: "I think the three-strikes law should only be applied to a defendant whose criminal history, including his last offense, demonstrates that he needs to be taken off the streets because he poses a realistic threat to the health and safety of the community" (*Corrections Professional*, 2003). A deputy district attorney stated: "The nonviolent felony provision—it offends the common citizen's sense of justice—'steal a piece of pizza . . . life term'" (personal interview). Some third-strike cases have involved relatively minor offenses, including petty theft with a prior and drug possession. For example:

- A man was charged with stealing $5 worth of meat.

- A homeless man whose only possession was a bicycle was charged with stealing a $2 bicycle lock.

- A severely retarded 34-year-old woman who was homeless and living in a park was charged with possession of a $5 rock of cocaine.

- A man who allegedly bought a crushed macadamia nut from the police was charged with attempting to possess drugs.

In other cases, defendants with a history of more serious priors were convicted and sentenced under three-strikes for minor current charges:

- A man was convicted of stealing a carton of cigarettes from Target. His priors, 15 years earlier, included burglary and assault.

- A woman whose priors included robbery, burglary, and prostitution was convicted for taking a $5 cut in a cocaine deal.

- A man was convicted for receiving stolen property—a 1985 Cadillac. His priors included burglary and drug possession and a robbery that involved a pack of cigarettes taken from another inmate.

Some jurors have expressed regret over their vote for conviction or requested leniency for the defendant after discovering the severity of the penalty. A juror who voted to convict a three-strikes defendant of petty theft told the defense attorney: "I'd be glad to talk to the judge and ask for a lighter sentence" (Krikorian et al., 1996). After the panel realized the possible punishment for the burglary conviction, two jurors filed declarations with the court. One juror stated in court documents: "This is stupid, I don't think this benefits anyone. Personally, I don't think the three-strikes should apply to nonviolent crimes" (Lynch & Cekola, 1995). In the case of a woman convicted for buying $5 worth of cocaine, a juror, who wished that he had held out for a mistrial, expressed his chagrin after he discovered the verdict would send a chronic drug user to prison for life:

> I felt deceived by the court. They should have let us know this was a
> three-strikes case. I'm a firm believer in "don't do the crime if you can't
> do the time," but this was just ridiculous. (Lynch & Cekola, 1995)

In one dramatic courtroom scene, Henry Jackson Jr., who had four previous felony convictions, was found guilty of possession of rock cocaine. After the verdict was announced, Jackson shouted, "I want you all to know you put me away for 25 years" (Sherwood, 1995). The jurors were polled after the outburst and a mistrial was declared after two refused to affirm their previous decision to convict. In San Francisco, a jury refused to continue deliberations when they learned the defendant would be sentenced under the three-strikes law (Cox, 1996).

Juror Ben Sherwood (1995) described his experience in a three-strikes case that resulted in a hung jury. The charges involved two men who were accused of selling 5.3 grams of marijuana to an undercover cop. According to Sherwood:

> The judge instructed us neither to pity the defendants nor to consider
> their possible punishment. In our first straw poll, nine jurors voted to
> convict. Three "not guilties" were worried about the dire consequences
> the defendants faced.

In Silicon Valley, Joe Louis Lugo, who had confessed to possessing a small amount of crack cocaine, was acquitted because the jury disagreed with the three-strikes law. According to Public Defender Edward Nino, "compassion overcame punitive sanctions." He stated:

> All of the jurors could not—or had a real difficult problem with the fact
> that they were—that a conviction in this particular case would send
> this man away for the rest of his life. This is an example of jury nulli-
> fication, because the evidence was extremely strong. (Gonzales, 1995)

A jury's right to nullify is firmly entrenched in common law and viewed by many as a legitimate part of the legal process (Reed, 1996). Jurors nullify the law when they acquit defendants despite sufficient evidence to convict. Gormlie (1996) notes that nullification experienced a revival in the 1990s because of the media attention given to high-profile cases. Proponents of nullification argue that its purpose is to promote justice by informing jurors that they have the power to act mercifully, if applying the law to the defendant's act would lead to an unjust result (Dorfman & Iijima, 1995).

The controversy often focuses on whether jurors should receive nullification instructions. Brody (1995) believes that jurors should be informed of the right to return a verdict of not guilty, despite evidence of guilt. The reluctance of trial courts, with the exception of Georgia, Indiana, and Maryland, to formally implement instructions has promoted grassroots movements to apprize jurors of the available options. The Fully Informed Jury Association, a national, nonprofit organization, promotes nullification through newsletters, a Web site, and handbills (http://www.fija.org). Prosecutors and judges, however, have pursued charges of contempt, obstruction, or tampering against distributors of nullification propaganda (King, 1998). Some courts have dismissed or replaced jurors who advocate nullification. The Second Circuit Court of Appeals ruled that judges have the duty to dismiss jurors who intend to nullify (*United States v. Thomas*, 1977).

The majority of courts agree that mandatory sentencing laws are insufficient justification for instructions on nullification. In 1996, Dennis Baca filed an appeal after he was found guilty of two counts of petty theft with a prior and sentenced under the three-strikes law. The appellant argued that he "had an absolute right to have the jury made aware of the harsh sentence which the court would be required to impose if he were convicted, and to have the jury acquit him if they felt that the sentence was too harsh, regardless of the strength of the evidence of his guilt" (*People v. Baca*, 1996). The California Court of Appeals rejected Baca's claim that he was entitled to have the jury instructed on the doctrine of nullification. The court, although it acknowledged a jury's right to nullify, rejected suggestions that the "jury be informed of that power, much less invited to use it." The court revisited the nullification issue in *People v. Williams* (2001) and determined that the practice is "contrary to our ideal of equal justice" because it permits the "prosecution's case and the defendant's fate to depend on the whims of a particular jury."

Judges in California have expressed concern over possible nullification in three-strikes cases. One judge commented:

> Generally speaking: Petty theft or minor personal possession of drugs should NOT result in 25 to life in prison. Jurors on these kinds of cases are becoming concerned and reluctant to convict even when guilt is certain. (personal interview)

Jury speculation over punishment has resulted in problematic outcomes in other cases, as well. San Francisco Superior Court Judge Lucy Kelly McCabe noted:

> We have had two cases in our system already where the jury thought it was a third strike, although it wasn't, and they hung, because people are unwilling, faced face-to-face with the defendant, to give somebody life for a bad check. (Alegria, 1994)

Judges rarely allow lawyers to mention possible sentencing, and standard jury instructions prohibit jurors from considering punishment. The majority of courts agree that information about punishment is the exclusive domain of the judiciary except in death penalty cases. Requests by defendants to inform juries of the sentencing consequences of a guilty verdict have been routinely denied and deemed as "inappropriate and distracting" (*United States v. Patrick*, 1974). Courts have consistently refused to grant requests that would allow the jury to consider punishment (King, 1998).

> A Kentucky court rejected the defendant's claim that he should have been able to tell the jurors that, while convicting on the principle offense, they could refuse to find persistent felony offender status in order to avoid triggering a mandatory sentence enhancement if they concluded that the sentence enhancement was too severe. (*Medley v. Commonwealth*, 1985)

> The Sixth Circuit court upheld a district court's refusal to allow defense to inform the jury of the sentence if the defendant is found guilty, and of nullification power. (*United States v. Calhoun*, 1995)

> The First Circuit court rejected efforts by defense attorney to inform the jury of the severity of the punishment as an indirect attempt to provoke jury nullification. (*United States v. Manning*, 1996)

In California, trial judges' responses to issues surrounding juries and the three-strikes law have varied widely. One judge, for example, declared a mistrial after discovering mid-trial that four jurors disagreed with the three-strikes law (*Jones v. Hennessey*, 1995). A few California judges, however, now allow lawyers to question potential jurors about their views of three-strikes during voir dire. One deputy district attorney suggested that full information for jurors may not be a bad thing. She spoke to jurors after a three-strikes conviction and was told that the jurors had considered that fact but had ". . . convicted anyway, we knew the judge could sentence the defendant to less than life under the *Romero* decision" (personal interview). Nonetheless, the great majority of judges and prosecutors attempt to keep the fact that the defendant faces severe punishment from the jury.

Defense lawyers are discovering that the introduction of prior record evidence, contrary to past research, may work in favor of their client. A California district attorney stated:

> The defense now tries to communicate to the jury that their client has suffered prior nonviolent felony convictions, hoping that the disproportionate punishment of a life term will create renegade jurors who refuse to convict. (personal interview)

Baseball analogies are frequently included in opening and closing statements. A defense attorney may simply state, "Let's play ball" or "We're on third base." Lawyers are using arguments that tell the jury to disobey the law. A lawyer who has promoted nullification in several cases says that sophisticated arguments offer jurors a "hook." This tactic gives juries an option and "lets them off the hook for disobeying the judge's instructions" (personal interview). Judges have responded by threatening severe sanctions if the defense attorney informs the jury of the defendant's strike status. "I make no bones about it. I let them know they'll (defenders) go to jail if they mention the three-strikes law" (personal interview). Nonetheless, the baseball analogies still abound in strike cases.

Researchers, however, have consistently found that under a variety of circumstances the introduction of prior record information results in increased conviction rates by mock jurors (Borgida & Park, 1988; Doob & Kirshenbaum, 1972; Greene & Dodge, 1995; Hans & Doob, 1976; Wissler & Saks, 1985). Horowitz (1985, 1988) notes that nullification arguments by defense lawyers promote the consideration of social norms in the decision-making process. Mock jurors, for example, were more lenient in euthanasia and possession cases. Mandatory sentencing has increased defense lawyers' arguments that the imbalance between crime and punishment should lead to an acquittal (Gormlie, 1996; Morvillo, 1994).

In rare instances, judges have allowed defense attorneys to disclose a client's criminal record. Attorney Michael J. Cassidy revealed a client's prior record at trial. Jurors, though troubled by the conviction, felt obligated to obey the judge's instruction to follow the law. Cassidy commented on the case:

> I tried to impress upon the jury that the people who voted for three-strikes thought it was only for people who committed violent crime, and I tried to tell them this particular case didn't fit the bill of goods that they were sold. It didn't work. (Lynch & Cekola, 1995)

Defense lawyers are also choosing to forego bifurcation in hopes that by introducing prior convictions during the guilt phase jurors will consider punishment in deliberations and be less likely to convict. This tactic, however, is not always successful. Courts may order bifurcation over the objection of defense counsel in strike cases, when the prosecutor requests it to prevent the specter of jury nullification (*People v. Cline*, 1998). In *Cline*, the court of appeal commented: "Here, the court noted that it had presided over two trials in which the jury apparently had refused to follow the law and had found the defendants not guilty of offenses falling under the three-strikes law."

Prosecutors are opposed to attempts to introduce three-strike information at trial. Several attorneys believe that the possibility of nullification is greater if the jurors discover the nature of the case before the verdict and start guessing about a defendant's priors. A prosecutor expressed concern about "jurors being allowed to hear [and therefore consider] the penalty or punishment in a particular case" (personal interview). A number of California deputy district attorneys expressed similar sentiments: "Jurors become reluctant to convict or find priors to be true if they learn it is a three-strikes case." Another claimed, "In terms of jury nullification the worst thing that happened to prosecutors was the third strike" (personal interview). This is also true in jurisdictions where jurors, particularly African American jurors, are perceived to be sympathetic to defendants. One deputy district attorney said a problem with the three-strikes law was "racial nullification by black jurors of black defendants regardless of race of victims."

The draconian punishments imposed for relatively minor current offenses under California's three-strikes law has made jury nullification a central concern of the state's trial courts. The common wisdom is that jurors will balk at severe punishments for minor offenses. Jury expert James P. Levine (1997) notes:

> So, whereas mock jurors agree with current policies which penalize recidivists more stringently than first-time offenders and even accept in principle the idea of life imprisonment for habitual offenders which has been approved by the Supreme Court, they resist imposition of draconian punishments when the repeat offenses are relatively trivial; in their minds, "enough is enough."

Despite the relatively few reported cases of acquittal, the possibility of nullification or hung juries is a concern of prosecutors and judges and an area of continuing interest for defense counsel. This has, undoubtedly, led to prosecutors dismissing prior allegations in some cases, though others resist this response. As one prosecutor proudly recollected, "Our jurors will follow the law. One jury came back and convicted—they had tears in their eyes, but they convicted" (personal interview). Nonetheless, the potential for nullification is a common subject of comment and concern (Marder, 2002).

The exact number of three-strikes nullification cases is unknown. Incidents of nullification may begin to diminish as a result of the *Romero* decision. Initially, the decision appeared to have had little impact on trials (Legislative Analyst's Office, 1999; Clark, Austin, & Henry, 1997), though recently the number of three-strikes convictions has dropped as district attorneys become more selective in prosecutions and apply a higher level of discretion that shapes the use of the law around the principle of proportionality (Bowers, 2001; Greenwood & Hawken, 2001). If the possibility of judicial discretion becomes widely known, it may influence jurors and lead to conviction, even when they have concern over application of the law.

In November of 2002, the United States Supreme Court scrutinized California's three-strikes law in two cases that claimed sentences were unconstitutional based on the cruel and unusual punishment clause. Gary Ewing was sentenced to 25 years in prison on his third-strike offense of stealing three golf clubs valued at $399 apiece (*Ewing v. California*, 2002). Ewing's previous felony convictions included three burglaries and a robbery. Leandro Andrade's third offense was the theft of videotapes from two K-mart stores that resulted in a 50-year sentence without parole, despite the Ninth U.S. Circuit Court of Appeals ruling that the sentence was "grossly disproportionate" to the crime (*Lockyer v. Andrade*, 2002). In a 5–4 decision the Supreme Court affirmed the sentence deferring to the legislature's responsibility to impose penalties for state criminal law violations. In his dissenting opinion, Justice David Souter commented: "if Andrade's sentence is not grossly disproportionate, the principle has no meaning."

Despite the concern of the courts and arguments of legal scholars, there is as yet little systematic research concerning nullification in three-strike cases. Judicial and advocate approaches to the issue remain *ad hoc* and without firm social science support or analysis. Further research efforts should include the identification and analysis of cases that have resulted in hung juries and known nullification. Juror questionnaires should assess whether juror knowledge of prior conviction, known to increase the probability of conviction, is counteracted by knowledge of severe punishment for a minor current offense. Interviews with jurors in identified nullification cases may also help to understand the phenomenon.

It may be time to rethink judicial approaches to jury nullification. Current responses to the issue emphasize maintaining jury ignorance and suggest that juries are not to be trusted. Perhaps such responses engender the kind of haphazard pattern of nullification that all in the justice system find frustrating and many find inequitable. Jurors in some states already give sentencing recommendations. Providing the jury with all of the facts and a voice in sentencing may lead to greater consistency in application of the law. It may also provide for a greater sense that justice is being done.

References

Alegria, I. (1994). "California Judge Refuses to Enforce Three-Strikes Law." *National Public Radio.*

Applegate, B. K., Cullen, F. T., Turner, M. G., & Sundt, J. L. (1996). "Assessing Public Support for Three-Strikes-and-You're Out Laws: Global Versus Specific Attitudes." *Crime and Delinquency*, 42:517–534.

Blumstein, A., & Cohen, J. (1980). "Sentencing of Convicted Offenders: An Analysis of the Public's View." *Law and Society Review*, 14:223–261.

Borgida, E., & Park, R. (1988). "The Entrapment Defense: Juror Comprehension and Decision Making." *Law and Human Behavior*, 12:19–40.

Bowers, J. D. (2001). "The Integrity of the Game is Everything: The Problem of Geographic Disparity in Three Strikes." *New York University Law Review*, 76(4):1164–1202.

Brody, D. C. (1995). "Sparf and Dougherty Revisited: Why the Court Should Instruct the Jury of It's Nullification Right." *American Criminal Law Review*, 33:88–122.

California Department of Corrections (2003). "Second and Third Strikers in the Institution Population by Offense Category, Offense Group, and Admission or Return as of December 31, 2002." http://www.corr.ca.gov (Accessed December 5, 2003).

Clark, J. Austin, J., & Henry, D. A. (September 1997). "Three Strikes and You're Out: A Review of State Legislation." *National Institute of Justice*.

Corrections Professional (25 July 2003). "9th Circuit Judge Bucks California's 3-Strike Rule."

Cox, G. D. (29 May 1996). "Jurors Rise Up Over Principle and Their Perks." *National Law Journal*, A1.

Department of Corrections State of California (August 2003). "Second and Third Strikers in the Institution Population." Sacramento, CA. http://www.corr.ca.gov/OffenderInfoServices/Reports/OffenderInformation.asp (Accessed December 5, 2003).

Doob, A., & Kirshenbaum, H. (1972). "Some Empirical Evidence on the Effect of S. 12 of the Canada Evidence Act Upon the Accused." *Criminal Law Quarterly*, 15:88–96.

Dorfman, D. N., & Iijima, C. K. (1995). "Fictions, Fault, and Forgiveness: Jury Nullification in a New Context." *University of Michigan Journal of Law Reform*, 28:861–877.

Ewing v. California, No. 01-6978 [U.S. Nov. 5, 2002].

Gonzales, E. (1995). "Simpson Case Focuses Attention on Jury Nullification." *National Public Radio*.

Gormlie, G. F. (1996). "Jury Nullification: History, Practice, and Prospects." *National Lawyers Guild Practitioner*, 53:49–70.

Greene, E., & Dodge, M. (1995). "The Influence of Prior Record Evidence on Juror Decision Making." *Law and Human Behavior*, 19:67–78.

Greenwood, P., & Hawken, A. (2001). "Assessing the Impacts and Effectiveness of California's Three-Strikes Law." A Conference Report Prepared for the RAND Three Strikes Policy Roundtable, Santa Monica, CA.

Hans, V., & Doob, A. (1976). "Section 12 of the Canada Evidence Act and the Deliberations of Simulated Juries." *Criminal Law Quarterly*, 18:235–253.

Horowitz, I. A. (1985). "The Effect of Jury Nullification Instruction on Verdicts and Jury Functioning in Criminal Trials." *Law and Human Behavior*, 9:25–36.

Horowitz, I. A. (1988). "Jury Nullification: The Impact of Judicial Instructions, Arguments, and Challenges on Jury Decision Making." *Law and Human Behavior*, 12:439–453.

Jones v. Hennessey (1995). U.S. Dist LEXIS 19540 1, 3-6 (N D Cal).

King, N. J. (1998). "Silencing Nullification Advocacy Inside the Jury Room and Outside the Courtroom." *University of Chicago Law Review*, 65:433–500.

Krikorian, G., O'Neill, A. W., Corwin, M., Boyer, E. J., & Abrahamson, A. (1 July 1996). "Front-Line Fights Over 3 Strikes." *Los Angeles Times*, p. 1.

Legislative Analyst's Office (1999). "The Three Strikes and You're Out Law: An Update." http://www.lao.ca.gov/default.asp (Accessed December 5, 2003).

Levine, J. P. (1997). "Review Essay—Jury Wisdom." *Criminal Justice Ethics Journal* 16(1):49–56.

Lockyer v. Andrade, No. 01-1127 [U.S. Nov. 5, 2002].

Lynch, R., & Cekola, A. (20 February 1995). "3 Strikes Law Causes Juror Unease in OC." *Los Angeles Times*, p. 1.

Males, M., & Macallair, M. (1999). "Striking Out: The Failure of California's 'Three Strikes and You're Out' Law." *Stanford Law and Policy Review*, 11:65–74.

Marder, N. S. (2002). "Juries, Drug Laws and Sentencing." *The Journal of Gender, Race, and Justice*, 6(2):337–380.

Medley v. Commonwealth (1985). 704 SW2d 190,191 (Ky).

Miller, J. L., Rossi, P. H., & Simpson, J. E. (1991). "Felony Punishments: A Factorial Survey of Perceived Justice in Criminal Sentencing." *Journal of Criminal Law and Criminology*, 82:396–422.

Morvillo, R. (7 June 1994). "Jury Nullification." *New York Law Journal*, p. 3.

People v. Baca (1996). Cal. App. LEXIS 838.

People v. Cline (1998) E019186, (Super.Ct.No. FSB09681), Fourth Dist., Div. 2.

People v. Superior Court of San Diego City ex rel. Romero (1996). 13 Cal. 4th 497, 504, 917 P.2d 628,630.

People v. Williams (2001). 25 Cal. 4th, 441, 21 P.3d 1209; 106 Cal. Rptr. 2d 295.

Reed, J. T. (1996). "Penn, Zenger, and O.J.: Jury Nullification-Justice or the 'Wacko Fringe's' Attempt to Further its Anti-government Agenda?" *Duquesne University Law Review*, 1125, 11602.

Samuel, W., & Moulds, E. (1986). "The Effect of Crime Severity on Perceptions of Fair Punishment: A California Case Study." *Journal of Criminal Law and Criminology*, 77:931–948.

Sherwood, B. (12 February 1995). "Deciding Guilt in a Three-Strikes Case." *Los Angeles Times*.

Shichor, D., & Sechrest, D. K. (1996). *Three Strikes and You're Out: Vengeance as Public Policy*. Thousand Oaks, CA: Sage Publications.

United States v. Calhoun (1995). 49F3d 231, 236 (6th Cir).

United States v. Manning (1996). 79, F3d 212, 219 (1st Cir).

United States v. Thomas (1977). 116 F3d 606, 617 (2d Cir).

United States v. Patrick (1974). 494 F.2d 1150, 1153 (D.C. Cir).

Wissler, R. L., & Saks, M. J. (1985). "On the Inefficacy of Limiting Instructions: When Jurors use Conviction Evidence to Decide on Guilt." *Law and Human Behavior*, 9:37–48.

Zimring, F. E., Hawkins, G., & Kamin, S. (2001). *Punishment and Democracy: Three Strikes and You're Out in California*. New York: Oxford University Press.

22

Normal Homicides, Normal Defendants
Finding Leniency in Oklahoma's Murder Conviction Machinery

DAVID KEYS

Introduction and Literature Review

The late ethnomethodologist David Sudnow (1965), in his classic paper "Normal Crimes: Sociological Features of the Penal Code in a Public Defender Office," analyzed a broad range of criminal offenses. He found that public defenders and prosecutors worked in a coordinated and complimentary fashion, coupling charge reductions with guilty pleas for a quick disposal of cases. In a similar study of jury deliberations, Garfinkel (1956) found that panel members, in the face of opposing views on a given defendant's guilt, formed what he called "common-sense considerations that anyone could see" to arrive at the necessary unity in their verdict (240–241). Sudnow's work looked at the interactions of supposed adversaries that were, in reality, cooperative relationships and vital to the smooth operation of a criminal court. Sudnow (1965) documented opposing counsel's considerations of the "typical manner in which the offenses are committed, the social characteristics of the persons who regularly commit them, the features of settings in which they occur, and the types of victims often involved" as key organizing concepts in understanding and explaining the normality of a given homicide (256). Out of these concepts Sudnow constructed the idea of *normal crimes,* or an array of offenses whose typical features (e.g., manner of occurrence, characteristics of the people who

Prepared especially for *Courts and Justice.*

commit them) both the defense and prosecution could agree merited mutually beneficial legal compacts, thus dispensing with trials. Garfinkel (1967) observed jurors working across what could have been significant disagreements, using a body of commonsense knowledge and a range of procedures and considerations that permitted the finding of unanimous verdicts. Garfinkel (1956) found that jurors worked through a number of challenging distinctions (e.g., "fact versus opinion," "what the evidence shows and it says to each of us," "what was reasonable doubt") in arriving at unified decisions (241).

Both studies examined emerging and functional patterns of agreement within *commonsensemaking* procedures that any ordinary member of society would understand and use. Sudnow and Garfinkel sought out organized patterns of interaction, institutionalized treatment of circumstances, and constructions of order in the everyday business of the courts. It is within these existing interactional constructions that the "usual and ordinary" sharply contrast with the abnormal and unusual, that the unwritten rules of normality become dominant, and that stock interpretations produce what appears to be, and is subsequently treated as, objective reality. Both Sudnow and Garfinkel, in very different settings, outlined how seemingly disparate interests actually work together to achieve a mutually acceptable and essentially efficient conclusion to their respective business.

These ideas of norm formation in the operation of justice are applicable in Oklahoma's circumstances as an execution state. Although Oklahoma is second only to Texas in total number of executions since 1976 and maintains the highest death sentence rate in the post-*Furman* period (1972–present), a majority of homicide prosecutions in Oklahoma never proceed to trial. Of those intentional homicides (first- and second-degree murders), 61% end in plea-bargaining, where charge reductions and/or sentence decreases are the norm. Clearly, if prosecutors and defense attorneys in Oklahoma were not disposed to make such concessions, the state's criminal courts would be overwhelmed. It bears asking: how do opposing attorneys, in what appears to be a highly adversarial system, come to such vital and frequent agreements on a weighty issue such as homicide? How are *normal* cases selected for plea bargains, and how are the requisite reductions in charge and sentence arrived at? In essence, what constitutes a *normal homicide* and a *normal defendant,* or how does the *normalization* process operate within Oklahoma's murder conviction machinery?

Data Description and Methodology

Data were collected from a multitude of sources, the primaries being: (1) the Oklahoma Offender Database (OOD) for the years 1973–2005, (2) Oklahoma Indigent Defense System records, and (3) crime reporting collected from 44 local newspapers covering cases charged as "capital" and "second-degree" homicides. This period spanned the first 32 years of Oklahoma's current, post-*Furman* capital sentencing law with 7,662 reported homicides in the state. Complete case information amounted to 32.8% (n = 2,516) of the total. Offender information data systems, appellate documents, and newspaper accounts carried varied information (e.g., name, department of corrections number, age, ethnicity, years of education completed, criminal record, and eligibility for parole if applicable) and some circumstances of the crime (newspapers usually carried a narrative description of the events, method, and weapon used as well as victim information such as age, ethnicity, and possible relation to the offender). Records from the Oklahoma attorney general's office and the Oklahoma Criminal Court of Appeals included statutory aggravators, legal representation of the defendant, and accompanying facts of the crimes.

Normal homicides were assumed to have specific predictive factors leading to the lighter, less harsh sentencing for *normal defendants.* Using interviews with prosecutors and defense attorneys (n = 16), it was possible to extract the typical features of a *normal homicide* and *normal defendant,* as well as predict with reasonable certainty the final sentences of the cases considered *normal.* It was also possible to determine the most highly predictive variables (e.g., typical relationships of victim to offender, weapon used) in explaining the interactions of prosecutors and defense attorneys in attaining a reasonable compromise. Officers of the court (four prosecutors, ten public defenders, and two private defense attorneys) working across the two most *homicide-active* judicial circuits were interviewed as to their procedures in "handling a typical homicide." The interviews were conducted in an unstructured fashion and were taped and transcribed. The interviewer endeavored to direct an open-ended discussion with each subject as to the following points:

- What constitutes a typical homicide in this jurisdiction?
- Do such cases have typical offenders and typical victims?
- Are there typical circumstances that persistently reoccur (e.g., weapon used, offender-victim relationship)?
- What is the most common outcome or legal disposition of such cases?
- Which format (television, radio, newspaper) is typically used by the local media?

Inverting the premise that "the selection of homicide defendants for death is the cumulative result of a series of decisions and evaluations" by state's attorneys and juries (Radelet and Pierce 1985: 617), examinations of defendants and the circumstances of their offenses were done in order to understand which factors have reasonable predictive power in the construction of a *normal homicide,* or the kind of crime that meets the norms in its details (e.g., weapon employed, victim selection, overall race, age, and social congruency of assailant and assailed) that could, accordingly, be disposed of without seemingly undue investigation, court time, or public notice. Qualitative findings were analyzed and coded in an effort to understand the normalization process: in essence, the prosecutor's and defense attorney's joint determination of eligibility for a lesser sentence or lesser charge of second-degree homicide. In addition, the findings of the interviews were checked against empirical data (n = 2,516) to confirm or deny the actual existence of the *normal homicide* and the *normal defendant.*

Follow-up interviews were conducted with attorneys (four prosecutors and four defense) via telephone after quantitative analyses were finished. After presentation of the quantitative findings, they were asked the following questions:

- Does the decision to pursue a particular defendant depend on that person's race or the race of the victim?

- Do the results of the quantitative data analysis change your feelings about the fairness of the present system of plea bargaining and sentencing?

Table 1 on the following page summarizes the answers of the officers of the court (n = 16).

Normal Procedures in the Normal Homicide

In every interview of court officers, a set process emerged. Prosecutors provided details of the crime in the original complaint, with the most prominent facts brought forward at arraignment, bail hearings, and any evidentiary proceedings. If necessary, that is, if the two sides cannot fast track a plea agreement immediately following indictment, the prosecutor will turn over to the defendant's attorney evidence gathered in anticipation of a trial. Pretrial conferences between prosecution and defense counsels will work to establish the normality of the crime, where offenders "receive their due" (Sudnow 1965: 264). The defense will accordingly stipulate its client's guilt, while agreeing or disagreeing with specifications of the charges, with the express goal of arriving at a plea agreement and a satisfactory sentencing recommendation. In many cases, the specifications of the crime and the resulting sentencing memo, which is returned to the court, are the most serious points of contention between prosecution and defense since they directly affect the eligibility and circumstances (e.g., evidence of remorse, future dangerousness, possibility of recidivism) of the eventual

Table 1   Attorneys' Views on the Attributes of *Normal Homicides*

Typical Attributes of a Normal Homicide	Public Prosecutor		Public Defender		Private Defense Attorney	
	Yes	No	Yes	No	Yes	No
Homicide Characteristics						
a "neighborhood thing"	x		x		x	
with associated felony		x		x	x	
Offender Characteristics						
male	x		x		x	
young (under 22)	x		x		x	
non-white	x		x		x	
gang affiliated	x		x		x	
poor		x	x			x
with prior convictions		x		x		x
Victim Characteristics						
male	x		x		x	
young (under 22)	x		x		x	
non-white	x			x		x
gang affiliated	x			x	x	
poor		x	x		x	
Crime Circumstances						
weapon—firearm	x		x		x	
motive—money		x		x	x	
motive—passion/revenge	x		x			x
offender-victim same race	x		x		x	
multiple victims		x		x		x
Case Outcome						
capital murder		x	x		x	
plea bargain	x		x			x
Media Attention/Notice						
television		x		x		x
newspaper		x		x		x
radio		x		x		x

parole of a given offender. After analyzing court officers' interviews, the *normal crime* emerges as one with origins and motives in the neighborhood, involving young, male offenders and victims of the same race, usually motivated by passion/revenge, done with a firearm, and experiencing little media exposure. Attorneys agreed that *normal offenders,* i.e., offenders that are likely to realize a reduced charge of second-degree homicide and/or realize significant reductions in sentence, would probably not possess records containing prior felony convictions, involving multiple victims, or cases receiving public attention. Prosecutors indicated that they would not entertain leniency or forgo requests for the death penalty for what appeared to be career criminals committing multiple homicides, as there existed

> a great deal of public pressure orchestrated by media coverage to get tough on these sorts of people . . . and that the [state] legislature reflected the public will to do so in their revisions of the homicide laws over the past two decades. I mean, all murders are bad, but some are worse than others.

In contrast, the same assistant district attorney appended his previous statements by saying:

> The public has accepted the fact that crime-ridden areas of [the city's name] experience this sort of violence on occasion and there is little public outrage or even public knowledge when a charge is reduced or the death penalty waived in the process of getting someone bad off the streets for a very long time.

To establish a *normal homicide* and *normal offender*, prosecutors and defense counsels labored to link the act of murder with the *normal* category of homicide as it was understood. It was generally accepted in nearly every case that this relationship precluded the possibility that the defendant might not be guilty, that the victim might have been a party to his/her own death, or that the homicide was justifiable—all conditions that would have mitigated the seriousness of the crime or closed any prosecution. A public defender revealed:

> These guys are guilty 99% of the time and they are anxious to get a deal. They know that the possibility of getting a harsh sentence for killing another banger [gang member] is pretty small or is not even going to trial.

Another public prosecutor indicated:

> It is very hard to get a jury to sentence a young man to death when the crime involves a drug deal gone bad or a domestic feud . . . death penalty trials call for serious resources to undertake, and it is a commitment we do not take lightly and hardly seems worth the time and money. *Our defendants* and victims are very similar types of people and it's hard to press a jury for a death penalty in these cases. (emphasis added)

Juries were considered obstructions when the prosecution had to press a hard-nosed agenda intent on getting a death sentence.

> You might think that in a conservative state like Oklahoma juries would be anxious to hand down more death sentences, but I can tell you, it's tough for common folks, unfamiliar with capital justice, to look in the face of a young person, in their twenties, or younger sometimes, and say, "We are taking your life."

A public defender that was often an adversary of the prosecutors quoted above put it succinctly, commenting, "Typical murder—typical defense. These sorts of killings happen too often to go to the mat [i.e., employing every available resource] every single time." The typing of cases, in fact, is done very early in the process, as one urban police force has stated, "Homicides are broken down into the following categories in Oklahoma City: gang-related, domestic, robbery, self-defense, officer-involved, argument, child abuse, accidental, other and unknown, which are typically unsolved" (McCool 2008). In that both prosecutors and public defenders have limited resources to devote to heavy caseloads, the impetus for employing serious hours of investigation, research, and strategy making must come from someplace other than the fact that a homicide has been committed. A public defender, accompanied by a prosecutor at lunch, told the interviewer, "Every so often, a victim's family will inspire some press coverage that will make a done-deal null and void." The prosecutor then interjected:

> I have witnessed a defendant's family and friends whip up the idea that their boy is getting a raw deal, you know, railroaded into a life sentence. It's rare, but sometimes the newspapers like that kind of story and it will spoil a compromise they we [pointing to his lunch companion] have already made. It usually ends up bad for the defendant.

The emphasis on the normality of a given case, as it fits cases already decided and conditions already determined, strongly implies that the defense attorney and prosecutor know beforehand the conditions (i.e., commonsense situations whose features are largely taken for granted) under which they will request/grant a plea bargain.

> He [the prosecutor] has always agreed to these circumstances and the conference this afternoon is a formality. Their office does not need a run-of-the-mill murder clogging up the pipeline of putting away the really bad guys.

At the same time, prosecutors were aware of the priorities of their colleagues across the aisle, saying,

> The IDS [Indigent Defense System] in Oklahoma, I am sure, has an informal setup on the kinds of homicides it will vigorously defend and those they need not worry about. If a defendant gives it up [agrees to confess] and gets a break on the sentence, how much more can his lawyer do? Some private attorneys will fight everything down to the wire, but they are charging their clients for those billable hours, right? I don't have a lot of respect for those kind. They make everyone go to all kinds of ends to prove facts that are already in evidence, object to normal procedures, and end up giving their client a bunch of false hope.

This statement parallels Sudnow's (1965) observation that, "To put on a fight is a disconcerting task for persons who regularly work together as a team" (275). The agreed upon circumstances usually entail a homicide where a young person, more often than not an African American male, has killed another young African American male, where offender and victim know each other or share a situation where circumstances connect them in some way (e.g., gang rivalry, personal jealousy, revenge for a past wrong). In doing so, the defendant has committed a personal crime, commonly without endangering the lives of others, and usually does not have a lengthy or serious criminal record.

A public defender stated, with a prosecutor nodding her agreement in the background, "This black kid on black kid sort of killing does not make for much public outrage because those cases do not get a lot of press." In these "low-visibility" cases, prosecuting attorneys felt no pressure to request the death penalty and processed them with minimal resources. Defense attorneys and prosecutors, having agreed on the types of cases and the character of defendants with whom they would be willing to compromise, essentially program the process of bargaining in the incidence of what can be a *normal homicide*. Again, Garfinkel (1967) expressed the crux of the issue, saying that the "outcome comes before the decision" (114). In the final assessment, prosecutors were responsible to the public if a given case realized subsequent publicity, which can be expressed by Garfinkel's idea that the "decision maker's task of justifying a course of action" (114) is a factor that all prosecutors take to heart. At the same time,

> We try to make justice as speedy a process as possible, which means having some predictable set of circumstances at hand to get things moving. I respect the court's task of bringing out the individual details of a homicide, but frankly the sorts of murder I normally see, and would be willing to [plea] bargain on, are pretty much standard stuff.

Consequently, as defined by the lawyers involved, a *normal defendant* is a male offender, non-white (most often African American), with no serious criminal history, and has victimized other young, non-white men. In a *normal homicide*, the weapon most likely used was a firearm, and the offender was linked or was very similar to the victim in some personal, social, or economic circumstances. There did seem to be considerable differences in the descriptions of normalness made by private counsels contrasted to public defenders (and prosecutors), but the divergence seemed to be explained by the poor economic circumstances that clients of public defenders endure when they cannot afford private counsel.

Normality Emerging from the Quantitative Data Set

In Oklahoma, one of the conclusions that emerged from the interviews regarding the *normal offender* and *normal homicides* was the same race/ethnicity in the victim-offender relationships. However, widely accepted empirical studies in Maryland found that "state's attorneys were approximately twice as likely to file a notification to seek a death sentence and not withdraw that notification when the homicide victim was white rather than black" (State of Maryland 2000). A later report found that "blacks who kill blacks and homicides involving 'other' combinations of offender's and victim's race are significantly less likely to have a death notification 'stick' than homicides involving black offenders and white victims" (State of Maryland 2000: 37). Applying the inverse and considering the racial variety in Oklahoma (e.g., African Americans, Latinos, Asians, and Native Americans), the data set should show crimes involving non-white offenders and victims in Oklahoma receiving more leniency, i.e., charges of second-degree homicide or charges of first-degree homicide with a waiver of death penalties, including the possibility of parole.

The following hypotheses outline each of the factors found in Oklahoma that support *normal offenders* and *homicides*. Data are provided in order to support or reject the validity of each factor. Lenient treatment is defined as a charge of second-degree homicide or a charge of first-degree homicide with the death penalty waived while harsh treatment included a request for the death penalty. The expected frequencies of each hypothesis are shown in italics.

Hypothesis 1

Non-white offenders will exceed statistical expectations in lenient treatment when victims are non-white.

Table 2   Offender/Victim Combinations and Plea Bargaining

		White Victims	Non-White Victims	Totals
White Offenders[a]	**Lenient**	816 *(828.6)*	171 *(159.4)*	987
	Harsh	408 *(395.4)*	63 *(75.6)*	471
Totals		1,224	234	1,458
Non-White Offenders[b]	**Lenient**	192 *(284.7)*	488 *(395.3)*	680
	Harsh	251 *(158.3)*	127 *(219.7)*	378
Totals		443	615	1,058
		1,667	849	2,516

[a] Chi^2 = 3.69; sig. = 0.055.
[b] Chi^2 = 145.4; sig. = 0.00.

Table 2 shows that the raw counts for white offenders/white victims are in line with the expected frequencies, demonstrating no systematic statistical link existed between race and prosecutors' decisions to accept guilty pleas in exchange for charge reductions to second-degree homicide or death waivers. For non-white offenders the raw counts are significantly different from the expected frequencies. The combination of non-white offenders and white victims shows that prosecutors request the death penalty much more frequently than expected, while non-white offenders and non-white victims are treated with greater leniency (93 more waivers and fewer death sentences than expected). Considering offender/victim combinations, *normal homicides* tend to be *non-white offenders* assailing *non-white victims* as described by attorneys' interviews. Hypothesis 1 must be accepted.

Hypothesis 2

In an analysis across all ethnic categories (white, African American, Latino/a, Native American, and Asian), offenders and victims with the same race/ethnicity are more likely than expected to be successful in attaining *lenient treatment*, i.e., to make guilty pleas in exchange for charge reductions to second-degree homicide or death waivers, as opposed to offender-victim pairings of different race/ethnicity, who were hypothesized as receiving *harsh treatment*, i.e., sentences of life without parole or death at trial.

Table 3   Victim/Offender Same Ethnicity and Prosecutorial Bargaining

	Victim/Offender Same Ethnicity		
	Yes	No	Total
Lenient Treatment	1,071	365	1,436
	(1,027.9)	*(408.1)*	
Harsh Treatment	730	350	1,080
	(773.1)	*(306.9)*	
Total	1,801	715	2,516

Chi² = 14.8; sig. = 0.00.

Cross-tabulation shows that leniency is linked to victim and offender being the same race/ethnicity. Hypothesis 2 is accepted.

Hypothesis 3

Offenders with no previous felony convictions are more likely than expected to be successful in attaining *lenient treatment*, i.e., to make guilty pleas in exchange for charge reductions to second-degree homicide or death waivers, as opposed to receiving *harsh treatment*, i.e., sentences of life without parole or death at trial.

Table 4   Previous Felony Convictions and Prosecutorial Bargaining

	Previous Felony Convictions		
	Yes	No	Total
Lenient Treatment	532 (600.1)	870 (801.9)	1,402
Harsh Treatment	521 (452.9)	537 (605.10)	1,058
Total	1,053	1,407	2,460

Chi² = 31.44; sig. = 0.00.

Cross-tabulation shows that the existence of previous felony conviction was indeed connected to harsher treatment and offenders were less likely to be treated as *normal defendants*. Hypothesis 3 must be accepted.

Hypothesis 4

Cases that receive significant pretrial publicity are less likely to receive leniency and will not be treated as *normal homicides*.

Table 5   Media Attention and Felony Homicide Cases (1973–2005)

	Received Media Attention Before Trial		
	Yes	No	Total
Lenient Treatment	175 (498.8)	1,261 (937.2)	1,436
Harsh Treatment	699 (375.2)	61 (74.8)	1,080
Total	874	1,322	2,516

Chi² = 750.432; sig.= 0.00.

Hypothesis 4 must be accepted, as cross-tabulations show that lenient treatment is less likely in cases that realize significant pretrial publicity. *Normal homicides* are not well-publicized before trial.

Hypothesis 5

Cases involving firearms are more likely to receive leniency and be treated as *normal homicides*.

Table 6   Weapons Used in Oklahoma Homicides (1973–2005)

	Blunt Instrument	Firearm	Personal	Knife	Other	Total
Lenient Treatment	92	392	71	80	46	623
	(94.8)	*(383.1)*	*(73)*	*(92.6)*	*(42.1)*	
Harsh Treatment	34	1,155	228	294	124	1,893
	(34.2)	*(1,163.9)*	*(225)*	*(281.4)*	*(127.9)*	
Total	126	1,547	299	374	170	2,516

Chi^2 = 4.76; sig. = 0.445.

Hypothesis 5 must be rejected, as cross-tabulations show that lenient treatment is not linked to any specific weapon type and *normal homicides* are not linked to firearm type. The Chi-square value exceeds the critical value of 1.61 (at 1 df), but no clear indication exists as to where a systematic bias might be located.

Conclusions

The prosecutors and defense lawyers that were interviewed indicated that individuals (both offenders and victims) experience a simplification of their identities. Offenders' identities were diminished much in the same fashion that patients become their disease, developing the *master status* of "the lung cancer patient" or "the amputation" as opposed to being Mr. Jones or Ms. Smith within the normal institutionalized functioning of a hospital (Goffman 1961). Offenders in particular, undeserving as it were of an individual identity, were referred to as "the gang shooting" or "the domestic killing" while occupying a spot on the court docket in a given week. These identities, and their associated charges and sentences, were negotiated, usually without undue perspiration, by respective counsels, with a settlement that legally confirmed the *normalness* of the crime and criminal. Analyses (table 2) show that the incidence of leniency (or harshness) was not systematically connected to the presence of white victims. By contrast, for non-white offenders, leniency was systematically related to the non-white condition of their victims. Although prosecutors denied in their interviews that non-white offenders realized harsher treatments when their victims were white, analysis shows that assailing white victims precipitated more harsh punishments. Analysis of the data set indicated that non-whites' crimes would be more likely to be *normalized* if their victims were also non-white. Attorneys' beliefs that prior felony convictions posed a significant obstacle to leniency were substantiated by the quantitative data analysis. Overall, one of the strongest predictors of a *normal homicide* was a similarity of offender to victim in personal and social senses. From both the interviews of court officers (n = 16) and the data set (n = 2,516), it is clear that homicides across race/ethnic divisions offend the racial etiquette of those communities, while same-race homicides are treated as *normal.*

The only exception to a one-to-one correlation between attorney interviews and the quantitative examination of the state data set was the issue of weapon. Prosecutors and defense attorneys assumed that homicides involving firearms were more likely to be considered *normal.* The state data set did not bear out this assumption.

When asked about the fairness of bargaining pleas and sentences, both defense counsels and prosecutors defended the idea, saying "no justice would be possible if every case went to trial." This reasoning sets up what Garfinkel (1967) called *incorrigible propositions,* i.e., a continued belief in the face of objective contradictions. When follow-up interviews were conducted and interviewees were presented with the empirical finding that races of victims and offenders were key elements in the determination of leniency/harshness, they resisted the belief that some systematic bias was at work. Appropriately, defense attorneys resisted the idea that non-white offenders were *normalized* when their victims resembled them. Prosecutors in turn denied that they were tougher on the assailants of white victims, and less vigilant when non-whites were victimized. Both groups denied that a racial etiquette, prohibiting and systematically sanctioning interracial homicides, as well as *normalizing* homicides and offenders in same-race crimes, was at work in Oklahoma.

The data set confirmed the categories and types of crimes that afford negotiation, that is, men of color accused of assailing other men of color realized the highest probability of obtaining leniency and exercised significant power of choice in whether they would be offered a plea bargain or go to trial. The chances of receiving harsher penalties, a life sentence without the possibility of parole or death, were further decreased if the offender had no prior felony convictions.

In conclusion, the concepts of *normal defendant* and *normal homicide* are empirically verifiable in the case of Oklahoma, operating within a particular legal culture and social conditions that structure decision making and trial outcomes for the most serious of crimes—homicide.

References

Garfinkel, Harold. 1956. "Conditions of Successful Degradation Ceremonies." *American Journal Sociology* 61: 240–244.

———. 1967. "Some Rules of Correct Decision Making That Jurors Respect." Pp. 104–115 in *Studies in Ethnomethodology*. Englewood Cliffs, NJ: Prentice-Hall.

Goffman, Erving. 1961. *Asylums: Essays on the Social Situation of Mental Patients and Other Inmates*. New York: Anchor Books.

McCool, Steven. 2008. "In Oklahoma City Murder Trend is Hard to Spot." *The Oklahoman* 8 January, 3.

Radelet, Michael L. and Glenn L. Pierce. 1985. "Race and Prosecutorial Discretion in Homicide Cases." *Law & Society Rev.* 19: 587–621.

State of Maryland. 2000. *Capital Punishment in Maryland 1978–1987: A Report by the Maryland Public Defender on the Administration of Capital Punishment*. R. Paternoster, Principle Investigator.

Sudnow, David. 1965. "Normal Crimes: Sociological Features of the Penal Code in a Public Defender's Office." *Social Problems* 12: 255–276.

Questions to Consider

1. When an appellate court reverses a lower court's decision in a criminal matter, this new decision usually means that some ruling made against a defendant has been changed to favor the defendant. In approximately one-half of these cases, the prosecution still ends up obtaining some type of conviction against the defendant. Was this your understanding of how court reversals worked? If this was not your understanding, how did you arrive at your original opinion?

2. What type of attorney would you wish to represent you if you were charged with a crime? Does this answer depend on how much money you have? How does this affect your opinion about what type of attorney should be provided for others?

3. As you watch one of the many sensational jury trials on TV, you may see efforts to pick jury members who have heard or seen nothing about major political events. Do you think one has to be substantially ignorant about an issue in order to be unbiased? What would such a group of jurors be like? Would they really represent us? What do we potentially lose by selecting such a jury? Can there be bias not only when one is too close to an issue but also when one is too far from an issue?

4. As you read David Keys' article on plea bargaining, what elements of bias did you see entering into these decisions? If the prosecutor is the primary decision maker in these "bargains," which represent the vast majority of cases, to what extent is this individual even more powerful than a judge? To what extent can or should we fault defense attorneys in acceding to prosecutorial norms and decisions?

5. Originally, we asked juries, who used a collaborative decision-making model, to decide most of the factual and legal problems involved with courts. As we have become more judge centered in our courts, we have lost this collaborative decision making except in the highest appellate courts. Many judicial systems in Europe utilize multiple judges, both lawyers and nonlawyers, to decide cases. What does such a system offer that our system does not?

6. If depending on the multiplicity of a jury seems to be a better way to achieve justice than simply relying on one individual, what has happened as the power of the jury to make decisions has slowly eroded over the years?

Section VI
The Future of Courts
Thinking Outside the Lines

The final section focuses on two issues that potentially affect all of us. The first two articles talk about the ever-present issue of gender and how this fundamental difference is, or is not, being addressed by our courts. To what extent do women have a say in our court process, and are they being served equally? The next two articles substantially expand this underlying theme of ownership and service and look at recent trends that seem to show an increasing loss of ownership of the courts not only by the citizenry, but also by the professionals who have been charged with managing our courts.

Gender justice is a concept that reflects the democratic principle of broad participation in our societal decision making. Just as a variety of viewpoints are important in obtaining fair jury decisions, a variety of viewpoints are also important in achieving better overall justice from judicial decisions. Early studies indicate that including women's perspectives may not greatly change the outcome pattern of current court decisions; rather, the new and varied participatory styles of women may change the way courts conduct everyday business. New styles in conducting the everyday business of courts become important especially when considering the prevalence of gender bias in such everyday business. Studies in more than thirty states make it clear that gender bias is quite prevalent, an unsurprising result as court personnel share in the prevailing attitudes of the larger society. This raises the question of what it really means to be a woman professional within the court system. If such professionals are to be given power and discretion, what obligations do they have toward those whom they serve? To what extent can we expect more from court professionals other than a simple reflection of prevailing social biases? In addition, we are faced with the broader question of how we protect ourselves from abuses of power while giving judges the power and independence to do justice.

Democracy, which asks that citizens involve themselves in our societal decision making, requires that our citizenry be informed so that they can make appropriate decisions. However, a potentially problematic trend in our court process involves increasing secrecy and the steady acquisition of control over the courts by the executive branch of government.

John Gibeaut documents an increasingly pervasive secret justice system that allows litigants to use public courts, but to hide the process and outcome from public scrutiny. Such secrecy becomes problematic as public access to all aspects of our court system, either in person or through the media, has been an essential ingredient in holding courts responsible for their actions. The trend towards secrecy has accelerated since September of 2001, with a substantial increase in the executive branch's efforts to gain control of the court process, often through similar efforts at secrecy. Baker and Gregware detail efforts to limit public control of courts through the institution of secret searches and holding secret the location and identity of those detained by the executive. At the same time, professional power over courts has been reduced through the implementation of material-witness warrants and enemy combatant designations. Totally new courts, called military tribunals, are being set up under total executive control and without independent court professionals or juries.

To what extent do such controversial actions involve the courts in a larger political process? Answers to that question will also impact our central question: who does, and who should, own our courts? These are not abstract academic questions. They go to the core of our constitutional democratic system of governance, and to the system of justice on which that system depends.

23

Gender Bias in the Courts
A Review of the Literature

CRAIG HEMMENS, KRISTIN STROM, and ELICIA SCHLEGEL

In theory, all persons involved in court proceedings are supposed to be treated equitably. A number of states have conducted studies which indicate that in actuality men and women receive differential treatment in court. As is the case in many aspects of American society, women are most often victims of gender bias (Schafran 1990b; Washington 1989). Female litigants face an uphill battle in pursuing their cases in both civil and criminal courts. Gender bias can take several forms. Gender discrimination often affects domestic violence, divorce, and sexual assault cases. Gender bias can also affect everyday courtroom interactions and operations. Gender bias is harder to detect than in the past because it is more subtle, but it continues to exist (Belknap 1996; Moyer 1992).

In the 1980s, a program called the National Judicial Education to Promote Equality for Women and Men in the Courts (NJEP) was formed by the National Organization for Women Legal Defense and Education Fund, which then invited the National Association of Women Judges to become a cosponsor of the program (Wikler 1980; Schafran 1990a). The NJEP promoted the creation of task forces to study gender bias in the courts. By 1989 thirty states had established gender bias task forces (Schafran 1990a). State task forces were established by state bar association or state court administrative offices and funded largely through donations and research grants (Roberts and Knoebel 1989). In 1989 the National Conference on Gender

Reprinted with permission from *Sociological Imagination*, 35(1): 22–42 (1998).

Bias in the Courts was held in Virginia, and the results of the nine completed bias task force reports were made available for national dissemination. The majority of task force reports discovered gender bias in virtually every stage of the justice system (Schafran 1990b).

This article presents a comprehensive review of the state gender bias studies. While at least thirty states have conducted gender bias research, to date there has been no effort made to examine these studies in toto. Consequently these studies have been examined in isolation, without any effort to explore commonalties among the various states. This article attempts to fill this gap in the literature.

Defining Gender Bias

Before determining the impact of gender bias on the courts, the term "gender bias" must first be defined. There are many different definitions of gender bias, but all share common traits. Gender bias is "actions or attitudes that negatively impact an individual or group primarily because of gender" (Washington 1989:3). Gender bias occurs when decisions are made or actions taken based on stereotypes about men and women (Hawaii 1989). The Utah task force (1990) noted that stereotypes affect society's attitudes about the value of men's and women's work. Gender bias can also involve insensitivity towards certain aspects of men's and women's lives that are genuinely different and may require the inclusion of gender as a factor in decision making (Wisconsin 1991).

Bias can additionally be "intentional and reflect ill will" (California 1996:27). Intentional bias, according to the California report, is the easiest to understand but also the least likely to occur. Biased treatment can further be defined as differential treatment of the sexes in situations where gender should not be considered (Colorado 1990). Gender bias is often based on "misconceptions about the economic and social realities of women's and men's lives manifested in judicial decision and court interaction" (Texas 1994:13). One report defined gender bias as conduct which reflects attitudes and behavior based on stereotypical beliefs about the sexes' "true natures" and "proper roles" rather than independent evaluation of each individual's abilities, life experiences, and aspirations (Louisiana 1992:40).

Surprisingly, several of the state task force studies of gender bias do not explain what the term "gender bias" means. Failure to operationalize the term makes it difficult to determine what is meant by "gender bias."

Bias in Domestic Violence Cases

The state task force studies found that one of the areas in criminal justice where gender bias is most common is domestic violence cases. All of the state task force reports found that women are victims of domestic violence far more often than men. Ninety-eight percent of domestic violence victims are women (Nebraska 1994). Nationwide, 28% of female homicide victims are killed by former husbands or boyfriends, whereas only 5% of male homicide victims are killed by former wives or girlfriends (Wisconsin 1991). Domestic violence is the number one cause of physical injury to women in the United States (Utah 1990).

Gender biased treatment is often based on stereotypes about how domestic violence cases should be handled. Courtroom actors often believe that domestic violence is a private, family matter and should not be dealt with by the courts (Washington 1989). Domestic violence situations are often minimized relative to comparable incidents involving strangers (Utah 1990). In Massachusetts, juries expect more physical injuries to domestic violence victims than to victims of other violent crimes (Massachusetts 1989). In Maryland, 51% of the male attorneys and 68% of the female attorneys believed that judges sometimes failed to view domestic violence as a crime (Maryland 1989). The misconceptions that victims of domestic violence provoke the offender, or that the victim must like it or they would leave, are also a problem (Washington 1989). A state trial court judge commented, "I have difficulty finding where this defendant's [the husband] done anything wrong, other than slapping her [his wife]. Maybe that was justified" (Utah 1990:44). The Massachusetts study revealed that some victims report improper or irrelevant questions during court proceedings. Over three-fourths of the responding attorneys said judges sometimes allow questions as to what the victim did to provoke the battering. Comments made by judges included, "Why don't you get a divorce?" and "Why are you bothering the court with this problem?" (Massachusetts 1989:90).

Bias Towards Victims of Domestic Violence

Female victims of domestic violence encounter many problems when they enter the court system because of biased opinions about domestic violence. The California (1996) task force found that 53% of the male court personnel surveyed "agreed" or "strongly agreed" that declarations of abuse are often exaggerated. Only 26% of the female court personnel surveyed felt this was the case. Additionally, 40% of the men felt that domestic violence cases should be diverted or that counseling should be used rather than criminal prosecution, compared to only 21% of the women surveyed (California 1996).

Iowa's (1993) study found that 45% of the females were only "somewhat confident" or "not that confident" that they would be treated fairly by the court system if they were victims of domestic violence. Their fears appear justified by the Washington (1989) study, which found that 57% of the respondents believe that while police "rarely" or "never" handle domestic violence cases informally, and the perpetrator is usually arrested or cited, prosecutors "rarely" or "sometimes" prosecute domestic violence cases vigorously. Even when the offender is arrested it is unlikely he will spend any time in prison (Illinois 1990). In most cases, the guilty party is merely required to attend counseling sessions (Illinois 1990).

Prosecution When Victim Withdraws Complaint

Further problems in the prosecution of domestic violence cases are created when a victim withdraws her complaint. The Wisconsin (1991) task force found that when victims recant, 32% of the cases are dismissed, 39% of the cases are prosecuted, and 29% are diverted. Victim cooperation is viewed as essential to the prosecution, which often makes the victim responsible for the survival of the case (Minnesota 1989). Holding victims responsible, even indirectly, for the prosecution of a domestic violence case is completely contrary to the principles of the criminal justice system, according to the Minnesota (1989) task force.

Protection Orders

Female victims of domestic violence also have problems obtaining protection orders. The Nevada task force (1988) found that 43% of the attorneys and judges believed that seriously endangered victims of domestic violence are not always granted protection orders. In many cases women are given no assistance in filing protection orders and court personnel may even discourage women from obtaining protection orders (Nebraska 1994). The New Mexico task force (1990) found that 44% of the attorneys surveyed believe court personnel do not provide adequate assistance to women who attempt to get protection orders. This finding is significant because nearly a third of the service providers in the Washington (1989) survey said that victims "usually" or "frequently" had problems completing the paperwork required to obtain a protection order. The Michigan task force (1989) found that there may be a long delay between the granting of a protection order and the protection order becoming effective. The Missouri task force (1993) reported that many times a petitioner attends protection order proceedings underrepresented. Of the judges surveyed, almost half said a petitioner was seldom, if ever, represented by counsel when seeking a protection order (Missouri 1993). This lack of representation may affect the chances of success for female litigants.

Enforcement of Protection Orders

Even when a victim of domestic violence can obtain a protection order, there is no guarantee it will be enforced. According to the Washington (1989) study, 45% of the respondents "usually" or "frequently" violate the "no contact" provisions of protection orders. In the Nebraska (1994) study, only 47% of the attorneys questioned said that misdemeanor violators of protection orders were sentenced to jail. Texas (1994) attorneys said that sanctions, including civil commitments, are only "rarely" or "sometimes" used when protection orders are violated. Maryland (1989) found victims of domestic violence had difficulty receiving protection during divorce proceedings. Although violence often escalates after a victim attempts to leave the batterer, 4 of 10 judges responded that protection order petitions are sometimes or always rejected when other domestic relations cases are pending (Maryland 1989).

Another problem is the inadequate enforcement of protection orders. Police fail to arrest, district attorneys fail to prosecute, and judges fail to adequately punish men who commit crimes against their spouses or violate court orders (Louisiana 1992). In Missouri, 65% of the female attorneys and 64% of the male attorneys believe judges are reluctant to use criminal sanctions in domestic violence cases. In one example, a judge fined a woman $500 and sentenced her to two years probation for shoplifting cigarettes and in the next case only fined a husband $35 for breaking his wife's nose by kicking her in the face (Missouri 1993). This implied to many attorneys that domestic violence cases are not accorded high priority in Missouri courtrooms.

Mutual Protection Orders

Mutual orders for protection imply that both parties are abusive, even when there is no proof of wrongdoing by the petitioner (Michigan 1989). Granting mutual orders for protection can also create problems because police often arrest both parties when called to enforce the protection orders even when only one of them is abusive (Minnesota 1989). The issuing of mutual protection orders also encourages the idea that victims are responsible for their abuse. Granting mutual protection orders proves to women that the court is not serious about holding the abuser accountable for his behavior (Minnesota 1989). Victims of domestic violence who have not committed acts of violence are embarrassed and confused by mutual protection orders (California 1996).

A further problem with the issuance of protection orders is that the majority of judges grant mutual protection orders, even when only one party petitioned for the order (Nebraska 1994). The Texas (1994) task force found comparable results. Approximately 80% of the lawyers surveyed said that mutual protection orders were issued even when only one party had presented evidence of abuse. The Missouri task force (1993) reported that 64% of the female attorneys and 48% of the male attorneys agreed that the issuance of mutual protection orders without evidence of joint fault was at least sometimes the practice in Missouri courts.

Bias in Sexual Assault Cases

Another area in which women experience bias is sexual assault. Much like domestic violence, there are many misconceptions about sexual assault. A study of 1,500 Rhode Island junior high school students found some surprising results about their understanding of sexual assault. The students were asked when a man was justified in having sexual intercourse with a woman who did not consent. Fifty-seven percent of the boys and 39% of the girls said the act was justified if the woman allowed the man to touch her above the waist. Sixty-five percent of the boys and 47% of the girls said that rape was acceptable if the two had a long-term dating relationship. Finally, 24% of the boys and 16% of the girls said the act was reasonable if the man had spent a lot of money on the date (Rhode Island 1987). Although these opinions do not necessarily reflect the attitudes of criminal justice professionals, they do indicate that, among certain segments of the public at least, there is a lack of sensitivity to gender equality issues.

Bias Against Victims of Sexual Assault

Stereotypes about females being responsible for their victimization permeate the criminal justice system, reflecting larger societal perceptions (Belknap 1996). Attitudes of criminal justice personnel often affect whether or not a victim reports sexual assault. As a result of biased attitudes, women seldom report sexual assault (Washington 1989). The misconception that sexual assaults are crimes of passion, not violence, often leads to bias against sexual assault victims (Michigan 1989). As one judge remarked: "Rape is simply a case of poor salesmanship" (Minnesota 1989:894). The New Mexico (1990) task force survey found that 30% of the males and 50% of the females believe that judges sometimes believe that women invited sexual assault by their appearance or behavior.

The main reasons why women do not report sexual assault, according to the Texas (1994) task force report, are fear that the police either will not believe the victim or will blame the victim for the assault. Victims of sexual assault often are not considered believable by criminal justice workers. Half of the female attorneys surveyed in Texas reported that police officers "sometimes" or "frequently" accord less credibility to victims of sexual assault than to victims of other types of assaults (Texas 1994). Forty percent of the female lawyers felt that judges and prosecutors also believe that sexual assault victims are less credible (Texas 1994). Police may feel that they are doing other criminal justice agencies a favor by making judgments about a victim's credibility (Utah 1990).

The Massachusetts task force (1989) also reported bias against sexual assault victims by court employees and courtroom actors. Of the responding district attorneys and public defenders, 47% believe that juries accord less credibility to sexual assault victims than victims of other felonies. Sixty-four percent of these attorneys agreed that juries are less likely to convict if the defendant does not have any physical injuries (Massachusetts 1989). Almost three-fourths of the attorneys and 63% of the judges surveyed in one state agreed that gender stereotypes are commonly used to discredit victims of sexual assault cases (Vermont 1991).

Connecticut (1991) reported that 26% of the responding judges believed that a woman's character and past sexual behavior were relevant to the sexual assault charges to determine the seriousness of the charges. Thirteen percent of the judges believe that provocative dress or the actions of the victim could have provoked the attack (Connecticut 1991). The Washington (1989) task force found that 24% of the judges surveyed believe that victim attire or behavior "sometimes" or "frequently" precipitates sexual attacks. This finding is rather ironic, because rape by definition is forced or coerced sexual intercourse (Klotter 1994).

Prior Relationship with the Perpetrator

The predominant cultural stereotype of "real rape" remains the violent stranger hidden in the shadows (Minnesota 1989). However, one-third of all reported rapes do not fit this stereotype (New Mexico 1990). Sexual assaults are most often committed by family members, friends, coworkers, employers, neighbors, or other acquaintances (Minnesota 1989). These "acquaintance" rapes are often considered less serious than "real" rapes by the criminal justice system. In the Washington (1989) survey, 68% of the attorneys indicated that they believe judges give shorter sentences in acquaintance rape cases. The Nebraska task force (1994) had similar findings. Eighty-three percent of the attorneys surveyed said that "date rape" defendants receive lighter sentences than "stranger rape" defendants. Sixty-six percent of the female attorneys and 40% of the male attorneys surveyed in Colorado (1990) felt that judges inappropriately reduce charges in acquaintance rape cases on some occasions. Seventy-two percent of the attorneys questioned in the Utah (1990) survey said that conviction is "always" or "often" less likely when the victim knew the defendant. Attorneys in the Texas (1994) survey felt that in sexual assault cases involving acquaintances, the offenders receive more lenient sentences than when the victim and assailant were strangers.

The Nebraska task force (1994) found that 85% of the female attorneys believe bail is set lower in cases where the parties know one another. Police are also more likely to take sexual assaults seriously when they are committed by a stranger (Texas 1994). Attitudes regarding the victim's relationship to the offender are significant because 80% of sexual assaults are perpetrated by someone known to the victim (Nebraska 1994).

Ninety percent of the judges surveyed in Missouri (1993) believe juries are less likely to convict in a sexual assault case in which the victim has been sexually active. Eighty-one percent of the judges, 87% of the female attorneys, and 85% of the male attorneys believe that acquaintance rape offenders receive shorter sentences than offenders who had no prior relationship with the victim (Missouri 1993). Similarly, in the state of Vermont (1991), 78% of the attorneys and 47% of the judges believe shorter sentences are given to offenders who had a prior relationship with the victim.

Treatment of a Victim Who Reports a Rape

If a woman decides to report her rape she may face the possibility of being re-victimized by the courts. In the Texas (1994) survey, 37% of the male judges, compared to only 8% of the female judges, agreed that the victim's sexual history is relevant to the issue of her consent. A woman who does not conform to society's expectation that she be chaste and virginal must have been asking to be raped (Michigan 1989). Ninety-two percent of the female attorneys and 76% of the male attorneys in the Nebraska (1994) survey believe that defense attorneys use stereotypes such as "women say no when they mean yes" to discredit victims.

In Nebraska (1994), 62% of the attorneys and 60% of the judges responded that during trial "date rape" victims are questioned beyond what is necessary to present a consent defense. Minnesota (1989) found that 75% of the attorneys surveyed felt defense attorneys "always," "often," or "sometimes" used stereotypes to discount sexual assault victims. The attorney may badger or harass the victim witness (Michigan 1989). When asked how often judges intervene when there is improper questioning about the victim's sexual history, 33% of the attorneys surveyed in Colorado (1990) felt that judges "never" or "almost never" intervene.

Bias in Divorce Cases

Divorce cases are, for obvious reasons, an area in which the possibility of gender bias looms large. There are several issues which arise, including alimony, division of property, child support, and child custody. All state task force reports are unanimous in their findings that women suffer from gender bias in all areas of divorce cases. Several studies also found that men suffer from gender bias in regard to child custody issues.

Alimony Awards

A major issue in divorce cases is whether to grant alimony. Popular belief about divorce is that men are generally the most affected economically. Many divorced men claim that their ex-spouse received the majority of their personal belongings and was awarded a substantial amount of alimony (New York 1986). Research shows that this perception is false. The Georgia (1992) study concluded that it is women who experience a dramatic decrease in their standard of living following a divorce. This is especially true when the woman is a homemaker and has put aside further education and training for marriage. When the marriage ends in divorce, the woman is forced to enter a work force where her earning capacity is extremely low (New York 1986). The Nebraska (1994) survey found that 55% of the attorneys believed that judges are more likely to sacrifice the current lifestyle of the wife when determining the amount of maintenance awards. The Florida (1990) survey found that men were routinely awarded over half of the marital assets, even when women were awarded custody.

The failure of the courts to provide adequate support has resulted in significant economic variation between former husbands and wives which greatly disadvantages women (Iowa 1993). The average awards issued to women in one state are completely insufficient and provide a standard of living close to the poverty line (California 1996). In another state, fathers experienced a 73% *increase* in their standard of living after a divorce, while the wives who retained custody of the children experienced a 32% *decrease* in theirs (Utah 1990).

Part of the problem is due to the fact that judges do not have a realistic understanding of the future earnings of a homemaker who has not worked outside of the home for a significant amount of time (Nebraska 1994). Another reason for this problem is the lack of enforcement of alimony awards may result in a long-term reduction in a woman's standard of living (New Mexico 1990). The Missouri task force (1993) also found that maintenance or alimony is detrimental to custodial women. Their research found that women with children following a divorce are the fastest growing poverty group. The percentage of children in poverty almost doubles from

19% to 36% after their family splits up. Other research found indicated that judges often decide the amount of alimony based on the amount the ex-husband could afford without altering his standard of living.

In Maryland (1989) 30% of the judges, 20% of the male attorneys and 44% of the female attorneys responded that upholding the husband's current lifestyle is often or always a deciding factor when deciding the amount of alimony awarded. Half of the female attorneys and 20% of the male attorneys in another state believe judges seldom or never have a realistic understanding of the likely future earnings of a longtime homemaker (Missouri 1993). Without a realistic understanding of a woman's earning capacity, a judge is unable to grant an appropriate alimony settlement. The District of Columbia (1992) report found that 35% of the attorneys believe judges rarely or never grant sufficient alimony awards.

Division of Marital Property

The division of marital property is an area where most would believe women generally benefit. Such is not the case, however. A majority of the attorneys surveyed in Nebraska (1994) felt that judges believe husbands are entitled to a greater share of the marital property when the wife's primary contribution has been that of a homemaker. This finding reflects the notion that "whoever earns it, owns it" and neglects the contribution female homemakers provide (Nebraska 1994). In New Mexico (1990) 63% of survey respondents felt the division of property generally results in a long-term reduction in the standard of living for women but not for men. Forty percent of the female attorneys in Hawaii believe women are at a disadvantage in division of property, as compared with only 23% of the male attorneys (Hawaii 1989). Property division and alimony are often treated as a package, which also creates problems for women (Colorado 1990).

Child Support Awards

Women also face problems with child support awards. While 90% of children in divorced families reside with their mother (Kentucky 1992), only 45% of the lawyers surveyed in Washington (1989) believe that child support awards realistically reflect the cost of raising children. The Nebraska (1994) study found that 37% of the attorneys felt that judges' awards for child support "rarely" or "never" reflect the costs of actual child rearing.

Judges also have a tendency to follow child support guidelines that do not adequately reflect the needs of children (Minnesota 1989). Judges rarely give mothers more money than the guidelines recommend. If the judge deviates from the guidelines at all, it is usually to grant less child support than is suggested (Minnesota 1989). This practice is problematic because child support guidelines were designed to be the floor for determining support levels, not the ceiling (Minnesota 1989). Following child support guidelines "often" or "always" leads to a reduced standard of living for women and children after a divorce, according to 49% of respondents in the New Mexico (1990) survey.

Enforcement of Child Support

Even when suitable child support is awarded, it may not be enforced by the courts. In 1990, the Census Bureau reported only 44% of children nationally receive the court-ordered child support payments (Vermont 1991). Failure to pay child support is one of the most blatant violations of court orders (California 1996). In Minnesota (1989) child support agencies said they collect on their cases about 40% of the time. In Nebraska (1994) only 15% of the child support payments due were collected. Many fathers do not pay child support because they receive no punishment from the court system. The Washington (1989) task force found that half of the lawyers surveyed said judges "never" use jail as a sentence for failure to pay child support. However, 81% of attorneys in the Nebraska (1994) survey said that judges are willing to use the court's contempt powers to enforce child support. The majority of attorneys (73%) also believe judges are willing to jail non-payers of child support, which indicates that some states are willing to use sanctions to enforce child support awards (Nebraska 1994). Although 51% of the judges in Maryland reported entering earnings withholdings orders on delinquent child support payments, 62% of the female attorneys and 56% of the male attorneys regarded this statement as rarely or never true (Maryland 1989).

Massachusetts has used wage assignments to enforce support payments since 1986. Wage assignment involves deducting the child support payment directly from the non-custodial parent's paycheck (Massachusetts 1989). This procedure was later adopted as a model for national legislation. Several other states argued that in theory this is an effective measure, but too many judges fail to use it. Attorneys reported to the Kentucky task force (1992) that some judges do not use wage assignments because they fear doing so will jeopardize a man's job or embarrass him in front of his coworkers.

Child Support as a Bargaining Chip

An additional problem with child support is that it is often used as a bargaining chip in custody hearings. "Many fathers threaten a custody battle (even though they do not want custody) to browbeat their wives on economic issues—i.e., accept low support or I'll go after custody. Unhappily, it works. Women feel so powerless and frightened, they will allow their ex-husbands to reduce them and their children to poverty, just to preserve custody of their children" (Utah 1990:25). Sixty-one percent of the lawyers and 71% of the judges in the Washington (1989) survey believe that women "occasionally" or "usually" accept lower child support.

Bias Against Courtroom Actors

Female court employees and lawyers also suffer from gender bias, often at the hands of other courtroom actors. The Nevada task force summarizes the existence of gender bias in the courts very well: " . . . from time to time male judges, lawyers, and other participants in the legal system have conducted themselves in a manner that is offensive and intolerable to women participants in the legal system" (Nevada 1988:67). Seventy-four percent of the lawyers and 54% of the judges surveyed in Washington believe that gender bias is present in the courts (Washington 1989). Between 20% and 40% of respondents perceived bias in some form in Hawaii's legal system (Hawaii 1989). The perception of the existence of bias is clearly related to gender, however. Forty-four percent of the female lawyers as compared to only 11% of the male attorneys surveyed in Texas believe that bias is widespread (Texas 1994). The Colorado task force (1990) found similar results. Four of ten of the female attorneys compared to just 6% of the male attorneys felt that bias was widespread. The Nebraska task force (1994) found that 48% of the male attorneys surveyed believe bias was nonexistent in the courts, while only 3% of the female attorneys felt this was the case. Clearly, males and females in the courts have different opinions about the existence of bias in the courts.

Bias Against Female Attorneys

Females working in the courts perceive much more gender bias than male actors do (Colorado 1990). Bias was most often reported by female attorneys (Nebraska 1994). Eighty-two percent of the female attorneys in Texas reported that they experienced biased behavior from opposing counsel, and 64% experienced bias from male judges (Texas 1994). Rhode Island (1987) identified male attorneys as being responsible for the majority of discrimination against women in the courtroom. Male attorneys were identified as being responsible 45% of the time, while judges were identified 31% of the time. In the Missouri task force survey (1993), 42% of the female attorneys admitted hearing demeaning remarks about women by judges, either in the courtroom or in chambers (1993). Female attorneys in New Jersey reported similar experiences. Seventy-six percent of the female attorneys reported being treated disadvantageously by judges because of their gender. Eighty-six percent of the female attorneys and 49% of the male attorneys reported incidents of discriminatory treatment of female attorneys by their fellow male attorneys in the courtroom (New Jersey 1984).

Maryland (1989) surveyed attorneys on the different types of gender bias behavior they had observed. Fifty-seven percent of the female attorneys reported judges giving less credibility to the statements of female attorneys than statements of male attorneys. Fifty-six percent of the female attorneys, compared to 20% of the male attorneys, were repeatedly asked by judges if they are attorneys. Fifty-four percent of the female attorneys have experienced comments about their personal appearance. In one case, a female attorney was assigned to an adoption case. When she entered the courtroom the judge looked at her and said: "They don't make the stork like they used to!" (Maryland 1989).

Not only are male attorneys not exposed to the types of gender bias that female attorneys report, they are often not even aware that it exists (Ninth Circuit 1993). As noted above, male lawyers consistently report fewer observations of gender bias than female lawyers (Kansas 1992). A comment from one male attorney is instructive: "This sounds to me like someone fishing for problems that don't exist. In eleven years, I have never seen a judge treat a woman with less respect than a man" (Utah 1990:94).

The most common form of gender bias mentioned was the practice of judges and attorneys addressing female attorneys in a demeaning manner (Kansas 1992). Many females reported that judges would refer to them by their first name during court procedures while addressing male attorneys by their formal names. Many female attorneys reported being addressed by familiar terms such as "sweetie," "little lady lawyer," "pretty eyes," and "dear" (Michigan 1989:927). Female attorneys in Missouri reported being addressed by judges in familiar terms twice as often as male attorneys (Missouri 1993). Fifty percent of the female attorneys in Nebraska said they were addressed in familiar terms by attorneys (Nebraska 1994). The New Mexico task force (1990) found that 48% of the female attorneys said that counsel sometimes addressed females in an inappropriate manner while only 12% of the male attorneys said this sometimes happened.

Another common form of gender bias suffered by female attorneys is sexist remarks or jokes (New Hampshire 1988). When asked if inappropriate jokes about their sex had been made in their presence, 21% of the female attorneys in the Iowa survey reported that it had occurred on many occasions, while only 1% of the male attorneys said it occurred frequently (Iowa 1993). Half of the female lawyers surveyed in California said that they had heard jokes or remarks demeaning to women from fellow attorneys. In addition, 45% of the females indicated that they had heard judges make such comments at least occasionally (California 1996).

Females are also often asked whether or not they are attorneys while men are not questioned (Nebraska 1994). Seventy percent of the female attorneys responding to the Minnesota (1989) survey said they were sometimes asked if they are attorneys. "When I accompany a senior partner to court, I am often asked if I am his daughter (by attorneys, judges), I am not assumed to be a competent associate attorney working on a case." (Utah 1990:97). Female attorneys may also endure comments about their personal appearance (Washington 1989). Just over half of the female attorneys in the Nebraska survey responded that comments had been made about their personal appearance by other attorneys. Further, female attorneys may experience bias if they attempt to act aggressively (Nebraska 1994). "I have found that if I don't immediately agree to something the other side wants, they consider me a 'bitch' and difficult to work with. . . . If a man says no to a demand, he is being an aggressive litigator" (Nebraska 1994:9).

Gender bias also often affects the hiring and promotion of female attorneys (Kansas 1992). Thirty-five percent of the females surveyed in New Mexico felt that women have trouble being hired, while only 10% of the male respondents felt that females have trouble getting hired (New Mexico 1990). California (1996) found that 62% of the female attorneys believed they had less chance for advancement than men and 96% of the females said they had more trouble balancing work and family than male attorneys. Over half the women surveyed by the Ninth Circuit Court task force believe that promotion is tilted in men's favor (Ninth Circuit 1993). The types of law female attorneys practice may reflect bias as well. Judges may believe that capital cases or major drug cases are too difficult for female attorneys. Unfortunately, because women are rarely involved in major cases, it is difficult for them to establish a reputation as being a good criminal attorney (Michigan 1989).

Female attorneys are also paid less than male lawyers for the same work. "It is my perception that the partners believe that women will work at least as hard as men and will accept lower salaries" (Ninth Circuit 1993:38). The New Mexico task force (1990) found that the average mean income of male lawyers was always higher than that of female attorneys in similar types of practices. After twenty years in practice male lawyers can expect to earn, on average, $92,000 while female attorneys make approximately $66,100 a year (New Mexico 1990). Female lawyers, on average, earn $100 less per case than male attorneys (Michigan 1989).

Bias Against Female Judges

Female attorneys are not the only actors in the court system that experience bias. Many female judges also report encountering gender bias. Several judges in the Minnesota survey reported being addressed in familiar terms and even referred to by their first names by court personnel, bailiffs, and janitors (Minnesota 1989). Half of the female judges responding to the Colorado (1990) survey said that they were sometimes treated with less respect by counsel. Additionally, 35% of the female judges surveyed in Colorado said they were treated with less respect than their male counterparts (Colorado 1990). "Difficult white male judges are referred to as 'irascible' while female judges are characterized as 'bitches'" (Michigan 1989:87).

The most common gender bias perceived by female judges was the hiring practices and placement of female judges (New Hampshire 1988). Women are greatly underrepresented on the bench. The Minnesota task force (1989) found that women made up only 10% of the state's judiciary. In Louisiana (1992), the task force found that of 525 judicial appointments made in three years, women received only 15% of the available appointments. In Vermont, in 1991, only 5 out of the 33 appointed judges were women. In Missouri, 75% of the male attorneys and judges, and 96% of the female attorneys felt that gender was a significant factor in judicial nominations. Eighty-four percent of the female attorneys and 36% of the male attorneys believe that a court will not nominate another female or minority member if one has already been selected.

Female judicial applicants are sometimes asked inappropriate questions by male judicial commission members (Vermont 1991). The female applicants may be asked who will care for their children if they are appointed or how they would handle their job if they had children (Nebraska 1994). Twelve percent of the female attorneys responding to the Iowa survey indicated they had been asked during interviews for judgeships if they intended to have children, while none of the male attorneys said they had been asked that question (Iowa 1993).

Do Judges Intervene to Stop Biased Behavior?

Because gender bias is present in the courts it is important to know how often judges intervene to stop the behavior. Judges have a great deal of influence on the conduct of courtroom actors. Judges who intervene when bias occurs have a lasting impression and may encourage others to follow suit (Michigan 1989). Unfortunately, 81% of the females and 62% of the males surveyed in Texas said that male judges "rarely" or "never" intervene when court personnel make comments demeaning to women (Texas 1994).

Only 9% of the female attorneys in the New Mexico survey said judges intervene to correct biased conduct. The majority of attorneys (both male and female) surveyed by the Colorado task force (1990) felt that judges "rarely" or "never" intercede when biased behavior takes place. However, the majority of judges felt they "always" or "almost always" reprimand counsel or court personnel for behaving in a manner demeaning to women (Colorado 1990). A survey in New Jersey (1984) found that only 18% of the female attorneys and 7% of the male attorneys have seen judges intervene to correct discriminatory behavior. According to the Vermont task force (1991), 70% of the female attorneys surveyed reported that judges rarely, if ever, intervene in the demeaning or differential treatment of women.

The Effect of Gender Bias on Case Outcome

When judges do not attempt to stop bias in the courtroom the case may be affected by it. Twenty-five percent of the females and 8% of the males responding to the New Mexico survey felt that gender bias does affect the outcome of the case (New Mexico 1990). Fifty-nine percent of the female attorneys and 30% of the male attorneys surveyed in Texas believe that the gender of the attorney affects case outcome (Texas 1994). Over one-third of the female attorneys responding to the Colorado survey believe that male judges assign more weight to arguments made by male attorneys (Colorado 1990).

Bias Against Men

Bias against men does exist in the courts. However, the extent to which men experience biased behavior is not clear. Two areas in which there is evidence that men routinely suffer from gender bias are child custody cases and criminal sentencing (Daly 1987; Price & Sokoloff 1995).

Child Custody

The area in which men most often experience gender bias is child custody. A father who wants to pursue custody faces stereotypes about who should raise children. The Georgia (1991) task force collected research on gender bias in child custody hearings. The data indicated that, in most cases, mothers are given the sole custody of their children after a divorce. In the majority of cases women receive sole (61%) or joint (27%) custody of their children, while fathers receive sole custody only 13% of the time according to the Washington (1989) survey. The Nebraska (1994) task force found that half of the attorneys surveyed felt judges assume that children belong with their mothers. In Iowa's survey an even greater percentage (72%) of attorneys said judges presume mothers should receive custody (Iowa 1993). A judge in a custody dispute was quoted as saying, "I don't buy that the father is better for a 22-month old girl than the mother. And I can't swallow it. I'm going to vomit on it. I can't handle it" (Michigan 1989:62). Less than one-fourth of the attorneys in the Texas (1994) survey believe judges give serious consideration to fathers who seek custody. Thirty percent of the attorneys in Nebraska (1994) said they discourage fathers from seeking custody because they believe judges will not give the father's petition fair consideration.

The Georgia (1991) study found several biased attitudes which influence a judge's custody decision. These include the belief that a father is not as good a parent as the mother, and the belief that children need to be with their mothers. Missouri (1993) found that 86% of the female and 94% of the male attorneys felt that judges indicated, by action or statement, that young children should be with the mother. The Maryland task force (1989) reported similar assumptions in 49% of judges, 79% of female attorneys, and 95% of male attorneys.

Sentencing

Another area in which bias against men is perceived to exist is criminal sentencing (Curran 1983; Daly 1987). Jail sentences are imposed less often on women, and when women are sent to jail they serve less time than men (Minnesota 1989). However, women are usually convicted of property crimes, which are considered less serious than crimes against persons under sentencing guidelines (Minnesota 1989). Approximately 103,000 men and 7,000 women were convicted of violent felonies in 1986 (Wisconsin 1991). The smaller number of women in prison is explained by the distribution of offenses (Minnesota 1989). Defendants with similar criminal histories, charged with similar crimes, receive like sentences, regardless of gender (New Mexico 1990).

Although many of the studies found women's and men's sentences to be comparable, the perception exists that women receive lighter sentences. Sixty-three percent of the judges questioned in the Texas (1994) survey believe men are "frequently" treated more harshly by the criminal justice system than women. Forty-two percent of the attorneys in the Texas (1994) survey believe women receive lighter sentences than men convicted of similar crimes. The largest area of biased sentencing appears to be probation (New Mexico 1990). Seventy-nine percent of respondents in the New Mexico (1990) survey believe women are more likely to receive probation than men. Judges in the Washington (1989) study said they do consider gender related issues in sentencing. For example, judges are reluctant to sentence women with small children to prison (Washington 1989).

Conclusion

Clearly women experience gender bias in the courts of this country. While a review of the state task force reports makes the extent and prevalence of the problem clear, the solution is not so obvious to determine or easy to achieve. A major problem in dealing with gender bias is that it is not a practice created by the court system. Rather, it is a reflection of prevailing attitudes in society. The implication of gender bias is that women are still not being viewed as equal to their male counterparts. Although current laws and affirmative action plans have furthered women's equality, they cannot by themselves change the attitudes of individuals. It is the individual attitudes that require change if gender bias is to be eradicated.

One of the most important recommendations for change mentioned by all the studies is education. It is extremely important that courtroom actors develop a better understanding of how gender bias affects the justice system. Another recommendation was extending greater sensitivity to victims of sexual assault and domestic violence. These two crimes are particularly degrading to victims and must be handled with a great deal of compassion. Additionally, judges must develop a better understanding of economic issues facing women after a divorce.

The task force reports on gender bias provide strong evidence that gender bias exists in all aspects of the court system, and in virtually all courts. The reports also indicate that there is a wide variation in the perception of the existence of bias, depending on the gender of the observer. Females perceive much more bias than do males. While it is possible that this is due to females being overly sensitive to the issue, the evidence suggests it is the males who misperceive the situation. Remedying gender bias requires convincing those most often guilty of it that they are acting in a biased fashion. If this can be accomplished, a major step will have been taken.

Task Force Reports

California. 1990. *Achieving Equal Justice for Women and Men in the Courts: The Draft Report of the Judicial Advisory Committee on Gender Bias in the Courts.*

Colorado. 1990. *Colorado Supreme Court Task Force on Women in the Courts, Gender and Justice in the Colorado Courts.*

Connecticut. 1991. *Gender, Justice and the Courts: Report of the Connecticut Task Force.*

District of Columbia. 1992. *District of Columbia Courts Final Report on Racial and Ethnic Bias and Task Force on Gender Bias in the Courts.*

Florida. 1990. *Report of the Florida Supreme Court Gender Bias Study Commission.*

Georgia. 1991. *Gender and Justice in the Court: A Report to the Supreme Court of Georgia by the Commission on Gender Bias in the Justice System.*

Hawaii. 1989. *Achieving Gender Fairness: Designing A Plan to Address Gender Bias in Hawaii's Legal System.*

Illinois. 1990. *The 1990 Report of the Illinois Task Force on Gender Bias in the Courts.*

Iowa. 1993. *Final Report of the Equality in the Courts Task Force.*

Kansas. 1992. *Report of the Kansas Bar Association Task Force on the Status of Women in the Profession.*

Kentucky. 1992. *Kentucky Taskforce on Gender Fairness in the Courts: Equal Justice for Women and Men.*

Louisiana. 1992. *Louisiana Task Force on Women in the Courts: Final Report.*

Maryland. 1989. *Report of the Special Joint Committee on Gender Bias in the Courts.*

Massachusetts. 1989. *Gender Bias Study of the Court System in Massachusetts.*

Michigan. 1989. *Final Report of the Michigan Supreme Court Task Force on Gender Issues in the Courts.*

Minnesota. 1989. *Minnesota Supreme Court Task Force for Gender Fairness in the Courts.*

Missouri. 1993. *Report of the Missouri Task Force on Gender and Justice.*

Nebraska. 1994. *Nebraska Supreme Court Task Force on Gender Fairness in the Courts, Final Report.*

Nevada. 1988. *Justice for Women: First Report of the Nevada Supreme Court Task Force on Gender Bias in the Courts.*

New Hampshire. 1988. *Report of the New Hampshire Bar Association Task Force on Women in the Bar.*

New Jersey. 1986. *Second Report of the New Jersey Supreme Court Task Force on Women in the Courts.*

New Mexico. 1990. *Final Report of the New Mexico State Bar Task Force on Women and the Legal Profession.*

New York. 1986. *Report of the New York Task Force on Women in the Courts.*

Ninth Circuit. 1993. *The Effects of Gender in the Federal Courts: The Final Report of the Ninth Circuit Gender Bias Task Force.*

Rhode Island. 1987. *The Final Report of the Rhode Island Committee on Women in the Courts: A Report on Gender Bias.*

Texas. 1994. *The Gender Bias Task Force of Texas Final Report.*

Utah. 1990. *Utah Task Force on Gender and Justice: Report to the Utah Judicial Council.*

Vermont. 1990. *Gender and Justice: Report of the Vermont Task Force on Gender Bias in the Legal System.*

Washington. 1989. *Washington State Task Force on Gender and Justice in the Courts.*

Wisconsin. 1991. *Wisconsin Equal Justice Task Force Final Report.*

References

Belknap, J. 1996. *The Invisible Woman: Gender, Crime, and Justice.* Cincinnati: Wadsworth.

Curran, D. 1983. "Judicial Discretion and Defendant's Sex." *Criminology* 21:4158.

Daly, K. 1987. "Discrimination in the Criminal Courts: Family Gender, and the Problem of Equal Treatment." *Social Forces* 66:152–175.

Klotter, J. 1994. *Criminal Law.* Cincinnati: Anderson.

Moyer, I. L. 1992. *The Changing Roles of Women in the Criminal Justice System: Offenders, Victims, and Professionals.* Prospect Heights, IL: Waveland Press.

Price, B. R., and N. S. Sokoloff. 1995. *The Criminal Justice System and Women: Offenders, Victims, and Workers.* New York: McGraw-Hill.

Roberts, A. and W. Knoebel 1989. "National Conference on Gender Bias in the Courts." *State Court Journal* 13:12–21.

Schafran, L. H. 1990a. "Overwhelming Evidence: Reports on Gender Bias in the Courts." *Trial* 26:28–35.

Schafran, L H. 1990b. "Gender and Justice: Florida and the Nation." *Florida Law Review* 42:181–207.

Wikler, N. J. 1980. "On the Judicial Agenda for the 80s: Equal Treatment for Men and Women in the Courts." *Judicature* 64:202–209.

24

Making a Difference
An Overview of Gender and the Courts

SUSAN LENTZ

Introduction

In our complex society and legal system, the issue of gender and the courts is often controversial. Our understanding of sex and gender roles all impact expectations and behaviors in law and the courts. In turn, law itself has had a significant impact on such expectations. The constitutional debate regarding rights and statutes promoting equality has tackled discrimination, stereotypes, and bias. Bias may be for or against, well intentioned or bigoted, purposeful or quite unconscious (e.g., Hemmens et al., 2009). However, defining equality is not a simple matter. At its heart perhaps is our understanding of difference. In regard to gender, this understanding is not only an issue about the degree to which men and women differ, but the degree to which they appropriately and legally may be treated differently. From women's first entry into the legal profession, gender difference has been debated regarding bias in the law and legal system and, most significantly, the probable impacts of women's presence in the legal profession and on the bench.

In order to better understand the issues of gender and the courts today, this chapter is divided into several sections. First, it is essential to introduce the long-standing debate regarding the roles of nature and nurture in defining gender. It is definitions of man and woman, their roles, characteristics, and differences, that historically have shaped women's and men's experiences in the world of work, government, and law. Historical background is provided in order to understand our present and envision the future, including women's entry into the public world, their progress, and the chal-

Written especially for *Courts and Justice*.

443

lenges of gender bias in the courts. From an overview of such issues, an introduction to feminist legal theory will set the stage for examining current issues and research regarding gender and the courts. For women in the courts, acknowledging difference may be critical to making a difference.

The Nature of Woman and Man

The nature-nurture debate regarding what is male and female and their appropriate roles in society has challenged and often perplexed philosophers, theologians, and scholars since ancient times. It is an appropriate starting point to note that the great thinkers who expounded on these issues in the past were, with few exceptions, male. Their debate is also an appropriate starting point for our understanding of gender in the courts, as historically women were largely excluded from public life, including the world of commerce and politics. As man ruled the state, so too was he largely defined as the head of the family. According to Law (1987: 24–25), "the male headed family—not the individual—was the basic unit of political interaction" at the founding of this country. She quoted historian Carl Degler that women were thought of as "supportive assistants—necessary to be sure, but not individuals in their own right" (25). Following the founding of this country, Kerber (1980: 152–53) observes that their place in the courts remained as plaintiffs, defendants, and witnesses—"recipients, rather than dispensers, of justice."

For political philosophers, from Aristotle to Rousseau, as well as many theologians, man was the natural ruler. The reasons given for the subordination of women were multifaceted, but focused on firm beliefs regarding woman's nature. According to Rousseau, "the disadvantages peculiar to woman . . . as they necessarily occasion intervals of inaction, this is sufficient reason for excluding them from this supreme authority" (in Agonito, 1977: 119). Although Rousseau does not further explain these disadvantages, monthly menstrual cycles and motherhood have been woman's particular burdens.

Beyond such biological burdens, women have been viewed as the weaker sex not only physically but also intellectually and emotionally. This too was seen to justify men's rule. In 1677, Dutch philosopher Benedict de Spinoza, in concluding his *Political Treatise,* directly asked the question "whether women are under men's authority by nature or institution? For if it has been by mere institution, then we had no reason compelling us to exclude women from government. But if we consult experience itself, we shall find the origin of it is in their weakness." De Spinoza went on to assert that if women and men were equal, there would be nations where both sexes ruled or where men were ruled by women. Holding that no such nation could be found, he concluded "that women have not by nature equal right with men" (in Balz, 1937: 196).

That women had largely been denied education and, thus, opportunities outside the home was deemed largely irrelevant. That women were taught to be good wives and mothers was simply seen as reinforcing their natural roles. Moreover, as women were traditionally considered to be less evolved than men, their nature was more physical, not of the soul but of the body (e.g., Aristotle, Darwin). From this followed a need to control women's sexuality. For example, Rousseau argued that man's rule in the family was necessary so that he would know that his children were truly his (in Agonito, 1977: 119). Teaching women modesty and a disdain for sex itself was, thus, also more than just a matter of nature (e.g., Hume, in Agonito, 1977).

During the nineteenth century, when many women were beginning to demand full citizenship and participation in the public world of commerce, politics, and the courts, such beliefs persisted. Charles Darwin, writing on the origin of sexual differences in his *Descent of Man*, also suggested that woman's nature destined her to inequality, noting that "the chief distinction in the intellectual powers of the two sexes is shewn by man's attaining a higher eminence, in whatever he takes up, than can woman—whether requiring deep thought, reason, or imagination" (in Agonito, 1977: 260). Yet, there were men who joined women in challenging their second-class status. English philosopher John Stuart Mill in *The Subjection of Women* wrote, "That the principle which regulates the existing social relations between the two sexes—the legal subordination of one sex to the other—is wrong in itself," an obstacle to human improvement, and "ought to be replaced by a principle of perfect equality, admitting no power or privilege on one side, nor disability on the other" (in Agonito, 1977: 225).

The Entry of Women Into the Public World of Law

Although there are records of women practicing law in the courts dating back to the seventeenth century, the first woman licensed as an attorney was admitted to the Iowa bar in 1869; the first black woman was admitted to practice in the District of Columbia in 1872 (Berkson, 1982). Quite simply, lawyers were expected to be male. In *Bradwell v. Illinois* (1872), the U.S. Supreme Court ruled that practicing law was not a privilege under the U.S. Constitution, and states could restrict licensure to males. Justice Bradley's concurring opinion added that the Creator had ordained woman's destiny in the home as a wife and mother (Murray, 1990). Beyond woman's domestic role, in 1875 the Wisconsin Supreme Court declared that a female candidate who was educationally and legally qualified to practice law was still unfit, reasoning, "The peculiar qualities of womanhood, its gentle graces, its quick sensibility, its tender susceptibility, its purity, its delicacy, its emotional impulse, its subordination of hard reason to sympathetic feeling are surely not qualifications for forensic strife" (in Eich, 1986).

In addition to the perceived natural disabilities of their sex, women, particularly married women, were still generally denied property rights and an independent legal status necessary to the practice of law well into the nineteenth century. As women obtained these rights, the next step was for them to begin "thinking of themselves as persons exercising authority" (quoted in Bernat, 1992: 309; see generally Morello, 1986). In 1870 the first woman briefly sat on the bench in the Wyoming territory, yet by 1900 only five women had served in some judicial capacity (Murray, 1990; Berkson, 1982). In the 1870s women also briefly served as jurors in the Wyoming and Washington territories. However, both territorial courts quickly withdrew the privilege (Lentz, 2000a).

For generations, progress was undeniably slow. Even after the Nineteenth Amendment guaranteed women the vote in 1920 and women in many states became eligible for jury service, they were systematically excluded from juror selection. Here too, women's nature justified such exclusion as opponents were not only concerned about protecting women from the crudeness of the courtroom but also in women being too lenient because of their emotions. One newspaper article questioned whether women could ever be impartial given their "sensitiveness, sympathies, predilections, jealousies, prejudice, hatreds" (quoted in Lentz, 2000b).

Civil Rights and the Women's Movement

Since the courtroom was not seen as a suitable place, at least, for a respectable woman well into the twentieth century, many law schools continued to exclude women, and those women who were accepted often faced being ridiculed by male professors and fellow students alike (Murray, 1990). It was only during the civil rights era, beginning in the 1960s, that the legal system first addressed discrimination in education and employment based on race, religion, national origin, and sex. Title VII of the Civil Rights Act of 1964 and its amendments have been most significant in regard to women's progress in the legal profession.

One hundred years after the first women were licensed to practice law, Sassower (1974) would report that in 1969, there were just over 8,000 women attorneys and only about 200 females judges. But, things were changing as sex discrimination lawsuits followed the enactment of federal and state discrimination statutes and the women's movement spurred women to seek not only economic and professional advancement but also to challenge old biases regarding women's roles and abilities. During the 1970s, law schools began to open their doors to women and the number applying began to grow dramatically. Estimates regarding the proportion of female lawyers in 1970 ranged from as little as 2.8 percent to 4.7 percent of the legal profession. In a decade, that percentage had risen to about 13 percent, or nearly 59,000 (Berkson, 1982; also "Different Voices," 1990).

The legal profession was also rapidly growing: by the mid-1980s, it was reported that there were about 122,000 female lawyers, but their proportion of the attorney population had only reached about 17 percent (Bernat, 1992; see also Fossum, 1983). Minority representation also grew but at a troubling pace, with not even 6,000 black women attorneys reported in 1987 (Bernat, 1992). As the numbers of women grew in the profession, it was anticipated that women's presence in the judiciary would also increase. By 1980 it was estimated that there were over 500 women sitting as judges on state courts and by the early 1990s that number had more than doubled, but their percentages were not significant (Carbon et al., 1982; Murray, 1990; "Different Voices," 1990; Martin, 1993b).

Gender Bias in the Courts

Eich wrote in 1986 that sexual stereotyping was "institutionalized in the practice of law," adding that the business of judges was traditionally "the business of men." And, as a result, it had "always suffered from men's stereotypical views of women" (340, 341). Wikler reported in 1980 that the examination of sexism in the courts, that is, unsupported assumptions about women's "individual capabilities, interests, goals and social roles on the basis of sex differences," embedded also in social institutions, had only just begun (202).

Gender myths and biases have impacted the courts' treatment of both men and women. For example, in regard to criminal defendants, women have been widely perceived as being treated chivalrously, but closer examination suggests that some women are treated favorably and others harshly based to a degree on sex-role expectations. Women who fulfill traditional roles may fare better than women whose crimes are unfeminine (Wikler, 1980). However, a respectable woman can loose the protective care of society or the courts. For example, Judge Johnson (2002), reflecting in 1993 on gender bias, pointed to how the media can turn even a middle-class, white woman into a "vengeful female," the "woman scorned" (236). Intersecting stereotypes and expectations regarding race, class, and gender have perhaps had the harshest impact on women of color (e.g., Johnson, 2002).

Women who are in the courtroom as judges, attorneys, jurors, witnesses, victims, or plaintiffs have also faced sexual stereotyping regarding their nature and abilities. Being seen as a "good victim" in rape or domestic violence cases can make a difference regarding whether a case even goes forward. Modern scholars have noted that throughout much of history, women's perceived sexual nature has created a dichotomy of the madonna and the whore, the "good woman" and mother who is virtuous and nurturing and the temptress who is sexually provocative, seductive, even predatory (see, e.g., Schafran, 1985). In addition, the devaluing of women's intellectual abilities has been reflected in their being viewed as less credible (e.g., Schafran, 1987). While rooted in historical views of women as being more deceptive than men, such assumptions can have a devastating impact in the courtroom.

Where such preconceptions or prejudices have been deeply ingrained in society, they have influenced men and women. Empathizing with a female victim may be difficult. Bias has also been more blatant as judges have been criticized for viewing female victims as the seductive woman in cases addressing sexual assault and sexual harassment (see, e.g., Bohmer, 1974; Eich, 1986; Schafran, 1990, 1991). Labeling women as sexually accessible not only impacts victims and witnesses but, in the not too distant past, has turned female attorneys into "pretty things" that are not to be taken too seriously (Eich, 1986). Referring to female attorneys by their first name and male attorneys by Mr. So-and-So treats a woman with less respect and greater familiarity, impacting her credibility in the courtroom (e.g., Schafran, 1985; Eich, 1986). Sexism has also been used as a trial tactic without consideration that female witnesses or attorneys have been demeaned or humiliated (e.g., Schafran, 1987; see also Johnson, 2002).

With a growing presence of women in the law, new organizations, from women's bar associations to the National Association of Women Judges (NAWJ), began to advocate for change (e.g., Klein, 1980). Most significantly, the NAWJ, founded in 1979, worked with the NOW Legal Defense and Education Fund's National Judicial Education Program in training judges and encouraging the establishment of task forces addressing gender bias in the courts. By 1997, 34 states and federal circuits had issued reports covering issues of divorce, child custody, rape, domestic violence, civil litigation, prostitution, prison conditions, sexual harassment, and the status of court personnel (Schafran, 1993; Kearney and Sellers, 1997; for an overview of task force reports, see Hemmens et al., 2009). In their examination of laws, rules, policies, and behaviors, it was evident that the nature-nurture debate goes beyond the obvious physical or biological differences impacting historic roles. Gender bias was found to be a significant problem throughout the judiciary from judicial decision making to the interactions of attorneys, judges, litigants, witnesses, and court personnel (Schafran, 1993).

Responses to Bias

In response to such evidence of bias, task forces, joining with the courts and bar associations, have sought to recommend and implement change.

For example, in 1990 the American Bar Association (ABA) proposed in its Model Code of Judicial Conduct that judges be required to intervene to stop attorneys' sexist conduct and to refrain themselves from verbal or physical harassing behaviors (Schafran, 1993; Jackson, 1997). By the 1990s appellate cases successfully began to challenge verdicts that were likely impacted by biased behaviors in the courtroom. For example, the South Carolina Supreme Court reversed a criminal conviction where the trial judge referred to the defendant's attorney as "a pretty girl" or a "nice girl," adding that it was doubtful that he would have addressed a male lawyer as a nice or handsome boy. The court found prejudicial error, ruling that the trial judge had undermined defense counsel's credibility and, thus, her ability to represent her client effectively (Jackson, 1997: 16–17).

Women's progress in the courts itself has reflected "social change in attitudes about women and changing attitudes of women about themselves and others" (Kaye, 1990: 53). Given that women have only recently entered the courts as lawyers and judges in significant numbers, it is not surprising to find ignorance, discomfort, or bias on the part of male attorneys who mostly grew up in a stridently male-dominated profession (e.g., Schafran, 1990). Early studies consistently found a "gender gap" in the perception and understanding of bias with male judges and attorneys generally less conscious or concerned regarding inequality than women (Jackson, 1997). Wikler (1990) suggests that sexism in courtroom interactions is more easily remedied because it is likely to elicit less resistance from judges. Misconduct by attorneys may only require a verbal reprimand; judges facing one comment or complaint, or even reading one article on gender bias, will be much more cognizant of their own behaviors. Whether male or female, judges are likely to see themselves as important role models.

Gender bias in substantive law and judicial decision making is more subtle and complex. In considering a future of enormous potential for social change through law, Kaye (1990) emphasized the importance of women's growing presence in the courts, particularly as attorneys and judges. Such women not only teach people the "absurdity" of stereotyping but also encourage and inspire other women. Their presence heightens sensitivity to problems particularly affecting women and ultimately increases opportunities to effect "pervasive change in the law" (54). Kaye (1990) also notes that women have contributed to the law in their willingness to express divergent views.

In this overview of women's early experiences in the courts, it is their different nature, roles, and abilities that justify different treatment. Later in confronting bias, it is such different treatment that is largely seen as discriminatory. Eliminating overt sexist remarks in the courtroom does not necessarily eliminate the underlying bias in stereotypes and assumptions about the nature of man and woman, or the nature of law itself. While men may have been denied certain employment opportunities historically, more doors were closed to women. This approach to bias implicitly, if not explicitly, suggests that gender discrimination is different treatment "from men" and equality may be defined as treating women the same as men. Yet, the equal treatment of women and men may be quite different.

Feminist Legal Theory: Sameness and Difference

Following quickly on the heels of the women's movement, feminist legal theory grew out of women's experiences in law schools, courtrooms, and the legal system. As Dalton notes (1987/88: 2), to "be engaged in feminist legal thought is to be a feminist who locates both her enquiry, and her activity, in relation to the legal system." Thus, feminist legal thought examines women's historical "place" in society in order to bring about change.

Defining Gender Neutrality and Sameness

The focus of many feminists and court cases in the 1970s was on the elimination of overt legal distinctions based on sex. While there are several important federal and state civil rights laws that address sex or gender, Title VII of the Civil Rights Act of 1964 has perhaps had the deepest impact on our understanding of bias. The core provisions of Title VII, 42 U.S.C. section 2000e-2, declare that it is an unlawful employment practice to discriminate with respect to the terms or conditions of employment, including firing or a refusal to hire, because of an individual's race, color, religion, sex, or national origin. In its language, the law suggests that sex, or gender, a term more commonly used today, should be irrelevant to an employment decision. It demands gender neutrality or gender blindness; the goal is essentially to treat men and women alike. Dalton (1987/88: 4) adds that this strategy has to a degree taught men, and women, how to refocus their vision, "to see women's sameness where before they had seen difference."

While such a strategy bought important gains, its limitations were soon apparent. Ignoring stereotypes, myths, and biases that have been pervasive in our society has not proven to be an easy task. In a public world traditionally dominated by men, male institutions, and masculine organizations, neutrality could become simply "treating women like men." According to Dalton (1987/88: 5), "The equality model proposed, for strategic purposes, that what women wanted was access to a world already constituted."

Problems with the gender neutral approach to equality were brought to the attention of the gender bias task forces of the 1980s. Family law is one of several areas where the negative impacts of gender neutral laws focusing on treating men and women the same have been recognized (see, e.g., Binion, 1993). By the 1980s it was acknowledged that apparently fair treatment in divorce, particularly in dividing economic responsibilities for children, had often resulted in women being in much worse economic positions than their husbands. As Eich (1986) notes, "equal treatment" in divorce is fair only if men and women have access to "equivalent resources" (343), and this is often not the case.

Recognizing Unequal Impacts

Gayle Binion (1993) in her article on the nature of feminist jurisprudence identifies several stages in the development of the law and feminist discourse. In response to the limitations of the first stage of equality focusing on gender neutrality, feminists recognized that gender blind laws or policies are not necessarily neutral or equal in their impacts. This was particularly observed when the U.S. Supreme Court held in *General Electric v. Gilbert* (1976) that an employer's discrimination against pregnancy in regard to disability benefits was not sex discrimination. After all, only women can become pregnant and not all women are pregnant at any one time, so such a policy was considered gender neutral. As Binion (1993: 141) observes, "Superficial gender neutrality only renders women invisible, not equal." Dalton (1987/88: 5) adds that such equality has tended to suppress "the concrete ways women's lives tend to be shaped differently than men's."

The sameness-difference debate also has deeper meaning in the justice workplace itself. Challenging and breaking down stereotypes may occur in a variety of ways. For example, becoming a lawyer or judge in the 1970s and 1980s was still stepping outside traditional roles. Yet, such women also faced a profession and judiciary that were masculine not only in composition but in culture and organization. Martin and Jurik (1996), among other scholars, have noted that when women have entered a male-dominated work environment or profession, they may adapt in different ways. Some may feel that they are expected to behave in certain ways (i.e., masculine); others may strive to maintain their femininity. Men face similar pressures as they enter professions traditionally dominated by women, such as nursing. What is expected of me? How should I behave? Moreover, that men and women may have similar career goals, attitudes, and behaviors in the workplace does not necessarily mean that everything is equal.

Understanding Difference

Facing such contrasting, and perhaps conflicting, theories, the women's movement became split "on whether to continue to urge equality, or instead to concede difference" (Dalton, 1987/88: 5). As historically perceived, or imposed, differences had been used to justify discrimination against women, many rights advocates feared such a recurrence and this discouraged women, according to Dalton, from "insisting that the law take account of their reality" (5). Moreover, arguing difference in some cases led to the criticism that women were seeking special treatment rather than equal treatment. Yet, difference feminists have been particularly important in addressing gender in the courts and applying Carol Gilligan's (1982) "different voice" or cultural feminism to women's participation in the legal profession, suggesting that woman might transform the adversarial nature of law (see, e.g., Bowman and Schneider, 1998).

Significantly, difference to a degree has been acknowledged in the law. For example, in response to the *Gilbert* decision noted above, Congress in 1978 enacted the Pregnancy Discrimination Act, which declares that pregnancy and related medical conditions fall under the protection of Title VII. By contrast, Supreme Court interpretations of the Fourteenth Amendment equal protection clause, first applied to gender in the 1970s, continue largely to define equality as neutrality.

The debate regarding the limits of neutrality and the problems of difference leads to a stage of jurisprudence that Binion (1993) terms progressive feminism, which asks whether the law can truly serve women and recognize their experiences. In regard to such possibilities, some feminists remain unconvinced as they would argue that the law and the legal system remain male centered. Theorists such as Catharine MacKinnon caution that incorporating women's experiences may be misplaced because women remain defined by their subordination and, thus, their true "nature" cannot perhaps be known (in Binion, 1993). Ultimately, questions of neutrality, difference, subordination and experience do not represent linear stages but rather coexisting points of debate (Binion, 1993; Martin, 1993b).

Acknowledging Diversity

Within feminism and feminist legal theory, diversity is not simply a matter of identifying women's and men's experiences. Dalton (1987/88) stresses that no single feminist theory should see itself as speaking "univocally for *all* women" (7). For Razack (1990/91: 455), feminism must confront the reality that sexism does not exist in isolation; there are "interlocking systems of domination" including race, class, and gender. For example, "When sexuality is identified as central to women's oppression, as it is in cases involving rape, there is little room left for understanding the experience of women equally oppressed by racism," and, "little space for understanding that sexuality itself is constructed along racist lines" (455). Razack adds that when "white middle-class women have argued in court, it is from their own experiences as women that they have spoken, obscuring in the process the complexities of oppression as it is experienced by poor women and by women of color" (442).

Given that there are differing viewpoints among feminists about significant and controversial gender issues in the law, the impact of feminism on law and the courts may be questioned. By studying sex or gender cases before the U.S. Supreme Court in the 1970s and 1980s, George and Epstein (1991) suggest that feminist organizations with quite disparate views were able to find common ground. Yet, differences do exist and to the degree that some viewpoints may seem irreconcilable, consensus on important issues such as pornography and prostitution may be difficult to achieve. As a consequence, debate may be muted, and the status quo reinforced. Many questions also remain regarding the impact of women in the legal workplace. Bowman and Schneider (1998) emphasize the interaction of practice and theory "in which feminist practice has generated feminist legal theory, theory has then reshaped practice, and practice has in turn reshaped theory" (249).

Martin (1993b) distinguishes the notions of a different feminine voice and a different feminist voice, the former largely reflecting women's experiences and the latter representing divergent views on gender and law as represented by feminist legal theory. It is these distinctions of difference that perhaps frame our understanding of gender and the courts.

Making a Difference

Bringing difference and recognizing diversity have been central issues in research on gender and the courts, and particularly on judges and judging. Thus, as women become lawyers and judges in greater numbers, do they gravitate to certain specialties by choice or are they directed, if subtly, to certain paths? Will the workplace also change in regard to being family friendly? in regard to acknowledging different leadership styles? or, going even further, to reject hierarchal models? Will advocacy in the legal system become less adversarial? How will gender and racial diversity on the bench impact issues brought before the courts, and judicial decision making itself? Is a critical mass necessary to make a difference? While these are important questions, their answers may not be apparent for some time. From the first women to seek the bench, difference has been an issue.

Women's First Experiences on the Bench

Understanding the paths and experiences of the first women who became judges introduces the complexity of the sameness-difference debate in the courts. It was during the late 1800s that middle- and even upper-class women began to enter the justice system in a variety of roles. In addition to lawyers and a handful of judges, women began to serve as prison and police matrons, and later probation officers. In 1910 the first police woman with arrest powers was hired. To a degree such careers were accepted as an extension of the domestic sphere of the wife and mother. In general, such women sought to bring guidance and protection to largely poor and immigrant women and children, to save them from lives of violence, intemperance, and godlessness (Schulz, 1995; Cook, 1993).

While women who entered the courtroom as lawyers and judges, as well as matrons, police or probation officers, encountered rigid sex roles, they generally won the tolerance of the male legal world by accepting traditional sex-role values. To a degree this perhaps reflects a double standard of white middle-class women seeking authority for themselves while imposing traditional sex roles on the women who came before them in court. Although they did not directly challenge male domination, they found themselves segregated in what might be termed a "women's public sphere" (Cook, 1993). Beverly Cook examined the career of Georgia Bullock, California's first female judge. It was a male judge who in 1914 first appointed her to assist him with largely misdemeanor cases involving women and children. He then proposed a separate lower court for such cases with a female judge. It was not until 1924, however, that Bullock sat on the bench without a male judge by her side.

Throughout her experience on the Women's Court, Bullock emphasized the importance of her gender identity. While she sentenced a young wife to six months in jail for impersonating a man in order to get a job as a truck driver, she also began to speak out about women's legal and economic inequalities. When she first ran for office in the Superior Court, which handled felonies and civil cases of greater value, Cook (1993: 155) notes, the "rhetoric of gender sameness and equality" was necessary to demonstrate her competence. Although Bullock lost that election, she was eventually appointed to the Superior Court and was reelected. While her career there spanned 25 years, her assignments remained domestic relations, adoptions, or juvenile cases.

The segregation of women in the courts and justice professions largely continued until it was challenged in the civil rights era of the 1960s. With women entering the legal profession in greater numbers, it was anticipated that they would no longer be tokens in a male-dominated world.

The Path to the Bench

As the path to becoming a judge is more complex and arduous than practicing law, the decision to pursue such a career is not made lightly. According to Cook (1983), the traditional path to judicial office, which requires experience in litigation, professional recognition, and political credentials, was a barrier to the first modern generation of women seeking judicial office. Of course, definitions of merit and eligibility in this path are a reflection of the law also being traditionally a white male-dominated profession. In one survey asking several female judges what prepared them for the bench, motherhood was stressed not only because of the many decisions mothers must make, but also in teaching you to be "patient, to listen, to be firm, and to be fair" (quoted in Miller and Meloy, 2007: 713). A survey of the 500-plus female state court judges in 1980 by Carbon et al. (1982) found that this generation had less political experience and was more likely to have reached the bench by appointment rather than election.

As Martin (1987) suggests, expanding the eligible pool of candidates for judicial posts in the late 1970s and early 1980s required looking for different (rather than traditional) career characteristics for the federal bench. For example, President Carter nominated women who had a lower level of political activism but a higher level of judicial experience at the state level (see also, Martin, 1982). Slotnick (1984), in noting that traditional definitions of political activism (such as holding party or political office) most often benefited white males, added that women were to a degree redefining political activity to include other forms of public service. While nontraditional paths to the bench were applied to female and minority applicants as early as the 1970s, it was, and still remains, unclear whether such nontraditional paths would become normative for the selection process generally (for Clinton appointments, see Beiner, 2005; Goldman and Saronson, 1994).

Given traditional obstacles to the bar and bench, it is not surprising that those women seeking and achieving judicial office have sought to make a difference. This simply may be a matter of establishing a place for women in the third branch of government as well as becoming role models (see, e.g., Martin, 1993a). It also may demonstrate a desire not only to bring a woman's perspective to the bench but to advance issues of particular interest to women, including a feminist agenda.

Researching Difference

Research regarding gender difference has included comparing the attitudes of female and male judges in regard to discrimination, work, and family. For example, early research suggested that women seeking federal positions were most likely to be supportive of women's equality (Cook, 1983). In a study on Carter appointees to the federal bench regarding experiences and attitudes, Martin (1990: 208) concluded that in general "women have certain experiences and attitudes that are not the same as men." While men were generally supportive of women's changing political and judicial roles, a much higher percentage of women judges expressed "strong support." In other studies, similar results had been found in regard to state judges and legislatures. This generation of women also revealed that they had to over-come various forms of sex discrimination from a belief that women's place is in the home and from the view that women simply can't do the job as well as men.

In a comparison of Carter and Reagan female appointees to the federal district and appellate courts, different attitudes also were apparent. In the Reagan selection process a strong emphasis was placed on a judicial phi-losophy supportive of traditional "family values," particularly in areas of equal rights and abortion rights. Thus, it would not be surprising that Reagan's female appointees were much less supportive of the women's rights movement; moreover, they were less supportive than other Republi-can women politicians. The Reagan appointees also saw greater conflict between career goals and family responsibilities, which, in part, may explain their lower support for the changing roles of women (Martin, 1987).

In addition to research on judges' attitudes, scholars have focused on judicial decisions and decision making in the appellate courts where a judge may write or join the majority, concurrence, or dissent. Of course, even in examining the positions a justice takes on issues in opinions may not truly represent a personal or philosophical position. Collegiality often produces consensus. Concerns about being perceived as neutral decision makers may particularly impact women and minorities whose numbers reflect a minority, or even token, status. Numbers may make a difference.

In general, such research has focused on comparing the voting behaviors of male and female judges on particular topics coming before the courts such as discrimination or criminal law. Research on voting patterns, how-ever, does not necessarily get to the heart of either judicial attitudes or pro-cess. Courts remain bound by precedent, among rules of decision making. Adding new issues or perspectives depends on attorney arguments as well as a judge's own background, experience, and philosophy. In order to address these issues, research has begun to include examination of the background and life experiences of female judges as well as in-depth anal-yses of opinions, particularly concurring and dissenting opinions of women on appellate courts (e.g., Beiner, 2005).

Studies of voting patterns generally suggest that on certain issues, such as discrimination and family law, female judges are strongly "pro-woman," despite differences in political party affiliations; thus, to a degree the stud-ies supported the findings of attitudinal surveys (Maule, 2000/01). In early studies on the federal courts, for example, female judges more often than males supported employment discrimination claimants (Davis et al., 1993). Why such support has existed, however, is not a clear cut issue: women may themselves have experienced discrimination, be able to identify with marginalized or disadvantaged groups, and/or be more concerned about relationships (Davis et al., 1993).

Studies of the first modern generation of state judges have also tended to confirm that these women reflect a more "representative role" incorporating a woman's viewpoint on a broad range of issues impacting women (Allen and Wall, 1993; Martin, 1993a). On other issues, however, such as criminal defendants, voting patterns at the appellate level were more likely to reflect political party affiliation or experience (Allen and Wall, 1993; Maule, 2000/01). To date, gender difference appears limited. Anecdotal evidence from this generation has also suggested that female judges may be more empathetic in regard to many issues facing women from accessing child care to being a crime victim (Miller and Meloy, 2007). In this, women play an important role in challenging gender stereotypes and raising the consciousness of their fellow judges. This role is also evident in the unique life experiences they bring to the bench as wives, mothers, minorities in many workplaces, or even breast cancer survivors (e.g., see discussion, Kruse, 2005). In regard to employment discrimination cases, for example, research has suggested that having even one woman on an appellate panel will impact the voting of male judges (Farhang and Wawro, 2004).

Finding a Voice

While it is unclear that more women on the bench would result in the courts hearing more cases addressing issues of particular concern to women, Maule (2000/01: 315) found that as the number of female justices increased on the Minnesota Supreme Court (they became a majority in 1991), so too did "their willingness to express themselves." Perhaps a more diverse court became a "safer place for women to express dissonance" (315). This safer place may be most evident when women write concurring or dissenting opinions in nonunanimous decisions. By contrast, women on the bench may eschew a semblance of gender difference where they remain a distinct minority. For example, is collegiality on a male-dominated court more likely to encourage the adoption of a "masculine" approach to decision making? Or, are male justices themselves likely today to be more open to and encouraging of diversity? Moreover, that men and women may reach the same decisions does not necessarily mean that they get there in the same way (e.g., Miller and Meloy, 2007).

Despite personal experience with sex discrimination, U.S. Supreme Court Justices Sandra Day O'Connor and Ruth Bader Ginsburg have made statements generally denying that their life experiences or gender are factors in their decision making. Certainly the notion of objectivity or neutrality in judicial decision making would support, even require, such expressions. Former Justice O'Connor has stated that "the important thing is not that [she] will decide cases as a woman, but that [she is] a woman who will get to decide cases" (Kruse, 2005: 997–98; for additional research on Justice

O'Connor, see Davis, 1993; Bodine, 1983). Yet, the findings of Kruse (2005: 998) suggest that in sex discrimination cases "involving primarily female victims," O'Connor and Ginsburg have ruled in the woman's favor and in other Title VII cases also supported the broadening of such discrimination law. Their decisions, to a degree, may demonstrate not only a feminine voice in their empathy but a feminist voice in supporting such expansion.

It is perhaps unrealistic to expect that a person's background and experiences will not influence decision making, even indirectly, as certainly everyone is a product of their life experiences. In the sameness-difference debate, gender neutrality reflects concerns regarding difference, largely as a matter of nature, leading to sexism and discrimination. If gender neutrality means that no one should use the g-word (gender) much less the f-word (feminism) then women most especially are silenced. Ignoring gender is particularly problematic in the face of a history of white male domination over other people, including women and minorities. If continuing issues of inequality cannot be discussed, or even raised, how can equality itself be assumed? The future of gender in the courts will continue to be impacted by the women on the bench and in the courtroom.

Conclusion: A Glass Half Full

Beiner (2005: 847) concludes that women judges, "through their careers and the body of law they have created, have made the courts more hospitable to those who are outsiders to the system." Whether they bring a distinctly feminine or feminist voice will continue to be researched and debated. Significantly, women's minority status on the bench itself will impact this debate and its conclusions. In this regard, it is important to acknowledge that the future of women on the bench is tied to that of women in legal practice generally.

Progress But Not Equality

In 1990, some female lawyers reported that bias had not disappeared, it had just gone underground (Swanson). According to Swanson (1990: 47), statistics demonstrated that the experiences of women from the classes of 1974 and 1975 differed greatly with their males classmates, "outstripping us professionally in all categories, particularly as partners in major law firms." Central questions were asked regarding the "feminization" of the profession, that is, the likely impacts of growing numbers of women on the professional workplace, on the performance of legal tasks, and substantive law. If women are generally more empathetic or more focused on consensus, might the legal system itself be transformed from its competitive, adversarial nature ("Different Voices," 1990)?

A panel of men and women in 1990 agreed that women in the legal profession and on the bench have raised concerns that were not just women's issues and have created more choices generally. As one female panelist noted, "the mommy track" is not just a concern of women but an issue regarding the structure of the business of law that impacts men as well. The female participants in particular saw that women brought different styles. The Honorable Fern Smith, a federal district court judge, stated that she did not think that women looked at fairness and justice differently, but she added, "I do think that ethnicity and race and socioeconomic status change people's perception of fairness and justice and that's a very important issue. . . . I think that the presence of women expands the areas in which justice and fairness is now applied" ("Different Voices," 1990: 143). A male justice, however, suggested that as more women come to the bench, it would become evident that men and women are not so different.

To a large degree these issues and questions remain. In 1990, based in part on the number of women in law school, it was projected that women would "constitute 35 to 40 per cent of the profession" and maybe even higher by 2000 ("Different Voices," 1990: 138). In 2006, women comprised just over 30 percent of the legal profession and in 2003 under 17 percent of law firm partners, reflecting progress from 1994 when women represented a reported 23 percent of the profession (*A Current Glance*, 2006; *Charting Our Progress*, 2006).

Yet, a glass half full is also one that is half empty. This is perhaps most evident in a 2000 *ABA Journal* survey where only 56 percent of women reported that they were treated equally with men in their organizations. Some women indicated they were treated differently, including lower salaries, less responsibility, and fewer prospects for advancement (Samborn, 2000). Women's fewer networking and mentoring opportunities further serve to maintain glass ceilings (Durant, 2004). These obstacles are greater for minority women (*Visible Invisibility*, 2006). Such issues will not be resolved by men standing on the sidelines, but if they have few experiences in common with women or see themselves as having no stake in women's success, a gender gap will remain (e.g., Herring, 2003).

The *ABA Journal* poll in 2000 also suggested that in some respects women were even losing ground. For example, in a similar 1983 survey only 38 percent of women said that they had to work harder than men to get the same results, where in 2000 the number had risen to nearly 57 percent (Carter, 2000). A recent report from the ABA's Commission on Women in the Profession noted that the stereotypes and gender issues raised in the task force research in the 1980s remain relevant today. Imagine a female attorney being called "baby," and female attorneys still being perceived, at least by some, to be either too aggressive or not aggressive enough, or to be too strident, emotional, and bossy (*Charting Our Progress*, 2006).

In addition, the percentage of women and men in 2000 who believed that it is realistic for women to do it all—lawyer, wife, and mother—also decreased significantly from 1983 (Samborn, 2000). Instead of the private practice becoming more family friendly, competition has increased the number of expected billable hours in the private sector, expanding the "mommy track" and blunting the potential for flex time, part time, day care, and other accommodations only won in recent years, and potentially benefiting men as well as women (Carter, 2000; see, e.g., *Advancing Women*, 2007). As one female partner stated, "I think the work ethic in law firms is still the one that was designed for working men who had stay-at-home spouses" (Carter, 2000: 36). Most importantly, the impact on the profession of high female law school enrollments is diminished when women leave the practice of law due to work-life pressures (for a detailed discussion, see Durant, 2004; also *Advancing Women*, 2007).

The Future of Women on the Bench

Work-life issues and glass ceilings also impact the pool of women likely to become judges when women are prevented from reaching top leadership positions or opt out of more traditional legal careers that to a significant degree remain a path to the bench (Durant, 2004). According to the ABA, in 2006, women comprised less than 25 percent of female federal judges and approximately 30 percent of the justices on state courts of last resort (*A Current Glance*, 2006). These data do not present a complete picture, however, as variations within the country and the status of women on the lower courts is not included, and is perhaps unavailable. Yet, to increase, or even maintain, the reported percentages, women must continue to serve in the lower courts throughout the country.

Although some may see equality as numerical parity, our understanding of equality in law and society is much more complex. The degree to which women or men are viewed or treated primarily on the basis of their sex or gender remains an important issue, an issue that will be debated, and to a degree answered, in the courts. Perhaps the central question in regard to gender in the courts, to our understanding of difference and equal treatment and the roles and opportunities of women and men in society, is who will define and shape that debate. Will women make a difference?

References

Advancing Women in the Profession: Action Plans for Women's Bar Associations (2007). MIT Workplace Center.

Allen, David and Diane Wall (1993). "Role Orientations and Women State Supreme Court Justices," *Judicature*, Vol. 77, No. 3 (November–December): 156–165.

Beiner, Theresa (2005). "Women of the Courts Symposium: Female Judging," *University of Toledo Law Review*, Vol. 36: 821–847.

Berkson, Larry (1982). "Women on the Bench: A Brief History," *Judicature*, Vol. 65, No. 6 (December–January): 286–294.

Bernat, Frances (1992). "Women in the Legal Profession," in I. Moyer, ed. *The Changing Roles of Women in the Criminal Justice System*, 2nd ed. Long Grove, IL: Waveland Press.

Binion, Gayle (1993). "The Nature of Feminist Jurisprudence," *Judicature*, Vol. 77, No. 3 (November–December): 140–143.

Bodine, Laurence (1983). "Sandra Day O'Connor," *ABA Journal*, Vol. 69 (October): 1394–1399.

Bohmer, Carol (1974). "Judicial Attitudes toward Rape Victims," *Judicature*, Vol. 57, No. 7 (February): 303–307.

Bowman, Cynthia Grant and Elizabeth M. Schneider (1998). "Feminist Legal Theory, Feminist Lawmaking, and the Legal Profession," *Fordham Law Review*, Vol. 67: 249–271.

Bradwell v. Illinois, 83 U.S. 130 (1872).

Carbon, Susan, Pauline Houlden, and Larry Berkson (1982). "Women on the Bench: Their Characteristics and Attitudes about Judicial Selection," *Judicature*, Vol. 65, No. 6 (December–January): 294–305.

Carter, Terry (2000). "Paths Need Paving: Although Trailblazers Have Led the Way for Women, the Road Ahead is Still Bumpy and Under Construction," *ABA Journal* (September): 34–39.

Charting Our Progress: The Status of Women in the Profession Today (2006). ABA Commission on Women in the Profession.

Cook, Beverly Blair (1983). "The Path to the Bench: Ambitions and Attitudes of Women in the Law," *Trial* (August): 49–55, 101.

Cook, Beverly Blair (1993). "Moral Authority and Gender Difference: Georgia Bullock and the Los Angeles Women's Court," *Judicature*, Vol. 77, No. 3 (November–December): 144–155.

A Current Glance at Women in the Law (2006). ABA Commission on Women in the Profession.

Dalton, Clare (1987/88). "Where We Stand: Observations on the Situation of Feminist Legal Thought," *Berkeley Women's Law Journal*, Vol. 3, No. 1: 1–13.

Darwin, Charles. "The Descent of Man," 2nd ed. rev. (1874), Part 3, Ch. 19 in R. Agonito, ed. *History of Ideas on Women: A Source Book*. New York: Perigee Books.

Davis, Sue (1993). "The Voice of Sandra Day O'Connor," *Judicature*, Vol. 77, No. 3 (November–December): 134–139.

Davis, Sue, Susan Haire, and Donald Songer (1993). "Voting Behavior and Gender on the US Court of Appeals," *Judicature*, Vol. 77, No. 3 (November–December): 129–133.

"Different Voices, Different Choices? The Impact of More Women Lawyers and Judges on the Justice System" (1990). *Judicature*, Vol. 74, No. 3: 138–146.

Durant, Leah. (2004). "Comment: Gender Bias in the Legal Profession: A Discussion of Why There Are Still So Few Women on the Bench," *Margins Law Journal*, University of Maryland School of Law, Vol. 4 (Spring): 181–205.

Eich, William (1986). "Gender Bias in the Courtroom: Some Participants are More Equal Than Others," *Judicature*, Vol. 69, No. 6 (April–May): 339–343.

Farhang, Sean and G. Wawro (2004). "Institutional Dynamics on the U.S. Court of Appeals: Minority Representation under Panel Decisionmaking," *The Journal of Law, Economics, and Organization*, Vol. 20, No. 2 (October): 299–330.

Fossum, Donna (1983). "Women in the Law: A Reflection on Portia," *ABA Journal*, Vol. 69 (October): 1389–1393.

General Electric v. Gilbert, 429 U.S. 125 (1976).

George, Tracey and Lee Epstein (1991). "Women's Rights Litigation in the 1980s: More of the Same," *Judicature*, Vol. 74, No. 6 (April–May): 314–321.

Gilligan, Carol (1982). *In a Different Voice: Psychological Theory and Women's Development.* Cambridge, MA: Harvard University Press.

Goldman, Sheldon and Matthew Saronson (1994). "Clinton's Nontraditional Judges: Creating a More Representative Bench," *Judicature*, Vol. 78, No. 2 (September–October): 68–73.

Hemmens, Craig, Kristin Strom, and Elicia Schlegel (2009). "Gender Bias in the Courts: A Review of the Literature," in G. L. Mays and P. R. Gregware, eds. *Courts and Justice: A Reader*, 4th ed. Long Grove, IL: Waveland Press: 423–442.

Herring, Jacob (2003) in D. Rhode, ed. *The Difference "Difference" Makes: Women and Leadership*. Stanford, CA: Stanford University Press.

Hume, David (1977). "The Conventional Origin of Female Virtues," from *A Treatise on Human Nature*, in R. Agonito, ed. *History of Ideas on Women: A Source Book*. New York: Perigee Books.

Jackson, Vicki (1997). "What Judges Can Learn from Gender Bias Task Force Studies," *Judicature*, Vol. 81, No. 1 (July–August): 15–21, 38.

Johnson, Justin (2002). "'Flotsam on the Sea of Humanity': A View from the Bench on Class, Race, and Gender," in C. Reasons, D. Conley, and J. Debro, eds. *Race, Class, Gender, and Justice in the United States*. Boston: Allyn & Bacon: 232–239.

Kaye, Judith (1990), "Women and the Law: Creating Profound Social Change," *Trial* (February): 52–56.

Kearney, Richard and Holly Taylor Sellers (1997). "Gender Bias in Court Personnel Administration," *Judicature*, Vol. 81, No. 1 (July–August): 8–14.

Kerber, Linda (1980). *Women of the Republic: Intellect and Ideology in Revolutionary America*. New York: W.W. Norton & Co.

Klein, Joan Dempsey (1980). "Women Judges Join Together," *The Judges Journal*, Vol. 19, No. 2 (Spring): 4–6.

Kruse, Brenda (2005). "Women of the Courts Symposium: Women of the Highest Court: Does Gender Bias or Personal Life Experiences Influence Their Opinions?" *University of Toledo Law Review*, Vol. 36: 995–1022.

Law, Sylvia (1987). "Family, Gender & Sexuality: What the Founding Fathers Had to Say," *The Judges Journal* (Summer): 23–27, 56–57.

Lentz, Susan (2000a). "Without Peers: A History of Women and Trial by Jury Part One—From the Women's Sphere to Suffrage," *Women & Criminal Justice*, Vol. 11, No. 3: 83–106.

Lentz, Susan (2000b). "Without Peers: A History of Women and Trial by Jury Part Two—The Law of Jury Service in the Twentieth Century," *Women & Criminal Justice*, Vol. 11, No. 4: 81–101.

Martin, Elaine (1982). "Women on the Federal Bench: A Comparative Profile," *Judicature*, Vol. 65, No. 6 (December–January): 306–313.

Martin, Elaine (1987). "Gender and Judicial Selection: A Comparison of the Reagan and Carter Administrations," *Judicature*, Vol. 71, No. 3 (October–November): 136–142.

Martin, Elaine (1990). "Men and Women on the Bench: Vive la Difference?" *Judicature*, Vol. 73, No. 4 (December–January): 204–208.

Martin, Elaine (1993a). "The Representative Role of Women Judges," *Judicature*, Vol. 77, No. 3 (November–December): 166–175.

Martin, Elaine (1993b). "Women on the Bench: A Different Voice?" *Judicature*, Vol. 77, No. 3 (November–December): 126–128.

Martin, Susan Ehrlich and Nancy Jurik (1996). *Doing Justice, Doing Gender.* Thousand Oaks, CA: Sage Publications.

Maule, Linda (2000/01). "A Different Voice: The Feminine Jurisprudence of the Minnesota State Supreme Court," *Buffalo Law Journal*, Vol. 9: 295–316.

Mill, John Stuart (1977). From *The Subjugation of Women*, in R. Agonito, ed. *History of Ideas on Women: A Source Book.* New York: Perigee Books.

Miller, Susan and Michelle Meloy (2007). "Women on the Bench: Mavericks, Peacemakers, or Something Else?" in R. Muraskin, ed. *It's a Crime: Women and Justice*, 4th ed. New Jersey: Pearson Prentice-Hall: 707–722.

Morello, Karen Berger (1986). *The Invisible Bar: The Woman Lawyer in America 1638 to the Present.* New York; Random House.

Murray, Florence (1990). "Women and the Law: Have We Really Come a Long Way," *The Judges Journal* (Winter): 18–23, 48.

Razack, Sherene (1990/91). "Speaking For Ourselves: Feminist Jurisprudence and Minority Women," *Canadian Journal of Women and Law*, Vol. 4: 440–458.

Rousseau, Jean Jacques (1977). "Paternity and the Origin of Political Power," from *Discourse on Political Economy*, in R. Agonito, ed. *History of Ideas on Women: A Source Book.* New York: Perigee Books.

Samborn, Hope Viner (2000). "Higher Hurdles for Women," *ABA Journal* (September): 30–35.

Sassower, Doris (1974). "Women and the Judiciary: Undoing 'The Law of the Creator,'" *Judicature*, Vol. 57, No. 7 (February): 282–288.

Schafran, Lynn Hecht (1985). "How Stereotypes About Women Influences Judges," *The Judges Journal* (Winter): 12–17.

Schafran, Lynn Hecht (1987). "Documenting Gender Bias in the Courts: The Task Force Approach," *Judicature*, Vol. 70, No. 5 (February–March): 280–290.

Schafran, Lynn Hecht (1990). "Overwhelming Evidence: Reports on Gender Bias in the Courts," *Trial* (February): 28–35.

Schafran, Lynn Hecht (1991). "Interview—Update: Gender Bias in the Courts," *Trial* (July): 112–118.

Schafran, Lynn Hecht (1993). "Gender Equality in the Courts: Still on the Judicial Agenda," *Judicature*, Vol. 77, No. 2 (September–October): 110–114.

Schulz, Dorothy Moses (1995). "Invisible No More: A Social History of Women in U.S. Policing," in B. Raffel Price and N. Sokoloff, eds. *The Criminal Justice System and Women: Offenders, Victims, and Workers*, 2nd ed. New York: McGraw-Hill: 372–382.

Slotnick, Elliot (1984). "The Paths to the Federal Bench: Gender, Race, and Judicial Recruitment Variation," *Judicature*, Vol. 67, No. 8 (March): 370–388.

Spinoza, Benedict de (1937). *Political Treatise*, in A. G. A. Balz, ed. *Writings on Political Philosophy by Benedict de Spinoza*. New York: D. Appleton-Century Co.

Swanson, Victoria (1990). "The More Things Change," *Trial* (February): 44–47.

Visible Invisibility: Women of Color in Law Firms (2006). Executive Summary. ABA Commission on Women in the Profession.

Wikler, Norma (1980). "On the Judicial Agenda in the 80s: Equal Treatment for Men and Women in the Courts," *Judicature*, Vol. 64, No. 5 (November): 202–209.

Wikler, Norma (1990). "Gender and Justice: Navigating Curves on the Road to Equality," *Trial* (February): 36–37.

25

Secret Justice

JOHN GIBEAUT

It cost plenty for reporter Kirsten B. Mitchell and her newspaper to tell readers about a $36 million secret settlement of an environmental lawsuit between Conoco Inc. and residents of a mobile home park in Wrightsboro, N.C.

U.S. District Judge W. Earl Britt found Mitchell and the Wilmington, N.C., *Morning Star* in civil contempt and ordered them to pay the oil company $500,000. Then, Britt fined Mitchell another $1,000 in late February for criminal contempt.

Her offense: Obtaining the settlement figure from a sealed file inadvertently handed her by a court clerk.

"I've never seen a case like this, where you're held in contempt for looking at a document the government gives you," says George Freeman, assistant general counsel for the newspaper's parent corporation, The New York Times Co.

Media lawyers say Mitchell is a casualty of an increasingly pervasive secret justice system that allows well-heeled or famous litigants to make private use of the public courts while the travails of ordinary citizens are revealed for all to see.

"That's an example of how bizarre things can get," says lawyer Jane E. Kirtley, executive director of the Reporters Committee for Freedom of the Press in Arlington, Va. "I would say it's reaching epidemic proportions."

But while Mitchell and the *Morning Star* may pay a high price, the cost of secret justice to the public ultimately may be even higher. Whether judges seal files, close courtrooms or allow anonymous jurors to hear cases, critics complain such practices erode public oversight and confidence in the system, and reduce accountability for some protected wrongdoers.

"People who can afford to buy secret justice do, and that's just not what our system's about," says lawyer Kelli L. Sager, who represents media interests in Los Angeles.

In the long run, critics say, such secrecy creates a two-tiered justice system, one for the rich and famous, and a second one for everyone else. And sometimes, as in the Conoco case and others, major public safety and consumer concerns are swept under the rug.

"There's this concern that public figures get to clean their laundry in a private or semiprivate cubicle while everyone else has to use the Laundromat," says St. Paul, Minn., lawyer Paul R. Hannah, who concentrates on media and entertainment law. "If, in fact, justice is the great leveler, you no longer see a system that protects the weaker against the strong."

Concerns about secrecy are not just from nosy reporters and cranky editors trying to mind everyone's business but their own. New York lawyer Eugene R. Anderson recently filed an amicus brief on behalf of United Policy Holders, a public interest group that wanted to know what's contained in voluminous sealed files in litigation between the 3M Co. and its insurers over coverage for the company's potential liability for silicone-gel breast implants. "I don't [care] about the media," Anderson says. "We represent policyholders. The insurance industry is the most secret industry in the world."

Still, media lawyers primarily form the front line. Although no figures are available, media lawyers across the country report increased problems in obtaining access to criminal and civil court proceedings and documents. Judges, often unaware of serious constitutional and other legal requirements, frequently close the system to public scrutiny, often simply because the parties to a case want it that way.

Sometimes celebrities don't even have to ask a court for help. Los Angeles prosecutors listed Steven Spielberg as "John Doe" in a case against a man accused of stalking the filmmaker, although Sager says there was no indication Spielberg requested anonymity.

Also in Los Angeles, a state judge partly closed a 1996 civil trial in which actress Sondra Locke accused her former lover Clint Eastwood of fraud. "Neither Eastwood nor Sondra Locke requested that the trial be closed," says Sager, who represents the *Los Angeles Times* and *California Community News* in an ongoing appeal on the access issue to the California Supreme Court.

As for Locke and Eastwood, they settled for—you guessed it—an undisclosed amount of money as jurors deliberated.

Notorious criminal defendants, too, can get some of the same advantages as celebrities when courts decide their fair trial rights are special enough to trump First Amendment rights. Convicted Oklahoma City bomber Timothy McVeigh and co-defendant Terry Nichols were able to hide from view chunks of documents that routinely would have become public in other cases.

Money Talks

Perhaps the most troubling aspect of the latest wave of secrecy springs from cases involving large corporations that want to control costs and maintain solid public images while taking advantage of the finality of res judicata that only a public court can offer.

"I'm seeing this a lot," says Minneapolis lawyer Mark R. Anfinson. "I think it's becoming standard operating procedure, especially in complex commercial litigation."

While the U.S. Supreme Court has long held that the public has a nearly unqualified First Amendment right to attend all phases of criminal proceedings, it has issued no specific pronouncement regarding court files themselves or civil trials.

Thus, lower courts are all over the map when it comes to files and civil matters, with some finding varying degrees of First Amendment rights in individual areas, more limited common-law rights in others, and, in still others, no rights at all.

The California Supreme Court, however, is expected to decide this year whether a specific First Amendment right exists to attend civil trials in the Locke-Eastwood case. *KNBC-TC v. Superior Court*, No. S056924.

But the Minnesota Supreme Court in early March refused to hear arguments to unseal the 3M case. *State Insurance Co. v. Minnesota Mining and Manufacturing Co.*, Nos. C0 97-2257, C4 97-1872. Media lawyers were uncertain what they would do next in the case.

"If they rule there is no First Amendment right, we'll continue in a helluva mess until we get a definitive statement from the U.S. Supreme Court," says lawyer Richard M. Schmidt Jr. of Washington, D.C., counsel for the American Society of Newspaper Editors.

Observers and participants say the California case is especially important because the government, which is supposed to ensure openness, is pressing for secrecy instead of the parties. And the sheer scope of the Minnesota case starkly illustrates its public interest, they say.

"It's just astounding," says Anfinson, who represents the Minneapolis *Star Tribune* in the case against St. Paul-based 3M and the insurance companies. "It's far and away the most astonishing example of secret justice

I've ever seen. It's truly mind-boggling. This is big-time litigation with lots of consequences for lots of people."

Different Drummer

Lawyers seeking closure for corporate clients pack a different agenda. Although legal arguments for closure typically center on the need for secrecy as an incentive to settle and courts' traditional deference to the parties' wishes, money lurks at the bottom.

In the Conoco case, 178 mobile home residents claimed leaks from one of the company's gas stations had polluted their drinking water. The deal in the case was struck last summer after a public trial that lasted more than a month and after the jury had found Conoco liable for the pollution. Jurors were considering punitive damages when the settlement came. Conoco lawyer Jonathan D. Sasser of Raleigh, N.C., says the *Morning Star*'s disclosure of the settlement amount will cost the Houston-based company a pile because it's involved in about 50 similar cases.

"It increases the expectations of other plaintiffs and other plaintiffs lawyers," Sasser says. "We were harmed to the tune of millions of dollars. It will raise the value of settlements in the future and raise the costs of defending these cases."

The judge declined other requests by Conoco to find *Morning Star* reporter Cory Reiss in contempt and force him to identify two confidential sources who gave him the same information on the settlement figure. But it was the publication of Mitchell's information citing court documents that really stung, Sasser says. "That adds a degree of credibility to it." Although Judge Britt wrote in his Jan. 21 civil contempt order that "this matter is not about the freedom of the press, but about the respect that any citizen, individual or corporate, should have for an order of the court," he also echoed Conoco's complaints. *Ashcraft v. Conoco, Inc.*, No. 7:95-CV-187-BR(3) (E.D.N.C.).

Although irrelevant to the contempt proceeding, newspaper lawyer Freeman says Conoco overlooks one significant factor: "None of this would have happened if the settlement hadn't been sealed in the first place."

Freeman, co-chair of the ABA Litigation Section's First Amendment and media committee, says Mitchell had no reason to believe the settlement wasn't public because the clerk had pulled a different sealed document from the file before handing it to her.

Minneapolis lawyer Dale Larson, who represents 3M in the insurance case, tells of concerns similar to Conoco's. The 3M court file has to remain sealed, he says, because it contains privileged attorney work-product information, including strategy and defense costs in the separate breast-implant litigation. The insurers have a right to that information, but the plaintiffs in the underlying case do not, Larson says.

"If the insurance case was open while your suit was pending, the other party would have all your privileged and confidential information," Larson says.

He's especially steamed that one of those seeking access is Mealey Publications Inc., a suburban Philadelphia newsletter publisher that distributes dozens of titles dealing mostly with the insurance industry and litigation. As part of its service, Mealey sells copies of court documents to its readers. Some of those readers include plaintiffs lawyers, who Larson says aren't entitled to know 3M's secrets.

Give me a break, says Mealey's lawyer, Lee Levine of Washington, D.C. "The fact that readers of Mealey Publications include plaintiffs lawyers, who 3M assumes are evildoers, is basically irrelevant," Levine says. "They have no less right to information than anyone else."

Even accepting that 3M must surrender and keep secret some privileged materials, *Star Tribune* lawyer Anfinson wonders why it had to file them with the court in the first place. He has an even harder time swallowing the idea that the voluminous file is so rife with legitimately confidential stuff that it can't be weeded out.

Moreover, he says, the case also deals with the court's refusal to release transcripts of some hearings. Although the court maintains that those hearings were public, the docket scheduling them was not.

"That's one of the Alice-in-Wonderland aspects of this whole thing," Anfinson says.

Blame for the Bench

Still, critics don't blame secrecy all that much on lawyers seeking closure. For example, they say, a criminal defense lawyer runs a risk—albeit remote—of giving ineffective assistance by failing to ask for protective orders and other measures to guard his or her client's Sixth Amendment rights.

Judicial ignorance probably plays the most crucial role in expanding secrecy, critics say. They place much of the blame directly on judges who often agree to requests to seal off the system without even acknowledging the competing and, indeed, sometimes conflicting public interest in openness.

Closure orders typically arise out of stipulations reached by the parties and presented to unsuspecting judges who may not know any better, lawyers say.

That criticism is just too brutal, says Judge Michael G. Harrison, chair of the National Conference of State Trial Judges.

"Why is it so difficult to believe that a judge isn't familiar with something?" asks Harrison, a circuit judge from Lansing, Mich., who says he only rarely orders closure himself. "There are thousands of issues that come up. You can't expect a judge to know about them all."

The system's pressure on judges to keep the docket moving and speed civil cases toward settlement also is key, says St. Paul lawyer Hannah, who waged an unsuccessful battle for newspapers and television stations in the Twin Cities area trying to lay their hands on a lawsuit involving the personal life of Minnesota Vikings coach Dennis Green.

"I hear more and more judges mumble that these are two private parties," Hannah says. "The feeling I get is that judges tend to look upon individual lawsuits as a dispute resolution process and not as an exercise of the power of the court."

Obtaining access is even harder these days because courts commonly close the system first without public notice and only entertain questions later. Although the bulk of First Amendment jurisprudence presumes an open system and places the burden on the party seeking closure, the presumption and the burden often are flipped once a courtroom is closed or a document sealed. Making things even more difficult, lawyers trying to pry open cases often don't know exactly what they expect to find. "Rarely do we know what we are looking for," Hannah says. "Our arguments are very general, and the response is much more specific."

"In the Dennis Green case, I felt I was tilting at windmills." All the same, some news outlets are venturing into uncharted territory.

In Southern California, a coalition of influential media entities is trying to use an unusual feature in state law to unseal grand jury transcripts of an aborted criminal investigation of Merrill Lynch & Co. in connection with the 1994 Orange County bankruptcy.

In upstate New York, the 35,000-circulation Glens Falls *Post-Star* is appealing a federal judge's refusal to release documents from settlement discussions in an environmental case involving a town government and General Electric Co.

The New York case concerns allegations that GE dumped 452 tons of hazardous waste from 1958 to '68 at a disposal site in the town of Moreau, just north of Albany, and contaminated the town's drinking water. The newspaper tried to learn more last year when it heard a settlement may be near. But the parties, including town officials, already had agreed to keep both negotiations and draft settlement documents secret, although they had publicly discussed the talks. That was enough for U.S. District Judge Lawrence E. Kahn to keep the paper out of settlement conferences and from getting hold of the documents, which were given to the court clerk's office but not filed. Settlement negotiations and documents tradi-tionally have been private affairs, and few cases ever would settle if the parties had to deal publicly, Kahn wrote last September in *United States v. Town of Moreau*, 979 F. Supp. 129 (N.D.N.Y.).

Despite the inherent secrecy of settlement talks, a significant First Amendment card comes into play when they involve elected officials, says the paper's lawyer, Thomas F. Gleason of Albany. The case is pending before the 2nd U.S. Circuit Court of Appeals in New York City.

"The reason we thought it was important is because the settlements that were being bandied about, like million-dollar payments and a new water supply, have long-term implications for the town," Gleason says. "An essential tenet of our argument is that it was public officials acting."

In Orange County, news organizations are trying to use a provision of California law that allows release of grand jury transcripts once an indict-ment is issued.

The local district attorney began a criminal investigation after the 1994 bankruptcy, which cost cities, schools and county agencies $1.64 billion. As one of the county's financial advisers, Merrill Lynch was a target of the probe.

Sealed Settlement

But as a grand jury considered the case, Merrill Lynch and the district attorney reached a $30 million settlement in June 1997 that included a multimillion-dollar payment for costs to the prosecutor's office. The investigation ended and the grand jury records were sealed, until a trial judge ordered them opened in September.

The state supreme court spurned Merrill Lynch's protest and shipped the case to an intermediate appellate court, where it remained in late Feb-ruary. *In re Request for Transcripts of Phase Three Grand Jury Proceedings*, No. G022076 (Cal.Ct.App. 4th Dist.).

Although California normally does not release grand jury materials in cases that don't result in indictments, the Merrill Lynch case is different because of the settlement with the state, says media lawyer Sager.

"Here, the grand jury didn't get a chance to decide whether to issue an indictment," Sager says. "And here, Merrill Lynch paid millions of dollars, which suggests something was wrong. And the district attorney's office cut them a deal."

Meanwhile, the Wilmington *Morning Star* and the New York Times Co. are taking the *Conoco* contempt case to the 4th U.S. Circuit Court of Appeals in Richmond, VA.

As for Reporter Mitchell, she carried a copy of the novel *Midnight in the Garden of Good and Evil* to her sentencing, perhaps in anticipation of hard time ahead.

But, besides the hefty fine, she got little else for her trouble. Her information accounted for only a tiny portion of the published story. She didn't even get a byline.

26

Citizens, Professionals, or the Executive
Who Owns the Courts?

NANCY V. BAKER and PETER R. GREGWARE

The history of courts in the United States has been a history of contestation between at least two competing perspectives. One perspective sees the courts as being ultimately accountable to the people, who are responsible for their system of governance. This approach recognizes the large citizen role in governance, reflected in the incorporation of grand juries and trial juries in the actual decision-making process. Also consistent with this perspective is the fact that many state court judges are subject to selection and retention by a vote of the people.

A counterperspective focuses on the role of the courts as the impartial arbiter of disputes, with professionals—lawyers and judges—given the task of devising appropriate rules to ensure fairness. Over the centuries, the ability of professionals to create new rules on a day-to-day basis, and their singular ability to define and "safeguard" the role of the people in the court process, have resulted in these professionals garnering additional powers at the expense of public power. This clearly raises the question of who should ultimately be making the decisions.

Recently, we have seen the emergence of a powerful third contender for control of the court process. The political branches of government have always been a minor contender in this process, with President Roosevelt's attempt to "pack" the Supreme Court as one of the more salient examples, as well as more recent congressional efforts to limit judicial discretion with mandatory sentencing laws. Since the terrorist attacks of 2001, this trend has accelerated, and this time it is the federal executive branch that is seek-

Written especially for *Courts and Justice*.

ing—and gaining—extensive power over court processes. This expanded executive authority comes at the expense of both the citizenry's ability to oversee the process and court professionals' ability to control the courts.

Minimizing the Role of the Public

Tension has long existed between government officials and us, the citizenry, over the right to know what the government is doing. "The natural tendency of government officials is to hold their meetings in secret. They can thereby avoid criticism and proceed informally and less carefully" (*Detroit Free Press et al. v. Ashcroft* 2002, p. 20). Against government's preference for confidentiality is a strong presumption of openness in a democratic society, which is based on the idea that "an informed public is the most potent of all restraints upon misgovernment" (*Grosjean v. American Press Co.* 1936, p. 250), and that the citizenry "alone can protect the values of democratic government" (*New York Times v. United States* 1971, p. 728). Reflecting this presumption, the courts have usually halted or diminished governmental attempts at secrecy related to legal process. Since 9/11, however, there has been a concerted effort to hold secret a whole range of legal processes. As an unelected body, with their own seemingly professional self-interest compromising their position, the judiciary have found it more difficult than in the past to stand up to executive claims that a national emergency necessitates greater secrecy.

Secret Searches

Public control of the government's search and seizure powers rests primarily on the requirements of the Fourth Amendment to the Constitution, which permits only reasonable searches by the state, with reasonable defined as probable cause to believe a crime has been committed, as evaluated and authorized by a neutral magistrate. For almost a century at the federal level and 50 years at the state, evidence seized in violation of the Fourth Amendment has been excluded from criminal trial.

Despite the formal constitutional requirements, the government has engaged in spying on citizens who were involved with domestic opposition groups or political dissent. Congressional investigations in the 1970s uncovered intrusive government surveillance of civil rights leaders and peace activists; in response to this abuse, Congress enacted in 1978 the Foreign Intelligence Surveillance Act (FISA). Surveillance for national security intelligence purposes could continue without regular court oversight, but only with the approval of a secret federal tribunal known as the Foreign Intelligence Surveillance Court, also known as the FISA court. Investigators seeking intelligence related to agents of foreign powers were able to ignore normal Fourth Amendment requirements because any evidence gathered would not be used at a trial. Over the years, the frequency with which federal investigators used the FISA court increased, and with it, concern over the extension of federal power without adequate oversight. This controversy has increased substantially with the expansion of federal powers under the 2001 Patriot Act, and the commingling of foreign intelligence activities and domestic criminal processes.

The FISA court is composed of senior federal judges, but it operates beyond public oversight. It meets in secret in an office in the Justice Department and considers only the government's position. It also defers to executive requests for warrants; in the first 23 years of its existence, it denied only one federal warrant application, and that was because it lacked jurisdiction (Sanders 2001). On only one occasion was its decision subject to judicial review—by an even more secret appeals court.

Under FISA, because evidence pertaining to criminal activity and intelligence is kept separate and the volume of intelligence cases is relatively small, most consider the threat to judicial and public oversight to be relatively minor and an appropriate balance was made between security and constitutional rights. This changed with the Patriot Act, which amended FISA to permit greater interaction between law enforcement and intelligence officers. No longer is foreign intelligence the sole purpose of a FISA investigation; instead, it merely has to be "a significant purpose" of the investigation (USA Patriot Act 2001). This language opens the door to the use of FISA warrants for "nonintelligence" related investigations. Critics of these secret surveillance powers argue that targets of FISA searches have lost their traditional right to examine government evidence used to justify the initial warrant (Lane 2002). The Patriot Act also expands the government's surveillance authority through emergency foreign intelligence warrants, which may be issued by the attorney general or by a type of administrative subpoena called a national security letter (NSL). Recipients of NSLs—which may include libraries, clinics, businesses, and schools—are required to turn over all personal information on the individual named in the letter. They are barred from telling anyone except an attorney. Due to the secrecy surrounding such requests, there is no way to determine how many NSLs have been issued (USA Patriot Act 2001). Such secrecy, without any review, arguably keeps both citizens and the courts from monitoring administrative actions, and many have voiced concern about the potential for abuse of authority and the loss of privacy (Eggen and O'Harrow 2003).

These are not abstract concerns. In March 2007, the Justice Department Inspector General issued a report documenting extensive misuse of national security letters. Most of the more than 1,000 potential violations involved the FBI's unauthorized collection and retention of Americans'

Internet and phone data. From 2003 to 2005, the FBI had substantially underreported possible violations to Congress, as well as underreported the total number of requests for NSLs. Glenn Fine, the inspector general, noted that he considered the errors to be unintentional; even so, he told senators: "The FBI's failures, in my view, were serious and unacceptable" (Office of Inspector General 2007).

A greater challenge to citizen oversight of government surveillance arose in connection with the National Security Agency (NSA). In December 2005, the *New York Times* broke the story that, since September 11, the NSA had conducted a secret wiretapping program tracking Americans' international telephone calls and e-mails. Later news reports revealed that the spy agency had analyzed the records of millions of Americans, all without a search warrant, even one issued by the FISA court (Cauley 2006). The program was authorized by a secret executive order issued by the president in 2002, with the president reauthorizing it every 45 days (Abramson 2006). Several citizen lawsuits were filed against the telecommunications companies that had turned over their records to the NSA, although some were dismissed because the parties could not show they had suffered a legal injury and therefore had standing to sue (Goldstein 2007).

The executive branch resisted pursuing any statutory authorization until after May 2007, when the FISA court ruled that the government needed a court warrant whenever it tapped a fixed wire on U.S. soil. The decision restricted the government's ability to tap foreign communications that pass along wires and through switching stations located in the United States. The ruling made it clear that statutory authority was necessary to cover the NSA program (Warrick and Pincus, 2007). In August 2007, Congress passed a statute authorizing NSA eavesdropping of Americans' international phone and e-mail communications, as long as the actual target of the search was the person overseas. No notice or search warrant was required. The law recognized a role for the FISA court, but only to review surveillance procedures after the fact, not to review individual search requests. All oversight rested with the executive branch, specifically the attorney general or the director of national intelligence. Telecommunications companies could be forced to cooperate, and they were immunized from citizen lawsuits for their cooperation. The law had a six-month sunset and had not been reauthorized at the time of this writing. However, other wiretapping bills have been introduced (Risen 2007).

Central to this controversy is how the potential for abuse by the executive should be overseen and checked. Administration officials argue that the main check on executive power is and should be political; that is, if the public perceives the president's approach is excessive or ineffective, they will vote him out of office (Lane 2002). Critics of such broad executive power argue that secrecy makes any public check on such powers virtually impossible (Kiefer 2002, Elsner 2002), and that the courts—under the doctrine of separation of powers—have a constitutional mandate to balance executive as well as legislative claims of authority (Tribe 2000).

Identity and Location of Detainees

Through the control of information, the federal government is also securing the increased ability to influence court processes. A particularly significant example occurred in the months following the 9/11 attacks, when the federal government arrested at least 1,200 people and refused to disclose their names, locations, and charges, if any. Initially, the Justice Department disclosed how many were detained but stopped providing that number in November 2001 (Goldstein and Eggen 2001). This not only affected the access of the press and public to that information, but families of the detained and defense attorneys also were disadvantaged, sometimes unable to locate a person in detention for weeks. Because this was seen as a violation of the Sixth Amendment's right to counsel, the American Bar Association condemned the secrecy surrounding the detentions at its annual meeting in 2002 (*Washington Post* 2002).

Under the rationale of security need, many judges have complied with executive claims of power. In one case, 19 organizations sought to compel disclosure of the names and locations of the detainees through the Freedom of Information Act (FOIA), a statute providing for the release of most non-classified government records when requested by the public. When the Justice Department denied their request for information, the groups brought a lawsuit. The district judge gave a mixed ruling, ordering the government to release the names of the detainees and their attorneys, but not the detention locations (*Center for National Security Studies et al. v. Department of Justice* 2002). But the DC Circuit Court of Appeals upheld the government's position, accepting the Justice Department's argument that the information fell under an FOIA exemption, on the grounds that "revealing it could reasonably be expected to interfere with enforcement proceedings" (Bridis 2003).

One state judge in New Jersey, citing state laws requiring disclosure, issued a deadline by which the Justice Department had to release the names of those held in New Jersey county jails on a contract with the Immigration and Naturalization Service (Edwards 2002). In response, the Justice Department issued a rule banning any state or local government from releasing information on any immigration detainee held under federal contract on the grounds that immigration matters fall within the federal sphere of authority. The Justice Department rule asserts that "the courts . . . are ill-equipped to become sufficiently steeped in foreign intelligence matters to serve effectively in the review of secrecy classifications in that area." Furthermore, "application of state law in this area has the potential to threaten the Attorney General's [national security] mission" (INS Rule 2002). The state high court then deferred to national executive authority, and overruled the state judge.

The rationale for almost total secrecy regarding the 1,200+ individuals who were detained following the attacks of 9/11 was that they were likely involved with terrorism. Of note is that—while 762 eventually were charged with immigration violations—not one was ever charged with a crime related to terrorism (Inspector General Report 2003).[1]

Minimizing the Role of Court Professionals

As part of the general trend toward centralizing power in the White House during a national emergency, the judicial branch has experienced a significant lessening of its authority under the antiterrorism measures of 2001 and 2002, resulting in an expansion of executive power. Both legislative actions—particularly the Patriot Act—and executive measures have weakened the ability of court professionals to oversee searches, including detentions, "intelligence" searches discussed in the previous section, and administrative rules relating to attorney-client contact for some federal inmates. Court professionals are largely excluded as well from participation in the military tribunal process, even at the appellate level (Baker 2002). Finally, in the application of material witness warrants and the designation of individuals as enemy combatants—both of which will be discussed in greater depth below—the executive has restricted the role of judges and attorneys in the legal process.

Material Witness Warrants

The application of material witness warrants in the war against terrorism has diminished the ability of court professionals to engage in oversight, in this case limiting how long the executive branch can detain a person without court approval. Under the Material Witness Statute of 1984, a judge may order the detention of a reluctant witness whose testimony is shown to be material to a criminal proceeding and when a subpoena is not practical. The detention is limited to a "reasonable period of time until the deposition of the witness can be taken."

The 9/11 attacks altered how that law is interpreted and applied. FBI agents—and not judicial officials—claimed the authority to arrest and jail U.S. citizens and residents. The actual number of detentions is unknown since these cases were shrouded in secrecy. According to a 2006 report, Human Rights Watch identified 70 people who had been detained without judicial approval, many of them willing to testify and some already cooperating with the FBI's antiterrorism investigation. The government eventually released 42 without any charges and issued apologies to 13 for wrongful detentions (Human Rights Watch 2006). Conceding that most of the detained were innocent of any crime, the government argued that their detention was essential because—even unwittingly—they might hold a small piece of the larger terrorism puzzle. Michael Chertoff, at the time the assistant attorney general for the criminal division, called the Material Witness Statute "an important investigative tool in the war on terrorism" (Fainaru and Williams 2002).

The law apparently was employed to hold not just potential witnesses but also people about whom the FBI was suspicious when there was not sufficient probable cause for either a search or an ordinary arrest. Supporting this is the fact that many never testified before either a grand jury or a court. In December 2002, almost half of those still in custody—20 out of 44—had never been called to testify (Fainaru and Williams 2002). A report in June 2005 found that 30 people out of the 70 arrested had never been called (Human Rights Watch 2005). Material witness arrests enabled federal agents to search the detainees' homes, which sometimes uncovered evidence that the government later used to bring criminal and immigration charges against them (Baker 2006). Seven of the 70 eventually were charged with providing material support to a terrorist organization, and 20 were charged with other criminal or immigration violations (Human Rights Watch 2006). These cases did not follow regular criminal procedures or Fourth and Fifth Amendment requirements. The judiciary was shut out of its oversight role.

Other court professionals, notably defense attorneys, also have found their role circumscribed in material witnesses cases. Some were denied access to the warrants for the arrest of their clients as material witnesses; others to the affidavits that supported the warrants. Defense counsel as well as family members were under gag orders; almost all court proceedings were closed and documents sealed. Notice of most of the hearings was expunged from court dockets (Human Rights Watch 2005). This level of secrecy also eliminated the public's capacity to engage in oversight of the criminal justice system, further enhancing executive control.

Without the safeguards of a judicial process, the power to detain someone as a material witness is open to abuse. One obvious concern relates to the length of such detentions. The Justice Department reported that half were detained 30 days or less, but many of the others were held three months and even longer, including one detention of more than 430 days (Fainaru and Williams 2002). Also problematic were the conditions of their arrest and confinement. For example, many were not read their Miranda rights at the time of their arrests, and some were denied access to counsel for weeks (Liptak 2004). Classified as high security inmates, they faced harsh treatment, from leg and waist shackles to repeated strip searches and solitary confinement. One U.S. citizen held as a material witness called it a "terrifying and humiliating ordeal," where he was ordered "to sit in a small cell for hours and hours and hours buck naked" (Liptak 2004). Under the stress of such confinement, some material witnesses made misstatements that later became the basis for prosecutions against them. For example, Egyptian graduate student Abdallah Higazy became so confused and upset during his detention in the aftermath of 9/11 that he falsely confessed to owning a ground-to-air radio transceiver found in a hotel across from the World Trade Center. The radio transceiver appeared to link him to the terrorist attack. He was exonerated only when an American pilot who had been staying at the hotel came forward to claim it.

Despite the potential for abuse, the judicial branch largely deferred to expansive executive use of the material witness statute. In only one case—involving a Jordanian student named Osama Awadallah—did a court find that the law had been inappropriately applied. While being held as a material witness, Awadallah gave contradictory testimony to a grand jury about knowing one of the 9/11 hijackers and was subsequently charged with perjury. His attorney argued that his initial arrest as a material witness was illegal and therefore any testimony resulting from that arrest was inadmissible in his criminal trial. A federal district judge agreed and dismissed the indictment against Awadallah. The FBI had erred in two ways: the agent who had signed the affidavit for Awadallah's arrest was also a grand jury witness, and the law applied only "to those whose testimony is material" and at the pretrial stage, not the grand jury (*United States v. Awadallah* 2002). On appeal, a three-judge panel of the Second Circuit Court of Appeals disagreed and reinstated the indictment (*United States v. Awadallah* 2003). In November 2006, five years after his material witness arrest, a jury acquitted Awadallah of all charges (Shenon 2007).

In no other instance did the judiciary question this use of the material witness statute in the months following September 11.

The ability of the judiciary and the legal bar to control this detention process is clearly limited. Critics in Congress introduced a bill in 2005 to "ensure that the material witness law is used only for the narrow purpose that Congress originally intended, to obtain testimony, and not to hold criminal suspects without charge when probable cause is lacking" (Leahy 2005). The bill (sponsored by Senator Patrick Leahy of Vermont) would restore the judiciary's role in several key ways. First, there would have to be a pending grand jury proceeding or criminal trial before warrants could be issued. In addition, it would require a higher showing that a potential witness is a flight risk and limit the time someone could be detained. Those held as material witnesses would be informed of the basis of their arrest and their right to counsel, and be held in the least restrictive conditions possible, preferably separate from those charged with a crime. Finally, the bill would mandate an annual Justice Department report on the numbers of those detained and the average length of detentions (S. 1739). After its introduction, the bill was referred to the Senate Judiciary Committee but as of this writing, no further action has been taken.

Civil litigation may provide an avenue for judges to reassert their oversight role, as in the case of Portland attorney Brandon Mayfield. Mayfield was held for two weeks while the FBI sought to build a case against him for complicity in the Madrid terrorist bombings of March 2004. Insisting that his fingerprint matched a partial print found by Spanish investigators on a bag of detonators, the FBI seized items in his home and office under the Patriot Act's delayed notification provision (called "sneak and peek") and then put him in indefinite custody as a material witness. Three weeks prior to his arrest, however, Spanish authorities had told the FBI that the fingerprint match was faulty, but the FBI rejected their conclusions and did not release Mayfield until after the partial print was definitively traced to another man. The FBI then apologized (Associated Press 2004). Mayfield filed a lawsuit against the FBI for violating his civil rights with the wrongful arrest, and the FBI settled for almost $2 million in November 2006 (Eggen 2006). Mayfield's lawsuit challenging parts of the Patriot Act was permitted to continue and, in September 2007, two provisions used in Mayfield's case were struck down as unconstitutional. U.S. district judge Ann Aiken specifically criticized the role of the executive branch, "In place of the Fourth Amendment, the people are expected to defer to the executive branch and its representation that it will authorize such surveillance only when appropriate" (*Mayfield v. United States* 2007).

Enemy Combatant Designation

Nowhere is the shift away from court professionals more striking than in the enemy combatant cases. The executive branch has asserted that the president alone, acting in his commander-in-chief role, has the authority to classify individuals as enemy combatants, and that this authority extends to indefinite detention without counsel. Furthermore, the executive has argued that courts lack the authority to review such a classification. In the words of one Justice Department brief, "the Court may not second-guess the military's enemy-combatant determination. At the very most . . . a court could only require the military to point to some evidence that supports its determination. Either way, no evidentiary hearing is required" (Brief for Respondents-Appellants 2002). In effect, declaring someone, citizen or not, an enemy combatant keeps courts from engaging in their normal role with an accused.

The illegal enemy combatant classification did not exist prior to 2001. In the past, the categories of criminal and enemy soldier were conceptually distinct, subject to different handling by the state. The first fell under regular criminal law, including the protection of criminal procedural rights. The second fell under international law and the laws of war. The executive has in effect instituted a new classification in which neither set of rules apply.

In his first term, President Bush classified three men as enemy combatants. Two of them, Yaser Hamdi and Jose Padilla, were U.S. citizens; the third, Ali Saleh Al-Marri, was a national of Qatar living legally in the United States. Padilla and Al-Marri were picked up in the United States and initially held on material witness warrants before being transferred to military custody. Hamdi was captured by Northern Alliance troops in a combat zone in Afghanistan in November 2001.

Yaser Esam Hamdi was born in Louisiana of Saudi parents. Once U.S. authorities ascertained his American citizenship, he was transferred from Guantanamo Bay to the naval brig in Norfolk, Virginia, where any court involvement would eventually go to the Fourth Circuit, a court that had historically made favorable decisions supporting expanded executive power. His father filed a habeas corpus petition as Hamdi's "next friend." Ruling with Hamdi, the district court for the Eastern District of Virginia appointed a public defender and ordered that Hamdi be permited to meet with counsel without military authorities present. The government immediately appealed to the Fourth Circuit, arguing that Hamdi could be detained for the duration of hostilities with no constitutional right of access to counsel. The appeals court found that the district court had not shown proper deference to the serious national security and intelligence interests advanced by the government. While not dismissing the case as the government sought, the judges reversed the district court's order mandating access to counsel and remanded the case for further proceedings (*Hamdi v. Rumsfeld* 2002a). The district court found that Hamdi's Fifth Amendment due process rights were violated by his indefinite detention without counsel and without charges. Furthermore, the court held that the two-page affidavit by a Defense Department official used by the government as the basis for his classification as an enemy combatant was insufficient. The government was ordered to provide additional material as sealed documents (*Hamdi v. Rumsfeld* 2002b). The government again appealed to the Fourth Circuit. The three-judge appellate panel reversed the district court, finding that the government affidavit was sufficient to establish grounds for Hamdi's continued detention as an enemy combatant. Writing for the court, Chief Judge Harvie Wilkinson found that the president's authority rested on his powers under the Constitution and the Authorization for the Use of Military Force (AUMF) passed by Congress in September 2001. In terms of the district court's efforts to secure more information regarding Hamdi's initial capture and classification, Wilkinson wrote, "The cost of such an inquiry in terms of the efficiency and morale of American forces cannot be disregarded. . . . The logistical effort to acquire evidence from far away battle zones might be substantial. And these efforts would profoundly unsettle the constitutional balance" (*Hamdi v. Rumsfeld* 2003).

Hamdi's father appealed to the Supreme Court. The decision was announced in June 2004. Different majorities in the case found, first, that the AUMF provided sufficient legal authority for the president to detain a citizen as an enemy combatant; second, that the detainee had the right to know the factual record on which he was detained and challenge it before a neutral decision maker and, therefore, for this limited purpose, had to have access to counsel. The neutral decision maker, notably, need not be a regular court, but could include a "properly constituted military tribunal." Responding directly to the White House claim of unilateral constitutional authority in this area, Justice O'Connor wrote:

> We necessarily reject the Government's assertion that separation of powers principles mandate a heavily circumscribed role for the courts in such circumstances. Indeed, the position that the courts must forgo any examination of the individual case and focus exclusively on the legality of the broader detention scheme cannot be mandated by any reasonable view of separation of powers, as this approach serves only to condense power into a single branch of government. We have long since made clear that a state of war is not a blank check for the President when it comes to the rights of the Nation's citizens. (*Hamdi v. Rumsfeld* 2004, pp. 535–536)

Three months following the decision, the U.S. government sent Hamdi to Saudi Arabia on the conditions that he renounce his U.S. citizenship, stay in Saudi Arabia, and report any terrorist activity (CNN.com 2004).

The facts surrounding Jose Padilla's arrest differ from Hamdi's. Padilla was not an enemy soldier captured on a battlefield. Instead, he was arrested in May 2002 in Chicago as a suspect in a plot to detonate a radioactive "dirty bomb." Government officials conceded the criminal case against him was not strong; the plot was only in the planning stages and Padilla did not have access to radioactive materials (Hays 2002). Instead of charging him, the government opted to hold him as a material witness in a grand jury probe of al Qaeda. A month after that, after he refused to testify before the grand jury, he was designated an enemy combatant and transferred to military custody (Mintz 2002). The government based his transfer on the president's authority under the commander-in-chief clause of the Constitution and the congressional resolution authorizing use of force that was passed by Congress soon after the attacks of 2001 (Brief for Respondents 2003). He remained in secret detention for almost four years.

As an enemy combatant, Padilla was removed from regular judicial oversight. Like Hamdi, he had not been charged and had no access to counsel.

After many lower level court decisions, his case was appealed to the Supreme Court. However, in April 2006, just as the government was slated to respond to Padilla's cert petition, prosecutors brought a criminal indictment against Padilla. The justices voted 6–3 that the enemy combatant case was now moot, since Padilla was being transferred to civilian court. In her dissent to the denial of cert, Justice Ginsburg pointed out that the government could decide later to transfer him again to military custody. Justice Kennedy, concurring in the denial of cert, noted that the court would review his habeas petition if that occurred (*Padilla v. Hanft* 2006).

Padilla was tried in Florida with two other men on charges of providing material support of terrorism and conspiracy to murder, kidnap, or maim people in a foreign country. His attorneys tried to have him declared incompetent on the grounds that the coercive interrogation techniques used in military detention had left him incapable of trusting his attorneys and assisting in his own defense. According to three psychological reports filed by his defense attorneys, Padilla suffered severe psychological damage resulting from long-term isolation, sensory deprivation, and stress positions (Richey 2007). Government attorneys insisted that he had not been abused, and the court refused to find him incompetent. In August 2007, Padilla and the others were convicted (Goodnough and Shane 2007). Despite the Justice Department's argument that Padilla should receive a life sentence, he was sentenced to 17 years; the federal judge took into account his harsh treatment during his years in the military brig (Whoriskey and Eggen 2008). The successful prosecution of Padilla, according to some legal observers, illustrates that terrorism cases can be handled by civilian courts, and that military commissions and the enemy combatant designation are not necessary (Goodnough 2007).

Al-Marri, a Qatari graduate student studying in Illinois, is the third person classified an enemy combatant. He was arrested in Peoria in 2001 and held initially as a material witness, then faced charges in Illinois for credit card fraud. Just before his trial was to start, he was designated an enemy combatant in June 2003 and transferred to a military brig in South Carolina, where he remains as of this writing. He was held incommunicado and without counsel for 16 months. His attorney filed a petition for a writ of habeas corpus, denied by the district court and appealed before the Fourth Circuit Court of Appeals (Anderson 2003, Petition for a Writ of Habeas Corpus 2003). The government again asserted that the judiciary's role was limited. Eventually, in June 2007, a Fourth Circuit panel rejected the government's authority to detain him without charge, finding that he had a right to bring a habeas corpus claim before a court. That did not mean that he had to be released. For the majority, Judge Diane Gribbon Motz explained, "Al-Marri can be returned to civilian prosecutors, tried on criminal charges and, if convicted, punished severely. But the Government cannot subject al-Marri to indefinite military detention" (*al-Marri v. Wright* 2007). The government petitioned for a rehearing en banc, which the Fourth Circuit granted. The nine judges heard the case in October 2007. Many of their questions focused on the government's claim that the president has the legal authority to order the military to indefinitely detain people captured in the United States. Government attorneys cited the AUMF passed by Congress in September 2001. Four months later, and over six years after his arrest, the decision is still pending (Liptak 2007).

The direct question about the constitutionality of this power claim has yet to be resolved by the Supreme Court.

The expanded military/executive role in legal affairs raises another issue: it provides the executive branch with leverage to gain compliance from judges hearing terrorism cases. The case of Zacarias Moussaoui provides an interesting case study of this. Moussaoui is on trial in Virginia as the possible twentieth hijacker in the attacks of 2001. He has admitted to links with al Qaeda but denies involvement with the 9/11 attacks. Acting as his own defense counsel, he sought to compel testimony from a man named bin al-Shibh who did coordinate the 9/11 attacks and was captured in Pakistan by the U.S. military. A federal district judge—citing the Sixth Amendment and a long line of precedent—twice ruled that Moussaoui had a right to any testimony that could support his defense. The government twice defied the order. The Justice Department argued that the government has no obligation to provide access to an enemy combatant held overseas, and the military has made it clear that it will not permit Moussaoui to question bin al-Shibh. Ordinarily, such defiance would result in the judge dismissing the indictment. However, if the judge did this, the administration said it would simply transfer Moussaoui out of the civilian judicial system to the Department of Defense (Shenon 2003). The judge sought a middle path in order to keep the case in civilian court. She dropped the possibility of the death penalty and limited the case to the broader issue of Moussaoui's involvement with al Qaeda, not 9/11 (Markon 2003). At the time this is going to press, the government is appealing both decisions and has not dismissed the possibility of transferring the case to a military tribunal.

Excluding Professionals and the Public: Military Tribunals

The potential problems of the executive controlling the adjudicatory process can be seen in the recent attempts by the executive to prosecute, via military commissions, the detainees at Guantanamo Bay.

Military commissions are new courts established by the military order issued by President Bush on November 13, 2001, as an alternative to the regular judicial system. Under it, not simply those captured on the battlefield but "certain non-citizens" could be detained and tried "for violations of the laws of war and other applicable laws." The military order was explicit that the military commissions would not follow "the principles of law and the rules of evidence generally recognized in the trial of criminal cases in the United States district courts" (Bush 2001).

The president claimed an inherent constitutional authority to create military tribunals without any congressional authorization. In contrast, numerous constitutional scholars and legislators argued that such courts fall under Article III of the Constitution, to be created by Congress as federal courts inferior to the Supreme Court.

Under the military order, the executive branch—specifically the president and Defense Department—dominates the entire adjudicatory process, from selecting defendants to hearing any appeals. The defense secretary sets the regulations, procedures, place, and time of any trial. The trials would be secret. Evidence could be kept from the defense and the accused. The judges, prosecutors, and—to a large degree—defense attorneys are military. Only one of the three judges is required to have legal training. There are no juries and no judicial review. Because the order applies broadly to "non-U.S. citizens," up to 18 million people could be subject to its authority (Fisher 2003).

The executive branch argued that these military courts would replicate the fairness of civilian courts while preserving information that could compromise the war on terrorism. The fairness and utility of military tribunals are subject to debate. In six years, while most of the accused waited in prison, only one war-crime case had been completed. In addition to numerous complaints from civilian and military defense attorneys (Swift 2008), the chief prosecutor for the Office of Military Commissions, Col. Morris Davis, resigned, claiming that the adjudicatory process had become "deeply politicized." Davis charged that the executive has intermingled judicial and prosecutorial roles, creating a rigged process stacked against the accused. He also argued that the total secrecy mandated at these trials was unnecessary. "Telling the world 'trust me' will not bolster our standing as defenders of justice" (Davis 2007). He subsequently agreed to testify for defendants being tried by military tribunals about the politicized influence of government officials over the trial process (Glaberson 2008).

Summary

At issue here is who owns the courts. The executive is asserting that in order to protect us from terrorists, it must have secrecy in many areas of our criminal process so that potential terrorists will not know what it knows (*Detroit Free Press et al. v. Ashcroft* 2002). Opponents of such secrecy assert that the "framers did not trust any government to separate the true from the false for us" (*Detroit Free Press et al. v. Ashcroft* 2002). Similarly, the executive argues that it must keep court professionals out of the process because only it knows the true nature of the terrorist threat, and that to allow such professionals into the process would only inhibit their efforts to wage war on terrorists (Brief for Respondents-Appellants 2002). Even the generally deferential Fourth Circuit rejects this position, arguing in one case that "the mere assertion of national security concerns by the Government is not sufficient reason to close a hearing or deny access to documents . . . rather we [judges] must independently determine whether and to what extent the proceedings and documents must be kept under seal" (*United States v. Moussaoui* 2003).

Several questions emerge from this review of the government's antiterrorism measures. Will the federal courts be able to maintain credibility and the perception of fairness when court process is veiled from public oversight? Will the shift in authority from court professionals to the executive be temporary, or a fixture of the permanent war against terror? Is the very nature of the constitutional system thereby altered and, if so, does that matter? Perhaps it is too soon to have answers, but we are not too early to start asking questions.

Note

[1] Zacarias Moussaoui was in custody before September 11 and his case will be discussed later in the chapter.

References

Abramson, Larry. 2006. "Q & A: The NSA's Domestic Eavesdropping Program." National Public Radio. May 4. Available at www.npr.org/templates/story/story.phg?storyId=5187738.

Anderson, Curt. 2003. "Qatar Man Named al-Qaida Enemy Combatant." Associated Press. June 23. Available at news.findlaw.com.

Associated Press. 2004. "FBI Apologies to Lawyer Held in Madrid Bombings." May 25. MSNBC. Available at http://www.msnbc.msn.com/id/5053007/.

Baker, Nancy V. 2002. "The Law: The Impact of Antiterrorism Policies on Separation of Powers: Assessing John Ashcroft's Role." *Presidential Studies Quarterly.* December, pp. 765–778.

Baker, Nancy V. 2006. *General Ashcroft: Attorney at War.* Lawrence: University Press of Kansas.

Bridis, Ted. 2003. "U.S. Doesn't Have to Name 9/11 Detainees." Associated Press. June 17. Available at news.findlaw.com.

Brief for Respondents. 2003. *Padilla ex rel Newman v. Bush.* "Respondents' Reply in Support of Motion to Dismiss the Amended Petition for a Writ of Habeas Corpus." U.S. District Court for the Southern District of New York.

Brief for Respondents-Appellants. 2002. *Yaser Esam Hamdi et al. v. Donald Rumsfeld et al.* U.S. Court of Appeals for the Fourth Circuit. No. 02-6895. Available at http://www.news.findlaw.com/hdocs/docs/hamdi/hamdirums61902gbrf.pdf.

Bush, George W. 2001. "Detention, Treatment, and Trial of Certain Non-Citizens in the War Against Terrorism." Military Order. November 13. White House Office of the Press Secretary.

Cauley, Leslie. 2006. "NSA Has Massive Database of Americans' Phone Calls." *USA Today,* May 11, p. A1.

CNN.com. 2004. "Hamdi Voices Innocence, Joy about Reunion." October 14. http://www.cnn.com/2004/WORLD/meast/10/14/hamdi/.

Davis, Morris D. 2007. "Military Justice Goes AWOL." *LA Times.* December 10. Available at http://www.latimes.com/news/opinion/la-oe-davis10dec10.0.2446661. syory.

Edwards, Jim. 2002. "Judge Orders End to Secret Detention of Federal Inmates in County Jails, Ruling Stayed While U.S. Department of Justice Appeals." *New Jersey Law Journal.* April 1.

Eggen, Dan. 2006. "U.S. Settles Suit Filed by Ore. Lawyer." *Washington Post.* November 30, p. A03.

Eggen, Dan and Robert O'Harrow. 2003. "U.S. Steps Up Secret Surveillance." *Washington Post.* March 24, p. A01.

Elsner, Alan. 2002. "Bush Expands Government Secrecy, Arouses Critics." Reuters. September 3. Available at news.findlaw.com.

Fainaru, Steve and Margot Williams. 2002. "Is the Law Being Bent? The Material Witness Statute Keeps Detainees in Jail, But Many Have Never Testified." *Washington Post National Weekly Edition.* December 2–8, pp. 29–30.

Fisher, Louis. 2003. *Nazi Saboteurs on Trial.* Lawrence: University Press of Kansas.

Glaberson, William. 2008. "Ex-Guantanamo Prosecutor to Testify for Detainee." *New York Times.* February 18, p. A14.

Goldstein, Amy. 2007. "Lawsuit Against Wiretaps Rejected." *Washington Post.* July 7, p. A01.

Goldstein, Amy and Dan Eggen. 2001. "U.S. to Stop Issuing Detention Tallies." *Washington Post.* November 9, p. A16.

Goodnough, Abby. 2007. "After 5 Years, Padilla Goes on Trial in Terror Case." *New York Times.* May 15. Available at http://www.nytimes.com/2007/05/15washington/15padilla.html.

Goodnough, Abby and Scott Shane. 2007. "Padilla is Guilty on all Charges in Terror Trial." *New York Times.* August 17. Available at http://www.nytimes.com/2007/08/17/us/17padilla.html.

Hays, Tom. 2002. "Attorney Says Alleged Terror Suspect Held Unconstitutionally." *Washington Post.* June 11. Available at http://www.washingtonpost.com/ac2/wp-dyn.

Human Rights Watch. 2005. "Witness to Abuse: Human Rights Abuses under the Material Witness Law Since Sept. 11." June. Available at http://hrw.org/reports/2005/us0605.

Human Rights Watch. 2006. "Preventing Abuse of Material Witness Detentions: S. 1739 and Companion Legislation in the House of Representatives." January 3. Available at http://hrw.org/English/docs/2006/01/03/usdom12354_txt.htm.

INS Rule. 2002. "Release of Information Regarding Immigration and Naturalization Service Detainees in Non-Federal Facilities." *Federal Register*, Vol. 67, No. 77. April 22, pp. 19508–19511.

Inspector General Report. 2003. "The September 11 Detainees." Office of Inspector General. U.S. Department of Justice. April 29.

Kiefer, Francine. 2002. "Backlash Grows Against White House Secrecy." *Christian Science Monitor*. March 25, p. 03.

Lane, Charles. 2002. "In Terror War, 2nd Track for Suspects." *Washington Post*. December 1, p. A01.

Leahy, Senator Patrick. 2005. "Statements on Introduced Bills and Joint Resolutions." Congressional Record, September 21 (Senate), pp. S10296–S10303. Available at http://www.fas.org/irp/congress/2005_cr/s1739.html.

Liptak, Adam. 2004. "For Post 9/11 Material Witness, It is Terror of a Different Kind." *New York Times*. August 19. Available at http://www.nytimes.com/2004/08/19/politics/19witness.html.

Liptak, Adam. 2007. "Court Takes Second Look at Enemy Combatant Case." *New York Times*. November 1. Available at http://www.nytimes.com/2007/11/01/us/01combatant.html.

Markon, Jerry. 2003. "Judge Bars Death Penalty for Moussaoui." *Washington Post*. October 2. Available at www.washingtonpost.com/ac/wp-dyn.

Material Witness Statute. 1984. 19 U.S.C. 3144.

Mintz, John. 2002. "Al Qaeda Suspect Enters Legal Limbo." *Washington Post*. June 11, p. A10.

Office of Inspector General. 2007. "A Review of the Federal Bureau of Investigation's Use of National Security Letters." Department of Justice. March. Available at www.usdoj.gov/oig/special/s07036/final.pdf.

Petition for a Writ of Habeas Corpus Pursuant to 28 U.S.C. section 2241. 2003. *Al-Marri v. Bush*. U.S. District Court for the Central District of Illinois. Available at www.findlaw.com.

Richey, Warren. 2007. "Padilla Interrogation, No Checks or Balances." *Christian Science Monitor*. September 4. Available at http://www.csmonitor.com/2007/0904/p02s01-usju.html.

Risen, James. 2007. "Bush Signs Law to Widen Reach for Wiretapping." *New York Times*. August 6. Available at http://www.newyorktimes.com/2007/08/06/washington/06nsa.

S.1739. 2005. "To Amend the Material Witness Statute to Strengthen Procedural Safeguards, and for Other Purposes." Introduced September 21, 109th Congress, 1st session.

Sanders, Edmund. 2001. "The Court That Wields the Wiretaps." *Los Angeles Times*. September 30. Available at www.latimes.com/news/nationworld/nation.

Shenon, Philip. 2003. "Hearing to Affect Government's Ability to Try Terror Suspects in Civilian Courts." *New York Times*. June 2. Available at www.nytimes.com/2003/06/02/politics.

Shenon, Philip. 2007. "Post-9/11 Cases Fuel Criticism for Nominee." *New York Times.* September 24. Available at http://www.nytimes.com/2007/09/24/washington/24mukasey.html.

Swift, Charles. 2008. "Why Now." *Slate.* February 15. Available at http://www.slate.com/id/2184476.

Tribe, Laurence. 2000. *American Constitutional Law,* 3rd ed., Vol. 1. New York: Foundation Press.

USA Patriot Act. 2001. PL 107-56.

Warrick, Joby and Walter Pincus. 2007. "How the Fight for Vast New Spying Powers Was Won." *Washington Post.* August 12, p. A01.

Washington Post. 2002. "ABA Opposes Secret Custody in 9/11 Probe." August 14, p. A10.

Whoriskey, Peter and Dan Eggen. 2008. "Judge Sentences Padilla to 17 Years, Cites His Detention." *Washington Post.* January 23, p. A03.

Cases

Al-Marri v. Wright. 2007. U.S. Court of Appeals for the Fourth Circuit. No. 06-7427. Available at http://pacer.ca4.uscourts.gov/opinion.pdf/067427.P.pdf.

Center for National Security Studies et al. vs. Department of Justice. 2002. 215 F. Supp. 2d 94; 2002 U.S. Dist. LEXIS 14168.

Detroit Free Press et al. v. John Ashcroft. 2002. U.S. Court of Appeals for the Sixth Circuit. 2002 ED App. 0291P (6th Cir).

Grosjean v. American Press Co. 1936. 297 U.S. 233.

Hamdi v. Rumsfeld. 2002a. 296 F.3d 278.

Hamdi v. Rumsfeld. 2002b. 243 F. Supp. 2d 527.

Hamdi v. Rumsfeld. 2003. 316 F. 3d. 450; 2003 U.S. App. LEXIS 198.

Hamdi v. Rumsfeld. 2004. 542 U.S. 507.

Mayfield v. United States. 2007. Opinion and Order. U.S. District Court for the District of Oregon. Civil No. 04-1427AA. September 26.

New York Times v. United States. 1971. 403 U.S. 713.

Padilla v. Hanft. 2006. 547 U.S. 1062.

United States v. Osama Awadallah. 2002. U.S. District Court for the Southern District of New York, 2002 U.S. Dist. LEXIS 7536.

United States v. Osama Awadallah. 2003. 349 F. 3rd 42, U.S. App. LEXIS 22879.

United States v. Zacarias Moussaoui. 2003. Order. U.S. Court of Appeals for the Fourth Circuit. No. 03-4162. May 13.

Questions to Consider

1. Not surprisingly, studies have indicated that the individual characteristics of any woman who becomes a judge is the most important predictor of the decisions they make, not necessarily the fact that they are
   female. Given this, why should we be concerned that we have more
   female judges?

2. If one is not represented in the courts, does this impact one's sense of
   ownership? How important is it that we have as many of our citizens
   as possible claiming ownership of our democratic institutions? To what
   extent does having people in decision-making roles serve as models
   and inspiration for others?

3. First Amendment freedom of the press significantly helps us to know
   what is going on in public life. Authoritarian governments put significant effort into controlling the flow of information. What aspects, if
   any, of public courts should be kept secret? Explain. What are the dangers of creating more secrecy?

4. To what extent does court secrecy breed the perception that the underlying process is unfair or rigged? How much do you trust the government to always be fair and just?

5. To what extent is an act of terrorism just another type of crime, or is it
   so different that it must be handled in special executive courts in
   secret? If it is somehow different from normal criminal proceedings,
   how do we know if the executive is acting justly if everything is secret?